CW01024297

THE WORLD'S FIRST RAILWAY SYSTEM

The World's First Railway System

Enterprise, Competition, and Regulation on the
Railway Network in Victorian Britain

MARK CASSON

OXFORD
UNIVERSITY PRESS

OXFORD

UNIVERSITY PRESS

Great Clarendon Street, Oxford OX2 6DP

Oxford University Press is a department of the University of Oxford.
It furthers the University's objective of excellence in research, scholarship,
and education by publishing worldwide in

Oxford New York

Auckland Cape Town Dar es Salaam Hong Kong Karachi
Kuala Lumpur Madrid Melbourne Mexico City Nairobi
New Delhi Shanghai Taipei Toronto

With offices in

Argentina Austria Brazil Chile Czech Republic France Greece
Guatemala Hungary Italy Japan Poland Portugal Singapore
South Korea Switzerland Thailand Turkey Ukraine Vietnam

Oxford is a registered trade mark of Oxford University Press
in the UK and in certain other countries

Published in the United States
by Oxford University Press Inc., New York

© Mark Casson 2009

The moral rights of the author have been asserted
Database right Oxford University Press (maker)

First published 2009

British Library Cataloguing in Publication Data

Data available

Library of Congress Cataloging in Publication Data

Data available

Typeset by SPI Publisher Services, Pondicherry, India
Printed in Great Britain
on acidfree paper by
CPI Antony Rowe, Chippenham, Wiltshire

ISBN 978–0–19–921397–9

1 3 5 7 9 10 8 6 4 2

In memory of John Dunning, who gave me my first (and only) job, and provided me with advice and support throughout my career

Contents

Preface and Acknowledgements

This study of the evolution of the British railway network, 1825–1914, investigates claims that the network was overcapitalized due to excessive duplication of lines. A counterfactual network is constructed to represent the most efficient alternative network that could have been constructed given what was known at the time. This is the first counterfactual of its type ever constructed. Comparison of the actual and counterfactual networks suggests that the actual network was even more inefficient than is commonly alleged. The roots of this inefficiency can be traced to excessive competition between towns which national government was too weak to control, and to the strategies employed by competing companies to disrupt each other's operations. Parliament was too weak to regulate excessive competition because members of Parliament were reluctant to put national interests ahead of the local interests of the towns they represented. Whilst localism and competitive individualism generated substantial economic benefits in certain economic sectors, they proved to be a weakness in the context of the railway system.

This research was financed by a grant from the UK Economic and Social Research Council. I am grateful to their advisers for comments on the original proposal, and also on the final report. Previous versions of this book have been presented at the Annual Conferences of the Economic History Society, the Association of Business Historians, and the Historical Geographical Information Systems Conference, University of Essex; also at Cardiff University Business School; Business History Unit, London School of Economics; Queen Mary Business School, London; and the Institute of Railway Studies, University of York; on each occasion very useful feedback was received. I am also grateful to the Leverhulme Trust for awarding me a fellowship that has allowed me to follow up some of the themes of this book as part of a wider study into the economics of networks.

A large amount of primary source material has been collected for the purposes of this study, and I therefore have great debts to librarians and archivists. I wish to mention particularly the staff at the places where I have spent most time: the Bodleian Library, Oxford (especially the Map Room and the John Johnson Collection) and the county record offices at Reading, Oxford, Buckingham, Northampton, Warwick, Worcester, London Metropolitan, Winchester, Woking, Chichester, Norwich, Hawarden, Wakefield, Northallerton, Durham, and Newcastle. The staff of the West Register Office in Edinburgh were also most helpful, although I did not have enough time to make full use of all the valuable material held there.

In addition to the extensive primary sources alluded to above, a large number of secondary sources have been used in this study. As a lifelong railway enthusiast, I have drawn freely on the enthusiast's literature. Although some academics have in the past made rather disparaging remarks about this literature, I have always found it most illuminating, and the factual accuracy is often greater than in the academic literature. The Business Enterprise Heritage Trust has a unique collection of this literature, and I am very grateful to them for providing access. The Ford Railway Collection of the University of Lancaster Library, Search Engine at the National Railway Museum, and the rare book and pamphlet collections of the British Library of Political and Economic Science at the London School of Economics have also proved very useful in this respect.

It is not really practical to cite all the primary and secondary evidence that bears on each fact or interpretation offered in this study. To compensate for this, a classified bibliography has been provided. A reader seeking confirmation of some fact or observation in the text can locate its provenance by identifying the literature relating to the particular company and/or the particular region concerned.

To simplify some very complex stories, not all the stages in the transfer of the ownership of lines are recorded, nor are all the different steps in the opening of lines distinguished—for example, opening for freight, opening for passengers, construction of stations after the line has been opened, and so on; judgement has been used to focus on those events that were of the greatest importance from a strategic point of view. The names of the companies have also been simplified—in particular, the Manchester Sheffield & Lincolnshire is referred to throughout as the Great Central, even though its name change occurred only in 1897.

A number of scholars have taken an interest in this work and have provided advice and support; in particular Mike Anson, Tony Atkins, Nick Crafts, Robert Crawshaw, Colin Divall, Carolyn Dougherty, Roy Edwards, James Foreman-Peck, Terry Gourvish, Ian Gregory, Tim Leunig, Teresa da Silva Lopes, Paloma Fernandez Perez, John Poulter, Mary Rose, Robert Schwartz, Leigh Shaw-Taylor, David Stirling, Brian Turner, Jonathan Tyler, and Tony Wrigley. Jill Turner, Jean Teall, and Lorna Earnes provided valuable administrative suport. I would also like to thank George Muir of the Association of Train Operating Companies for inviting me to join the Passenger Demand Forecasting Council as an Associate Member; attending informal discussions relating to the contemporary privatized railway system has helped to inform my understanding of what may have happened on the privatized Victorian system, although there is no intention to draw explicit parallels between the two systems in this book.

Chapter 1 is loosely based on a paper published in *Networks and Spatial Economics*, 2008, whilst Chapter 2 is the basis for a joint chapter with Andrew Godley in a forthcoming book published under the auspices of the Kauffman Foundation, to whom we are grateful for financial support.

Finally, I should also like to thank David Musson and Matthew Derbyshire of Oxford University Press for their patience in awaiting the final delivery of this manuscript, and my wife and daughter for their patience and putting up with me whilst I was finishing it off.

List of Illustrations
(between pages 220 and 221)

List of Figures

List of Tables

List of Abbreviations

BMR	Brecon & Merthyr Railway
CLC	Cheshire Lines Committee
CR	Caledonian Railway
DNSR	Didcot Newbury & Southampton Railway
FR	Furness Railway
GCR	Great Central Railway
GER	Great Eastern Railway
GJR	Grand Junction Railway
GNR	Great Northern Railway
GNSR	Great North of Scotland Railway
GSWR	Glasgow & South Western Railway
GWR	Great Western Railway
HBR	Hull & Barnsley Railway
ICE	Institution of Civil Engineers
ILN	Illustrated London News
LBR	London & Birmingham Railway
LBSCR	London Brighton and South Coast Railway
LCDR	London Chatham and Dover Railway
LMR	Liverpool & Manchester Railway
LNWR	London & North Western Railway
LSR	Leeds and Selby Railway
LSWR	London & South Western Railway
LTS	London Tilbury & Southend Railway
LYR	Lancashire & Yorkshire Railway
MGNR	Midland & Great Northern Railway
MR	Midland Railway
MSJAR	Manchester South Junction and Altrincham Railway
MSWJR	Midland & South Western Junction Railway
NAHR	Newport Abergavenny and Hereford Railway
NBR	North British Railway
NER	North Eastern Railway
NLR	North London Railway
NSR	North Staffordshire Railway
NSWJR	North & South Western Junction Railway
NUR	North Union Railway
OAGBJR	Oldham Ashton & Guide Bridge Junction Railway
RR	Rhymney Railway
SDJR	Somerset & Dorset Joint Railway
SDR	Stockton & Darlington Railway

1

Introduction and Summary

1.1. THE EFFICIENCY OF THE VICTORIAN UK RAILWAY NETWORK: AN UNRESOLVED ISSUE

A key issue in the history of the UK railway system—and the major focus of this study—is the question of whether the railway system was an efficient response to the traffic requirements of the economy (Simmons and Biddle 1997). While the efficiency question applies to both the construction and the operation of railways, the efficiency of operation is heavily constrained by the structure of the system, and so the construction of the system is the key topic in this chapter.

The study encompasses England, Wales, and Scotland, and excludes Ireland, partly because it is geographically separate, and partly because the political and economic factors that impinged on railway development there were very different from the rest of the UK. The Isle of Wight is included and the Isle of Man excluded because the former is included in the official railway statistics for England and Wales and the latter is not. Underground railway systems, such as the London tube lines, are not included.

The main period of railway construction was 1825–1914, and so this was the period selected for study. Prior to the opening of the Stockton and Darlington Railway (SDR) in 1825, railways were normally powered by horses rather than steam locomotives, conveyed traffic consigned by their owners rather than by the public, and carried mainly minerals—especially coal. The SDR was the world's first steam-powered public passenger–carrying railway, and was quickly followed by the world's first inter-urban trunk railway—the Liverpool and Manchester (LMR), opened in 1830, which operated scheduled express services on which businessmen could make a return journey within a day.

By 1914 three major railway-building booms had come and gone, and the construction of trunk lines had ended (it did not restart until the Channel Tunnel Rail Link of the 1990s). The railway's monopoly of long-distance inland transport, based on its superiority to the canal, was being eroded by road competition—first from the tram, and then from the coach, lorry, and motor car. The Railway Grouping of 1923 terminated much of the inter-company competition that characterized the 1825–1914 period, as the Big Four companies formed at the grouping turned their attention to fighting road competition instead.

The UK railway system was constructed entirely by private enterprise, with minimal state subsidies. The efficiency of the system is therefore, indirectly, a judgement on the performance of private enterprise. Although Simmons (1991),

Turnock (1985), and other transport historians have pointed to apparent inefficiencies in the structure of the system—in particular, the duplication of main lines—no one has so far spelled out in detail what an efficient railway system would have looked like. If the efficient system looked just like the existing system but without the duplication of main lines then the degree of inefficiency could be deemed quite modest. If the efficient alternative was completely different, however, then the inefficiencies could be very large.

This study suggests that the inefficiencies were not only large but also larger than anyone has ever suggested before. In 1914 the railway system comprised approximately 20,000 route miles of track. This study suggests that equivalent social benefits could have been obtained with only 13,000 miles of track. The method of calculation is explained in detail below.

The explanation for the result lies partly in the fact that it was not only main lines that were duplicated but also lines to and from mining areas, ports, and industrial centres. There was an excessive density of lines in lightly populated rural areas. Many railway hubs were located at relatively isolated locations, such as Crewe and Ashford, rather than at major centres of population nearby, such as Stoke-on-Trent and Trowbridge. This resulted in duplication of hub facilities, and required additional lines to serve the hubs. Great cities such as London, Manchester, and Leeds did not fulfil their potential to be major hubs because passenger routes did not join up there: each railway company, or group of companies, had its own terminus in the city.

Although private enterprise was wasteful, it is always possible to argue that state planning would have been no better, or even worse. Evidence suggests, however, that state planning would in fact have resulted in a much better outcome, though not a perfectly efficient one. The Railway Committee of the Board of Trade published detailed recommendations regarding the future structure of the network in 1845, based on over 20 detailed regional plans. Railways that did not conform to these guidelines would not have been authorized by Parliament. After following the Committee's guidance for just one year, Parliament decided to dispense with its services in future, for reasons explained below. Had the Board of Trade's guidance been accepted, the number of railways constructed would have been much lower, and many of the routes would have followed better alignments, and served larger populations along the way.

1.2. THE CONCEPT OF A RAILWAY NETWORK

The defining characteristic of any network is connectivity. A network may be characterized in terms of

- the nature of the elements connected up,
- the number and diversity of these elements,
- the nature of the connections between them, and
- the configuration of the linkages—in particular the pattern of hubs.

The UK railway system connected numerous local settlements (e.g. towns and cities). The spatial division of labour dictated that different towns specialized in different industries, and this specialization was increased through the improved transport links provided by the railways themselves. Track and trains forged the connections. The configuration of the network was dictated by the locations of the junctions between the various lines. Railway hubs emerged where several lines met. Engine sheds, goods yards, and engineering works were often sited at these hubs.

The UK railway system was part of an international inter-modal transport system. The UK is an island with considerable entrepot potential, sited between northern Europe and North America. Its victory in the Napoleonic Wars meant that by 1830 the British navy controlled the Atlantic Ocean, the Mediterranean, and the North Sea. From the 1840s, free trade and fiscal prudence was national policy. Emigration fuelled imperial expansion, and London banks expanded to finance international trade and investment.

Early railways were promoted with international trade in mind. The LMR, linking the Atlantic port of Liverpool to the textile centre of Manchester, handled imports of raw cotton and exports of finished cotton goods. A chain of tracks quickly developed across the Pennines as the lines expanded eastward, linking the West Coast port of Liverpool to the East Coast port of Hull. The Newcastle and Carlisle Railway—another early promotion—was specifically built as a 'land bridge' to convey Scandinavian timber imported through the East Coast port of Newcastle, to Ireland; it was exported through ports to the west of Carlisle.

When trunk lines to London were promoted, it was ports that often took the lead. Liverpool and Bristol competed for the Atlantic trade; Liverpool promoted the Grand Junction Railway (GJR), and Bristol promoted the Great Western Railway (GWR). Isambard Kingdom Brunel promised Bristol a superior broad gauge line, but Liverpool triumphed because Bristol's port silted up. Southampton became one of the most successful Atlantic ports, thanks mainly to another early scheme—the London and Southampton Railway (which developed into the London and South Western Railway (LSWR)). Railway companies acquired shipping lines serving Ireland, the Continent and the Channel Islands. They invested in port improvements and built hotels to offer a fully integrated service to seagoing passengers.

British railway engineers built railways in Continental Europe—lines which often connected with the British railway companies' shipping routes. British experience was also exploited in the Empire; British managers, engineers, and financiers played an important part in developing colonial railway systems. Latin America also attracted substantial British railway investment.

Some of lessons from the British system were applied overseas. In India, for example, the imperial government was determined not to repeat the mistakes that had been made in Britain, and India obtained a better railway system than Britain as a result. Other lessons were not learned, however; in Australia, for example, three different gauges were used for trunk line railways in the various states, repeating Brunel's mistake in adopting a non-standard gauge. The failings of the

British railway system had international repercussions. While the present study is confined to the UK, it has implications for other countries which should be pursued in future research.

1.3. CONSTRUCTING A COUNTERFACTUAL: BASIC REQUIREMENTS

Counterfactuals are widely used in economic history. If it is asked 'Why was the railway system the way it was?' the answer is 'Because it was not the way that it might have been'. There are many possible 'might have beens', but economic theory suggests a natural scenario—namely that the system was the most efficient possible.

An efficient system is defined as one that meets a given set of traffic requirements at minimum cost. These requirements are defined only in general terms, as described below. If the counterfactual system were required to generate exactly the same mix of services as the actual system then, apart from eliminating duplications, it would perforce be very similar to the actual system. By specifying traffic requirements in general terms, significant differences in the configuration of the actual and counterfactual systems can emerge. Investigation of these differences provides insights into why the actual system adopted the particular configuration that it did.

Because of the emphasis on railway construction, the focus of this study is on the costs of construction and maintenance, which depend mainly on the number of route miles. Costs of operation are also considered, and it can be shown that the counterfactual network would have been a much easier system to operate than the actual network. Better routes with fewer bottlenecks would have been selected, and the system of hubs would have been organized more rationally.

The traffic requirements are assumed to be those that might reasonably have been estimated at the birth of the railway system. The aim of this study is therefore to construct a counterfactual railway system that minimizes the route mileage required to meet traffic requirements as they would appear about 1840. This includes meeting additional traffic requirements which could reasonably have been foreseen at this time. Since railways were long-term investments, built with considerable spare capacity at the outset, traffic growth was clearly envisaged by their promoters and engineers. The counterfactual therefore allows for an estimated rate of economic growth which would lead to a correction prediction of the aggregate growth of traffic that occurred up to 1914. In effect, therefore, it is 1914 traffic requirements that are used in the study. This assumes that investors in 1840 successfully anticipated the structural changes that occurred over the subsequent 74 years—such as the growth of London as a world financial trade, the expansion of imperial shipping, and the growth of the coal export trade. In fact, company prospectuses and journalistic commentaries suggest that these developments were foreseen in general terms, and were reflected in heavy investment in serving London, the Atlantic ports, and the major coalfields near them.

Overall traffic requirements can be specified using either a 'bottom up' or 'top down' approach. In a bottom up approach, individual requirements are specified for the conveyance of a given type of traffic between a given pair of locations with a given quality of service. The requirements of all types of traffic between all pairs of locations are then aggregated up to determine overall requirements. This approach is too data-intensive, and too demanding of computation; with over 6,000 stations on the actual network in 1914, a detailed analysis of individual traffic flows is not viable.

This study therefore adopts a 'top down' approach which specifies traffic requirements at a high level of aggregation. A number of different types of traffic are identified which flow between different types of towns and cities— for example, mining towns to ports, or rural towns to provincial agricultural centres. Some types of traffic are inherently local, some are long-distance, and others are a mixture of the two. Some traffic flows link major centres, some link minor centres to major centres, and some link minor centres to each other. The overall performance of the system is assessed by how well it accommodates the needs of each type of traffic. The basic requirement is that, on average, the counterfactual system should meet these requirements just as well as the actual system.

The counterfactual was designed initially to equal the average performance of the actual system across all types of traffic. In order to determine average performance, however, it is necessary to know how much weight should be attached to each type of traffic. The derivation of appropriate weights is a potentially controversial exercise, for even if there were accurate figures for the different types of traffic on the actual network it would not follow that the weights should be based upon these figures, because an optimal network might carry a different mix of traffic. It was therefore necessary to carry out a sensitivity analysis, employing a variety of different weights. It soon became apparent, however, that with only minor enhancements a counterfactual could be constructed that unambiguously dominated the actual system in the sense that it equalled the performance of the actual system in respect of every type of traffic, and exceeded it in most cases. It is this 'dominating' counterfactual that is reported here. It should be emphasized that this counterfactual is not superior for every conceivable consignment of traffic, but only for a typical consignment of a certain type of traffic.

The counterfactual system is developed from a 'blank sheet of paper'—almost literally—and not by simply exploring variations to the configuration of the actual network. It is constructed using an iterative process, as explained below. To avoid the need for a full evaluation of the performance of the network after each iteration, a set of simple criteria were used to guide the initial formulation of the model. These criteria represent conditions that the counterfactual would almost certainly have to fulfil if it were to stand any chance of matching the performance of the actual system.

The criteria are that:

- All towns of a certain size must be served by the network, and every such town must be accessible from every other.
- All pairs of nearby towns which specialize in complementary activities—for example, mining and shipping—must be connected by a direct route.
- All towns must be connected to their nearest major provincial centre and to London by a reasonably direct route.
- All towns must be connected to neighbouring towns of similar size by a reasonable route.

The actual network met the first two of the four criteria extremely well. The third criterion was not consistently met: while some towns were well connected to London, and some to their provincial centres, many were not well connected to both and a few were not well connected to either. The fourth criterion was not satisfied at all in many cases, because there were many dead-end branches, and towns located at the terminus of a single dead-end branch can be accessed from only one direction.

The railway network conveyed six main categories of traffic: passengers, perishable freight (e.g. livestock, dairy products), ordinary freight, parcels, mail, and troops. Passengers, parcels, and freight were the most important in economic terms, although mails and troops were important for social and political reasons. Lines suitable for passengers are generally suitable for parcels and freight, but not vice versa. Parcels, mail, and some perishables were often conveyed by ordinary passenger trains. The counterfactual is therefore specified in terms of its passenger-carrying capabilities. An exception concerns heavy mineral traffic, where it is recognized that lines may have to be designed to cope with intensive freight traffic even though passenger traffic is light.

A certain degree of scepticism can be expected regarding any counterfactual that claims to be optimal. It is a well-known precept that actual systems should be compared to practical alternatives and not to highly idealized ones. To this end, the counterfactual has been constructed on very conservative assumptions, which are elaborated below. The engineering assumptions are very conservative relative to actual railway practice, while the use of detailed land surveys and large-scale maps means that major infringements of local parks and amenities have been avoided.

1.4. PERFORMANCE METRICS: DISTANCE AND TIME

Two main performance metrics are used in this study: journey distance and journey time. The most obvious metric by which to compare the actual and counterfactual systems is by the route mileages between pairs of towns. This metric is not quite so useful as it seems, however. For many types of traffic, including passengers, mail, troops, and perishable goods, it is the time taken by the journey that is important and not the distance per se. Second, journey distances are difficult to compute for the actual system because the shortest route was often not the route actually used by most of the traffic. This is because the most direct route involved switching between rival companies' networks at an intermediate point, perhaps involving a change of station, or a long wait for a connecting train. In many cases the shortest route was a highly contrived route that involved reversing at junctions or using connecting spurs with steep gradients that were designed for only occasional use.

Since the distance metric is so imperfect, the time metric is the main metric employed in this study. It must be emphasized, however, that the time was not the only consideration so far as passengers were concerned. Convenience (determined by the number of changes of train and the quality of terminal facilities) and comfort (determined largely by class of travel and the degree of overcrowding) mattered too. The issue of convenience is addressed in this study, though not by the use of formal metrics; comfort, however, lies outside its scope.

To convert from a distance metric to a time metric, it is necessary to know average speeds, which depend partly on the speed of the trains and partly on the time spent joining and leaving the train, or waiting for connections. The speed of a train is limited by the quality of the track—in particular, the ruling gradient, and whether double track is provided. (Minimum radius of curvature is also important, but its impact is difficult to assess, as curvature is often highest at junctions where the train is likely to be running slowest, and so this factor has been excluded from the analysis.)

Four levels of track quality are distinguished, and each is associated with a particular average speed. At the time the first inter-urban railways were constructed, many engineers correctly foresaw that steam locomotive technology would continue to improve radically, and so the speeds we assume are those that were actually achieved in the 1850s and 1860s. The four levels of track quality determine four categories of route:

- Trunk: heavy traffic at high speed (40 mph; ruling gradient 1/250; double track throughout).
- Primary: moderate traffic at reasonably high speed (40 mph; ruling gradient 1/150; double track throughout).
- Secondary: moderate traffic at moderate speed (30 mph; ruling gradient 1/75; double track for heavily used portions, and single track elsewhere).
- Local: light traffic at low speeds (20 mph; ruling gradient 1/40; normally single track).

The quoted speeds allow for the fact that trunk lines will normally carry passenger expresses and local lines will normally carry stopping trains. The ruling gradients are expected to apply to at least 98 per cent of the route.

Journey time has been calculated using a specially constructed national timetable—a sort of 'Bradshaw's Guide' to the counterfactual system. To keep the timetable to a manageable size, it was decided to specify a fixed interval service on each route. While this has the disadvantage that train frequency does not increase during the morning and evening peaks, it has the great advantage that the entire daily service in each direction can be inferred from the timing of a single train.

The counterfactual timetable used in this study assumes that trains run on each route at two-hour intervals. They run at the maximum speed permitted by the quality of the track (as specified above). Where routes share the same section of track, however, frequency may be higher, and for obvious reasons it may be higher in suburban areas too. Two hours corresponds roughly to the intervals between trains on many of the trunk lines that were opened in the 1830s and 1840s. Frequency later declined on some routes, partly because companies sought to reduce their operating costs by consolidating traffic onto fewer trains, and partly because, as the early trunk lines lost their monopolies, inter-urban traffic became spread over several competing routes. Given that the counterfactual network turns out to be much smaller than the actual network, it is appropriate to assume that there would be a greater concentration of traffic on any given route, and that a frequency of two hours (or more) is therefore warranted.

The timetable approach is implemented exclusively for passenger trains (which are also assumed to carry parcels and mail). Passengers are allowed five minutes to change trains. It is assumed that interchange stations on the counterfactual system are laid out in a manner that facilitates connections, along the rational principles employed on the actual system at stations such as Nottingham Victoria and Edinburgh Waverley. The five-minute allowance is consistent with actual operating practices at the end of the nineteenth century (as indicated by contemporary timetables).

When estimating passenger journey times, the time incurred by passengers in travelling to and from the stations at the start and finish of their journey is ignored. Provided that both the actual and counterfactual systems serve the same towns (as is normally the case) the time taken should be the same in each case (except where the counterfactual station is better located, in which case there should be a time advantage to the counterfactual system).

Using the timetable, passenger journey time can be calculated in two ways. It can be assumed either that passengers turn up just before the advertised departure time of their train or that they turn up at the time at which they want to depart and then catch the first available train (or, strictly speaking, the next available train that will get them to their destination at the earliest possible time). In the first case the journey time is independent of the frequency of trains, while in the second case it reflects the frequency of services as well as the actual travelling time. The second approach is used by modern railway professionals, and it is the approach used in this study.

1.5. IMPLEMENTATION OF THE PERFORMANCE CRITERIA

Given the substantial fixed costs of railway construction, there is a minimum size of town which is necessary in order to warrant its connection to the railway network. Main line railways were built to serve the needs of industry and commerce rather than the needs of agriculture, with many agricultural market towns being bypassed by the early railways. While the early railway builders assumed that major urban centres would continue to thrive, they believed that where smaller towns were concerned, the traffic would tend to follow the railway rather than the other way round: markets would shift to railway centres, so market towns bypassed by the railway would naturally decay. It was mainly the branch lines built late in the nineteenth century that were intended to serve agricultural needs. This suggests that in the counterfactual model the minimum size of town to be served by the railway should set fairly high. After inspecting the regional distribution of population, a threshold population of 3,000 was set.

Towns with a population in the region 1,500–2,999 were also included if they were actually served by a railway in 1914. The existence of a railway may indicate a specific local need—for example, a local quarry or a large estate suitable for a dairy herd. Requiring the counterfactual to serve these towns also neutralizes a potential criticism—namely that its mileage is low simply because its service to rural areas is unacceptably poor.

Census data for 1831 was used to identify qualifying towns (large parishes with high population but no discernable centre of population were excluded). Census data collected in 1831 was the latest information available to promoters making decisions about the railway system in 1840. Many towns and villages with very small populations will be served by a railway by accident rather than by design, because they happen to lie along a trunk or primary route. It is inefficient to deviate a trunk route to serve a small village, but local branch lines have been allowed to deviate to serve small communities which, on their own, would not merit a separate rail connection. The limits of acceptable deviation are set by the requirements specified earlier.

Eighteen major provincial centres were identified. Several are major ports, for reasons explained above. Other criteria for selection are the size of population, administrative status, and the geographical extent of the area served. They are Glasgow, Edinburgh, Newcastle, Leeds, Hull, Manchester, Liverpool, Holyhead (for Dublin), Nottingham, Birmingham, Swansea, Cardiff, Bristol, Norwich, Plymouth, Southampton, Brighton, and Dover.

A simple gravity model was used to construct indicators of the traffic potential between these centres. The coefficients of the model are set so that traffic is directly proportional to the population of each town and inversely proportional to the distance between them (distance being measured by the shortest available land-based route in 1914). The results were then adjusted in the light of more specific information on economic structure—in particular, the nature and extent of traffic through nearby ports. This exercise indicated relative (but not absolute) volumes of traffic; the larger traffic flows identified by this exercise were deemed to require trunk links.

Simple gravity models also ignore special circumstances affecting local traffic flows between smaller centres. When applied to the Cardiff Valleys, for example, they suggests large flows between adjacent valleys rather than large flows down the valleys to the ports, which is what is actually required. The need to adjust traffic estimates in the light of local circumstances suggested using local information to classify towns by their principal activity, and to base traffic estimates on whether neighbouring towns played complementary roles in the economy. Suitable evidence was available from Victoria County Histories, the Phillimore and Tempus series of illustrated local histories, and other sources in the local studies libraries which were visited as part of this study.

The requirements imposed on the counterfactual may therefore be summarized as follows:

- All towns which either had a population of over 3,000 or had a population of over 1,500, and were actually served by a railway, should be served by the counterfactual system.
- Long-distance traffic between pairs of large towns, and other long-distance traffic flows deemed to be large, must be handled by trunk routes.
- Other traffic flows should be handled using routes that were sufficiently direct and fast that the system as a whole could equal or surpass the performance of the actual system in handling the relevant type of traffic.

1.6. SOLVING THE OPTIMIZATION PROBLEM: THE ROLE OF HEURISTICS

No one has ever constructed a counterfactual railway network; at any rate, a literature search failed to reveal any similar study. The social savings approach, pioneered by Fogel (1964) and Hawke (1975), and recently refined by Leunig (2006), involves a counterfactual expansion of alternative transport modes—notably canals—but no change in the railway system itself. The present exercise is, to some extent, a refinement of these exercises, as the counterfactual allows the route mileage of the railway system to be optimized, rather than just equated to the status quo. On the other hand, what is missing from the present study is any explicit analysis of the impact of the counterfactual railway system on other modes of transport.

A network is inherently complex. There are many possible configurations for even a very small network. There is no easy way of searching out an optimal network from a large set of possible networks. Solving a network optimization problem for a system as large as a national railway is a challenging task.

The computational problems involved in the construction of counterfactual networks have never been fully addressed. While Fogel refers to the use of linear programming in network optimization, he acknowledges that he has not actually implemented the technique (Fogel 1964, p. 26). The method by which his counterfactual canal system was derived is not fully explained in the Appendix, and his estimate of its performance is based on guesswork (p. 38).

Network optimization cannot be effected by linear programming, as Fogel mistakenly suggests. Making a connection between two locations involves a binary decision: the two locations are either connected or they are not. Network optimization is therefore an integer programming problem, and problems of this kind encounter combinatorial explosion: the number of possible network structures increases at an accelerating rate as the number of locations to be served rises.

An additional complexity arises from the fact that the optimal location for a railway junction may be in the middle of the countryside rather than at a town. Constraining all junctions to be at towns may reduce the performance of a network quite considerably. As indicated above, the actual network made extensive use of rural junctions, at places such as Crewe, Swindon, and Eastleigh, and lesser-known centres such as Evercreech, Broom, and Melton Constable. Introducing rural locations as potential junctions increases the dimensions of the problem: indeed, since rural areas were far more extensive than urban ones in the nineteenth century, the dimensions of the problem are considerably increased. Formulating the optimization of the railway network as an integer programming problem is therefore not viable unless the dimensions of the problem are artificially constrained, and this makes integer programming unsuitable for this study.

The precise methods used to solve for the counterfactual, and the details of the solution, are presented in Chapter 3. The core of the solution, however, is the Steiner Principle, which describes the way in which the total route mileage involved in connecting up a set of towns is minimized. According to this principle, an efficient solution either links adjacent towns directly, by a straight-line connection, or it links them indirectly by a three-way junction. It is a remarkable mathematical property that at any three-way junction each of the lines makes an angle of $120°$ with the other lines. In other words, the junction is symmetric with respect to each of the lines. In some cases the route between two towns may involve a succession of three-way junctions.

The Steiner Principle alone cannot be made the basis of the counterfactual, however, because it pays no attention to the distance of a journey between any particular pair of towns; in the interests of minimizing overall route mileage, the Steiner Principle can generate some very convoluted routes between individual pairs of towns. It must therefore be combined with other principles if a system to rival the performance of the actual system is to be devised.

There are two main ways of modifying the Steiner Principle in order to produce more direct routes between particular pairs of towns. One is to 'soften' the effect of the $120°$ junction, which turns the direction of travel of everyone passing through the junction by 30°; the natural way to do this is to replace the junction by a triangle, allowing travellers to change direction on average by only 15°. In other words, the point of intersection is spread out over space, being distributed across the three vertices of a triangle which is centred on the original intersection. When the triangle become very large then any three adjacent towns become directly connected to each other by the sides of the triangle. This modification of the Steiner Principle therefore encourages the evolution of railway network constructed out of interlocking triangles.

The second approach is to compensate for the indirectness of certain routes by putting in additional links. This may be termed a 'cut off' principle. Adjacent towns that are connected by very devious routes are given additional direct connections of their own.

Both of these two approaches introduce 'redundancy' into the counterfactual network. Because it minimizes overall route mileage, the pure Steiner Principle eliminates all redundancy; if any one link breaks then the system is fractured. Where triangles and bypasses are used, alternative routes become available, namely, the other two sides of the triangle, or the bypass, or the original route.

The introduction of redundancy into the network has important strategic implications, as explained in Chapters 3 and 6. Redundancy means that there is potential competition between alternative routes. In a pure Steiner system with no redundancy every linkage is complementary to the other linkages, but once redundancy has been introduced linkages can become substitutes for each other.

A number of other principles are also employed in the construction of the counterfactual. These principles mainly concern the way that regional networks are designed and the way that they are integrated into a national system. The principles suggest that, where appropriate, regional sub-systems should be constructed from interlocking coastal loops, and that connections between adjacent systems should be based at bridging points on prominent river estuaries. The towns located at these bridging points therefore emerge as natural hubs on the counterfactual network.

1.7. OBJECTIONS TO COUNTERFACTUAL EXERCISES

Counterfactual exercises are vulnerable to a number of criticisms (as indicated earlier). It is often alleged that:

- It is not possible to specify the counterfactual in sufficient detail to permit a reliable comparison with the actual situation.
- The counterfactual is not feasible because it ignores certain physical or technological constraints.
- While the counterfactual may have been feasible in technological terms, there was never any opportunity to pursue it, because the social and institutional obstacles were insurmountable.

- The counterfactual has been constructed by imposing modern concepts on the past. These concepts would have been completely alien to an earlier generation. The counterfactual is irrelevant because it could never have been conceived by those who needed to conceive it.

None of these criticisms has any force with respect to the present study.

The counterfactual railway system is detailed: it has been mapped to a scale of 2.4 miles to the inch. The distances between all major stations on each route have been computed, allowing for the line to follow the contours of the landscape and avoid major geological obstacles in the way. The quality of track on each section of the network has been specified. The main long-distance through services have also been specified, making it possible to identify the particular hubs at which passengers on various journeys will need to change trains.

Considerable care has been taken to ensure that the counterfactual is feasible in engineering terms. In so far as the counterfactual is just a truncated version of the actual network, the feasibility of the network is assured by the fact that its lines are just a subset of lines actually built. There are more fundamental structural differences, too, however. There are about 2,000 route miles where the counterfactual follows routes that were never built. It is important to be sure that these alternative routes are feasible.

During the course of the nineteenth century almost every conceivable railway route was promoted at one time or another, and engineering plans exist for all those schemes submitted to Parliament, including many lines which were never built. Almost all of the missing 2,000 miles can be reconstructed from a combination of such lines, or minor variations of them. Plans for many of these lines have been consulted as part of this study; between them, they cover all parts of England and Wales, and are comprehensive for many parts of the country.

In some cases, however, the counterfactual requires a route to be built to a higher standard than that originally envisaged. Fieldwork surveys have been carried out to assess the viability of such upgrades. A cautious approach has been taken, so that if an upgrade appears dubious, an alternative route has been selected instead.

The counterfactual network would have been completely intelligible to early railway promoters. Prior to 1825, a number of visionary writers had set out the benefits of an integrated national railway network. Some visualized wooden rails and others iron rails; some assumed horse power and others steam power, but they were all aware of the benefits of connectedness, which is the defining characteristic of a network.

Network externalities were understood at both an intuitive and practical level. Thomas Gray set out a plan for a national system involving a north–south spine and various east–west branches. Some early mineral railways were designed as small networks; the Stockton and Darlington Railway of 1825, for example, involved feeder lines from collieries, and branches to ports at Croft and Yarm, as well as to the main line terminus at Stockton.

There is even evidence that the Steiner Principle was intuitively understood. Robert Stephenson's London and Birmingham Railway (LBR) turned west near Rugby, from which branches were later thrown off north to Leicester, and north-west to Nuneaton. Francis Giles's London and Southampton Railway turned south-west at Basingstoke, from the point at which it was planned to construct a branch to Bath, and from which a later line to Salisbury and Exeter was built. I. K. Brunel's GWR turned from north to west at Didcot, at the point from which the Oxford (and later Banbury) line was built. Such alignments are consistent with the view that the engineers concerned took account of options for later extensions when planning their routes, and that they optimized the line they built with respect to the line(s) that they planned to build in future.

Finally, it is possible to identify a potential historical turning point at which the evolution of the railway system could have taken a different path, as explained in more detail below.

1.8. THE STRUCTURE OF THE COUNTERFACTUAL NETWORK

There is a great deal that can be learned about the actual system by comparing it, region by region, with the counterfactual. A detailed discussion is presented in Chapter 4, and only the main points are summarized here. It was noted in the introduction that the counterfactual system eliminates duplication of routes, not only for inter-urban trunk lines but also for access lines to mining areas and ports. In some cases the counterfactual simply eliminates a surplus route, leaving the rest of the system unchanged, while in other cases the entire configuration is changed as a result.

One of the 'highlights' of the counterfactual is that a single trunk line runs from London to the north, branching near Rugby to serve Birmingham (to the west), Lancashire and Scotland (to the north-west) and Leicester, Nottingham and Leeds (due north). Scotland is served by a variant of the Caledonian Railway (CR) route from Carlisle to Glasgow, which had a branch from Carstairs to Edinburgh and Motherwell to Stirling, Perth, and Aberdeen. The Glasgow and South Western (GSWR) line through Kilmarnock, and the North British (NBR) Waverley route are downgraded from trunk line status. Hawick and Galashiels are served by a cross-country primary route from Newcastle to Glasgow. The East Coast main line from London to York is downgraded, and altered to run via Spalding and Lincoln, on an alignment proposed in the early 1840s, which better meets the needs of local traffic. There is no trunk line to Birmingham via Banbury. London to Bristol traffic is served by a trunk line spur from the main line between London and Plymouth, while South Wales traffic is routed via Oxford, Cheltenham, and Gloucester.

The routes that are eliminated from the counterfactual are generally the later constructions. This illustrates a general pattern: that earlier routes generally follow better alignments than later competing routes. Being first in the field, their promoters had the widest choice, although there are some cases where the first mover did not appear to choose wisely. A similar pattern was evident in the selection of the Beeching cuts of the 1960s: the lines that were first to be closed were often those that were the last to be constructed, suggesting that they followed inferior alignments.

The counterfactual trunk line system has a striking similarity to the modern motorway network. The lines from London to the north, for example, replicate the M1, M6, and M45 motorways, while the down-grading of the East Coast route is reflected in the relatively lowly status of the A1 road. It is also interesting to note that the counterfactual cross-country system has some affinities with the old Roman Roads—in particular, the Fosse Way. Canal routes are also significant: the London to Bristol line, mentioned above, follows the direct route of the Kennet and Avon Canal rather than more roundabout route of the Wilts and Berks Canal that was favoured by Brunel.

1.9. ENGINEERING FEATS AND OTHER POTENTIAL IMPROVEMENTS

It would be very easy to improve on the performance of the actual network through a number of spectacular engineering feats, such as a Humber Bridge, improving connections from Hull to the south, or a tunnel under Shap Fell, allowing the West Coast main line to pass through Kendal. Such feats would be very costly, however. Although costs of construction are not explicitly considered by the counterfactual, there are specific restrictions on heavy engineering works which are designed to avoid any 'cheating' in the counterfactual specification.

The actual network contains three engineering feats of its own: the Severn Tunnel, north of Bristol, the Tay Bridge, near Dundee, and the Forth Bridge, north-west of Edinburgh. These are all late additions, from the 1870s onwards. At the time the system was being developed in the 1830s and 1840s it was unclear whether such feats would become feasible. Indeed, the first Tay Bridge collapsed, and construction of the Severn Tunnel was nearly abandoned because of water problems. The Forth Bridge was so expensive that four railway companies had to form a partnership to build it. The Severn Tunnel and the Forth Bridge have incurred substantial maintenance costs ever since they were built.

The counterfactual avoids spectacular engineering feats such as the Severn Tunnel and Forth and Tay bridges. It involves only two tunnels through the Pennines, at Standedge and Woodhead, in comparison with the four actually built (the others being Littleborough and Dore and Totley). The only other notable engineering work is a tunnel at Llangurig, east of Aberystwyth. It carries a direct line from Aberystwyth to London via Gloucester. A tunnel at Llangurig was actually proposed, and the approach line partly built, by the ill-fated

Manchester and Milford Railway. The tunnel is not sufficiently long, however, to qualify as a major engineering feat.

If the Severn Tunnel and the Forth and Tay bridges had been included in the counterfactual then local services in the areas concerned—Bristol, South Wales, and Fife—would have been significantly improved, but 'knock on' benefits for the rest of the system would have been relatively small. The configuration of neighbouring parts of the counterfactual system would have changed quite significantly, as a result of 'fine tuning', but the improvement in overall performance would have been surprisingly small. This is consistent with the view that some of the major engineering feats on the railway system were driven by the engineering profession's desire for public recognition and by companies' concerns to build shorter routes than their competitors; Parliament was happy to authorize these schemes because they were privately financed and brought political benefits through enhanced national reputation for engineering excellence, even though the public benefits were fairly modest.

There are other improvements which could have been made but which are objectionable on environmental grounds. A London Central station would have improved London's performance as a passenger hub, but valuable amenities such as Hyde Park or Regent's Park would have been destroyed in the process. While the counterfactual rationalizes the provision of termini in large towns and cities, it avoids environmentally destructive schemes. Indeed, by concentrating traffic on a smaller number of better-used lines and reducing the number of hubs, the counterfactual ameliorates the negative environmental impact of the railway system as a whole.

1.10. EXPLAINING THE INEFFICIENCIES OF THE ACTUAL SYSTEM: EXCESSIVE COMPETITION

Given that 20,000 miles of railway were constructed when only 13,000 miles were required, a considerable waste of resources was incurred. The capital invested in the 7,000 surplus miles could have been put to other uses. Given the finite capacity of the construction sector, a small network could have been completed more quickly than a large network, generating transport benefits sooner. Once construction had been completed, workers could have been redeployed to other uses. Canals and coastal shipping could have enjoyed a longer life, and roads could have been improved at an earlier stage.

The reduction in route mileage effected by the counterfactual is reflected in lower estimated construction costs. However, the reduction in construction costs is somewhat lower than the reduction in route mileage because, although the counterfactual employs a smaller proportion of trunk lines than the actual system, it also employs a lower proportion of purely local lines. This is because many rural lines in the counterfactual form part of cross-country through routes, and are therefore engineered to convey through traffic at a reasonable speed. Estimates of construction cost for different types of line can be obtained from evidence relating to the actual system: engineers' reports, contractors' tenders, and final construction costs as reported in annual company accounts. Allowing for estimation error, it seems likely that the cost per mile of constructing the counterfactual would have been, on average, no more than 10 per cent higher than the cost per mile of the actual system. Thus substantial capital cost savings, of the order of 25 per cent or more, could have been achieved.

The social savings approach, which has dominated previous studies of railway investment, is mainly concerned with investigating, and then de-bunking, exaggerated claims about the impact of railways on the macroeconomy. It passes judgement on the railway system, with early studies claiming that the equivalent of only a few year's annual economic growth was generated by railway investment. Later assessments, however, that take account of time savings and benefits to the location of industry, are more favourable (Leunig 2006). The objective of the present study, however, is not merely to pass judgement, but to explain how and why the railway system evolved in the way that it did.

Had the actual system been shown to be efficient, it would be easy, in principle, to explain the result in terms of a well-functioning market system. Explaining the enormous waste is more problematic, however. A detailed comparison of the actual and counterfactual system reveals a single systematic factor that explains most of the waste: namely, excessive competition. 'Excessive', in this context, means competition which is so intense that it generates significant social costs.

The roots of competition lay in the towns. Although an urban elite was sometimes divided into factions by religion or party allegiance, a common set of economic interests, combined with a pragmatic outlook, often sustained a united front at the local level. Provision of local infrastructure—water, sewage, gas, bridges, harbour improvements, regeneration of slums—all required cooperation, and provision of a railway was just another example of this (Chalklin 1998). Some towns, such as Chester, Shrewsbury, and York, showed great initiative in attracting lines which would turn their city into a railway hub; in some cases they even provided land for a joint station to facilitate this.

The promoters of the earliest trunk lines, such as the L&MR, GJR, GWR, and the LBR, were interested mainly in intercity traffic, and in the traffic of the region as a whole. They paid little head to towns of modest size, because they planned to access traffic through the railheads along their route. The LMR bypassed Warrington and St. Helens, the LBR bypassed Northampton, the GJR bypassed Stoke-on-Trent, and the GWR bypassed the textile district around Trowbridge. A high proportion of towns were therefore left off the early 'railway map'.

The cheapest remedy for a bypassed town was a branch line, but towns which were not satisfied with a branch could promote their own intercity route, passing through their town, on which trunk traffic would supplement purely local traffic. A large number of dissatisfied towns led to a large number of such proposals, and that is how the Railway Mania of 1844 got underway.

At the time of the Mania, Parliament and the Board of Trade were well aware that the duplication of railway routes was wasteful. But MPs were reluctant to choose between rival schemes, for fear of favouring one town over another. When they refused to authorize any scheme from a set of competing schemes, as they often did at the outset of a contest, the rival promoters were encouraged to merge their interests. This stimulated cooperation between neighbouring towns and encouraged ambitious integrated regional schemes for serving them all. Under the leadership of Edward Denison, MP, for example, towns in Lincolnshire successfully merged their interests into the Great Northern Railway (GNR). The GNR illustrates clearly the benefits to be achieved from inter-urban cooperation when it could be made to work.

In 1845, as the Mania approached its height, the Railway Committee of the Board of Trade, under Earl Dalhousie, the future Governor-General of India, published a set of recommended regional railway systems, which were compiled by selecting a small proportion of the many schemes submitted to Parliament that session. Initially MPs followed the recommendations of the Railway Committee, but when they realized how unpopular their decisions had become—because of the large number of schemes they rejected—they changed their attitude. They challenged the impartiality of the Railway Committee, denounced its members as arrogant bureaucrats, and resolved not to take such advice in future. As a result, in the following year MPs authorized far more schemes than they would have done had they followed the principles adopted by the Railway Committee.

The simplest explanation of MP's behaviour is that they tacitly colluded to reject proposals which would have denied railway access to important towns, or placed some towns at a serious disadvantage relative to their neighbours. In a classic 'log-rolling' manoeuvre, they collectively protected their local reputations as champions of the local railway schemes in order to safeguard their electoral popularity. In doing so, they sacrificed both national and regional interests to local populism. For, following the collapse of the Mania, many towns failed to get the railways that they had been promised.

The failure of Parliament to ration the number of railways authorized meant that the burden of effective rationing fell upon the capital market (Lewin 1936; Parris 1965). A crisis in the short-term capital market, aggravated by other factors, such as the Irish famine, meant that many shareholders in the new railway companies could not afford to pay their calls. Had they done so, there would not have been enough navvies, or sufficient supplies of construction materials, to carry out the work. Many companies failed, most scaled down their plans, and a few completed their plans but with considerable delay (up to 10 years). All that was salvaged from many ambitious regional schemes was a branch from the largest town to the nearest existing line. This legacy explains why so many trunk lines in the UK passed through a succession of country junctions at which short branches deviated to serve nearby towns.

As the surviving Mania lines were completed, competition between routes began to intensify. A fundamental feature of any transport network is that as the number of individual linkages increases, the number of alternative routes between pairs of locations increases too. Railway routes that originally enjoyed monopoly power began to acquire competitors. Because the early trunk lines were often built as 'direct lines', they generally remained the shortest, but longer alternatives were often perfectly adequate so far as freight traffic was concerned. The longer the route, the greater the range of alternatives: thus the CR, which thought it had a monopoly of Anglo-Scottish traffic when authorized in 1844, soon found that it faced competition from both the GSWR and NBR companies (Gourvish 1972).

By 1860 most towns with a population of 3,000 or more were served by a railway. But substantial inequalities remained in railway provision. In particular, towns that were served by two or more railway companies had lower fares and freight charges than those served by a single company. While Poole was well served by railways, for example, its inhabitants were aggrieved at the high fares charged by the LSWR; they envied the inhabitants of towns such as Salisbury which were served not only by the LSWR but also by the GWR (Popplewell 1986). Demand for a second railway encouraged the promotion of cross-country routes to supplement the trunk lines and branches already constructed; the proposed cross-country lines intersected main lines radiating from London and helped to join up isolated branches to each other.

Most cross-country lines were not a commercial success, however (Popplewell 1986). The builders of a cross-country route were often confronted by obstruction from established companies in the areas they planned to serve. The established companies sought to deny the cross-country lines access to their regional hubs, and thereby increased their costs by forcing them to build their own system of local lines as well. If the invading railway could not afford to do this then it was effectively starved of local traffic.

Once the boom of 1861–66 had subsided, the companies turned their attention to alleviating bottlenecks on the busier parts of the network, and improving their stations in the major urban centres. Shortly before the main line system achieved maturity in 1914, the GWR improved its main lines to Birmingham and the west of England, and the Great Central Railway built its London extension. By the end of the epoch, the companies had returned to their original strategy— defending regional monopolies and competing with each other for the London traffic.

1.11. LINES THAT WERE NEVER BUILT

While excess competition may offer a plausible account of why excessive mileage was built, it is not immediately obvious how it explains the fact that some highly desirable lines were never built. The counterfactual implies that 11,000 miles of the 13,000 miles that should have been built corresponded to lines that were actually built: the remaining 2,000 miles correspond to lines that ought to have been built but never were. In fact, the excess competition thesis can explain this inefficiency too.

The basis of the explanation is that Parliamentary Select Committees found it very difficult to make correct decisions between rival schemes. Competition created confusion, and members' judgements were often flawed. MPs strove to maintain an appearance of competence and integrity in dealing with complex issues, but in practice they usually fudged the issues in a predictable way. The established railway companies understood the biases in Parliamentary judgements, and exploited them wherever possible. It was not the merits of individual schemes, but the sophistication of a promoter's Parliamentary tactics, that often won the day.

Experienced companies understood that bills that were unopposed would usually be passed, but that contested bills would rarely pass at the first attempt. Where opposition to a railway scheme came purely from landowners, an experienced promoter with 'deep pockets' would buy off all the opposition in advance (Brunel 1843). The promoter would know how much to pay in the light of the saving of time and expense in Parliament the following year. Inexperienced promoters, and those with limited capital, would argue their case in Committee, but if their advocate was inexperienced, and their opponent an aristocrat, their prospects would be poor.

The promoter might do better at a second attempt, but by then other promoters could have spotted the same opportunity. A profitable promotion would therefore attract competitors, and only an unprofitable scheme would remain unopposed. Based on the degree of opposition, therefore, an unprofitable scheme was more likely to succeed in Parliament than a profitable scheme. The survival of the unprofitable helps to explain why paternalistic aristocrats were able to build uneconomic rural branch lines—and to lose a lot of their money in the process. At the same time, profitable schemes were lost through rivalries which enriched the engineers, solicitors, and advocates, but produced no useful outcome (Kostal 1994).

Exploiting the same principle, an established company threatened by an invading scheme would put up a 'me-too' bill to confuse the issue. The established company would argue that they should be authorized to build the line in order to maximize network externalities—they could connect the line more easily to the lines they already operated. If they won the argument, they would refuse to build the line, because their strategy was just to stop the invader and not to serve the district better. When the LBR attempted to expand towards Cheltenham, into GWR territory, for example, the GWR put up a me-too bill. The GWR's scheme was authorized, but never built. Although a line from Oxford to Cheltenham is a trunk-line component of the counterfactual network, and part of the main line from London to South Wales, such a line was never built despite repeated attempts. The GWR already had a line from London to Cheltenham via Swindon and Gloucester, and had no intention of building another line that would, in the words of its Chairman, just 'compete against itself' (Gooch 1972).

1.12. HUBS IN THE WRONG PLACES

It was noted above that the concept of network externalities was well understood by early railway promoters. During the Railway Mania a number of very ambitious schemes were promoted—such as the Welsh Midland Railway from Swansea to Birmingham via Leominster—which are better regarded as regional networks than as single lines. The ambitious scope of a Mania proposal is often indicated by its name. Many of these schemes involved systems with a central hub.

Robert Stephenson produced a number of regional schemes. He often placed a four-way hub at the centre of his network; most of his plans are Steiner-compliant, in the sense that the hub has a distinctive orientation and the lines cross at about 60° rather than 90°. Despite his eminence, Stephenson's plans were not particularly successful. Some lost out to rival schemes, and others had to be scaled down because they were too ambitious. Perhaps the best example of his work was the York–Driffield–Selby–Hull system in East Yorkshire, which had a four-way hub at Market Weighton. It was eventually built in full, although most of it was closed down during the Beeching cuts of the 1960s.

The construction of integrated regional schemes was encouraged by the Railway Committee of the Board of Trade, although this did no good for the promoters of such schemes for, as we have seen, Parliamentary support for the Railway Committee soon evaporated. Some of these schemes were seen, rather cynically, as just an attempt to monopolize a region by courting favour with the Board of Trade. Had they been pursued, however, the results would certainly have improved upon what actually occurred.

A feature of these integrated schemes is that they often involve hubs in relatively isolated places. Market Weighton is not the obvious place to site a hub, and neither are some of the other hubs that Stephenson proposed, such as Verney Junction, in the heart of rural Buckinghamshire. The obvious explanation is that Stephenson was considering a private hub that would be monopolized by a particular company, rather than a public hub shared by independent users.

A private hub is, of course, a rational way for a private company to extract economic rent from network externalities. It is therefore not surprising that the isolated monopoly hub was widely used in practice: for example, at Crewe, Swindon, and Ashford. This desire for monopoly also explains why companies sought to deny other companies access to their hubs: thus while the GWR obtained access to Crewe, via Market Drayton, it was against the wishes of the London and North Western Railway (LNWR), which was the dominant company at Crewe.

Another practical reason for locating hubs in isolated areas was that more logical locations for hubs could not be made to work. Many of the great industrial centres, such as Manchester, Leeds, and Birmingham, are natural hubs. Indeed, they became great centres because of their hub potential in the age of roads and canals. But none of the railway companies was able to monopolize them. As great centres they attracted rival companies, and the interests of the town lay in cultivating competition, as explained above. Each company drove independent lines into the city and built its own terminus, or shared a terminus with its smaller allies. Manchester had four major stations, Leeds three, and Birmingham two. Each major company wanted to control its own station in order to promote its image and to avoid direct competition with other companies' trains. The costs of making connections between different stations discouraged passengers from changing trains at major urban hubs. This suited the railway companies, because it allowed them to control a passenger's journey, by ensuring that they changed to another of the company's trains at a monopolized hub.

1.13. THE SIGNIFICANCE OF CROSS-COUNTRY LINES

A major strength of the counterfactual system is that it provides a far better set of cross-country lines than the actual system. The actual system required many cross-country passengers to travel up to London to make connections. Passengers could have completed a cross-country journey by switching from one company's lines to another's, but their journey would have been a difficult one. Connections were not timetabled in a convenient way, changes of station at intermediate towns would be required, and many of the trains would have been slow.

The weaknesses of the cross-country system in the UK are easy to explain. The earliest trunk lines naturally sought to monopolize the most profitable traffic, and for many promoters this meant the last 50 miles or so of a route into London. Several major trunk line schemes of the 1830s approached London from different points of the compass. Once they had secured their entry into London, they expanded their systems with feeders, to lengthen the catchment area from which they could gather traffic, and built branches to broaden the catchment areas to either side of their line.

So far as these companies were concerned, any project that drew off traffic from their network before it reached London was to be resisted at all costs. The network existed to channel traffic onto this crucial section of track from which the bulk of the profit would be made. Cross-country schemes would do just this. As trains approached Watford on the LBR, Reading on the GWR, or Basingstoke on the LSWR, traffic might be siphoned off instead of continuing through to London. If there was one thing on which all the major companies were agreed, it was that cross-country schemes promoted by independent companies should be opposed. It has already been noted that opposition was normally sufficient to delay a scheme; concerted opposition from a number of established companies was normally sufficient to kill it off.

The principal long-distance cross-country line prior to 1860 was the Midland Railway (MR) line from Bristol to Leeds via Birmingham and Derby. After 1860 a number of other cross-country routes were constructed, though to a more modest specification. As already explained, the attitude of the towns was crucial to this. They wanted cheaper fares, and believed that a second railway serving their town was the answer. Parliament agreed with the need for more competition, but wished to avoid the duplication of lines. Cross-country routes were the obvious solution. They would intersect the trunk lines radiating from London, rather than replicate them. They could link up rural towns and subsidize local traffic by carrying long-distance traffic too.

The companies were sympathetic because they saw cross-country routes as a means of gaining access to additional traffic: it was not so much the traffic along the route that appealed to them as the traffic at the end of it. The MR's support for the Somerset and Dorset Joint Railway (SDJR), for example, was stimulated by the prospect of holiday traffic to the South Coast, while the GWR's support for the Didcot Newbury and Southampton Railway (DNSR) was based on the expectation of access to Southampton docks traffic.

Companies recognized that invading each other's territories would invite reprisals. The SDJR was an invasion of GWR territory, while the DNSR was an invasion of LSWR territory. The companies took the view that, with mergers ruled out by Parliament, competition was inevitable and they simply could not help themselves. Each company's strategy was to compete more fiercely than its rivals.

Nevertheless, the financial results, as might be expected, were rather poor. While the MR expanded successfully in the 1870s and 1880s, some of its schemes were better conceived than others. The SDJR linked the Midland main line to Bristol with the LSWR network near Poole, giving the two partners a bridge to each other's network. The SDJR bridged hostile GWR territory, however, and so had no connection to the GWR main line that it crossed, and was obliged to replicate parts of the GWR network. The line also served the Somerset coalfield, however, and, though expensive to operate, carried a reasonable amount of traffic.

When the MR and GNR invaded Great Eastern Railway (GER) territory on the north Norfolk coast neither partner had access to a local network, and so they had to create their own system of branches to serve the principal towns and holiday resorts, at considerable cost. The only compensation was that most of the traffic originated in the Midlands rather than in Norfolk, so that poor connections to the GER were not a serious issue.

Independent cross-country lines in which the major companies had no stake tended to fare much worse because they had no guaranteed access to traffic at either end of the line. The independent Midland and South Western Junction Railway (MSWJR), for example, was entirely dependent on the MR for connecting traffic at Cheltenham, and on the LSWR for traffic at Andover. The Stratford-on-Avon and Midland Junction Railway (SMJR) was in an even worse position, because it was dependent on the MR for traffic from the Bedford direction to the east and the Gloucester direction from the west. Unfortunately, the Midland has its own line from Bedford to Gloucester too; the only advantage to the SMJR was that its line was much shorter than the Midland link via Birmingham.

The promoters of cross-country lines seem to have anticipated some of these problems. The lines were often built with only single track, though the earthworks sometimes provided for two. Few expresses were run, and stopping trains were extremely slow, so that passengers gained little time over going via London. In the counterfactual system, the cross-country lines are built to a higher standard, in the expectation of greater traffic, which would be attracted by the higher speed that is possible.

A modern reader, looking at a Bradshaw map of the railway network in 1914, and seeing a dense web of lines criss-crossing the country, might conclude that provision for cross-country travel was much better than what has been suggested above. Close examination of the timetable would reveal, however, that many of the cross-country links were not actually connected up. For example, the LNWR and Great Northern Railway (GNR) branches to Dunstable met end-to-end, but there was no through service for many years; the small village of Ramsey, near Huntingdon, had two separate branch lines, leaving the village in different directions, one owned by the GNR and the other by the GER, each with its own terminus; and so on. Railway companies were so keen to defend their regional frontiers that if a neighbouring company built out a branch towards their territory they would build out in the opposite direction towards their rival's territory. The branches met in order to neutralize each other, and not to provide a through service. A through service was the last thing the companies desired, as it would have given each company's captive customers access to an alternative route.

1.14. PATH DEPENDENCY

The evolution of networks is often described as a path-dependent process, in which the network gets 'locked in' to a particular trajectory of development. Could path dependence, rather than excessive competition, explain the inefficiency of the UK railway system?

Network externalities mean that it is natural for the promoter of a new line to connect their line to the system that already exists. To leave their line isolated could deny it access to a great deal of traffic. It is, however, possible to design a railway to connect with another railway that is about to be built. This was quite common at the time of the Railway Mania: many Mania schemes were predicated on connecting up to other Mania schemes. Furthermore, it is also possible to build a railway in anticipation of future railways that will be built. We have already seen that the promoters of early trunk lines, such as the LBR and the GWR, built in 'real options' for the extension of their networks. This was perfectly natural as there were no other railways in the area with which they could connect their lines.

The obvious disadvantage of building a line to connect with a future railway is that the railway concerned may never be built. Even if it were built, there could also be delays in its completion, so that revenue from feeder traffic would be delayed. This was, indeed, the fate of many Mania lines. Path-dependence therefore emerges as a consequence of individual insurance policies, where new lines are built mainly to connect with existing lines.

If railway lines were liable to close down almost as soon as they were built, then connecting to an existing line would offer only limited insurance, however. But British civil engineers built their lines to last—their lines were not just strategic transport links, but monuments of empire and testaments to personal engineering skill. The construction costs were sunk—they could not be recovered if the line was closed (apart from iron bridges, which were used for scrap). As the network expanded, some lines became obsolete, however—for example, the Birmingham and Derby Junction line from Whitacre to Hampton-in-Arden—but most were simply downgraded to local use rather than closed altogether. It was not until the Beeching cuts of the 1960s that wholesale closures occurred. Closures were so unusual that promoters could count on existing railways staying open—indeed, building a connection to a line would improve its chance of survival by bringing extra traffic to it.

Path dependence can explain the alignments of many branch lines. It has already been noted that many branches were built in the aftermath of the Railway Mania to salvage something from more ambitious schemes. The branch was built to the nearest trunk line, and so the alignment of the branch is determined by the alignment of the trunk line that was built before.

The early trunk lines, in turn, were built to connect the major urban centres. Because these lines avoided some important towns en route, hubs developed at some distance from these towns. But had these towns been on the line from the start, and prospered more, traffic congestion might have required a bypass, which could have followed the alignment of the direct route. Thus the direct lines might still have been built, but at a later date. Indeed, the counterfactual provides several bypasses of this kind, although not so many as the actual system. Path dependence may therefore alter the sequence in which lines are constructed, but it does not necessarily alter the final outcome.

Because the resources available for railway construction were limited at any one time, railway construction was inevitably a sequential process. It was efficient to construct the system by developing new connections from the lines already built. But it does not follow that initial choices of alignment completely dictated the system's final form. These initial choices may have affected the sequence of construction, rather than the selection of lines that were finally built. Path dependence can explain a number of local features of the network, but it cannot explain why the network was so much larger than it needed to be. The trunk lines that formed the basic skeleton to which Mania lines were added were an adequate solution to inter-urban traffic needs of the country. It was the competition between the towns, reinforced by competition between the major companies, and not path-dependence, that explains why the network grew as large as it did.

1.15. REGULATORY FAILURE: THE POLICY ISSUES

Given the enormous waste that was incurred in developing the railway system through private enterprise, it is tempting to suggest that planning would have been a much better solution. Nationalization of the railway system was an option provided for in Gladstone's Railway Act of 1844. There are a number of well-known arguments against the state planning of the railway system, but their force is easily exaggerated (Gomez-Ibanez 2003). The issues are examined in detail in Chapter 6, and only the main points are noted here.

Parliamentary rhetoric at the time emphasized the British genius for private enterprise. By contrast, state planning was the method favoured in France. Cultural commentators today often suggest that what may work in France will not work in Britain, but in the 1830s and 1840s the argument was rather different. France had been defeated in the Napoleonic Wars, and its state apparatus had been shown to be deficient. Even if its methods could be transferred to Britain, there was no point in doing so, because the French system had been shown to be inferior to the British one.

Some railway historians have suggested that the use of state planning would have delayed the establishment of the railway system, and thereby retarded the growth of the economy. It is certainly true that early projects such as the LMR would probably not have gone ahead without private capital. But by 1840 many people had come round to the view that railways were the technology of the future. It was pointed out in Parliament that while the promoters of the first railways had earned their high returns by shouldering serious risks, after 1840 many of these risks had disappeared. Few doubts were expressed that the industrial system required a railway network, and that railways were superior to both roads and canals for carrying heavy loads (Alderman 1973). Steam locomotive technology was no longer in the experimental phase: the only question was how much further improvement it was capable of. This analysis suggests that while private enterprise may have been important in 'kick-starting' the railway system, it was unnecessary for its subsequent development. Railways could have been nationalized in 1844 (or later) without adverse effects, provided that state purchase of existing railways had been made on reasonable terms.

Provided the railways had broken even after interest charges had been paid, there would be no burden on taxation. Government borrowing would have increased, but private borrowing would have diminished by a similar amount. Private individuals could have invested in additional government stock instead of railway shares, providing them with much greater security. The redistribution of income from naïve investors to street-wise lawyers, which occurred at the time of the Railway Mania, would have been avoided.

Another objection to state planning is that the configuration of the railway system would have been dictated by military needs. There is no direct evidence to support this view, however. Military considerations influenced the structure of the network anyway. The importance of linking up the naval ports along the South Coast was mentioned by promoters of relevant private schemes. The Chester and Holyhead Railway was offered a subsidized mail contract in order to promote improved communication between England and Ireland—partly to encourage Irish MPs to attend Parliament in London, and partly to expedite the movement of troops to Ireland in case of unrest. The Admiralty imposed restrictions on the building of bridges over estuaries where they believed that they could impede naval traffic (and commercial shipping). The proposals made by the Board of Trade did not attach undue emphasis to military requirements, and there is no reason to believe that a more formal planning system would have done so either.

1.16. RELATIONS BETWEEN PARLIAMENT AND THE BOARD OF TRADE

It should not be inferred, however, that the entire system of railway promotion was flawed. The system of appraising railway projects through Select Committees was a tried and tested system that had been used previously for turnpike trusts and canals. Parliament was broadly sympathetic to innovation, but interference with private property rights through compulsory purchase of land was a serious business, especially when it was to be done for private profit. Parliament needed to be certain that a major infrastructure project like a railway would benefit the public. It is not unduly fanciful to suggest that Committees attempted an early form of social cost–benefit analysis. Before recommending a project they needed to be sure that the project was adequately capitalized (so that construction could be completed), that it would be profitable (so that its operation would continue) and that the public would benefit (so that charges must be capped to prevent the undue exploitation of monopoly power). Nothing would be worse than to authorize an interference with private property only to leave a legacy of unfinished or derelict works. Once Parliament was satisfied about the benefits, MPs were happy to override objections from landowners and other interested parties.

The flaw in the system was specific—not general. MPs did not fully understand that because of network externalities, the net benefits of different lines are not simply additive (Klein 1998). Parliament was committed to a process of examining one project at a time, or at most grouping bills into directly competing sets. This procedure is adequate when projects are independent, and their benefits additive, but not otherwise.

The Board of Trade Railway Committee wanted to change this process to take account of a whole range of potential interdependencies between alternative schemes by considering them simultaneously. The Railway Mania provided a wonderful opportunity to do this, since almost every plausible scheme was proposed at that time. But Parliament was committed to its legal traditions, which required hired advocates to present each contested case and then to cross-examine the witnesses of the other party. This process was far too tedious, and expensive, to permit a simultaneous examination of all the leading schemes.

MPs described the procedures of the Board of Trade as 'secretive' because the Board conferred with parties who had not yet submitted their plans while declining to be lobbied by those who had already submitted their plans. No provision was made for the used of hired advocates. The MPs argued, in effect, that inarticulate entrepreneurs were being penalized because they could not hire a legal advocate to explain the merits of their schemes to the Board, or the shortcomings of rival schemes. The Board, of course, argued, quite correctly, that they did not have the time to listen to all these explanations and to write their reports as well. The Board preferred written evidence to oral evidence, while MPs took the opposite view.

Finally, it must be recognized that even after the passage of the Reform Act of 1832, MPs were still predominantly local landowners and country gentleman, who often had limited interests in wider issues of national policy. They seem to have thought of their own constituency as a relatively self-contained community, which needed to be in contact with London, for reasons of political representation, but which did not really need to be in contact with other local towns, which were often seen as rivals in the provision of local markets. The intellectual elite of mathematicians, statisticians, and engineers who were recruited to the secretariat of the Board of Trade adopted a rationalistic view of national policy that was alien to many local MPs. While there were strong political leaders in Parliament, these leaders were not always able to promote a national view of railway policy. They were often preoccupied with other issues, and had to buy support for their positions on these issues by sacrificing national policy interests on more minor issues of local policy such as the authorization of railway bills. Even if the railway system had been nationalized, as Gladstone wanted it to be, the parochial outlook of MPs might still have dictated railway policy. While nationalization would undoubtedly have strengthened the administrative powers of the Railway Committee of the Board of Trade, MPs would have remained free to meddle in railway affairs through Parliamentary debate, and to subordinate national interests to local ones.

1.17. CONCLUSION

The Railway Mania was a time of missed opportunities. Almost every railway built in the UK between 1844 and 1914 was submitted to Parliament, in one form or another, at the time of the Mania. Nearly all the schemes proposed in later years were anticipated by one or more Mania schemes. Some were direct derivatives, based on reworking the earlier plans and sections; many branch line proposals, for example, were drastically scaled-down versions of earlier more ambitious schemes.

Had the discipline of social cost–benefit analysis been adopted systematically at the time of the Mania, a much more efficient railway system would have been created. Parliamentary Committees struggled to implement these principles, but their methods, based on oral testimony and adversarial cross-examination, were unsuited to the task. It was difficult to appreciate how railway schemes in different regions complemented one another when schemes were considered on a local basis.

MPs were unwilling to take tough decisions on rival schemes when the interests of different towns were at stake because they wished to preserve their popularity with their local constituents. MPs rejected the opportunity to take advice from the Railway Committee of the Board of Trade on a regular basis because, they said, they distrusted intellectual bureaucrats and disapproved of the secrecy of the Committee's deliberations. The Committee were concerned with an overarching national interest, while MPs were concerned with the reconciliation of conflicting local interests. The Committee saw the selection problem as a technical issue, to be decided by applying rational principles to documentary evidence, while MPs believed the issue should be resolved by persuasion, involving public debate conducted through hired legal advocates.

After the collapse of the Railway Mania in 1846, commentators highlighted the capital losses sustained by shareholders, and the enormous expenditure on legal fees. They denounced Mania schemes as dishonest, whereas, in fact, most of the schemes were honest attempts to meet the commonly agreed requirements of the regions they planned to serve. The term Mania created a misleading impression, suggesting that the schemes were foolish and that investors were stupid.

This study suggests that the failings of the Railway Mania were political and cultural rather than purely psychological. It was bad decision-making, rather than financial speculation, that was the most serious problem. The Railway Mania represented a turning point in the history of the UK railway system. It provided an opportunity for politicians to authorize the planning of a national railway system, and to harness private enterprise for its construction. But Parliament was too weak to reconcile conflicting local interests, and the opportunity was lost. MPs were simply not up to the job of choosing between alternative schemes, and in particular alternative routes between major towns, in terms of national interest. The collapse of the Railway Mania caused private misery for many private investors, and financial ruin for some, but the real tragedy lay in the events that led up to the collapse. The failure of Parliament to establish an integrated national system was the permanent and most serious aspect of the legacy. The counterfactual constructed in the study reveals the enormity of the social cost involved.

2

Railways in the Victorian Economy

2.1. INTRODUCTION

This chapter examines the wider economic and social context in which the Victorian railway system was developed. There is an immense literature on this subject, and so the treatment is necessarily selective, focusing solely on those issues that had a direct bearing on the evolution of the railway system. Because the development of railways was such an important aspect of the Victorian economy, however, both in terms of the resources that it used—land, labour, capital, and technology—and in terms of the amount and variety of the traffic it carried, it is still necessary to cover quite a lot of ground.

There has been considerable controversy over the Victorian economy, with some writers hailing it as a great success and others condemning it as a partial failure. Those who proclaim success often point to the benefits conferred by free markets and liberal economic policies, while those who perceive failure often highlight social rigidities, resistance to innovation, and a preoccupation with the family. Evidence relating specifically to Victorian railways suggests that neither laissez faire economics nor social conservatism were dominant factors. Commitment to free markets was pragmatic rather than ideological, while social conservatism was linked to the quest for status within the local community.

Free market ideology was most important in the early and most intensive phase of railway building, up to 1866. Commitment to free markets was based on the notion that they were well suited, in some sense, to the British character. There was no ideological commitment to the absolute supremacy of private property rights, since railway building relied heavily on state-sponsored compulsory purchase of land.

During the early phase of railway building, social conservatism manifested itself mainly in a preoccupation with local interests, and with the importance of each person playing their appointed role within the local community. This allowed people from very different walks of life to come together to promote a railway for local benefit, each person contributing finance, expertise, or influence according to their social position.

It was not just the expansion of the factory system in manufacturing industries that was the driving force in the growth of railway traffic but also the expansion of the Empire. The consequent growth of international trade encouraged the promotion of railways to link up ports with the major manufacturing and consumption centres.

As the Empire expanded, so attitudes towards it changed. By 1870 the British railway system was approaching completion, and capital which had flowed into domestic railway construction was diverted into investment in Empire instead (Roth and Dinhobl 2008). Along with railway technology, a number of important British institutions were exported to the Empire—law, parliamentary democracy, and the 'British way of life'. The British social elite began to think of themselves less as traders and entrepreneurs and more as imperial administrators. Their socially conservative values were transformed into a system of 'civilization' to be exported to other countries. This concern with civilization may have undermined the dynamism of the earlier entrepreneurial economy, but if so, it came too late to affect the development of the British railway system.

A recurrent theme in Victorian culture is the possibility of improvement—both in economic efficiency and in society. Improvement was effected through a wide variety of different types of project, and the key question was which projects should be undertaken and, in particular, which should be undertaken first. In this context, economic freedom meant the freedom to undertake a project at one's own expense if it seemed worthwhile. If other people believed that they would lose from the project and they refused compensation then Parliamentary authority would have to be obtained.

Pragmatism and localism were the driving forces in project selection. While free trade ideology supported the notion that railways should be privately promoted, it had little influence on which particular schemes were actually built.

Once the railway system had matured, the ideology of imperialism came to the fore. The focus of improvement was no longer the domestic economy but the Empire as a whole. Furthermore, improvement was increasingly understood in cultural rather than economic terms. The promotion of domestic infrastructure projects gave way to the promotion of projects overseas. These overseas projects were increasingly viewed as monuments to British civilization rather than just pragmatic ways of improving the quality of life. In relative terms, domestic manufacturing stagnated, but on the other hand the export of services substantially increased. Enterprise increasingly focused on promoting and financing overseas projects of cultural as well as economic value.

2.2. VICTORIAN INNOVATION

While the factory system was the major technological innovation of the Industrial Revolution (1760–1830), the introduction of railways, and the switch from sail to steam in ocean-going shipping, were the major technological innovations of the Victorian period (1830–1900). It was not so much in manufacturing, but rather in infrastructure, and most particularly in transport and communications systems, that Victorian Britons made their mark.

Steam power was the principle moving force at the end of the Victorian period, just as it was at the beginning, and horses still provided the major motive power on the roads. Although the principles of electromagnetism were discovered in Britain before the Victorian period, it was only after the end of the period that large-scale urban electrification—let alone rural electrification—got under way. Apart from the electric tram, little systematic use was made of electrical power until the very end of the nineteenth century.

It was not only technological innovation that was important in the early Victorian era but institutional innovation too. Entrepreneurial attitudes were not confined to the private business sector; they were also evident in ambitious political leadership, and in the rapidly growing professional civil service.

The Victorians were immensely proud of Britain's (unwritten) political constitution. They created an empire which exported British institutions to many parts of the world—most notably the Indian subcontinent and the large settler economies of Canada and Australia. Having 'learned their lesson' from the American Revolution of 1776, when their principal colonial foundation declared independence, successive British governments administered their empire in a relatively decentralized manner. Although access to imperial markets was restricted, trade within the Empire was largely based on the principles of free trade enunciated by Adam Smith (Mitchener and Weidenmier 2008). The Empire therefore constituted an enormous captive export market for British manufacturing firms, which they accessed through the transport linkages provided by rail and sea. The steady growth of the imperial population, through both natural increase and territorial expansion, coupled with rising incomes in the settler economies, encouraged product innovations. By the end of the Victorian period, British firms exported an enormous range of trade-marked products, especially in sectors such as steam-powered machinery and metal household goods.

Private entrepreneurs did not enjoy particularly high status in Victorian Britain. Indeed, the owners of small firms were often classed as 'tradesmen' and looked down upon by middle class professionals and those with inherited wealth. On the other hand, setting up a business was easy, as regulations were few. A business partnership between a wealthy investor and an enterprising artisan became a widely accepted and very successful business model. But other avenues of wealth accumulation were possible too. The ever-shifting imperial frontier provided potentially 'rich pickings' for soldiers and bounty-hunters. Furthermore, many young men of great ability chose to enter the church in search of spiritual rather than material rewards, with the entrepreneurial risk-takers opting for missionary work overseas.

The principle of partnership was extended during the Victorian period through a series of reforms to company law which made it much easier for large businesses to be incorporated as joint stock companies with limited liability for their shareholders. This in turn increased liquidity in stock markets by making it easier for ordinary people to buy and sell shares in small denominations. This in turn facilitated the growth of large firms.

However, little trust was placed in the law as a means of resolving business disputes. The law had a bad reputation for being slow, complex, and extremely expensive. Many businesses, including quite large businesses, therefore relied on local people to subscribe capital. The family was an important unit of business organization: it was not only the 'moral bedrock' of Victorian society but also a device for building trust between partners in a business. Many large businesses remained under the control of family dynasties, and 'marrying the boss's daughter' was a reliable way of securing promotion in many firms. This illustrates the general point that Victorians invested heavily not only in political institutions but in social and moral institutions too.

2.3. BACKGROUND: KEY FEATURES OF BRITISH ECONOMIC AND SOCIAL DEVELOPMENT, 1825–1914

The period 1825–1914 was a time of considerable political and social change. It began badly: following the end of the Napoleonic Wars in 1815, the economy had entered a serious depression. There were riots in Manchester and other cities. The Duke of Wellington, the hero of the Battle of Waterloo, soon became a most unpopular Prime Minister.

The political situation improved after 1832, when the Reform Act extended the franchise and removed some of the 'rotten boroughs'. But new problems emerged. In Ireland the mismanagement of the famine stimulated calls for Home Rule. Population grew rapidly (see Figure 2.1), and rural poverty was rife. The great industrial cities were insanitary and, as a result, health became a major Victorian obsession. Millions left the land and emigrated to Australia, New Zealand, North America, and elsewhere.

Nevertheless, in comparison with other European countries, the UK remained remarkably stable. The Victorian notion of paternalism encouraged local elites to be responsive to local needs, and many successful businessmen became social reformers. Religion was very important to the Victorians. It provided a bond

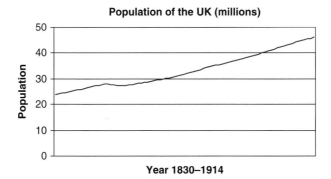

Figure 2.1. Population of the UK: 1830–1914
Source: Officer (2005).

between members of different social and economic classes, particularly in the non-Conformist churches, where artisans and small businessmen could take on responsible roles as pastors. Although there was conflict between different denominations, the Christian ethic was a potent unifying force, promoting relatively high standards of behaviour in both public and private life.

The performance of the economy was steady, if unspectacular, by modern standards. But compared to the relative stasis of medieval and early modern times, growth appears to have been remarkably high. Gross domestic product per head rose from £1,672 in 1830 to £3,911 in 1900 (at 2003 market prices), an average compound percentage growth of just over 1.2 per cent per year (Figure 2.2). Prices were steady throughout the period, apart from cyclical changes caused by periodic booms and slumps (Figure 2.3). The stability of prices helped to sustain relatively low rates of interest. Long-term interest rates were rarely above 3.5 per cent, and in the 1890s fell to below 2.5 per cent (Figure 2.4), although short-term rates were far more volatile, particularly at times of financial crisis, such as 1846 and 1866.

Figure 2.2. Gross domestic product per head in the UK: 1830–1914
Source: Officer (2005).

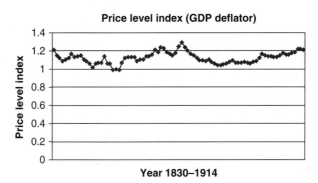

Figure 2.3. Price level in the UK: 1830–1914 (1851 = 100)
Source: Officer (2005).

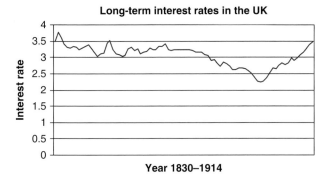

Figure 2.4. Long-term interest rates in the UK: 1830–1914
Source: Officer (2005).

The combination of low inflation and low interest rates encouraged long-term investment. The Victorians were great builders—in almost every sense of the word. They built grand public buildings, which were symbolic of national pride, such as the new Houses of Parliament and, at a local level, they built numerous town halls, and clock towers too. They built institutions—reforming local government and creating numerous local charities; they built an Empire, on which they believed that 'the sun would never set', and—most importantly for this book—they built a massive infrastructure of ports, railways, urban gas and water systems, and so on. This infrastructure supported the evolution of major agglomerations of factories—the specialized industrial districts later described by Alfred Marshall (1923). Thus, despite the apparently modest levels of growth in national income they attained, the Victorians left a valuable and impressive legacy. Although much of this legacy was squandered in the twentieth century in fighting two world wars and defending the Empire overseas, the Victorians built so well that a significant amount of their infrastructure—both social and physical—has survived to this day.

As the Victorian era progressed, entrepreneurs increasingly focused their efforts on promoting large infrastructure projects. This was because factory production became less profitable and infrastructure projects more profitable. In the late eighteenth century, at the start of the Industrial Revolution, infrastructure projects were often undertaken mainly as an adjunct to factory-building. Entrepreneurship was focused on the innovation of the water-powered (and later steam-powered) factory. The building of canals, and the conversion of roads into turnpikes, was useful to entrepreneurs because it reduced transport costs and thereby widened the market for their mass-produced factory goods. Many factory masters therefore invested in canal projects (Pearson and Richardson 2001). By the start of the Victorian period, however, the first major wave of factory-building had come to an end. After the final defeat of Napoleon in 1815, Britain was the master of the seas, and there were major opportunities to extend maritime trade. This encouraged investments in ports and harbours instead.

To realize their full potential, however, ports needed to be connected to the great industrial centres, and canals were proving inadequate for this purpose; they dried up in summer and iced up in winter. Railways were the answer. But it soon turned out that railways could do much more than carry freight; they could carry mail and passengers at unprecedentedly high speed as well. New opportunities for tourism, commuting, and the development of a national system of banking were opened up. Infrastructure projects acquired a life of their own. Cities began to develop as information hubs as well as industrial centres—a function that they had always performed, but which they could perform more easily once long-distance communication had been speeded up.

The social tensions alluded to earlier led to difficult industrial relations in many factory-based industries. British workers valued autonomy—a status very much associated with the skilled artisan—and resented the military-style discipline of the factory. If labour had been cheap then factory owners could simply have ignored the wishes of their workers, but their workers had alternatives to factory employment; not only emigration, but employment in service industries such as transport, retailing, and banking. Factory production became steadily less economic as a result.

Infrastructure, on the other hand, prospered. The British Empire was growing fast, and everywhere there were new opportunities for development. Ports, railways, telegraphs, and urban investments were the key. It was not so much the factory as the engineering workshop that became the hub of British manufacturing. While the factory remained dominant in the textile trades, engineering workshops, and 'yards' were responsible for producing most of the sophisticated machinery that was exported overseas; in particular, ships and steam locomotives, and the pre-fabricated bridges and pipework that were exported for use in overseas projects. By the end of the century the Victorian economy was economically driven by—and dependent upon—the project of Imperialism.

When the Age of Imperialism came to an abrupt end in 1914, the legacy of Victorian enterprise largely ended with it. A whole generation of budding entrepreneurs was wiped out in the trenches of the First World War. Furthermore, the international political instability created by the post-war settlement at Versailles undermined the system of international trade on which the Empire was built. It was not the fault of individual British entrepreneurs that they became locked in to such a vulnerable Imperial system. If there was a failure, it was an over-optimistic belief, encouraged by Britain's political leaders, that the project of Empire would continue indefinitely without disruption.

2.4. ECONOMIC POLICY IN VICTORIAN BRITAIN

It is often mistakenly suggested that Victorian Britain was committed to a policy of *laissez faire*. According to this view, there was a popular belief that the pursuit of profit, constrained only by free competition, would lead to benefits for all;

consequently, state interference was rejected as meddlesome. Under this regime of *laissez faire*, entrepreneurship thrived; the fetters of government regulation were discarded, and the economy 'took off'. But then trade unions appeared, the story goes, and they began to monopolize the supply of labour. Using the political power of the Independent Labour Party, they crushed the spirit of enterprise. The Victorian British economy went into decline, and the responsibility carrying the torch of free enterprise passed to the United States.

There are a number of difficulties with this story. The first involves a question of dates. For a significant period prior to 1830 Britain was at war with Napoleonic France. During this period, government had an active role in stimulating demand for both textiles (e.g. military uniforms) and engineering products (e.g. guns and armour), and when this demand ceased at the end of the war a serious recession ensued. Indeed, some military historians turn the argument around, and maintain that military procurement, by setting challenging targets for entrepreneurs, stimulated investment and innovation in precision-made factory products.

Furthermore, Free Trade was not official government policy until the repeal of the Corn Laws in 1846, and the Prime Minister, Robert Peel, who pushed through this reform, split his political party in the process. Although Richard Cobden, John Bright and other members of the 'Manchester School' had been vociferous lobbyists for Free Trade, it was neither their free market ideology nor the prospective benefit to industry that finally swayed Peel and his followers, but the benefits to the workers themselves. Peel was concerned that the benefit to workers of any reduction in the price of corn would be neutralized by lower wages, and it was only when he was persuaded that wages would remain high because of buoyant product demand that he agreed to the reform (Prest 2004).

Another reason for government involvement in the economy was that many of the major industrial projects in Victorian Britain involved the compulsory acquisition of land. Far from defending individual property rights unequivocally, government presided over a system in which large amounts of private land were acquired, subject to arbitration, on the authority of the state. It is a mistake to assume that, as in the United States, land could simply be acquired by pushing forward the frontier of settlement. By 1830 Britain was already a relatively mature and densely populated country, and government regularly authorized the subordination of private property rights to the public interest.

If there was a governing principle in early Victorian society, it was that advances in technology created the potential for sustained improvement in the standard of living. Unlocking this potential required good institutions, and since not all institutions were fully rational, institutional reform was required. The liberalization of markets emphasized by Smith was only one of the reforms required. It was also important to ensure that the benefits of improvement were fairly distributed between different members of society. Political reform in support of a more just distribution of the benefits of progress was an important aspect of legislation 1830–50.

There was disagreement, however, about how radical the reforms should be. Some people argued that existing institutions must already be rational, in the pragmatic sense that they had 'stood the test of time'. Others argued that they were irrational legacies from the medieval period. Radical populists such as Marx and Engels (both of whom lived in England in the 1840s) argued that technological improvements, by liberating workers from the back-breaking toil of agricultural labour, should allow them to spend more time in rewarding and creative craft production. But factory work was anything but creative and rewarding, they observed—it was repetitive, highly disciplined, and alienating. Having escaped from the tyranny of the local squire, the worker was now tyrannized by the local industrial capitalist instead. Marx and Engels predicted a worker's revolution, but in practice the Chartist Revolution of 1848 quickly fizzled out.

In the 1870s democratic socialists promoted trade unions. The idea was that the trade union would neutralize the power of the capitalist by exercising a countervailing monopoly power through control of the labour supply. The trade union movement gained considerable support after 1880—initially among skilled workers and later among the unskilled as well. By 1900 several industries had become dominated by large and powerful trades unions, some of whose leaders sought to use strike action not only to improve wages and conditions of employment but also to challenge the traditional rights of employers over their workers. In manufacturing, mining, and transport, wage rates rose, basic hours of work fell, and productivity growth stagnated (Broadberry 1997, 2006).

Labour disputes began to polarize political opinion. Some employers turned to confrontation, locking workers out before a strike could take effect, and hiring strike-breakers, while others agreed to conciliation. Some embraced novel forms of profit-sharing and part-ownership with employees, while others emphatically asserted their absolute rights as employers. Government began to legislate over worker's rights and trade union representation, leading to high-profile court cases which resolved the immediate issues but often left more ill-feeling between the parties than there had been before.

By 1900 many aspects of economic life were tightly regulated, and an increasing number of activities, such as education and local transport, were coming under local government control. If there was a period of *laissez faire* in Britain then it was certainly a very short one—say between 1850 and 1880—and even then the economic freedom prevailing in Britain was nowhere as great as the freedoms that existed at this time in the United States.

2.5. DECLINE IN LATE VICTORIAN BRITAIN: MYTH AND REALITY

The zenith of Britain's technological leadership is commonly said to be 1851—the year of the Great Exhibition in Hyde Park, London. The key innovators, it is said, were artisan entrepreneurs who, from the late eighteenth century, had pioneered the mechanized factory system (Deane 1979; Mokyr 2004). International exhibitions became popular attractions in the nineteenth century, attended by increasing numbers of the general public, and after 1851 the success of British entrepreneurs in winning prizes went into decline, while that of United States and continental European entrepreneurs rose.

Not everyone agrees that the decline of Victorian entrepreneurship can be conveniently dated to some time in mid-century, however. An emphasis on economic performance rather than the pace of technological innovation suggests dating decline to the end of the Mid-Victorian Boom and the onset of the Great Depression in 1873 (Church 1975; Saul 1969). Crafts (1985) has taken a more radical view. He argues that the impact of the 'industrial revolution' on British productivity growth in the first half of the nineteenth century has been exaggerated. Mass production was mainly confined to the textile industries of the north: cottons in Lancashire and woollens in Yorkshire. More generally, Pollard (1997) has argued that throughout European history innovations in manufacturing have been concentrated in marginal agricultural areas such as the north of England, where local families combined mixed farming with proto-industrial pursuits. Crafts' view suggests that there was greater continuity between the two halves of the nineteenth century than the traditional view suggests, with a modest rate of productivity growth being sustained throughout.

It is possible that while Victorian enterprise was sustained for longer than previously thought, its direction shifted. As suggested earlier, there was a major shift from developing the resources of the domestic economy into imperial development. Around mid-century growing numbers of the 'middling sort' who aspired to fame and fortune, emigrated to the 'settler economies' within the empire, such as Australia and New Zealand, while the more highly educated joined the growing colonial civil service. On this view, the dynamism of the late Victorian economy shifted to the 'frontier of empire'. Some aristocratic families made a smooth transition into merchant banking, helping to fund the growth of imperial trade and investment from its London hub. The rapid growth of financial services, together with artisan emigration, drew resources away from manufacturing industry. Over-crowding and insanitary conditions in the industrial cities reduced the quality of the manufacturing labour force, fuelled labour discontent, and accelerated the spread of trade unionism to unskilled workers. As a result, the rapid industrialization of the United States, Germany, and other continental European countries exposed the weaknesses caused by low manufacturing productivity growth in Britain.

Schumpeter's (1939) analysis of long waves in the world economy leads to similar conclusions regarding structural change, but by a different route. According to Schumpeter, Britain pioneered not one but two major innovations: first the factory system and then the railways. Since the overseas diffusion of the railway system was a feature of the second half of the nineteenth century rather than the first, this suggests that Britain may have continued to be entrepreneurial, but switched its focus from manufacturing to transport infrastructure and utilities (Broadberry 2006). While early transport investments focused on the domestic economy, later investments were mainly concerned with supporting international trade. Railway technology pioneered in Britain was exported to the colonial frontier. Overseas railway investments were supported by investments in shipping lines, whereby steam-powered vessels provided regular communications with harbours served by local railway. The growing influence of infrastructure investment, and its international orientation, is reflected in the growth of British coal exports to overseas bunkering stations, and the declining proportion of coal output supplied to domestic heavy industry (Church 1986).

Chandler (1990) suggests a different perspective on British decline, however. He claims that British entrepreneurs were slow to make 'three-pronged' investments in marketing, professional management, and organized research that were required for successful mass production. A conservative attachment to the institution of the family firm, and a cult of amateurism in management, made British firms unable to respond to US and German competition in high-technology industries in the late nineteenth century.

An alternative view, however, would suggest that British entrepreneurs neglected investment in mass production manufacturing industry because they perceived more profitable opportunities elsewhere. Economies of mass production, as exemplified by the Chicago meat-packing industry, benefited from cheap unskilled immigrant labour and abundant land—both factors that were missing from Britain, where land was scarce, towns were congested, and most workers aspired to artisan status. Because the territorial area of the UK is so much smaller than that of the United States, British entrepreneurs were more concerned to expand internationally. They needed to invest overseas in a range of colonial markets, many of which were relatively small at the time. As a result, they evolved more flexible managerial forms than the hierarchical Chandlerian enterprise. A good example of a flexible form is the 'free-standing firm', whose operations were based wholly overseas—often in a single country—and which were controlled from a small head office, usually in London (Wilkins 1986; Wilkins and Schroter 1998). A constellation of several free-standing firms provided greater flexibility than would a single hierarchical firm on the US model, managing overseas operations through national subsidiaries. By incorporating each major project as a separate company, financial transparency was increased, allowing shareholders rather than salaried managers to decide whether profits should be re-invested in new schemes.

Olson (1982) offers yet another perspective on the subject. He argues for the institutionalization of collusion as a general cause of economic decline in nations, and he uses Britain as an exemplary case. His focus is on two types of horizontal combination: combinations of workers—namely trades unions—and combinations of firms—namely trade associations and cartels. These combinations are designed to raise wages and prices by eliminating competition; in other words, they are generated by 'rent seeking' rather than 'efficiency-seeking' behaviour (Baumol 1994).

According to Olson, lengthy apprenticeship schemes and restrictive practices reduced occupational mobility. The labour market became segmented into distinctive crafts, with particular types of job reserved for members of particular unions. A social hierarchy of crafts developed, analogous to an Indian caste system. So far as firms were concerned, government became increasingly willing to listen to demands for the protection of domestic and colonial markets. As the international competitiveness of British labour declined, so trade associations became increasingly vociferous. Government failed to take a tough line with firms in mature manufacturing industries that had switched from efficiency-seeking to rent-seeking activities.

2.6. CULTURAL EXPLANATIONS OF ENTREPRENEURIAL DECLINE

Decline in late Victorian Britain is popularly attributed to premature gentrification. In the second half of the nineteenth century, it is claimed, the social gulf between artisans and aristocrats widened. Self-employed artisans and the owners of small family firms could no longer aspire to the 'fame and fortune' which had motivated earlier generations. Wealthy industrialists no longer challenged the aristocracy for political power, but bought into it by investing in country estates.

Wiener (1981) claims that from about 1850 Victorians became increasingly concerned about the adverse moral and social consequences of rapid industrialization. Talented young men preferred to make a career in Church or State rather than 'trade'—religious zeal and social reform provided them with greater emotional satisfaction than what was perceived as the venal pursuit of personal profit. The most prestigious schools and universities in England taught classical studies rather than science and technology, because a knowledge of the Greek and Roman empires was considered to be more relevant for careers in the army, Church, or colonial service. As private enterprise was drained of talent, entrepreneurship declined, the rate of profit diminished and investment was reduced.

Cain and Hopkins (2002), however, believe that the contrast between entrepreneur and gentleman is overstated. They claim that gentleman entrepreneurs have a played a continuous role in British trade and investment from the seventeenth to the twentieth century. They emphasize that the moral and social aspirations which govern gentlemanly behaviour impinge not only on the desirability of a career in trade but also on the way that trade itself is conducted. The gentleman trader likes to trade with people who come from the same social class—who were educated at the same school, served in the same regiment, and whose families are related, if only distantly. A gentleman can enlarge his social circle by being introduced to other gentlemen by a reputable third party. This third party acts as a 'bridge' between the two social circles to which the respective gentlemen belong. High-status women are well qualified to act as 'bridgers', as they have both the opportunity to cultivate social networks and the capacity to offer hospitality on a large scale.

There is a minimum amount of wealth (or credit) that is required to sustain a gentlemanly lifestyle, and marriage to a wealthy heiress—such as the daughter of successful gentleman trader—can augment capital within the business community. Bridgers can therefore play a useful role as marriage brokers.

Gentlemanly capitalism is related to, though not identical with, what Chandler (1990) calls 'personal capitalism'. But while Chandler emphasizes the negative aspects of personal capitalism, Cain and Hopkins emphasize its positive features. Investment in social networks, they suggest, reduces transaction costs. Gentlemanly capitalism was particularly well adapted to the conduct of maritime trade, because merchants required a network of trusted agents in all the major ports with which they were connected. While some cultures were forced to rely on kinship ties to sustain trust, gentlemanly capitalists could rely on regimental loyalty and 'the old school tie' instead (Jones 1998, 2000). Overseas agents could be recruited not just from the extended family but from the wider expatriate community. The honesty of local agents was reinforced by peer-group monitoring within the expatriate community, based around 'the club'.

Gentlemanly capitalism had its political uses too. The values of the gentleman were useful in ensuring integrity in colonial administration. A gentleman had obligations to his social inferiors, which meant that gentlemanly administrators were more likely to pay attention to local needs than officials who saw themselves simply as bureaucrats employed by a colonial power. These values of self-restraint in the exercise of power assisted the growth of empire, allowing it to extend (to some degree) through agreements with native leaders rather than by military conquest.

2.7. THE LEGAL FRAMEWORK OF BUSINESS

The framework of company law within which entrepreneurs operated changed significantly over the Victorian period. In early Victorian Britain firms could obtain joint stock status and limited liability only by Act of Parliament, following the precedents set by the early chartered trading companies. All canal and railway promoters, for example, had to apply to Parliament if they required these privileges. These companies were typically incorporated with a large authorized capital, because additional capital could only be raised by a further Act. Thus most large firms were 'born large'—they did not grow from small beginnings, as happened later. Most small firms were started as partnerships or family businesses, and although they could grow by increasing the number of partners, or extending the family through marriage, etc., there were limits to how far and how fast they could grow. By the end of the century, however, companies could incorporate as joint stock limited liability companies through a simple act of registration. This allowed small firms to grow into large industrial enterprises without a major reconstruction of their capital.

Nevertheless, many family firms remained suspicious of diluting ownership by flotation on a stock exchange. They were also reluctant to delegate entrepreneurial decisions to professional employees, especially, it would seem, when the professional specialists were better qualified than the family members themselves. The predominance of close-held family firms impeded the operation of the market in corporate control alluded to above. The owners of many family firms adopted a dynastic view—treating the firm as they treated their land; as an asset to be maintained under family ownership and control and held in trust for future generations. The eldest son had a customary right to run the business, and an obligation to exercise this right, irrespective of his inclination or his competence. This created an endemic 'succession' problem (Rose 1993), made famous as the 'Buddenbrooks syndrome' of 'rags to rags in three generations'.

2.8. PROJECT PROMOTION AND FINANCE

Projects played a crucial role in the Victorian economy—from small projects such as new factories to large projects such as railways and mega-projects such as new ports, and holiday resorts, and their associated towns. Projects are much more heterogeneous than ordinary economic activities of the kind described in basic economics textbooks—no two projects are ever alike. They have a minimum efficient scale and substantial set-up costs, and a distinctive life cycle of start-up, consolidation, maturity, and decline. Projects are risky, because the set-up costs cannot be recovered if a project fails. While individuals may be able to diversify risks using share portfolios, society is still exposed to systemic risk if a major project fails.

Throughout the Victorian period the projects undertaken by British entrepreneurs became increasingly ambitious. Even the early railway schemes had impressive titles, such as 'Great Western Railway' and 'Grand Junction Railway', and architectural allusions to the Roman Empire and the Egyptian Pharaohs were exceedingly common. While the pace of technological progress in Britain may have diminished as the century progressed, the diversity of the projects, and the locations in which they were based, increased dramatically as the Empire expanded. Victorian enterprise became increasingly focused on managing and financing a range of projects in infrastructure, urban development, shipping, and financial services. These projects involved the use, not only of British resources but also of the resources of colonies, dominions, protectorates, mandates, and independent countries under British influence, all around the world.

These imperial projects were based on domestic blueprints. Transport, communications, utilities, and public services developed in Britain were transferred abroad, being adapted incrementally to foreign conditions. Although these overseas projects sometimes foundered because local conditions were unexpectedly different from those in Britain, the performance of overseas projects often surpassed that achieved in Britain because lessons had been learned from mistakes made in the domestic environment. The Indian railway system, for example, was developed along lines designed to avoid the problems created in Britain by the Railway Mania, and the defective system of government regulation at that time.

Table 2.1 reports the number of Acts of Parliament authorizing large projects over the period 1800–1910. It shows the number of relevant Acts—so-called Local and Personal Acts—classified by type of project. The data presented consist of 10-year averages; the evidence is summarized using a bar chart in Figure 2.5. The table provides an approximate measure of the level and direction of project-centred entrepreneurial activity. No entrepreneur could compulsorily acquire land, or otherwise interfere with property rights, without such an Act. Not all applications for Acts were successful, as opposition from landowners, and the promoters of rival schemes, was often acute. The numbers should be doubled, at very least, to allow for the number of unsuccessful applications. Nor were all the authorized projects successfully completed—many failed, or were scaled down, because of lack of capital.

The table indicates the flow of new projects rather than the stock of existing projects. However, since it also includes authorized amendments to schemes in progress, and changes to the capital stock of existing schemes, the flow at any one time reflects to some extent the accumulated stock. This in turn reflects the fact that entrepreneurship becomes a continuing activity when projects run into difficulties, because judgement must continue to be applied in order to rescue the project from failure.

Prior to 1830, large projects focused on the enclosure of commons and the extension of agricultural estates, together with road improvements effected by turnpike trusts and the building of canals. These reforms improved the productivity of the land, and the local transport infrastructure, providing increased traffic that could be fed into, or distributed by the railway system. Town improvements—such as new slaughterhouses and cattle markets—also helped.

Railway projects 'took off' in the 1830s, with a peak in the 1860s. The first Railway Mania year occurred in the period 1844–46. The railways promoted during this period were authorized with a one-year lag in the period 1845–47. There were 119 railway Acts in 1845, 263 in 1846, and 187 in 1847. Many small investors lost their life savings in the speculation that surrounded the Mania. It was a long time before the public regained its confidence in railway investment, but when it did, a second—less virulent—Mania developed. It began in 1861, when 160 railway schemes were authorized. The number rose to 251 in 1865, falling slightly to 199 in 1866. The Mania ended with the collapse of Overend Gurney bankers in 1866—an apparently respectable firm that had been heavily involved in railway finance.

During the Second Railway Mania, many of the schemes that had failed in the first Mania were re-launched under new names and new management. Some of the schemes were supported by towns that had missed out on the railway altogether,

Table 2.1. Number of Local and Personal Acts of Parliament 1800–1910, classified by type of project, 10-year averages

2.1.1. Projects relating to inland transport

	Railway	Tramway	Road	Canal	River	Drain	Bridge
1800–09	1.2	0	48.9	5.9	2.9	3.4	3.1
1810–19	1.5	0.1	50.6	5.3	1.9	3.5	4.8
1820–29	5.2	0	63.7	3.7	2.8	1.6	6.8
1830–39	18.4	0	41.4	3	2.6	2.5	5.9
1840–49	82	0	13.4	3.8	3.2	3	2.3
1850–59	73.1	0.2	18.8	1.3	4	2.7	2.7
1860–69	144.6	1	11.7	1.4	2.9	4	5
1870–79	81.7	11.7	1.2	1.8	3.4	5.9	4.2
1880–89	70.4	17.9	1.8	1.2	3.2	5.3	4
1890–99	64.1	13.4	0.6	4.1	3.7	3.2	2.7
1900–09	40.4	20.9	0.1	1.4	2.2	3.4	1.4
1910–14	21.8	7.6	2.2	1.4	2.6	5.6	1

2.1.2. Other projects relating to external trade, urban infrastructure, and social improvement

	Harbour	Water	Gas	Electricity	Towns	Social	Other
1800–09	6.4	1.6	0.1	0	9.7	6.3	52.2
1810–19	5.3	2.3	2.2	0	15.4	8.6	55.8
1820–29	5.6	3.1	8	0	16.6	5	11.1
1830–39	8.5	4.4	3.8	0	12.1	3.9	14.2
1840–49	13.7	7.4	7.8	0	18.4	4.7	14
1850–59	10.3	14.7	12	0	17.5	2.2	10.6
1860–69	13.5	19.3	19.8	0	16.3	3.9	10.7
1870–79	15	19.6	22.5	0.1	21.6	12.6	18.5
1880–89	13.5	18.5	12.5	2.4	23.6	15.2	28.6
1890–99	15	25	17.5	11.3	32.6	13	32
1900–09	11.5	20.9	27.2	15	41.3	11.2	30.5
1910–14	10.6	16	24.8	9.2	34.4	8.4	29.8

Source: Compiled from UK Law Commission and Scottish Law Commission (1996) *Chronological Table of Local Legislation: Local and Personal Acts, 1797–1994*, 4 vols, London: HMSO.

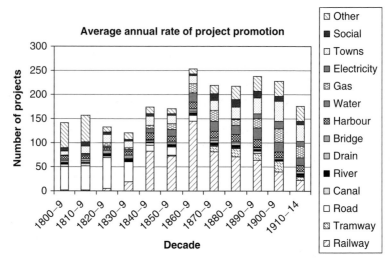

Figure 2.5. Promotion of large projects requiring statutory authorization in the UK, 1800–1914

while other towns encouraged new schemes in the interests of greater competition, which they believed would lead to lower fares and freight rates.

New canal projects were still in progress at the time that the first inter-urban railway—the Liverpool and Manchester—was completed in 1830. This explains the intensity of opposition from canal interests in the early years of railway development. By 1840, however, most canal schemes were either for merger and rationalization or for the conversion of canals into railways. Canal building revived at the end of the century with the construction of the Manchester Ship Canal.

From the seventeenth century onwards, river navigations made a significant contribution to freight transport in Britain, by allowing river traffic to penetrate further inland, thereby connecting the industrial heartlands to the coast. In East Anglia river navigations also assisted the drainage of the fens. The importance of maritime trade to an island such as Britain is underlined by the significant number of port and harbour improvement schemes that were promoted throughout the nineteenth century. The statistics for harbours also include piers built to develop tourism at seaside resorts.

The various types of transport schemes were complementary to each other. Roads fed traffic to the railways, and the railways fed traffic to the ports. The rapid extension of maritime trade in the age of 'high imperialism' after 1870 allowed parts of the railway system to act as a land-bridge between traffic between the North Sea ports on the East Coast, the Channel ports on the South Coast and the Atlantic ports on the West Coast. Even the canals, which competed most directly with the railways, could take slow-moving heavy traffic off the railway and free up railway capacity for higher-value loads.

The social problems of rapid urbanization had become acute by mid-century, not just in the industrial Midlands and north, but in London too. Victorian moral revulsion, particularly at child poverty and the incidence of disease, was translated into practical action in the form of schemes for the piping of fresh water into city centres. These were often allied to river and drainage schemes to carry sewage out to the coast. Control of crime was aided by street lighting. A ready supply of coal, facilitated by the railways, encouraged lighting by gas, both in the streets and in the home. Electrical power was slow to develop, although the switch from horsepower to electric power made the tram an important competitor to the railways so far as suburban transport was concerned.

The concept of 'town improvement' had been a well-established concept in Britain since Norman times (Chalklin 1998). In the eighteenth century spa towns like Bath and Cheltenham, and fashionable resorts like Weymouth, were improved by large-scale property development in the 'Georgian' style. In the early part of the nineteenth century, the provision for the poor, the sick, and elderly, through the construction of workhouses and infirmaries, became a priority. Early railway stations were often on the margins of towns, on low-value marshland, for example, close to cattle markets, gas works, asylums, and gaols. As stations penetrated further into the heart of cities, they became agents of slum clearance (Kellett 1969). Some of the workers expelled from the slums were relocated to new working class suburbs from which they commuted in special workmens' trains. Municipal socialism, which began to flourish in the 1870s, gave an added impetus to town improvement. New urban facilities which had previously been promoted by individual Acts were increasingly promoted with the framework of Local Government Acts, as statutory orders approved by Parliament. Towns and cities extended their administrative boundaries, and often took the initiative for promoting projects away from private enterprise. Many of these towns and cities were controlled by business elites, who used their influence to extend the boundaries of their town and applied the local rates to investments in public facilities which would improve the competitiveness of their town relative to its rivals.

The 'other' category which appears near the bottom of the table contains a diverse and changing mixture of schemes. In the first half of the nineteenth century financial institutions—particularly mutual assurance societies—predominate, while in the second half investment trusts and large industrial enterprises—including several steamshipping lines—come to the fore. Industrial patents and educational institutions are the subject of some Acts. The growing amount of local government legislation described above is also included in this category when it cannot be attributed to any single sector mentioned elsewhere in the table.

The Local and Personal Acts are mainly concerned with projects based wholly in Britain. Projects concerned with colonial development were authorized by the colonial governments, or the Colonial Office, and are not included except in special cases. The substantial growth of overseas projects owned and managed from Britain can be readily documented from other sources, however. Wilkins (1989), for example, offers a comprehensive account of British enterprise in the

Table 2.2. Free-standing railway companies controlling overseas operations from the UK, 1913

Country	Number
Empire	
India	18
Africa	7
Canada	5
Australia	1
West Indies	1
Total Empire	32
Latin America	
Argentina	18
Brazil	9
Chile	7
Uruguay	7
Mexico	6
Colombia	6
Cuba	3
Other (Bolivia, Ecuador, Costa Rica, Peru, Paraguay, El Salvador)	9
Total Latin America	65
Other countries	
Spain	5
Others (one each: United States, China, Burma, Philippines, Turkey, Egypt, Sweden)	7
Grand total	109

nineteenth-century United States. The global spread of Victorian enterprise can be assessed from other sources. Thus Bradshaw's Railway Manual (see Table 2.2) indicates that by 1912 no fewer than 109 large overseas railway systems in 29 countries were owned and managed from Britain; 32 were in the Empire and 65 in Latin America (Bassett 1913, Parts II–IV; a somewhat higher figure is given by Corley 1994). Many of these companies made huge investments, although, because they often acquired control through state concession, they did not always enjoy ownership in perpetuity as with conventional manufacturing investments.

2.9. MINING AS A PROJECT-BASED INDUSTRY

Mining is a classic example of a project-based industry. Coal was a crucial source of power for the Victorian economy, and the UK had abundant reserves of coal. Sinking a new mine was a classic Victorian project.

The Romans mined gold and lead in Wales when they occupied the country. Coal was mined as a substitute for charcoal in medieval times—albeit on a small

scale (Hatcher 1993). The iron-masters of the early Industrial Revolution generated a huge demand for coal and coke, and this stimulated mining on an
industrial scale. Many of the earliest mines were driven horizontally into hillsides,
making it easy to bring out the minerals. Indeed, some of the key components of
railway technology originated in the mining industry, where wooden tramways
were used to transport minerals out of the mine and down to a river or coastal
port.

Even before the Industrial Revolution, coal shipped from Newcastle, in the
north-east, had been widely used for brewing ale and heating the home—especially by wealthy Londoners (Nef 1932). The discovery of iron ore nearby gave a
huge boost to this industry. The Staffordshire coalfield developed as the Midlands
town of Birmingham expanded its speciality metals trades.

Once mineral deposits near the surface had been exhausted, it was necessary to
go further down. Shafts were sunk, and winding gear installed. Pumps were
necessary once the mine went down beneath the water table. The stationary
steam engine was ideal for providing power to a mine—especially in a coal
mine, because the mineral extracted could be used directly as the fuel.
Mounting a stationary steam engine on a colliery wagon was one of the earliest
inspirations for the railway locomotive.

The aristocratic owners of large estates asserted rights to the minerals underneath their land. During the eighteenth and early nineteenth centuries the
aristocracy began to exploit their mineral reserves in a highly organized way
(Ashton and Sykes 1929). Increasingly, the sinking of a coal mine became a major
project. A large tract of land would be required, with not only mineral rights but
also surface rights to facilitate access to the mine, to accommodate spoil heaps,
and to provide washing and processing facilities for the coal. A large amount of
expensive machinery would have to be installed. In remote locations, workers'
housing and village facilities would have to be provided too.

There was no guarantee that the mine would be a success. In the early
nineteenth century the science of geology was in its infancy, and so the volume
of the deposits, as determined by the dimensions of the seams, could not be
known in advance. Unexpected geological faults could always emerge, causing the
mine to flood or the tunnel passages to cave in.

The mineral industry therefore required project-centred entrepreneurship of a
high order. The scale of the investment required meant that coal mining was not
an industry for the 'self-made man' operating on a small scale (Mitchell 1984).
Only a wealthy aristocrat could afford to 'go it alone'—and even such persons
would find their personal resources stretched. For this reason wealthy people
often formed partnerships—sometimes with family members, creating a dynastic
ownership structure. In other cases they made alliances with other families.

Since no single person could possess all the technical expertise required to
operate a large mine, it was the usual practice for the owners to hire professional
managers—the colliery viewers. Viewers were often self-taught, had plenty of
practical experience, and needed entrepreneurial qualities. A successful viewer

was someone who could improvise effective solutions to unexpected problems. Because they were so versatile, colliery viewers often moved around the country, helping to start up mines in new areas. They also transferred their skills to other industries too—thus several viewers from the north—east transferred their skills to the railway industry. The most prominent example was George Stephenson. He took with him not only his familiarity with steam technology but also his ability to recognize the mineral potential of any district in which he worked. One of the skills that commended Stephenson to railway promoters was his skill in assessing the mineral potential of the district through which a railway was intended to pass.

As steamships replaced sailing ships on the main ocean shipping routes, a demand was created for a network of bunkering stations around the world. Ships, like railway locomotives, needed top-quality steam coal, which was only available from a limited number of sources. South Wales was the main source of steam coal. Initially coal was mined in Wales to support the iron industry (centred on Merthyr Tydfil), but as iron ore deposits became exhausted, the coal was increasingly exported to bunkering stations instead. It was this development that led to the enormous expansion of Cardiff (and later Barry) as a port (Church 1986).

In the late Victorian period important coal deposits were identified in South Yorkshire around Tickhill, near the railway town of Doncaster (Buxton 1978). A huge amount of investment went into this coalfield, including the building of several new railway lines. At a time when the British manufacturing industry was losing its global market share, Britain was becoming increasingly specialized in the coal export trade. It is, to some extent, indicative of the relative decline of British manufacturing in the late Victorian period that so little of the newly discovered coal was consumed by domestic industry, and so much of it was exported instead. Because coal of different grades is found in different parts of the world, there is no economic objection to a country exporting coal of one grade and importing coal of another. At the end of the nineteenth century, however, British coal was following British capital in leaving the country. Rather then being channelled into domestic manufacturing, it was employed to support the country's imperial linkages instead.

2.10. RAILWAY ENTREPRENEURSHIP

The railway industry is an excellent example of the finance and management of large projects by Victorian entrepreneurs. Many ambitious railway schemes were developed through visionary foresight. The vision was implemented by entrepreneurs who showed considerable perseverance under difficult conditions. A basic chronology of early railway development is presented in Table 2.3.

It is possible to distinguish five main visions of the railway system in early Victorian Britain.

Table 2.3. Basic chronology of early railway development

Type of railway	Traction	Examples	Date open
Wagon way	Horse	Surrey Iron Railway	1804
Freight railway open to public	Horse	Middleton Railway	1812
Railway with steam traction	Geared locomotive	Stockton and Darlington Railway	1825
Railway open to passengers and freight	Horses plus ordinary locomotives on level plus rope-hauled inclines		
Trunk line: inter urban railway with scheduled passenger service	Ordinary locomotives on level plus rope-hauled incline at terminus	Liverpool and Manchester Railway	1830
Branch line from trunk line to important town		Warrington and Newton Aylesbury Railway Chester and Crewe	1831–40
Connecting line to create long-distance network, but involving change of station and train	Exclusive use of ordinary locomotives running on standard gauge track	Grand Junction Railway from Birmingham to Warrington	1837
Trunk railway from city to metropolis	Ordinary locomotives on level plus rope-hauled incline at terminus	London and Birmingham Railway	1838
Connecting line designed for through running		Birmingham and Derby Junction Railway Midland Counties Railway	1839–40
High-speed trunk railway from city to metropolis	Ordinary locomotives running mostly on almost level track with no tight curves	Great Western Railway from London to Bristol	1840
Extension to lengthen trunk lines		Lancaster and Preston Junction Lancaster and Carlisle Bristol and Exeter	1840–6

(continued)

Table 2.3. (Continued)

Type of railway	Traction	Examples	Date open
Merger of competing lines		Midland (Birmingham and Derby Junction with Midland Counties)	1844
Merger of lines meeting end-on		Midland (Midland Counties with North Midland)	1844–5
		Midland (Birmingham and Gloucester with Bristol and Gloucester)	
		London and North Western	
Extensions to trunk line to create regional networks		Great Western lines to Gloucester, South Wales, Oxford, Banbury, Worcester and Wolverhampton	1844–54
Sideways extensions		Northampton and Peterborough	1845–57
		Wilts Somerset and Weymouth (Chippenham–Yeovil–Weymouth)	
		South Eastern Railway extensions	
Cut-offs		Trent Valley	1847–59
		Churnet Valley	
		Portsmouth Direct	
		Manchester and Leeds (Heywood–Bury–Wigan–Liverpool)	
Long-distance railway network planned from scratch		Caledonian Railway	1848–52
		Great Northern Railway	

- The notion of an integrated national network organized around a central north–south spine was set out by the artisan philosopher Thomas Gray (1825). The proposed technology was not very futuristic, however, being based on the existing mineral railways of the time.
- George Stephenson—the 'father of the railways'—discovered the key combination of components which made possible the modern railway: straight routes on easy gradients, steam locomotive power, and double tracks of iron rails. As a colliery engineer, however, Stephenson always attached considerable weight to the carriage of freight rather than passengers, and the carriage of coal in particular. It was said that Stephenson always looked out for signs of coal deposits when surveying a new line of railway. His vision for the British railway system was once unkindly described as a glorified coal distribution system.
- Brunel provided the grandest vision of the railway system: a high-speed luxury transport system for the social elite (Rolt 1957). The elite would travel over land by rail, and overseas by steam-powered iron-built liner ships, which would connect with trains at the ports.
- Robert Stephenson, George Stephenson's son, believed that every part of the country should have access to a railway. He was interested in the railway as an agent of rural development, and not just as a means of serving industry and commerce (Addyman and Haworth 2005; Bailey 2003). Stephenson's approach was very influential in other countries, but in Britain many of his regional projects achieved only limited success.
- Finally, there was a political vision of a UK bound together by rails. Railways were seen as important in allowing Scottish and Irish Members of Parliament to take up their places in Westminster, and to carry the policies enacted there back to their provincial constituencies. Government therefore intervened to ensure that London was well connected by rail to Dublin and Edinburgh.

Before 1825 the typical railway project involved a short line of wooden rails from a coal mine or quarry to a neighbouring port, river quay, or canal dock, where the cargo would be transferred to water (Lewis 1970). All of this had changed by 1830. Between 1830 and 1860 the promotion of a railway was usually undertaken by a small group of local citizens, anxious to connect their town to a local port or industrial city, or to connect their port or city to London. They would obtain advice on the route from a reputable engineer, and consult a local solicitor about the purchase of land. They would organize a public meeting, chaired by a local dignitary, at which a motion supporting the railway scheme would be proposed. Opponents, such as local landowners, canal proprietors, turnpike trustees, or the promoters of rival schemes, would often turn up and attempt to disrupt the meeting. In this case the outcome could well hinge on a timely intervention from the engineer—a role in which showmen such as Brunel excelled.

A provisional committee would be formed with a mandate to secure an Act of Parliament, until which time the committee would act as a 'shadow' Board of Directors. A 10 per cent deposit paid by investors who had been accepted as prospective shareholders provided these investors with saleable scrip—a tradeable option. Because options were so much cheaper than shares, even household servants and labourers could afford to invest their meagre savings in railway speculation. Once the first trunk lines to London had opened by 1840, it was clear that towns that were bypassed by a railway were destined to decline. Railway promotion now became a civic duty, and towns vied with each other to get themselves 'on the railway map'.

Although the social elites in many towns were split along religious and party lines—for example, Church of England and Non-Conformist, Whigs and Tories—civic pride and collective self-interest were sufficiently strong to unite them. Most of the competition was between towns rather than within towns; where competition arose within towns it was usually because of speculators moving in from outside, as in the case of the London to Brighton line.

Parliament took the view that public benefit was the only reason for interfering with landowners' private property. A railway project afforded a potential 'improvement', and there was a long-standing tradition, derived from earlier forms of improvement, such as land enclosures and canal projects, that the benefits of an improvement should be distributed fairly between the different groups involved. No one should lose out; thus if a loss were sustained, the person concerned should be compensated. The benefits should be shared by the shareholders who financed the railway and bore the commercial risks, and the local communities whose members used the railway.

In presenting a Bill to Parliament, the promoters had to prove that the prospective benefits were substantial. Promoters made traffic surveys along roads and canals to establish the existence of demand, and proposed schedules of maximum fares and freight rates to ensure that much of the benefit of the railway would accrue to the public. At the same time they had to show that their construction costs were reasonable, and their estimates robust. If their scheme was financially unsound then the countryside might be dug up for no good purpose.

With so many lawyers sitting in Parliament as MPs or Lords it is not surprising that cross-examination by hired advocates was the preferred way of presenting evidence to a Parliamentary committee (Kostal 1994). To ensure compliance with standing orders, Parliamentary agents were hired. When rival schemes were argued before a committee many technical 'knock-outs' were achieved, and often the knock-outs were mutual, so that all the schemes failed. When a scheme failed, the engineers, solicitors and Parliamentary agents would submit their claims for fees, sometimes using up all the deposits and leaving nothing for the shareholders. If the scheme succeeded, then the newly established Board would make calls on the shares so that construction could begin. Contracts for separate sections of line would be put out to tender. Although the process was nominally competitive, some contractors might have friends on the Board; indeed, they might be involved in the promotion of the line, and effectively award the contract to themselves. In common with many construction projects, initial estimates were often too low, and so the project would either have to be scaled down, and part of the route abandoned, or additional capital would have to be raised. This would require further application to Parliament, as an Act limited both the amount of capital and the time in which it could be raised.

Once a line was opened, competition for traffic would begin (Reed 1969, 1975). In many cases, the strongest rivalry came from an alternative railway route. As the network developed, so the number of alternative routes between any two places increased (Turnock 1998). Mergers provided an obvious solution, but from the mid-1850s Parliament became increasingly concerned about their monopolistic tendencies, and only approved then in exceptional cases. In the 1840s and early 1850s, however, major speculative gains could be made from the promotion of mergers. The 'Railway King' George Hudson, a draper from York, made his name by engineering the merger that created the Midland Railway (Arnold and McCartney 2004). He eliminated competition between Derby and London, and between Leeds and Hull. The tradition of 'railway politics' was continued by the 'Second Railway King', Sir Edward Watkin, who coordinated the management of different companies through an interlocking chairmanship (Hodgkins 2001). His grand design was for a through line from Manchester to Paris via a Channel Tunnel. He was successful in gaining financial support from shareholders and political support from government, but engineering problems and the costs they created defeated him in the end.

Popular mythology recognizes the railway engineers—men such as George and Robert Stephenson, Joseph Locke, and Isambard Kingdom Brunel—as the true entrepreneurs of the railway system. Samuel Smiles' (1862) hagiography portrays Victorian engineers not only as technocrats but also as the strategic thinkers behind the new industries that they helped to create. Detailed evidence on company promotion, such as Brunel's Letter Books (1836), suggests that this assessment is correct. It was not so much the owners of the railways as their consultant engineers who masterminded strategy in the early years. The reason is quite straightforward: the principles of railway strategy were specific to railways—a new type of network industry with a very costly infrastructure—but common across all locations. While shareholders were often endowed with good local knowledge, they had limited experience of the railway system as a whole. Consulting engineers, however, would have experience of several schemes, from which they could identify general patterns.

Consulting engineers also socialized with each other. They met as peers at meetings of the Institute of Civil Engineers and other professional associations, and as adversaries before Parliamentary Committees on Railway Bills. Although Brunel and Robert Stephenson could not even agree on the best gauge for a railway—Brunel favouring the broad gauge and Stephenson the standard gauge—they remained the best of friends. They fought an intense battle in Parliament over lines in the West Midlands, which Brunel won; yet they dined together, and even died at about the same time! Both men advised their respective companies on strategy—the Great Western and London and North Western— planning routes that would block rival lines, devising trunk line routes to maximize the potential for profitable branch line traffic, and helping to monopolize key ports.

By mid-century it was the company secretary who was becoming the major strategic thinker in the railway sector, together with the company chairman. In the second half of the nineteenth century the most successful railway entrepreneurs were those who combined practical experience of the industry with a wide range of general interests—such as Samuel Laing, the chairman of the London Brighton and South Coast Railway, who was a former official with the Railway Department of the Board of Trade and who became a popular writer on philosophical issues.

2.11. CONCLUSION

The importance of the railways—and infrastructure in general—to the Victorian economy illustrates the danger of placing undue emphasis on manufacturing industry when evaluating entrepreneurship in Victorian Britain. Railway promotion was a highly entrepreneurial activity. Railway companies were born large. Sales growth occurred mainly through long-term traffic growth fuelled by the gradual expansion of the economy, rather than by bidding traffic away from other companies. Shareholders took most of the risks, but specialist entrepreneurs took the strategic decisions: initially the consulting engineers, and later the company secretaries and chairmen.

At the time of their construction, most railway lines were projected as civic enterprises, representing a single town, or a coalition of towns along the route. Civic enterprise was particularly notable in some of the old county towns, like Chester, Lincoln, York, and Shrewsbury, which sought to renew themselves as railway hubs. The most spectacular example of a coalition of towns creating a new trunk railway was the Great Northern Railway—one of the most successful of the Mania schemes. This was a merger of rival schemes, based upon a common interest in serving country towns in Bedfordshire, Huntingdonshire, and Lincolnshire. Because of its length, it connected London directly to York and Edinburgh, by a junction near Doncaster, and because of its breadth, achieved by a loop line, it was able to serve the agricultural districts of Lincolnshire too. The merger was organized by Edmund Dennison, MP for Doncaster. He used his political influence to serve his constituents by insisting that the railway terminate near Doncaster, thereby transforming a declining gentrified horse-racing town into a prosperous railway hub.

The railway system was just one of the many innovations exported from Britain to the Empire in the Age of High Imperialism (Dumett 2008). Professional governance, which had evolved steadily since the Norman Age, was exported through systems of colonial administration. This provided a framework of law and order within which various types of large project could be exported too. While many of these projects were first developed in Britain, others—such as river navigation, drainage, and water supply systems—involved refinements of technologies developed elsewhere.

Overseas projects involved the export not only of British technology and management but British capital and labour too. Much of the labour was highly skilled. Many of the civil engineers who left Britain for the colonies in the second half of the nineteenth century never returned to Britain. There were so many opportunities for engineers on the colonial frontier that there was little incentive for them to return. It was mainly the senior professionals, who ran consulting practices from London, who remained in Britain. Many of these consultants became involved in high finance and political negotiation, as foreign monarchs and ministers came to Britain to negotiate for railway schemes. The engineer Sir John Fowler, for example, received his knighthood not for his engineering expertise, but for the political assistance he rendered to the British government during the war in Sudan.

One of the key aspects of entrepreneurship is that it facilitates structural change. It is a mistake to infer that entrepreneurship declined in late Victorian Britain just because Britain failed to maintain its industrial lead over Germany and the United States. Victorian entrepreneurs may well have been slow to recognize the magnitude of scale economies in heavy industries, and to appreciate the commercial benefits of organized industrial research in well-equipped laboratories. But in a small and increasingly crowded country, this was not where national comparative advantage lay.

The late Victorian economy is an example of what is now called the knowledge-based economy. Its comparative advantage lay increasingly in the export of knowledge-intensive services, such as public administration, trade, shipping, finance, and engineering consultancy. These services were mainly delivered in packages relating to major projects for colonial and overseas development. Each project required inputs of several of these knowledge-based services for its successful completion. The whole process depended on specialized institutions such as the London Stock Exchange, an agglomeration of scientific and professional institutions, and the 'free-standing' overseas company.

The twentieth century saw enormous geopolitical changes, most of which disadvantaged British entrepreneurship, and undermined the Victorian legacy. War, followed by the collapse of international trade and global demand, more war and then the loss of Empire, all reduced the scope for large complex project-based entrepreneurship coordinated through traditional British institutions such as the London stock market. The notion of an Empire based on trade in agricultural products and knowledge-intensive services was replaced by the notion of an Empire based on large-scale high-technology manufacturing industry. Economic logic now favoured the hierarchical multinational firm rather than the free-standing firm. It is a mistake to suppose, however, that the loss of Empire, and twentieth-century economic failure, can be blamed on the deficiencies of Victorian enterprise. Entrepreneurship was a vibrant force in Britain throughout most of the Victorian era, and its classic manifestation was in the railway sector.

3

The Counterfactual Network

3.1. INTRODUCTION

This chapter explains how the counterfactual network was derived and compares it with the actual network (statistics for the actual network are presented in Table 3.1). The main finding has already been highlighted in Chapter 1: namely that 13,000 miles of track on the counterfactual equal the performance of 20,000 miles of track on the actual system. This chapter presents the analysis that underpins that finding; further details are presented in Appendices 3–6.

The counterfactual represents the best available alternative to the actual system—or at least an approximation to it. It also represents a viable alternative—that is, an alternative that might have been implemented had circumstances been a little different. More specifically, it is a counterfactual that could well have been implemented at the time of the Railway Mania in 1845, and that might have been championed by the Board of Trade, had Parliament given it the appropriate mandate (which it failed to do).

The first part of this chapter identifies the general factors governing the demand for railway transport in Victorian Britain. It discusses the advantages and disadvantages of railways relative to other modes of transport. In the Victorian context, this means comparing railways with roads, canals, and shipping. The development of steam power in the early nineteenth century shifted the balance of advantages from roads and canals to railways and shipping. By increasing speeds, steam power enlarged the range of traffic that could be transported—for example, perishable goods—and also stimulated existing demands—especially for passenger travel. As a result, railways began to specialize in carrying a distinctive type of traffic, in which they had a strong comparative advantage; this had important implications for the way that the railway network needed to be configured.

The second part of this chapter discusses the techniques that were used to derive the counterfactual. They comprise a set of nine heuristic principles which achieve reasonably direct linkages between major traffic centres with the lowest possible route mileage. The heuristics also inform the design of the regional sub-systems, and indicate how these systems can be interlocked into a national system. Finally, the heuristics indicate how geographical constraints imposed by an irregular coastline, inland mountain ranges, and circuitous river valleys can be accommodated efficiently.

Table 3.1. Actual railway mileage, 1911, from Board of Trade Railway Returns

Company/category	Double track (miles)	Single track (miles)	Total route mileage	Total length of track (miles)
England and Wales				
Great Western	1,621	1,385	3,006	6,645
London and North Western	1,541	425	1,966	5,502
North Eastern	1,235	493	1,728	4,842
Midland	1,134	398	1,532	4,852
Great Eastern	667	466	1,132	2,540
London and South Western	663	301	964	2,218
Great Northern	663	193	856	2,655
Great Central	640	117	757	2,252
South Eastern and Chatham Man. Cttee	555	74	629	1,588
Lancashire and Yorkshire	552	39	591	2,194
London Brighton and South Coast	355	99	454	1,234
Cambrian	9	274	283	377
North Staffordshire	156	60	216	501
Midland and Great Northern Joint	79	115	194	337
Cheshire Lines	124	18	142	419
Furness	86	48	134	369
Taff Vale	72	52	124	387
Somerset and Dorset	45	61	106	179
Hull and Barnsley	74	17	91	295
London Tilbury and Southend	66	13	79	222
Stratford-upon-Avon and Midland Junction	2	66	68	78
Barry	64	2	66	287
Midland and South Western Junction	35	30	65	115
Brecon and Merthyr	27	32	59	107
Rhymney	44	7	51	162
Other railways with under 50 route miles	195	570	765	1,504
Electric lines	131	10	141	351
Total: England and Wales	10,835	5,365	16,200	42,212
Scotland				
North British	518	21	1,339	2,652
Caledonian	601	471	1,072	2,713
Highland	72	413	485	636
Glasgow and South Western	320	146	466	1,104
Great North of Scotland	78	255	333	523
Portpatrick and Wigtownshire Joint	3	79	82	98
Other railways with under 50 route miles	7	31	38	47
Total: Scotland	1,599	2,216	3,815	7,773
Grand total: England, Wales, and Scotland	12,434	7,538	20,015	50,982

The third part of this chapter compares the actual and counterfactual systems. The key factors contributing to the superiority of the counterfactual system are identified. Particular attention is paid to the role of hubs. While many hub locations are common to both networks, there are important differences regarding the location of the major trunk line hubs. A paradox is identified: namely that the actual system appears to have many more hubs, and much larger hubs as well. On closer examination, however, it turns out not only that many of these hubs were badly designed for the interchange of traffic but also that the companies never intended them to be used for this purpose, and often did their best to obstruct the interchange of traffic at them. These strategies were a direct result of competition between the companies, as it was played out under the Parliamentary 'rules of the game'. The same competitive forces that led to the duplication of trunk lines, and the proliferation of lines converging on ports and coalfields, also led to a proliferation of ineffective hubs.

3.2. THE IMPACT OF STEAM POWER ON INTER-MODAL COMPETITION

In the early 1820s when the Stockton and Darlington Railway (SDR) was being promoted, there were five main methods of powering transport and two main ways of distributing that power. The main power sources were people, animals, wind, gravity, and steam. People and animals converted food into energy while steam derived energy from fossil fuels, and in particular coal (wood was too expensive to use as a commercial fuel). Wind power was applied mainly to sailing ships, while gravity was applied both directly to downhill traffic and indirectly by harnessing the flow of a river or the pull of the tide.

Until 1825 steam power was mainly applied to railways through rope-worked inclines; it was stationary power, based in an engine house at the top of an incline, rather than locomotive power applied by an engine pulling a train. Inclines could also be worked by gravity, with loaded wagons descending hauling empty wagons up—an operation that was suited mainly to mineral lines connecting hill-side mines to sea-level ports. While the SDR was the pioneer in applying steam locomotion to passenger travel, it was the Rainhill Trials on the Liverpool and Manchester Railway (LMR) in 1829 that demonstrated the superiority of steam locomotion over stationary power—particularly in regard to speed. While 'Locomotion' on the SDR was just that—an early locomotive, the 'Rocket' on the LMR, as its name suggests, was the first successful high-speed locomotive.

Steam power can in principle be applied to almost any form of transport, but it was railway transport that was revolutionized rather than the other modes. Shipping was slow to embrace steam because of the large amount of coal that needed to be carried on a long voyage—a problem eventually solved by more efficient power units using the compound principle, larger ships, and bunkering stations located at strategic points along international shipping routes. Wooden ships also faced a fire hazard with the use of steam: the switch to iron hulls in mid-century facilitated both larger and safer ships.

So far as inland transport was concerned, steam had only a limited impact on canals and roads. Barges, like locomotives, could be refuelled regularly, so that coal supplies were not so great a problem. The main problem was the wash created by the barge, which eroded banks and disturbed passing traffic—particularly on the narrow canals that had been built in the eighteenth century. The application of steam to roads proved problematic too. Long trains were not viable without tracks, and without a train each vehicle needed to be separately powered. Vehicles could not be too large or they would obstruct the highways. The answer was to scale down the size of the power unit. High-pressure boilers were part of the answer, but this increased the risk of explosion, as iron plate was prone to fracture and rivets often burst. Despite the best efforts of William Murdoch and other pioneers, steam road vehicles remained heavy and clumsy. They damaged roads, frightened horses, and were difficult to steer. They were uneconomic because they required the same amount of manpower as a steam locomotive hauling a train. The pioneering public services were on long straight roads, such as Paddington to the City of London, and Cheltenham to Gloucester, but even then regular starting and stopping proved to be a problem. They needed to be taken off the public highways, given tracks and a train to pull, and run for long distances without a stop; in other words, steam locomotion required a railway.

When the first main lines were built, local stage coach and mail coach services disappeared almost overnight, and roads were relegated to the role of feeders to the railway system. Because of the inconvenient siting of many stations, however, local carters and carriers continued to ply a reasonable trade—so much so that some railway companies sought to profit from it by franchising carriers who were awarded privileged access to their stations. So far as the counterfactual network is concerned, therefore, it is necessary to appreciate that, like the actual network, it is a part of an inter-modal system and is fed by local roads.

Canals were more serious competitors to the railways. Indeed, some early railways—such as the Cromford and High Peak in Derbyshire—were built as adjuncts to the canals. Canals evolved from river navigations; they cut off river bends, and extended river systems further inland. It was difficult, however, to connect adjacent valleys without an expensive tunnel, as a long flight of locks was difficult to operate. A railway based on a rope-hauled incline was therefore an attractive proposition. But once a railway had been built, it was reasonable to ask whether the canal was still needed, or whether the railway should be extended to take its place. Unlike canals, railways did not freeze up in winter, nor run dry in summer, nor need expensive reservoirs to store the water. A railway could continue running throughout the year so long as it had a good supply of coal. Once steam locomotion arrived therefore, canals were in jeopardy.

Water has a great advantage, however, in supplying natural buoyancy; railways must obtain similar support through the ballasting of the track, which requires the digging of ballast pits. Because speeds are slow, canals can accommodate sharp bends, allowing them to follow the contour of the land; this avoids the deep cuttings, high embankments, and other expensive engineering works characteristic of railway lines. With less intrusion in the landscape, there is less objection from local landowners, and less compensation to be paid as a result. Canals were therefore a cheap method of conveying slow-moving traffic, and were well suited to handling small consignments of heavy freight, such as stone and minerals. After the coming of the railways, canals retained a niche role for certain types of traffic. The counterfactual recognizes this by providing, where appropriate, for the interchange of traffic at canal basins.

While railways were generally substituted for roads and canals so far as long-distance traffic was concerned, they were very much complementary to shipping. Just as roads and canals became feeders to the rail network, so railways—right from the outset—became feeders to the shipping network. There was some competition with shipping, it is true, for example, the coastal shipping of coal from the north-east to London—but this was the exception rather than the rule. As British overseas interests increased, so the notion of railways as links in an imperial inter-modal network of transport and communication took root. The diffusion of railway-building overseas—in particular to the settler economies— was one manifestation of this, and the linking of railways with ports within the UK was another.

The early promoters of trunk lines appear to have had a very clear view of the internal transport links required by an imperial power. They understood in an intuitive way the concept of the spatial division of labour, which created highly specialized locations, notably ports, mining areas, manufacturing districts, and administrative centres that needed to be linked to one another.

Within these categories they recognized a hierarchy, ranging from the ocean port near the mouth of a major estuary, down to a local port near a creek used by coastal tramp shipping; and from London—the great metropolis—down to a local market town and centre of judicial administration, serving a rural area. They also recognized the growing importance of fashionable residential centres and holiday resorts, including established inland spas such as Bath, Cheltenham, and Leamington, and seaside resorts such as Brighton and Scarborough. Following the introduction of weekly holiday entitlements for workers, railway promoters came to play an important role in developing new resorts such as Blackpool, Bournemouth, and Skegness. The counterfactual reflects a similar view of the railway system and its role in connecting up different types of traffic centre that emerge within a growing economy.

3.3. CONSTRUCTION OF THE COUNTERFACTUAL: COVERAGE OF CITIES, TOWNS, AND VILLAGES

The counterfactual system is required to serve all towns and villages that had a population of 3,000 or more in 1831. This date is chosen as the date of the most recent census that was available to promoters and government officials at the time of the Railway Mania. For the purposes of this analysis a town or village is defined as a place with a significant clustering of population around relevant amenities such as churches, public houses, and shops. Since population census data is reported by parish, and some parishes are very large and dispersed, contemporary maps have been used to assess whether or not a large parish was associated with a town or village of the appropriate size.

It would be impossible for the counterfactual to match the national coverage of the actual system, however, unless it served a number of smaller towns and villages that were also served by the actual system. It is therefore required in addition that the counterfactual serve every town or village with a population of 1,500 or more that was served by the actual system. The counterfactual also serves many villages much smaller than this, but this is only as a consequence of having to serve larger settlements and so pass through smaller settlements on the way. In fact, counterfactual lines are often routed deliberately through small villages in order to enhance the overall service provided, even though the service to these small villages is not formally included in the metrics by which performance is judged (as explained below). As a result, the counterfactual serves several towns and villages that were not served by the actual system at all.

It is sometimes difficult to tell from a printed railway map whether a railway line actually served a particular town or village because railway stations were often named after towns some distance away. Sometimes the remoteness of the town is indicated by the name of the station—for example, Wallingford Road near Moulsford or Bodmin Road near Llanhydrock, but in other cases, such as Burford station, near Brize Norton, the problem is disguised. In all such cases maps have been used to determine which towns were actually served by the railway and which were not; a town or village more than two miles from the railway line is deemed not to be served by the railway.

Although it is assumed that the counterfactual was devised in 1840, the actual date of comparison is 1914, which is the time at which the actual system reached its zenith. Between 1840 and 1845 a huge range of railway plans were 'on the table', and most schemes that were subsequently built were based on schemes that appeared at this time. Although some of the main trunk lines had already been built, it would have been perfectly possible to modify the trunk line system by building cut-offs and extensions at that time—and indeed, this actually happened some time later, but too late to have any material effect on the rest of the system. In practice the counter-factual system, being smaller, would have been completed much earlier than the actual system, assuming that the pace of construction had been the same. Thus the average working life of the counterfactual system would have been longer—another advantage which is not formally included in the comparison.

3.4. CONSTRUCTION OF THE COUNTERFACTUAL: PERFORMANCE METRICS

To compare the performance of the actual and counterfactual systems a set of 250 representative journeys was examined. Ten different types of journey were distinguished, and sub-samples of 25 journeys of each type were generated. Performance was measured for each type of journey, and an overall measure of performance, based on an arithmetic average, was constructed.

To begin with, a sample of 25 journeys was constructed using the Index to Bradshaw's Guide. Fifty towns appearing at the top of each page were identified and paired at random; since larger towns have multiple entries, this method weights towns by size to some degree; it is also easy to replicate. Two long-distance samples were then constructed, one involving journeys from the centre of London and one involving cross-country travel. The destinations involved both large and small towns—because large towns typically act as hubs for small towns on the counterfactual, distinguishing between them is somewhat artificial. Finally, seven regional samples were constructed—reflecting the fact that most journeys on any railway system tend to be relatively short. Comparing the results for different samples illustrates how well the actual system served different types of traffic and different parts of the country.

The counterfactual network was constructed using an iterative process. The performance of the actual system was first assessed. This proved to be a most illuminating process, indicating that the actual performance of the system for many categories of traffic was much inferior to what has often been suggested—particularly in the enthusiasts' literature. An initial counterfactual system was then constructed, using only a limited number of local lines, and its performance compared with the actual system. The main discrepancies between the actual and counterfactual were then determined, and the counterfactual was then revised, increasing the mileage to eliminate the observed deficiencies.

Iteration continued until a counterfactual route mileage of just over 12,000 was reached. At this point the average performance of the counterfactual equalled the average performance of the actual system, although performance was inferior for certain types of traffic. It was decided, nevertheless, to refine the counterfactual further. The reasoning was that critics could challenge the equal weighting that had been applied to the different types of traffic, arguing that the counterfactual was weakest on the most important types of traffic. With a little further refinement, it seemed possible that the performance of the counterfactual could equal or exceed actual performance for every type of traffic, and this would provide a much more robust result. In addition, there seemed to be a strong social case for investment in some additional lines; thus an augmented counterfactual would be close to what seemed intuitively to be a network of approximately optimal size.

Once the counterfactual had expanded to about 13,000 route miles the enhanced level of performance was attained. A new set of 250 journeys was then developed—to combat a possible criticism that the refinements to the counterfactual had been targeted on problems unique to the sample journeys and not to problems endemic to the network as a whole. The results of the final exercise are shown in Table 3.2.

The table reports the results for two metrics: a distance metric and a journey time metric. The distance metric relates to the shortest route and the time metric to the fastest route. On the actual system the shortest possible route was not

Table 3.2. Performance of the counterfactual network relative to the actual network

Sample	Distance metric	Time metric
Bradshaw	102.4	92.6
London	102.4	97.2
Cross-country	100.8	87.6
Wales	94.1	77.6
Scotland	99.0	86.0
North	100.9	84.5
East	98.5	75.8
Midlands	99.4	76.8
South and south-east	98.1	68.5
South-west	86.0	74.0

Note: The performance of the actual network is normalized to 100. Superiority of the counterfactual network is indicated by a value of less than 100, which represents a shorter distance or a shorter journey time.

usually the quickest route, so different routes may be used for the two calculations. Furthermore, the shortest route sometimes involved complex manoeuvres, such as shunting trains backwards over junctions before proceeding forwards again. The results for the actual system allow for up to two reversals at an intermediate hub.

To assess the journey time on the counterfactual system it is necessary to have a counterfactual timetable, and so a timetable was developed specifically for this purpose (see Appendix 6). The focus of the timetable is passenger trains. Although in practice many freight trains ran to timetables, speed does not carry such a premium for freight (except for perishables). Furthermore, mineral traffic, which was dominant in the nineteenth century, was usually timetabled in response to specific local needs. Finally, it has always been difficult to predict overall journey times for freight traffic, even with timetabled trains, because delays caused by shunting in marshalling yards mean that connections between trains are often missed.

Passenger trains are assumed to travel over the counterfactual system at the same average speeds that they travelled on an equivalent route on the actual system. Passengers are allowed a minimum of five minutes to change trains; although this seems quite short, it is actually less than was often allowed on the actual system, where two minutes was sometimes deemed sufficient. Allowing longer would weight the results unduly against the counterfactual system.

Train speeds and connection times were estimated from Bradshaw's Guide. The principal source was a Bradshaw's Guide for 1911; although a Guide for 1914 would have been more appropriate, a Guide for 1911 has been reprinted and is therefore more accessible.

To avoid unnecessary complications, the counterfactual system employs a fixed interval service with a normal interval of two hours. This gives a daily frequency service on main lines that is broadly comparable to that on the actual system. Fixed interval (or 'cyclic') timetables are often considered to be a modern innovation, but in fact many of the earliest railway companies used schemes of roughly this kind. But as competition developed throughout the system there was a tendency for companies to compete with each other by scheduling rival expresses at peak times; these peaks were at breakfast time, lunchtime, and late afternoon–early evening, with slower trains sometimes running at intervening times. So far as service frequency is concerned, the counterfactual generally offers higher frequency on local lines. This is because counterfactual operations exploit the greater connectivity of the counterfactual network by maintaining regular connections with main line trains, and with intersecting local services, through-out the day. This is achieved, not by using extra locomotives and carriages, but rather by using them with greater intensity.

The statistics presented in the first column of the table show the distance by the counterfactual as a percentage of the distance by the actual system for each of the 10 types of traffic. The second column shows the journey time on the counter-factual as a percentage of the journey time on the actual system. These statistics are unweighted averages of the percentages computed for each of the 25 sample journeys included in each category; this means that a given percentage reduction in distance or journey time is regarded as being of equal value whether the overall distance or journey time is short or long.

The counterfactual is superior to the actual according to the time metric in every case. It therefore dominates the performance of the actual system on this metric. On the distance metric the counterfactual is superior in 6 out of 10 cases but marginally inferior in 4—London traffic, cross-country traffic, the north of England, and the Bradshaw routes.

Overall the statistics indicate that the advantage of the counterfactual is great-est where local and short-distance cross-country traffic is concerned, and is lowest where trunk line traffic to and from London and long-distance country traffic is concerned. Its advantage is greater in terms of time than distance—reflecting the fact that the counterfactual is designed to provide punctual con-nections at all hubs whereas the actual system is not.

3.5. CONSTRUCTION OF THE COUNTERFACTUAL: ESTIMATING POTENTIAL TRAFFIC FLOWS

Two main types of location on a railway system are identified: traffic-generating centres and hubs. As these names suggest, a traffic-generating centre functions mainly as an origin or destination for traffic while a hub focuses on the inter-change of traffic. If a traffic-generating centre is an intermediate station on a line between other centres then a substantial proportion of traffic may be through traffic, and only if it is also a hub will the through traffic be interchanged there.

A traffic-generating centre is defined in relative rather than absolute terms; namely by the fact that its main purpose is the origination and destination of traffic rather than its interchange. Thus it is quite possible for a traffic-generating centre to be small—for example, a market town at the terminus of a short dead-end branch.

All traffic-generating centres—however large or small—were classified into one of the following categories:

− Ports
  • Ocean (e.g. Liverpool)
  • Ferry (e.g. Holyhead for Dublin, Dover for the Continent)
  • Coastal (e.g. Newcastle)
  • Naval (e.g. Plymouth)
− Mining (e.g. Cardiff Valleys)
− Industry (e.g. Manchester)
− Commercial and administrative centres (e.g. London, Norwich)
− Resorts (e.g. Brighton)
− Agricultural market centres
− Other towns

Particular attention was paid to the role of ports as centres of transhipment and processing, recognizing their potential importance as hubs on inter-modal international transport systems. Similarly, the need for agricultural market centres to feed into local road and river systems was allowed for in the analysis. A classification of the largest towns and cities in 1831 according to these principles is presented in Table 3.3.

Significant local traffic was imputed to links between mining areas and nearby ports, mining areas and nearby industrial districts, and industrial districts and nearby ports. The same requirement was applied to lines connecting ports, mining areas, or industrial districts to nearby commercial and administrative centres, and connections from any of these types of town to resorts. Effective connections were also required between neighbouring industrial towns, to allow for 'industrial district' agglomeration effects on traffic flow. Links between neighbouring agricultural market centres and 'other' towns are allowed to be of only local quality (despite the potential for arbitrage between market centres to stimulate local trade).

The actual volume of traffic generated at any traffic-generating centre is assumed to be proportional to the size of its population. The amount flowing along any given link to some other traffic-generating centre will be proportional to both the population of the origination centre and the population of the destination centre. The amount of traffic will also depend upon proximity, with larger flows between centres a short distance apart. These effects are captured in a simple gravity model of traffic flow in which the traffic between any given pair of traffic-generating centres is directly proportional to the population of each centre and inversely proportional to the distance between them. This study, however, applies the gravity approach on a case-by-case basis—that is, in the context of the particular type of traffic likely to flow between the centres, given their role within the spatial division of labour described above. The study also takes into account the suitability of the traffic for carriage by rail; thus if canal transport is likely to

Table 3.3. Principal towns and cities in England, Wales, and Scotland 1831

Rank Town or City	Principal functions	Total population 1831
London + Middlesex	Admin, Port	1,358,200
Manchester	Manufacturing	270,961
Glasgow	Manufacturing, Port	202,426
Liverpool with Toxteth	Manufacturing	189,242
Edinburgh	Admin, Port	162,156
Birmingham	Manufacturing	146,486
Leeds	Manufacturing	123,393
Bristol + Clifton	Admin, Port	103,886
Sheffield	Manufacturing	91,692
Bradford	Manufacturing	76,996
Plymouth	Port	75,534
Norwich	Admin, Manufacturing	61,166
Aberdeen	Port, Manufacturing	58,019
Paisley	Manufacturing	57,466
Nottingham	Manufacturing, Admin	50,680
Portsea + Portsmouth	Port	50.389
Newcastle-upon-Tyne with Gateshead	Port, Mines	47,837
Hull (with Sculcoates)	Port	46,426
Dundee	Manufacturing, Port	45,355
Bolton	Manufacturing	41,195
Brighton	Resort	40,634
Leicester	Manufacturing	39,063
Bath	Resort	38,063
Stoke-on-Trent	Manufacturing	37,220
Preston	Manufacturing	36,336
Ashton-under-Lyne	Manufacturing	33,597
Exeter	Admin	32,404
Oldham	Manufacturing	32,381
Sunderland (with Bishop Wearmouth)	Port, Mines	31,522
Huddersfield	Manufacturing	31,041
Eccles	Manufacturing	28,995
Jarrow (with South Shields)	Port, Mines	27,995
Greenock	Manufacturing	27,571
Blackburn	Manufacturing	27,091
Coventry	Manufacturing	27,070
Rochdale	Manufacturing	26,404
Stockport	Manufacturing	25,469
York	Admin	25,359
Tynemouth	Port	24,778
Wolverhampton	Manufacturing	24,732
Greenwich	Port	24,553
Wakefield	Manufacturing	24,538
Derby	Manufacturing	23,607
Macclesfield	Manufacturing	23,129
Dudley	Manufacturing	23,042
Cheltenham	Resort	22,942
Lancaster	Admin, Port	22,294
Merthyr	Mines	22,083
Chester	Admin	21,363
Shrewsbury	Admin	21,227

Table 3.3. (Continued)

Rank Town or City	Principal functions	Total population 1831
Yarmouth	Port	21,115
Cambridge	Admin	20,917
Kidderminster	Manufacturing	20,865
Sedgley, Staffs	Mines, Manufacturing	20,577
Ipswich	Admin, Port	20,454
Oxford	Admin	20,434
Perth	Admin, Port	20,016
Carlisle	Admin	20,006
Dewsbury	Manufacturing	19,854
Deptford	Port	19,795
Southampton	Port	19,324
Warrington	Manufacturing	19,155
Worcester	Manufacturing, Admin	18,610
Kilmarnock	Manufacturing	18,093
Woolwich	Manufacturing, Port	17,661
Dunfermline	Manufacturing, Admin	17,068
Barnsley (Silkstone)	Mines, Manufacturing	16,561
Chatham	Port, Manufacturing	16,485
Colchester	Admin	16,167
Saddleworth	Manufacturing	15,986
Reading	Admin	15,595
Mottram	Manufacturing	15,536
Maidstone	Admin	15,387
Halifax	Manufacturing	15,382
Northampton	Manufacturing, Admin	15,351
West Bromwich	Manufacturing	15,327
Kingswinford	Mines; Manufacturing	15,156
Bury	Manufacturing	15,086
Walsall	Manufacturing	15,066
Tipton (Wolverhampton)	Manufacturing	14,951
Bilston (Wolverhampton)	Manufacturing	14,492
Canterbury	Admin, Resort	14,463
Middleton (Rochdale)	Manufacturing	14,379
Inverness	Admin	14,324
Ormskirk	Manufacturing	14,053
Leyland (Preston)	Manufacturing	13,871
Swansea	Port	13,694
Kings Lynn	Port	13,370
Bedminster (Bristol)	Manufacturing	13,130
Falkirk	Manufacturing	12,743
Burslem (Stoke)	Manufacturing	12,741
Gosport (with Alverstoke)	Port	12,637
Croydon	Admin	12,447
Frome	Manufacturing	12,240
Montrose	Port	12,055
Gloucester	Admin, Port	11,933
Dover	Port	11,924
Lincoln	Admin	11,892
Dumfries	Admin	11,606

(*continued*)

Table 3.3. (Continued)

Rank Town or City	Principal functions	Total population 1831
West Ham	Manufacturing	11,580
Doncaster	Admins, Resort	11,572
Bury St. Edmunds	Admin	11,436
Wrexham	Manufacturing, Mines	11,408
Whitehaven	Port	11,393
Batley	Manufacturing	11,335
Boston	Port	11,240
Taunton	Admin	11,139
Loughborough	Manufacturing	10,969
Trowbridge	Manufacturing	10,863
Bedwelty (S. Wales)	Mines	10,637
Rotherham	Manufacturing, Mines	10,417
Tonbridge	Admin	10,380
Margate	Resort	10,339
Hereford	Admin	10,280
Pontypool (with Trevethon)	Mines	10,280
Bradford-on-Avon (Wilts)	Manufacturing	10,102
Hastings	Resort	10,097
Kirkheaton	Manufacturing	10,020
Kendal	Admin, Manufacturing	10,015

Note: The table excludes large parishes which have no significant centre of population and are mere agglomerations of many small townships scattered over a wide area. In some cases a township is reported in place of a parish of the same name, if it is judged that the other townships are not suburbs of the main town.

Source: British Parliamentary Papers (HC348, 1831) Population: Comparative Account of the Population of Great Britain in the Years 1801, 1811, 1821, and 1831.

be competitive, the imputed flow will be lower than the flow if all the traffic were likely to go by rail.

Finally, additional sources of information have been used to estimate traffic flows in cases where they happen to be available. Victorian County Histories, local histories, histories of local lines, and the history of passenger carriages and goods wagons all provide evidence on the size of certain traffic flows. In addition, many railway bills presented to Parliament cited evidence of traffic already carried by turnpikes and canals, and witnesses to Parliamentary Committees often testified to the amount of traffic being carried by existing modes. Even more detailed estimates could, in principle, be obtained from consulting the records of individual railway companies in the Public Record Office, and from a detailed analysis of the Annual Railway Returns and other statistical reports on the railways published in British Parliamentary Papers. The volume of information is so huge, however, that it was impossible to use these sources systematically for the purposes of this study.

As explained in Chapter 1, four categories of rail linkage are distinguished:

- Trunk: heavy traffic at high speed
- Primary: moderate traffic at high speed
- Secondary: moderate traffic at moderate speed
- Local: light traffic at low speeds

The greater the amount of traffic expected to be carried, the more important it is that a line be built to a high standard. Thus trunk lines will be required to link large traffic-generating centres to each other, while at the other extreme local lines will suffice to link small traffic-generating centres to each other. The specification of the counterfactual identifies the category of every single linkage on the system.

In order for the counterfactual to match the actual system, it is necessary not only that lines are built to adequate standards but also that communication between traffic-generating centres is relatively direct. Direct communication between any two traffic-generating centres requires both that individual linkages are direct (there are not too many twists and turns in the route) and that if the route passes through intermediate hubs then it should not change direction too much between entering and leaving the hub.

It is not necessary to specify rigid requirements for directness, because if such requirements are not satisfied when the system is considered as a whole then the performance criteria will not be met. The main exception relates to routes that confront natural geographical obstacles, where the actual system will be handicapped in its performance as well. However, to simplify the algorithm for constructing the counterfactual it is useful to have some simple criteria, and it has therefore been determined that trunk lines should be built as direct as possible, using tunnels and viaducts as necessary whereas, at the other extreme, local lines are allowed to follow the contours of the landscape, provided that these are not too devious. It is also required that where trunk lines pass through intermediate hubs, they should not change direction by more than $20°$, whereas no such restriction is imposed on local lines. Secondary lines are treated as an intermediate case, and allowed to turn by up to $35°$.

3.6. CONSTRUCTION OF THE COUNTERFACTUAL: HEURISTIC PRINCIPLES

The number of possible counterfactual configuration is enormous. There are thousands of traffic-generating centres—cities, towns, and villages—to be connected up, and therefore millions of pairs of origins and destinations. In addition there are tens of thousands of places at which hubs can be sited. Hubs do not have to be sited at traffic-generating centres; although it is often efficient to locate a hub at a traffic-generating centre, and natural hubs often develop as traffic-generating centres in their own right, there is no logical necessity for this coincidence, and indeed they often did not coincide on the actual system.

Any pair of traffic-generating centres can be connected either directly or through a hub—or, indeed, through a sequence of different hubs. The number of different permutations by which routes can be constructed is therefore formidable. It is thus essential to have some set of heuristic principles which can reduce this complexity to manageable proportions.

Nine main heuristics have been employed:

- the Steiner principle,
- the traffic-weighting principle,
- the triangle principle,
- the cut-off principle,
- the bypass principle,
- the contour principle,
- the concavity principle,
- the loop principle, and
- the space-filling principle.

These are all optimization heuristics, which serve to minimize the total route mileage involved in meeting the traffic requirements set out above. The first five principles are mainly concerned with the optimal configuration of hubs, while the remaining four are mainly concerned with optimal adaptation to physical constraints such as the coastline or mountains.

3.6.1. The Steiner principle

When confronted with the basic problem of how to connect up a given set of locations by minimizing the total length of the linkages involved, intuition suggests that a single continuous line linking up adjacent points might provide an appropriate basis on which to begin. To minimize the total length of the line it is necessary to construct it from straight-line segments, since a straight line minimizes the distance between any pair of adjacent points. It is also necessary that the line does not intersect itself, since this implies a wasteful solution. The route of minimum length can be found, if desired, by an analogue method in which the locations are represented by pins and the route by a piece of string that winds around the pins. Figure 3.1 illustrates this approach using just a small number of major towns and cities distributed fairly evenly across the UK.

The problem with this approach is obvious: the route between any two towns that are not directly connected can be very circuitous. Furthermore, there is another problem with the line shown in the figure: it is not geographically feasible. It ignores the boundary constraints imposed by the coastline, and consequently takes the railway across part of the sea—for example, across the widest part of the Severn Estuary between Bristol and Cardiff. Once the boundary conditions are changed, the route is changed quite substantially; between Bristol and Cardiff there is detour to Birmingham, while Nottingham is now directly connected to Norwich (see Figure 3.2). This illustrates a general feature of a 'shortest distance' problem; namely that the solution is highly sensitive to changes in constraints. The issue is not that the total distance increases substantially when the constraints are changed by a small amount, but rather that the configuration of the line can change substantially even though its overall length does not.

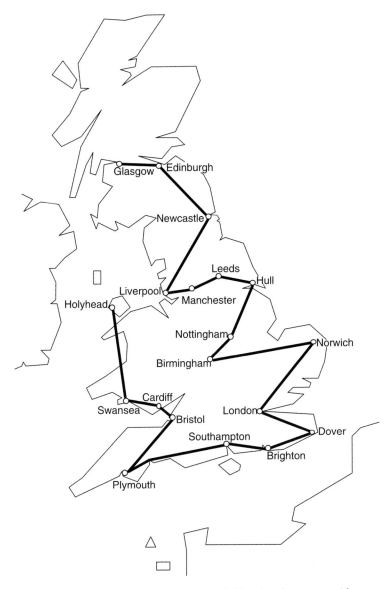

Figure 3.1. A continuous linear trunk network linking key locations, with no coastal constraints

There is no reason to suppose that a continuous line represents the best solution, however. A main line with branches is a more general solution, as it contains the single continuous line as a special case in which the number of branches is zero. When Thomas Gray articulated his vision of a national railway

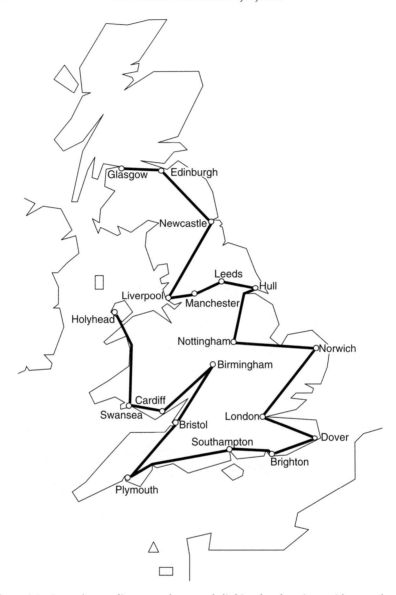

Figure 3.2. A continuous linear trunk network linking key locations with coastal constraints

network he proposed a north–south spine with branches, similar to (but not identical with) the configuration shown in Figure 3.3. There is a central spine running from Edinburgh to Southampton with ribs, or branches, serving towns and cities on the east and west coasts.

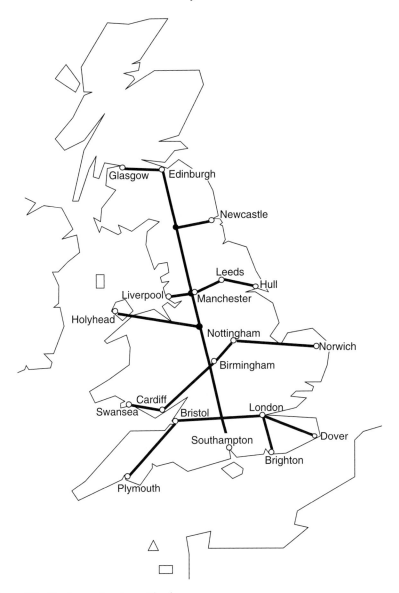

Figure 3.3. North–south spine with ribs

There is no necessity for the spine to be absolutely straight, however. It is possible that overall distance could be shortened by allowing the main line to shift from side to side in order to shorten the lengths of the branches. This is the basis of the Steiner solution which is shown in Figure 3.4. The key

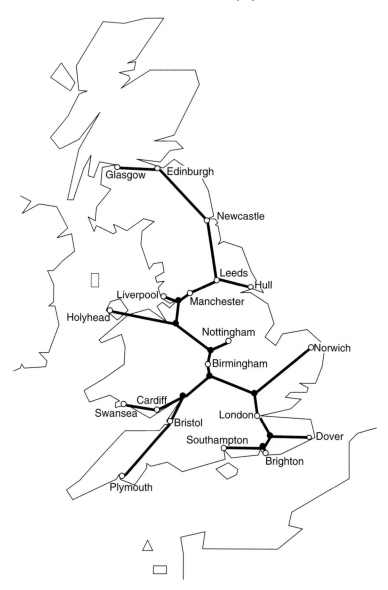

Figure 3.4. Steiner solution

properties of the Steiner solution is that adjacent linkages meet either at a town or at a hub; at a hub, three lines meet at 120° exactly, while at a town which is not a hub two lines meet at an angle greater than 120°. Further details are given in Appendix 3.

3.6.2. The traffic-weighting principle

The Steiner principle needs to be adjusted when the volume of traffic along different routes varies significantly. Under these conditions it is more appropriate to weight the distance along each linkage by the volume of traffic it carries, and to minimize total traffic-weighted distance. This modification implies an adjustment to the angles at which the lines meet at a hub. It involves straightening out routes which carry relatively heavy traffic, thereby requiring traffic on the more lightly loaded routes to make a sharper turn. For economic efficiency the angles are adjusted up to the point at which the marginal saving (in time or distance) on heavier traffic running on higher quality track is just offset by the additional cost imposed on light traffic running on lower quality track.

The application of the traffic-weighting principle is illustrated in Figure 3.5. The figure represents the case in which traffic flows to and from major centres such as London are heavier than to smaller centres such as Nottingham, Norwich, and Holyhead. The ranking of centres is very important; when traffic diverges to London and Birmingham, the route to London is shortened and the route to Birmingham is lengthened, but when traffic diverges between Birmingham and Nottingham, the route to Birmingham is shortened instead.

3.6.3. The triangle principle

Even when the Steiner Principle has been applied, the routes between two distant towns can still be very indirect. This is most readily understood in the absence of traffic-weighting. If two neighbouring towns are linked through an intermediate hub then traffic will change direction by $60°$ as it passes through the hub. If the hub is very near to one of the towns then this will not add much to the length of the journey, but if the hub is midway between the towns then the distance travelled will be significantly increased. The problem is potentially much greater where distant towns are concerned, for in this case it is likely that several hubs may intervene. The route may zig-zag to left and right through successive hubs, or it may form an arc to one side or the other of a direct line.

Because of the symmetry inherent in the unweighted Steiner solution, the problem facing traffic at a hub is the same from whichever direction it approaches—namely that it turns through $60°$. The natural solution to the problem is to replace the hub with a triangle, so that traffic along any route can effectively 'cut off' the hub. The single hub is replaced by a set of three hubs—its function is distributed, with each new hub having a specialized role in separating traffic between a specific pair of routes. Because of symmetry, the triangle is equilateral and the angle at each of its vertices is $60°$. This is the triangle principle. Applying the triangle principle means that through traffic now turns through only $30°$. Although the traffic has to turn twice, so that it turns $60°$ in total, it cuts off the sharp $60°$ turn at the original hub. The triangle principle trades off additional

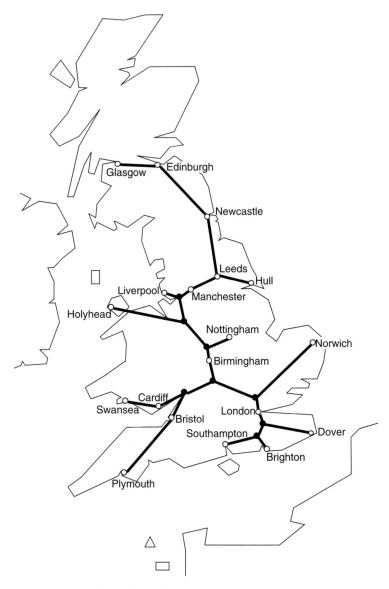

Figure 3.5. Steiner solution with traffic-weighting

route mileage against improved operating performance, and thereby helps the solution to meet the performance targets laid down above. The triangle principle can also be combined with traffic-weighting; some of the angles in the triangle will become more acute and others more obtuse.

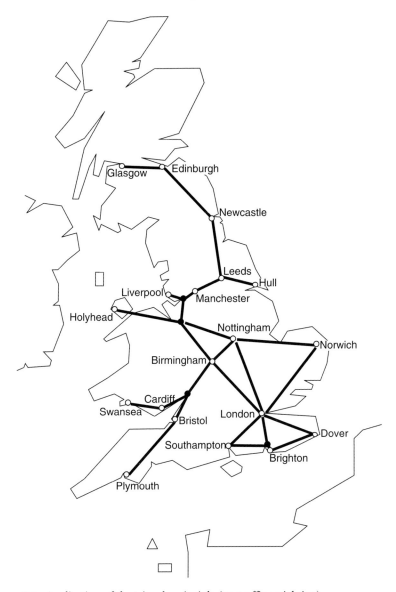

Figure 3.6. Application of the triangle principle (no traffic-weighting)

If the triangle principle were exploited fully, the dimensions of each triangle would be extended until one of its vertices either met a vertex of an adjoining triangle or touched one of the towns. In the first case, where two triangles adjoin, the routes along the sides of the triangles will meet at a four-way hub. The triangle principle therefore helps to explain why three-way hubs do not dominate the counterfactual system as the pure Steiner Principle would suggest. Its application is illustrated in Figure 3.6.

According to the pure Steiner principle it is inefficient for lines to cross at 90°: thus according to this principle, even the corners of a square are connected by a pair of three-way junctions at 120° rather than by intersecting diagonals at the centre of the square. This suggests that a four-way junction derived from the triangle principle will have a distinctive orientation, determined by the relative position of adjoining triangles. The importance of this result is confirmed by the fact that a distinctive orientation has been a feature of some of the most popular railway junctions on the actual railway system throughout its history. The converse of this is that 90° junctions are of little value, as interchange traffic has to turn so sharply that its journey becomes very indirect. This is also confirmed by the operation of the actual system: 90° junctions tend to be little used, and in some cases no station is even provided in recognition of this. Apart from one or two special cases, where other considerations intrude, the counterfactual system involves no 90° junctions at all.

3.6.4. The cut-off principle

The triangle principle is a special case of the more general cut-off principle. The cut-off principle is to avoid a switch of direction at some intermediate point along a route by connecting two points either side of the point by a direct line. Unlike the triangle principle, which applies just to a single three-way hub, the cut-off principle applies to any sequence of towns or three-way hubs at which traffic changes direction. The cut-off principle can be used to shorten the distance between any pair of towns by avoiding an intermediate town or hub that lies off the direct route between them. The application of the cut-off principle is illustrated in Figure 3.7.

3.6.5. The bypass principle

The bypass principle is used to avoid congestion at intermediate points. It can be applied to intermediate towns at which some trains stop while others run through. If a bypass is built as a direct line around a congested hub then it may also be a cut-off, in the sense that it shortens the route of through traffic. A bypass is not necessarily a cut-off, however, because it may actually be indirect, looping round a point of congestion through which traffic can pass without change of direction. Conversely, a cut-off is not necessarily a bypass as the town or hub that is cut-off is not necessarily congested.

A collection of cut-offs can form a bypass when, for example, they create an orbital system. An orbital system allows some traffic to cut-off a point of congestion as well as to bypass it, while other traffic bypasses the point of

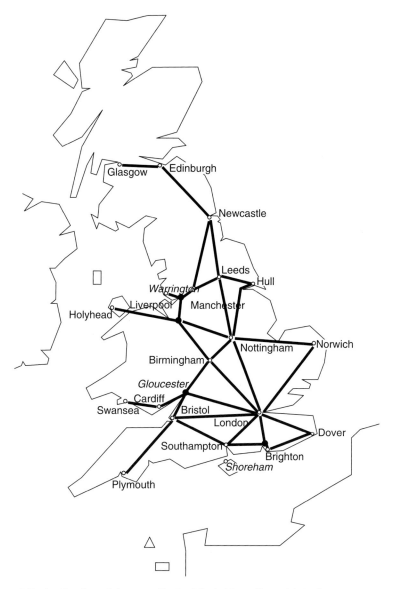

Figure 3.7. Application of the cut-off principle (with traffic-weighting)

congestion but uses a more circuitous route. The counterfactual network uses the bypass principle to provide avoiding routes round major centres such as London, Birmingham, Manchester, and Leeds. Bypasses are particularly useful when a network operates at close to capacity; they avoid chain reactions in which queues build up outside busy hubs, preventing traffic from entering or leaving other centres which feed into these hubs.

3.6.6. The concavity principle

The remaining principles are concerned mainly with the impact of geographical constraints on network optimization. It has already been noted that the optimization of a railway network is constrained by the shape of the coastline. (Where the border of a country is a territorial border rather than a coastline, as with many Continental European countries, it is the border rather than the coastline that mainly constrains the network.)

If the interior of the country were convex, coastal boundaries would have little impact on the structure of the network. Any straight-line route between two urban centres would lie entirely within the country (the only problem would arise if geological obstacles forced a detour outside of the country). In practice, though, river estuaries create numerous indentations in the UK coastline which only expensive bridges and tunnels can overcome. The resulting concavities in turn generate natural hubs on both road and rail systems. Traffic between towns on either side of an estuary will cross the estuary at the first available bridging point, which then becomes a hub. A wide variety of traffic which cannot follow a straight-line route because of the concave boundary 'turns the corner' at the hub in order to follow the shortest available interior route. Since traffic on different routes has to turn the same corner, the corner becomes a natural hub.

In Figure 3.7, for example, six corner hubs figure in the counterfactual system; three are also traffic-generating centres—namely London, Southampton, and Newcastle–and three are specialized hubs–namely Gloucester (the junction for Cardiff and Bristol), Warrington (the junction for Liverpool), and Shoreham (the junction for Brighton). Further examples of corner hubs are presented in Table 3.4.

3.6.6.1. *The core and periphery principle*

If these corner hubs are connected up to their immediate neighbours by straight-line links, then a core of the country will be created as the area enclosed by these links. In some cases the core may be convex, depending on the overall shape of the country. In the case of the UK the core is almost convex, but not entirely so, because the country as a whole is concave—for example, Edinburgh, on the East Coast, lies to the west of Bristol on the West Coast. This explains why long-distance traffic in the UK tends to follow a West Coast route rather than an East Coast route.

Efficient transport within the core normally requires that each of the corner hubs has good links to every other hub, whether it is a neighbour or not. The hubs also need to have good links to the major traffic-generating centres—in the case of the UK, to London and the major provincial centres identified above.

Table 3.4. Examples of natural hubs

Estuary/Firth/Bay	Other rivers	Primary hub	Type	Secondary hub	Type	Other hubs
Thames		London	First bridge	Oxford	Major crossing	Reading
Wash	Nene, Great Ouse, Welland	King Lynn	Ferry	Peterborough	Major crossing	Wisbech, Huntingdon
Humber		Hull	Ferry	Goole	First bridge	Grimsby, York, Gainsborough, Newark, Nottingham
Tees		Middlesbrough	Ferry, transporter bridge	Stockton	Earliest bridge	Darlington
Tyne		Newcastle	Ferry, later bridges	Gateshead	Opposite Newcastle	North Shields, South Shields
Forth		Edinburgh/Leith	Ferry	Stirling	First bridge	
Clyde		Glasgow	First bridge	Lanark	Waterfalls	Motherwell
Solway	Eden	Carlisle	First bridge	Stranraer	Natural harbour	Dumfries
Morecambe	Lune, Kent	Lancaster	First bridge	Kirkby Lonsdale	Major crossing	
Ribble		Preston	First bridge	Clitheroe	Major crossing	
Mersey		Liverpool	Ferry	Birkenhead	Opposite Liverpool	Runcorn, Widnes, Warrington, Stockport
Dee		Chester	First bridge			
Bristol Channel	Severn, Avon	Bristol	Natural harbour	Gloucester	First bridge	Tewksbury, Worcester, Stourport, Shrewsbury, Welshpool
Tamar		Plymouth	Ferry, later bridge			
Exe		Exeter	First bridge			
Test		Southampton	First bridge			
Adur	Wey	Shoreham	First bridge			

Table 3.5. Fourteen major peripheral areas in the UK

Peripheral area	Estuaries	Natural hubs at bridging points	Major ports, resorts	Administrative centres
North of Scotland: Highlands, Grampian, Kintyre and Strathclyde	Clyde, Tay	Glasgow, Perth	Aberdeen, Dundee	Inverness
Fife	Tay, Forth	Perth, Stirling	Kirkcaldy	
Northumbria and Midlothian	Forth, Tyne	Stirling, Newcastle	Leith (Edinburgh)	Edinburgh
Wearside	Tyne, Tees	Newcastle, Stockton	Sunderland	
East Yorkshire	Tees, Humber	Stockton, Snaith	Hull Scarborough	York
Lincolnshire	Humber, New River	Snaith Spalding	Grimsby, Boston	Lincoln
East Anglia	Ouse, Thames	Kings Lynn, Cambridge, London	Yarmouth, Harwich	Norwich, Ipswich
Kent and Sussex	Thames, Test	London, Southampton	Dover, Brighton	Canterbury, Guilford
South-west	Test, Severn	Southampton, Gloucester	Bristol, Plymouth, Weymouth	Exeter, Yeovil, Truro
Wales	Severn, Dee	Gloucester, Shrewsbury, Chester	Cardiff, Swansea, Milford Haven, Holyhead	Aberystwyth
Wirral	Dee, Mersey	Chester, Warrington	Birkenhead	
Merseyside: west Lancashire and Fylde Coast	Dee, Ribble	Warrington, Wigan, Preston	Liverpool	
Lake District	Ribble, Eden	Preston, Carlisle	Barrow, Whitehaven	Kendal
Galloway	Eden, Clyde	Carlisle, Glasgow	Stranraer, Ayr	

Note: Each peripheral area can, in principle, be subdivided further using minor estuaries: for example, the north of Scotland and Merseyside can be subdivided into smaller areas using the River Lochy (bridged at Fort William), and the Moray Firth (bridged near Inverness), but these additional divisions are of little value, because the bridging points they identify already appear as ports, resorts, or administrative centres. Note also that the peripheral areas are not the only areas with coastline. The core has coastline along The Wash between Spalding and Kings Lynn.

Outside the core lie the peripheral areas. Fourteen major peripheral areas are distinguished in Table 3.5. These have been constructed by rationalizing 18 areas defined by major river systems, through merging the less industrialized and more sparsely populated areas into larger neighbours; the original 18 areas are illustrated in Figure 3.8. Each peripheral area is coastal, and is bounded by a pair of river estuaries.

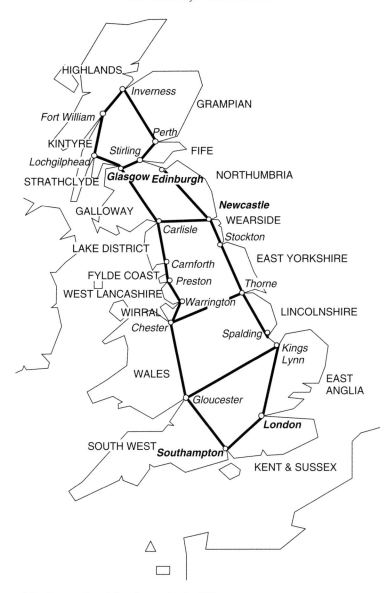

Figure 3.8. Core and peripheral areas in the UK

There are four main types of urban centre within a typical coastal peripheral area:

- The corner hubs at the estuary bridging points, as described above;
- Other entry and exit points—in particular, points roughly midway between the estuaries, and suitable for traffic entering the heartland of the peripheral area;

- A commercial centre in the heartland, serving the needs of both coastal and inland towns; and
- Towns along the coastline, further out along the estuaries. These may include fishing ports, deep-sea ports, seaside tourist resorts, and retirement areas. Coastlines are often well-populated, and may evolve into linear 'service' districts, analogous to the industrial districts of manufacturing areas.

The corner hubs, and the other entry points between them, constitute the interface between the periphery and the core. Each corner hub typically serves two peripheral regions—one on either side of the estuary—while the other entry points serve only one. The need for additional entry points depends on the distance between the estuaries, for where this distance is small, the corner hubs will be close together.

Coastal ports will consign much of their traffic through the nearest corner hub. It is therefore natural to connect coastal ports to their corner hubs by a coastal route. This coastal route should have a connection to the heartland centre (if it exists). In addition, the heartland centre should have links to the corner hubs and the other entry points. This provides a recipe for equipping each peripheral area with a local system that is efficiently connected to the central core.

3.6.7. The loop principle

The loop principle asserts that where traffic is reasonably heavy a loop is better at making connections than a dead-end branch. Consider two dead-end branches connected to different hubs on the national system. Traffic on each branch can only make connections by leaving town in one direction—towards the hub. But if the ends of the two branches are connected up, a loop is formed, and traffic from any town can access hubs at either end of the line. The amount of traffic on the new connection will depend on whether different journeys from a given town benefit from being routed through different hubs. If there is only a small amount of traffic on each branch and the ends of the branches are far apart then the completion of the loop may not be viable.

A simple application of the loop principle is to the coastal lines described above. If there are two lines, running alongside adjacent estuaries, then it may be useful to link up their termini. Traffic from one estuary may be routed along the loop to a hub on the other estuary, in order to shorten its journey to destinations in that direction.

The loop principle can also be employed in inland areas. Trunk lines between major urban centres may have to deviate considerably from a direct route in order to take in all the intermediate towns. Local traffic needs may best be met by a loop which takes in all the intermediate towns and feeds into the trunk system through hubs at either end. This has operational advantages too: express trains on the trunk line are not delayed by local traffic at intermediate towns. In this context, the inland loop represents an extension of the bypass principle. Inland loops are particularly useful when one end points towards London and the other towards a local provincial centre.

3.6.8. The contour principle

Geographical constraints impinge on network optimization not only through the shape of the coastline but also through obstructions in the interior. In the UK the principal internal obstacles are mountains and hills, although in some countries lakes may also be a constraint. To avoid steep gradients and expensive bridges and tunnels, railways must accommodate themselves to the contours of the land. In an island country like the UK, many railway lines start or finish on the coast, where it pays to start the railway at sea level in order to meet the needs of port traffic. Railways therefore tend to follow valleys inland, provided the sides are not too steep and the river does not meander too much; the railway climbs slowly along the valley floor, tunnelling through to an adjacent valley, and then descending to the coast on the other side of the country. As a result, new types of hub are created where valleys intersect: more than three lines may meet, and when there are just three lines they may not meet at 120° (Jackman 1962).

In principle, these new types of hub could be rural hubs, but in practice they tend to be urban hubs because their natural commercial advantages will have been recognized and exploited before the railway arrives. As urban centres, they would need to be served by the network anyway. Practical application of the contour principle to the location of hubs does not therefore lead to a radical revision of the results presented above.

The application of the contour principle is illustrated in Figure 3.9. Some of the mountains within the UK have limited impact on the linkages between the largest towns because no direct trunk links would pass through them anyway. The exception is the northern Pennines, which block a direct route from Liverpool and Manchester to Newcastle. This in turn lengthens the detour involved in reaching Glasgow via Newcastle, and strengthens the case for a direct line from Warrington (the hub serving Liverpool and Manchester) to Glasgow along the West Coast, as illustrated in the figure. This reinforces the argument made above about the role of geographical fundamentals in favouring a West Coast route to the north, despite the commercial advantages of a route via Newcastle.

3.6.9. The space-filling principle

When the railway system caters only for towns above a certain size, some parts of the country may get left 'off the map' altogether. Although population density may be low in such areas, their extent may be so great that there is still some traffic potential. It may therefore be efficient to drive a branch into the heart of the country, with stations spaced at equal intervals to act as railheads for traffic brought to them.

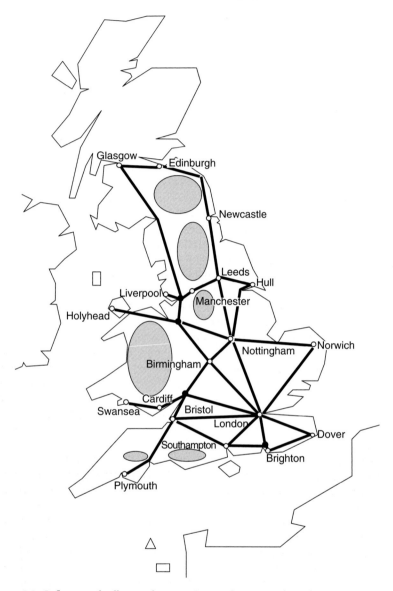

Figure 3.9. Influence of valleys and mountains on the counterfactual system

The space-filling principle asserts that the best way of meeting such needs is by a dead-end branch driven into the area from a convenient hub in such a way that the maximum distance from any point in the area to any point upon a railway (whether on the branch or not) is a minimum. This principle can determine both the length of the branch and the route that it follows.

The space-filling principle exploits the fact that the dead-end branch is the cheapest way of filling space. Although a loop would offer greater flexibility, through access to a second hub, the additional mileage may not be warranted when traffic is extremely light. The dead-end branch will meet the needs of small farmers who require supplies of coal and lime, and the conveyance of cattle and crops, but it will not meet the needs of people who need to travel regularly: they will have to live elsewhere in order to benefit fully from the railway system.

3.7. CONSTRUCTING THE FIRST TRIAL SOLUTION

The first trial solution of the counterfactual was developed using a three-stage procedure. In the first stage, a provisional network of long-distance lines was specified, to form a skeleton around which short-distance lines could be configured. At this stage it was left open as to whether these are trunk or primary routes. The centres connected by the skeleton network comprised London and the major provincial centres mentioned earlier, together with the three types of centre associated with the peripheral areas, and listed in Table 3.5.

Connecting up these centres using the Steiner, triangle cut-off and bypass principles identified a number of hubs within the core. Prominent core hubs include Melrose, Darlington, Kirkby Lonsdale, Huddersfield, Wetherby, Stoke-on-Trent, Derby, Leicester, Northampton, Reading, and Trowbridge. While some of these locations, such as Darlington, Derby, and Reading, are recognized railway centres, others are not. Some of the centres are close to better known centres—for example, Kirkby Lonsdale is near to Carnforth, Wetherby is near to York, and Trowbridge to Westbury. By contrast, other hubs—for example, Melrose— acquire importance because of fundamental structural differences between the actual and counterfactual networks.

The second stage was to specify the local lines. Wherever possible, local lines feed into the hubs identified at the first stage. By concentrating interchange traffic at a limited number of hubs, the number of stops that long-distance trains need to make for connection purposes is reduced. At the same time, the power of hubs to act as a 'one-stop shop' for local connections is increased. An iterative process was then followed to fine-tune the interfaces between trunk and local networks.

The final stage is based on the counterfactual timetable. The preparation of the timetable provides an opportunity to assess whether upgrading certain links to permit higher speeds would improve connections. Connections are improved when speeding up one link relative to others allows trains entering a hub from the accelerated link to make connections with trains that they would otherwise miss. The main effect of this exercise is to upgrade a number of local lines to secondary status.

It could be argued that this upgrading process is unhistorical, in the sense that timetabling issues of this kind would not have been anticipated when the network was under construction. In practice, however, many routes were upgraded after

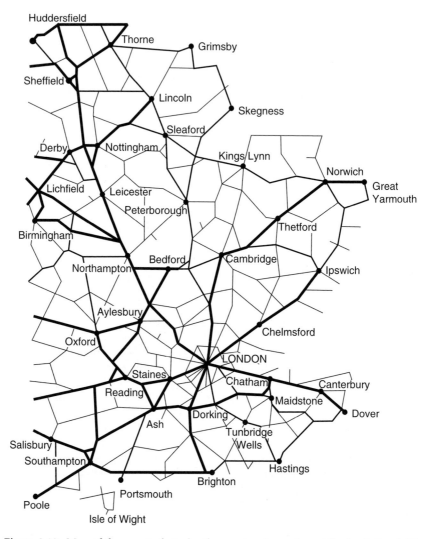

Figure 3.10. Map of the counterfactual railway network: south-east England, East Midlands, and East Anglia

they were constructed, and indeed many routes were built with an option to upgrade (e.g. double-track bridges and tunnels were built on single-track lines). Although there is little direct evidence that timetabling factors alone led to the upgrading of routes, it seems reasonable to suppose that they may have been a contributing factor in certain cases.

The spatial configuration that results from this process is illustrated in Figures 3.10–3.12, while details of all the routes are given in Appendix 4.

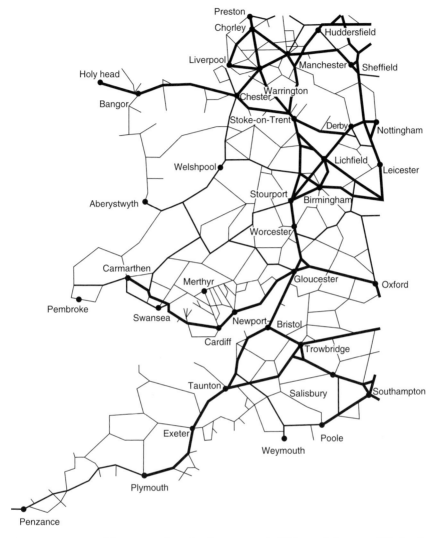

Figure 3.11. Map of the counterfactual railway network: Wales and the west of England

3.8. THE OPTIMALITY OF THE COUNTERFACTUAL SYSTEM

Having described the heuristics by which the counterfactual was derived, we turn to the question of how we know that the result is optimal. The short answer is that we do not. In Simon's (1983) terms, the application of heuristics represents

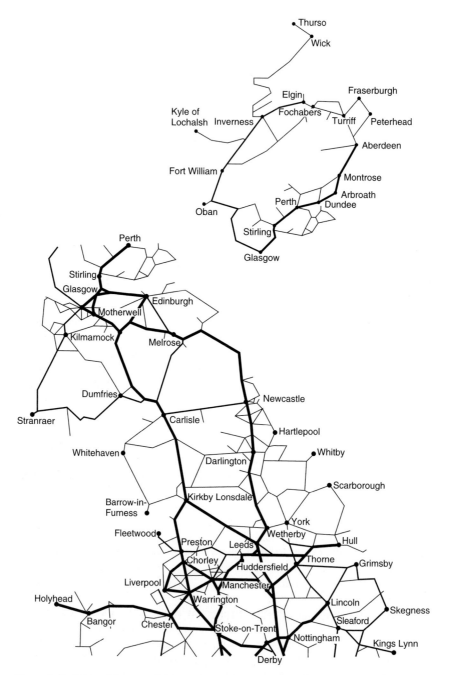

Figure 3.12. Map of the counterfactual railway system: Scotland and the north of England

'procedural rationality' rather than 'substantive rationality'. The appropriate way to test whether the result is optimal is by sensitivity analysis. This involves specifying a range of alternatives and investigating whether a better result can be obtained. It has proved impossible so far, after extensive experimentation, to obtain a better result than the one reported in this study.

In the light of this, it is our contention that it is difficult (but perhaps not impossible) to find a network which meets the criteria set out above with a smaller total route mileage. Furthermore, if a better network were found, it would have a total route mileage very similar to the one reported in this study, because any improvement would be marginal. Moreover, the discovery of such a network would only reinforce the conclusion that the actual network was inefficient by showing that the best alternative is even better than we have claimed. The conclusions are therefore quite robust.

What cannot be claimed, however, is that any improvement in the network would involve only a marginal change in its configuration. For example, a local adjustment in one part of the network—say the Midlands—might tip the balance away from a West Coast main line to Scotland in favour of an East Coast main line, resulting in radical change to the rest of the network too. Although the reduction in route mileage might only be marginal, the impact on structure could be immense. While this would not affect the overall conclusion that the actual network was inefficient, it could affect the analysis of more specific failings in the system.

This problem was recognized from the outset, and so in constructing the counterfactual a number of radically different options were considered, in addition to the localized variations that are considered in conventional sensitivity analysis. While the radical variations already considered are definitely inferior to the structure proposed, there always remains a possibility, in complex problems of this kind, that some other configuration which has not been considered could have a marginal advantage over the configuration proposed.

For reasons explained above, the specific outputs of the counterfactual system—in terms of the quality of service on particular routes—are very different in some respects from those of the actual system. Had the counterfactual system been introduced, the type of traffic carried by the railways would have been rather different. For example, cross-country travel would have been much easier, and as a result, cross-country traffic would have increased. In comparing the outputs of the two systems, therefore, there is an 'index number' problem. Comparing performance on the basis of the traffic carried by the actual system will favour the actual system, while basing the comparison on the probable traffic conveyed by the counterfactual system will favour the counterfactual system. Where the performance of the two systems is finely balanced, each will tend to perform best in respect of its own type of traffic. Because we have deduced the traffic requirements from general considerations, as explained above, and explored the sensitivity of the solution to variations in these requirements, the 'index number' problem does not directly affect our results. It is important to bear the problem is mind, however, when considering wider policy implications.

3.9. THE CONFIGURATION OF HUBS

The performance of a network of any kind is significantly influenced by the structure of its hubs. Given the marked superiority of the counterfactual network, it is natural to seek an explanation in terms of its superior pattern of hubs. Indeed, given the importance of the Steiner principle in the derivation of the counterfactual, it is plausible to suppose that the precise location of the hubs, and the geometry of the system around each hub, contributes significantly to its strong performance.

Although this point is valid, the demonstration of it is not so simple as it might appear. The problem does not lie so much with the counterfactual system, where the identification of hubs and their description is quite straightforward, but rather with the actual system. The issues are examined in detail in Appendix 5. The gist of the problem is easily stated, however: namely that many of the hubs on the actual system were unintended hubs so far as the railway companies were concerned, and in many cases they were unwanted hubs as well.

The fact that a hub was unintended does not mean that it occurred at random or that its existence cannot be explained. Quite the contrary, in fact: these hubs arose as a direct consequence of the wasteful duplication of routes created by competition between the companies. The unintended hubs arose at frontiers between rival railway networks, where invaders encountered established local companies. The established companies excluded the invaders from their existing hubs and did their best to prevent new hubs from emerging at points where the invading lines crossed established ones.

A Victorian traveller who consulted a Bradshaw map of the railway system would be most impressed, at first sight, by the number of hubs on the actual system. They would infer that a cross-country journey could be accomplished very comfortably using a variety of possible routes. On closer examination, however, the traveller would discover that many of these routes were not viable. Where the map suggested a junction, there would be actually a crossing: two lines would intersect with no connection between them. At other places, connection would be possible, but the traveller would have to transfer between stations some distance apart. Even where there was a junction station, the timing of the trains might be inconvenient; throughout the day, trains might leave just before connecting trains arrived. After examining the various options the traveller might well conclude that the quickest and most reliable route was via London—even though the other routes were much shorter.

Figure 3.13 shows the relative frequency distribution of hubs on the counterfactual system. Hubs are distinguished by the number of different lines converging on them. The minimum size of a hub is three, since this is the smallest number of lines required to form a junction. Many of these hubs are composite hubs; that is, they comprise a number of different junctions in a particular area that are centred around a station, or group of stations in the same town, where

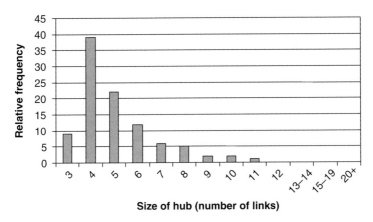

Figure 3.13. Size distribution of hubs on the counterfactual system

interchange of traffic can take place. As explained in the appendix, this is the most useful way of defining a hub for the purposes of this exercise. There are a total of 293 hubs. There are 27 hubs with only 3 lines and 2 hubs with as many as 11 lines. The most common size of hub is four and the average number of lines per hub is 5.04.

By comparison, the actual system has a larger number of hubs—495—and, on average, a larger numbers of lines per hub as well—5.95. This is statistically possible because the actual system is far larger in terms of route miles. The relative frequency distribution of hubs is shown in Figure 3.14.

This comparison reveals three distinct (though related) issues. First, the actual system contains many more hubs than the counterfactual one; second, it contains a relatively small number of small hubs and a relatively large number of large hubs; and third, the large hubs are very much larger than the large hubs on the counterfactual system.

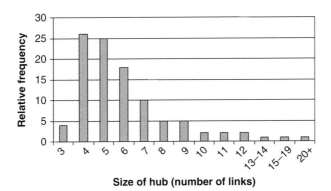

Figure 3.14. Size distribution of hubs on the actual system

The simplest way of explaining these results is that the actual system is very wasteful. Because it has many lines, it has lots of intersections, which in turn means lots of potential hubs. These hubs, moreover, are much larger than they need to be: thus small hubs become large and large hubs become even larger. The problem then becomes to explain how this waste arises.

The problem can also be stated the other way round, using mirror images of the preceding results. First, the counterfactual employs only a small number of hubs; this is partly because it has a much lower route mileage, and partly because the hubs are more effective. Second, the counterfactual system has hubs that are relatively small; this is only to be expected from the Steiner Principle, which prescribes three-way hubs, and the triangle principle which suggest that four-way hubs will emerge when cut-offs are built around the three-way hubs. Third, the counterfactual has large hubs that are relatively small; these large hubs are mainly traffic-generating centres, which is why the angles between the lines converging are small. Even so, the number of lines directly entering the hub is reduced by the use of satellite hubs at which approaching lines merge and orbital lines diverge. Thus the size of the hub is much less than it might otherwise be.

So why does the actual system not exploit the same efficient principles? The answer has already been summarized in Chapter 1 and is spelled out in greater detail in Chapter 6. It is because the hubs on the actual system did not function properly, and so additional hubs emerged to take over their roles. These additional hubs did not work well either—they were often badly sited because they were 'second best' locations. Furthermore, dominant companies often did their best to disrupt the working of hubs used by rival companies to prevent 'captive' passengers from switching to the rival networks. Because of the disruption of hubs, companies had to tap into traffic by building direct lines into the heart of traffic-generating centres, instead of accessing existing hubs. They built their own termini in the traffic-generating centres to market their own services. The large number of lines converging on independent termini turned traffic-generating centres into very large but ineffective hubs.

Because traffic-generating centres could not function as effective hubs, companies built their main interchange facilities elsewhere—often on greenfield sites. This created even more hubs. Companies knew that they could not expect to monopolize a large traffic-generating centre, as local interests were strongly in favour of competition, but they could monopolize isolated hubs where local interests were weak. Connections were therefore made, not at places people wished to visit, but at places that they did not.

These outcomes can be explained more fully using a simple stylized model that lends itself to diagrammatic illustration. A hexagonal configuration of towns is assumed, with a metropolis at the centre of the hexagon. In a UK context, a hexagonal configuration is exemplified by major provincial centres such as Dover, Brighton, Bristol, Birmingham, Nottingham, and Norwich, and the metropolis is, of course, London.

An intuitive way of connecting up these towns is illustrated in Figure 3.15. It is a 'hub-spoke-rim' configuration reminiscent of a bicycle wheel. The principal

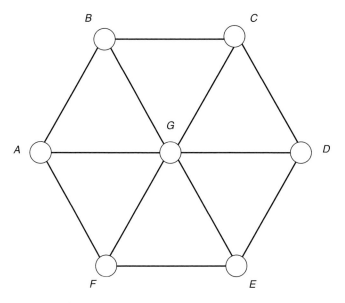

Figure 3.15. Hub analysis for a symmetrical system with a metropolis surrounded by equidistant large towns

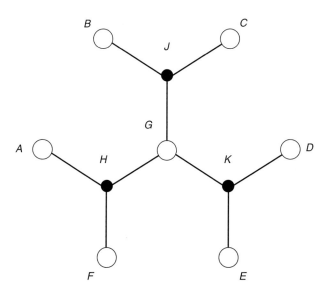

Figure 3.16. Steiner solution for the symmetric system

towns are labelled A–F and London is labelled G. Each provincial town has two equidistant neighbours and is linked to each of these neighbours and to London. Each provincial town is therefore a three-way hub, while London is six-way hub. There are seven hubs altogether and the average number of links per hub is 3.43.

When the Steiner principle is applied three satellite hubs appear (see Figure 3.16); these are labelled H, J, and K. Each provincial town is the terminus of a dead-end branch and so is not a hub. Only London remains a hub, but with three links to its satellites instead of six links to the towns. There are four hubs and each has three linkages.

The application of the Steiner principle produces very indirect routes, as noted earlier, which is why it needs to be supplemented by a cut-off principle. The most indirect routes are A to B, C to D, and E to F. Introducing cut-offs between these towns generates three loops with a common point at G (see Figure 3.17). This is a stylized version of the system of coastal loops that is used in the counterfactual. There are still just four three-way hubs; the only difference is that the dead-end spurs have disappeared in the course of creating the loops. Thus, even when combined with the cut-off principle, the Steiner principle reduces both the number of hubs and the number of linkages per hub.

Now consider the actual system. Suppose that it begins with the construction of main lines from London to the provincial towns. This produces a single six-way hub in London (see Figure 3.18). Each town is connected to every other town, but only via London. Suppose, furthermore, that each main line is owned by a separate company that claims a regional monopoly; the regional areas are radial and their boundaries are indicated by the dotted line in the figure. If

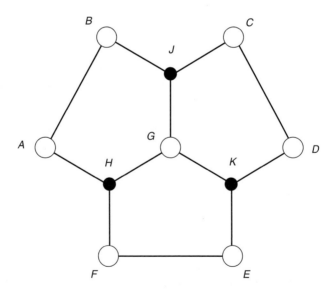

Figure 3.17. Application of the cut-off principle to the symmetric system

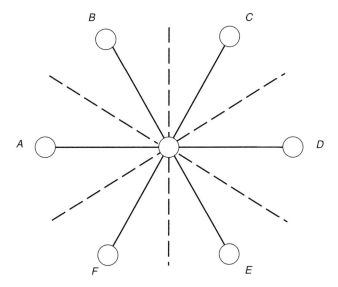

Figure 3.18. A radial main line system for the symmetric network, built by private companies aspiring to regional monopolies

demand for cross-country travel is confined to a small wealthy elite then these boundaries are impermeable; it is easy for the companies to collude by routing all cross-country traffic via London. When a new market for popular cross-country travel opens up—for example, for excursions and holidays—independent lines will be built if the established companies do not build them first. Competition therefore develops as the companies invade each other's territories.

Suppose that neighbouring companies are on bad terms with each other and therefore cannot cooperate, but that non-neighbours can cooperate to build joint lines. Non-neighbours cooperate to invade the territories of their common enemies, which are the companies that border each of their regions. In the hexagonal system, each company has two enemies, one on either side of their territory, and two allies, each on the opposite side of the enemy's territory. They invade the enemy territory by building a link across it. It is assumed that this link is a direct line between the respective provincial towns.

The outcome of this process is shown in Figure 3.19. The figure shows a 'spider's web' that involves a massive proliferation of hubs. Twelve new hubs are created, labelled L–X; each is a four-way hub because it represents the intersection of two lines. The provincial centres each become three-way hubs, while London remains a six-way hub. There are now 19 hubs altogether, and the average number of links per hub is 3.79.

Despite the proliferation of hubs, however, the system is difficult for the traveller to use. This is because each of the four-way hubs involves lines operated by different companies. At six of the hubs both the intersecting lines are joint

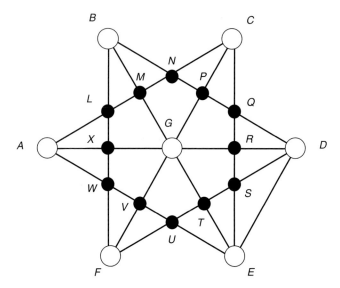

Figure 3.19. Cross-country linkages on the symmetric network, built by invading companies

venture cross-country routes, and the companies involved in each line are quite distinct, though none are enemies. At the remaining six hubs, however, the cross-country line intersects the main London line of the company whose territory it is invading. Relations between the companies will be particularly poor. The most serious conflict of interest arises from the fact that cross-country passengers from the provincial town can switch from the London line to the cross-country route at an intermediate point. This induces the main line operator to break connections with the cross-country lines from the provincial centre, rather than to facilitate connections in the interests of network flexibility.

Finally, suppose that the cross-country lines are built by independent companies instead. This may lead to an even greater proliferation of hubs. Where joint lines are constructed by main line companies, the companies can take measures to avoid their joint lines competing with their own main lines (even if they use them to compete with their rivals' main lines) whereas when the cross-country lines are owned by independent companies they can be used to compete with any established main line.

Suppose therefore that each main line company has a local competitor that initially operates a purely local network in and around the provincial town. It is this competitor that seizes the opportunity to build an independent line. It hopes that the independent line will help it to 'break out' of the locality in which it has hitherto been confined. The local companies build out alternately to the left and the right of the main lines. The local competitor at A builds a cross-country line to C, the local competitor at C builds a line to E, and E builds to A; B builds to F, F to D, and D to B. These cross-country lines intersect at the hubs L–X as before. So far there is no difference from the scenario above, apart from the ownership of the cross-country lines.

Unlike their main line rivals, however, the independent local companies are still unable to serve London, as their cross-country lines run only to other provincial centres. Although each cross-country line intersects a main line to London, the main line concerned is operated by a company whose region has been invaded, and which is therefore an enemy. As part of their plans for cross-country lines, therefore, the independent companies may decide to build independent lines to London as well. Direct replication of their local competitor's existing main line will be unacceptable to Parliament and, in any case, economy of construction suggests that the line should be built from a junction with the cross-country line. The question is then where the junction should be situated.

One possibility is to situate the junction at an intersection with another cross-country line. Each cross-country line intersects two other cross-country lines, but only the intersection nearest to the provincial town provides a route to London that is sufficiently direct to be viable. Furthermore, building a line from this intersection suggests that it could be built jointly with the owner of the other line. Thus in Figure 3.20, the line from A to C, owned by the local competitor at A, intersects the line from B to F, owned by the local competitor at B, at the point L. A and B then join forces to build a line from L to G which both companies can use to access London. A practical example is the Great Central–Great Western Joint Line from Ashendon Junction near Bicester, which the Great Central used to

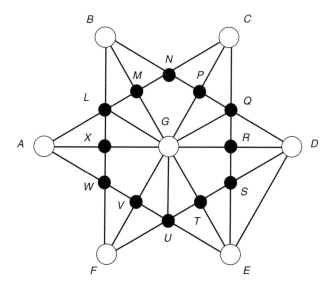

Figure 3.20. Symmetric network in which invaders collaborate to build lines to the metropolis in competition with the local main line companies

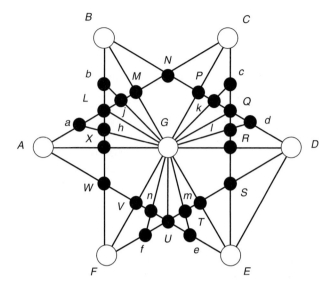

Figure 3.21. Symmetric network in which invading companies build their own competing lines to the metropolis

compete with the Midland route from Nottingham to London and the Great Western used to compete with the London and North Western route from Birmingham to London. This outcome changes the hubs at L, Q, and U from four-way to five-way hubs, and raises London from a six-way hub to a nine-way hub, thereby raising the average number of links per hub from 3.79 to 4.10.

There are two difficulties in the path of achieving this cooperative outcome, however. The first is that the two companies need to be aware of each other's plans, and to coordinate these plans so that the intersection occurs at a mutually convenient point. Second, the deviation that each company must accept in its route to London in order to share the use of a line may be deemed too great to permit effective competition with the established main line. In this case each company will build its own main line into London from a point nearer to the provincial town it serves, as illustrated in Figure 3.21. This line will then intersect the other cross-country route, creating six new four-way hubs, a–f, in addition to six three-way hubs, h–n, where the London line diverges from the cross-country route. As a result, London is 'upgraded' to a 12-way hub. The total number of hubs increases from 19 to 31 and the average size of hub falls back to 3.87—lower than before, but still higher than without any competing London lines.

Like any simple model, however, there are certain limitations that need to be recognized. Because of the symmetrical treatment of all the provincial towns, whatever happens in one region happens in every other region, so that a commitment to building cross-country lines has a dramatic effect within the model.

In practice, not all regions were as attractive as others, and so proliferation tended to be not so serious in poorer areas. Despite its limitations, however, the model is useful in explaining the proliferation of hubs not only at the national level but at the regional level too. For example, if the model is re-scaled down to the regional level, then it can be used to explain the proliferation of hubs around Birmingham by identifying Birmingham as the central hub, and Northampton, Worcester, Stafford, Derby, and Nottingham as the provincial towns.

It must be emphasized that underpinning this entire analysis is the view that rival companies not only could not cooperate in the operation of hubs but could not cooperate in the operation of lines either. In practice this meant that running powers conferred by Parliament over other companies' lines were difficult to enforce without the goodwill of the other companies. As the growth of a mass market stimulated competition, companies were forced to abandon their strategy of simply exploiting a regional monopoly. But they were unable to develop comprehensive cooperative strategies to respond to the competitive conditions. The only way to achieve full cooperation was through merger, and Parliament ruled this option out so far as mergers between major companies were concerned. The most that companies achieved was to cooperate in fighting a common rival. Some of the companies became quite adept at this—particularly the Midland and Great Central.

Cooperative invasions of rival companies' territories was a means of expanding a company from a local or regional 'player' into a potentially national 'player'. The companies that were most anxious to achieve this national status were local companies that operated cross-country lines but had no direct access to London— specifically the two companies mentioned above. By contrast, the companies that had developed main lines at an early stage were content to refine their defensive strategies to defeat the attempted invasions of expansionist companies. The larger the region that was controlled, the more content was the company—thus the Great Western, which controlled an enormous area, was for many years a very defensive company, and only after the broad gauge was abandoned did it become more aggressive. By contrast, the London and South Western, which controlled a much smaller area—certainly an area that was small compared with the aspirations suggested by its name—was more expansion minded. Even defence companies could be expansionist when attack was the best form of defence. A defence company that threatened a counter-attack might be obliged to go through with its attack if its bluff was called.

3.10. CONCLUSION

This chapter has explained how the counterfactual network was derived. A counterfactual system of this type has never been constructed before, to the best of our knowledge. The counterfactual represents the best railway network that could reasonably have been achieved by 1914 had it been planned on the advice of the Board of Trade Railway Committee, or some other enlightened body, at the time of the Railway Mania. This was a propitious time to devise a national railway system, as almost all the feasible plans for railway routes were 'on the table' at this time. It would not have been necessary for the railways to have been nationalized in order to implement the counterfactual, but it would have been necessary for Parliament to accept specialist advice when authorizing private railway promotions—which it was ultimately unwilling to do. Furthermore, to exploit the resulting system properly, Parliament would have had to require the shared use of stations and cooperation between companies over the interchange of traffic at hubs—neither of which it was prepared to do.

The counterfactual network equals or exceeds the performance of the actual network for all types of traffic so far as journey times are concerned, and for most types of traffic so far as distances are concerned. The weighting of the criteria does not affect the main result so far as time is concerned; it could only be undermined if the types of traffic were further subdivided and some specific subdivisions were identified where journey times were longer. Even then, it would be necessary for a critic to show that the relevant types of traffic were more important than all the other types of traffic on the system.

Four different standards of railway route have been distinguished. The standard of route, and the direction of the linkages, reflect the anticipated volumes of traffic. Traffic volumes have been estimated from a variety of sources, including statistics on the population and industrial structure of leading towns and cities and the distances between them. Information on specific traffic flows has also been collected from secondary sources and used in the analysis. The accuracy of these traffic estimates does not have a direct bearing on the results, so long as the individual linkages have sufficient capacity to cope with the volume of traffic that they need to carry, whatever that happens to be.

The costs of constructing the different types of route have not been considered in detail in this study. If the optimization performance were reformulated in terms of minimizing construction cost, or minimizing total cost (inclusive of operating costs), then accurate estimation of specific traffic flows would become much more important, and more complicated calculations would be required.

4

Regional Comparisons

4.1. INTRODUCTION

The national railway system may be regarded as a collection of regional systems. These regional systems interface at hubs along their boundaries. They are served by lines radiating from London, and are connected to each other by cross-country lines, some of which run from coast to coast. On the actual system most of the lines radiating from London are trunk and most of the cross-country lines are secondary, while on the counterfactual the distinction is much less sharp: both trunk and primary lines radiate from London and both primary and secondary lines provide cross-country links.

This chapter presents a detailed comparison between the actual and counterfactual systems, disaggregated to a regional level. Nineteen regions are discussed in turn, with both the actual and counterfactual networks being examined in each case. Each region is treated as a separate entity, although its connections with neighbouring regions are fully discussed. The historical evolution of the actual system in each region is summarized, based on the secondary sources presented in the appropriate sections of the classified bibliography. Each section has been written so that it can be read on its own without reference to the rest of the chapter. Readers who have no special interest in the regional dimension may wish to proceed directly to the next chapter.

The sequence of regions corresponds to an anti-clockwise circuit of England and Wales, beginning in East Anglia, to the north-east of London, and concluding with Kent and East Sussex to the south-east of London. London and the Home Counties are then discussed, and finally the regions of Scotland. The English and Welsh sequence runs anti-clockwise because it permits the discussion to focus on some of the most isolated regions first, with the regions that are more strongly integrated into the national system being discussed later. Scotland is considered separately because the Scottish system is relatively self-contained, with north–south routes crossing the ancient border near Hadrian's Wall at just two main points—Newcastle and Carlisle. Taking a detour into Scotland half-way through the tour round England and Wales would disrupt the chapter's continuity.

The regional subdivisions are summarized in Table 4.1, which also indicates the coverage of each region by references to the principal administrative units—the counties—as they were in the mid-Victorian period.

Table 4.1. The regions of the network employed in the comparison of actual and counterfactual systems

Region	Constituent areas
East Anglia	Norfolk, Suffolk, Cambridgeshire, and Huntingdonshire
South Midlands	Oxfordshire and Gloucestershire, and adjoining parts of Buckinghamshire, Somerset, Wiltshire, and Worcestershire
The Shires	Northamptonshire, Leicestershire, Rutland, Bedfordshire, and Buckinghamshire
Lincolnshire	Lindsey, Kesteven, City of Lincoln
Yorkshire	North Riding, West Riding
Humberside and Cleveland	East Riding of Yorkshire and Cleveland
North-east	County Durham and City of Newcastle
North Pennines	Westmoreland and adjoining parts of Cumberland and County Durham
North-west and Cumbria	Lancashire (including the Furness district), Cheshire, and Cumberland
North Midlands	Derbyshire and Nottinghamshire
West Midlands	Warwickshire, Staffordshire, Worcestershire, and adjoining parts of Shropshire
Wales	Anglesey, Brecknockshire, Caernarvonshire, Cardiganshire, Carmarthenshire, Flintshire, Glamorgan, Merionethshire, Monmouthshire, Montgomeryshire, Pembrokeshire, Radnorshire, and adjoining parts of Shropshire
South-west	Devon, Cornwall, and adjoining parts of Somerset
Somerset and Dorset	Somerset, Dorset, and adjoining parts of Hampshire and Wiltshire
South Coast	Hampshire, the Isle of Wight, and adjoining parts of Sussex, Berkshire, and Surrey
Kent and East Sussex	Kent and adjoining parts of Sussex and Surrey
London and the Home Counties	Surrey, Middlesex, Berkshire, Hertfordshire, Essex, and the City of London
Scottish Lowlands	
Central Scotland and the Highlands	

4.2. EAST ANGLIA

East Anglia comprises the two large counties of Norfolk and Suffolk and the smaller counties of Cambridgeshire and Huntingdonshire. The county of Essex lies between Suffolk and London. The cathedral city of Norwich is its principal commercial and administrative centre. It was the second greatest city in medieval England, after London and ahead of York, and it still possesses the greatest collection of medieval churches in north-western Europe.

East Anglia was a large and prosperous agricultural area in the Victorian period, but in railway terms it 'led to nowhere', in the sense that lines radiating north into East Anglia terminate about 100 miles north of London on the north Norfolk coast. There was no reason to build a railway through rural East Anglia in order to connect London with major industrial centres elsewhere. As a result, East Anglia was relatively late to develop railways, and many of its lines were built mainly to satisfy local needs.

However, East Anglia contains a number of ports that are well positioned for trade with northern Europe and the Baltic. In Victorian times mail packets sailed from Harwich in Suffolk to Zeebrugge in Belgium, while Great Yarmouth had a substantial herring fishery. General commodity trade was handled at Ipswich and Lowestoft. This encouraged the development of the East Suffolk Railway from London, running through Essex to Colchester, and then parallel to the coast through Manningtree (for the Harwich branch), Ipswich, Beccles (for the Lowestoft branch), and Yarmouth. The Great Eastern Railway (GER), which was formed by the amalgamation of a number of East Anglian lines in 1862, invested heavily in Harwich as a port, close to London, that was well suited to all the main forms of traffic: passengers, mail, and freight.

The main entry points to East Anglia from the rest of England lie along its eastern border, from Kings Lynn in the north to London in the south. Kings Lynn is a natural corner point where the River Ouse enters the Wash. The shortest route from the Midlands and the north to Norwich passes through Kings Lynn. London—the first bridging point of the River Thames—is a natural corner point lying on the shortest route to Norwich from Kent, Sussex, and the south to Norwich.

The university town of Cambridge is the main intermediate entry point on the counterfactual network, conveying traffic from the south Midlands and south-west to Norwich, and traffic from the East Midlands and north to Bury St. Edmunds, Ipswich, and the Essex coast. But the small cathedral town of Ely, about 16 miles north of Cambridge, became the main hub on the actual network.

Considered in railway terms, Cambridge was a failed hub. Unlike Ely, which was owned and operated wholly by the GER, Cambridge station was shared between the GER and London and North Western (LNWR) companies. The LNWR's cross-country line from Oxford could have been a useful feeder to a Cambridge hub, but in practice it was just a solitary extension of the LNWR's network into alien territory. It was the east–west axis of Robert Stephenson's scheme for the Buckinghamshire Railway. It had the potential to become an outer-orbital line around London, though it probably appealed more to the LNWR board because it could be used to 'block' lines into London from the Midlands and the North that would compete with the LNWR's main line through Rugby. It failed in this objective, though, for the London Extension of the Midland Railway (MR) was built over it at Bedford. Because the two companies' stations at Bedford were some distance apart, the LNWR's line was not particularly useful as a feeder for traffic from the Midlands into Cambridge.

The MR had alternative access to Cambridge via a cross-country line from Kettering, which could have been used as a feeder for traffic from Leicester and the East Midlands. But the MR portion of the line stopped short at Huntingdon, where it connected with a jointly owned GER line as far as St. Ives, which in turn connected with a wholly owned GER line into Cambridge. The MR crossed the

Great Northern (GNR) main line from London to Doncaster at Huntingdon, and could therefore have acted as a useful feeder for traffic from the north and east, as happens in the counterfactual system. But connections were poor because separate stations were used, and so astute MR passengers from the Leicester area would use the alternative MR line through Stamford and connect with the Great Eastern at Peterborough instead. This would feed them in to East Anglia via March and Ely rather than via Cambridge.

Cambridge was also the point at which two routes from London converged. The Northern and Eastern Railway, as its name suggests, had great ambitions to connect London to the north via Cambridge. It selected a route from London up the Lea Valley, and then via Ware (junction for Hertford), Broxbourne (for Buntingford), Bishops Stortford, and Audley End (for Saffron Walden). But a route via Cambridge was too much of a deviation for northern interests, as journey times would have been lengthened by the detour. The serious money was diverted to the GNR scheme—a merger of previous rival schemes for a direct East Coast route to the north through Huntingdon and Peterborough. The GNR proposed to serve Cambridge by a branch from its main line to the north at Hitchin. This alternative line completely undermined the Northern and Eastern's intended monopoly of Cambridge traffic, as it was straighter and flatter than the Northern and Eastern line. The Northern and Eastern route was eventually completed by another company, and became part of the GER in 1862.

But the GNR did not get everything its own way. Conflict between the rival schemes was resolved by dividing the Hitchin—Cambridge line into two portions which met at the village of Shepreth. Although the GNR reached Cambridge, it did so only by the exercise of running powers over its rival's portion of line, and it never got further into East Anglia using this route. The company's aspirations for territorial expansion led it to make further forays into East Anglia, however. These included the line from Huntingdon to St. Ives, mentioned above, and a line from Bourn, near Stamford, run in conjunction with the MR, as described below. There was also a successful invasion from South Yorkshire and Lincolnshire, also described below.

The regional centre of Norwich, situated 20 miles inland from Great Yarmouth, at the confluence of the rivers Yare and Wensum, was a natural hub for local and regional lines. The most obvious trunk route between London and Norwich is via Cambridge, Newmarket, Thetford, and Wymondham, crossing flat heathland for much of the way, and taking in major urban centres en route. But this was not the route selected by the early railway builders. Norwich was served instead by a branch from a line between London and Bury St. Edmunds. The London terminus was at Shoreditch, just north of the present-day Liverpool Street station. It ran parallel to the Essex coast through Romford, Chelmsford, Colchester, and Ipswich, before turning inland to Stowmarket, where the Norwich branch commenced, and Bury. The case for building a coastal route between London and Ipswich was impeccable, as traffic could be generated both from the intermediate towns and from branches to nearby centres such as Maldon, Braintree, Clacton, Sudbury, and Harwich. In an area with low population density, intermediate traffic of this sort could not be overlooked. Continuing the line from Ipswich to Bury reflected the entrepreneurial enthusiasm of Bury citizens in raising the necessary funds. But the most economical way to serve Norwich was by a joint line to Yarmouth, leaving the main line at Ipswich, and dividing somewhere between Halesworth (as on the counterfactual system) or Haddiscoe (as later built).

Instead, however, a direct line was built from north of Stowmarket through empty countryside around Diss. Diss was basically a meeting point of five roads, and a collecting point for traffic from a large sparsely populated area. This route to London was never superseded, and remains the main trunk route to this day. In fact, the natural rail route, which follows the modern A11 road, was never built in full. Thetford and Cambridge are connected only by a detour through Ely, and Thetford itself lies on a curious detour from Brandon to the south. Although a line was later built from Cambridge in the direction of Thetford, it went only as far as Mildenhall, and passed through Fordham rather than Newmarket.

It is unlikely that this 'gap' in the network was an accidental oversight by GER management. As noted above, the GNR had effective control over a route from London to Cambridge via Hitchin, and had Cambridge been well connected to Norwich the GNR might have obtained running powers to Norwich. Thus had the Cambridge to Norwich line been improved by an 'Ely cut-off', the GNR might have had a better line to London than the Great Eastern.

Considering its low population density, and the relative failure of the Cambridge hub, East Anglia was surprisingly well served by railways by 1914. Part of the explanation lies in another competitive front that was opened up by the GNR in the 1880s. Both the MR and the GNR were interested in developing the tourist potential of the north Norfolk coast between Hunstanton, north of Kings Lynn, and Great Yarmouth. Holiday traffic from the industrial East Midlands and South Yorkshire was potentially large (see below). As originators of the traffic, the two companies aspired to keep most of the profits, but in East Anglia they were confronted by an established regional monopolist. They set out to break this monopoly by exploiting, and later acquiring, the independent Eastern and Midland Railway, which linked Bourn, north of Stamford, via Spalding and Sutton Bridge (where a branch from Peterborough joined) to South Lynn, near Kings Lynn. The Eastern and Midland took over the Lynn and Fakenham Railway as part of a 'push' into the heart of GER territory. The isolated village of Melton Constable, south of the small fishing port of Blakeney, developed into a miniature railway hub, with a four-way junction between lines to South Lynn, Cromer, Norwich, and Great Yarmouth, and its own railway workshops.

This attack on its regional monopoly spurred the GER to promote additional lines, including an improbable line from Wroxham through Aylsham to County School—another isolated spot, some 6 miles north of East Dereham. This line is best understood as a defensive 'rampart' designed to prevent the Midland and Great Northern (MGNR) from penetrating further into the Norwich area. To protect its Yarmouth traffic, the GER also made a number of improvements in the Norwich and Yarmouth area.

Eventually the GER came to terms with the MGNR and, as the Norfolk and Suffolk Joint Railways, it promoted a loop line between Cromer and North Walsham through the would-be resort of Mundesley-on-Sea. This line was never a commercial success. Moreover, despite the collaboration, there was no rationalization: there remained two stations at Cromer and two at North Walsham—not to mention two at Fakenham, and separate stations at Kings Lynn and South Lynn. Although an expensive connecting line between the two systems was built at Great Yarmouth, there remained three separate stations there—Southtown, Beach, and Vauxhall (the only survivor).

East Anglia also benefited from local initiatives. Although agricultural prosperity in Britain declined after the repeal of the Corn Laws in 1846, and the onset of the 'Great Depression' in 1873, Norfolk and Suffolk, having better soil fertility and proximity to London, fared better than most regions. They were able to 'trade up' to higher value-added products such as vegetables. Local initiatives for connecting nearby market towns to one another allowed Sudbury, Bury, Thetford, Dereham, Wymondham, and Swaffham to become small hubs.

However, many East Anglian lines were built quite late. The holiday line to Mundesley was not completed until 1902. East Anglia was one of the main areas in which light railways were promoted after 1890. The aim was to 'infill' areas between existing lines in order to bring the railway closer to the farm gate. While some of the more ambitious schemes failed, railways were completed to Laxfield, Southwold, Thaxted, Tollesbury, and Upwell. The promoters failed to anticipate the rise of road transport after 1918, however; army surplus lorries were well suited to carrying agricultural produce, and motor buses ran to and from the centres of towns and villages, while railway stations remained on the outskirts.

4.3. THE SOUTH MIDLANDS

The South Midlands comprises the counties of Oxfordshire and Gloucestershire, together with adjoining parts of Buckinghamshire, Somerset, Wiltshire, and Worcestershire. Its heartland is Cotswold hills. To the east lies the university city of Oxford, on the River Thames, and to the west are the old industrial towns of Trowbridge and Devizes. Bath and Bristol lie on the edge of the region, bordering on the south-west. Bath is an exclusive spa town, developed on Roman foundations by eighteenth-century property speculators, while Bristol is an ancient port which traded across the Atlantic to the West Indies and America, and across the Severn estuary to South Wales.

The South Midlands is part of the Heart of England. It is one of the most crucial of the core areas of the country, as described elsewhere. East–west traffic flows connect London to Bristol, the south-west and South Wales, while north–south flows connect the Midlands and the north to the South Coast. The configuration of the railway network in this area has a major influence on the topology of the railway network as a whole.

While east–west traffic routed through the area has a number of options, North–South traffic faces a major dilemma: whether to head due south, crossing first the Cotswold Hills and then the Berkshire Downs and the hilly plateau of Salisbury Plain, or whether to pass to either side—through Gloucester and Bristol to the west, along the Severn estuary, or through Banbury and Oxford to the east, along the Cherwell valley.

So far as east–west traffic is concerned, there are two crucial differences between the actual and counterfactual networks in this region. First, while the main line from London to Bristol, as selected by Brunel, takes a northerly route through Didcot, Swindon, and Chippenham, the counterfactual line takes a southerly route through Newbury, Hungerford, and Devizes. Second, the counterfactual route involves no Severn Tunnel: all traffic from London to South Wales is routed via Gloucester instead.

Brunel's choice of the northerly route is often hailed as an enlightened decision. It is said that the route was straighter and flatter than the southern alternative, which Brunel considered and rejected. It is, however, a longer route. Furthermore, although the 'billiard table' section through the Vale of the White Horse between Didcot and Swindon is level, the descent from Chippenham into Bath through Box Tunnel is steep. The alternative route through Devizes, which was chosen by the builders of the Kennet and Avon Canal, avoids this steep descent and tunnel, at the cost of sharp curves through the river gorge near Bradford-on-Avon; but apart from this section, the route is also straight and flat. The mail coaches also followed the southern route for most of the way.

A great advantage of the southern route used by the counterfactual is that Bristol is served by a branch from the main line to the south-west, which connects Exeter and Plymouth directly to London. Prior to the construction of the Castle Cary cut-off in 1902, Great Western (GWR) passengers to Exeter took a detour through Bristol, and on their way to Bristol they took a detour through Didcot and Swindon. It not for nothing that the GWR was also known as the 'Great Way Round'.

A final advantage of the southern route is that it passes through the heart of the west of England cloth-making district—a cluster of small industrial towns centred on Trowbridge (where the Bristol line diverges)—and runs close to the north Somerset coalfield. Although in decline in the 1830s, this district was still sufficiently important for Brunel to propose a special branch to serve it. This branch becomes much shorter when the main line is re-routed.

There are two factors that may explain why Brunel rejected the southern route. The first is that at the time that he surveyed the two routes, he was convinced that friction was the single most important obstacle to high speed (see Chapter 7). High speed requires low friction, and low friction implies big wheels. Because big wheels cannot cope with sharp curves, straight track is required. On this view, the curves through the Avon Gorge may have been an insuperable obstacle that ruled out the southern route.

The second factor concerns what modern writers refer to as a real option effect. Brunel was not only a highly original engineer but, as his Letter Books testify, a

highly original strategic thinker too. Brunel realized that every main line generated options for branches, and that different routes afforded different options.
Brunel assumed that there would be a single main line to the west, and so he had
to decide whether the southerly options afforded by the southern route were
more valuable than the northerly options afforded by the northern route. To the
south lay the South Coast near Weymouth, and the south-west beyond Exeter.
Weymouth was a smart seaside resort and ferry port, while the south-west
possessed important tin and copper mines. But the north, arguably, offered
even greater riches. Oxford, Gloucester, and Cheltenham could be easily served
by branches from the northern route, and these were quickly built. Gloucester
then became the gateway to South Wales, with its huge reserves of coal and iron—
an area already familiar to Brunel because of his work for the Taff Vale Railway.
Beyond Oxford, across the Chilterns, lay Worcester and the industrial West
Midlands, and beyond Worcester lay the Welsh coast. The coast itself had little
significance for Brunel (except perhaps as a tourist area) but he had great
ambitions to build a port for the Irish mails on the Lleyn Penninsular at
Porthddinlleyn, by extending the line from Worcester.

When Brunel considered the competition, he would have had to reckon with
the London and Southampton Railway (subsequently the London and South
Western Railway (LSWR)) to the south. In the early 1830s they were a serious
rival. Their trunk line was one of the first in the south, and they planned to
capitalize on their lead by building a line to Bath as a branch from Basingstoke.
Brunel and his GWR colleagues defeated their scheme, however, by persuading
the people of Bristol and Bath that they needed their own railway to serve their
own interests, and not a mere branch railway controlled by the rival port of
Southampton. By supporting the Bristol and Exeter scheme as a complementary
project, the GWR board could count the West Country traffic as already won. To
make doubly sure, they built a branch through Westbury to Weymouth, cutting
across the LSWR's proposed westward extension. Although the LSWR eventually
reached the West Country, it never achieved a substantial share of the traffic.

When Brunel looked north, he saw a much more serious competitor—the
London and Birmingham Railway, engineered by his great friend and rival the
redoubtable Robert Stephenson. It would be a simple matter for the London and
Birmingham to expand westwards into the West Midlands, cutting off the GWR
at Worcester and pinning it into the area to the south. The London and
Birmingham could (and did) make branches to Oxford and Banbury, which
could be further launch-pads for attacks on GWR territory. If a pre-emptive
strike was to be made therefore, it should certainly be made to the north rather
than the south. This may be the reason why the northern route was retained even
once Brunel had realized that in engineering terms the southern route might be
just as good.

The second key difference between the actual and counterfactual systems in
respect of east–west traffic concerns the Severn Tunnel. While the actual route
from London to South Wales tunnels under the Severn just north of Bristol, near
the site of the second M4 suspension bridge, the counterfactual route follows the

traditional mail coach route through the first bridging point on the Severn—the cathedral city of Gloucester.

If the counterfactual network had been designed purely to minimize network length at any cost then it would obviously have included a Severn Tunnel. On today's system, for example, the journey from London to Cardiff, the Welsh capital, is almost 20 miles shorter via the Severn Tunnel than via Gloucester.

To allow for the counterfactual network to include a Severn Tunnel would, however, be incompatible with the premises on which the counterfactual has been constructed. The counterfactual represents an integrated system which could, in principle, have been designed at the time of the Railway Mania. Furthermore, because it is smaller than the actual network, it could have been completed more quickly and would therefore have enjoyed a longer economic life. The cost of this approach, however, is that the whole network has to use technology that was available at the time of the Railway Mania, or shortly afterwards, and this does not include tunnelling under a major river.

The penalty to network performance incurred by the omission of the Severn Tunnel is much lower than might be expected, however, for a number of reasons.

To begin with, the operational benefits turned out to be rather modest. The GWR was short of funds at the time of its construction, and would probably not have constructed it at all if it had not been for the South Wales coal owners, who threatened to build their own railway from the coalfields to the capital and employ a rival railway company to operate it (as happened in South Yorkshire too). Because the approaches to the tunnel were steeply graded, and speed through the tunnel was restricted to reduce vibration, coal trains took a long time to complete their journey through the tunnel. Because the tunnel was signalled as a single block, with only one train in the tunnel in each direction, the frequency of trains that the tunnel could handle was relatively low. This frequency became even lower when special paths had to be reserved for express passenger trains, travelling at a different speed from the rest of the traffic. As a result, coal trains continued to be diverted by Gloucester after the tunnel had been built.

Even the passenger trains were not greatly accelerated. There was traffic congestion not only around the tunnel but in the Bristol and Bath area to the east of the tunnel too. To alleviate the bottleneck, the GWR had to invest in a complementary project—the Badminton line—which bypassed Bath and Bristol to the north.

The Severn Tunnel has always been very expensive to maintain. Geological problems bedevilled its construction, and the entire area around the tunnel remains prone to flooding. Brunel's original proposal for a Severn Bridge south of Gloucester, though opposed by the Admiralty as an obstruction to shipping, would have been a more economical proposition; indeed, a railway bridge was subsequently built across the Severn further south at Sharpness (though this was built to low standards and was not particularly successful—see below).

The Severn Tunnel was only completed in 1886, and so was not available for much of the Victorian period. The Badminton line was only completed in 1903;

while much valued by the twenty-first–century traveller to Bristol Parkway or Cardiff, it was completed too late to benefit the Victorian traveller.

The most important reason why the Severn Tunnel is not really required, however, is that on the actual network the entire approach to the Severn estuary from London is wrong. On the actual system South Wales is served by a branch from the Bristol route, while on the counterfactual system it has its own dedicated line. This line runs direct from London to Gloucester via Oxford and Cheltenham, and then down the north bank of the Severn estuary to Newport and Cardiff, throwing off branches to the north on its way. Brunel's northern route from London to Bristol is thus replaced, in the counterfactual, by two routes—a southern route to Bristol, which also serves the West country, and a route to the north of Brunel's northern route which serves South Wales.

The crucial link in the counterfactual network that is missing from the actual network is a direct trunk line between Oxford and Cheltenham, which feeds into a London line at its eastern end and into a Gloucester line at its western end. This route along the Windrush Valley, through Burford and Northleach, is that followed by the Welsh cattle drovers, the turnpike builders and the mail coaches of the eighteenth century—and also by the modern A40 trunk road. The GWR itself ran an express bus service along this road in the 1930s because its own route from Oxford to Cheltenham was so indirect.

The GWR served Cheltenham and Gloucester by a branch from its Bristol main line at Swindon, opened in 1841. This was one of the options that Brunel exploited in connection with his northern route. It was built by the Cheltenham and Gloucester Union Railway and backed by Cheltenham interests—probably because they wanted to defend their town's position as a spa against competition from Bath. This line cut across the Cotswold escarpment at Sapperton, using a long tunnel approached by steep grades. Brunel had always envisaged that South Wales traffic would use this line—indeed, he had proposed a Severn Bridge near Stonehouse precisely for this purpose. But compared to the Bristol line, it was built on the cheap, and was never really fit for purpose as a trunk line. Indeed, passengers continued to cross to South Wales by ferry from the Bristol area until the Severn Tunnel was completed.

If Brunel had adopted the Oxford to Cheltenham line then the operational difficulties associated with the Sapperton incline would have been avoided. The South Wales coal owners would have had a perfectly satisfactory freight service, and there would have been no need for a Severn Tunnel. In fact, Brunel devised an Oxford to Cheltenham line which was presented to Parliament in the Mania year of 1845. It did not follow the Windrush Valley route, however, but branched off an Oxford to Worcester line near Shipton-under-Wychwood. The GWR board supported this line, however, only to fend off a proposal by the London and North Western Railway (LNWR) (successor to the London and Birmingham Railway) to 'invade' their territory. Daniel Gooch, the locomotive engineer, and subsequently chairman of the GWR, wrote later that he opposed the idea of building the line as the GWR would only be 'competing against itself' (i.e. against its Sapperton line) for a fixed amount of traffic. Thus although a direct line was authorized, it was never built. The GWR, which was nearly always strapped for cash, and especially so in the 1850s, put its own short-term financial interests ahead of the long-term interests of the South Wales industrialists.

The actual and counterfactual systems also differ in their provision for north–south traffic. The counterfactual system is committed to avoiding hilly ridges wherever possible, and to making maximum use of valleys, so long as they are reasonably straight. Hilly ridges mean either tunnels, bridges, and viaducts, which are expensive to build and maintain, or steep gradients, which slow down traffic, limit loads, and increase operating expenses. As a result, the counterfactual system routes all north–south traffic through either Gloucester and Bristol or Banbury and Oxford. Since east–west trunk traffic also passes through Gloucester and Oxford, these cities become major hubs.

Traffic from Wolverhampton and the north-west that is taking the western route via Bristol and Gloucester feeds into the main line from Birmingham to Gloucester at Kidderminster. Traffic from the north-east via Lichfield is fed in at Stourbridge, while traffic from Chester and Shrewsbury feeds in at Stourport. Traffic from Leicester and the East Midlands feeds in at Tewkesbury, having bypassed Birmingham through Leamington, Stratford, and Evesham. At Bristol all traffic for the south-west continues to Exeter via Taunton, while traffic for the South Coast continues via Bath and the Avon Valley to Trowbridge. Traffic for Weymouth is routed via Frome and Yeovil, while traffic for Southampton and Portsmouth is routed via Salisbury and Romsey.

Traffic for Brighton, Dover, and the south-east uses the eastern route down the Cherwell Valley. Traffic from the north-west via Birmingham and from the north-east via Leicester is consolidated at Leamington for forwarding to Oxford, where it joins traffic from South Wales to London as far as Wallingford, where it either diverges south for Newbury and Southampton, or continues south-east as far as Wokingham, where it diverges south for Guildford and Dover.

Because north–south trunk traffic avoids the Cotswolds, an issue arises regarding provision for local traffic. In line with the general principles of the counterfactual, local traffic is accommodated mainly by cross-country loops. Their routes are somewhat more irregular than those of the trunk lines, as part of their rationale is to connect up neighbouring market towns.

A key east–west secondary route runs from the main line from Oxford to London at Radley, through Abingdon, Wantage, and Lechlade to Cirencester, where it connects with a north–south secondary line from Stratford-on-Avon (for Birmingham and Leamington) to Northleach (for Cheltenham). From Cirencester the east–west line continues to Stroud and Gloucester, while the north–south line continues to Chippenham and Bath. The Cotswold system is completed by a line from Chippenham to Witney (for Oxford) via Lechlade, which connects at Swindon with a line from Newbury to Cirencester, thereby creating mini-hubs at both Swindon and Lechlade.

In contrast to the counterfactual, the GWR's own rural system relied heavily on dead-end branches from main-line junctions. Each town tended to be connected to the nearest main line. There were several small junctions stretched out along the Bristol main line serving towns that had been bypassed as part of Brunel's original design. Passengers between these towns had to change twice at the junctions, and as few main line trains stopped at these small junctions the service was poor. In some cases neighbouring towns had junctions with different main lines. Thus Fairford and Lechlade were served by a branch from Oxford, while the neighbouring town of Cirencester was served by a branch from Kemble on the Cheltenham line. To reach Cirencester, passengers from Lechlade would have to travel via Oxford, Didcot and Swindon—a very circuitous route. On the counterfactual, by contrast, a direct service is available between all these towns.

4.4. THE SHIRES

The Shires lie north of London and extend towards the East Midlands. They handle a lot of traffic from London to the North, together with cross-country traffic from Wales and the South-west to East Anglia and Lincolnshire. The principal city is Leicester, although the town of Northampton is an important centre too. There are numerous market towns in the region, including the county towns of Bedford and Aylesbury, the former county town of Buckingham, and the cathedral city of Peterborough.

The counterfactual railway system in the Shires is radically different from the actual one, and exemplifies many of the advantages of the counterfactual system over the actual one. Although the counterfactual mileage is smaller, it meets the needs of the long-distance traveller much more effectively. This is because the main trunk line from London serves a variety of towns and cities without the use of connecting services, while cross-country lines are built to higher standards and make better connections with the regional systems that lie at either end.

The most striking feature of the counterfactual system is that there is a single trunk line from London to the Midlands and the north as far as Crick, near Rugby. The route to Crick follows the general line of the London and Birmingham Railway, engineered by Robert Stephenson, through Harrow, Watford, Tring, Leighton Buzzard, and Bletchley, and completed in 1838. It passes Northampton, unlike the actual system which by passes it. After passing through the Watford Gap the line divides into three at Crick.

The central line serves Scotland and the north-west, following the route of the London and North Western (LNWR) Trent Valley main line, through Nuneaton and Tamworth to Rugeley. From Rugeley it proceeds to Stoke-on-Trent (rather than Crewe), where branches to Manchester and Chester diverge, before continuing to Warrington (for Liverpool), Preston, Lancaster, and Carlisle to Glasgow.

The western line runs to Birmingham, Wolverhampton, and Shrewsbury, where there are connections for Welshpool and Aberystwyth. The route follows the line of the London and Birmingham Railway as far as Birmingham, and then the route of the Great Western (GWR) Shrewsbury and Birmingham and Shrewsbury and Welshpool Railways as far as Welshpool (parts of which was jointly owned by the LNWR—see below).

The eastern fork is the most interesting. It serves the East Midlands, Derbyshire, Yorkshire, and the north-east. It heads first for Leicester via Lutterworth. At Leicester it connects with two cross-country lines, described below. Following the route of the Midland Railway (MR) main line, it proceeds through Loughborough, where branches to Derby and Nottingham diverge, and then up the Erewash Valley to Chesterfield, Sheffield, and Leeds. From Leeds it uses a variant of the North Eastern (NER) system to reach Newcastle. The eastern fork therefore supplants the East Coast trunk line of the actual system. Although the counterfactual includes a primary route from London to Wetherby via Peterborough and Lincoln which resembles some of the early schemes for an East Coast main line, this is not the main trunk line to Newcastle, as on the actual system. The main trunk line to Newcastle run through the industrial heart of Yorkshire and the East Midlands, connecting Crick to Wetherby, and putting the north-east in direct connection, not only with London, but with the East Midlands too.

This eastern fork connects up a number of lines which in practice were owned and operated as separate entities. The MR's original main line from Derby to Leicester and London ran via Rugby, where it made a junction with the London and Birmingham line, but disagreements with the LNWR, which took over the Birmingham line in 1846, led to the MR switching its custom to the Great Northern (GNR) which in 1850 opened its East Coast main line into London. The MR built an alternative main line from Leicester to Hitchin, opened in 1857, where London traffic was fed on to the GNR main line. Once again, however, friction with the other company followed, and the MR finally built its own London Extension from Bedford to London St. Pancras, opened in 1868. By this time the original MR line from Leicester to Rugby had become redundant as a trunk line, and had been downgraded to a branch. It was finally closed in the 1960s.

In the 1890s the Great Central (GCR) invaded MR territory with its own London Extension, opened in 1898, which began between Sheffield and Nottingham and terminated at Marylebone station, London. The GCR duplicated the old MR line between Leicester and Rugby, choosing a route closer to Lutterworth, as used by the counterfactual system.

This concept of serving both the north-east and north-west from a common trunk route through the Midlands was previously adopted by the canal system. The Grand Union Canal, like the counterfactual trunk line, followed a westerly route out of London, and near Rugby it divided into three. The Grand Union main line continued west to Birmingham, a branch to the Coventry Canal led north-west through Stoke-on-Trent, while a Leicester branch ran due north to a junction near Long Eaton, where it connected with Nottingham and the north-east via the River Trent. As in the counterfactual system, there was no East Coast trunk line.

Similar observations can be made about the modern motorway system. The M1 motorway follows the general route of the trunk line as far as the Watford Gap, where once again three routes diverge: the M45 turns west to serve Birmingham via Coventry, the M6 runs north-west along the route of the West Coast main line to Carlisle, while the M1 itself serves Leeds via Leicester and Sheffield. North of Leeds, near Wetherby, the M1 connects with the A1 to serve Newcastle. There is no 'East Coast main line' on the motorway system, although the A1 road, which follows roughly the route of the old Great North Road, is being progressively upgraded to motorway standards.

Several cross-country routes traverse the Shires. The key link in the counter-factual cross-country system is an east–west line from Bedford to Cambridge. Cambridge is a major hub for traffic entering East Anglia from the west, as described earlier. Bedford funnels two streams of traffic into this link.

Traffic from the Midlands and the north-west is fed in through the Watford Gap, where the three lines described above converge. From Northampton it proceeds due east to Bedford. Traffic from the South Wales, the south-west, and the South Coast is funnelled into Bedford along a line from Aylesbury, where routes from Oxford and Newbury converge. Oxford feeds in traffic from South Wales via Gloucester, while Newbury feeds in traffic from Southampton, Bristol, and Exeter. The line from Aylesbury to Bedford crosses the main trunk line from London at Leighton Buzzard, giving travellers from Southampton connections for the East Midlands and the north-east.

All these counterfactual lines are built to trunk line standards in order to expedite the movement of cross-country traffic. There are also secondary cross-country lines that serve intermediate towns and afford alternative routes in the case of accidents, congestion, or repair works. These include an east–west line from Birmingham through Leicester to Peterborough, and a line from Oxford to the Lincolnshire coast via Towcester, Northampton, and Peterborough.

Analogues of some of these cross-country lines exist on the actual system, but none of them were operated as trunk lines. Most of these lines represented one company's attempt to invade another company's territory, which meant that the two companies controlling the networks at either end of the line refused to cooperate. In some cases the line was built to a high standard but operated as though it were a branch, with a stopping service rather than an express service, while in other cases the line was built on the cheap because money had run out, so that it could not be used for expresses anyway.

Although the LNWR made a serious attempt to promote long-distance traffic on its Oxford to Cambridge line, it was hampered by the fact that all the traffic feeding in at its western end—Oxford—was controlled by its rival the GWR, apart from traffic originating in Oxford itself. The MR was also interested in boosting traffic on its line from Birmingham to Peterborough, but the company controlling the eastern exit from the line—the Great Eastern (GER)—was on bad terms with the MR because of the latter's involvement with an invasion of its territory further north (see above). With the exception of the LNWR, none of the companies was all that bothered by the dislocation of cross-country travel as a result of their rivalries, as they expected passengers to travel via London instead, and therefore pay both companies a higher fare than their share in the revenue from a cross-country ticket.

4.5. LINCOLNSHIRE

Lincolnshire is a large county that borders the North Sea, to the east of the Midlands, and north of East Anglia. It is separated from East Anglia by The Wash—a broad inlet near Kings Lynn. The River Humber forms the northern boundary of Lincolnshire, with the ancient fishing port of Grimsby on the south bank of the river standing almost opposite the even larger port of Hull, in the East Riding of Yorkshire, on the north bank.

The main feature of the counterfactual in Lincolnshire is that the county town of Lincoln lies on a main line to Yorkshire and the north-east, rather than off the main line to the east, as in the actual system. As noted earlier, the counterfactual trunk line to the north-east runs through the industrial East Midlands, to the west of the actual East Coast main line. But there is also a main line loop which takes in towns in Lincolnshire that would otherwise be 'off the map'. This main line loop follows (approximately) the route of the present East Coast main line as far as Peterborough, and then runs via Spalding, Sleaford, Lincoln, Gainsborough, and Selby to a junction with the trunk line at Wetherby.

At Spalding there is a connection with a coastal loop line through Boston and Grimsby which rejoins the main line at Thorne, north of Gainsborough. This line serves the coastal resorts of Mablethorpe and Skegness and the town of Louth on the Lincolnshire Wolds. Thorne, the terminus of the loop, is a major hub, playing a role equivalent to those of Doncaster and Stainforth in the actual system, and providing connections for Barnsley, Sheffield, Knottingley, and Leeds.

These loops are intersected by three cross-country lines. One runs due west from Nottingham to Boston via Newark and Sleaford, with connections at Sleaford for Spalding and Kings Lynn. From Newark a branch continues north-east to Grimsby via Lincoln and Market Rasen, with a branch from Market Rasen to Louth. A third line, of a purely local nature, serves the vast tracts of rich agricultural land around Horncastle at Woodhall. It runs from Metheringham, on the main loop line south of Lincon, to Alford, near Mablethorpe, on the coastal loop, and provides convenient access to the urban consumption centres of Lincoln and London (via Metheringham) and the ports of Grimsby and Boston (via Alford).

The actual railway system was very generous in its provisions for Lincolnshire. The Great Northern (GNR) was the dominant force in local railway provision, although the Great Central (GCR) was also significant in the north of the county. Part of the GNR's generosity undoubtedly stemmed from its desire to exclude the GCR from expanding south and the Great Eastern (GER)—the dominant force in

East Anglia—from expanding north. Saturating rural areas with local lines was a good way of blocking entrants by undermining the Parliamentary case for additional lines.

But unlike the GER, which was also quite generous in its provisions in East Anglia (see above), the GNR constructed a very rational system. The difference seems to be explained mainly by the fact that the GNR was initially promoted as a single integrated regional system, which provided a 'skeleton' on which later development could be grafted, while the GER was a merger of various unsuccessful trunk line schemes and impoverished local schemes. The GNR was able to defend its monopoly proactively, on the basis of its quality of service, while the GER defended its monopoly responsively by fighting invaders whenever they appeared.

In contrast to many other parts of the country, it is therefore quite a challenge for the counterfactual to improve upon the actual local system. Indeed, because the East Coast main line is shifted westwards, away from the Lincolnshire coast, the counterfactual cannot rely to the same extent as the actual system on connections with this line, and therefore needs to be more self-sufficient in local provision. This issue is addressed mainly by taking a loop line built by the GNR and upgrading it into a primary route.

Lincolnshire was ignored by many of the early railway promoters because railways were seen as part of the infrastructure of an industrial economy rather than an agricultural economy. Landowners soon appreciated, however, that railways could benefit agriculture by bringing in coal and lime and carrying away produce. They could also promote the cattle trade—the analogy between cattle and ordinary passengers was not lost on early third-class railway travellers. In general, railways could promote inter-regional specialization in agriculture based on differences in soils, with each area exporting those specific agricultural products in which it possessed comparative advantage.

The simplest way to justify a main line through an agricultural area remained, however, the idea of linking great urban and industrial centres at either end of the route, and treating agriculture as a source of intermediate traffic. This was the philosophy of the GNR promoters who, at the time of the Railway Mania, argued that Lincolnshire could be served by an East Coast main line from London to Scotland. They faced two major difficulties, however.

First, many people—including the members of a Parliamentary Committee—thought that the country needed only one main line to the north. A West Coast main line was in the process of completion, and the shareholders of the newly formed Caledonian Railway from Carlisle to Glasgow—who thought that they had acquired a monopoly of Anglo-Scottish traffic—were incensed at the idea of a competitor. But the wealthy landowners of Lincolnshire were willing and able to put up most of the money, and they lobbied most effectively for their line.

The second problem arose because of local differences of opinion regarding the route. Lincolnshire is a very large county, and no single direct line to the north could take in all the important towns. The answer was to build both a main line—the present East Coast main line—and a loop line that follows roughly the route of the counterfactual main line described above. The main line ran through the market towns of Grantham, Newark, and Retford, while the loop line ran from Peterborough, south of Grantham, through Boston and Lincoln, to rejoin the main line at Doncaster. This compromise between rival local interests was engineered by Edmund Denison, MP for Doncaster. It had the dual virtue of keeping all the major landowners happy, and turning his own constituency into a railway hub. It also transformed Doncaster races from a local event in a decaying market town into a major national attraction.

Lincolnshire did not remain aloof from industry for long, however. The development of the South Yorkshire coalfield to the east of Doncaster created a demand for coal transport to the coast at Grimsby, and also to the South. The GCR controlled most of the traffic to Grimsby, which used its line through Thorne and Barnetby, while the GNR controlled much of the traffic to the South. But the GNR's main line was congested, particularly south of Hitchin, where until 1868 it was used by Midland Railway (MR) traffic too. The GER had designs on the London coal traffic; an early ambition of one of its constituent companies had been to build a main line to the north through Cambridge, and it had spare capacity on its routes into London. To head off the GER, the GNR was forced to build a Boston cut-off on its loop line, running direct from Spalding through Sleaford to Lincoln and to offer a half-share in this line to the GER (as explained in Chapter 5). This line corresponds to one of the key portions of the counterfactual system. However, the GNR did not fully exploit the potential of this line for passenger traffic, although it was used by a boat trains to Harwich (for Hook of Holland). Another 'cut-off'—a direct line from Lincoln to Grantham—was more clearly aimed at passengers; the connection at Grantham enabled London passengers to avoid a detour through Newark (using an MR line), Sleaford, or Boston.

Overall, the counterfactual system matches the local performance of the actual system with a somewhat smaller mileage of track. The saving in track mileage occurs not only in the rural areas but also in the more populous north of the country, where the GNR faced competition from the GCR, and to a lesser extent the MR. This resulted in wasteful duplication of lines; in particular, the county town of Lincoln was served by all three companies using two separate stations, which reduced its effectiveness as a hub.

4.6. YORKSHIRE

Yorkshire is a very large county which is divided into three Ridings for administrative purposes—the North, centred on Northallerton, the West, centred on Wakefield, and the East, centred on Beverley. It developed a very complex railway system, which is best discussed on a sub-regional basis. This section describes the central and western parts of the county—the East is discussed in a separate section on Humberside and Cleveland, as it has a distinctive geographical character.

The physical geography of Britain makes the area around Wakefield and Doncaster a natural hub of a national railway system. It occupies relatively flat country on the western edge of the Pennines, from which major rivers flow down to the Humber: the Aire from Leeds, the Calder from Mirfield, and the Don from Sheffield and Doncaster. These river valleys facilitate excellent rail communications with, respectively, the Furness district of the north-west via Skipton, Liverpool and Manchester via Huddersfield or Todmorden, and Birmingham via Sheffield and Derby. Facing east, the plains around the confluence of the rivers provide a gateway to Humberside and Cleveland to the north, and Lincolnshire to the south. Routes leading south from Tyneside, Teesside, and Weardale enter from the north down the Swale and Ouse valleys, and proceed towards London through the Trent valley to Newark and then along the edge of the Cambridgeshire fens through Peterborough.

On the actual railway system Doncaster has always functioned as a major hub, where the routes from London to Leeds, York, and Hull diverge, but on the counterfactual system the corresponding hub is at Thorne, about 10 miles north-east of Doncaster. Today, Thorne is an important junction on the motorway system, as well as being a minor hub on the railway system. The shift of the hub from Doncaster to Thorne is induced by the eastward shift in the primary east coast route to pass through Lincoln rather than Newark. The desire to compete for traffic to Leeds, and to turn Edmund Denison's constituency into a railway hub, probably explained why the actual system was pulled away from Lincoln towards Newark, and away from Thorne towards Doncaster.

York is another important hub on the actual system and, like Doncaster, its importance is much diminished on the counterfactual system. Its role is taken over by Wetherby, further west. The counterfactual trunk line to the north-east enters the North Riding from Leeds rather than Doncaster, and so places York well off a direct line to Newcastle. The East Coast loop line enters Wetherby from Thorne via Selby and Tadcaster. The counterfactual also provides a loop line to Wetherby through Wharfedale, serving the resorts and commuter dormitories of Ilkley and Otley, and affording a convenient bypass around Leeds for traffic from Skipton. From Wetherby, trunk traffic proceeds north through Knaresborough (junction for the spa town of Harrogate) to the cathedral town of Ripon. The trunk line then continues north through Darlington and Durham to Newcastle, while another line heads off west down Wensleydale to a junction with the West Coast main line near Sedbergh. A third line heads off in the opposite direction to Thirsk and Middlesbrough. The market town of Thirsk and the county town of Northallerton are served by a loop from Ripon to Catterick, on the Darlington line, from where a short branch to Richmond diverges.

The counterfactual lines resemble the road system. Wetherby lies on the historical Great North Road near the point where the M1 motorway from London via Leeds joins the A1 trunk road. By contrast, York is only a minor hub on the road system where the Doncaster to Middlesbrough road crosses a road from Leeds to Scarborough. There is a main road down Wensleydale, analogous to the counterfactual main line, but on the actual system there were only a couple of branches owned by different companies that met in the middle at Hawes.

The woollen textile towns of Leeds and Bradford are major traffic-generating centres in West Yorkshire. Leeds was the commercial centre of the trade, with manufacturing concentrated in Bradford and its satellites, including Halifax, Huddersfield, Dewsbury, and Keighley. The Lancashire and Yorkshire (LYR) and the Great Northern (GNR) fought over access, with the London and North Western (LNWR) and Midland (MR) getting involved as well. The LYR was the first main line to enter the area, approaching from Manchester along the Calder Valley through Todmorden. But the LYR neglected to consolidate this early lead, preferring to develop its network around Manchester and Liverpool instead. This let in its rivals. Later, in a vain attempt to recover its position it proliferated branches to out-of-the-way places such as Meltham (opened in 1869), Stainland (1875), Clayton West (1879), and Rishworth (1881). Unlike most other companies, it also developed alternative routes to its own lines, having no fewer than three routes between Bradford and Dewsbury, for example, through Halifax, Bailiff Bridge, and Liversedge. But all of these developments came too late.

The invaders played a similar game, and caught up with the LYR. The GNR, for example, not only developed a triangular trunk line system linking Wakefield, Leeds, and Bradford but also built loops to serve Deswbury and Pudsey, as well as branches to Shipley, Stourton, and Hunslet. A triangular station was built at the desolate township of Queensbury, from which radiated lines to Bradford, Keighley, and Halifax; the tortuous route between Keighley and Halifax was the only one that did not replicate another company's more direct route.

In their pursuit of freight traffic, the various companies proliferated dead-end branches from their own network to towns already served by rival companies. In some cases these lines were built simply to block routes proposed by their rivals. As a result, some towns such as Dewsbury were served by all four of the major companies. To begin with the companies were reluctant to cooperate in any way, but as the formidable cost of the expansion became evident a number of cost-sharing schemes were introduced—such as a joint GNR/LYR station at Bradford (Exchange). On balance, however, the legacy of railway competition in West Yorkshire was a fragmented network composed of numerous branches radiating from company-specific hubs that were not 'joined up' in any coherent way.

The LYR and GNR routes are not replicated by the counterfactual system, with one or two exceptions. The core of the counterfactual system is an analogue of the LNWR main line from Manchester to Leeds via Huddersfield and Dewsbury, opened in 1848. The counterfactual adopts an analogue of the MR main line from Leeds to Skipton via Keighley, and its branch to Bradford via Shipley. The GNR main line from Wakefield to Leeds is also used; in addition, its route from Bradford to Halifax is preferred to the LYR one, as it facilitates an end-on connection with the Shipley line at Bradford. Although the LYR Calder Valley main line is not the main trans-Pennine route in the counterfactual, it provides a useful link from Wakefield to the West Coast main line at Preston, via Todmorden and Burnley.

To substitute for the maze of lines described above the counterfactual provides a major hub at Deighton, near Huddersfield, where the Manchester to Leeds main line intercepts the Calder Valley, and a line from Sheffield via Penistone enters from the south-east. At Greetland, west of Deighton, the Halifax and Bradford line feeds in too. Suburban traffic is catered for by a circular line that runs around the hills in the Pudsey and Batley area west of Leeds.

In North Yorkshire matters were somewhat better, but by no means perfect. By 1862 the North Eastern Railway (NER) had acquired, through a series of mergers, an effective monopoly. The price of expansion by acquisition, however, was that many of the lines were not well integrated, as they had been promoted initially as independent and sometimes rival schemes. For example, the NER operated two main lines from Leeds to the north-east—via York and via Harrogate.

To defend this monopoly it then built additional lines. It made a serious attempt to rationalize its network through incremental adjustments. Thus it built new lines around Harrogate to improve connections between the various lines it had acquired. Mini-hubs such as Starbeck, Pilmoor, and Melmerby were developed, but they saw little traffic because the lines they connected served little useful purpose. Towns with direct connections by road were connected by rail using convoluted routes, such as that from Tadcaster to Leeds.

Overall, Yorkshire was poorly served by the railway system. Being a natural 'national crossroads' and a major industrial district it attracted a huge amount of railway investment, but the proliferation of routes did not result in a coherent integrated regional network, which was what the industrial district required. Neither did competition result in low fares and charges, because the companies were forced to collude on price to some degree in order to cover the enormous capital costs incurred by their profligate expansion. Initially the local traders were dissatisfied with their local monopolies, and so they encouraged the construction of competing lines. But the proliferation of lines did not produce the anticipated reduction in fares and improvements in quality of service. By the 1880s the system had become extremely dense, but dissatisfaction with the service was still rife. The counterfactual network delivers a service that would have been equally as good at a mere fraction of the capital cost. Even without the benefits of competition, a regulated rational system with lower capital costs would have afforded better value for money.

4.7. HUMBERSIDE AND CLEVELAND

The east coast of England north of the River Humber and south of the River Tees is dominated by the Yorkshire Moors. It lies 'off the beaten track' to the east of the Great North Road through Wetherby. Its natural hub and traditional commercial and religious centre is York. This area was well served by railways. They developed at an early date and spread quickly over the region. George and Robert Stephenson engineered some of the key lines, and George Hudson of York, the 'Railway King', promoted several of them.

The fishing port of Hull on the north bank of the Humber attracted a lot of interest from railway promoters, and the Hull and Selby Railway was completed as early as 1840. Once a bridge had been built across the River Ouse at Selby, an end-on junction was made with the Leeds and Selby Railway. This completed a 'land bridge' across the South Pennines connecting the North Sea at Hull to the Atlantic port of Liverpool via Milford, Normanton, Wakefield, and Manchester.

The Yorkshire Moors are rich in ironstone. The Whitby and Pickering Railway was opened in 1836, connecting the market town of Pickering to the fishing port of Whitby further up the coast from Hull. Like some other early railways, it contained vestiges of an old mineral railway—in this case an inclined plane (later bypassed) by which trains descended from the Moors to the banks of the River Esk.

At the time of the Railway Mania Robert Stephenson produced a number of plans for integrated regional railway systems, one of which related to Humberside. He visualized two cross-country routes intersecting at a hub: one ran south-east from York to Hull, and the other north-west from Selby, south of York, to Driffield, north of Hull. They met at Market Weighton. Some of Stephenson's schemes involved hubs at very remote locations, and so having a hub at a market town—albeit a small one—was very useful. Most of Stephenson's regional plans foundered, but this one was built—eventually. One of his difficulties was that in trying to accommodate the needs of all the towns in a district, he could be out-manoeuvred by more parochial schemes which gave one particular town an advantage over the others and thereby sucked away local support from the integrated scheme. Another problem was that his schemes were very expensive, and in the aftermath of the Railway Mania, with capital very scarce, most of the bigger schemes had to be scaled down or abandoned altogether. His Humberside schemes seem to have survived because they had powerful backing from Hudson and the town of York; it certainly took much longer to complete the line from Selby to Driffield than it did the line from York to Hull.

This compact network was embedded in a wider network that included not only the Hull and Selby railway along its southern boundary but also a coastal line from Hull to Scarborough via Bridlington in the east. Scarborough—an up-and-coming seaside resort—was connected to York by a main line that ran through to Leeds and that formed the northern boundary of the local system.

This highly rational structure was later dissipated by a profusion of minor branches, however. The North Eastern Railway, which acquired all the Stephenson lines—decided to consolidate its monopoly by filling up the spaces that remained between the existing lines. A rather pointless line was built between Driffield and Malton—a market town on the York to Scarborough line, passing through empty countryside near Sledmere House. This line was extended via Gilling to Pilmoor, from where an adventurous traveller could continue their journey to Harrogate. Alternatively, the passenger could return by an alternative route: from Gilling there was a cross-country branch line to Pickering via Helmsley, with connections to Seamer on the Scarborough line.

North of Scarborough a similar network of lines could be found. There was a very expensive heavily engineered route to Whitby, which crossed the River Esk at Whitby on the impressive Larpool Viaduct—the remains of which can still be seen today. This line continued along the coast to Middlesbrough, a major industrial centre on the River Tees, while another line to Teesside ran inland through Eskdale, with connections to the Rosedale Mines from Battersby. There were two routes to Brotton: a coastal route passing near the popular resort of Saltburn, and an inland route via Guisborough. The proliferation of lines in this area was caused by rivalry between the NER and the Cleveland Railway over access to the ironstone district. The NER replicated lines until the Cleveland Railway was hemmed in on every side, and then took them over by making them an offer that they could not refuse.

The counterfactual sticks to the approach of Robert Stephenson and eschews the profusion of lines later created by the NER. It is similar to the actual system in many respects, but lacks 'the frills'. Hull is served by an east–west main line from Leeds via Knottingley and Goole. A line from Thorne and the south feeds into this main line at Goole, and a line from Selby to York at Balkholme—an arrangement similar to that in use today. From Hull the main line loops round along the coast, using the Driffield route to Scarborough and the Esk Valley route to Middlesbrough. There is a direct line from York to Scarborough, with a branch to Pickering and Whitby. At Crathorne (south of the present hub of Thornaby) the Esk Valley line joins a line from Thirsk to Middlesbrough which completes the coastal loop. A traveller from Selby can then return home via the direct line through Thirsk.

4.8. THE NORTH-EAST

The north-east claims a special place in railway history as the 'Cradle of the Railway Revolution'. It was here that George Stephenson engineered the Stockton and Darlington Railway—the first railway in the world to use steam power and to offer a scheduled service to passengers. Like many lines in the north-east, the Stockton and Darlington (SDR) was designed to carry coal from mine to port. Its name is misleading. It begins near Bishop Auckland, the ancient residence of the prince Bishops of Durham, on the Durham coalfield. Several colliery branches feed traffic into the main line, which then cuts across from the Wear Valley to the Tees Valley at Stockton by means of inclined planes. This reflects the early philosophy of mineral railways, which often linked collieries or quarries in one valley with a downstream port in an adjacent valley, avoiding difficult roads and expensive canal locks in between.

The SDR did not cut across to Stockton in a straight line, however, but made a detour to the south through Darlington. The prominent Quaker banker, Edward Pease, and his associates resided in Darlington, and since they put up the money they expected their town to be on the route. This was the first recorded instance of the general principle of railway finance that intermediate towns would be served by detour if (and sometimes only if) they raised sufficient funds to cover the additional capital cost.

This detour proved to be a serious weakness. No sooner had the SDR been opened than a direct line to the coast—the Clarence Railway—was promoted. This ran due east to the coastal port of Hartlepool rather than the river port of Stockton. It was better equipped on all counts to carry heavy traffic: a shorter route, no inclines, and access to a seaport rather than a river port. Later railway promoters also learned their lesson from this: to deter competitors it is best to build a direct line. Put another way, intermediate towns must compensate promoters not only for the construction cost of a detour but also for the additional expense of carrying through traffic by a longer route and the heightened risk of competition from another line. This approach encouraged railway promoters to ignore the interests of intermediate towns and to require these towns to build their own branches to the direct line. While this was often good competitive strategy, it was poor network economy because it led to a proliferation of dead-end branches served by minor hubs strung out along a direct line.

The consequences of this approach in the north-east was that a series of largely independent east–west lines were built to carry coal from the Pennine foothills to the coast or to a convenient river estuary. These independent lines crossed the route of the main north–south trunk line from Newcastle to York via Darlington, but made little connection with it. One set of lines carried coal at slow speed and the other carried passengers at high speed. At Darlington, for example, the main line crossed the SDR line on the level, just north of the main line station at Bank Top and east of the SDR station at North Road. It was a crossing point, but not an effective hub.

The counterfactual system integrates these two sets of lines. Between Darlington and Durham there are powerful hubs at Newton Aycliffe (connections for north-bound traffic from Middlesbrough and south-bound traffic from Weardale), Spennymoor (connections for north-bound traffic from Bishop Auckland), Durham (connections for the Consett loop line and the East Coast), and Chester-le-Street (connections for Sunderland and Stanley). On the actual system, Durham was the only passenger hub of note, and here were two separate stations (rationalized down from three).

The situation at Newcastle is better than at Durham, because there is a single station, built jointly by some of the companies that merged to form the NER. One of these was the Newcastle and Carlisle—a venerable company operating one of the oldest trunk lines in the country, opened throughout in 1838. Designed as a 'land bridge' between the ports on the Tyne (facing the Baltic) and the Solway Firth (facing Ireland), the promoters predicted a large trade in Scandinavian timber destined for Dublin. Part of the route, between Hexham and Newcastle, was later used by the North British Railway to 'invade' Newcastle, and undermine the NER monopoly of the East Coast main line south of Berwick. The Carlisle line is an important component of the counterfactual, although the NBR line from Rillington Junction has no role in it.

Overall, it must be recognized that both the actual and counterfactual systems are strongly influenced by the geography and the geology of the north-east. In each case the railway system resembles a rib cage, with branches shooting off from the spine (the north–south main line) to link collieries with ports. Both systems link up the ports with a coastal line, but the counterfactual also provides convenient links between the inland colliery areas which the actual system generally neglects to do.

4.9. NORTH PENNINES

The railways across the North Pennines present a sorry spectacle to anyone who might have hoped for a rational social provision of railways. With so much empty space waiting to be opened up, it is disappointing to see how much the railways, even in this bare territory, were bent on duplicating one another's routes rather than putting isolated communities on the railway map.

The railway prospects for the north Pennines could have been considered quite promising in the 1850s, as they were bordered on either side by Anglo-Scottish trunk lines. To the west, the London and North Western (LNWR) main line ran from Lancaster through Carnforth, Tebay, and Penrith to Carlisle (reached in 1846), while to the east the North Eastern Railway (NER) main line ran from York to Newcastle via Northallerton and Darlington. The NER line joined the Great Northern main line to London just north of Doncaster, and the North British (NBR) main line to Edinburgh just south of Berwick. It was progressively improved, reaching Newcastle via Boldon in 1844, via Usworth in 1849, and by a direct line through Durham in 1868.

The most notable line through the North Pennines is another north–south line running in the middle—the Settle and Carlisle line of the Midland Railway (MR). This line was promoted for strategic reasons that had nothing to do with the area through which it passed: its logic was to link London and Glasgow via Leeds. As explained elsewhere, the MR felt 'boxed in' by its powerful neighbours. It first promoted an independent route from the Midlands to London St. Pancras, completed in 1868. It then turned its attention to bidding for Anglo-Scottish traffic. It acquired the 'Little North Western' line from Leeds to Lancaster via Skipton in 1871, from which there was a branch to Ingleton, where an end-on junction was made with an LNWR branch that gave access to Carlisle via a junction with the West Coast main line at Low Gill, south of Tebay. Running powers over the LNWR would allow the MR to connect with the Glasgow and South Western (GSWR) main line to Glasgow at Carlisle, and also with the North British 'Waverley Route' to Edinburgh. To 'soften up' the LNWR for negotiating purposes the MR proposed an independent main line from a junction with the Little North Western just south of Settle to a junction with the NER's Newcastle and Carlisle line near Carlisle. The LNWR took an inflexible stance and so the MR obtained an Act of Parliament to build its line. The LNWR then offered concessions, which the MR wished to accept, but Parliament would not allow the MR to back out of its plan, and so the line was constructed—at enormous cost both financially and in loss of workmen's lives.

The Settle and Carlisle line climbs northwards to a summit at Blea Moor Tunnel and then descends through Kirkby Stephen and Appleby. At Kirkby Stephen the route could have joined the NER's South Durham and Lancashire Union line from Barnard Castle to Penrith, or later on at Appleby, the county town of Westmoreland, where the routes actually cross. But these options were rejected in favour of giving the MR total control of every mile of its route up to the junction at Carlisle. There were thus two parallel routes between Kirkby Stephen and Appleby, operated independently, while other pairs of neighbouring towns, such as Sedbergh and Kirkby Stephen, had no direct connection at all.

The counterfactual system feeds northbound traffic from Leeds into the West Coast main line at Kirkby Lonsdale, well south of Carlisle, and thereby avoids the duplication of lines. North of Lancaster, the counterfactual main line follows the Lune Valley, east of the actual line, thereby avoiding the 1 in 75 gradients of the route over Shap Fell. Appleby and Kirkby Stephen are both served by a secondary loop from Sedbergh to Carlisle—a much cheaper solution affording a better local service.

There were two East–West routes across the Pennines. Both were secondary routes, and neither has survived as a through route. The first was the South Durham line across Stainmoor, already mentioned, which is replicated in the counterfactual by a line from Barnard Castle to Penrith via Brough. It was mainly used for heavy freight from Workington to Teeside. The second is a line through Wensleydale, comprising two separate branches that met head-on at Hawes. These branches carried purely local traffic. In the counterfactual both lines are upgraded for express passenger trains, and provided with better connections to the rest of the system, particularly on their eastern flanks. As a result, both these lines can be used for long distance Trans-Pennine passenger traffic linking North Lancashire, Furness, and the Lake District to Tyneside and Teeside. The two lines are also connected by a link from Sedbergh to Brough, thereby creating an integrated regional system linking the principal market towns.

There were plans to create other Trans-Pennine links. One was a link from Alston, the terminus of a branch from the Newcastle and Carlisle line, to Wearhead, the terminus of a branch from Bishop Auckland. Another was a westward extension of the branch from Barnard Castle to Middleton-in-Teesdale. Neither plan came to anything—which is probably just as well because, apart from lead mining, there was very little industry or population in the area. Neither of these lines figures in the counterfactual system.

4.10. THE NORTH-WEST AND CUMBRIA

The popular image of the north-west is based on the factory system that developed in the Lancashire textile industry. Manchester, on the River Irwell (a tributary of the Mersey) was the commercial centre. The availability of water power from the Pennine Hills, the damp climate, and the scarcity of agricultural employment all favoured this development. By 1824 vast quantities of cotton were being imported along the Bridgewater Canal from Liverpool to Manchester for distribution to factories in neighbouring towns, and finished fabrics were being exported in the opposite direction. The Duke of Bridgewater had an effective monopoly because the only alternative means of freight transport—the Leeds and Liverpool Canal and the Mersey and Irwell Navigation—were much slower. In any case, all canals were prone to disruption by ice in winter and shortage of water in summer.

A railway was a natural solution, and the Stockton and Darlington (SDR), engineered by George Stephenson and opened in 1825, seemed to be a suitable model. The pragmatic Stephenson was invited to re-survey a line proposed by the visionary eccentric William James. There were key differences between the Liverpool and Manchester (LMR) and the SDR, however. The distance was greater, the countryside was flatter and the freight was more valuable. Speed was important for commercial reasons, and it was also possible because of the flat terrain. Technology was able to deliver. Robert Stephenson equipped his experimental (and aptly named) Rocket locomotive with a multi-tubular boiler, allowing it to reach a speed of 30 mph in public trials. Father George was still thinking in terms of inclined planes, but rope-hauled inclines were no longer necessary to supplement steam locomotive power. The real problem was crossing water-saturated ground at Chat Moss. On the opening day in 1830, William Huskisson, President of the Board of Trade, was knocked down and killed by Rocket, and there were fears that the workers would riot when the Prime Minister, the Duke of Wellington, arrived in Manchester. But the railway itself was an immediate commercial success. Furthermore, an unexpected market in inter-urban business travel was revealed.

Stephenson's route avoided intermediate centres of population such as St. Helens, Widnes, and Warrington. Opposition from landowners is part of the explanation, and the coolness or ambivalence of town authorities towards the railway may have been a factor too. But it is worth noting that many of these early railway schemes were designed to further the commercial interests of the merchants and manufacturers who promoted them rather than to benefit intermediate towns. Early railway promoters appear to have viewed their company as a kind of club from which the members would receive not only dividends but also benefits in kind—such as cheap rates for their freight. Only those who joined the club by subscribing capital were entitled to the commercial benefits on this view. Excluding other towns was also a means of eliminating competition. Both

Widnes and Warrington are on the Mersey, and had the railway served them ships might have passed Liverpool by and unloaded upstream. A few years later, similar thinking seems to have persuaded the Gloucester proprietors of the Birmingham and Gloucester Railway to bypass the important city of Worcester because it was a rival port on the Severn.

A consequence of local dissatisfaction with Stephenson's route was that another line was subsequently built through Widnes and Warrington, but this could not be operated as a trunk line because it used a suburban branch from Manchester for part of its route. Another route was opened up through Wigan—which again was indirect. The best route—and the last to be built—was the Cheshire Lines route which ran direct but provided loops into Warrington and Widnes. A variant of this line is used in the counterfactual system, and substitutes for the assortment of lines described above.

The industrial district around Manchester and the hinterland of the port of Liverpool is only a small part of the north-west in geographical terms. To understand the wider regional network within which Manchester and Liverpool are embedded, it is important to recognize that the north-western coastline of Britain is highly irregular. There is a succession of important river estuaries, including the Dee at Chester, the Mersey at Liverpool, the Ribble at Preston, the Lune at Lancaster, and the Solway at Carlisle. In between these estuaries are distinctive areas—the Wirral, Merseyside, the Fylde peninsular, and the Furness district. The first three of these areas are flat, but the last is mountainous—the Furness district, which adjoins the tourist area of The Lake District. The natural rail hubs of these areas are the towns and cities that form the first bridging across these rivers: Warrington (the Mersey), Preston (the Ribble), Lancaster (the Lune), and Carlisle (the Solway). The exception is the ancient city of Chester, whose river has long silted up.

Deep-sea ports lie on the seaward side of the these bridging points: Birkenhead on the Wirral, Liverpool on Merseyside, Fleetwood and Heysham on the Fylde, and Barrow-in-Furness. The natural access to these points is through the corresponding bridging points. Further inland to the east lie the foothills of the Pennines, oriented north to south. The watersheds that determine the routes of the rivers that create the bridging points also determine the valleys that can be used by trans-Pennine trains. These geographical fundamentals are common to both the actual and counterfactual systems, and the tight constraints that they impose dictate that the two systems are quite similar in terms of the wider picture.

The spine of the north-west railway network is the West Coast main line, which connects up the bridging points on a north–south orientation. It runs north from Staffordshire, through Cheshire and Lancashire to the Scottish border just north of Carlisle. The alignments through Warrington, Wigan, Preston, and Lancaster are broadly the same, but between Lancaster and Carlisle they diverge. The actual line makes a detour to the west through Oxenholme, allowing it to serve the manufacturing town of Kendal and the resort of Windermere, while the counterfactual pursues an easier route up the Lune Valley. At Kirkby Lonsdale it crosses a trunk line from Leeds to Barrow-in-Furness, which also feeds north-bound traffic from Yorkshire into the main line. In the actual system the connections with Leeds and Barrow are made further south at Carnforth, which makes the route from Leeds to the north less direct.

Although the actual system provides a cut-off for north-bound traffic through Ingleton, this route was little used because of a frontier dispute between the Midland (MR) which controlled the route from Leeds and the London and North Western (LNWR) which controlled the route onwards to Carlisle (as explained above). It was this stalemate that led to the MR to build its Settle and Carlisle line from Leeds to the Scottish border. No such line is necessary on the counterfactual system.

For the benefit of trans-Pennine traffic from Teesside to the Furness district the counterfactual provides a route through Wensleydale from Leyburn to the West Coast main line at Sedbergh, north of Kirkby Lonsdale. To the east of Leyburn this line divides, the northern branch serving Teesside and the southern branch serving Yorkshire and Humberside. The analogue of this route on the actual system is a line between Garsdale Head and Northallerton, which was only built to branch line standards and carried little through traffic.

On both the actual and counterfactual systems the border city of Carlisle is a major hub. Furthermore, both systems provide a coastal route from Carlisle to Barrow via the ironstone district around Workington and the port of Whitehaven. Further south, Preston too is an important hub on both systems. Warrington is also a hub on both systems, but is less important on the actual because Liverpool is connected to Crewe and the south by a bridge at Runcorn—an expensive engineering feature which the counterfactual avoids—rather than through the hub at Warrington.

On the Fylde peninsular, however, some significant differences are to be found. The emphasis of the counterfactual is on a coastal route from Preston to Garstang via Blackpool, with a branch to Fleetwood, while the actual system prioritizes traffic from Preston to Blackpool—there were no less than three routes between the two towns, with two separate terminals in Blackpool.

Proliferation of routes also occurred around Wigan in the heart of the Lancashire coalfield. Competition for coal traffic between the Lancashire and Yorkshire and the LNWR led to a maze of lines in and around Wigan, and even the Great Central Railway became involved. The counterfactual rationalizes these lines considerably, focusing on links to Southport via Ormskirk, to Liverpool via St. Helens, and to Manchester, Bury, and Rochdale via Bolton.

Manchester is an important hub on the counterfactual system. This is in line with one of the general principles on which the counterfactual is constructed—namely that important centres of traffic generation should also 'double up' as hubs. Manchester is a natural hub because it is near a point at which several Pennine valleys emerge onto the north Cheshire plain. On the actual system, however, Manchester was a failure as a railway hub. By 1914 it had four separate main line stations: London Road (now Piccadilly), Central (now closed), Victoria, and Exchange (now merged and used mainly for local traffic). Although there were connecting lines that provided opportunities for flexible working, they were not fully exploited, because of rivalries between the companies concerned.

Concentrating too much traffic on Manchester could lead to congestion, and so the counterfactual also provides Manchester with bypass routes, such as the Stockport to Stalybridge link to the east, the Bolton–Bury–Rochdale line to the north, the Warrington to Stockport line to the south and the West Coast main line to the west. All these lines are replicated on the actual system, but there is a proliferation of other lines as well.

In contrast to Manchester, Liverpool is not a natural hub, because it lies on the Merseyside peninsular. As an important port it naturally attracted a lot of railways, as noted above. On the actual system it was served by three separate termini—Lime Street, Central, and Exchange—whereas on the counterfactual, lines fan out from a single station to the principal inland hubs to the north and east of the city.

4.11. NORTH MIDLANDS

The North Midlands comprises Derbyshire and Nottinghamshire. As the home of Richard Arkwright, inventor of the water-powered loom, the county town of Derby was the site of early textile factories, and Nottingham developed as a lace manufacturing centre too. By the nineteenth century large coalfields were being exploited in the Erewash Valley between Derby and Nottingham, and in Charnwood Forest, to the south near Loughborough. To the north-west lies the scenic Peak District around Bakewell and Matlock, and in the north-east Sherwood Forest.

The North Midlands has a natural transport hub midway between Derby and Nottingham. It is here that the River Trent, wending its way east from Stoke, past Stafford and through the brewery town of Burton, to Nottingham and Lincoln, crosses a north–south route from Leeds and Sheffield to Leicester and London that passes through the Erewash Valley. This valley was used by the Midland Railway (MR) for part of its main trunk line from Leeds to London, and it forms part of the counterfactual trunk line from Leeds to London too. When the MR was created in 1844, by merging the North Midland, Midland Counties Railway, and Birmingham and Derby Junction, its route to London, south of Leicester, was via Rugby and the West Coast main line. This original route—rather than the later alignments (first through Hitchin and then Luton)—is the one used by the counterfactual (see above).

In both the actual and counterfactual systems the Trent Valley forms part of a cross-country main line from Birmingham through Burton to Nottingham, Newark, and Lincoln. This line feeds traffic from the south-west into the main line to Leeds and the north-east near Derby. In the actual system the junction is at Long Eaton, while in the counterfactual it is further north at Ilkeston. The counterfactual makes it easier for trains using the Erewash Valley to call at

Derby en route. On the actual system trains calling at Derby must use a parallel line to Sheffield, which is a wasteful duplication of track.

The actual and counterfactual systems also use different routes from Birmingham to Burton. These routes intersect the West Coast main line at Tamworth and Lichfield respectively, making the counterfactual route the shorter of the two. As the intersections are at right-angles they are of limited use for long-distance traffic, but in a local context the cathedral city of Lichfield makes the more useful hub.

Subject to these minor differences, the counterfactual system is broadly similar to the MR network in the area. The difference lies not in the configuration so much as in the total mileage of track. Compared to the counterfactual, the actual mileage is very high because the Great Central (GCR) and Great Northern (GNR) also built extensive networks in the area—duplicating, and sometimes triplicating, MR routes. The GCR duplicated the MR main line with its own line from Sheffield to London via Nottingham and Leicester, while the GNR invaded at a number of points from the east—most extravagantly by building a branch from Nottingham, through Derby to Stafford on the West Coast main line. Duplication was endemic in the mining area between Sheffield and Nottingham; further south, the Burton area was served by no less than five different companies.

The comparison between the two systems illustrates vividly the waste incurred by the actual system in replicating both inter-urban trunk lines and branch line access to mining areas. The basic configuration of both networks is heavily constrained by physical geography (as in many other parts of the country), but the duplication of lines along the permissible routes that occurs in the actual system is mainly a product of competitive private construction.

4.12. WEST MIDLANDS

The West Midlands comprises the counties of Warwickshire, Staffordshire, and Worcestershire. Its natural commercial centre is Birmingham. In the nineteenth century Birmingham was England's 'second city' after London, though closely challenged by Liverpool, Manchester, and Leeds. In Scotland, only Glasgow was of comparable size. The area was famous for artisan manufacture—from the nail manufacturers of the Black Country around Dudley, Walsall, and Wolverhampton, to the jewellers, gunmakers, and watch-makers of Birmingham itself.

The West Midlands is a natural cross-road for north–south and east–west traffic. While it would be most convenient if this cross-road were at Birmingham itself, in practice Birmingham lies slightly to the south of the natural West Coast route from London to the north. Furthermore, the country around Birmingham is quite hilly, and it is therefore advantageous for long-distance traffic to pass to either side. Finally, since local traffic is quite heavy because of industrialization, it pays through traffic to bypass Birmingham in order to minimize congestion. Thus while Birmingham is a natural local hub and major traffic-generating centre, it is not ideal as a major national hub. It is advantageous for through traffic to bypass it wherever possible.

This suggests that as major routes approach Birmingham, they should diverge, with one route heading for the city centre and the other avoiding it. The points where city centre and bypass routes diverge constitute natural satellite hubs. Connecting up the satellite hubs will create a ring route round the city and thereby promote economic links between different satellite locations. The counterfactual system exploits this network structure more effectively than does the actual one.

Since Birmingham is a major traffic-generating centre in the interior of the country it is only natural that lines should radiate from it in all directions. The radial pattern is manifest in both the actual and counterfactual systems. In both the actual and counterfactual systems the main line to London proceeds through Coventry to the West Coast main line near Rugby. Moving clockwise, a line runs south through Leamington and the Cherwell Valley to Oxford, replicating the original Great Western (GWR) main line into Birmingham from the south; this line handles traffic for Southampton and the South Coast. On the counterfactual system traffic for Bristol and the south-west leaves Birmingham via Stourbridge and Kidderminster—the GWR route to Worcester—rather than via Bromsgrove on the Midland (MR) route—thereby avoiding the Clent Hills and the infamous Lickey Incline. There is also a loop line through Redditch that joins the Bristol line near Tewkesbury—replicating an MR branch.

A main line to Wales leaves Birmingham via Wolverhampton to Shrewsbury, whence it proceeds to Aberystwyth, following the old GWR and Cambrian Railway routes as far as Newtown. Wolverhampton is also the gateway to the north-west, with a connection to the West Coast main line. In the counterfactual this connection is made at Stone, near Stoke-on-Trent, whereas on the actual system it is made further south at Stafford. The north-east is served by a line through Burton to Derby (see above), while East Anglia is reached via Nuneaton and Leicester—as on the actual system.

Bypasses are provided on both systems. There are more bypasses on the counterfactual system than on the actual system, but the major difference is that the potential bypass lines are connected up better on the counterfactual system than the actual system because there is no fragmentation of ownership between rival systems. On both systems the West Coast main line bypasses Birmingham to the north, through Nuneaton and Lichfield, for reasons described above. There is a north-western bypass on both systems too, between Stourbridge and Walsall via Dudley, based on the route of the South Staffordshire Railway. There is also a western bypass along the Stour Valley between Kidderminster and Wolverhampton, following the route of a GWR line built after World War I.

A major innovation in the counterfactual is a southern bypass between Evesham and Leamington via Stratford-on-Avon. At Evesham connections are available for Worcester (for Central Wales) and Tewkesbury (for Bristol and the south-west). At Leamington, connections are available for Coventry, Nuneaton, and Leicester (for the north-east) and Daventry and Northampton (for East

Anglia). Most of this route was actually developed by the railway companies, but the segments did not join up in a coherent manner. While the GWR provided a link between Evesham and Leamington, the tortuous route comprised five separate sections, involving connections at Honeybourne, Stratford-on-Avon, Bearley, and Hatton. At Leamington a passenger would need to transfer to the LNWR station to continue their journey to Leicester or Northampton. An alternative for Northampton passengers would be to take the MR to Broom and the Stratford-on-Avon and Midland Junction to Blisworth, where they could change to the LNWR.

Taken together, the bypasses on the counterfactual system provide a ring of rails around Birmingham linking up a string of satellite hubs: Northampton, Leamington, Evesham, Kidderminster, Wolverhampton, Stoke-on-Trent, Lichfield and Nuneaton, and various smaller hubs between them. The ring not only expedites the passage of long-distance traffic through a congested region but also contributes to the economic development of the region through the links between the satellite hubs. It gives passengers a choice of routes, and an opportunity to develop flexible itineraries. It also provides operational flexibility through diversionary routes.

Inside the ring, there are benefits from having a single station too. Prior to 1854 Birmingham was served by a single joint station—New Street—owned by the LNWR, MR, and North Staffordshire Railway. The GWR, however, as a fierce competitor of the LNWR, built its own station half a mile away at Snow Hill. The site was cramped, and the GWR later built an additional station for suburban traffic at Moor Street, which made it difficult for commuters to connect with north-bound services from Snow Hill. Weaknesses in the satellite system were therefore reproduced as weaknesses in the central hub.

4.13. WALES

The railway system of Wales illustrates very clearly the commercial drivers of railway investment: long-distance passenger traffic and the exploitation of minerals. Wales spans the main routes from London to Ireland. The North Wales port of Holyhead, on the tip of the Isle of Angelesey, served Dublin via Dun Laoghaire, while the South Wales ports of Neyland and Fishguard served Waterford and Limerick, in the south of Ireland, via Rosslare. As a result, two trunk lines developed, both running East–West.

The Chester and Holyhead line, engineered by Robert Stephenson, ran along the North Wales coast, and was opened in 1848. At Chester it connected with a line to Crewe, which in turn connected with the West Coast main line to London. The line was notable for its two tubular bridges—one across the River Conway beneath Conway Castle, and the other across Menai Strait, giving access to Anglesey from Bangor. It was operated as part of the London and North Western (LNWR) system and was formally acquired by that company in 1879.

The Holyhead line benefited from a lucrative government mail contract because of its strategic role in conveying Irish MPs to Westminster. It also had the potential to transport British troops to Ireland to quell political unrest.

The other main line—the South Wales Railway—was engineered by Stephenson's great friend and rival, Brunel, and was built to the broad gauge (opened in 1850). Unlike the Holyhead line, its major purpose was not to carry the Irish traffic but to tap into mineral resources along the way. South Wales was famous for its deposits of high-grade steam coal, which was used by railway locomotives and steam ships at home and abroad. There was a small coalfield near Wrexham in North Wales too. A variety of metal ores could be found, including the famous copper mountain at Amlwch, near Holyhead, and the iron ore deposits concentrated around Merthyr Tydfil.

Mineral railways preceded the development of main line railways in South Wales (as they did in many other parts of the country). The Pen-y-Daren Railway, near Merthyr, was the scene of a notable experiment in steam locomotion by the Cornish engineer Richard Trevithick in 1804. One of the most important mineral lines, that ran from Cardiff to Merthyr—the Taff Vale—was engineered by the young Brunel, who built it on George Stephenson's standard gauge. When he became famous as an advocate of the broad gauge, his critics unkindly drew attention to his previous commitment to the standard gauge; Brunel replied that the standard gauge was fine for mineral railways, but quite unsuitable for passenger-carrying trunk lines.

The South Wales Railway ran from a junction with the Great Western (GWR) Cheltenham line at Gloucester along the north bank of the Severn Channel through Lydney to Newport, where it connected with a line from Abergavenny and Hereford down the Usk Valley. It continued through Cardiff and Swansea. The line was extended to Carmarthen in 1852 and Milford Haven in 1863 (the date on which the GWR formally acquired the South Wales Railway). Fishguard was initially served by a lightly built branch; the main line only reached the port in 1906. The broad gauge adopted by the South Wales Railway integrated it into the GWR system and facilitated through running to London, but it created problems too. Gloucester was also served by the Midland Railway trunk line from Birmingham to Bristol, which was on the standard gauge, and it became notorious for the inconvenience caused by 'break of gauge'. Furthermore, most of the mineral lines were standard gauge too, so that getting mineral traffic onto the line was just as difficult as getting it off again at Gloucester.

These difficulties encouraged the LNWR to invade the GWR's territory in South Wales. It was in a good position to transport coal in standard gauge wagons to the industrial centres of the Midlands and north. It could also deliver coal to London—albeit by a roundabout route. It promoted a line along the 'Heads of the Valleys' from Abergavenny, north of Newport, via Tredegar and Dowlais, to the heart of the South Wales coal and iron industries at Merthyr. At the same time, however, the LNWR made a serious error of judgement in allowing the GWR to enter North Wales through its acquisition of the Shrewsbury and Chester Railway. This gave the GWR access to the North Wales coalfield at Wrexham, and ultimately to the port of Birkenhead. While the LNWR remained dominant in the north, and the GWR in the south, competition for the mineral traffic led to significant duplication of lines in both areas. Competition was further complicated by the presence of a third company based in Mid-Wales—the Cambrian Railway. It is in Mid-Wales that the differences between the actual and counterfactual systems are most pronounced.

In accordance with the economic logic set out above, the major companies initially ignored Mid-Wales. It is hilly country—and so expensive territory in which to build a railway. Sheep farming makes the best of poor soil and a damp climate, but supports only a small population. The landed gentry supported a local railway—the Cambrian—which came under the influence of speculators interested in developing the tourist potential of the coast around Barmouth and Aberystwyth. The Cambrian built a line from Whitchurch, on the LNWR line from Crewe to Shrewsbury, through Oswestry, Welshpool, and Machynlleth to Aberystwyth (opened in 1863). A coastal branch was later completed from the Dovey estuary near Machynthlleth to Pwllheli in the Lleyn Peninsular of North Wales.

The tourist trade developed only slowly at Aberystwyth, but eventually the GWR decided to compete with its own line from Ruabon, on the Chester to Shrewsbury line, to Dolgellau, where it connected with a Cambrian branch to Barmouth on the Pwllheli line. The GWR line, through Llangollen and Bala Junction, was well suited to holiday traffic from Liverpool and Manchester that was previously funnelled onto the Cambrian at Whitchurch by the LNWR.

The GWR also invaded the Mid-Wales coast by taking over the operation of the ill-fated Manchester and Milford Railway. Like another grand scheme described below, its promoters believed that profitable long-distance traffic could cross-subsidize sparse local traffic. The optimism of the Manchester and Milford promoters rested on the idea that textiles from Manchester could be exported from ports in south-west Wales, while coal from South Wales could fuel the mills of Manchester. The only portion of the line ever built was a section from Aberystwyth to Pencader, which was later extended by other companies to connect with the South Wales trunk line at Carmarthen. The whole line was taken over by the GWR to act as a feeder to its main line at Carmarthen.

The final link in the railway system of Wales was a north–south line along the Welsh border from Chester through Shrewsbury, Ludlow, Hereford, and Abergavenny down to Newport. The Shrewsbury to Hereford portion was jointly owned by the GWR and LNWR, and all the rest was owned solely by the GWR, although the LNWR had extensive running powers. The jointly owned portion represented a frontier between LNWR-dominated territory in the north and GWR-dominated territory in the south (see Chapter 5).

According to the guiding principles of the counterfactual system, Wales may be regarded as a very long and broad peninsular projecting from England into the Irish Sea. As such, it should be served by a combination of different types of line. The skeleton system should comprise a coastal line and an inland line across the base of the peninsular, to which is added a grid of lines linking points on the coast to hubs on the inland line. These intersections of these lines create a set of additional hubs. The system is completed by secondary lines feeding traffic into local hubs strung out along the main lines.

The major ports on a large peninsular often lie at its extremities, and are served by trunk lines from the inland hubs. This is the case with Wales. The location of the major Irish ferry ports dictates that both the actual and counterfactual systems are built around coastal trunk lines in the north and south. Traffic from the interior is fed onto these lines down valleys that terminate at minor hubs strung out along the main lines. Parallel valley lines can be turned from dead-end branches into through routes by building a line across their heads, as the LNWR did in South Wales, provided that geography permits it. It may also be possible to connect adjacent valleys in the middle, as the GWR did with its line from Pontypool to Neath. Given the expense, such connections are warranted only if substantial traffic is likely to flow out of the valleys, or between one valley to the next. This condition is satisfied only in South Wales—where, in consequence, the counterfactual provides analogues of the LNWR and GWR lines.

On both the actual and counterfactual systems the two coastal trunk lines are joined up to form a continuous loop by a line from Bangor to Carmarthen. On the actual system this route had four distinct portions, separated by hubs at which trains reverse directions—Afon Wen, near Pwllheli, Dovey Junction near Machynlleth, and Aberystwyth. Three separate companies owned the line: the LNWR, the Cambrian, and the GWR. The sections north and south of Aberystwyth were operated almost entirely independently. On the counterfactual, by contrast, the entire coastal loop, including the trunk line portions, can be operated as an integrated entity.

The inland line on both the actual and counterfactual systems links Newport to Chester via Hereford and Shrewsbury, but there is a difference in the route between Shrewsbury and Hereford. The counterfactual takes in the Ironbridge district in the Severn Valley, whereas the actual proceeds directly across the hills through Craven Arms.

The major difference between the actual and counterfactual systems, however, lies in the interior of the country. On the counterfactual the intersecting lines across Central Wales are realigned, and the hubs are re-sited, in order to improve connections. This expedites communication with England and Wales and—most importantly—improves communication within Wales as well. Coastal towns benefit substantially—especially those between Bangor and Carmarthen.

The counterfactual provides a direct connection from the main administrative centre at Aberystwyth to London via Llangurig, Builth Wells, Hereford, and Gloucester. This link is much shorter than the actual routes from Aberystwyth through either Shrewsbury and Birmingham or Carmarthen and Cardiff. Part of this route follows the path of the Cambrian's Mid-Wales line from Moat Lane Junction, near Newtown, to Three Cocks Junction near Brecon, but the counterfactual line is better oriented for east–west traffic and is built to main line standards.

Crossing this main line at Builth Wells is another main line linking Swansea to Warrington via Llandovery, Welshpool, and Chester. This line provides connections from South Wales to Liverpool, Manchester, and Scotland via the West Coast main line. It shares the route of the other main line between Builth Wells and Llangurig. This southern portion of this route has an analogue in the LNWR's Central Wales line from Swansea to Craven Arms, south of Shrewsbury, which crossed Mid-Wales at Builth Road, just north of Builth Wells.

The Mid-Wales main line system is completed by a line from Carmarthen to Birmingham via Llandovery, Brecon, Leominster, and Stourbridge. It joins the Swansea to Warrington line from the west at Llandeilo, and diverges at Llandovery. It makes a junction with a secondary line from Neath at Sennybridge, and then joins the Abersytwyth to Gloucester main line at Three Cocks Junction near Hay-on-Wye. It diverges north from this line at Willersley, picks up traffic from Ludlow at Woofferton, and joins the main trunk line from Gloucester to Stoke-on-Trent at Stourport. It turns off this line at Kidderminster to reach Birmingham. There is no close analogue of this line on the actual system, although part of the route was used by the Midland Railway line from Hereford to Brecon and its continuation—the Neath and Brecon Railway. The closest analogue is actually a Railway Mania scheme that was never built, the Welsh Midland Railway which, as it name suggests, set out specifically to link South Wales—and Swansea in particular—to the West Midlands via Mid-Wales. Like the Manchester and Milford, optimism collapsed at the end of the Railway Mania. Although the scheme was never revived, some portions of the line were subsequently built by other companies.

Comparing the actual and counterfactual systems shows that railway provision was adequate—and indeed often overgenerous—where ports and mining areas were concerned. The main deficiency lies in the lightly populated and hilly inland areas where capital needed to be conserved. Instead of building a few well-thought out main lines that intersected at useful hubs, private companies promoted under-funded schemes based on ambitious ideas for carrying trunk line traffic. When these schemes foundered, under-provision of railways resulted. The completion of lines was delayed, and although connections were sometimes put in once lines were built, the alignments of these lines did not reflect any coherent plan. As a result, many towns in Wales remained isolated from their neighbours because they were served by different lines owned by different companies whose main concern was to feed traffic into their own systems rather than provide an integrated system for the benefit of the local economy.

4.14. THE SOUTH-WEST

The south-west, comprising Devon, Cornwall, and West Somerset, is a long peninsular pointing out into the Atlantic Ocean, which progressively narrows as it approaches Lands End, just west of Penzance. The southern coast line is hilly and irregular, with numerous small and inaccessible fishing ports.

The River Tamar divides Devon and Cornwall. Although Cornwall was a thriving copper and tin mining district during the late eighteenth and early nineteenth century, the difficulty of bridging the Tamar made it quite remote. Brunel's Saltash Bridge, completed in 1859, altered the transport geography of the country quite dramatically, but came too late to save the fortunes of the Cornish mining industry.

High moorland dominates the interior of the south-west—the most extensive areas being Bodmin Moor in Cornwall and Dartmoor and Exmoor in Devon. Railways must thread their way around the edges of these moors in order to avoid steep gradients. As the desolate mining areas declined, so population shifted to the coast where tourism was expanding, particularly in the quaint fishing ports. This was particularly evident in south Devon, where from the beginning of the nineteenth century sandy beaches and temperate climate attracted growing numbers to the 'English Riviera'. The rise of tourism is clearly reflected in the evolution of the local rail system. Tourist potential makes a southern trunk route along the peninsular much more viable than a northern one.

The natural gateway to the south-west is the cathedral city of Exeter. Once a major port, Exeter has long been the administrative capital of Devon. While it is possible to enter the peninsular to the north at Taunton, and head due west to Minehead or Barnstaple, the Quantock Hills, Brendon Hills, and Exmoor create a serious barrier for anything other than a branch line railway. Both the actual and counterfactual systems therefore enter the peninsular at Exeter.

The Great Western (GWR) reached Exeter in 1844 thanks to its associate company the Bristol and Exeter Railway, although it was not until the rebuilding of Bristol Temple Meads station that direct travel from London became easy. The South Devon Railway opened from Exeter to Plymouth in 1848. However, Brunel had engineered it as a single track broad gauge railway operated on the atmospheric principle, and had constructed viaducts out of wood instead of brick. All these features had to be replaced, although it was not until 1892 that the broad gauge finally disappeared.

A further extension—the Cornwall Railway—reached Truro in 1859. The GWR was again behind the project and Brunel was again the engineer. From Truro the West Cornwall Railway took over for the final leg to Penzance. It passed through the mining district around Carn Brae and the mining towns of Redruth and Camborne—an area catered for by mineral lines which operated few scheduled passenger services.

The lightly populated north of Devon was of limited interest to profit-seeking railway promoters. Crediton, a small market town north of Exeter, was connected to the county town in 1851, on the initiative of its local elite, and this line was quickly extended to Barnstaple—the 'capital' of north Devon—in 1854. Initially the line was operated on the broad gauge, to facilitate connection with the GWR, but in 1865 it was taken over by the London and South Western Railway (LSWR) and converted to standard gauge in 1877. Further north, the West Somerset

Railway had been opened from Norton Fitzwarren, near Taunton, to the small port of Watchet in 1862, which also handled traffic from the independent West Somerset Mineral Railway.

The loss of the Barnstaple line to the LSWR prompted the GWR to build an alternative line to Barnstaple from Norton Fitzwarren via Dulverton which gave superior connections for London, and they also extended the Watchet line to Minehead. A direct line was constructed from Exeter to Tiverton, avoiding the need for changes at Tiverton Junction, and this line was then extended north to meet the new Barnstaple line near Dulverton. This defensive 'space filling' did not, however, deter the LSWR from extending its Barnstaple line northwards to the resort of Ilfracombe, and eastwards to Bideford and Torrington. This was part of a larger expansion through which the LSWR achieved its long-standing ambition of an independent route from London to Plymouth. Its line to Plymouth diverged west from the Barnstaple line at Yeoford, near Crediton, and skirted round to the north of Dartmoor via Okehampton, where a line to Padstow diverged. The extensions came very late, however—Plymouth was not reached until 1890 and Padstow until 1899—and never seriously challenged the GWR's dominance of the area.

A prominent feature of the counterfactual system in the south-west is the systematic use of coastal loops. Most of the population is concentrated on the coast, for reasons noted above, and it is therefore appropriate to provide good connections between adjacent settlements on the coast. By contrast, the GWR used dead-end branches and not loops to serve towns off its main lines. There were branches to Ashburton, Bodmin, Brixham, Falmouth, Fowey, Helston, Kingsbridge, Kingswear, Launceston, Looe, Minehead, Moretonhampstead, Newquay, Princetown, St. Ives, and Yealmpton. The only qualification to this is that Newquay and Fowey were served by branches from two different hubs, and could therefore be thought of as being on a loop. However, the lines were not operated as loops, and reversal would have been necessary to use the branches in this way.

A journey by GWR between neighbouring coastal towns would therefore normally involve two changes—often on isolated country junctions. By contrast, in the counterfactual system a direct service is often available. Furthermore, the loops converge on a limited number of hubs on the main line, and thereby reduce the number of intermediate stops that main line expresses need to make. Most hubs serve more than one loop, so that only one change is required even between quite distant towns. Average distances are shorter because passengers have greater choice over direction of travel, since they can exit a loop at either end.

The GWR's preference for dead-end branches cannot be explained purely by geographical limitations imposed by the coastline, because it used the same strategy in inland areas where these constraints do not apply. It seems rather to reflect a company philosophy in its early years that as a main line company it provided main line trains, and that local communities were responsible for providing local trains. They should make their own arrangements to connect with the main line network by building and operating individual branch lines at their own expense. The GWR would operate the branches for them, and even purchase them, but only on terms that made it attractive to the company (which normally meant a loss for the local promoters).

Loops emerged on the actual system, but more by accident than design. Thus the LSWR main line from Exeter to Plymouth functioned as an inland loop as it joined up with the GWR main line at either end. A northern coastal loop was also formed as a result of an LSWR junction at Wadebridge, which made it possible for passengers from Exeter to return via Bodmin and the GWR main line. Although these loops provided a certain amount of flexibility, they were inefficient because they both duplicated portions of the GWR Plymouth to Launceston branch.

On balance, therefore, competition between the GWR and LSWR did not materially improve the provision of railway services, except in north Devon, where the GWR was stimulated to make improvements by the loss of its Barnstaple line. Both the GWR and the LSWR perceived rural towns as mere feeders to their trunk line systems. They constructed dead-end branches whose role was to help in the development of the tourist trade rather than to promote mobility for local residents. It is possible that more tourists might have settled locally, and permanently boosted the economy, had the overall quality of local transport been improved. This would have required loop lines to replace dead-end branches as the preferred method of local provision, as exemplified in the counterfactual system.

4.15. SOMERSET AND DORSET

Somerset and Dorset constitute a large and mainly rural area, bounded to the north by Bristol and Bath, on the River Avon, and to the south by Weymouth and Swanage on the English Channel. To the west lies the Devon border, which passes near to Taunton, the county town of Somerset, while to the east lies the border with Wiltshire near Shaftesbury.

On both the actual and counterfactual systems, traffic from the south-west is funnelled into Exeter, the county town of Devon, along various routes. Traffic from the north and Midlands enters via Bristol, the regional metropolis, and proceeds to Exeter via Bridgewater and Taunton. Traffic from London has a choice of routes; road traffic has tended to take the shortest route via Salisbury, while most rail traffic takes a more northerly course. The counterfactual main line from London to Exeter follows the course of the Great Western (GWR) direct line (completed in 1906) which skirts the Wiltshire Downs and passes south of the Mendip Hills between Frome and Castle Cary.

The rugged coastline of the English Channel near Lyme Bay, between Bridport and Sidmouth, makes it difficult to build a railway line to Exeter along the South Coast. Traffic from Portsmouth, Southampton, and Poole must therefore be routed north through Yeovil. The counterfactual network feeds traffic from the South Coast into Yeovil along two routes: from Southampton via Poole, Blandford

Forum, and the Blackmore Vale, and from Weymouth via Dorchester, the county town of Dorset. From Yeovil, west-bound traffic joins the London–Exeter main line at Langport, and this in turn merges at Taunton with traffic from Bristol and the north.

The South Coast resorts of Lyme Regis, Seaton, and Sidmouth are served by branches from a secondary line that connects Yeovil and Exeter via Axminster and Honiton. This is the analogue of the London and South Western railway (LSWR) main line built in the 1860s; in the counterfactual, however, this line is downgraded to secondary status for most of its length, and deviates to serve intermediate towns such as Wincanton and Shaftesbury. This avoids the duplication of main lines that occurred on the actual system.

The counterfactual system makes good provision for traffic from the Midlands and north to the South Coast. A link along the Parrett Valley between Bridgewater and Langport routes traffic from Bristol into Yeovil, from whence it has a choice of routes to the South Coast—west to the resorts of Lyme Bay, south to Weymouth, or south-east to Southampton and Poole.

Yeovil was also a hub on the actual system—but a very poor one. It had no less than three stations. The GWR's Taunton service (started in 1853) ran into the Town station, while its Weymouth service (started in 1857) ran into Pen Mill. The LSWR's main station was Yeovil Junction, south of the Town, although it served the Town station too by a short branch. While the GWR ran a through service between Bristol and Weymouth via Yeovil, it followed a roundabout route via Frome and Castle Cary. This was a legacy of the Wilts, Somerset and Weymouth Railway scheme promoted by the GWR at the time of the Railway Mania, as a successful attempt to delay the extension of the LSWR to the west. Once this route was opened in 1857, the GWR saw little advantage in building a Langport link simply for the convenience of its customers. A bizarre legacy of this situation remains today, for it is sometimes quicker to travel from Bristol to Yeovil via Taunton, with a reversal of the direction of travel, than to take a through train via Frome instead.

Another option for the north–south traveller in Victorian Britain was the Somerset and Dorset Joint Railway (SDJR), opened throughout in 1874. Reaching Bath from a junction with the Midland Railway (MR) Birmingham–Bristol main line at Mangotsfield, the traveller could transfer to a train for Poole and Bournemouth via Templecombe. This train followed a tortuous route through Combe Down Tunnel, south of Bath, to the mining town of Radstock—a route necessitated by the fact that the GWR already occupied the more convenient route along the Avon Valley. Crossing the GWR Weymouth line at Bruton, no connection was offered; passengers were meant to use a connection further south at Templecombe instead. Here they could join the Exeter line of the LSWR—the MR's partner in the SDJR. The GWR did not want a connection at Bruton either in case its passengers switched to the MR or LSWR networks at that point. The same policy was pursed at Bath, where there was no connection between the two lines either.

This lack of cooperation between the GWR on the one hand and the SDJR, MR, and LSWR on the other impeded local traffic. As a result, the counterfactual affords local travellers much better service with fewer miles of track. The counter-factual provides a useful hub for north Somerset at the cathedral town of Wells— another point at which separate stations were built by the GWR and SDJR. The counterfactual hub lies on a through line from Weston-super-Mare to Frome, providing connections for Bristol at Weston and for London at Frome. A branch runs due south to a hub at Langport which provides connections for Bridgewater, Exeter (via Taunton), and Weymouth and Southampton (via Yeovil). Radstock and Midsomer Norton can be accessed by a branch to Bath from Shepton Mallet—the next station along the line to Frome.

Temple Meads station at Bristol, originally opened in 1840, is one of the most impressive features of the railway system in the area—and not just because of the Brunel heritage and the splendid architecture. It is one of the few examples of a single railway station serving an entire city—albeit in a rather inconvenient location, which led to later abortive proposals for a more convenient central station. Perhaps the most impressive feature is that it is joint between the two great rival companies: the GWR and the MR. This is not quite so impressive as it seems, however. The MR acquired its interest only in 1845, by taking over another company—the Bristol and Gloucester, which the GWR thought (wrongly) was its ally at the time that the station was originally built. The GWR and the MR, however, made the most of their alliance by jointly operating some local railways too. There was still some replication, however. The two companies ran independ-ent lines between Bristol and Yate and Bristol and Bath; the counterfactual elim-inates this duplication by eliminating the MR system, with its hub at Mangotsfield, and also eliminates the MR Thornbury branch by putting Thornbury on the Gloucester main line.

If all the rival lines constructed by the various companies had been linked up by connecting spurs and through trains had been run between the different com-panies' lines, then the area would have possessed an outstanding railway system. It would have been difficult to improve upon it except by eliminating duplication as described above. But the fact that cooperation was largely confined to the Bristol area meant that the local service actually offered was quite poor. In contrast with other rural areas where local monopoly prevailed—parts of East Anglia, for example, or County Durham—the connectivity of local services was very poor. Inter-company rivalry not only led to over-building but reduced operational flexibility, and so reduced the contribution to the rural economy that the railways were able to make.

4.16. THE SOUTH COAST

The South Coast borders the English Channel, opposite the Normandy coast of France. The area examined here lies between Poole and Brighton, and includes

Hampshire, the west of Sussex, together with parts of Wiltshire and Dorset, and the Isle of Wight. Most commercial activity in the area takes place on or near the coast. Southampton has been a major port since Saxon times, and the neighbouring cathedral city of Winchester, a major administrative centre, was once the capital of the Kingdom of Wessex. Portsmouth is famous for its naval dockyard, and as the ferry port for the short crossing to the Isle of Wight. To the east, between the cathedral city of Chichester and the fashionable resort of Brighton, due south of London, lies a string of smaller resorts, much developed by the railway, including Worthing and Bognor. There are also many small ports, such as Shoreham on the River Adur and Littlehampton on the River Arun.

Near Southampton is the New Forest which, like several other forest areas, has a distinctive form of local self-government. Near Poole, the resort of Bournemouth, with its extensive sands, was developed in the 1860s and 1870s as a speculative property development, facilitated by the expansion of the railway network.

Inland lie a number of wealthy aristocratic estates and prosperous market towns, such as Wimborne, Romsey, and Arundel. Although there was considerable rural poverty in the aftermath of the Napoleonic Wars in 1815, the agrarian economy as a whole was relatively strong in this area because of its proximity to London. In addition, the relatively warm climate and the natural beauty of the coastline have always made the area attractive to the leisured classes, such as retired London merchants.

The basic philosophy of the counterfactual railway network is to serve coastal areas with a continuous coastal line. In most areas the coast route takes the form of a loop, because the coastline bulges out between estuaries at either end. The relevant stretch of the South Coast is relatively straight, however. This means that the coast line is also the main line through the region, running from Brighton in the east to Poole in the west through Chichester, Southampton, and Bournemouth.

There are a few wrinkles in the coast, however. As a result, ports such as Portsmouth and Lymington, and resorts such as Bognor, lie off the direct line to the south. Lymington is served by a loop from the main line between Southampton to Poole, which links Brockenhurst to Christchurch, while Bognor is served by a loop between Worthing and Chichester via Littlehampton. The loop principle cannot be applied to Portsmouth, however, because it lies at the end of the very narrow Portsea Island. While a loop could, in principle, have been constructed between Chichester and Fareham by bridging various harbours, such schemes were not acceptable to the Admiralty because of the potential obstruction to naval vessels.

The coastal system as built is fairly similar to the counterfactual. The desirability of a coastal main line between Brighton and Southampton was quickly recognized. The London and Southampton Railway—later renamed the London and South Western (LSWR)—built out eastwards from Eastleigh towards Portsmouth, reaching Fareham in 1841 and Cosham in 1848, while the London and Brighton Railway—later the London Brighton and South Coast Railway

(LBSCR)—built out westwards from Hove towards Chichester (reached in 1846). They met at Cosham in 1848, and shared a line to Portsmouth.

The original main line from Southampton to Poole ran inland through the market towns of Ringwood and Wimborne; it was known as 'Castleman's Corkscrew' in homage to its promoter and recognition of its circuitous route (opened in 1847). The counterfactual line takes a more direct route through Lyndhurst and Christchurch, where it connects with a cross-country line from Ringwood to Salisbury. By running closer to the coast, this line serves Bournemouth too.

London is a natural hub for towns and cities on the South Coast. In the absence of a coastal line and other links, passengers would have to travel up to London and back out again in order to reach another coastal town. This is not so onerous as it sounds, because London makes a convenient meeting point with many cultural attractions. The area is sufficiently prosperous, however, to warrant both direct lines to London and a coastal link as well.

The counterfactual provides four main links to London—from Southampton, Portsmouth, Arundel, and Brighton. The main line from Southampton runs via Winchester, Alton, and Farnham, which is a more direct route than the actual main line via Basingstoke. The route via Basingstoke is also more hilly—probably it would not have been chosen had the London and Southampton not planned to build a branch from Basingstoke to Bath, and also to create a railhead there for coaches on the Salisbury and Exeter road.

Portsmouth is served by a direct line through Havant, Petersfield, and Farnham, where it joins the Southampton main line. The tortuous route of the actual direct line north of Petersfield, which runs through Haslemere to Guildford, is avoided.

The South Coast centres of Chichester, Bognor, Littlehampton, and Worthing are served by a direct line from Arundel (a hub on the coastal main line) up the Arun Valley through Pulborough to Horsham, where it joins the main Brighton line, and continues north through Dorking and Leatherhead along the Mole Valley. A similar route is still in use today, although the hub is at Ford, south of Arundel, and the line through Dorking is not the Brighton main line.

The fourth line is the Brighton main line itself, which runs up the Adur Valley from Shoreham to Horsham and enters London via Leatherhead and Epsom.

Comparison of the actual and counterfactual networks shows that the counterfactual provides a single route from Southampton to London, while the actual provides two: a main line via Basingstoke and a secondary route through Alton along the route of the counterfactual main line. It also provides a single route from Brighton to London, while the actual system provides two: a main line through Redhill and a secondary route through Horsham and the Mole Valley along the route of the counterfactual main line; this route is now closed south of Horsham, but is heavily used north of it. A line from Botley to Petersfield provides an analogue of the Meon Valley line between Fareham and Alton.

The counterfactual does not effect a major economy in local provision because neither of the local companies—the LSWR and the LBSCR—were prone to the proliferation of defensive lines. The only excess construction of branches occurred at their frontier—for example, at Midhurst, which was served by two LBSCR branches (opened in 1866 and 1881) and one LSWR branch (opened in 1864).

Matters are different where north–south linkages are concerned, however. Here competition between the LSWR and the Great Western (GWR) led to a significant proliferation of lines. On the counterfactual system there are just three main routes that connect the South Coast to the Midlands and the north. Traffic from Poole, Bournemouth, and Christchurch can head north via Ringwood, Salisbury, Trowbridge, and Bristol. Traffic from Southampton can join this route at Salisbury, or run due north through Winchester and Whitchurch, reaching Oxford via Newbury. Traffic from Portsmouth and Chichester can reach Oxford via Petersfield, Ash, and Reading, while traffic from Brighton and Worthing can feed into this route at Ash via Horsham and Guildford.

The actual system provided variants of these three routes and more besides. The first line, via Ringwood, involves a combination of three separate LSWR lines: a branch from Christchurch to Ringwood (opened in 1862), a section from Ringwood to West Moors along Castleman's Corkscrew, and a line from West Moors to Salisbury (opened in 1866). These three lines were never operated as an integrated cross-country line, however.

The second line is the GWR's Didcot Newbury and Southampton (DNS) line. The GWR line never reached Southampton, however, but joined the LSWR main line at Shawford, south of Winchester, which meant that the GWR could never really compete with the LSWR for Southampton dock traffic (opened to Winchester in 1885 and Shawford in 1891). Although originally planned as a major trunk route, financial exigencies meant that it was only built to light standards—particularly on the steeply graded portion over the Berkshire Downs between Didcot and Newbury. This line was much improved during World War II in order to handle military traffic, but it was never a commercial success. The counterfactual line avoids the steep sections across the Berkshire Downs by taking a route along the Kennet Valley and Thames Valley through Pangbourne, but it follows the actual route through the Litchfield gap south of Newbury.

The third route runs from Redhill, on the Brighton main line to Oxford via Guildford and Reading. A major complication was that access to Reading was provided by the South Eastern and Chatham (SECR) which was a rival of both the LSWR and the LBSCR. Furthermore, interchange at Reading was inhibited by the fact that the SECR had its own station there.

There are two actual routes that have no direct counterparts on the counterfactual system. One is a line from Mottisfont, north of Romsey, to Andover, where it joins the independent Midland and South Western Junction (MSWJR) line to Cheltenham via Marlborough and Cirencester (opened throughout in 1891). One of the unusual features of this line is that it served Swindon—best known as the GWR hub, but also the administrative headquarters of the MSWJR. Needless to say, the MSWJR had its own station at Swindon in the heart of the old town, over a mile away from the GWR station in the new town, although a connection between the two stations was provided by a short spur at Rushey Platt. Like the DNS line, the MSWJR was lightly engineered. It crossed three sets of hills in succession: Salisbury Plain, north of Andover, the Berkshire Downs north of Marlborough, and the Cotswolds north of Swindon. North-bound passengers could connect with Midland Railway (MR) expresses to Birmingham at Cheltenham Lansdowne (one of three major stations in the town), but they faced a long and tiresome journey getting there. MSWJR trains were slow, and its daily express faced regular disruption from the GWR at Marlborough until it built its own station in the town in 1898.

The other north–south link is the Somerset and Dorset Joint Railway (SDJR) discussed in the previous section. Like the MSWJR, however, the line was steeply graded, especially near Bath, where grades of 1 in 50 were used to cross the Mendip Hills. Also like the MSWJR, it fed into the MR at its northern end. Unlike the MSWJR, however, the SDJR was jointly owned by the MR and LSWR, and these two companies tended to route their traffic over the SDJR at the expense of the other line.

All of these failed cross-country routes have one thing in common—they were all perceived as invaders by the dominant company in the area. They were forced to choose uneconomic steeply graded routes through lightly populated country because the established company had already taken the best routes along the river valleys. They were then disrupted and starved of traffic by their powerful rival. Both the MSWJR and the SDJR were deeply resented by the GWR, and this made it difficult for them to provide good connections for local passengers in an area dominated by the GWR. Conversely, the GWR suffered at the hands of the LSWR as its DNS line was starved of traffic at its southern end by the LSWR.

Overall, therefore, while the actual South Coast system provided good local services in the areas dominated by the LSWR and LBSCR, the competitive lines that entered from the north did little to improve quality of provision. The LSWR and LBSCR concentrated their own lines on populous areas and connected them using a coastal main line. They also provided good connections to London. Many of their lines were built early, and are still in use today, so that they have had a very long economic life. Although some of the lines across the South Downs were expensive to construct—for example, the London to Brighton main line—the high volume of traffic carried at high speed has provided a good return on investment, though not such a good return as the more economical counterfactual routes would have done. By contrast the later cross-country lines were generally failures: they were expensive to construct, because of the hilly terrain, but slow and expensive to operate. The connections they made with the rest of the local system were poor. They proved useful for summer excursions and holiday traffic, but seem to have won only a small share of regular north–south traffic. Many passengers preferred to travel via London—a less direct but often faster and more reliable route.

4.17. KENT AND EAST SUSSEX

Kent, a large county to the south-east of London, is known as the 'Garden of England' and the 'Gateway to the Continent'. It is bounded on the north by the Thames Estuary and on the south by the English Channel. Its favourable climate and proximity to London make it an ideal location for market gardens, orchards, and hop-fields. In medieval times the Cinque Ports of Hastings, New Romney, Hythe, Dover, and Sandwich, together with the ancient towns of Rye and Winchelsea, were major centres for the import of wine and luxury goods from France. By the early nineteenth century, however, Dover had become Britain's leading port for the continent, and the others of the Cinque Ports had long gone into decline. Dover had also become a major military stronghold, while Folkestone was developing as both a port and a major resort. The North Downs between Epsom and Rochester became popular as a recreational and residential area for well-to-do Londoners.

On the counterfactual system there are three main routes entering Kent from the west: one from London—the first bridging point of the River Thames—another from Dorking, a country town, and hub on the London to Brighton line—and the third from Brighton itself—the most accessible South Coast resort from London and in the early nineteenth century a very fashionable resort with royal patronage. There is also secondary route entering Kent via Horsham, a market town south of Dorking and also on the Brighton line.

A coastal loop line is the natural way to serve a large peninsular such as Kent, and this is the approach adopted by the counterfactual system. Geology reinforces the case, for the South Downs blocks a direct line from London to the heart of Kent around the spa town of Tunbridge Wells. The main line from London to Dover is therefore routed along the Thames Estuary through Dartford, Gravesend, and Chatham to Faversham and Canterbury—along the actual route used by the London Chatham and Dover Railway (LCDR).

A loop from this line between Faversham and Dover serves the coastal towns of Whitstable, Ramsgate, Sandwich, and Deal. In fact, this is a double loop because there is also a direct connection from Sandwich to Canterbury. This connecting line continues through Canterbury to Ashford, where it crosses a line from Maidstone to Dover. It proceeds through the market towns of Tenterden and Cranbrook to Tunbridge Wells, thereby connecting mid-Kent directly with the north Kent coast.

Traffic from Poole, Southampton, and the South Coast resorts enters Kent via Brighton, and continues along the coast through Lewes (for Newhaven and Sleaford), Polegate (for Eastbourne) to Hastings. From Hastings it proceeds through Rye to Folkestone and Dover. A variant of this route also exists on the actual system. Traffic for north Kent can leave the South Coast line at Arundel, west of Brighton, and proceed through Horsham and East Grinstead to Tunbridge Wells, from where a range of onward connections is available.

There is also an orbital route to the south of London through Reading, Ash, and Guildford, which feeds traffic into Kent through Dorking on the Brighton line. The route continues through Godstone, Oxted, and Otford to Chatham, where it joins the main line from London to Dover. At Godstone traffic for Tunbridge Wells and Hastings diverges to the south-east. At Otford the route is joined by a line from London and Orpington, which diverges further east at West Malling to Maidstone, and then continues to Ashford, Folkestone, and Dover, providing useful connections for the country towns of mid-Kent. The portion of this route between Reading and Godstone is replicated on the actual system by the South Eastern (SER) line from Reading to Tonbridge. The divergence beyond Godstone is accounted for by the fact that Maidstone, the county town of Kent, is a major hub on the counterfactual system, and takes over the role that Tonbridge plays on the actual system.

There are also good connections between London and the south coast of Kent and East Sussex. Traffic from London to Hastings leaves London via Croydon and Godstone. This is one of only two routes to the south of London that pierce the South Downs—the other being the Orpington line described above. At Godstone traffic for Eastbourne continues due south through East Grinstead and the Ashdown Forest to Uckfield (for Lewes), Hailsham, and Polegate (for the coastal line). Traffic for Hastings turns east through Oxted and Tunbridge Wells and then south through Hurst Green.

By contrast, four lines cross the North Downs on the actual system. In particular, the portion of the SER main London to Dover line between Chiselhurst and Tonbridge (opened in 1868) was built at great expense to 'cut off the corner' that was created when the very first main line to Dover was built as a branch from the Brighton line at Redhill. When the SER's great rival, the LCDR, began to develop an alternative route to Dover the SER felt compelled to improve its own main line at any cost.

The most important difference between the actual and counterfactual systems lies in mid-Kent, however, The SER main line ran very straight through largely empty countryside between Tonbridge and Ashford; Hawkhurst was served by a dead-end branch (opened in 1893), while Rolvenden and Tenterden were served only by the independent Kent and East Sussex Light Railway (opened in 1905); and places such as Lamberhurst had no rail service at all. By contract, the counterfactual provides a network of through routes meeting up at hubs in local market towns, which receive a far superior service as a result. As in other rural areas, the ability of the counterfactual to provide an integrated system of rural railways linking adjacent market towns is one of is its main advantages over the actual system.

4.18. LONDON AND THE HOME COUNTIES

London was by far the largest city of the United Kingdom in 1825, and it was still as large relative to other cities in 1914—notwithstanding the growth of northern industrial cities. Its growth was fuelled by the expansion of specialized business services, and by 1914 it had become indisputably the world's largest financial centre. It is therefore an exceptional case so far as both the actual and counterfactual systems are concerned.

The actual system was exceptional in four main respects. First, London's railways were on average built much earlier than those in other parts of the country. Although South Wales, Cornwall, and the Forest of Dean each had several mineral lines before 1825, they were not as quick as London to develop passenger railways. Only the north-east matched London in this respect, partly due to the enthusiasm of George Hudson, the 'Railway King'. Even before 1825, the horse-powered Surrey Iron Railway (opened in 1804) had connected the Croydon area to the River Thames at Wandsworth, and a Commercial Railway had been projected to connect the City with the East India Docks. Following the early success of the Liverpool and Manchester Railway, a wave of trunk line railway schemes promoted connections between London and provincial towns and cities, including Dover, Brighton, Southampton, Bristol, Birmingham, Cambridge, and Norwich, and most of these lines were completed by about 1840.

The development of suburban traffic was another prominent feature of London's railways. The London and Greenwich—sometimes called the world's first suburban railway—opened as far as Deptford in 1836. During the 1840s other suburban lines were opened—mainly as branches from the newly built trunk lines. These included a branch to West Croydon from Norwood Junction on the Brighton line (opened in 1839, and extended to Epsom in 1847); a branch from Edmonton, on the Northern and Eastern Railway's Cambridge line, to Enfield, opened in 1849; and a branch from Clapham Junction, on the Southampton line, to Richmond and Windsor (also opened in 1849). The development of suburban railways continued relentlessly from the 1860s to the 1890s. Additional stations were built to improve access from new residential areas springing up beside the lines, and high-frequency services were introduced—especially in the inner suburbs—to compete with trams. Eventually, however, electric trams and tube railways took away much of the inner suburban traffic, although rush-hour road congestion meant that the railways remained major carriers of commuter traffic. The rapid growth of the outer suburbs, where road competition was less intense, provided a compensating source of revenue growth, however.

The third characteristic of London was that many routes bifurcate as they enter the suburbs in order to serve different parts of the city. The city centre has a number of distinctive zones: business services are concentrated in the 'square mile' of the City, shopping is centred in the West End, government and administration in Westminster, and commercial activity in the Docks. On the south bank of the river, around Vauxhall, Southwark, and Deptford, there were entertainment and recreation facilities, and also the Surrey Docks. The early trunk lines simply terminated on the outskirts of London facing the provincial region that they served. They were kept away from the centre on environmental grounds, and the companies were broadly content with this policy because it saved them from purchasing more expensive land. So long as all the railways were kept out, it seemed that the companies faced a 'level playing field'. But as the trunk line networks expanded, the companies increasingly found themselves competing for traffic in provincial areas they had expected to monopolize. The siting of their London terminus then became an important issue. The companies therefore sought to extend their termini into the heart of the city. The companies with termini to the south of the river felt particularly disadvantaged. The London and South Western (LSWR), which served Southampton, extended northwards from Nine Elms to Waterloo, directly opposite a river bridge, while the South Eastern (SER), which served Dover, actually crossed the river from its London Bridge station to a new station at Charing Cross right by Trafalgar Square. On the north bank, the Great Eastern (GER), which served Cambridge and Norwich, extended from Bishopsgate into Liverpool Street.

Companies entering London from the east were well placed to serve the City but poorly placed to serve the West End, while the converse applied to those entering from the west. Companies entering from the north and south faced a dilemma as to which part of the city to serve. The answer was to serve all parts of the city by dividing their routes as they approached London. For passenger traffic, one fork typically served the City and the other the West End and Westminster. The docks were served by special freight lines, as described below. The SER built two new termini on the north bank—at Charing Cross (for the West End, opened 1864) and Cannon Street (for the City, opened 1866). Its rival, the London, Chatham and Dover Railway (LCDR) served Ludgate Hill (for the City, opened 1864) and Victoria (for Westminster and the West End, opened 1867) from a junction at Herne Hill. The London Brighton and South Coast Railway (LBSCR) divided its lines as far south as Croydon, where the Victoria line (opened in 1839) turned north-west to Clapham Junction while the old main line continued due north to London Bridge, a station shared with the SER on the south bank opposite the city.

The early underground railways represent another attempt to solve this dilemma. Reliance on underground lines is London's fourth distinctive characteristic. Unlike the later tube railways, which were built by tunnelling deep through the London clay and were electrically powered from the start, the early lines— notably the Metropolitan and the Metropolitan District—were essentially extensions of the overground system and were built immediately under the streets using a cut-and-cover method. Suburban steam trains ran through from the suburbs to the far side of the city, often burrowing underground as they approached the main line terminus on the near side of the city. There was an east–west link from Paddington to Aldgate (opened as far as Farringdon in 1863), serving main line stations at Euston, Kings Cross, and Liverpool Street en route. To the south, another east–west link built under the new Thames Embankment, linked Kensington to Whitechapel via Aldgate (opened as far as Mansion House in 1871 and extended to West Ham in 1902).

There were north–south underground lines as well. The Metropolitan Line between Kings Cross and Farringdon was modified to allow through trains from the northern suburbs to run through to the LCDR at Ludgate Hill, while the East London Line (opened in 1876), connected the SER at New Cross and the LBSCR at New Cross Gate to Liverpool Street; it used Brunel's old Thames Tunnel to take passengers from the southern suburbs to the City.

The Docks were served by both passenger lines and freight lines. The rope-hauled London and Blackwall Railway, based on the early Commercial Railway scheme, was opened in 1840, but only became part of the main line system later. A branch from Stratford, the original junction of the Cambridge and Norwich lines, was opened to North Woolwich in 1847, while on the south bank a loop line to Dartford via Woolwich was opened by the SER in 1849. In 1851 the East and West India Dock and Birmingham Junction Railway opened from the London and Birmingham Railway at Camden to Poplar; it carried large amounts of freight traffic from the Midlands and north for export, and became the core of the North London Railway system in 1853.

London also shared a number of features with other major cities. Two in particular merit attention. One was the proliferation of independent main line terminals. The huge potential size of the London passenger transport market meant that companies felt unable to rely on terminals operated by other companies—and by potential rivals in particular. Because London was a major source of long-distance first-class passenger traffic, a terminus needed to make an architectural statement highlighting the pretentions of the company. Hence the Midland Railway's extravagant Gothic fantasy at St. Pancras (opened 1868)—a controversial building whose splendour and affluence contrasted sharply with the slum dwellings that had been demolished to make way for it. As late as 1899 the Great Central opened an independent terminus at Marylebone—albeit on a more modest scale. Even where joint stations were employed, as at Victoria and London Bridge, each company had its own side of the station with an independent ticket office.

The proliferation of terminals was only a manifestation of a more fundamental factor—namely the perceived need for independent access to London. This meant independent tracks as well as independent terminals. Hence a large number of different lines converged on central London, creating a streetscape of bridges and arches in the inner suburbs—many of the arches being occupied by business units. Parliament attempted to rationalize entry into London in the 1830s and early 1840s, but eventually gave up. To the south of the city, the Croydon line shared a route with the Greenwich line, the Brighton line shared a route with the Croydon line, and the Dover line shared a route with the Brighton line. Operational conflicts quickly arose, however, particularly when the Croydon line adopted an atmospheric system of propulsion. Eventually the Brighton company acquired the Croydon company and the SER took over the Greenwich line and built a new line to Dover independent of the Brighton line. When Parliament abandoned its attempt at rationalization at the time of the Railway Mania, proliferation quickly developed—first of trunk lines and then suburban ones.

The counterfactual addresses these problems using a range of strategies. First, trunk lines and primary lines are consolidated as they approach the metropolis. This consolidation is effected at satellite suburban hubs. Between the hubs and the centre there are just eight main lines; on average, the angle between these lines as they approach London is 45°—far greater than on the actual system. In anti-clockwise order, the hubs are Dartford (Dover line), Bromley (Maidstone line), Croydon (Tunbridge Wells line), Epsom (Brighton line), Brentford (Bristol and Southampton lines), Wembley (Birmingham and Glasgow lines), Ponders End (Cambridge and Lincolnshire lines), and Barking (Norwich line) The positioning of these hubs reflects the Steiner principle, but allows for the fact that traffic flows mainly in the London direction. Thus the routes change direction by about 25° at a hub, rather than 60° as would occur if traffic flowed equally in all directions.

Second, the satellite hubs are connected to each other to create an orbital line running from Dartford through to Barking. This allows people to travel directly between suburbs without entering the centre, and thereby alleviates congestion on the main lines. It also enhances the London labour market by improving local mobility. There is no direct analogue of this orbital line on the actual system, although parts of the North London Railway performed this role.

In fact, there are three orbital lines in the counterfactual system. One is a line that joins the central terminals and the other is an outer orbital line. There are three main line terminals on the counterfactual: London South for Dover, Maidstone, Tunbridge Wells and Brighton, London north-west for Southampton, Bristol, Birmingham and Glasgow, and London north-east for Cambridge and Norwich. There are also stations at London West, serving a local line to Richmond, and London North serving a local line to Barnet. London South is in Southwark, near the present London Bridge station; London West is in Kensington, near the present Addison Road station, London North West is near Shepherd Bush, just west of the present Paddington station, London North is near the present Euston station, and London North East is at Shoreditch just east of the present Liverpool Street station. London North East serves the City, while London North and London West serve the West End. There is also an intermediate station at Vauxhall which serves Westminster. The only analogue of the inner orbital line is the West London line which links the Shepherds Bush area with Clapham Junction; in practice it has been underground lines like the Circle Line (made up of portions of the Metropolitan and Metropolitan District Railways) which have carried most of the traffic between London terminals. While underground systems are convenient (if somewhat unpleasant) for commuters, they are most inconvenient for long-distance passengers carrying heavy luggage.

The outer orbital line reflects the fact that not all lines entering London are consolidated at the hubs mentioned above; there are also outer hubs where some consolidation occurs before the main satellite hubs are reached. The outer orbital is built up from sections of cross-country lines that touch the London area tangentially and cross the main radial lines as they do so. The outer orbital runs from Chatham on the Dover line through to Brentwood on the Norwich line. Lines spin off at intermediate hubs—for example, from Dorking to Guildford and Oxford and from St. Albans to Stevenage and Cambridge.

There is no direct analogue of the outer orbital on the actual system, although there are some lines that perform a similar role; for example, the SER line from Reading to Redhill via Guildford and the LNWR line from Oxford to Cambridge via Bletchley. At the time of the Railway Mania there were numerous schemes for orbital lines, but they faced enormous opposition. The companies that had just completed their radial trunk lines into London wanted as much cross-country traffic as possible to be routed through London. They feared that passengers would switch to orbital routes to avoid the inconvenience of transfer between London terminals. The fact that the orbital lines crossed their property gave them *locus standi* as objectors. Even where orbital schemes were successful in Parliament, their ambitious nature made them costly; most of the finance available went into building branches to existing main lines rather than into complementing the radial lines with an orbital system.

The counterfactual system also rationalizes the provision of suburban lines. These lines are designed to fill up the interiors of the areas created by pattern of intersecting radial and orbital lines. This avoids the problem created by the actual system, where rival companies drove independent local lines into the heart of London. In some cases local towns had two lines into London via different routes, but poor connections to other towns nearby; Bromley, for example, had numerous routes into London but no direct routes to neighbouring towns such as Sidcup, Bexley, or Dartford.

Overall, therefore, the London railway system was a very wasteful one. Like other major traffic-generating centres, it attracted a disproportionate amount of railway capital, but there was no systematic attempt to rationalize railway provision. While the size of London merited substantial investment, network economies were not exploited to make the best use of the available funds. The excesses of terminal-building, notable in other major cities, was compounded in London by the fact that many companies wanted two independent terminals rather than one. Rail links between the different terminals were poor, except for underground services which were difficult for cross-country passengers to use. These passengers were forced into the city centre by the lack of orbital routes, and by the absence of collaboration in handling long-distance traffic over the few routes that were available.

4.19. SCOTTISH LOWLANDS

The Scottish Lowlands comprises the area lying between the Rivers Tyne and Solway to the south, which link the English cities of Newcastle and Carlisle along a route that follows Hadrian' Wall, and the Forth and Clyde Valleys to the north, which link the Scottish cities of Edinburgh and Glasgow. The Scottish border itself runs north-east, from Gretna, on the West Coast north of Carlisle, to Berwick-upon-Tweed, on the East Coast, roughly midway between Newcastle and Edinburgh. Between the border and the Tyne Valley lies the English county of Northumberland, with its ancient towns of Morpeth and Alnwick.

Until the Railway Mania got underway it was widely assumed that there would be just one railway route between London and Scotland, which would follow the West Coast through Lancaster and Carlisle. This route was promoted by the Caledonian Railway (CR) which, despite its Scottish-sounding name, was dominated by London interests who wished to secure a monopoly of Anglo-Scottish traffic. There were political as well as economic reasons for uniting London and Scotland with a high-speed rail line, and the London promoters believed that they were well attuned with government thinking on the subject.

In line with this general approach, the CR main line split into three south of Glasgow. At Carstairs, near the coal and textile town of Lanark, the main line to Glasgow forked left through Motherwell, using some upgraded mineral lines to gain access to the city. A branch to Edinburgh forked right along Breich Water and Gogar Burn, north of the Pentland Hills, while a central line ran due north from Motherwell through Coatbridge to join the Scottish Central Railway at Greenhill, near the modern town of Cumbernauld. This central line provided connections for Stirling, Perth, and Aberdeen. The lines to Edinburgh and Greenhill were completed in 1848, with immediate connection to Aberdeen, while the Glasgow line was completed in 1849.

The counterfactual main line follows broadly similar routes, although the line to Edinburgh diverges further south at Symington and runs to the south of the Pentland Hills through Biggar and Pencuik. In other respects, however, the counterfactual is very different from the actual system, because in practice competition soon led to a duplication of routes.

The CR's monopoly of Anglo-Scottish traffic was eroded on several fronts. To the east, the North British Railway (NBR) extended its Edinburgh to Glasgow direct line southwards from Edinburgh to Berwick, where it met a line running north along the East Coast from Newcastle through Morpeth and Alnmouth, which was later absorbed into the North Eastern Railway. This created an East Coast main line from Edinburgh to London via Newcastle which has rivalled the West Coast main line ever since.

To the west of the CR main line, the Glasgow and South Western Railway (GSWR) built an alternative route between Carlisle and Glasgow through Nithsdale, serving Dumfries and Kilmarnock on the way. This route had been rejected by the CR's promoters because, although it avoided a steep incline at Beattock, it did not provide the same options for spurs to Edinburgh and Stirling. However, by selecting the most direct route, the CR was able to maintain a strategic advantage over the GSWR which it would otherwise have lost. By way of compensation, the GSWR gained a dominant position in the Ayrshire coalfield, south-west of Kilmarnock, and at the port of Ayr.

To compound the CR's disappointment, the NBR then built its Waverley route from Edinburgh to Carlisle through the important textile towns of Galashiels and Hawick. This was a direct line that 'cut off the corner' of the CR's route via Carstairs. The CR, however, had an alliance with the London and North Western

(LNWR) which controlled the flow of West Coast traffic into Carlisle from the south. Neither the GSWR Glasgow line nor the NBR Edinburgh line had adequate feeders at Carlisle until the Midland (MR) reached Carlisle via Settle in 1876.

These developments occurred in quick succession, and precipitated a crisis in CR finances, from which it only recovered when its local mineral traffic began to grow. By the time the CR main lines were opened throughout in 1849, the East Coast route to Newcastle was already open, the Royal Border Bridge at Berwick having been completed the year before, while the GSWR Glasgow line was opened in 1850—only one year after the CR system. The Waverley route opened in 1862.

The counterfactual system avoids the waste associated with purely competitive lines. In line with CR thinking it concentrates long-distance trunk traffic north of Carlisle on an analogue of the CR main line. The NBR and GSWR lines fulfil important local functions, however, in providing through routes across important territories that would otherwise have to be served by dead-end branches. It is not necessary, however, that these routes be engineered to trunk line standards. The counterfactual therefore downgrades these lines, and in some cases—notably the East Coast main line—diverts them to take in additional centres of local population *en route.*

Kilmarnock and Ayr are served by a coastal line from Glasgow to Stranraer, the port for Irish traffic to Larne and Belfast, while Dumfries is served by a line along the Solway Firth from Carlisle to Stranraer via Kirkcudbright. These routes broadly follow the routes to Stranraer used by the GSWR from Glasgow (opened in 1877) and the Portpatrick and Wigtownshire Joint Committee from Carlisle (opened in 1861).

Further north, the counterfactual provides a complete coastal loop from Kilwinning (for Kilmarnock and Ayr) through Ardrossan and Largs to Greenock, Paisley, and Glasgow, which replaces a maze of duplicated lines built by the CR and GSWR in their struggle to occupy this territory. It also fills in a 'missing link' between the CR and GSWR systems between Wemyss Bay (reached by the CR in 1865) and Largs (reached by the GSWR in 1885).

Despite the competitive proliferation of lines, a direct trunk line was never built between the major industrial centres of Newcastle and Glasgow. On the actual system Glasgow could only be reached from Newcastle on main lines through either Edinburgh or Carlisle. (An enterprising cross-country traveller could, however, reach Glasgow along branch lines—for example, through Hexham, Reedsmouth, Riccarton Junction, Galashiels, Peebles, and Symington, using the tracks of three different companies—the NER, the NBR, and the CR— but it would take all day.) On the counterfactual system, a trunk line connects Newcastle and Glasgow, running north of the Cheviots and south of the Pentland Hills through Coldstream, Kelso and Melrose, from whence a connecting line serves Edinburgh. The line continues through Biggar to Symington, where it joins the West Coast main line to Glasgow.

The counterfactual system generates important hubs at Melrose and Symington. From Melrose the traveller has direct access to other major hubs at Glasgow, Edinburgh, Newcastle and Carlisle, with good local links to Galashiels,

Peebles, Selkirk, Hawick, Jedburgh, Coldstream, and Berwick. Symington also has direct links to Glasgow, Edinburgh, Newcastle and Carlisle, and good links to Dumfries, Lanark, Kilmarnock, and Ayr. Both Melrose and Symington are natural hubs as they are close to the confluence of rivers, but inter-company rivalry meant that their hub potential was not fully exploited by the actual system. On the actual system Galashiels is an analogue of Melrose, and Carstairs is an analogue of Symington, but neither of these hubs is as powerful as Melrose and Symington.

Redesdale and the Keilder Forest, north of Hexham, was an area contested by the NBR and the NER, and in consequence several unnecessary lines were built, which are avoided by the counterfactual. Although the two companies were allies in the East Coast route, there were always tensions between them as the NBR sought independent access to Newcastle. South of the border, in Northumberland, the NBR built invasion lines and the NER built defensive lines, neither of which served much useful purpose, as they did not connect up local towns in a coherent way. The NBR lines between Hexham and Riccarton Junction (opened in 1862), Reedsmouth and Morpeth (opened in 1865), and Scotsgap and Rothbury (opened in 1870) served heavily forested and lightly populated areas. While there may have been a case for logging railways, there was no economic case for passenger provision. The NER lines from Alnwick and Berwick to Coldstream (finally completed in 1887) were potentially more useful, but this potential was not realized as they only fed into the NBR system at Kelso, where onward connections were poor.

Overall, therefore, competition had a negative effect on the railway network in the area. Competition between the CR, GSWR, and NBR led to over-building of trunk lines, especially north of Carlisle, while competition between the NBR and the NER led to under-building of trunk lines and over-building of local lines in the parts of Northumberland north-east of Newcastle.

4.20. CENTRAL SCOTLAND AND THE HIGHLANDS

While central Scotland is quite densely populated, the Highlands, as its name suggests, is only sparsely populated. It is nevertheless useful to consider the two areas together because central Scotland is the gateway to the Highlands from the south. The low density of Highland population means that the duplication of lines is particularly wasteful. It also implies that routes must be designed to serve railheads for the surrounding country and not just the towns themselves.

The mountainous nature of much of the country, the highly irregular coastline and preponderance of lochs means that geographical fundamentals have a major influence on the structure of the railway network. This suggests that the actual and counterfactual networks will have substantial similarities. This is reflected in the fact that Glasgow, Edinburgh, Stirling, Perth, Aberdeen, and Inverness are all important hubs on both the actual and counterfactual systems. But at the same time there are important differences too.

Because the counterfactual avoids expensive engineering works, there is no Forth Bridge at Queensferry and no Tay Bridge at Dundee. The economic and engineering logic is fairly clear. The first Tay Bridge, engineered by William Bouch, collapsed with considerable loss of life in 1879. The Forth Bridge could only be built once the technology of steel tubes had been fully mastered. This highly specified bridge was extremely expensive to construct—the capital cost being shared by no less than four railway companies—and it has proved costly to maintain ever since. It did not open until 1890, and so it was operational for less than one-third of the total period covered by this study. In some respects, moreover, the costs of the Forth and Tay Bridges should be added together, since in terms of trunk line traffic one is not really viable without the other— the Tay Bridge without the Forth Bridge merely feeds traffic from Dundee into Queensferry, while the Forth Bridge without the Tay Bridge provides a direct line from Edinburgh to Perth, but no direct line to Dundee or Aberdeen.

The counterfactual routes East Coast traffic between Edinburgh and Dundee via Stirling and Perth. One advantage of this is that it avoids the steep climb to Glenfarg Summit encountered on the direct line across Fife that linked the Forth and Tay Bridges. Modern trains avoid Glenfarg by taking a circuitous route through Kirkaldy and Ladybank which obviates much of the distance advantage conferred by the 'direct' route.

Another big difference between the actual and counterfactual systems concerns access to Inverness from the south. No less than four separate railway companies were interested in serving the Highlands—two regional companies, the Highland (HR) and the Great North of Scotland (GNSR)—and two Scottish national companies—the Caledonian (CR) and North British (NBR). The HR main line ran due north from Perth to Inverness via Pitlochry and Aviemore. This line, opened in 1863, originally ran via Forres, but a cut-off between Aviemore and Inverness over Slochd Summit was opened in 1898. The line was steeply graded throughout and was single track for most of the way.

The GNSR built out from Aberdeen as far as Keith (reached in 1856), from whence HR tracks were required to reach Inverness (opened in 1858). The GNSR then extended to Elgin, an intermediate station on the HR line (reached in 1863). Thus the section between Elgin and Keith was duplicated, with the GNSR, as the late-mover, having the more circuitous route. The two companies continued to behave as rivals, making life difficult for through passengers between Aberdeen and Inverness.

A third approach to Inverness was made by the NBR, although it came very late and was never completed. This involved a combination of the West Highland line from Glasgow to Fort William (opened in 1894) and a branch from Spean Bridge, near Fort William, to Invergary and Fort Augustus at the southern end of Loch Ness (opened in 1903). A short and level line along the banks of Loch Ness would then have brought the NBR to Inverness. The simplicity of this route is indicated by the fact that prior to the coming of the railways it had been used for a water-based land-bridge—the Caledonian Canal between Fort William and Inverness.

The CR also seems to have appreciated the logic of this route. The CR controlled a line from Stirling and Dunblane through Callender to Oban (opened throughout in 1880). From Connel Ferry, near Oban, the company opened a line to Ballachulish in 1903. From Ballachulish Ferry this line could have been extended north-east to Fort William via Loch Linnhe and thence to Inverness.

The counterfactual rationalizes the provision of lines to Inverness by using just two of these routes: a West Coast route from Glasgow via Fort William and Loch Ness, following the route of the Caledonian Canal, and an East Coast route from Aberdeen through Keith and Elgin. The West Coast route leaves Glasgow via Dumbarton and follows the scenic banks of Loch Lomond to Tarbet and Crianlarich, where it is joined by a branch from Callander and Dunblane. At Connel Ferry a short branch runs due west to the important resort and ferry port of Oban, while the main line turns north-east to reach Inverness via Ballachulish Ferry and Fort William.

At Spean Bridge a loop line diverges west to Aviemore and Fochabers, where the line from Aberdeeen to Inverness is joined. Further on, at Invermoriston on the banks of Loch Ness, a branch turns north-west through Glen Shiell to Kyle of Lochalsh—the ferry port for the Isle of Skye. This line provides far better connections for Skye than does the actual route to Kyle, which loops round to the north of Strathconon Forest through Dingwall and Garve.

The East Coast route to Inverness from Aberdeen follows the HR line between Inverness and Elgin. Between Elgin and Aberdeen, however, it is diverted north of the GNSR line through Turriff in order to serve two coastal loops. The Peterhead and Fraserburgh loop runs north-east to the coast and rejoins the main line at Ellon, near Aberdeen, while the Banff and Buckie loop runs north-west to the coast and rejoins the main line at Fochabers, east of Elgin, where the Aviemeore loop also joins from the south. From Craigellachie, near Fochabers, there is a branch to Dufftown, one of the major centres of the whisky distillery area.

The double loops emanating from Turriff provide an efficient solution to the local transport needs in Morayshire and Aberdeenshire. In particular, fishing traffic can be loaded at successive ports along each loop and fed into the main line system in a consolidated manner. Although the GNSR provided a short coastal loop between Elgin and Cairnie Junction, near Keith, serving Willen and Portsoy, most coastal towns were served by dead-end branches instead.

North of Inverness the counterfactual follows the actual system in serving Wick and Thurso by a line through Dingwall and Helmsdale. North of Helmsdale, however, the route deviates from the HR line by following the coast through Lybster and Wick and then running alongside Loch Watten to Thurso. This provides a service to coastal settlements between Helmsdale and Wick and eliminates Georgemas Junction where the present lines to Wick and Thurso diverge. It also makes a separate line to Lybster unnecessary (opened in 1903).

Overall, therefore, the counterfactual system affords significant improvement in railway provision by connecting up various lines that were previously just dead-end branches—sometimes on the same system, but usually on different systems. It rationalizes main line provision by eliminating the HR main line from Perth to Inverness and concentrates traffic onto an extension of the NBR Glasgow to Fort William line instead. This delivers improved local services and a marginal reduction in total route miles.

4.21. SUMMARY AND CONCLUSIONS

The main conclusion is that competition between rival main line companies was almost always wasteful at the regional level. Although a 'second trunk line' proved quite useful in regions where the first trunk line bypassed important towns, it would often have been just as useful if it had been built as a secondary loop. Construction costs would have been lower, and the route would have been less likely to bypass other towns itself.

Where a dominant regional company built a local network from the outset, they sometimes adopted a rational structure of interlocking loops, but this was very much the exception rather than the rule. What normally happened is that they simply built dead-end branches from their main line, designed to block the paths of subsequent rivals. Where there were two rival companies, these dead-end branches did not normally join up, and so no integrated regional system emerged. Even if the rivals served the same town, there were often separate terminals, and sometimes there was no connection between them.

Joining up branches to create cross-country routes would have generated extra traffic for the companies, but the additional revenue was outweighed, in the view of railway managers, by the likelihood of lower fares resulting from fiercer competition.

Although lightly populated areas often had a quite high density of lines, local customers often had little choice of route because they could not easily access a rival network once they had commenced their journey at their local station. Densely populated areas enjoyed an even higher density of lines, but this conferred little benefit since many of the lines simply duplicated each other.

There is quite significant variation between regions in the performance of the actual network (see Table 4.2). Lincolnshire, Humberside, and the South Coast did well. Either a dominant company adopted a rational structure of regional routes from the outset, or local companies cooperated—usually by dividing the local territory between them. Other regions did badly: on the whole these were the more heavily industrialized regions to either side of the Pennines—where three or more companies often competed for the traffic. More competition led to more duplication, as each company drove branches into cities, manufacturing

Table 4.2. Summary of the regional comparisons

Region	Actual performance	Comments on actual system
East Anglia	Moderate	The dominant Great Eastern system was well integrated, except around Cambridge (a failed hub). There was a proliferation of defensive lines north of Norwich
South Midlands	Poor	No Oxford–Cheltenham line. Frontier territory in the gauge war. Severn Tunnel built late at great expense
The Shires	Moderate	Poor route selection. Failure to develop Northampton as a trunk line hub. Failure to follow the more rational examples of the earlier canals and later motorways
Lincolnshire	Good	The dominant Great Northern developed a rational system with integrated loops, but the routeing of the main line through Newark reduced the power of Lincoln as a hub
Yorkshire	Poor	The Lancashire and Yorkshire failed to construct a rational regional network to consolidate its early lead, thereby letting in numerous competitors—especially the Great Northern—who duplicated lines into the major 'woollen' towns
Humberside and Cleveland	Good	Due to the early influence of George Hudson and Robert Stephenson, an integrated system of lines was initiated at an early stage and was eventually completed
North-east	Moderate	Although the North Eastern Railway had an effective monopoly, this was achieved by acquisition. Most local lines were oriented east–west and most trunk lines north–south, and despite attempts at rationalization they were never fully integrated
North Pennines	Poor	Competition between the West Coast route, the East Coast route and the Midland Settle and Carlisle line led to a fragmented system which inhibited both east–west and local traffic flow. The hub potential of Kirkby Lonsdale was not exploited as the West Coast line was diverted towards Kendal
North-west and Cumbria	Poor	Competition to serve the cotton textile towns and the Lancashire coalfield led to wasteful duplication of east–west routes, and of terminals in the cities
North Midlands	Moderate	The Midland configured its trunk lines rationally but competition with the Great Central and Great Northern led to wasteful duplication of branches in mining areas
West Midlands	Moderate	Birmingham was a natural hub. Bypasses and satellite hubs were constructed, but their full potential was never realized because competition between the Great Western and the London and North Western discouraged interchange of traffic
Wales	Moderate	Although lightly populated, Central Wales attracted railways, but the structure of hubs was inefficient. Competition for holiday traffic between the Great Western, London and North Western and Cambrian led to undue emphasis on east–west routes

(*continued*)

Table 4.2. (Continued)

Region	Actual performance	Comments on actual system
South-west	Moderate	North Devon, though lightly populated, was eventually served by railways. A system of loop lines would have served the area well, but although some loops were constructed, integration failed because of trunk line competition between the Great Western and the London and South Western
Somerset and Dorset	Poor	The east–west trunk lines of the Great Western were poorly integrated with the north–south trunk lines from Cheltenham and Bath to the South Coast
South Coast	Good	The two rival companies—the London and South Western and the London Brighton and South Coast–agreed a division of territory and competed for the London–Portsmouth traffic to the benefit of passengers. Although the Great Western invaded, it was a failure
Kent and East Sussex	Moderate	Building two trunk lines to Dover was unnecessary. A single trunk line supported by a system of interlocking loops would have satisfied long-distance passengers and provided better local services
London and Home Counties	Moderate	A very dense network ensured good access to the system. A choice of terminals was often provided, but at great expense. A system of satellite hubs and orbital lines would have provided a better service with lower cost and less environmental damage
Scottish Lowlands	Poor	Trunk lines proliferated once Parliament undermined the Caledonian monopoly. Rivalry between the Caledonian, North British, and Glasgow and South Western undermined integrated provision of local services linking Ayr, Lanark, and Hawick
Central Scotland and the Highlands	Poor	There was no direct line along the route of the Caledonian Canal from Inverness to Fort William (from where connections to Oban and Glasgow could have been provided). The Highland main line through Aviemore was more for the benefit of tourists from London than the local economy. Coastal loops were lacking north of Aberdeen

districts, and mining areas in order to connect them to its main line. Overall connectivity within the region therefore suffered as each company concentrated purely on creating connectivity between the specific lines it owned. The greater the number of companies, the greater was the fragmentation of the regional network.

5

Joint Lines

5.1. INTRODUCTION

Of the 20,000 route miles of railways in 1914, about 1,000 miles were jointly owned. In many cases the owning companies were also rivals, being engaged in fierce competition elsewhere on the system. In addition to the track, stations and passenger carriages were also sometimes jointly owned. Does this joint ownership indicate that relations between railway companies were much friendlier than has been suggested above?

This chapter explores the issue by examining all the significant joint venture lines that were in operation in 1914. The only exclusions are local lines in the London area that came to form part of the London Underground system. The standard reference on the subject is Casserley (1968), from which an initial list of joint lines was obtained. Each line was then investigated using a mixture of primary and secondary sources. The secondary sources are listed in the bibliography; they comprise histories of the large companies and their constituents, of geographical regions and of individual lines. Most of the information has been sourced from at least two secondary sources, and primary sources have been used mainly to resolve disagreements between them. The method is not foolproof, because secondary sources often rely on each other (sometimes without acknowledgement), and so errors may be repeated. Many railway authors have a good reputation for accuracy, however, and many railway histories are written in a straightforward narrative style which makes the information easy to check.

The objective of this chapter is to evaluate the motives of the partners in joint lines and to examine the business strategies that they employed. The minute books of company boards do not usually give the reasons for the decisions that have been made, and so the imputation of motives from board minutes is necessarily somewhat subjective. Nevertheless, annual reports and press reports of shareholders' meetings give considerable insight into strategic thinking—although rhetorical flourishes can also mislead through exaggeration. Biographies of leading protagonists such as George and Robert Stephenson, Joseph Locke, George Hudson, Edward Watkin, George Bidder, and I. K. Brunel also provide insight into thinking at the time. In some cases, such as the Brunel Letter Books, we have direct insight into the strategic thinking of a major player. Finally there is the evidence presented by railway promoters to Parliamentary Select Committees, which although partial, records the results of rigorous adversarial cross-examination.

5.2. MOTIVES FOR JOINT VENTURES

General theories of joint ventures suggest a number of reasons why joint ventures may be formed (Shenkar and Reuer 2005), three of which are particularly relevant to Victorian railway lines.

Joint ventures can avoid a wasteful duplication of facilities where there are economies of scale. If both companies plan to construct identical lines then it is normally efficient for just one line to be constructed and shared between the companies. A jointly owned line therefore facilitates the rationalization of railway construction.

It would be possible for just one of the companies to construct the line and for the other to obtain running powers over it. Alternatively, the line could be constructed by an independent company and both the companies could have running powers over it. In practice, however, running powers were difficult to enforce. If one of the rival companies owned the track then they could use their control of the signalling system to obstruct the other company's trains, as the Great Western Railway did to its invader, the Midland and South Western Junction Railway, at Marlborough, Wiltshire. Where the company that owned the track ran no trains of its own, it could economize excessively on maintenance, as Railtrack did on the modern privatized railway system. Given that running powers were not an effective substitute for ownership, joint ownership was the most effective way of avoiding replication.

Joint ventures also economize on capital. Two railway companies might each aspire to own independent lines, but find that they cannot raise the capital to do so. They therefore share the outlay between themselves. Capital constraints are most likely to be binding at times when the financial markets are depressed, or where the railway industry has lost the confidence of investors. Typically this will occur following the collapse of a stock market boom.

Joint ventures allow complementary resources owned by independent companies to be combined without the companies being merged. There may be statutory obstacles to merger; alternatively, the resources concerned may be only a small part of the total resources owned by the separate companies, so that the administrative costs of merging the entire companies are disproportional to the benefits obtained. This suggests that joint lines will often be short lines owned by two or more very large companies.

The lines have been grouped according to the dominant motivation for the partnership. Within the larger groups, the lines have been further subdivided according to the size of the scheme.

Many joint ventures were formed for aggressive purposes: namely to invade another company's territory (see Sections 5.3 and 5.4). The high cost of the invasion encouraged companies to seek partners. Sometimes the partners were on the same side of the target territory, and sometimes they were on opposite sides, in which case the joint line was built right across it.

Other joint ventures were formed for mainly defensive reasons. Some lines were 'boundary markers', representing the agreed division of previously contested territory. Most of these involved just two companies, with territories on opposite sides of the line (see Sections 5.5.and 5.6). Typically each company would agree not to promote any new schemes on the opposite side of the boundary. Other defensive lines were 'truce lines': one company had succeeded in invading another company's territory and the two companies then agreed to act as partners in the line. The partnership signalled that the aggressor could go 'so far but not further' (see Section 5.7)

The remaining joint ventures represent attempts to rationalize railway provision in specific areas. In one case two companies had built a single route in the expectation of a merger but then found that a merger was impractical; joint ownership was introduced to avoid fragmenting the line into two parallel operations (see Section 5.8). In some cases rival companies already served an area and local interests wished to ensure that a new line connected with all the networks; to prevent the owner of the branch from denying access to rival networks, all the companies became owners (see Section 5.9). In large cities local lines were needed to interchange freight traffic. All the companies serving the city had an interest in this, and so they pooled their resources to construct joint lines (see Section 5.10). Finally, railways eventually realized that building duplicate lines in coalfields was very wasteful, and so when new coalfields were opened up towards the end of the Victorian period, joint lines were built in order to economize on capital (see Section 5.12).

5.3. JOINT INVASIONS: LARGE SCHEMES

5.3.1. Midland and Great Northern (MR and GNR)

The Great Northern (GNR) and Great Eastern (GER) were great rivals. In 1870 the GER monopolized East Anglia, controlling almost all the railways to the east of the GNR main line between London and Peterborough. The GNR, however, had a dominant position to the north in Lincolnshire.

The north Norfolk coast, from Hunstanton through Cromer to Great Yarmouth, had enormous potential as a holiday destination for workers in East Midland towns such as Leicester and Nottingham, but with a GER monopoly all this traffic would have to follow a circuitous route via Peterborough, with the GER taking a substantial share of the revenue while doing little to promote the traffic.

Much of the potential traffic originated on the Midland Railway (MR) and would inevitably cross GNR territory on its route to the coast. For some years the GNR had conveyed MR traffic for London using a junction at Hitchin that provided a connection from Nottingham and Leicester via Bedford. Although the two companies had experienced difficulties in working together, which led to the MR building its own line to London (St. Pancras), they faced a common obstruction in the GER.

The shortest routes for GNR traffic to the north Norfolk coast were via Spalding from the north and Peterborough from the south, while the shortest route for MR traffic was via a junction with their Syston–Peterborough line at Bourne. The two companies promoted the Midland and Great Northern Railway (MGNR) to carry all the traffic to the coast. MR traffic from Bourne was routed via Spalding to Sutton Bridge where a line from Peterborough converged. A trunk line then took traffic from Sutton Bridge, via South Lynn (a suburb of Kings Lynn) and Fakenham, to a hub at Melton Constable, deep in the heart of rural Norfolk. From Melton Constable the main line proceeded via North Walsham to Great Yarmouth, with a branch to Sheringham and Cromer, while a third line served the city of Norwich. Further branches were added later.

The system was built up in a number of stages over about 20 years (as explained in Section 4.2), mobilizing local landowners and business leaders to promote individual sections of the line through different companies. This conserved the capital of the partner companies (who could lease lines that others had paid to construct) and also assisted in obtaining Parliamentary approval. As local businesses were always suspicious of railway monopolies, support for the new line was considerable, although GER opposition was occasionally successful in causing delay. The network of associated companies was renamed the MGNR in 1893.

Although the MGNR was configured in the classic form of a trunk line system, unlike most trunk lines it had an east–west cross-country orientation, and was single line for most of the way. Despite the single line, however, the company ran daily expresses at fairly high speeds, although outside of the holiday season the frequency of the service was low.

5.3.2. Cheshire Lines Committee (GCR, MR, and GNR)

The Cheshire Lines Committee (CLC), formed in 1863, was a successful tripartite venture to invade the core territory of one of the leading railway companies of the time—the London and North Western Railway (LNWR). Formed in 1846 by a merger of some of the earliest trunk line railways, the LNWR controlled not only the West Coast route to Scotland but also the industrial heartland of England lying between Liverpool, Manchester, and Birmingham. Holding a dominant position in such a prosperous territory, the LNWR was not so expansion-minded as some of the smaller trunk line operators such as the GNR, but it was determined to defend the territory that it already held. Through the 'Euston Confederacy' (named after the company's London headquarters), the LNWR presided over collusive arrangements between the leading companies, including two of the companies that were to become partners in the CLC (and held negotiations with the third). By 1856, however, it was becoming clear that the LNWR regarded its co-conspirators as subordinates rather than equals, and had been making private deals with some that had not been disclosed to the others. It was obvious that other members of the Confederacy could only achieve their long-term objectives—in particular, access to the Atlantic port of Liverpool—if they broke with the Confederacy.

The GCR (or Manchester, Sheffield, and Lincolnshire, as it was known at the time) had long enjoyed access to Manchester from the east, and was, indeed, a partner of the LNWR in a local line—the Manchester South Junction and Altrincham Railway (MSJAR) (see Section 5.10.5). In 1857 it introduced its own express passenger service to London, competing with the LNWR. This service ran via Sheffield and Retford, and was operated in partnership with the GNR, whose East Coast main line joined Retford with London. But it was frustrated in its plans to reach Liverpool, since GCR running powers over a connecting line from the MSJAR were difficult to enforce. Under the influence of its new and energetic general manager, Edward Watkin, the GCR decided that an independent line from Manchester to Liverpool was necessary. As a former LNWR employee, Watkin believed that competition with the LNWR called for an aggressive strategy.

Both the GCR and GNR were expansion-minded, and the GCR consolidated its position by purchasing additional local lines in the Manchester area. In 1866 the MR reached Manchester through the Peak District from its hub at Derby. It connected with the GCR at New Mills, and entered Manchester by a rather circuitous route through Hyde. It used the terminus in Manchester that the GCR shared with the LNWR. Facing continued obstruction from the LNWR, the three companies then promoted an entirely new trunk line from Manchester to Liverpool, directly competing with the old Liverpool and Manchester line that was now the main east–west link in the LNWR system. But while the LNWR route passed to the north of the manufacturing centres of Warrington and Widnes, the CLC line, running to the south of the LNWR line, served both these centres by loop lines. In addition, the CLC built two new and very conveniently located termini in Liverpool and Manchester, which were known as the Central stations. The line was opened in 1873, although Manchester Central was not completed until 1880. In addition they built a line from Liverpool to Southport (opened in 1884) which, with the aid of a triangular junction at Halewood, allowed a Manchester to Southport service to operate as well. But the line was indirect compared to alternative routes, and never achieved the same success as the main Liverpool line.

The CLC also extended the MSJAR line south-west through Northwich to Chester. Indeed, the GCR went even further, going beyond Chester to serve the Wirral peninsular (on the opposite side of the River Mersey to Liverpool) and the North Wales coalfield at Wrexham. The GCR also had access to the Wirral by a CLC line from Mouldsworth, on the Chester line, to Helsby, which provided connections to Birkenhead. Passenger traffic from Liverpool to London was routed via Stockport, south of Manchester, from whence Midland trains ran via Derby and GCR and GNR trains via Sheffield.

The GNR was not involved in CLC operations to the same extent as the GCR and MR. Its main network only connected with the CLC via GCR tracks, and unlike the other two companies it never provided motive power. It maintained goods warehouses on the CLC system, however. The CLC was a profitable investment for the GNR, as it was for all the companies. The access it provided to major industrial centres in the north-west considerably enhanced the companies' reputations for national reach.

5.3.3. Great Northern/London and North Western Joint Lines in Leicestershire (GNR and LNWR)

This alliance enabled the GNR and LNWR to invade the territory of a common rival—the MR—which dominated traffic in Leicestershire. The GNR and the LNWR were unlikely partners, considering that the former operated the southern part of the East Coast route from London to Scotland, while the latter controlled the English portion of the competing West Coast route. Furthermore the GNR was a partner with the MR in the MGNR and, even more remarkably, in the CLC's invasion of the LNWR heartland, as described above. This illustrates the point that alliances were dictated by invasion tactics which varied from region to region, with an ally in one region being the invasion target in another.

In Leicestershire the GNR faced the MR to the west, while the LNWR faced it to the east, and pooling their resources enabled them to attack the MR more effectively. Until this time the fox-hunting landed gentry—led by the Duke of Rutland—had maintained the countryside relatively railway-free. But when valuable ironstone deposits were discovered in the area, the prospect of enormous mineral wealth appears to have changed the attitudes of the sporting aristocrats.

The GNR proposed to build a line from Newark, on its East Coast main line, to Leicester, crossing the MR line from Leicester to Peterborough at Melton Mowbray, and then taking a sharp right turn near Tilton to gain access to Leicester from the east. The right turn at Tilton was necessitated partly by the hilly nature of the country and the location of the ironstone deposits, but it was also suggestive of a plan to throw off a branch to the south to meet the LNWR line from Rugby to Peterborough near Market Harborough. This branch materialized once the LNWR became involved in the scheme.

Using the new branch in conjunction with its Northampton to Market Harborough line, the LNWR was able to create a new through route from London to the north-east of England, passing to the east of Leicester and Nottingham, and throwing off branches to both of them. In return, the GNR opened up a new route from Leicester to Peterborough by the use of the LNWR's Peterborough line.

The GNR incurred a risk in bringing in the LNWR, as the latter could siphon off traffic for the south onto the joint line at Newark, and thence onto its West Coast main line near Northampton, depriving the GNR of its Newark to London traffic. The risk was relatively small, however, and did not in fact materialize because the alternative route was too slow to compete for passenger traffic. Freight traffic— Yorkshire coal in particular—was more vulnerable, but as the GNR controlled the mining areas in which the coal traffic originated, it could normally control the route that the traffic would take. To set against this risk was the more certain prospect of ironstone traffic heading north to the industrial towns of Yorkshire, together with additional traffic from the LNWR's Northamptonshire lines.

5.3.4. Somerset and Dorset Joint Railway (S and DJR; MR; and LSWR)

This railway represents an invasion of Great Western (GWR) territory by the London and South Western Railway (LSWR) and the MR, who jointly acquired a regional network of lines from local interests. The primary objective of their invasion was not to steal traffic from the GWR, but rather to develop traffic that the GWR was ill-equipped to develop itself—namely holiday traffic from the Midlands and north to the South Coast. The MR controlled the source of the holiday traffic in the industrial towns while the LSWR controlled the major destination—the rapidly growing holiday resort of Bournemouth, which was being aggressively promoted by property speculators at the time.

The S and DJR's main line ran south from Bath (Green Park) to Broadstone and Wimborne, where it joined the LSWR system. Traffic from the north was fed into Bath by a junction with the MR's main line from Birmingham to Bristol at Mangotsfield, north-west of Bath. Although the S and DJR gave the LSWR access to Bath and Bristol, the main beneficiary was the MR, which was able to extend its network to the South Coast, thereby advancing its strategy of becoming a nation-wide company. The LSWR already operated a service from Portsmouth and Southampton to Bristol via Salisbury, in partnership with the GWR, and this route was much faster than the S and DJR. The benefit to the LSWR was mainly the opportunity to maximize the tourist potential of the local resorts that it served.

The MR scored an early success over the GWR in 1845 when it purchased the Birmingham and Gloucester and Bristol and Gloucester railways and thereby secured a through route from Leeds to Bristol via Birmingham, penetrating the heart of GWR territory. This early success was due to the GWR trying to drive too hard a bargain when bidding to take over the Gloucester companies. The MR's joint acquisition of the S and DJR was a natural means of consolidating and building upon this early success.

The SDJR system was created in 1862 by an amalgamation of two local companies: the Somerset Central, serving Highbridge and Burnham on the Bristol Channel, and the Dorset Central serving Wimborne, near Poole, on the south coast. Connecting up these two railways created a 'land bridge' between the Bristol Channel and the English Channel, allowing coastal shipping to avoid the circuitous and dangerous route around Land's End.

The coast-to-coast link fulfilled the Somerset Central's ambitions, but the Dorset Central's aim to link the Midlands to the South Coast was not so easily achieved. Traffic from the north via Bristol could change onto the SDJR at Highbridge, but this route involved a significant deviation. Furthermore, relations with the GWR, which controlled the mainline from Highbridge to Bristol, were not always good. The answer lay in a direct line to Bath, where a connection could be made with the MR that was entirely independent of the GWR. But the intervening country through the Mendips was very hilly; construction was so expensive that the local company ran out of funds. When it turned to the MR and LSWR, they provided financial support and became the joint owners of the line. When the main line from Bath was completed in 1874, the SDJR had two adjacent hubs—one at Evercreech Junction, where the lines from Bath and Highbridge diverged, and one at Templecombe, further south, where the LSWR main line from London to Exeter via Salisbury was crossed. The Templecombe link allowed MR passengers to reach Exeter (and later Plymouth) without ever travelling over the GWR.

5.3.5. Great Western and Great Central Joint Lines (GWR and GCR)

Although these lines can be construed as an invasion of LNWR territory, their objectives had little to do with capturing local traffic. The GCR sought independent access to London from the north, while the GWR wished to accelerate its service from London to Birmingham and Birkenhead. The GCR was seeking independence from the GNR and Midland, while the GWR was aiming to take express traffic between London and Birmingham away from the LNWR.

From a GWR perspective the joint line was a 'cut-off' that avoided a detour for Birmingham trains through Oxford, while from a GCR perspective the joint lines formed a 'loop' that allowed trains from the Midlands to bypass congestion on the lines approaching London that were shared with the Metropolitan Railway (MetR, see Section 5.4.4).

These joint lines were the last main lines of any length to be built on the railway system up to 1914. New construction of a similar scale in the UK was not witnessed until the Channel Tunnel rail link of the 1990s. The main line of the GCR London Extension from the Midlands, opened in 1899, took a south-westerly route, avoiding the territory already occupied by the MR main line. It crossed the LNWR main line at Rugby and intersected a succession of LNWR feeder lines: the Daventry and Leamington branch at Braunston, the Buckingham branch at Brackley and the Oxford to Cambridge line at Calvert. South of Calvert it joined the MetR line from Verney Junction and entered London (Marylebone) via Aylesbury, Harrow, and Neasden. A loop line was required to avoid congestion between Aylesbury and Neasden caused by local stopping trains. At the same time, the GWR was planning a direct line from London (Paddington) to Banbury in order to accelerate its Birmingham trains. The GCR proposed to use part of this cut-off as a loop. It built a link south of Calvert to the GWR at Ashenden, and another link from the GWR at Northolt to Neasden. The section between Ashenden and Northolt then became jointly owned. This section included part of the GWR's Maidenhead branch between Princes Risborough and High

Wycombe, but the rest was all new construction. The joint line was opened in 1905, although the GWR's new line to Banbury was not completed until 1910.

5.4. JOINT INVASIONS: SMALL SCHEMES

5.4.1. West Riding and Grimsby (GCR and GNR)

This line represents a joint invasion by the GCR and the GNR of Lancashire and Yorkshire (LYR) territory. The invasion was prompted by worsening relations between the GNR and the LYR, which were cleverly exploited by the GCR in a classic strategic manoeuvre of the sort characteristic of Victorian railway politics.

The LYR was a venerable company whose main line from Manchester to Wakefield, engineered by George Stephenson, was the first trans-Pennine line. It took a relatively level but circuitous route along the Calder and Hebble Valleys, and despite being known as the 'Manchester and Leeds Railway', never actually reached Leeds. At Wakefield the line divided, with a northern spur serving Leeds and York by means of connections with the North Eastern (NER) and MR railways at Normanton, while an eastern spur served the port of Goole on the River Aire.

The LYR had limited territorial ambitions in Yorkshire. From Knottingley it built a branch down to Askern, north of Doncaster, on the GNR, and also made connections with the GCR in the Barnsley area. Otherwise it concentrated its investments in Lancashire, with the result that much of its Yorkshire territory was invaded by other companies, including the GNR, GCR, MR, NER, and even the LNWR.

In the 1850s the GNR relied on the LYR line through Knottingley and Wakefield to serve the Leeds area. But when the GNR began to expand its operations around Leeds and Bradford by developing new suburban services in the area (see Section 5.7.6), relations between the two companies deteriorated. When the LYR joined forces with the GNR's rival, the GER, to promote a new freight line to London (see Section 5.5.3), the GNR decided that it had become imperative to fulfil its long-standing ambition to gain independent access from Doncaster to Wakefield, and thence to Leeds.

An independent company—the West Riding and Grimsby Junction—had obtained powers to build this line, opened in 1866, together with a line from Wakefield to the GCR at Thorne, from whence Grimsby would be reached. By taking over this line on a joint lease in the following year the GCR and GNR were therefore able to eliminate their common dependence on the LYR for access to Wakefield. Indeed, they acquired an entire system of lines which also gave access from Wakefield to Goole in direct competition with the LYR.

The two companies had already joined forces in Cheshire to attack the LNWR (see Section 5.3.2) and now they were able to exploit their partnership to gain independence from the LYR as well.

5.4.2. Sheffield and Midland Railways Joint
Committee (GCR and MR)

This partnership involved two of the three CLC partners—the GCR and MR—and was used to develop local lines in the Manchester area as an adjunct to CLC operations. The other CLC partner, the GNR, was not involved because it had no main line tracks of its own into Manchester, as noted above.

The GCR made an early entry into Manchester through its main constituent company, the Sheffield Ashton-under-Lyne and Manchester Railway, which linked the two cities by the spectacular Woodhead Tunnel under the Pennines. It shared Manchester (London Road) station (now renamed Piccadilly) with the Manchester and Birmingham Railway. However, the merger of the Manchester and Birmingham with the Liverpool and Manchester and other lines to form the LNWR undermined the GCR's status in Manchester, especially after the LNWR acquired a main line of its own across the Pennines, through Huddersfield to Leeds. The LNWR also built a connection from Stockport on the Birmingham line to Stalybridge on the Huddersfield line; this route crossed the GCR line to the east of Manchester, and allowed the LNWR to run an express service between London, Huddersfield, and Leeds.

When the MR entered Manchester with its main line through the Peak District from Derby, the GCR recognized that an alliance with the MR could help it to re-establish its position in Manchester (see Section 5.3.2). Formed in 1869, the partnership took over a GCR line from Hayfield to Manchester via New Mills and Romiley, part of which was used by the MR to gain access to Manchester. It initiated construction of a direct line from Romiley to Manchester via Reddish, opened in 1875, which expedited MR expresses. Two spurs were built to Stockport, connecting with an earlier GCR line from Godley Junction on its Sheffield main line. Stockport was an important industrial town near the confluence of several rivers, and Tiviot Dale station, adjacent to the Mersey, was far better situated than the LNWR station at the top of the hill.

The spur from Romiley to Stockport represented a major strategic move, as it gave the MR access to the developing CLC system to the west of Manchester. MR expresses from London could reach Liverpool via Stockport, Northenden and Glazebrook, with connections for Southport at Halewood. The MR (acting alone) capitalized further on this by building a new line from Stockport to the CLC's new Manchester Central station, thereby avoiding congestion at London Road. In 1902 it opened a Stockport bypass for its Manchester traffic through Hazel Grove and Didsbury.

In conjunction with these MR developments, the GCR opened a new South Manchester loop line between Guide Bridge, on its Sheffield line, and Manchester Central. This line provided a 'suburban circle' linking the Central and London Road stations and, together with the MR line, promoted residential development in the South Manchester suburbs.

As a consequence of these developments, the Joint Committee controlled 25 miles of suburban lines in the Manchester area which, together with the separate

GCR and MR lines, provided an impressive network serving an increasingly populous area. In a separate development, the Committee also constructed a loop line into Widnes from the CLC line to Liverpool when the GNR declined to contribute to the cost, opened in 1879. All of these developments helped the GCR to regain its earlier status in Manchester, and helped the MR to establish its position in the city too. As in many other cities, however, these suburban lines were adversely affected by the advent of trams and buses, while the complex of main lines and suburban lines around Stockport almost completely disappeared as a result of rationalization in the 1960s and 1970s, when operations were concentrated around the LNWR station there.

5.4.3. Macclesfield Committee (GCR and NSR)

As noted above, the GCR and MR were both expansion-minded companies. Both began operating cross-country routes in the industrial heartlands, and felt deprived by having no independent access to London. Both companies recognized the value of partnerships in extending their networks, but the GCR was particularly promiscuous in its partnering arrangements. This reflected the strategic vision of Edward Watkin. This strategy was valuable to the company so long as it remained on good terms with prospective partners, but was 'bad news' when (as sometimes happened with Watkin) it fell out with its partners (or prospective partners). GCR strategy is exemplified by its partnership with the North Staffordshire Railway (NSR) in the Macclesfield, Bollington, and Marple Railway.

In contrast to the GCR, the NSR was not an expansion-minded railway. Its territory, centred on its hub at Stoke-on-Trent, was hemmed in by the LNWR to the west and the MR to the east, and it normally showed little desire to 'escape'. Partly as a consequence of this, it was a prosperous little railway. It was locally owned and controlled, and focused on serving the 'Potteries' industrial district and the south Staffordshire coalfield. Because it originated most of its own industrial traffic, much of which was exported from the district, it could control the routes over which this traffic was consigned. It could therefore play off the big companies against each other to secure competitive rates.

Its main east–west route linked the MR hub at Derby to the LNWR hub at Crewe, but since these two big companies discouraged passengers from switching between their rival systems, there was not so much long-distance passenger traffic on this line as might have been expected. The NSR's main north–south route linked two parts of the LNWR system—the Manchester to Macclesfield branch to the north and the West Coast main line near Stafford to the south. The two lines intersected at Stoke, from where several local lines diverged. The north–south line offered the shortest express passenger route from London to Manchester, bypassing congestion at Crewe and serving Stoke *en route*. The LNWR ran some of its Manchester to London expresses via Stoke. This was to both companies' benefit: the NSR gained the additional traffic, while the LNWR gained a faster route that improved its competitive position relative to the MR and GCR. The NSR therefore maintained good relations with the LNWR.

In 1864 the GCR promoted a line south from Romiley, on its branch from Hyde to New Mills, to join the NSR near its end-on junction with the LNWR Manchester branch at Macclesfield. But this was no mere branch from a Manchester suburban system. It seems that Watkin was hoping to use the line to drive a wedge of suspicion between the NSR and the LNWR, and entice the NSR into the GCR 'camp'. The line gave the NSR access to Manchester that was entirely independent of the LNWR. Through Romiley the NSR could gain access to the entire GCR system while, conversely, the GCR gained direct access to the NSR system. A spur was also provided at Middlewood for NSR traffic to the MR main line through the Peak District, which provided a useful local link from Macclesfield to Buxton.

Having driven a wedge between the NSR and LNWR, the plan seems to have been to promote new railways south towards Birmingham. But the NSR was too prudent to antagonize its old ally the LNWR. While the new line strengthened its bargaining position with the LNWR regarding Manchester traffic, it refused to over-play its hand. It did not establish a new express service between Stoke and Manchester to compete with the LNWR, and consequently the Macclesfield, Bollington and Marple remained an essentially suburban line. The grand ambition of the GCR to enlist the support of the NSR in an invasion of LNWR territory came to nothing. The line appears to have been quite profitable, however, and was therefore justifiable as a modest and useful investment for the two companies.

5.4.4. Metropolitan and Great Central Joint Committee (MetR and GCR)

This Committee did not build any new lines, but rather operated a section of line that had already been built by the MetR and which became an integral part of the GCR main line into London. Edward Watkin, the 'Second Railway King', chairman of GCR from 1864, became Chairman of the MetR as well in 1872. The MetR operated an underground railway in London—not a 'tube line' tunnelling deep through the London clay, but a sub-surface line formed by the cut-and-cover method, and running below the streets. Its Moorgate station served the financial heart of the City. The line terminated initially in the north London suburbs, and was subsequently extended into rural Buckinghamshire. Property development was one of its main interests—London offices for clerical workers, and suburban housing estates from which they could commute. Watkin was invited to take the chair of the MetR when the company experienced a corruption scandal.

Watkin had a grandiose ambition to connect the industrial Midlands and north with the Continent via London and a Channel Tunnel. The section of the route south of London would be operated by the South Eastern Railway

(SER)—of which Watkin also became Chairman. Ideally, this plan required the MetR to be upgraded from a suburban railway into a main trunk line, but widening the tracks was difficult when so much of the area it served had already been built up. An alternative route into London was constructed (see Section 5.3.5), but this was more circuitous, and some GCR expresses still needed to use the MetR route. To avoid the GCR becoming a hostage of the MetR in the future, it was agreed that from 1906 the MetR would lease their line between Harrow and Verney Junction, north of Aylesbury, together with associated branches to Chesham and Brill, to a Joint Committee of the MetR and GCR. This arrangement was the result of independent arbitration following a period of great acrimony between the two companies which was only resolved by a change of staff. Despite the obvious conflict in the operation of expresses and suburban trains over the same route, subsequent relations appear to have been reasonably harmonious, probably because the agreement was carefully worded to protect the interests of each company.

5.4.5. Furness and Midland Joint (FR and MR)

This 10-mile line, opened in 1867, linked the MR route from Leeds to Morecambe via Lancaster with the Furness Railway (FR) main line from Carnforth to Barrow and Whitehaven. It commenced at Wennington, near Bentham, on the MR line, and terminated at Carnforth, where the FR main line connected with the LNWR West Coast main line.

The FR main line was coastal, and had once been considered as a potential Anglo-Scottish route, as it avoided the steep gradients of the LNWR route along the edge of the Lake District. It ran west along Morecambe Bay to Ulverston, serving the peninsular port of Barrow with a branch from Dalton, and then turned north to the ancient port of Whitehaven on the Irish Sea. At Whitehaven an end-on junction was made with the Whitehaven Junction Railway, which continued north through Workington to Maryport, where a further junction was made with the Maryport and Carlisle Railway. At Carlisle the West Coast main line was regained. The FR was a prosperous company run mainly by local interests, and served two areas rich in coal and iron ore—one around Barrow and the other near Whitehaven.

In the early 1860s the MR, frustrated by the LNWR monopoly of West Coast Anglo-Scottish traffic, was looking for an alternative route to Glasgow—the eventual solution being the expensive Settle and Carlisle line. One of the alternatives was to upgrade the FR main line by building a cut-off across the Duddon estuary, north of Barrow, and to make another short cut across the Solway Firth to join the Glasgow and South Western (GSWR) main line from Carlisle to Glasgow near Annan. The FR and the MR therefore formed an alliance to build the Wennington line as a part of a new Anglo-Scottish route. The plan fell apart, however, when the LNWR forestalled the FR by purchasing the Whitehaven Junction, thereby blocking the route north from Whitehaven to Carlisle.

The joint line was therefore obliged to fulfil more mundane, but quite profitable objectives. It provided a useful link between the extractive industries of the Furness district and the manufacturing centres of West Yorkshire. Passenger services to Bradford and Leeds benefited the Furness business community, while the MR gained access to the growing port of Barrow, in which Furness interests had invested heavily.

5.5. BOUNDARY MARKERS BETWEEN ESTABLISHED COMPANIES SHARING A FRONTIER: LARGE SCHEMES

5.5.1. Shrewsbury Joint Lines (GWR and LNWR)

An impressive system of joint lines radiating from Shrewsbury was jointly owned by the LNWR and GWR, comprising the Shrewsbury and Birmingham line as far as Wellington (opened 1849), the Shrewsbury and Hereford (opened 1853), and the Shrewsbury and Welshpool (opened 1862). Other railways converging on Shrewsbury included the Shrewsbury and Chester Railway (opened in 1848) and an LNWR line from Crewe (opened in 1858).

Thus, despite a relatively late start, Shrewsbury had become a major railway hub by 1860. Furthermore it possessed a grandiose neo-Gothic joint station built to rival the great joint station at Chester. It occupied a magnificent position underneath the Castle, opposite the Grammar School, and near the Market Place. The harmonious appearance is misleading, however, because in its early years Shrewsbury was the focus of bitter rivalry between the GWR and the LNWR for control of traffic in the West Midlands and Welsh Borders. The initiative for the joint station came from the mayor and corporation rather than the railway companies, and the joint ownership of the lines was due as much to local political pressure as to amicable relations between the companies.

Shrewsbury might never have developed as an important railway hub if there had not been a dispute between the London and Birmingham Railway and the Grand Junction Railway regarding the handling of through traffic between Liverpool and London. These railways made an end-on junction in Birmingham, at which passengers had to transfer between trains, and the railways could not agree on a fair division of the revenue for the two portions of the journey. To strengthen its bargaining position, each company encouraged the promotion of lines to rival its opponent's line. In particular, the London and Birmingham encouraged local interests around Shrewsbury to promote routes north of Birmingham that would compete with the Grand Junction's Liverpool line. When the two protagonists resolved their differences and merged with other companies to form the LNWR in 1846, they expected these rival schemes to founder. But they had underestimated the strength of the local interests, which persisted with their rival schemes.

During the dispute the Grand Junction had courted the GWR as a potential ally, and this company had resolved, as a consequence, to divert its proposed line from Oxford to Rugby to serve Birmingham instead. The GWR was therefore a natural ally of the Shrewsbury-based companies. An independent connection from Shrewsbury to Birmingham could feed traffic into the GWR line to London (Paddington) via Oxford. A link from Shrewsbury to Chester would connect with the Chester and Birkenhead Railway and, together with the Birmingham link, would create a new trunk line from London (Paddington) to the Mersey, terminating just across the river from Liverpool at the Woodside ferry terminal in Birkenhead. The constituent companies of the LNWR had, it turned out, 'shot themselves in the foot' by falling out among themselves. Although the GWR had never originally intended to serve Merseyside, it was now becoming a major player in the area.

The LNWR had a bad reputation in the Shrewsbury area because of the efforts of its General Manager, Mark Huish, to divert traffic away from the lines of the Shrewsbury-based companies—the Shrewsbury and Birmingham and the Shrewsbury and Chester—and funnel it through Crewe instead. The LNWR had an ally, however, in the Shropshire Union company—basically a group of canal proprietors who wished to salvage their failed canal investments by promoting a railway company that would purchase their canals at inflated prices and build railways over them at other people's expense. This company proposed, among other things, to build a railway from Shrewsbury to the LNWR main line to Stafford, thereby placing Shrewsbury on a branch of the LNWR system. Another group of promoters with more serious business interests wished instead to build a line from Shrewsbury to Birmingham, where they would have the option of joining up with both LNWR and the GWR lines. The two groups decided to join forces to promote a line between Shrewsbury and Wellington, where the Stafford and Birmingham lines would diverge. The Shropshire Union was subsequently acquired by the LNWR and the Birmingham company by the GWR so that the Wellington line became the joint property of the two companies. The arrangement worked surprisingly well. Huish resigned from the LNWR in 1858, over another issue created by his duplicity, and was succeeded by the more conciliatory Richard Moon. This encouraged the LNWR and GWR to seek cooperative solutions to other conflicts in the Shrewsbury area.

In 1860 the GWR merged with the West Midland Railway, and thereby acquired control of a considerable network of lines to the south of Shrewsbury. Like the other Shrewsbury-based companies, the Hereford company had good relations with the GWR, although it had remained independent, unlike the Chester and Birmingham companies. It employed the contractor Thomas Brassy to operate its line—which he did very profitably. The West Midland was developing an alternative route between Shrewsbury and Hereford via Worcester and Bewdley, however. Although indirect, the GWR, as the new owner, might prefer to route its traffic this way in future. This was important, because most of the long-distance traffic on the Hereford line was either originated on, or destined for, the GWR.

The LNWR saw an opportunity to come to the rescue of the Hereford company. The LNWR had big plans to expand into South Wales, and was already building a line south from Craven Arms on the Hereford line towards Swansea (see Section 5.7.7). Independent access to Hereford would bring it even closer to South Wales. But local sentiment was against either the LNWR or the GWR achieving a dominant position in the area, and under pressure from Parliament the two companies agreed in 1862 to operate the line jointly.

The last of the Shrewsbury Joint Lines was the Shrewsbury and Welshpool, which joined the Cambrian Railway main line From Oswestry to Aberystwyth at Buttington, just east of Welshpool. The Cambrian was an impoverished line serving Mid-Wales, and was anxious to develop holiday traffic to the coast. For this purpose it encouraged feeder lines to its system from the east. It already had a link with the LNWR Crewe line at Whitchurch, and a branch from the GWR Chester line at Gobowen fed into this link at Oswestry. Shrewsbury was a useful centre for consolidating traffic from the GWR at Birmingham and the LNWR at Stafford, and so the Cambrian was keen that the LNWR and GWR should both consign traffic over the Shrewsbury link. This was finally assured by joint ownership of the link agreed in 1865.

Overall, the Shrewsbury joint lines constituted a rational solution to the private provision of railway infrastructure in a thinly populated area with limited local commercial potential. Although both the GWR and LNWR contemplated additional construction, there were many demands on their capital for new lines in the main industrial areas—lines which were likely to be much more remunerative. The cooperative solution met the demands of local communities for an integrated railway service, and helped the companies to conserve their capital for use elsewhere.

Intermittent skirmishing continued, however, as the GWR pushed northwards towards Crewe via Market Drayton and the LNWR continued south to Swansea. Integration turned out to be a slow process too, with the companies operating their own trains over the joint lines, rather than single joint service, for a considerable time. The joint lines marked out a territorial boundary, although the border was porous to some degree. But while transgressions occurred, competitive construction of purely duplicate lines was avoided, and the role of Shrewsbury as a hub was safeguarded too.

5.5.2. Birkenhead Joint (GWR and LNWR)

The Birkenhead Lancashire and Cheshire Junction Railway operated a network of lines in the Wirral peninsular, north of Chester. It incorporated one of the earliest main line railways, the Chester and Birkenhead, opened in 1840. It also operated a main line from Chester to Warrington, where it linked with the LNWR West Coast main line. The mid-points of these two lines—Hooton and Helsby—were also connected, allowing traffic from Birkenhead to Warrington to bypass Chester. It was jointly acquired by the LNWR and the Great Western (GWR) in 1860. It subsequently opened a branch from Hooton to West Kirby—a popular residential centre on the Dee estuary.

The proprietors of the Chester and Birkenhead were mainly concerned to promote Birkenhead Docks, although some also wished to promote Chester as a railway hub. Birkenhead was a rival port to Liverpool on the opposite side of the Mersey estuary. It developed into a major shipbuilding and engineering centre, and handled a large amount of Irish cattle destined for abattoirs in major English cities. It also exported coal to bunkering stations around the British Empire. In the 1830s, however, it was still in the early stages of development.

Initially the Birkenhead company fed most of its traffic into the Chester and Crewe Railway, which in turn fed its traffic into the Grand Junction Railway at Crewe. The Grand Junction was a Liverpool-based company and to begin with did its best to divert traffic away from Birkenhead in favour of Liverpool, by making connections at Chester deliberately poor. However, the North Wales Mineral Railway (later to become the Shrewsbury and Chester Railway) fed considerable freight traffic for Birkenhead into Chester from the Wrexham area, and this more than made good any deficiency in the traffic from Crewe.

Once the LNWR had acquired the Grand Junction and the Shrewsbury company had allied itself with the GWR (as described in Section 5.5.1), the traffic dispute, which was already serious, escalated into a major confrontation. The LNWR took Liverpool's side, while the GWR supported Birkenhead. Using its Shrewsbury route, the GWR could divert traffic from London and the Midlands to Birkenhead. The LNWR successfully intimidated the Birkenhead company into obstructing Shrewsbury traffic at Chester, but the consequent loss of revenue, and the opposition of port interests, eventually forced the Birkenhead company to adopt a more neutral line. Stuck on the 'front line' between two warring factions, the proprietors seem to have favoured selling out to the highest bidder, but objections from the port proprietors meant that Parliament would approve only a joint acquisition. This would give Birkenhead access to both the LNWR and GWR networks on an equal footing. Thus just as with the Shrewsbury companies, two great rivals finished up as partners in a local railway system that spanned their frontier.

5.5.3. Great Northern and Great Eastern Joint Line (GNR and GER)

Despite its great length (123 miles) this line essentially marks a boundary between GNR and GER territory. The GER controlled the territory to the south, around Huntingdon, St. Ives and March, while the GNR controlled the northern end around Sleaford, Lincoln, and Doncaster. Portions of this line used former GNR routes while others were jointly built as new. While the earliest portions of the line date back to 1848, the final portions were not completed until 1867.

The GNR was the most ambitious of the Railway Mania schemes. It was one of many to be authorized, and one of relatively few to be built right away. It comprised a main line from London to Doncaster and a loop line to the east, from Peterborough to Boston and Lincoln, rejoining the main line at Doncaster.

Although many Mania schemes were resurrected later and built in a scaled-down form, the GNR was built at the time and was almost completed within five years.

The building of the GNR frustrated the ambitions of the LNWR and Caledonian (CR) to monopolize traffic from London to Scotland via the West Coast route, and it also frustrated plans to extend East Anglian railways further north. As early as 1835 it was proposed to extend the Northern and Eastern Railway from London to Bishop Stortford and Cambridge up past The Wash and into Lincolnshire, serving Sleaford and Lincoln on the way to York. This route had several advantages over the later GNR main line. It used the Lea Valley to enter London, avoiding the many tunnels on the GNR line north of London (Kings Cross); it served the university town of Cambridge; and it could be built straight, level, and cheaply across the Fens, avoiding the hilly country around Grantham. Ten years later, a variant of this route was the first choice of the Railway Committee of the Board of Trade for an East Coast main line. But due mainly to the political skills of Edmund Dension, MP for Doncaster, Parliament authorized the GNR scheme instead.

The Northern and Eastern line eventually became part of the GER, along with many other companies in the area. Although the GER achieved a virtual monopoly of East Anglia (subject only to the MGNR invasion) it still retained the aspiration to venture north in order to tap the traffic from Yorkshire to London. But while it had one of the best routes into London, it extended no further north than March and Kings Lynn. The company had potential allies in the north, however; namely, the competitors of the GNR: the MR, GCR, and LYR. In the 1840s the 'Railway King' George Hudson had proposed to link up the Cambridge line with his MR, while in the 1870s the 'Second Railway King', Sir Edward Watkin, had considered a link with his GCR. Both of these companies subsequently lost interest, however, when they planned their own lines into London through Bedford and Brackley respectively. This did not apply to the LYR, however, which was the only one of the Yorkshire companies not to have its own route into London, and was consequently reliant on the GNR.

In the 1860s the GNR invaded LYR territory around Bradford (see Section 5.7.6), and the LYR retaliated by seeking a new partner to handle its London traffic. Together with the GER it promoted a new specialized coal-carrying railway from the LYR's junction with the GNR at Askern, north of Doncaster, to Long Stanton on the GER line from St. Ives to Cambridge.

Schemes for coal-carrying trunk railways were popular with coal owners at the time, as a means of intimidating established railway companies into offering better freight rates and improved service. The GNR was vulnerable on this score, because its East Coast main line was used by both slow-moving coal trains and fast passenger expresses, and was consequently quite congested. Its loop line through Boston was less congested but quite indirect, and unsuitable for heavy traffic because part of it had been built over a defunct waterway. The natural solution was to bisect the area between the main line and the loop line with a new line—basically a variant of the scheme proposed in 1835. The loop line was also deviated north of Lincoln in order to connect with the GCR line from Grimsby to Sheffield at Gainsborough, and this involved building another new section of line, between Gainsborough and Doncaster.

The GNR offered to build the new lines itself, but to sell the GER a half-share in order to prevent further trouble from them. Once the line was completed, the GER ran trains north as far as Doncaster, but could not interchange traffic with the LYR there. The GNR improved its competitive position in the coal trade—especially in relation to the MR—by increasing the capacity of its routes to the south. In serving London via the joint line, it had a choice of consigning traffic over either its own main line from Huntingdon (using a spur from St. Ives) or the less-congested GER lines instead. Although the new line involved a substantial concession to the GER, it effectively neutralized that company's attempt to gain an even larger share of the Yorkshire coal traffic. Furthermore, while the GER was able to 'invade' Doncaster, the GNR hub, the GNR was able to invade the Cambridge area.

5.5.4. Swinton and Knottingley Joint (NER and MR)

The Swinton and Knottingley was opened in 1879 for the purpose of accelerating long-distance cross-country passenger trains from the north-east to the south-west over the section of their journey between York and Sheffield. It helped to develop a new market for luxury passenger travel at a time when railway competition on existing routes was becoming quite intense, and when passengers were substituting third class for first and second-class travel. The route connected with the NER main line from Newcastle at York, and with the MR main line to Derby, Birmingham, and Bristol at Sheffield.

In the 1840s the York and North Midland had worked closely with the North Midland Railway in developing through traffic between York, Sheffield, and Derby. York and North Midland trains from York joined the North Midland main line from Leeds to Derby at Altofts Junction, just north of Normanton station. Normanton was for a time a major hub, as the LYR line to Wakefield provided onward connection to Manchester. The York and North Midland was subsequently acquired by the NER, whose major hub was at York, while the North Midland Railway became part of George Hudson's MR empire based at Derby. As the MR expanded south, to Bristol in 1845 and London in 1868, so the potential for through traffic increased. Initially Sheffield was served only by an MR branch from Rotherham, but after 1870 it was on a loop line from Chesterfield, which made it possible for through expresses to call there.

The line from York to Sheffield via Normanton was indirect, however, and the importance of Normanton to the MR declined once passengers to or from the south could change trains at Sheffield. When the NER opened a new direct line from York to Doncaster in 1871 (to accelerate East Coast main line trains from London to York and Edinburgh) spare capacity on the old route from York via Knottingley became available. Continuing this line south from Knottingley to join the MR main line from Leeds to Sheffield at Swinton would provide a direct line from York to Sheffield that avoided Normanton.

The line from Swinton to Knottingley had other advantages too. The area was rich in coal. It crossed a number of important lines, including the GNR's main line from Doncaster to Leeds, and the GNR used the line between Moorthorpe and Church Fenton for London to Harrogate expresses via Tadcaster. Although this was not the shortest route between Doncaster and Church Fenton, it avoided using LYR tracks.

If the NER had built the line itself it could have been construed as an invasion of the Sheffield district, prompting a retaliatory MR invasion of York. Since the operation of through expresses depended on cooperation between the companies, however, a joint venture was a sensible strategy. As noted above, the two companies had a long tradition of working together to develop the cross-country traffic, despite their rivalries elsewhere, and this tradition almost certainly facilitated the negotiation of the joint venture arrangement.

5.5.5. Portpatrick and Wigtownshire Joint Committee (CR, GSWR, LNWR, and MR)

Galloway, in southern Scotland, is one of the most remote parts of Great Britain, forming a broad peninsular that projects out into the Irish Sea to the west of the Carlisle and to the south of Glasgow. Following the Protestant Plantation of Ulster in the seventeenth century, many Scots emigrated to the north of Ireland. The natural route between Scotland and Ulster was via Portpatrick, a small harbour at the tip of the peninsular. In the early nineteenth century the British Admiralty was keen to develop Portpatrick as an Irish Mail port, as part of a more general politically motivated strategy to strengthen economic and diplomatic ties with Ireland. While Holyhead concentrated on serving Dublin, Portpatrick would serve Belfast via Donaghadee (on the Belfast and County Down Railway).

The Portpatrick Railway was built to connect the port with the main line railway system at Dumfries, on the GSWR line from Carlisle to Glasgow. This link was of strategic importance to other railway companies too. The LNWR connected Carlisle to London, and later, on completion of its Settle and Carlisle line, the Midland (MR) became involved too. Much of the finance required to construct the railway was provided by other railway companies, because of the strategic importance of the line to the network as a whole. The GSWR was already building a line west from Dumfries to Castle Douglas (later extended to Kirkcudbright) and so the junction with the GSWR was made at Castle Douglas. Subsequently a branch was opened from Newton Stewart, an intermediate station on the Portpatrick line, to Whithorn—an ancient pilgrimage site—by an associated company.

The Caledonian Railway (CR) was also interested in the Portpatrick project, although it did not contribute funds. The CR controlled the West Coast main line north of Carlisle, and naturally had an interest in the area to the west of it, even though it was poor and lightly populated. The CR resented the GSWR building a line from Carlisle to Glasgow that competed with its own West Coast main line. It built a line to Dumfries from the West Coast main line at Lockerbie in order to gain independent access to Dumfries. Compared to the GSWR, the CR route from Dumfries to Carlisle was indirect, but its route from Dumfries to Glasgow was almost as good.

The Portpatrick line was opened as far as Stranraer, near Portpatrick, in 1861, and was completed in 1862. Stranraer soon eclipsed Portpatrick as the port for Ireland; the harbour was more sheltered and better suited to steamships, and the rail journey was shorter. The Stranraer ships took a more northerly route to Larne.

As a local company handling all the traffic east of Castle Douglas, and a major subscriber to the Portpatrick Railway, the GSWR expected to be asked to operate it, but its terms were so onerous that the Portpatrick board decided to operate the line themselves. In 1864 the CR completed its line from Lockerbie to Dumfries and was in position to take over the running of the Portpatrick line provided that it could get running powers between Dumfries and Castle Douglas. It offered very reasonable terms, and Parliament conferred the requisite powers.

The Portpatrick company soon discovered, however, that these reasonable terms came at a cost, as the CR made all sorts of unexpected demands. When the 21-year agreement expired, the Portpatrick board negotiated a sale to all the major companies that consigned traffic over its route, including the LNWR and MR. The interests of Galloway and its ports were protected by these arrangements as they avoided rail access being monopolized. Frictions remained, but they were confined to the managing committee in which two alliances confronted each other—the CR/LNWR alliance which controlled the West Coast main line, and the GSWR/MR alliance that consigned Anglo-Scottish traffic via the Settle and Carlisle line. None of the four companies was totally dependent on the Portpatrick line, as each operated other ports for Belfast.

Stranraer–Larne has remained popular as the short sea-route, Although the line from Dumfries has been closed, rail passengers can use an alternative route from Ayr—the Girvan and Portpatrick Junction—which was opened in 1877 by the GSWR.

5.6. BOUNDARY MARKERS BETWEEN ESTABLISHED COMPANIES SHARING A FRONTIER: SMALL SCHEMES

5.6.1. Preston Joint Lines: North Union Railway; Preston and Wyre; Preston and Longridge (LNWR and LYR)

Both the LNWR and the LYR served the industrial heartland of Lancashire. It might be expected that the two companies would be intense rivals, but this was not the case. For one reason, their systems complemented each other. They shared a hub at Preston—a regional manufacturing and commercial centre. The LNWR

West Coast main line, from Crewe to Carlisle, was oriented north–south, while the LYR main line from Manchester to Wakefield and Goole ran east–west. From Preston an LYR line ran east through Blackburn and Burnley to Todmorden, where it joined the main line from Manchester. So far as local lines were concerned, the LNWR was strong in the south, along the Mersey Valley and into the Cheshire Plain, while the LYR was strong in the north, along the Ribble Valley and into the foothills of the Pennines.

Another reason why they got on well was that their constituent companies in the area had a good record of cooperation. Two early lines—the Wigan Branch Railway and the Preston and Wigan—merged in 1834 to form the North Union Railway (NUR). Their end-on junction at Wigan allowed passengers from Liverpool and Manchester to reach Preston very conveniently via a junction with the Liverpool and Manchester Railway near Newton-le-Willows. Passengers to or from London could also change onto the Warrington line there. In addition, passengers from Bolton could reach Preston via a branch from Bolton to Kenyon Junction on the Liverpool line.

When the direct line of the Bolton and Preston Railway was promoted there was clearly scope for conflict, as Bolton passengers were likely to transfer from the NUR. Furthermore, the lines of the two companies approached Preston from the same direction. After some argument, the two companies agreed to merge. They used the same approach to Preston, avoiding wasteful duplication, and also avoided a 'fares war'. The only losers were passengers from Bolton to Preston who, despite a choice of routes, were confronted by a monopoly fare.

In 1846 the feeders into the NUR's Wigan line were merged into the LNWR, while the feeder into its Bolton line was taken over by the Manchester and Leeds Railway, which in turn became the LYR the following year. Both the LNWR and the LYR needed control over their entry to Preston, and so it was agreed that the portion of the NUR from Euxton Junction into Preston be jointly owned and the rest of the NUR be split between the two companies, the LNWR taking the Wigan line and the LYR the Bolton line.

The other two Preston joint lines were promoted by Peter Hesketh Fleetwood—a local landowner and entrepreneur. He inherited a large estate on the Fylde peninsular, north-west of Preston. Founder of the port of Fleetwood, which he built up from a mere 'rabbit warren', he was MP for Preston and an ardent social reformer. He promoted the Preston and Wyre Railway in order to improve access to the port—part of a successful integrated project of regional development. Steamships sailed from Fleetwood for Ireland, Scotland, and the Isle of Man, and also to Whitehaven on the Cumbrian coast. Until the completion of the Lancaster and Carlisle Railway, Fleetwood was in regular use for Anglo-Scottish travel by rail and ship.

Fleetwood erected two fine churches and several hotels at the port. As there was a convenient source of building stone at Longridge, north-east of Preston, he promoted the Preston and Longridge Railway too, which supplied stone, not only to Fleetwood but also to many growing towns and cities in the area. The proximity of Fleetwood to Blackpool sands encouraged the building of other railways to the Fylde coast. The resort of Blackpool, however, was built by speculative developers instead, and in consequence it came to resemble 'a Lancashire milltown without the mills'. Its popularity quickly eclipsed that of Fleetwood, however; while Blackpool took off as a major resort for local mill-workers, Fleetwood lost shipping business to ports with better docks, and eventually became a fishing port.

The Fleetwood line was opened in 1840, and the branch to Blackpool from Poulton was opened in 1846. Traffic for Blackpool and Fleetwood originated on both the LNWR and LYR systems, and so in 1849 the Preston and Wyre was vested jointly in the two companies, with the LYR taking the larger share, probably because it originated most of the excursion traffic on the line. The Preston and Longridge, which carried much less traffic, did not enter into joint ownership until 1866, however. To accommodate increasing holiday traffic, additional joint lines were built from Kirkham to Blackpool—the Lytham line in 1863 and the direct line in 1903.

5.6.2. Ashby and Nuneaton (LNWR and MR)

Ashby-de-la-Zouch is an historic town with an important medieval castle. Prior to the expansion of the Leicestershire coalfield, the railways showed little interest in it. It lay on a MR byway—an extension of the very early Leicester and Swannington Railway—which ran from Leicester, on the MR main line from Derby to London, to Burton-on-Trent, on the MR's Derby to Birmingham main line. These two main lines bordered the east and north of the Ashby area, respectively. To the south and west lay LNWR territory: the West Coast main line ran north-west from Nuneaton to Tamworth and onto Crewe, while from Nuneaton a branch ran east towards Leicester.

In the mid-1860s, during the Second Railway Mania, both the MR and LNWR promoted lines towards Ashby from Nuneaton. They were just two of a large number of schemes in the Midlands where the MR and LNWR were fighting each other for territorial advantage. Parliament favoured the MR plan but considered that the LNWR should also participate in the scheme, as it had such good connections at Nuneaton.

The system was Y-shaped, with a junction at Shackerstone, where the line from Nuneaton divided, one branch going to Overseal, west of Ashby, and the other to Coalville, east of Ashby, both on the MR Burton—Leicester line. It was opened in 1873. The LNWR subsequently extended the Coalville line to Loughborough—terminating in the smallest of the town's three stations, Derby Road.

As a result of the joint line, and additional running powers over the MR system acquired through political manoeuvring, the LNWR was able to run an express service over the line from London to Buxton via Nuneaton, Burton, Uttoxeter, and Ashbourne, in direct competition with the MR's main line to Buxton and Manchester through the Peak District. Apart from this express service, however, most of the other traffic was just local freight. The two companies also jointly owned a short freight branch from Narborough, east of Nuneaton, to Enderby. The area did not develop much as a result of the new lines, and the surviving part near Shackerstone is now operated as a rural byway by a heritage railway.

5.6.3. Otley and Ilkley Joint Line (NER and MR)

The harmonious relations between the NER and the MR that were evident in the case of the Swinton and Knottingley above were also evident 15 years earlier in the promotion of the Otley and Ilkley Joint Lines. Otley and Ilkley are two small towns in the Wharfe Valley that have long been considered suitable as residential areas for managers and professionals working in Bradford and Leeds. The air was pure, and there was good walking on the moors; indeed, by 1860 Ilkley was developing into a major hydrotherapy centre, and soon after the railway arrived in 1865 it was host to several luxury hotels.

Wharfedale also has a wider strategic significance from a railway point of view. It runs along an east–west axis north of Leeds and Bradford, and intersects the paths of trunk line railways running north from Leeds. One of these lines, owned by the MR, ran through the heavily industrialized Aire Valley, by way of Keighley to Skipton. This line connected at Skipton with the 'Little North Western' line to Ingleton, which in turn gave access to the LNWR West Coast main line at Low Gill.

At the other end of Wharfedale lay the route of the NER's Leeds Northern Railway from Leeds to Stockton-on-Tees via Harrogate and Northallerton. A railway through Wharfedale would allow the MR to invade NER territory going east, and also allow the NER to invade MR territory going west.

During the Second Railway Mania in the 1860s, the MR and NER were both fighting battles on many fronts—usually with other companies, but sometimes with each other. Both companies decided that Wharfedale was not worth fighting over, and so they came to an agreement which gave both companies access to Ilkley and Otley. The arrangement allowed the MR to have its own branch from Airedale to Ilkley, which joined the joint line at a triangular junction at Burley. This branch divided at Guiseley, south of Burley, providing links to both Leeds and Bradford which were suitable for commuter traffic. The NER had its own line to Otley, which made a triangular junction with its Leeds Northern line at Arthington. As a result, the MR obtained most of the Ilkley traffic and most of the traffic to Bradford, while the NER obtained most of the traffic from Otley to Leeds. A very grand station was built at Ilkley for joint use, most of which still survives as a shopping centre.

Both the MR and the NER were aware that further problems could arise if the NER attempted to build west from Ilkley towards Skipton, and so an agreement was made that neither company would promote this route without the other's consent. There was indignation among landowners when this agreement became public, as it was felt to be inimical to the economic development of Wharfedale.

Their fears were unwarranted, however, because the MR eventually built an extension to Skipton (with the NER's consent, it may be assumed) in order to consolidate its control of the area. This case illustrates the ambiguity of public opinion towards railway cooperation; while the lavish joint station at Ilkley was appreciated as a contribution to the tourist trade, the agreement not to build to Skipton was interpreted as a conspiracy against the local interest.

5.6.4. Croydon and Oxted Line and Woodside and South Croydon Line (SER and LBSCR)

The Croydon and Oxted line was built through a railway no-man's land of the 1870s. It lay between the SER main line from to Dover via Tonbridge and the London Brighton and South Coast Railway (LBSCR) main line from London to Brighton via Redhill, and was jointly owned by these two companies. The line was valuable to the LBSCR in feeding traffic from Oxted, East Grinstead, Tunbridge Wells, and Eastbourne through to London via Croydon. The value of the line to the SER is less obvious, because the company had agreed in 1848 that all the territory south of its Redhill to Tonbridge line and west of its Tunbridge Wells to Hastings line belonged to the LBSCR; as a result, most of the traffic that fed onto the line originated firmly in LBSCR territory.

The SER's motive appears to have been to forestall its great rival the London Chatham and Dover Railway (LCDR). The LCDR was already competing with the SER on its northern frontier. In 1862 it had opened a branch from its main line at Swanley to Sevenoaks, which was extended from Otford to Maidstone in 1874. If the Oxted line were not built by the SER then the LCDR, which was not bound by any agreement with the LBSCR, might build it instead. The route had already been surveyed and partly built by the defunct Surrey and Sussex Junction Railway, and it would be a relatively easy step to revive the scheme. The worst-case scenario, from the SER's point of view, would be that the LCDR built the line in order to get its hands on the SER's Hastings traffic.

The Woodside to Croydon line was built as a feeder to the Oxted line, in order to allow the SER to provide connections to the Oxted line via Lewisham and Beckenham. The service from Woodside was meagre, however, and the line was not very profitable. The LBSCR seems to have taken a stake in the scheme in case the SER should decide to use the line to invade its territory at a later date.

The rationale for the line appears to have been a desire by each of the companies to restrict the competitive options available to other companies in the future. The SER wanted to restrict the options available to the LCDR, and the LBSCR wanted to restrict the options available to the SER. Neither of the lines were particularly profitable, but there was some commercial benefit to the LBSCR from participation in the Oxted line scheme. Although the SER obtained a poor deal in revenue-generating terms, the outcome was almost certainly regarded as superior to losing territory to its great rival, the LCDR.

5.6.5. Portsmouth and Ryde Line, and Fratton and Southsea Line (LSWR and LBSCR)

This is a classic case of lines built along the border between the territories of two companies. The LSWR and the LBSCR were competing to serve residential areas along the South Coast and the major naval port of Portsmouth. The joint lines represented an eastern outpost of the LSWR and a western outpost of the LBSCR. The two companies operated other border lines as well: at Midhurst in rural Sussex, and between Epsom and Leatherhead, near London (see Section 5.6.6).

Because Portsmouth lies on a peninsular overlooked by high downland, there was no easy direct route from London. The LSWR originally proposed to serve Portsmouth with a branch from their main line from London to Southampton at Eastleigh (known as Bishopstoke at the time). But Portsmouth interests wanted their own direct line; they saw Southampton as a competing port. Since Portsmouth was closer to London than Southampton as the crow flies, this advantage should be preserved by the railway system, they thought. The hostility of Portsmouth interests persuaded the LSWR to build a line from Eastleigh to Gosport, on the opposite side of the river, serving Portsmouth by ferry (much as the GWR served Liverpool by the ferry from Birkenhead); it was opened in 1841.

At the time of the Railway Mania the LBSCR proposed to build a line along the South Coast from Brighton through Chichester to Portsmouth, entering Portsmouth through Cosham. Recognizing that the ferry crossing placed it at a competitive disadvantage relative to the Brighton route, the LSWR proposed to extend eastwards from Fareham, on the Gosport line, to Portsmouth via Cosham. This proposal was authorized at about the same time as both the Brighton line and another scheme (which subsequently foundered) that would also enter Portsmouth from the Cosham direction. Parliament required the companies to build a joint station at Portsmouth and, given this constraint, it was clearly in their interests to serve this station with a joint line from Cosham rather than to use three separate sets of tracks. The LSWR and LBSCR reached agreement on this basis in 1848. Subsequently two short joint branches were built; one from Fratton to Southsea, and another to the harbour, to serve the Isle of Wight ferry.

Joint operations never seem to have generated much trust so far as the companies were concerned, however. In the world of railway politics new lines were always being promoted—if not by the companies then by local interests— and it was inevitable that established companies would find many of these new schemes objectionable. This is evident in the case of the Portsmouth lines, where strategic rivalry continued alongside routine cooperation over the running of the lines.

Portsmouth interests later succeeded in obtaining a direct line to London via Guildford. This line, built as a speculative venture by the railway contractor Thomas Brassey, was opened in 1859. The aim was to sell or lease the line to the LSWR, as a southern extension of its London to Guildford line, but as this company was already serving Portsmouth via Fareham it was reluctant to acquire a new line that would simply divert some of the traffic it already carried. To encourage the LSWR to bid, the promoters made a contingency plan to link their new line with the SER at Guildford, instead of with the LSWR, and route their trains to London via Redhill. They also promoted a new line of their own from Guildford to London. These combined threats to the LSWR's Guildford traffic were sufficient to persuade it to purchase the line. As a result, the LSWR express service was re-routed via Guildford and Havant, approaching Portsmouth from the north-east instead of from the west as before, although the original route remained in use as well. A last-minute complication arose because the LSWR London expresses needed to use LBSCR tracks at Havant, and a dispute over running powers ensued. The result was the 'Battle of Havant' in which both companies resorted to physical violence before the issue was finally resolved.

Subsequently the LBSCR sought to counter the advantage of the direct line by extending its Horsham branch to Arundel (opened in 1863), cutting off the detour into Brighton, while the LSWR built yet another line—the Meon Valley—from Fareham to Alton (opened in 1903), which reached London via Aldershot. By 1905 Portsmouth had no less than four different routes to London (via Guildford, Horsham, Eastleigh, and Fareham) although only three were served by express trains.

5.6.6. Epsom and Leatherhead Line (LSWR and LBSCR)

This short line of 3.5 miles, linking two market towns on the fringes of London, is a veritable 'Hadrian's Wall' in terms of railway politics. It marks the border between the territory of the LSWR to the north and west and the territory of the LBSCR to the south and east. The newly built line was jointly acquired in 1859 as part of the truce that followed the Battle of Havant mentioned above.

The LBSCR reached Epsom from London via West Croydon and Sutton in 1847, and the LSWR arrived 12 years later via Wimbledon, just as the struggle for the Portsmouth traffic was reaching its climax. The LSWR was worried that the LBSCR was heading for Guildford—a prosperous county town that the LSWR already served with great success using the Guildford Junction line from Woking.

The LBSCR was even more concerned that the LSWR was planning a rival route to Brighton. During the 1830s no less than six different routes had been proposed between London and Brighton, with the most level route, proposed by Robert Stephenson (and surveyed by George Bidder), using the Mole Valley, which ran due south from Leatherhead to Dorking. At Horsham it entered the Adur Valley, and reached Brighton via Shoreham. Stephenson had planned to commence his route by a junction with the LSWR main line at Wimbledon. Parliament had selected a more direct but expensive line through Croydon and Redhill instead. However, the LSWR branch from Earlsfield to Epsom followed the first section of Stephenson's route. To make matters worse, Dorking was a natural town for which to aim, as it was still served only by the SER's cross-country route from Reading and Guildford to Redhill and Tonbridge. Horsham too was a natural target, as it lay at the head of the Arun Valley, which led down to aristocratic Arundel and the fashionable seaside resort of Bognor.

The LBSCR needed to develop the Horsham to Arundel route in order to compete effectively with the Portsmouth direct line that was nearing completion, and therefore could not allow the newly authorized Epsom to Leatherhead line to fall into the hands of the LSWR. Joseph Locke, the distinguished civil engineer who had long been associated with the LSWR, had surveyed a line to Brighton via Dorking in 1846, and in 1857 he was involved with a Wimbledon to Dorking project that could be used to revive the scheme.

Faced with the prospect of mutual invasion, the two companies backed off. They agreed to jointly acquire the independent company that had built the line. With the agreement of the LSWR, the LBSCR then set about constructing a new route from London to Portsmouth via Leatherhead, using a portion of the existing 'mid-Sussex' line between Horsham and Pulborough. When the new through route was opened in 1867, LBSCR trains ran through Leatherhead and only the LSWR trains terminated there. Having previously shared the use of a small terminus, the companies now built two independent but adjacent stations, with the result that LBSCR trains ran straight past the LSWR station to stop at their own station further south.

The LBSCR already had a route from Horsham to London through Three Bridges, and so passengers from Portsmouth to London could now be offered a choice of routes by changing at Horsham; they also had a choice of London stations—London Bridge or Victoria—while the LSWR direct line could offer only one station—Waterloo.

The LSWR eventually built a line from Leatherhead to Guildford via Effingham Junction, opened in 1885. This secured its monopoly of the Guildford to London traffic: there were three routes, via Woking, Surbiton, and Leatherhead, and all were controlled by the LSWR. Because of the subsequent development of commuter traffic, all three survive today.

As a result of these arrangements, both Epsom and Leatherhead became junctions, with a jointly owned line between them, forming a composite four-way hub. But unlike most four-way junctions, the routes never crossed. The LSWR and LBSCR through routes were merely tangential between Epsom and Leatherhead: LSWR territory lay to the north and west of the boundary line, and LBSCR to the south and east. Passengers could cross the boundary, but trains did not.

5.6.7. Tooting, Merton, and Wimbledon Line (LSWR and LBSCR)

Between 1860 and 1866 the Second Railway Mania, though less intense than the first, had a profound effect on the shape of the national railway system. Under political pressure from the towns, Parliament sought to strengthen competition by favouring new routes promoted by independent companies that opened up new territories. Alternative routes between major cities served towns that had been bypassed by the original trunk line schemes, while cross-country routes opened up rural areas. Around major cities, suburban lines propagated, filling up the gaps between existing lines converging on the city.

As an expanding metropolis, London attracted a large number of suburban railway projects. Many were promoted by property developers hoping to attract a wealthy middle class escaping the smoke and noise of the city centre. But suburban commuters increasingly demanded a choice between termini in different parts of London—some termini were suitable for shopping and others for work; and changing jobs was easier when all parts of the metropolis were accessible from home.

This demand for flexibility put pressure on established companies to link up their local networks—something that they had always resisted before (as in the case of the Epsom and Leatherhead line described above). If established companies did not build these links then new independent companies would step in to fill the gap. But any established company that unilaterally proposed a link into a rival company's territory would be branded an 'invader', and the response from the other company would be a rival scheme. Joint promotion was the obvious solution: it avoided retribution from the other company, while foreclosing independent entry. The main problem was that Parliament might consider the combination of established interests to be anti-competitive. A suitable strategy was to promote a nominally independent company whose line would be jointly leased to the partner companies once it had been built.

The Tooting, Merton, and Wimbledon lines represent a scheme of this kind. This short east–west loop line in the London suburbs linked Streatham on the LBSCR with Wimbledon on the LSWR main line. Trains from Streatham via Merton Abbey could continue through Wimbledon and return to Streatham via Haydon's Road, with trains running in both clockwise and anti-clockwise directions. The line was authorized as a joint scheme in 1865 and opened in 1868.

By changing at Wimbledon commuters could arrive at Waterloo, while by travelling in the opposite direction to Streatham they could arrive at either Victoria or London Bridge, and even Ludgate Hill. This flexibility made the Tooting area extremely popular with commuters—so much so that the Northern Line tube was subsequently built out through Tooting to Merton. The tube gave ready access to an even wider area of London, and together with electric tram competition, took away much of the commuter traffic. The southern part of the loop through Merton Abbey, which faced the stiffest tube competition, was subsequently closed, although the northern loop prospered, especially after it was electrified by the Southern Railway in 1929.

5.6.8. Glasgow and Paisley Joint Line (CR and GSWR)

Scotland had its own railway companies—two of largest being the CR and the GSWR. It might be thought that Scottish companies, sharing a common cultural identity, might be able to cooperate where English companies failed. Furthermore, as there were fewer Scottish companies, it should in principle have been easier for them to negotiate cooperative arrangements than the more numerous English companies. Finally, Scotland was on average a poorer country than England, and so the financial penalties from wasteful duplication were potentially much greater. But in practice none of these factors stopped the Scottish companies from competing aggressively against each other, just like the English ones. The Scottish companies were sometimes financed by English investors, and forged close partnerships with English companies—the CR with its West Coast partner the LNWR, the North British (NBR) with its East Coast partners the NER and GNR, and the GSWR with the MR. The competitive strategies that the Scottish companies pursued towards their local rivals were in part dictated by rivalries between their English partners. The main reason for Scottish companies being separate was almost certainly differences between the English and Scottish legal systems.

The CR was a notable example of a company controlled by English interests—its patriotic name being quite misleading in this respect. From the mid-1840s the CR fought both the GSWR—on its western flank—and the NBR—on its eastern flank—for control of central Scotland. It became a partner with the GSWR in the Paisley joint line when it acquired one of the companies that promoted the line and the GSWR acquired the other.

It was in the 1830s, prior to the formation of the two big companies, that the plan was made to build just a single rail route between Glasgow and Paisley. There were two companies proposing to build west from Glasgow, one intending to reach the coast at Greenock and the other at Ayr. They did not see themselves as competitors at the outset, and so, on the advice of the engineers Joseph Locke and John Errington, they built a joint line as far as Paisley, opened in 1840. But later developments changed the position. The CR saw the Greenock line as a useful feeder to its main line south to the border at Carlisle, while the Ayr line turned out to be part of a useful route into Glasgow from Carlisle via Dumfries and Kilmarnock—a route that rivalled the CR main line. As part of the development of this route the Ayr company was merged into the GSWR in 1850. The CR, to defend its interests in the area and secure the traffic from Greenock, acquired the Greenock company the following year.

Following the joint acquisition, the two rivals invested heavily in the line. When its textile trade went into decline because of competition from Lancashire, Paisley developed into a service centre for the shipyards along the Clyde. Branches were built to the Clyde near Govan (opened in 1868) and Renfrew (opened in 1902). Traffic on the main lines to the coast expanded rapidly, and to combat congestion the joint portion was widened to four tracks. It became a major artery of commuter traffic, and is now electrified.

5.6.9. Glasgow, Barrhead, and Kilmarnock Joint Line (CR and GSWR)

Collaborations never seem to run smoothly, and the two partners in the Paisley line (see above) soon became dissatisfied with the joint route. The GSWR was dissatisfied because Paisley lay off a direct line from Glasgow to Kilmarnock which would ideally be used by Anglo-Scottish expresses in order to cut the journey time to Carlisle and offer stiffer competition to the CR's West Coast route. The CR was dissatisfied because the GSWR had a virtual monopoly of traffic between Glasgow and the Ayrshire coast, including resorts such as Largs and Troon, the port of Ardrossan, and the Ayrshire coalfield. The best way to compete for this traffic was to build a direct line to the coast which would be shorter and faster than the existing GSWR route via Paisley. Like the GSWR direct line, the CR direct line would bypass Paisley to the south.

The CR had been slowly extending from Glasgow in the direction of Kilmarnock using an associated company—the Glasgow Barrhead and Neilston Direct Railway—which reached Barrhead in 1848 and Crofthead in 1855. In 1865 the GSWR was authorized to build a direct line all the way to Kilmarnock along a route that paralleled the Barrhead line for much of the way. The CR also obtained powers to extend its own line to Kilmarnock. The dramatic end of the Second Railway Mania in 1866 caused both companies to rethink this wasteful duplication of lines, and it was agreed to link the Kilmarnock end of the GSWR line to the Barrhead end of the CR line to form a single jointly owned route, with a branch to Beith. The line was opened throughout in 1873 and operated mainly by the GSWR.

5.6.10. Halesowen Railway (GWR and MR)

Halesowen is now a suburb of Birmingham with a motorway service station nearby. In the 1840s it was a small industrial settlement, served by the Dudley Canal, but bypassed by the railways. The Oxford Worcester and Wolverhampton Railway (later acquired by the GWR) ran to the west near Stourbridge, while the MR line from Birmingham to Bristol ran to the east through Northfield. There were various schemes to connect Halesowen to the rail system, and these intensified when a direct line from Stourbridge Junction to Birmingham was proposed, which reached Old Hill, close to Halesowen, in 1866. A GWR branch from Old Hill to Halesowen was authorized in 1862, but when an independent continuation of this line to Northfield—the Halesowen Railway—was projected in 1864, both the MR and GWR at first objected. After years of debate and procrastination, the GWR line from Old Hill opened in 1878 and the Halesowen Railway from Northfield in 1883. Between Halesowen and Northfield a modest passenger service was jointly provided by the two companies.

Traffic was light; much of the route was lightly populated, and in the urban areas competition from electric trams became severe. The journey to Birmingham via Northfield was indirect. The line was built cheaply, and even featured an old-fashioned tressle viaduct. There were several speed restrictions, including a 10 mph restriction over the viaduct, which made journeys very slow. The Halesowen company went bankrupt in 1904.

In 1906 the line was purchased by its operators—the GWR and MR—who also provided the connections at each end of the line. The line unexpectedly received a new lease of life when, about the same time, Herbert Austin established a successful motor car factory at Longbridge, near Northfield. But much of the factory's traffic soon went by road. The line was eventually closed, and the viaduct—a local landmark—was demolished to make way for the motorway.

5.6.11. Kilsyth and Bonnybridge line (CR and NBR)

This is a classic boundary-spanning scheme that connects a dead-end branch of one system to a dead-end branch of another system to form a through route linking the two systems. It ran just over 8 miles from Kilsyth, north-east of Glasgow, near the NBR centre of Kirkintilloch, to Bonnybridge, near the CR hub of Larbert, just south of Stirling. It was opened in 1888. It duplicated trunk routes between Glasgow and Falkirk operated separately by the two companies, and so was of no great strategic value to them. It simply enabled each company to extend the range of its local services. CR passenger trains could run through from Larbert to Kilsyth, while NBR trains could run through from Glasgow to Bonnybridge. By restricting operations to a local level, each company ensured that the other derived no substantial advantage from their share in the line. It also helped to undermine the other company's case for building additional lines in the area.

5.7. TRUCE LINES BETWEEN INVADER AND DEFENDER

5.7.1. Lancashire Union (LNWR and LYR)

One reason why agreements between neighbouring companies were so unstable, and invasions so common, was that independent third parties were always free to promote a scheme and then play off the established local companies against each other. Sometimes the independent promoters would ask for backing from the companies at the outset, before Parliamentary authorization had been obtained; sometimes they would invite them to take over their scheme once they had obtained Parliamentary approval, and sometimes they would wait until the line had been built and then ask the companies to either buy the line or operate it. Although the established companies could collude against the independent promoters and refuse to deal with them, one or other of the rival firms could not usually resist the temptation to make a deal behind the other's back. Thus independent promoters were often *agents provocateurs* in undermining trust between neighbouring companies.

   In some cases the independent promoter was a contractor—perhaps building a line in order to keep their key workers in employment during a recession. In other cases the promoters were property developers, usually developing new suburbs. In the case of the Lancashire Union (LUR) they were coal-owners seeking improvements in the transport of coal. Promoting a railway was an expensive business, which is why the coal-owners usually acted together. Their concern was sometimes just to obtain better service and lower rates from the established companies, rather than to build a new railway, and so they were willing to be 'bought off'. In other cases, however, congestion on the existing system was so serious that additional tracks were required, and when it was difficult to widen existing lines then a new line made good business sense.

In 1860 coal-owners around Wigan and St. Helens were dissatisfied with the rates and service offered by both their local companies, the LYR and LNWR. Their coal was much in demand by the steam-powered mills of north Lancashire and by the mill-workers resident in those towns. The route to Blackburn, Accrington, and Burnley was either through Preston to the north or through Bolton to the east. These were circuitous routes, and where charges were calculated on a mileage basis they were expensive. Given the competition from other coalfields, this additional cost was borne by the coal-owners in terms of a lower pit-head price. The answer was a direct route—specifically, a Preston 'cut-off' from Chorley on the Bolton–Preston line through to Blackburn, following the route of the Leeds and Liverpool Canal.

The LNWR supported the proposal, which turned it into an invasion of LYR territory. For defensive reasons the LYR then announced its own competing scheme. Parliament preferred the LYR proposal but encouraged the companies to collaborate. The LYR and the LUR became partners, and when the LNWR absorbed the LUR in 1883 the LYR and LNWR became partners instead. Two sections of joint line were built: one from Chorley to Blackburn, and the other from Boars Head, on the LNWR main line north of Wigan, to Adlington, south of Chorley. Both lines were opened in 1869. Together they provided a through route from Wigan to Blackburn, with the LUR and LYR making independent approaches to Wigan. Other parts of the scheme around Wigan were built by the two companies separately, and each company provided its own network of lines to the collieries, the LUR acting in concert with the LNWR. In fact the line from Chorley to Blackburn was not a great boon because its grades of 1 in 60–65 made it very expensive to operate with heavy coal trains. While the coal-owners got what they wanted, it was a poor deal for the railway companies involved.

5.7.2. Norfolk and Suffolk Railways Joint Committee (MGNR and GER)

An unusual feature of this joint venture is that one of the partners—the MGNR—was itself a joint venture; the Joint Committee was therefore doubly 'joint'. The MGNR's partner was its great rival the GER. Quite what prompted the dramatic transition from rivalry to partnership is unclear, though it is probable that the capital expense of their competing plans and the relatively poor returns from earlier investments in the region were a factor.

At the time it adopted its new identity in 1893, the MGNR was still relentlessly pursuing its plan to develop the north Norfolk coast, and to penetrate south of

Yarmouth into Suffolk. The GER was responding by promoting new lines of its own. The MGNR planned to serve the tiny resort of Mundesley by a continuation of its Cromer branch, while the GER proposed to serve Mundesley with a branch from its Norwich to Cromer line at North Walsham. The GER was also proposing to build a coastal line between Lowestoft and Yarmouth as an alternative to its inland route via the Haddiscoe junctions. This looks like an attempt to forestall the MGNR's push south, since its only advantage over the inland route was that it served the intermediate resort of Gorleston-on-Sea.

In 1897, however, the two companies agreed to pool the ownership of the new lines. The two Mundesley branches were joined in the middle at Mundesley to form a coastal loop line between Cromer and North Walsham, connecting at North Walsham not only with the GER but also with the MGNR Yarmouth line; the loop was completed in 1906. The Lowestoft line (opened in 1903) also became jointly owned, and an expensive connection was put in to the MGNR's station at Yarmouth Beach, allowing MGNR trains to reach Lowestoft by reversal at Yarmouth. The new lines serving Mundesley and Gorleston were not a great commercial success, however, and it is probably just as well that another scheme for a branch to Happisburgh was dropped.

5.7.3. Severn and Wye Joint (GWR and MR)

The Forest of Dean is one of Britain's oldest industrial districts, and was served by horse-drawn tramways well before the dawn of steam railways. These tramways ran downhill from coal mines in the heart of the Forest to ports and creeks along the northern bank of the River Severn south of Gloucester. The 'Foresters' who lived in this area had their own courts which safeguarded their traditional rights. The miners of the Forest were notorious for their militancy and this, together with rather primitive communications, made Forest coal relatively expensive compared to that produced by the South Wales coalfield to the west.

In the 1860s and early 1870s a local company, the Severn and Wye Railway, invested heavily in modernizing the old Forest tramway system that ran north from the port of Lydney to Park End, and from thence along separate branches to Colebrook and Lydbrook (on the River Wye). This independent network was 'imprisoned' within a web of GWR lines. Prior to the opening of the Severn Tunnel in 1886, the GWR's main line from London to South Wales ran along the north bank of the Severn through Lydney. Its Cinderford branch from Bullo Pill served the east of the Forest, while its Monmouth branch from Chepstow followed the River Wye northwards, forming the eastern boundary of the Forest. To the north, the GWR line from Monmouth to Ross ran through Lydbrook.

Developments at Gloucester, on the opposite bank of the Severn, promised liberation for the Severn and Wye, however. There were plans to build a large dock on the south bank of the river at Sharpness, which would be linked to Gloucester by rail. The link would be provided by extending a branch line from Berkeley on the MR trunk line from Birmingham to Bristol. This branch would bridge the Severn near Lydney, where it would connect both with the Severn and Wye and with the GWR. This extension, known as the Severn Bridge Railway, was authorized in 1872 and opened in 1879.

The Severn Bridge Railway promised to be more than just another outlet for Forest coal, however. It could also form a section of a new trunk line from London to South Wales which would rival the GWR main line. A bridge across the Severn south of Gloucester had been a key element of Brunel's plans for a South Wales trunk line back in the 1840s, but the Admiralty had blocked the proposal on the grounds that it would obstruct river shipping. (In fact, the Admiralty was quite far-sighted in this respect, for the nemesis of the Severn Bridge came in 1960 when a barge hit one of its piers.) Brunel had been forced to re-route his line through Gloucester, the lowest traditional bridging point on the Severn.

South Wales coal owners had always been dissatisfied with the GWR's handling of coal traffic to London, and their discontent surfaced periodically in their promotion of alternative routes. It was this pressure that led to the GWR promoting the Severn Tunnel which ran to the south of the bridge; work on the tunnel commenced the year after the bridge was authorized, and it was finally opened in 1886. With the prospect of a tunnel, the GWR had little use for the bridge. But it could not trust the MR not to use the bridge to siphon off traffic, either from the GWR at Lydney or from an extension of the Severn and Wye system into the South Wales coalfield.

In fact, the MR does not appear to have had great expectations from the bridge. It was only a modest single-track affair for a start. In addition, the MR already possessed access to South Wales through its Neath and Brecon line. However, when the Severn and Wye got into difficulties in 1894, the MR was prepared to come to its rescue. Fear of the consequences encouraged the GWR to participate in a joint acquisition. For the MR, it was a useful if rather minor invasion of GWR territory that attracted a modest amount of coal traffic, while for the GWR it made it possible to contain any future plans that the MR might develop for strengthening its access to South Wales.

5.7.4. Dumbarton and Balloch line (CR and NBR)

Although the CR built and operated the first major trunk line system in Scotland, stretching from the border at Carlisle to Aberdeen, with branches to Glasgow and Edinburgh, it was subsequently eclipsed by its great rival, the NBR, so far as serving local industries was concerned. By the 1880s the NBR had acquired a dominant position in the Fife coalfield and—even more annoying to the CR—on the north bank of the Clyde as well. Like most monopolists, however, the NBR had antagonized the local industrialists, and three very influential shipbuilding entrepreneurs joined forces with the CR to promote the nominally independent Lanarkshire and Dumbartonshire Railway, which would duplicate the NBR's main line along the north bank of the Clyde. For much of its route it would run between the NBR and the shipyards, bringing its tracks even 'closer to the customer' than the existing ones.

In a clever move, the CR also sponsored a continuation of this new line up to Loch Lomond, in competition with the NBR Balloch branch, which served a pier on the south bank of the Loch. Having obtained Parliamentary approval for its Dumbarton line, it then withdrew its plans for the Loch Lomond line and in return received a half-share of the NBR Balloch branch. By preventing the CR from building north of Dumbarton the NBR was able to protect its territory around Aberfoyle and ensure its monopoly of traffic between Dumbarton and Fort William when the West Highland line was built. But these were not major gains, because the traffic was light. It is quite likely that the CR would never have built the Loch Lomond line in any case. The CR was therefore the victor—but the spoils of victory did not last for long. The new railway did not open until 1896, and Clydeside went into permanent recession in 1921. Rationalization led to the closure of duplicating lines and left a legacy of rusting rails along the north bank of the Clyde—many of which still remain today.

5.7.5. Dundee and Arbroath Joint Line (CR and NBR)

The expansion of the NBR system (see Section 5.7.4) involved some grandiose schemes. One of the best known is the Tay Bridge near Dundee. This was a vital link in a chain of lines that eventually connected London to Aberdeen via an East Coast route through Edinburgh. The Tay Bridge collapsed in 1879 after having been open for traffic for less than two years. It was rebuilt in 1887, but remained of limited value until its companion, the Forth Bridge, was opened in 1890. Nevertheless the opening of the bridge signalled a shift in railway politics on Tayside. Passengers no longer crossed the Tay by ferry but entered Dundee across the bridge by train from Burntisland on the Firth of Forth, north of Edinburgh, and proceeded through Arbroath and Montrose on their way to Aberdeen, using running powers over the Caledonian (CR) system.

This marked a new chapter in the history of the Dundee and Arbroath Railway. The railway ran north-east from the 'jute metropolis' of Dundee along the North Sea coast to the port of Arbroath. Designed as a purely local railway (like other early railways around Dundee) it was opened in 1838 using a gauge of 5 ft. 6 in., and only later converted to standard gauge. When the railway from Perth arrived in Dundee in 1847 there were plans to integrate the two lines to form a through route from Perth to Aberdeen via Dundee and Arbroath, but this came to nothing. Integration finally occurred during the Second Railway Mania; the line was taken over by the Scottish North Eastern Railway in 1863, and this was in turn acquired by the CR in 1866.

In anticipation of the opening of the Tay Bridge the NBR obtained an Act authorizing it to take a half-interest in the Dundee and Arbroath line in order to guarantee a measure of control over East Coast express traffic north of Dundee. This arrangement also made sense, because the NBR was planning a separate line from Arbroath to Montrose and would therefore feed traffic from its own system onto the line at both ends (opened in 1883). As a result, the CR ceased to be the dominant railway company in Dundee, and the two companies became equal partners in the city. Even so, they did not fully rationalize their operations, as there were three separate stations in the city.

5.7.6. Halifax and Ovenden Railway and Halifax High Level Station (GNR and LYR)

This case is a very clear example of a boundary marker established between an invader, the GNR, and a defender, the LYR. The invader succeeded in extending its territorial coverage, while the defender prevented any further inroads in the future. The local business community gained because it obtained access to two networks rather than just one, and was able to play the two companies off against each other to keep freight charges relatively low.

In 1870 Halifax was the commercial centre of a large and prosperous industrial district spanning the Calder and Hebble valleys. It was difficult to serve by railway because of its hill-top location. As a result, it lay off the route of George Stephenson's Manchester and Leeds Railway, which became the backbone of the LYR system, and was served by the LYR's Bradford branch from Sowerby Bridge instead. This was particularly inconvenient for passenger travel.

The LYR had a bad reputation in Yorkshire for putting Lancashire interests first by investing more heavily in railways around Manchester and Liverpool than around Bradford and Leeds. Although the LYR was vulnerable because of both its poor service and lack of investment, it was difficult for other companies to exploit this weakness because of the high cost of building alternative lines through such hilly country.

This did not deter the GNR, however. Before the MR's London Extension to St. Pancras was completed, the GNR had effectively monopolized railway traffic between Yorkshire and London, and had become a highly profitable operation. Once the MR Extension opened, the GNR needed to generate additional traffic from Yorkshire to make good the loss, and so it decided to reinvest some of its profits for this purpose.

The GNR promoted a competitor to the MR line from Bradford to Keighley—the Bradford Thornton and Keighley Railway—which followed a circuitous route that took it through Queensbury, just 5 miles north of Halifax. Realizing the vulnerability of the LYR's position in Halifax, the GNR promoted a southern extension from Queensbury to join the Halifax and Ovenden Railway—a local scheme which ran from a junction with the LYR in Halifax to the suburbs of Ovenden and Holmfield, opened in 1874. The Halifax and Ovenden joined the LYR at the southern end and the GNR at the northern end, and it was therefore natural for it to approach both companies to lease the line. The GNR gained from the arrangement because, although it already had running powers into Halifax over the LYR, it now part-owned a line into the town, making access more secure, while the LYR gained because it secured a shorter route to Keighley.

Subsequently, some Halifax residents felt that the LYR station, used by both companies, was too far down the hill, and proposed an additional High Level station which was opened in 1890. Unfortunately the new station served only the Queensferry line, via a junction at Holmfield, and so was of little use for traffic over the LYR. The GNR and LYR, as joint owners of the Ovenden line, also became joint owners of the High Level line, even though it was of little use to the LYR. Indeed, it soon became of little value to the GNR too, as a convenient tram service was introduced between the High Level and LYR stations. It was unfortunate that the two companies failed to join forces in the interests of killing off the wasteful High Level scheme.

5.7.7. Vale of Towy Railway

The LNWR was not an expansion-minded railway like the MR, GNR, and GCR. It dominated railway provision in some of the most prosperous areas of the country and had possessed a trunk line connection to London from the outset. It devoted most of its effort to keeping other companies out of the areas it controlled rather than diversifying into less profitable ones. Nevertheless, there were certain areas that attracted its attention, and the South Wales coalfield was one of them. Its joint ownership of the Shrewsbury and Hereford line, connecting with its wholly owned line from Shrewsbury to Crewe, provided an important north–south link between two major industrial areas. From Craven Arms, between Shrewsbury and Hereford, the company had been promoting local lines that led in the direction of Swansea—a major South Wales port and metal-refining centre. When the line from Craven Arms, later known as the Central Wales line, reached Llandovery in 1868, it met up with the Towy Railway, whose line proceeded south to Llandeilo, where it connected with the Llanelli Railway. Up to this point the Llanelli Railway had effective control of the Towy Railway, as it was the only outlet for its traffic and held a short-term lease on it.

The Llanelli Railway was a local concern with a complex and sophisticated financial structure but weak management. It was one of several small South Wales concerns that the LNWR had cultivated in the past. Recognizing that the GWR's broad gauge main line through South Wales was incompatible with the standard gauge adopted by most of the local companies, the LNWR saw itself as a potential patron of these smaller companies—even if they did not see matters quite the same way themselves. It believed that it could perform an important service for these companies by connecting up their lines with each other and by giving them a better outlet for their traffic to the north. The GWR South Wales main line ran east–west, and traffic consigned to the north from the Swansea area by the GWR had first to go east to Newport or Pontypool. The Central Wales line was the direct connection that they needed.

The Llanelli management understood well that connecting up with the Central Wales line would bring additional traffic, and in anticipation of this they had built lines from Llandeilo to Swansea and to Carmarthen, the latter providing connections via the broad gauge for west Wales and the Irish Sea ports. Each of these two new lines was associated with a separate capital account. Although the LNWR was willing to finance these lines, the Llanelli company had employed independent contractors who, partly as a consequence of the Overend Gurney banking crisis of 1866, got into financial difficulties.

The date of the LNWR's arrival in Llandovery was also the date that the Llanelli company's lease of the Vale of Towy line expired. When the lease was renewed the LNWR and Llanelli became partners—an appropriate arrangement since the Llanelli made connection at one end of the line and the LNWR now made connection at the other. The near-bankrupt Llanelli also sold the LNWR running powers over its system, giving the LNWR access to Swansea, Carmarthen, and Llanelli at one go. The financial affairs of the company deteriorated further, however, and when it attempted to repudiate the running powers offered to the LNWR, Parliament intervened. In 1871 the company was effectively broken up along the lines indicated by its capital structure, with the LNWR taking the lines it most needed—to Swansea and Carmarthen—and the remainder of the system being acquired by the GWR in 1873. In this way the LNWR and GWR became partners in the Vale of Towy line.

5.8. DEFRAGMENTATION OF OWNERSHIP

5.8.1. Cheltenham and Gloucester Joint Line (GWR and MR)

The 6 miles of trunk line between Cheltenham and Gloucester was originally constructed by two companies that expected to work together and even to merge. But one of these companies was unexpectedly taken over by a rival of the other, and as neither of the rivals was willing to sell out to the other they continued as 'partners' in the line.

Cheltenham was a very fashionable Regency spa—similar to Bath and Leamington—and by the 1830s had become a large and prosperous town. Gloucester was an important port on the River Severn handling manufacturing exports from the Midlands, and was well served by canals. The wealthy elites of Cheltenham and Gloucester quickly developed an interest in railways, stimulated in part by the promotion of the GWR main line to Bristol which ran some 20 miles to the south. The Cheltenham and Great Western Union Railway (CGWUR) was promoted to link Cheltenham and Gloucester to the GWR at Swindon (opened throughout in 1845). Meanwhile, the Birmingham and Gloucester Railway was being promoted, following a similar alignment between Cheltenham and Gloucester (opened in 1840). South of Gloucester, the Bristol and Gloucester (opened in 1844) completed a triangle of lines whose base was the GWR Swindon–Bristol line, and whose east side was the CGWUR line.

The success of the Liverpool and Manchester Railway had convinced many canal and horse-tramway proprietors that their own technology had become obsolete, and so they were usually happy to sell out to railways that could make use of their routes. The CGWUR was able to acquire an old tramway that connected quarries near Cheltenham with the port of Gloucester. The Birmingham and Gloucester also had its eye on the tramway, and so the two companies agreed to joint construction of the new line. The CGWUR was to build the line and then sell half to the Birmingham company, but if construction was delayed then, to ensure timely completion, the Birmingham company would build the line instead and sell half to the CGWUR—which is what actually happened. The Bristol and Gloucester was meanwhile converting another tramway near Bristol, but with simpler arrangements.

The CGWUR was acquired by the GWR in 1843. The GWR was already operating the Swindon end of the line, opened in 1841, and the company was short of funds to complete the section into Gloucester. The Birmingham and Bristol companies were also interested in selling to the GWR. The GWR thought that it could drive a hard bargain with the Bristol company, however; it already owned two sides of the triangle with its routes to Swindon and it told the Bristol company that the third side of the triangle was consequently of little value to it. The Bristol company, however, considered that the notion of routing Gloucester to Bristol traffic via Swindon was absurd, and the Birmingham company, which was planning to consign through traffic from Birmingham to Bristol, does not seem to have been too impressed with the idea either.

In addition, the Birmingham and Bristol companies were aware that ownership by the GWR would imply operation on the broad gauge. However, Robert Stephenson's trunk line from London had reached Birmingham in 1838, and the standard gauge had since become the norm in the West Midlands, where most of their traffic would originate. In particular, the MR served Birmingham with a standard gauge line from Leeds via Derby, opened in 1842, and a continuation of this route from Birmingham to Bristol via Gloucester was an attractive proposition. Thus when the MR approached the two companies they accepted its offer with alacrity. Thus in 1845 the MR acquired, at a stroke, a through route from Leeds to Bristol and the GWR had, by over-playing its hand, allowed a major rival into the heart of its territory.

The Cheltenham–Gloucester route was now a vital link in the systems of two major rivals operating on two different gauges. Neither could afford to relinquish its stake in the line. It was therefore operated as a mixed gauge trunk line between two 'partners' whose interests were diametrically opposed—although each company continued to own its own tracks.

5.9. FEEDING INTO COMPETING LOCAL SYSTEMS

5.9.1. Weymouth and Portland Railway and Easton and Church Hope Railway (GWR and LSWR)

The Isle of Portland, in the English Channel, is connected to the mainland by a causeway to the port of Weymouth, Dorset. At the end of the eighteenth century

Weymouth was a fashionable seaside resort, patronized by royalty, although its popularity declined with the rise of Brighton, which was much nearer London. While Brighton obtained railway communication in 1841, Weymouth had to wait until 1857—and then two railways arrived at once. Both railways had been authorized at the time of the Railway Mania and had taken an inordinate time to complete. Weymouth was at the extremity of both, and was therefore the last town to be reached.

The Wilts Somerset and Weymouth Railway was a GWR protégé. It ran south from Chippenham, on the GWR main line, through Westbury, Frome, Yeovil, and Dorchester to Weymouth. Chippenham provided connections for both London (to the east) and Bristol (to the west), although both journeys were somewhat indirect. The Southampton and Dorchester was a LSWR protégé. It connected with the GWR Weymouth line at Dorchester, and had running powers over the GWR into Weymouth. It reached Dorchester in 1847 through Ringwood, Wimborne, and Wareham, with a short branch to Poole. It was not until 1857 that a through connection was made to Weymouth by running powers over the GWR line. The distance from Weymouth to London via the LSWR to Southampton was far shorter than the equivalent journey via the GWR.

The GWR and LSWR were enemies, as were most large companies serving neighbouring territories. However, the GWR seems to have had more enemies than most other companies. Part of this was a legacy of the gauge controversy which had isolated the GWR. But the GWR had played the gauge controversy to its advantage by arguing that only broad gauge branches should be built in broad gauge territory, and had thereby acquired a high degree of local monopoly which it was anxious to defend. It also had a large (if sparsely populated) territory which meant that it bordered on many different companies, rather than just on one or two companies as was normally the case.

As a highly skilled protagonist the GWR planned to make the most of its monopoly of lines in the Weymouth area. But the civic authorities were adamant that they wanted both the GWR and the LSWR to compete for traffic on equal terms. The GWR and the LSWR were already fighting over traffic elsewhere, and the residents of Weymouth seem to have wanted similar benefits from competition for themselves. The decline of Weymouth meant that there was not a huge amount of traffic to fight over, and so the two companies agreed to work together and share the use of the GWR station at Weymouth, although they maintained separate stations in Dorchester.

The Isle of Portland is famous for its stone, and well before the railways arrived in Weymouth there were two rope-hauled tramways on the island—the Merchants Railway and the Admiralty Railway—which brought stone down from the hills to the coast. Portland also has a prison and naval facilities. When a local scheme—the Weymouth and Portland Railway—was promoted, a major objective was to connect with both the main line networks, to ensure competition in long-distance traffic, and so both business and naval interests wanted the two companies to operate the connection jointly. As the GWR was broad gauge and the LSWR standard gauge, this required mixed gauge track. Although the two companies agreed to this, a squabble over the station at Weymouth, involving both the companies and the local promoters, delayed the opening until 1865. Furthermore, Board of Trade inspectors required the companies to install add-itional facilities so that each could operate their own trains independently of the other if they should fall out permanently.

Unlike the Weymouth and Portland Railway, the Easton and Church Hope Railway was never intended to be connected to the rest of the system. It was originally planned around a rope-hauled incline, but this was subsequently abandoned and a connection with the other railway substituted. Initial proposals were published in 1867, and it took 35 years and numerous 'rethinks' before these bore fruit. Just before the railway was opened in 1902 the GWR and LSWR took a joint lease so that it could be operated as an integral part of the Portland railway system. The establishment of this integrated joint venture owed much to lobbying by local interests and in particular to the power of the Admiralty which, as an important local customer with influence in government, was able to force the reluctant companies to cooperate.

5.9.2. Clifton Extension Railway and the Bristol Port and Pier Lines (GWR and MR)

This short line ran from Montpelier, a suburb of Bristol, through Clifton, to the port of Avonmouth, 8 miles down the River Avon from Bristol. There was a steeply graded branch from Sea Mills, south of Avonmouth, to the riverside at Hotwells, near Bristol Docks. At Montpelier the line divided, with one spur connecting to the GWR at Stapleton Road and the other to the MR at Fishponds.

Superficially this connecting line represents a joint venture by two companies to develop passenger traffic to the exclusive suburb of Clifton and to develop freight traffic to the new port of Avonmouth. Clifton was the preferred residence of Bristol's mercantile elite, and the new port of Avonmouth was their belated response to the silting up of the river close to the city. As usual with joint lines, however, this appearance of cooperation is deceptive.

By 1851 it had become clear that Brunel's broad-gauge line to London was not going to be sufficient to reverse Bristol's declining fortunes. Bristol would never become a transatlantic passenger port in competition with Liverpool unless the silting problem was finally addressed. But the citizens could not agree on the best response: to canalize the river, or to build a new port on the estuary. Nor could they agree where a new port should be built: one faction favoured Portishead on the south bank, while the other favoured Avonmouth on the opposite bank. Eventually both of these new ports were built, although neither was a great success at that time.

The Avonmouth faction built the Bristol Port and Pier Railway from Avonmouth to Hotwells, opened in 1865. It was initially unconnected with the national railway system—it simply brought goods downstream from Avonmouth to the site of the original port at Hotwells—at the bottom of the Avon Gorge and about 2 miles from the GWR Temple Meads station. Overlooking Hotwells from the top of the Gorge was Clifton.

Linking Hotwells and Temple Meads would mean driving a railway through the heart of the city, with consequent destruction of valuable property. Schemes of this type were promoted on the grounds that the GWR terminus could be relocated closer to the city centre. A cheaper and less disruptive option, however, was to tunnel through Clifton Down, from Sea Mills on the Port and Pier Railway to junctions with the GWR and MR networks to the east of the city centre. This would provide the residents of Clifton with a rail link to Temple Meads via the GWR and also with access to Bath via the MR.

The proposal for the Clifton Extension Railway was approved by Parliament in 1871. It was opened as far as Clifton Down in 1874, but thereafter progress stalled. Insufficient funds were available to complete the line through to Sea Mills—presumably the wealthy residents of Clifton lost interest once their own requirements had been met. The promoters appealed for capital to the GWR and MR jointly. Neither of the companies was particularly enthusiastic; both already served neighbouring ports—the MR at Gloucester and Sharpness, and the GWR at Lydney, Newport, and Cardiff. However, each seems to have feared what the other might do if left to its own devices, and so each invested as a means of monitoring and constraining its rival. They needed to hedge their bets in case Avonmouth became a successful port.

A passenger service from Bristol to Clifton and Avonmouth finally commenced in 1885 after numerous engineering and safety problems had been overcome, and joint ownership was effected in 1890. The GWR and MR operated independent services, as often happened on joint lines, with the GWR concentrating on Bristol traffic and the MR on traffic to Bath. The steep grades and sharp curves made the line unsuitable for heavy freight traffic, however, and once the Severn Tunnel had been competed the GWR found it easier to serve Avonmouth by an alternative route, opened in 1900 (with a cut-off built in 1910). This relegated the Clifton line to a suburban passenger role, which it maintains to this day.

5.10. URBAN FREIGHT LINES

In most large cities there was a need to transfer freight from one company's network to another's. Most trunk lines entering major cities were served by their own termini, and passengers seeking to make through journeys were left to make their own way between termini by foot or cab. But the same treatment could not be given to freight.

Long-distance cross-country freight could be handled by running trains from a hub on one company's network to a hub on another company's network. However, where freight needed to be distributed to a suburb on the other side of a city to the terminus and served by another company's system, a local cross-city link was required. Such links could also be used to transfer long-distance traffic between different systems too.

Where several different companies served the same city, an orbital freight line connecting all the converging lines would benefit all the companies. Such a line might not be economic for any single company to build, however, unless it could rely upon traffic generated by the other companies. The easiest way to secure this traffic, and to prevent the construction of competing lines, was for all the companies to share ownership of the line. This was equivalent to a 'forward purchase' by all the companies of their rights to use the line in future.

Given the lack of central organization in inter-company cooperation (with the exception of the routine matters handled by the Railway Clearing House), the onus normally lay with the company that had the greatest need for the line (as the originator of the largest amount of traffic) to make a deal with a sufficient number of companies to guarantee the viability of the new line. Once the line had been jointly built, other companies could be allowed to use the link at ordinary commercial rates. In this way the railways were able to provide intra-urban freight links as industry-specific 'public goods', while maintaining their competitive stance over other issues.

This seems to explain a common (though not universal) feature of joint urban freight lines—namely that the lines were owned by the companies that generated the traffic rather than the companies through whose territories they passed. Thus where trunk lines fed traffic into a centre city for distribution by a local company it was usually the feeder companies that jointly own the freight line rather than the local company that received the traffic.

5.10.1. West London Line (LNWR and GWR) and Extension (LNWR, GWR, and LSWR)

The West London (originally known as the Birmingham, Bristol, and Thames Junction Railway) was an independent line built to connect the London and Birmingham at Willesden with the GWR main line at Wormwood Scrubs and to connect them both with the Kensington Canal basin that gave access to the River Thames. Kensington was not so smart a place at that time as it soon became, and the railway emphasis was on freight traffic (although a basic and rather unreliable passenger service was provided).

The line was opened in 1844 and jointly leased by the London and Birmingham and GWR. At this time the rivalry between them was not so intense as it became once the Birmingham company became part of the LNWR. Relations were still rather cool, however, as the two companies had adopted different gauges and, partly as a consequence of this, had fallen out over a proposal to share the use of Euston station, as a result of which the GWR switched the site of its terminus to Paddington. Nevertheless, the two companies' lines ran very close to each other near Willesden, and both had a strong desire to interchange freight traffic with boats on the Thames. The line was therefore built as dual gauge.

The route was extended in 1863 across the Thames to Clapham Junction, where the lines of the LSWR and LBSCR ran through different sides of the station. The LSWR and LBSCR both took one-sixth of the shares in the extension, with the LNWR and GWR taking one-third each. By this time much of the GWR system was dual gauge. A good deal of coal traffic originated on the LNWR and the GWR, while the LSWR and LBSCR served a large area of south London where both the domestic and industrial demand for coal was high. There was also a suburban service, which for a time offered passengers from the north and west access to Victoria and Waterloo stations as well as to Euston and Paddington.

5.10.2. North and South Western Junction Railway (MR, LNWR, and NLR)

The North and South Western Junction Railway (NSWJR) was an independent line opened in 1853 to connect the LSWR Hounslow loop line at Kew, west London, to the LNWR at Willesden Junction, north of its Euston terminus. Beyond Willesden, access was available to London Docks via a junction between the LNWR main line and the North London Railway (NLR) at Camden. Originally known as the East and West India Dock and Birmingham Junction Railway, the NLR was a prosperous line that carried a large volume of export freight from the Midlands and north. The LSWR served mainly rural areas, however, and does not seem to have made much use of the line.

In the 1860s the NLR spotted the potential of the NSWJR as a commuter route linking the fashionable town of Richmond-on-Thames to the City, which was conveniently served by the NLR's Broad Street station (adjacent to Liverpool Street station, and now closed). The spare capacity of the line (opened in 1869) could be absorbed by the conveyance of wealthy bankers from the sylvan surroundings of Richmond to the bustle and smoke of the City.

The line's fortunes had already been boosted the previous year when the London Extension of the MR was completed. The MR generated enormous flows of coal traffic, and also of Burton beer, both of which required distribution throughout the London suburbs. As soon as it arrived in London the MR opened the Dudding Hill loop from near its freight yards at Cricklewood to the LNWR at Acton Wells. After a shaky start, the NSWJR had become of great strategic importance to the big companies. In 1871 the three companies jointly leased the line, probably to ensure that none of them would be able to monopolize the route in future. The emphasis switched from passengers to freight and, under new management, the line began to fulfil the aspirations of its original promoters.

5.10.3. Tottenham and Hampstead Joint Committee (MR/GER)

The Tottenham and Hampstead Junction Railway, opened in 1868, ran from the MR London Extension at Kentish Town, just north of its St. Pancras terminus, through Harringay (where it connected with the GNR main line) to a junction with the GER at Tottenham. It also connected with the LNWR at Gospel Oak, near Kentish Town (opened 1888). The main line was opened in the same year as the MR London Extension, and allowed south-bound freight from the Midlands to access East London. A spur was added at Tottenham which gave access to London Docks via Stratford. The railway also gave both the GER and the GNR access to North-west London. It became a joint line in 1902.

5.10.4. Tottenham and Forest Gate Railway (MR and LTS)

The MR orbital distribution system in north London, comprising the wholly owned Dudding Hill loop and the jointly owned Tottenham and Hampstead Railway, was completed by the Tottenham and Forest Gate Railway, opened in 1894. This railway extended the Hampstead joint line from Tottenham to Woodgrange Park, near Barking, on the London Tilbury and Southend Railway's (LTS) branch from Forest Gate. This branch made a triangular junction with the LTS main line at Barking, allowing freight traffic to reach both London Docks and Tilbury Docks. The LTS was a small independent system that operated an intensive suburban passenger service. It developed a close relationship with the MR and was eventually acquired by that company in 1912.

Given that the MR generated most of the traffic over both the Hampstead and Forest Gate lines, its motive for sharing ownership appears to have been to maintain cordial relations with the companies whose territories it was 'invading'. Although these companies were generally pleased to handle the additional traffic brought by the MR, they may have been suspicious about whether the MR intended to extend its influence in their area. In fact, as noted above, the MR did indeed succeed in reaching Tilbury and Southend, though by amicable acquisition rather than by building a competing line.

5.10.5. Manchester South Junction and Altrincham Railway (LNWR and GCR)

While the previous freight lines were London-based, the MSJAR was a Manchester-based concern. It began life as an urban freight link, but quickly transformed itself into a suburban passenger railway. This was because its main line, built to carry freight, was soon eclipsed by a branch that was designed to carry passengers.

The MSJAR was an early joint venture, promoted in the 1840s by two companies—the Manchester and Birmingham and the Sheffield, Ashton-under-Lyne, and Manchester—who shared the use of a Manchester station. They need to transfer traffic to the Liverpool and Manchester Railway to reach Liverpool. The Liverpool company had a separate station; and while passengers could be left to make their own way across the city, freight required a connecting line. There were plans to link the Manchester and Leeds line with the Liverpool line, and the Sheffield company was keen to build a similar link in order to maintain its competitive position in handling Yorkshire traffic.

The two companies built a short line from the east end of their joint station, through the Knott Mill area of Manchester, to Ordsall Lane, Salford, just west of the Liverpool company's terminus. An opportunity also arose to build a branch from Knott Mill to the market town of Altrincham, south-west of Manchester. Lord Egerton, whose family owned the Bridgewater Canal, was anxious, like many canal proprietors, to switch out of canals into railways. Freight traffic on the Bridgewater Canal had switched to the Liverpool railway—as was foreseen at the time that the railway had been built—but the canal operated a profitable passenger-carrying fly-boat service. It was agreed that Lord Egerton would make available land for the railway, and restrict competition from the fly-boat service, and in return receive shares in the MSJAR. Both the freight line and the passenger branch were opened in 1849.

When the Manchester and Birmingham was merged into the LNWR, and the Sheffield company was merged into the Manchester Sheffield and Lincolnshire Railway (which later became the GCR), the two partners in the MSJAR became rivals. As a result, the Altrincham branch acquired greater strategic significance than the original connecting line. The LNWR controlled the area to the south and west of Manchester, and the GCR decided to invade this area. It extended the Altrincham branch through Northwich to Chester (in partnership with the MR and GNR), and then built further extensions from Chester to Wrexham and Birkenhead (as noted in Section 5.3.2). The LNWR did its best to pre-empt further expansion by the GCR by operating a link from Timperley through Warrington to Ditton Junction, near Liverpool, but this did not prevent the GCR from eventually reaching Liverpool, although (with its partners) it was forced to build its own main line all the way from Manchester to Liverpool to do so. This illustrates the way that a joint line initially built for cooperative reasons could eventually become a strategic weapon in inter-company rivalry.

5.10.6. Oldham Ashton and Guide Bridge Junction Railway (LNWR and GCR)

The Oldham Ashton and Guide Bridge Junction Railway (OAGBJR) was another Manchester concern, jointly owned by the same two companies. The LNWR knew that the GCR had designs on its territory around Manchester, but was willing to cooperate with the GCR because they had a common rival in Oldham—the LYR. The two companies already shared the use of other lines in the area, for the LNWR exercised running powers over the GCR to connect its line from Stalybridge to Leeds with its network around Stockport and Manchester.

Oldham was a major centre of cotton textile manufacturing, and generated an enormous volume of freight traffic. The LNWR had reached Oldham in 1856 by a branch from Greenfield, to the east of Oldham on its line from Stalybridge to

Leeds, but it had no access from the south. The GCR had no access at all, even though its own main line from Manchester to Sheffield passed through Guide Bridge, only a few miles south of Oldham. An LNWR line from Stockport had reached Guide Bridge in 1849, and so a line built north from Guide Bridge would meet the requirements of both the GCR and the LNWR. The line made an end-on junction with the LNWR's Greenfield line at Clegg Street station, Oldham, thereby placing Oldham conveniently on a loop from the Stalybridge to Greenfield section of the line from Manchester to Leeds. It was opened in 1861 and leased to the two companies in 1862.

Since it is unlikely that Parliament would have approved separate lines for each company into Oldham, joint ownership avoided an expensive Parliamentary contest, and reduced the risk of a stalemate in which no new line was built at all. It also allowed these two mutually suspicious companies to keep a watchful eye on each other's operations in the Manchester area.

5.10.7. The Methley Joint Line (GNR, LYR, and NER)

This line allowed the growing GNR network around Wakefield and Leeds to tap into the existing LYR and NER networks in the area. It was a short line of 5 miles, which made a triangular junction with the GNR main line from Doncaster to Leeds just north of Wakefield, and ran due east to Methley, where it forked to join the NER line to Castlefield and York and the LYR line to Knottingley and Goole. It was opened in 1865.

It facilitated the interchange of local freight traffic between the GNR and the other two companies. The GNR also used the line for local passenger connections from Leeds and Wakefield to the NER at Castleford, where passengers could join NER trains from Normanton to York. So far as the NER and LYR were concerned, the line appears to have been a 'boundary marker', their joint ownership with the GNR signalling that they did not expect the GNR to expand any further to the north and east of its Leeds to Doncaster line, and in this respect the line proved successful.

5.11. LOCAL COALFIELD LINES

Two main groups of lines are discussed below: lines in South Yorkshire and lines in South Wales. A couple of local schemes elsewhere in the country are also noted.

5.11.1.   South Yorkshire Coalfield: Rationalization to avoid Duplication

Great Central and *Midland Joint Committee* (GCR and MR)
South Yorkshire Joint Line (GCR, GNR, MR, LYR, and NER)
Great Central, Hull and *Barnsley and Midland Joint Line* (GCR, HBR, and MR)

Great Central and Hull and *Barnsley Joint Line* (GCR and HBR)
Axholme Joint Committee (NER and LYR)

The early development of coalfields was a highly competitive affair, and many of the first coalfields opened up by railways—such as the Cardiff Valleys—had many duplicating lines. The South Yorkshire coalfield was one of the later coalfields to be developed, and by that time there were already a number of established railway companies operating in the area. If they had all built their own colliery lines then excessive duplication would have occurred. By this time, however, railway companies had learned to appreciate some of the benefits of cooperation—not least the economy of capital expenditure involved. Thus many of the joint coalfield lines are found in the coalfield areas that were among the last to be developed.

Nevertheless, cooperation in these fields was not always fully inclusive. While in some schemes all the railways with interests in the area cooperated on an equal footing, in other cases a dominant railway would attempt to exclude others from its area, and some of those excluded would then collude with each other to invade its territory.

Even before the development of the coalfield, South Yorkshire was well served by railways. It strategic inland position had turned it into a 'railway cross roads', with a range of hubs including Doncaster, Wakefield, Normanton, and Knottingley. Some of the lines were built to serve the great industrial centres of Leeds and Sheffield, while others connected more distant centres, such as London, Manchester, and Newcastle. The MR main line from Sheffield to Leeds via Normanton followed a north–south orientation along its western edge, while the GNR main line from Doncaster to Leeds was oriented north-west to south-east along the top edge. The GCR main line from Sheffield to Grimsby via Retford followed a similar orientation along the bottom edge, while the GNR East Coast main line between Retford and Doncaster formed the right-hand edge.

The NER had access to Leeds, Castleford, and Doncaster along the northern edge that was patrolled by the GNR, while the LYR cut across the middle through Wakefield with its east–west line from Manchester to Goole. A latecomer—the Hull and Barnsley Railway (HBR)—penetrated the area with three prongs, emanating from a junction near Kirk Smeaton just north of the GNR Doncaster to Leeds main line.

By the 1890s many of the best seams in the early British coalfields had been exhausted, but demand for coal remained high, and so deeper mines producing inferior coal became economic. Yorkshire industrialists had begun to exploit opportunities in the Sheffield–Doncaster–Retford triangle, and they were anxious for new colliery railways to be built. If the railway companies did not build them then they would build them themselves, as had often happened in the past. A rash of competitive lines connecting to different companies' systems would prove expensive for the railway companies, particularly at a time when many of them were already committed to major capital expenditure in upgrading their trunk lines. The urban freight lines that had been constructed around London (see Section 5.10) provided a suitable model for a cooperative solution to the problem. The main question was whether the railway companies would combine on the basis of rival teams or on an inclusive basis. The answer turned out to be a mixture of the two.

The epicentre of mining activity was Tickhill, between Doncaster and Worksop. The GCR was quick off the mark, persuading some of the key mining interests to support a scheme for a short branch from Shireoaks, near Worksop, to Dinnington and Laughton, south of Tickhill. The GCR brought in the MR as a partner. The MR had a branch from Worksop to Mansfield and Nottingham which could handle traffic for the Midlands and the south, leaving the GCR to handle the export traffic to the Humber ports. The GCR and MR already had a good understanding, being partners in the CLC (see Section 5.3.2). The line was opened in 1905.

The GNR, LYR, and NER also wanted a share of the traffic, however. In 1902 the LYR and NER jointly acquired the recently constructed Axholme Light Railway, which ran from the port of Goole (which both companies served) south to Haxey. This line had the potential to be extended south-west to Tickhill.

The HBR was also interested in the new coalfield. The HBR was 'the new kid on the block', and enjoyed the support of local industrialists because it had successfully challenged the NER's rail monopoly at Hull. The five established companies—the GCR, MR, GNR, LYR, and NER—therefore joined forces to block the HBR. They promoted the South Yorkshire Joint Line, which entered the coalfield from the north-east, via a junction with another GCR line near Thorne, where a number of routes converged. This provided a direct route to Hull for the LYR and NER, who then, as a result, lost interest in extending the Axhome Joint. It was opened in 1909.

The GCR and the MR seem to have believed, however, that it would prove impossible to keep out the HBR indefinitely, as the LYR and NER would have wished. The GCR and MR therefore decided to gain an advantage over their other partners by joining forces with the HBR as well. A new joint line of 4 miles was built from the original joint line at Laughton to Ravenfield, and thence, via a junction with a GCR–MR joint line, to junctions with the GCR and MR lines at Kilnhurst. This line was also opened in 1909.

Finally, the GCR decided to 'go it alone' and partner with the HBR without the involvement of the MR. It promoted a new 23-mile line from the GCR–MR joint line to the HBR main line near Snaith. This line was not opened until 1916. In effect, therefore, the GCR managed to achieve a dominant position in the coalfield by promoting four different lines with different sets of parties. By bringing the LYR and NER into one scheme and the HBR into two of the others it managed to dissuade them from building independent lines. It used as its main partner a local company—the MR—that had no direct access to a local port and was therefore not a direct competitor for local traffic. It avoided partnerships that involved direct enemies, such as the NER and the HBR, although its old rivals the GNR and LYR were partners in the most comprehensive of the schemes. The GCR generated so much additional traffic that it was able to finance a major development at Immingham Docks on the Humber estuary, thereby diverting much of the coal export traffic from Hull. It was also able to consign coal direct to London over its new London extension, opened in 1900, providing perhaps the only profitable traffic over this expensive route.

Joint developments on the South Yorkshire coalfield continued into the inter-war period, but lie outside the scope of this study.

5.11.2.   South Wales Coalfield: Joint Invasions, and Boundary Markers between Small Established Companies and Large Invaders.

The early coal industry of South Wales was established around places where coal outcropped on the steep valley sides. In contrast to the South Yorkshire coalfield, which was relatively flat, the South Wales coalfield was hilly, with valleys running southwards from the Brecon Beacons mountain range down to the Severn Channel ports around Newport, Cardiff, Neath, and Swansea. There was also a great deal of metallic ore in the area, which led to the development of metal refining industries that provided a local use for the coal. But when these mineral ores were depleted the emphasis changed to the export of coal. Some of the valleys produced top-grade steam coal, particularly suited for steamships, and much of this coal was exported to bunkering stations around the British Empire.

Horse-drawn tramways were well-established in South Wales by 1800, and were progressively converted into railways from 1830. Many of the railways up the valleys were independent concerns, and most remained independent until incorporated into the GWR at the Grouping of 1922–3. When the main trunk railways arrived in South Wales they naturally wished to tap into the coal traffic, and this led to tensions with the established local companies, such as the Taff Vale Railway (TVR) and the Rhymney Railway (RR). The Cardiff valleys in particular were targeted by the main line companies; they were nearest to London and the industrial Midlands and provided the best quality steam coal. The GWR entered the area from the east through its protégé the South Wales Railway (opened to Swansea in 1850), while the LNWR entered from the north in the 1860s, reaching Brynmawr in 1862. Although the LNWR and the GWR were rivals on many different frontiers (as explained above) it was their separate rivalries with the established independent companies that triggered joint ownership of lines in the South Wales coalfield. As a result, most of the joint lines were 'boundary markers' in which an established (often local) railway allowed an invader to enter so far—but no further—into their territory.

5.11.2.1. *Nantybwch and Rhymney Joint Line (LNWR and RR)*

Brunel's South Wales Railway was built on the broad gauge in order to integrate with the rest of the GWR system, but it was generally regarded as being poorly adapted to the carriage of coal. Broad gauge wagons were too large for a typical consignment of coal, while the track was too wide to permit the sharp curves required for contour-following railways in hilly country. Indeed, before building the GWR, Brunel had engineered the TVR from Cardiff to Merthyr on the standard gauge for precisely this reason. Standard gauge companies such as the LNWR were convinced that they could 'clean up' the market for the export of coal to other parts of Britain if only they could gain access to the area.

One of the LNWR's constituent companies—the London and Birmingham—had been involved in a Railway Mania scheme—the Welsh Midland—to link Birmingham with Swansea via Worcester, Hereford, and Brecon. The LNWR itself developed an interest in the Newport Abergavenny and Hereford Railway (NAHR, opened in 1853), which built a branch from its main line near Pontypool to Quakers Yard, north of Cardiff (opened in 1858). This branch was subsequently extended to Aberdare and Neath (reached in 1864). But the LNWR failed to support its associate when it was short of funds, and the company was acquired by the GWR instead. To retrieve the situation the LNWR then sponsored the Merthyr Tredegar and Abergavenny Railway, which ran westwards from the NAHR at Abergavenny, parallel to, and north of, the Quakers Yard line, along the heads of the valleys. By the time that the railway reached Nantybwch in 1864, rival schemes had emerged to challenge the company's entry into Merthyr. Nantybwch, however, was near the head of the Rhymney valley, down which ran the RR's line to Cardiff. If the LNWR could do a deal with the RR then it could reach Cardiff, and all the coal and iron destined for the industrial Midlands and north could be consigned from Cardiff by standard gauge. Instead of flowing down the valley to the GWR it would flow up the valley to the LNWR.

The RR, though small, was a sophisticated company with a head office in London, and it drove a hard bargain with the LNWR. To protect its interests, it insisted that the connection between the two systems at the head of the Rhymney valley was built as a joint line (completed in 1871). This proved to be an astute move, for a portion of the joint line subsequently became part of the through line to Merthyr (opened throughout in 1879).

The RR did not have matters all its own way, however. To increase its options, and strengthen its bargaining position, the LNWR also formed a partnership with the Brecon and Merthyr (BMR)—the RR's great rival. The LNWR also acquired a competing line down the adjacent Sirhowy Valley to Nine Mile Point, which gave access to Newport by running powers (opened in 1863 and acquired in 1875). In this way it steadily eroded the RR's bargaining power.

5.11.2.2. Brecon and Merthyr and LNWR Joint Line (BMR and LNWR)

Merthyr was one of the oldest, and certainly the greatest, of the mining and industrial towns of South Wales. Deposits of coal and iron were located side-by-side, making it a natural centre for iron production. Devoid of major public buildings, and lacking social infrastructure, Merthyr was a relatively lawless place with a transitory population. Except for the Crawshays, most of the industrial dynasties who made their money in Merthyr lived elsewhere, away from the smoke and noise. Indeed, much of the capital invested in Merthyr (as in South Wales generally) came from London.

The TVR, completed in 1841, was the first modern railway to enter Merthyr, and it chose the easiest route up the Taff Valley from Cardiff through Pontypridd. The LNWR and BMR were relative latecomers, arriving in the 1860s, and had to use alternative routes. The LNWR was heading slowly west towards Merthyr from Abergavenny, while the BMR was heading slowly south from a junction with the Mid-Wales Railway at Talyllyn Junction, near Brecon. It had a grand design to link Newport and Cardiff with the industrial Midlands and north through Mid-Wales. Its proposed route from Newport lay along the Rhymney Valley—which made the Rhymney Railway, which already served the valley, a natural enemy—and over the Brecon Beacons to Talyllyn Junction and Llanidloes. Merthyr was to be served by a branch from Pontstycill Junction, to the north-east, but because of the hilly terrain the branch would circle round Merthyr to the west and enter it from the south.

To begin with the BMR perceived the LNWR as just another enemy, as they both aimed to carry the same traffic. But the BMR was perennially short of money. Until its through route was completed it was reliant on local traffic, and given the mountainous terrain between Brecon and Merthyr, where its construction was focused, there was very little of that. The BMR's greatest asset was that it had parliamentary approval to build into Merthyr whereas the LNWR did not. Given their mutual difficulties in taking on the TVR, it was natural for them to bury their differences and collaborate, with the LNWR using the BMR's route to gain access to Merthyr. The LNWR financed half the cost of the BMR's Merthyr branch from the point at which its own line joined it. Both companies thereby gained access to Merthyr, at the expense of facilitating the other company's access too. Even so, there was continuous friction throughout the process. The joint line was completed in 1868 but it was not until 1879 that the LNWR was able to make full use of it.

5.11.2.3. *Quakers Yard and Merthyr Line and Taff Bargoed Joint Line (GWR and RR)*

These two joint lines in the South Wales valleys ran parallel to each other—one up the Taff Valley from Quakers Yard to Merthyr and the other from Llancaiach up Cwm Bargoed to Dowlais, a centre of the iron industry close to Merthyr. They were both branches from a line originally constructed by the NAHR as a link from Abergavenny to Neath via Quakers Yard. The LNWR was at one time interested in this line as a route to the valleys, but it was eventually acquired by the GWR (see Section 5.11.2.1). The line crossed the main line of the RR at Hengoed, east of Quakers Yard.

Both the GWR and the RR were interested in gaining access to Merthyr and Dowlais—already served by the TVR and the local tramways associated with it. In classic mode, the two aspiring invaders of TVR territory therefore joined forces in order to spread their costs and improve their chances of success in Parliament.

Their 'attack' involved a 'pincer movement' in which two separate lines converged from the south on the Merthyr area.

The Taff Bargoed was the first line to be completed, reaching Dowlais from Llancaiach in 1876. This 9-mile line ran through desolate country that generated little intermediate traffic, but access to Dowlais was the major prize. The Quakers Yard and Merthyr—a mere 6 miles long—was not completed until 1886. For much of its route it ran parallel to the TVR main line, about a mile away on the opposite side of the river—a classic example of the wasteful duplication that was so common in mining areas. The only positive factor is that in the absence of cooperation there might have been three lines up the valley instead of just two!

5.11.2.4. Brynmawr and Western Valleys Line (GWR and LNWR)

This short connection between the systems of two great rivals does not seem to have been regarded by them as being of any great significance. This was because each company had access to another more convenient route nearby by means of which they could achieve their main strategic objectives. It was local pressure that forced the companies into building the railway rather than any strategic imperatives of their own.

The line of just over 1 mile in length ran southwards from Brynmawr on the LNWR 'heads of the valleys' route to Nantyglo, terminus of a GWR branch from Newport. Although the LNWR could have used the route to gain access to the South Wales coast by acquiring running powers over the GWR, it already had access via the RR down an adjoining valley. Similarly, the GWR already had access to the north via its lines to Pontypool. Furthermore there was already a freight link between the two towns that served an important colliery. The line was built mainly to satisfy local demands for an improved passenger service between Brynmawr and Newport. A new line parallel to the colliery lines was therefore built and a passenger service commenced. It began in 1905 and ceased in 1962.

5.11.3. Elsewhere

5.11.3.1. Wrexham and Minera Extension (GWR and LNWR)

This short line gave the LNWR access to the North Wales coalfield at Brymbo, north-east of Wrexham. It also gave the GWR access to Mold, an important town between Chester and Denbigh. It marked the boundary between LNWR territory to the north and GWR territory to the south. The line commenced at Llanfynydd, terminus of a branch from the LNWR Chester to Mold line. This was the most southerly point reached by the LNWR network in the area immediately west of Chester. Opened in 1872, the line ran due south for 3 miles to Brymbo, where it connected with a GWR branch to Wrexham.

5.11.3.2. *Whitehaven Cleator and Egremont (LNWR and FR)*

The Bessemer process for making steel from haematite ore led to a major boom in the Whitehaven district of Cumbria in the 1850s. Whitehaven had long been an important commercial centre, with substantial exports of coal from the local Lowther estates to Dublin, on the opposite shore of the Irish Sea. Abundant local deposits of haematite boosted local industry as the coal was put to use in steel-making. The Whitehaven Cleator and Egremenot was established to support the steel trade. It was essentially an independent concern operating a local freight network, comprising a number of lines opened separately over the period 1856–81. The exhaustion of local coal deposits led to increasing amounts of haematite ore being consigned across the Pennines by rail to the north-east, where it was processed on Teesside and exported to continental Europe. Following the onset of the Great Depression in 1873, financial difficulties arose in the Whitehaven area, and so it was natural for the company to look to larger and better capitalized companies to take it over.

The LNWR was a natural candidate, as one of the country's largest joint stock companies, and the owner of two railways into the Whitehaven area: the Whitehaven Junction (see Section 5.4.5) and the Cockermouth Keswisk and Penrith. The FR, whose main line ran south from Whitehaven to Barrow and Carnforth, had much stronger links with the local business community, however, and consequently better local knowledge. Although the FR had periodic squabbles with the LNWR, relations between the two companies were generally harmonious—for no better reason than that the FR had little option but to 'toe the line'. Not only did the LNWR control the lines leading out from Whitehaven to the north and east, but it also controlled the FR's main outlet (though not the only one) to the south at Carnforth. The two companies took over the line in 1878. They agreed not to act independently, which meant that neither company would use the joint line as a springboard for invading the other's territory.

This joint venture is similar to the type of joint venture found in modern manufacturing industries, whose rationale is to combine complementary resources (in this case local expertise and infrastructure) without full integration of the two companies. It is quite probable that at this time the LNWR would have taken over the FR if Parliament would have allowed it. In this context the joint venture was an effective method of combining the resources of the two companies without the need for a takeover.

5.12. CONCLUSION

The inevitable conclusion from this discussion is that the appearance of cooperation between companies, suggested by the existence of joint lines, was an illusion. It was often mutual suspicion that brought companies together. Partners were often rivals. Joint lines allowed companies to restrict their rival's opportunities for expansion. They also allowed them to monitor their rival's activities. When genuine partnerships were concerned, they were usually formed just to attack some common rival; joint attacks often stood a better chance of success. Partnerships often emerged only after years of rivalry, and even then they sometimes had to be brokered by Parliament, in response to pressure from local civic authorities.

Joint lines were used for expansion. Companies tried to 'break out' of their territories, particularly when they felt 'imprisoned' by the neighbouring lines of rival companies. The GCR and MR both felt imprisoned in the heart of the country and deprived of access to ports and to London. Companies could also feel imprisoned in coastal areas where access to the rest of the country was cut off. The GER felt imprisoned in East Anglia by the GNR, while the LSWR felt imprisoned on the South Coast by the GWR. The feelings of imprisonment were often mutual. Thus while the MR felt imprisoned in the heart of the country and wanted to invade the north coast of East Anglia to develop holiday traffic, the GER felt imprisoned in East Anglia and wanted to expand inland to gain access to coal traffic.

Companies were quite accustomed to competing on one front while cooperating on another. Thus two companies who were rivals in one area could often cooperate quite effectively in some other area. Having a common enemy was a particular bond. There are some cases where rivalries became 'personal' and then cooperation of any kind became difficult so long as the people concerned remained in control of their respective companies. Managerial succession often solved these problems, however. Although shareholders seem to have been impressed with much of the rhetoric of inter-company rivalry, as articulated by the more aggressive general managers, they also became disillusioned when they realized the expense that was involved in implementing aggressive strategies.

Cooperation with other companies was a useful device for sharing costs. It also 'looked good'. Although Parliament was suspicious of cooperation between large companies—especially when it involved mergers—it recognized that cooperation at the local level was often the most appropriate way of avoiding wasteful duplication in the construction of lines. Local towns were aware of the benefits of joint stations as opposed to separate stations for each company: a single station on a convenient site was usually preferable to multiple stations on less convenient sites. In addition, the improved connections afforded by joint stations had the potential to increase through traffic, which in turn could encourage the provision of more frequent services.

ARRIVAL OF CHRISTMAS TRAIN, EASTERN COUNTIES RAILWAY.—DRAWN BY DUNCAN

E.C.R. Nº 23 LUGGAGE VAN

Illustration 1. A busy station scene, *ILN*, 21 December 1850

THE BRITANNIA TUBULAR BRIDGE.—ENTRANCE FROM THE BANGOR SIDE.

Illustration 2. Opening of the Britannia Tubular Bridge across the Menai Strait on the Chester and Holyhead Railway, engineered by Robert Stephenson, *ILN*, 23 March 1850

PNEUMATIC RAILWAY FOR PASSENGERS AT THE CRYSTAL PALACE.—SEE PRECEDING PAGE.

Illustration 3. Beyond the 'Atmospheric System': An experimental pneumatic railway at the Crystal Palace, South London, *ILN*, 10 September 1864

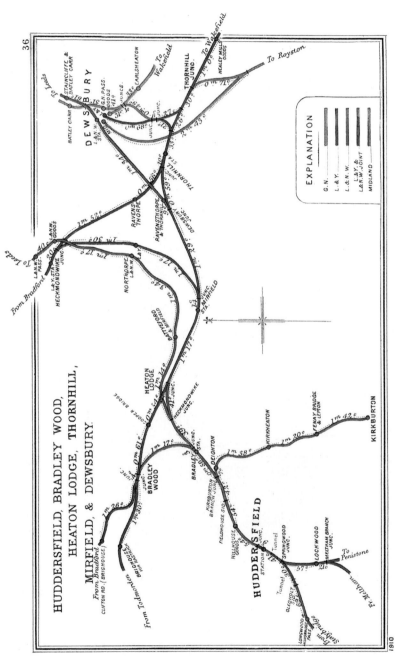

Illustration 4. Duplication of east-west routes in West Yorkshire, as illustrated in Railway Clearing House junction diagrams, 1914

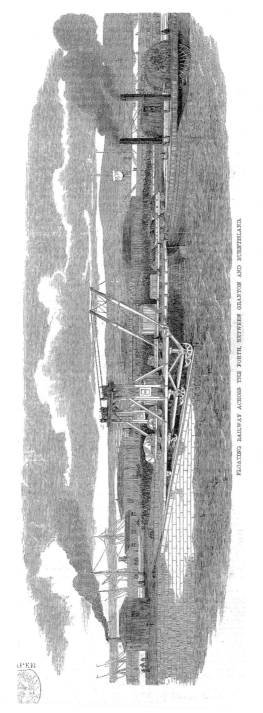

FLOATING RAILWAY ACROSS THE FORTH, BETWEEN GRANTON AND BURNTISLAND.

Illustration 5. Rail ferry north of Edinburgh, serving traffic to Dundee and Aberdeen, *ILN*, 16 February 1850

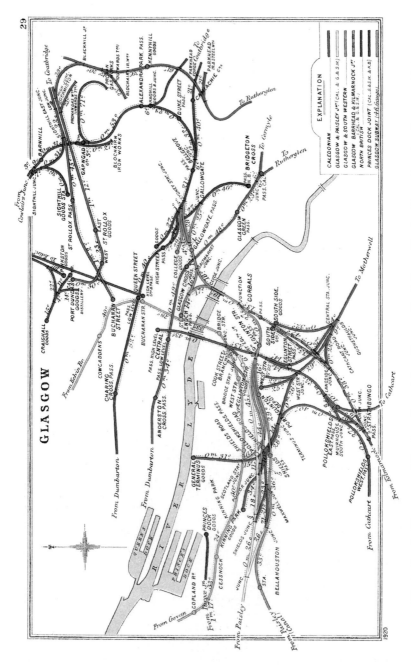

Illustration 6. Glasgow: proliferation of termini, as illustrated in Railway Clearing House junction diagrams, 1914

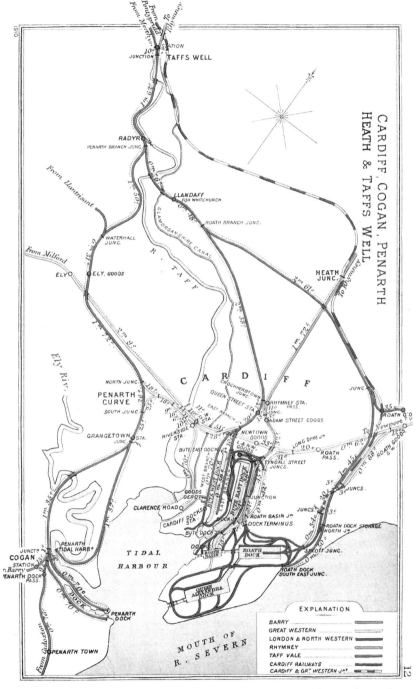

Illustration 7. Cardiff: proliferation of termini in a major port, as illustrated in Railway Clearing House junction diagrams, 1914

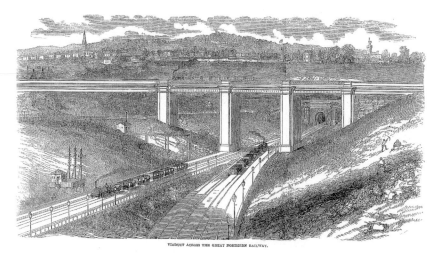

VIADUCT ACROSS THE GREAT NORTHERN RAILWAY.

Illustration 8. The North London Railway line crossing the Great Northern line north of King's Cross station, ILN, 15 November 1851

THE LONDON, CHATHAM, AND DOVER RAILWAY STATION AT BLACKFRIARS.—SEE NEXT PAGE.

Illustration 9. Blackfriars station of the London, Chatham, and Dover Railway on the north bank of the River Thames, *ILN*, 26 December 1863

THE GREAT CENTRAL RAILWAY STATION AT NEWCASTLE-UPON-TYNE.

Illustration 10. Newcastle Central station in 1850 (it is still much the same today), *ILN*, 10 August 1850

DEPOSITS OF RAILWAY PLANS AT THE BOARD OF TRADE.

OFFICE OF THE BOARD OF TRADE.—SCENE ON SUNDAY NIGHT.

Illustration 11. Office of the Railway Department of the Board of Trade at the time of the Railway Mania, *ILN*, 6 December 1845

THE BREAK OF GAUGE AT GLOUCESTER.

PASSENGERS AND LUGGAGE BEING SHIFTED FROM THE BROAD GAUGE TO THE NARROW GAUGE CARRIAGES

Illustration 12. Gloucester: Artist's impression of the inconvenience caused by the Break of Gauge, ILN, 6 June 1846

ARRIVAL OF THE WORKMEN'S PENNY TRAIN AT THE VICTORIA STATION.—SEE PRECEDING PAGE.

Illustration 13. A workmen's train arriving at London Victoria station,
ILN, 22 April 1865

RAILWAY BLOCKADE AT CLIFTON STATION, NEAR MANCHESTER.

Illustration 14. A Railway Battle: Blockade of the line at Clifton Junction, Manchester,
ILN, 24 March 1849

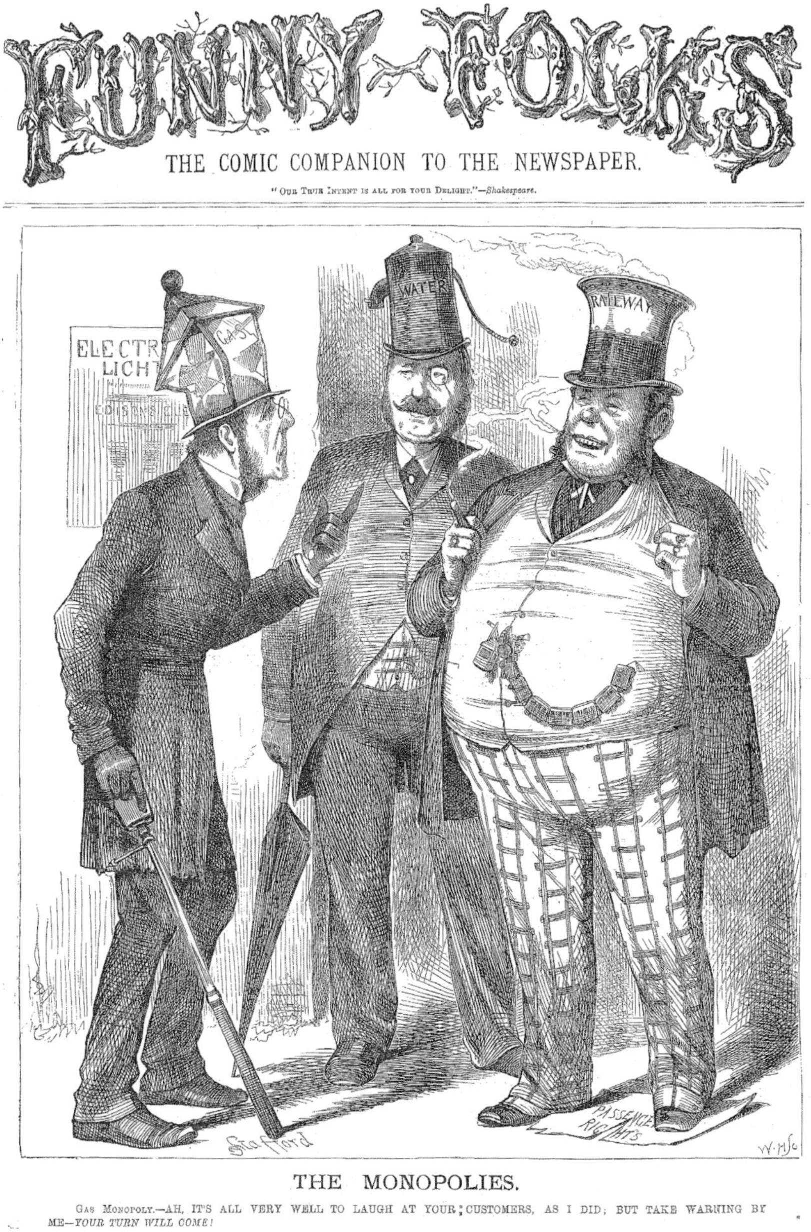
FUNNY FOLKS

THE COMIC COMPANION TO THE NEWSPAPER.

"OUR TRUE INTENT IS ALL FOR YOUR DELIGHT."—*Shakespeare.*

THE MONOPOLIES.

GAS MONOPOLY.—AH, IT'S ALL VERY WELL TO LAUGH AT YOUR CUSTOMERS, AS I DID; BUT TAKE WARNING BY ME—*YOUR TURN WILL COME!*

Illustration 15. The image of the railway proprietor in a comic weekly, Funny Folks, 11 January 1879

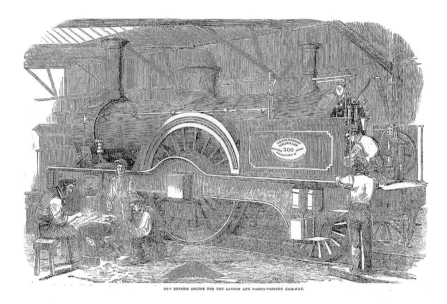

NEW EXPRESS ENGINE FOR THE LONDON AND NORTH-WESTERN RAILWAY.

Illustration 16. Crewe locomotive works on the London and North Western Railway, with male and female employees, *ILN*, 18 December 1852

6

Regulation

6.1. INTRODUCTION

The previous chapters have emphasized the adverse effects of competition on the structure of the railway network. In addition, it has been noted that an ideological commitment to the principle of competition hampered Parliament in selecting the railway schemes it authorized. This commitment led them to refuse to ration the number of railway schemes approved along the lines recommended by the Railway Committee of the Board of Trade.

This emphasis on the adverse effects of competition raises a number of important questions:

- Is competition always bad or is it only in railways and other network industries that it is bad?
- If competition is good in most industries but bad in railways, what are the crucial differences in industry characteristics that make competition good in some industries and bad in others? Does the explanation lie purely in the network externalities that characterize the railway industry, or are there other factors too?
- If competition is bad then should regulation be used chiefly to inhibit it? Or is competition bad only because of perverse incentives? If so, should regulation adjust the 'rules of the game' so that competition produces more desirable results instead? In other words, is the problem that the railway industry fosters the *wrong sort* of competition, and if so, should the regulator encourage the *right sort* of competition?
- Is nationalization, or some other form of social ownership such as municipalization, the simplest way of eliminating perverse incentives; or does the elimination of private ownership create perverse incentives of its own? In other words, will socialized ownership encourage competition to manifest itself in another form? Is it better, perhaps, to have transparent competition between rival companies rather than opaque competition between factions within a bureaucratic and politicized organization?

This chapter examines these issues in their historical context, with particular reference to the crucial period leading up to the Railway Mania. Sections 6.2 and 6.3 examine the basic principles of railway regulation and summarize the legislation through which it was implemented. Sections 6.4–6.5 examine in detail the activities of the Railway Committee of the Board of Trade in the crucial

Parliamentary session before the Railway Mania reached its peak. They examine the forces that led to its extinction—in particular the unpopularity of its recommendations with local towns.

Sections 6.6–6.10 examine the concept of competition as it applies to a railway network. It is shown that the different linkages that make up a railway network are both complements and substitutes for each other. Parliament and the Board of Trade tried unsuccessfully to distinguish between linkages that were purely complementary and linkages that were purely substitutes. Parliament allowed end-on linkages to be merged on the grounds that they were purely complementary. Parliament wrongly believed that the integration of end-on lines into a single company posed no significant threat to competition. It failed to anticipate that the integrated companies so formed had the power to block or disable substitute linkages that might be built in future. This gave the large firms regional monopolies. Because regulatory failure led to regional monopoly, competition became territorial, with each company defending its region against encroachment by its neighbours. To enter a rival region, competitors were obliged to build their own self-contained networks, thereby duplicating the network of the established company.

If the dominant companies had been able to merge, then the waste incurred by this duplication could have been avoided. But the towns were in favour of territorial competition—particulary along the frontiers—and so Parliament refused to authorize mergers. Although regional systems had a potentially complementary role in facilitating inter-regional travel, Parliament treated regional monopolists as potential competitors and encouraged them to invade each others territories. If Parliament had instead been willing to authorize mergers then a single integrated national company would almost certainly have been formed, and this would then have become a natural candidate for nationalization—some 80 years before nationalization actually occurred. Sections 6.11 and 6.12 consider the implications of this conclusion for the policy issues raised above.

6.2. PRINCIPLES OF REGULATION

The overall performance of an industry will reflect the quality of its regulation, and so any failure of regulation can have very serious consequences. A regulator is not a planner, who relies on subordinates to implement specific instructions. The regulator simply establishes the rules of the game, and independent actors then play the game. In the case of UK railways, the regulator was Parliament and the principal actors were the railway companies. Parliamentary policy was implemented through the Railway Department of the Board of Trade.

An effective regulator will review all the instruments at his or her disposal and consider how each of them might be deployed—both separately and together. He or she will anticipate how the actors will respond to each possible set of regulations—that is, each regulatory regime—and rank the outcomes in terms of the social benefit conferred. He or she will then implement the highest ranked regime.

The actors operating under a regulated regime can adopt two main attitudes. One is to be socially responsible: to abide by the spirit of the rules and to act responsibly to minimize the adverse consequences of any regulatory miscalculation. The alternative is to act purely selfishly: to abide by the letter of the rules when offences are likely to be punished, but otherwise to disregard them; furthermore, to make no attempt to abide by the spirit of the rules if there is private advantage to be gained by exploiting loopholes. By and large the railway companies took the latter approach. Indeed, it could be said that much of their entrepreneurial initiative went into 'playing the system' in order to get out of the system for themselves as much as the rules would allow.

When actors take a purely selfish view of their role within a regulated system, the regulator's role is easy in one sense, but difficult in another. It is easy in the sense that selfish actors are generally quite predictable in the way they will respond to any opportunity. If the regulator assumes the worst—namely that they will behave in an antisocial way if it pays them to do so—then he or she will normally be right. It is difficult in the sense that the regulator may not be able to anticipate all the opportunities that selfish entrepreneurial actors can identify. He or she may therefore find himself or herself confronted with perfectly legal but clearly antisocial 'scams' that the actors have developed to advance their own interests at the expense of others—and the expense of customers in particular. Furthermore, correcting the rules may prove politically difficult. The actors may claim that they entered the industry under a certain set of rules which they expected to see maintained, and that it is unfair of the regulator to change the rules once they have entered. They may even claim that they would never have entered the industry in the first place if they had been confronted with the modified rules that the regulator is proposing to introduce. If the industry is large enough to give the actors political influence—which was clearly the case with the railways—then they may be able to overturn the regulator's proposals through lobbying against them.

There can be no question that issues pertaining to railway regulation received significant attention from Parliament, even though many of the issues debated were not acted upon. The most high-profile issues related to the quality of service provided by the railway companies and the fares and freight rates that they charged for these services. Parliament needed to be satisfied that the public benefits provided by the railway system were commensurate with the inconvenience caused to the public by the compulsory purchase of land for railway construction and the noise, smoke, and steam generated by railway operations. Parliament was particularly concerned with health and safety—both of passengers and of railway employees. Excursion trains and troop trains were particularly liable to accidents as they did not run at regularly scheduled times, while shunters working in goods yards at night were often hit by wagons.

The overall quality of service provided by the railway system was strongly influenced by network infrastructure. The available infrastructure depended on which of the many railway schemes put forward were actually built. Parliament was dependent on private promoters to bring schemes forward since it rarely provided financial support itself. Only a few schemes ever received subsidies, and most of these involved modest loans to very early schemes which were eventually repaid (see Table 6.1).

Once schemes had been proposed, however, Parliament had a crucial role in deciding which of these it would approve. This created a policy feedback loop: in evaluating the performance of the network at any point in time, Parliament was indirectly evaluating the efficacy of its decisions on the selection of schemes. Parliament was somewhat lax, however, as it rarely blamed itself for the long-term consequences of its own erroneous decisions.

Potential problems with UK railway regulation can be seen at an early stage. Many Members of Parliament were lawyers and included railway companies among their major clients, while others were directors of railway companies. Most MPs would support the interests of railway companies that were major employers in their constituencies. The Railway Companies Association lobbied

Table 6.1. Public loans to railway companies up to January 1867

Company receiving advances	Total amount of advances (£000)	Dates of advances	Term (years)	Repayment
Hay	8	1817	20	Repaid
Llanvihangel	5	1817, 1820	3, 20	Repaid
North Stafford	8	1817	3	Repaid
Grosmont	5	1817	2	Repaid
Plymouth and Dartmoor	28	1820, 1823	20	£15,921 unpaid
Liverpool and Manchester	100	1827	20	Repaid
Heckbridge and Wentbridge	7.6	1827	20	£4,691 unpaid
Clarence	111	1832, 1833, 1835	20	Repaid
Newcastle and Carlisle	160	1833, 1834 (2), 1835 (2)	20 (4), 10 (1)	Repaid
Bodmin and Wadebridge	8	1834	20	Repaid
Sheffield, Ashton-under-Lyne and Manchester	50	1842	20	Repaid
Total: England and Wales			491	£20,612 unpaid

Note: Almost all loans were at 5%. Loans to Irish railways commenced in December 1842. A total of £2,545,096 had been advanced by 31 December 1867, on maturities of up to 20 years (mostly at the maximum period), of which £1,284,000 was unpaid. This includes many large advances from the 1840s which were still unpaid.

Source: Return ... of all Advances made by the Public Works Loan Commissioners to Railways ..., BPP, 1867, Vol. 62, Paper 140.

Parliament on behalf of the railway companies. The Association, however, mainly confined itself to non-competitive issues—that is, issues that affected all companies equally, and not one company at the expense of another. It therefore concentrated on issues such as the rating of railway premises rather than issues of monopoly and competition.

By and large, Parliament appears to have assumed that railway promoters would behave like 'gentlemen' even though their own experiences of using the railways would tend to persuade them otherwise. High fares, poor connections with other companies' trains, and lack of accommodation for third-class travellers, all pointed towards a strategy of calculated indifference to the interests of the travelling public. But by taking an optimistic view of promoters' behaviour, Parliament was able to justify its relatively lax approach to regulation. While government collected a considerable amount of statistical information about the railways, and held numerous inquiries into various aspects of railway regulation, it rarely persisted with legislative proposals to force rival railway companies to work together for the public good.

A basic chronology of Parliamentary regulation is presented in Table 6.2. The table shows that a wide range of measures were introduced throughout the nineteenth century in response to the reports of a variety of inquiries, Royal Commissions and Select Committees. A large amount of statistical material was collected from the railway companies on an annual basis, and simple performance indicators were constructed. Many inquiries were launched in response to events—such as major accidents—or public concerns—such as lack of punctuality—with specific interventions often being triggered by comment in the national press. Some concerns—such as high fares—were perennial, however, and were regularly re-examined.

Table 6.2. Chronology of key railway regulation affecting the construction and operation of the network

Date	Title/reference	Provisions
1831	BPP 1831 VIII, Cmd. 324	Select Committee on Steam Carriages criticizes the high tolls on steam carriages imposed by turnpike trusts (often over 10 times the tolls for stage coaches) but no action is taken to reduce them (see 2 and 3 William IV c. 120)
1834	4 and 5 William IV c. 25	First railway amalgamation Act, uniting the end-on lines of the Wigan Branch Railway and the Preston and Wigan Railway to form a through line from Newton-le-Willows to Preston, Lancashire
1838	BPP 1844 XI Cmd. 25	Select Committee on the State of Communication by Railways

(continued)

Table 6.2. (Continued)

Date	Title/reference	Provisions
		recommends, *inter alia*, that the Post Office should be able to run toll-free trains
1839	BPP, 1839, X Cmd. 222, 517	Select Committee on the State of Communication by Railways (two reports) refers to '…the difficulties that must arise from an extended inter-communication throughout the country, solely maintained by companies acting for their private interests, unchecked by competition, and uncontrolled by authority'.
1840	BPP, 1840, XIII Cmd. 50, 92, 299, 437, 474	Select Committee on the State of Communication by Railways (five reports) considers alternative routes from London to Dublin, Edinburgh, etc.
1840	4 and 5 Vict. c.7	First major railway acquisition. The York and North Midland Railway (YNMR) acquires the Leeds and Selby Railway (LSR). Passenger traffic is diverted from part of the LSR onto the YNMR.
1840	3 and 4 Vict. c. 97	An Act for Regulating Railways (Lord Seymour's Act) establishes the Board of Trade as the railway regulator, with powers to inspect railways, approve bylaws, and require statistical returns relating to traffic, etc.
1842	5 and 6 Vict. c. 55	An Act for the Better Regulation of Railways, and for the Conveyance of Troops allows the Board of Trade to arbitrate in disputes over joint traffic, and to require returns of serious accidents.
1842		Establishment of the Railway Clearing House
1844	7 and 8 Vict. c. 18	First major merger. An amalgamation of the YNMR, the Birmingham and Derby Junction Railway and the Midland Counties Railways, to form the Midland Railway, creates a through line under a single company from York to Birmingham and Rugby via a hub at Derby

Table 6.2. (Continued)

Date	Title/reference	Provisions
1844	BPP 1844 XI Cmd. 37, 79, 166, 283, 318, 524	Select Committee concerning New Provisions to be introduced into Railway Bills and Changes to be made in Standing Orders relating to Railways (Gladstone's Committee) (six reports)
1844		Establishment of the Railway Department of the Board of Trade: the 'Five Kings', led by Earl Dalhousie
1844	7 and 8 Vict. c. 85	Gladstone's Act gives the state the power to purchase railways authorized after the passage of the Act, although on terms very favourable to the companies and expensive for the state. These options were never exercised. All companies were obliged to run Parliamentary trains for the carriage of third-class passengers; this traffic was exempt from passenger duty.
1845	BPP 1845 X Cmd. 82, 135	Select Committee on Railway Bills suggests the classification of railway bills by a Special Committee
1845	8 and 9 Vict. c. 20	Railway Clauses Consolidation Act consolidates 160 clauses relating to railway construction, acquisition and use of land, provision of level crossings and other facilities for road traffic, and the working of mineral deposits under a railway, and other issues
1845	BPP 1845 XXXIX, Cmd. 279	Report of the Railway Department of the Board of Trade on proposed Amalgamations of Railways
1845	BPP 1845 XXXIX Cmd. 479	Minutes of the Lords of the Committee of Privy Council for Trade relative to the Constitution and Mode of Proceedings of the Railway Department
1846	9 and 10 Vict. c. 204	Decisive merger between the London and Birmingham Railway, the Grand Junction Railway (which had itself taken

(*continued*)

Table 6.2. (Continued)

Date	Title/reference	Provisions
		over the Liverpool and Manchester Railway the previous year) and the Manchester and Birmingham Railway to form the London and North Western Railway, with main line to London from Liverpool, Manchester, and Birmingham
1846	BPP 1846 XIII Cmd. 200, 275	Select Committee on Railways and Canals Amalgamation (Wilson Patten's Committee)
1846	BPP 1846 XIV Cmd. 590, 687	Select Committee on Railway Act Enactments (Morrison's Committee) (two reports)
1846	BPP 1846 XIII Cmd. 41, 61	Select Committee on Railway Bills (three reports)
1846	BPP 1846 XIII Cmd. 530	Select Committee on Railway Labourers
1846	BPP 1846 XIII Cmd. 489	Select Committee of the House of Lords on the Management of Railroads dealt with railway management, Private Bill procedure, speculation and the gauge question, and supported the proposal to establish Railway Commissioners. It sought to discourage purely speculative railway bills
1846	BPP 1846 XVI Cmd. 684, 699, 700	Commission on the Merits of the Broad and Narrow Gauge of Railways (Sir Frederick Smith, Sir George Airy (Astronomer Royal) and Peter Barlow) recommends standardization on the narrow gauge, as a gauge better suited to general goods traffic. Although the broad gauge is advantageous for high-speed passenger traffic, the gain is marginal. Standardization is strongly desirable, and narrowing the broad gauge is much easier than widening the narrow gauge, and there is only a fraction of the mileage to adjust
1846	9 and 10 Vict. c. 57	The Gauge Act requires future railways to be narrow gauge, but with crucial exceptions. Lines

Table 6.2. (Continued)

Date	Title/reference	Provisions
		already authorized, but not yet constructed, were exempted but, most critically, railways whose gauge was specifically mentioned in their authorising Act were exempted too. This exception allowed the Great Western Railway and allied promoters to continue to build broad gauge lines.
1846	9 and 10 Vict. c. 105	Following the closure of the Railway Department of the Board of Trade, the Railway Commissioners are established by an Act for Constituting Commissioners of Railways
1850	13 and 14 Vict. c. 33	The Railway Clearing Act clarifies the role of the Railway Clearing House (established 1842) and allows them to sue and be sued for outstanding balances with the member companies
1851	14 and 15 Vict. c. 64	An Act to repeal the Act for constituting Commissioners of Railways (of 1846) returns responsibility for railways to the Board of Trade. The Commissioners had received large salaries but had been given few responsibilities. Nevertheless, they produced very thorough commentaries and reports.
1852–53	BPP 1852–53 XXXVIII Cmd. 79, 170, 246, 310, 736	Select Committee on the Principal of Amalgamation as applied to Railway, or Railway and Canal Bills (Cardwell's Committee) (five reports)
1854	17 and 18 Vict. c. 31	Railway and Canal Traffic Act establishes trading standards with which railway companies must comply
1857–58	BPP 1857–58 XIV Cmd. 411	Select Committee on Railway and Canal Legislation recommends changes in Parliamentary procedure
1857–58	BPP 1857–58 XIV Cmd. 362	Select Committee of the House of Commons on the Causes of Accidents on Railways recommends that the Board of Trade

(continued)

Table 6.2. (Continued)

Date	Title/reference	Provisions
		should have the power to thoroughly investigate all serious accidents. Communication between guard and engine-driver should be improved, telegraphic block signalling should become standard, and companies should be discouraged from timetabling trains to run at excessive speeds. Legislation did not follow until 1868
1863	BPP 1863 VIII Cmd. 385	Select Committee of the House of Commons comments on the expense incurred by companies in complying with Private Bill procedures. The extension of the system has led to a proliferation of established lines that compete with any new proposal and therefore have *locus standi* to oppose
1863	26 and 27 Victoria c. 92	Railway Clauses Act reiterates the right of any railway which another railway subsequently joins to have absolute control of the junction, and makes other provisions
1864	27 and 28 Victoria c. 120	Railway Companies Powers Act allows the Board of Trade to sanction working agreements and other arrangements between companies, provided that other companies do not oppose. Not used in practice
1864	27 and 28 Victoria c. 121	Railways Construction Facilities Act allows branches and new works to be sanctioned by certificate, provided that other companies do not oppose. This attempt to reduce the cost of promoting new railways was never used because opposition was always anticipated
1865–67	BPP 1867 XXXVIII Cmd. 3844	The Royal Commission on Railways notes that there are 26 points at which the broad and narrow gauges interchange traffic, and there remained over 1,000 miles of broad gauge line.

Table 6.2. (Continued)

Date	Title/reference	Provisions
		A bland report that was widely criticized at the time because it fatalistically accepts current practices and their outcomes
1868	31 and 32 Victoria c. 119	Regulation of Railways Act requires trains to have an efficient means of communication between passengers and railway servants
1870	33 and 34 Victoria c. 78	Tramways Act stipulates that tramways are to be of standard gauge unless otherwise specified.
1871	34 and 35 Victoria c. 78	Regulation of Railways Act confers extensive powers of accident investigation on Board of Trade
1872		Large amalgamations are proposed: LNWR/LYR; CR/NBR; SER/LBSCR; NER/GNR; GWR/LSWR; MR/GSWR. None of those reaching Parliament is approved, although some joint working arrangements are authorized.
1872	BPP 1872 XIII Cmd. 364	The Joint Select Committee on Railway Companies Amalgamation makes various recommendations for strengthening inter-modal competition with canals and coastal shipping, but these were not put into effect
1873	36 and 37 Victoria c. 48	The Regulation of Railways Act puts the execution of the provisions of the Railway and Canal Traffic Act of 1854 into the hands of three Railway Commissioners (reversing the dissolution of the previous Railway Commissioners in 1851)
1877	BPP 1877 XLVIII Cmd. 1637	Royal Commission on Railway Accidents recommends that the Board of Trade be given extensive powers over railway operations; in particular, to require station enlargements, footbridges and pedestrian subways, interlocking points and signals, and speed restrictions

(*continued*)

Table 6.2. (Continued)

Date	Title/reference	Provisions
1882	BPP 1882 XIII Cmd. 317	Select Committee on Railways (Rates and Fares) recommends extending the powers of the Railway Commission, standardising the classification of goods, recognising and regulating terminal charges, and giving *locus standi* to trade associations and other representative bodies
1883	46 and 47 Victoria c. 34	Cheap Trains Act abolishes passenger duty on cheap fares and provides the Board of Trade with the power to mandate the provision of workmen's trains when there is evidence of unsatisfied demand
1888	51 and 52 Victoria c. 25	Railway and Canal Traffic Act provides elaborate schedules for setting freight rates and new procedures for resolving disputes between railway companies and their customers
1894	57 and 58 Victoria c. 54	Railway and Canal Traffic Act refines the agenda of the previous Act

6.3. THE RAILWAY COMMITTEE OF THE BOARD OF TRADE

The major failure of the railway regulation occurred at the time of the Railway Mania, when, after a short experiment, Parliament refused to accept advice on new railway schemes from the Railway Committee of the Board of Trade. This experiment originated with the most important of all the Select Committee Reports on Railways—the Fifth Report of the Select Committee of 1844. This insightful report was strongly influenced by William Gladstone, who had initiated the investigation as President of the Board of Trade (BPP, 1844, Vol. 11, Cmd. 318). Gladstone's father had been involved in the promotion of the Liverpool and Manchester Railway, and Gladstone was convinced that the railways would form a new national system of communication. Through careful study of the subject, he evolved a set of principles which he believed should guide railway policy.

According to the Select Committee:

'... Railway schemes ought not to be regarded as projects of merely local improvement, but ... each new Line should be viewed as a member of a great system of communication . . .' Furthermore, '. . . as railways multiply, the collision of interests between them becomes sharp and violent, and where the combatants on all sides are so powerful and opulent, a more than ordinary vigilance and firmness is demanded from Parliament for the protection of the public interests.'

This conclusion led the Committee to recommend a special procedure for the consideration of railway Bills presented to Parliament which deviated from the precedents governing the passage of ordinary Bills.

The Committee feel that . . . the ordinary machinery of Private Bill Committees is insufficient . . . It is to be expected, from the constitution of those Committees, that local interests will be chiefly regarded in their deliberations. It is almost impossible to hope, that . . . there should issue any distinct system of sound general rules, uniform in their foundation, and varying, where they do vary, in a strict and constant proportion to the actual peculiarities of the case.

It is, moreover, to be recollected, that new Lines of Railway are sometimes projected for the purpose, not of increasing, but of restricting Railway accommodation. Cases may occur in which a company, fearful of the competition of a parallel line, . . . may throw out a lateral Branch across the country to be traversed by such parallel Line, which although affording only circuitous communication with the terminus, may nevertheless materially increase the facilities of Parliamentary opposition . . .

As a result, the Report recommended the systematic scrutiny by the Board of Trade of all railway bills with respect to:

1. All questions of public safety.
2. All departures from ordinary usage of Railway legislation . . .
3. All provisions of magnitude which may be novel in their principle, or may involve extended considerations of public policy. For example, amalgamations and agreements between separate Companies; extensions of capital; powers enabling the railway Companies to pursue purposes different in kind from those for which they were incorporated; modification of the general law.
4. Branch and Extension Lines, in cases where upon the first aspect of the plan, a presumption is raised that the object of the scheme is to throw difficulties in the way of new, and probably legitimate enterprises.
5. New schemes where the Line taken presents a strong appearance of being such as to raise the presumption that it does not afford the best mode of communication between the termini, and of accommodating the local traffic.
6. Cases where a Bill of inferior merits may be brought before Parliament, and where a preferable scheme is in bona fide contemplation, although not sufficiently forward to come simultaneously under the judgement of Parliament according to its Standing Orders.
7. Any proposed arrangements with subsisting Companies which may appear as objectors to new Lines.

The Select Committee on Railway Acts Enactments concurred with this proposal (Second Report, BPP, 1846, Vol. 14, Cmd. 687, p. viii):

The example of foreign countries has shown that many inquiries with regard to railways can best be conducted on the spot . . . a properly-qualified Board, entrusted with railway affairs, would obtain more knowledge of the wants of the country, and of the best means of supplying them, than Committees, under the present system, can possibly possess. . . . the functions of the Board may, with safety, be extended to the supervision of existing railways, and the determining, in the first instance, . . . where lines should be constructed, and what projects should be entertained.

The recommended scrutiny procedure lasted for only one session of Parliament, however: namely the session 1844–45, during which the Railway Mania was approaching its height. The Mania peaked at the end of November 1845, when there was an enormous rush to submit Bills by the deadline for 1845–46. The scrutiny was implemented by the Railway Committee, whose members were known unofficially as the 'Five Kings'. The Committee was supported by a secretariat based in the Railway Department, which had been established earlier.

The Chairman of the Committee, Earl Dalhousie, was an intellectual as well as an aristocrat. Educated at Harrow and Oxford, he succeeded Gladstone as President of the Board of Trade in 1845. After the fall of Sir Robert Peel's government, he moved to India as Governor General, in which role he took an active part in the formulation of Indian railway policy; he signed a famous Minute on this subject in 1853, which defined the system of railway promotion in India. He was an active modernizer and reformer, and created social tensions in India through his determination to outlaw gangs and suppress suttee.

The other members of the committee were Samuel Laing, Charles Pasley, George Porter, and Donatus O'Brien. Laing was a brilliant mathematician and Fellow of St. Johns College, Cambridge. He was called to the bar in 1837 and served as Secretary to the Railway Committee of the Board of Trade from 1842 to 1846. He too went to India for a time, where he had a successful political career. He served two spells as Chairman and Managing Director of the London Brighton and South Coast Railway. He was a Liberal MP, financial secretary to the Treasury, 1859–60, and the author of best-selling philosophical and anthropological books.

General Charles Pasley FRS (as he later became) was a young military engineer who had served in Spain, Holland, and throughout the Mediterranean before he joined the Board of Trade. He lectured at a military college and was responsible for a range of innovations in telegraphy, mining, pontooning, and explosives.

George Porter was an economist, married to the sister of David Ricardo, MP (the classical economic theorist who was an opponent of Malthus and an advocate of free trade). He was an established figure with a high personal reputation at the time that he served on the Committee. He was the author of a monumental work on *The Progress of the Nation, in its Social and Economic Relations from the Beginning of the 19th Century to the Present Day*, which first appeared in 1836. He had already served for several years in senior positions in the Board of Trade. He played an active role in founding the Statistical Society, and became Head of the Board's Statistical Department in 1840. He believed strongly in the importance of economic fundamentals, and the need to measure them accurately. He was in favour of free trade, popular education, and other causes close to the heart of a classical economic liberal.

Donatus O'Brien had a more chequered career. As brother of the Chairman of the South Eastern Railway, he was alleged to have leaked confidential information from the Board of Trade to allow his brother to speculate in railway shares. The basis of the allegation was that his brother had bought shares in the South Eastern Railway just before the Committee reported in favour of one of its schemes, and although his brother claimed that he had bought the shares purely because he felt obliged to do so as a recently appointed chairman, the allegation was never convincingly rebutted. Unlike his colleagues, O'Brien failed to distinguish himself after he left his position at the Board of Trade.

The allegation of 'stock-jobbing' directed at the Five Kings was, however, only one of several criticisms directed at them. It seems likely that critics seized upon the stock-jobbing scandal simply to gain popular support for more fundamental political objections.

One criticism was that the Committee collected information on forthcoming schemes as well as schemes already submitted to Parliament. They held discussions with promoters in private, leaving the promoters of competitive schemes feeling excluded. On the other hand, they sometimes refused to see promoters who had requested an audience, on the grounds that the promoters merely wished to lobby for their schemes while the Committee wished to investigate them properly instead. The Committee's concern was to collect a large amount of detailed information on individual schemes as quickly as possible, rather than to share that information with other people. Although Parliament was informed of their recommendations, only a small part of the information that supported their recommendations seems to have been passed on.

Another criticism is that the Committee usurped the powers of Parliament by taking such a broad view of their mandate that they pronounced on issues that were none of their business. In order to ascertain the type of information they required, the Committee established a number of principles which they applied throughout their investigations, as explained in detail below. These principles, however, had not been agreed with Parliament, but simply emanated from the members of the Committee themselves. With the benefit of hindsight, it can be seen that these principles were very sophisticated, and that the judgements arrived at using these principles were broadly correct. But this was not obvious to Parliament at the time.

So far as many MPs were concerned, a bunch of ambitious young civil servants, led by senior people who should have known better, were telling older and more experienced MPs what decisions they should make, and indeed, effectively making these decisions themselves. Most MPs continued to favour the traditional Parliamentary procedure in which Bills were examined by Select Committees. These committees used tried and tested legal practices, in which each interested party—such as a railway promoter or their opponent—made their case in public and were then subjected to cross-examination by legal counsel. Experts, too, were subjected to cross-examination, from which they might emerge with much diminished reputation if they failed to answer questions satisfactorily. But instead of cutting experts down to size, as the traditional method did, the new method was creating additional experts out of civil servants—experts who could not be cross-examined by the Committees. Furthermore, many MPs were also lawyers, as noted above, and the civil servants at the Board of Trade were effectively encroaching on legal territory. By advising Select Committees on the decisions they should make, the Board of Trade was diminishing the input of the legal profession into the decision-making process.

But perhaps the single most important objection to the Board of Trade intervention was the one alluded to in the previous chapters. Many of the Railway Committee's recommendations were deeply unpopular at the local level. The Committee often suggested, for example, that local schemes should be deferred until the structure of the trunk network had been finally determined—a verdict that was unpopular with promoters and traders who want to put their local town on the railway map.

Furthermore, many MPs did not accept the principles of national policy by which the Committee arrived at their decisions. In any case, these principles were seen as too abstract, and too complicated, for MPs to explain to their constituents. As the product of high-powered intellects, it seemed obvious that they would be impossible to legitimate from a populist political perspective.

6.4. PRINCIPLES OF REGULATION ADOPTED BY THE FIVE KINGS

Given the criticism to which the Railway Committee was subjected, it might be expected that their advice was dogmatic, and that the principles they applied were of an ideological nature. In fact the situation was quite the opposite; the dogmatic opinions and appeal to simple ideology were more characteristic of their opponents than the Committee itself.

The Railway Committee produced 22 reports during its short life—a phenomenal output considering the small number of people involved. The Committee divided up all railway Bills into regional groupings, and then drafted reports on which set of schemes would best serve the needs of each region. Each region was viewed as an integral part of Britain as a whole. They also produced a thematic report on mergers.

Table 6.3 summarizes the general principles enunciated by the Committee in their publications. This parsimonious set of principles is congruent with the general principles that have been used to construct the counterfactual network in this study. A detailed study of the individual reports reveals a number of more specific principles which guided decisions in particular cases. These specific principles are summarized in Tables 6.4–6.6. The tables report numerous cases in which the Railway Committee made judgements on issues that were potentially controversial at the time, and in most cases these judgements appear, with the benefit of hindsight, to have been correct. For example, the Committee was very keen to promote national standards for the railway system that would facilitate inter-operability. It also favoured a conservative attitude to new technologies, arguing that newly promoted lines should not be used to experiment with novel technologies that were incompatible with the technologies employed on the majority of lines that were already built. Parliament, however, was more inclined to support technological novelties—such as atmospheric power and the broad gauge—and this was one of the main factors that underlay the major differences between Parliament and the Board when deciding on individual schemes.

The high quality of the Railway Committee's analysis of regional issues is exemplified by its pioneering analysis of the economics of industrial districts. In deriving its recommendations relating to Lancashire and the north-west (BPP, 1845, Cmd. 225) the Committee noted that:

Within a circle of 15 or 20 miles radius round Manchester, a population of upwards of a million and a half are concentrated, who are almost without exception either actively engaged in, or directly dependent upon, the great staple manufacture of cotton. The whole of this district may, in fact, be considered as one vast workshop, where production is constantly going forward on a scale hitherto unparalleled in the history of human industry. (p. 3)

Many circumstances have combined to render *time* an element of great and increasing importance in most of the operations connected with manufactures and foreign trade. By the establishment of lines of steam ships to America, the East and West Indies, the Levant, the north of Europe, and almost every point which affords an outlet for our manufactures, combined with the acceleration of communication by Railways in this and foreign countries, the period within which orders can be transmitted and returned has been greatly reduced, while by the great improvements in machinery and the different processes of manufacture, the time in which such orders can be executed has been equally shortened. The effect has been to introduce a considerable alteration in the old system, under which large quantities of manufactured goods were produced and forwarded a considerable time beforehand in anticipation of the probable demand of particular seasons and markets, involving a risk which is no longer necessary. The advantages of this change to all parties are obvious, both in the saving of interest on capital locked up in goods manufactured some time previously to their sale, and still more in reducing the risk of a fluctuations and loss arising from miscalculations as to the probable nature and extent of demand in distant markets. (p. 3)

One of the most marked effects of the progress of improvements in machinery and manufactures has been to introduce a continually increasing degree of subdivision of labour. This subdivision is now carried so far that the different processes of the same manufacture are frequently carried on not only in different establishments, but to a considerable extent in distinct localities. (p. 4)

The industry of one town or locality, owing to some combination of favourable circumstances, applies itself almost exclusively to spinning; that of another, to weaving; of a third, to bleaching or printing, and so forth: and thus the piece of cloth which is finally sold at Manchester and shipped at Liverpool for America or China, may be the joint product of the skill, labour and capital of Ashton-under-Lyne, Oldham, Bolton, Blackburn, and three or four different seats of manufacturing industry in the vicinity of the great emporium of Manchester. (p. 4)

It is evident that whatever favours this natural tendency towards a local subdivision of the processes of manufacture, must have the effect of increasing the manufacturing capabilities of the country, and its means of contending successfully with foreign competition. (p. 4)

A complete system of cheap and expeditious inter-communication, by which different processes of manufacture are enabled to follow out their natural tendency to settle themselves in the situations which natural or acquired advantages render most favourable, is obviously a permanent cause of manufacturing superiority of the same nature as the possession of cheap fuel or water power, and one to which the progress of scientific and mechanical invention, and the increasing perfection of the manufacturing system, is likely to add importance. (p. 4)

The general extension of Railway communication diminishes the tendency to an excessive accumulation of manufacturing establishments in large towns, and affords facilities for placing them under equal commercial advantage in situations more favourable for the moral and physical well-being of the operatives. (p. 4)

The introduction of Railways is also calculated, in many respects, to benefit the artisans in manufacturing districts, by affording them the means of cheap and expeditious transit, a benefit which is peculiarly apparent in the case of the handloom weavers, and other classes, whose work is given out at a central establishment, often at some distance from their residence, and much of whose time is lost to them when they are obliged to travel on foot. [. . .] Nor must we forget to mention . . . the opportunities afforded for keeping up family ties by visits to parents and relatives, for moving in search of employment, and for excursions for innocent and healthy recreation on holidays. (pp. 4–5)

In fact, it seems that individual Select Committees often found the Board of Trade's reports very helpful. Indeed, given the quality of the economic analysis that under-pinned these reports, as well as the voluminous evidence on which they were based, it is hardly surprising that individual committee members were enlightened by them. Furthermore, almost all of the recommendations of the Board of Trade were accepted by the Select Committees that they advised. To reconcile the helpfulness of the reports with the animosity they engendered, it is sufficient to note that the members of individual Select Committees were usually disinterested parties; the interested parties were only involved in debating the recommendation of the Select Committees when they reported back. The interested parties condemned the Board of Trade so vehemently because they recognized the influence that the Board had gained over the Select Committees it advised, and resented its interference in the schemes with which they were connected.

Table 6.7 summarizes all the Bills submitted to Parliament for the 1844–5 session and describes how each Bill fared at the hands of Parliament and the Board of Trade. In some cases different sources of evidence conflict—particularly regarding the reasons for the failure of the Bill—and so the table needs to be interpreted with caution. On key matters, however, the situation is very clear. A special report was produced on differences of opinion between Select Committees and the Board of Trade which shows that disagreements, where they occurred, were usually over a relatively minor issues. Thus even where a Select Committee rejected an argument put forward by the Board of Trade they did not necessarily arrive at a diffcrent decision on the railway scheme concerned. The substantive disagreements, as noted above, were mainly over standardization and technological issues where, with the benefit of hindsight, the Board of Trade was right.

Table 6.7 shows that, for one reason or another, many railway schemes were rejected in 1844–45. In several cases lines were rejected because they duplicated, in whole or in part, alternative schemes that were judged superior from a regional point of view. In other cases the Board recommended postponement of a decision on the grounds that better schemes were 'in the pipeline' and would be presented to Parliament in the following session. The table also shows that almost all of the lines that were authorized were actually built, and although some lines were delayed in construction, most were opened in full in a timely manner. Furthermore, most of these lines have survived in use down to the present day.

6.5. THE RAILWAY MANIA AND THE PARLIAMENTARY SESSION 1845–46

The Railway Committee had been disbanded by the time the postponed decisions came back to Parliament in the following session. Many towns had been upset by the fact that their schemes had been rejected in the previous session, and even where a decision had only been postponed, there was irritation because delay could be costly if other towns managed to get a lead. Promoters who were 'quick off the mark' should be rewarded, it was felt, even if their scheme was put together in haste.

The 'agenda' for 1846 therefore became to approve as many schemes as possible, and without the Railway Committee there was no effective check on Parliament. Despite the fact that many more schemes had been submitted than the previous session, the attitude to approval became more lenient. It seems that MPs were well aware of what they were doing. Many of the railway acts passed in 1846 specifically mention competing schemes which have also been authorized, and incorporate attempted checks on duplication, whereby part of one scheme could only be built if part of some other scheme were not. This is not only an explicit admission that duplicate schemes were being authorized, but also an implicit admission that many of the schemes that were authorized were unlikely to be built. Although provision for such contingencies had occasionally been made in earlier acts, it was never so common as it was in 1845–46. In addition to authorizing direct duplication, many schemes of indirect duplication were authorized, whereby two large cities already connected by a trunk route would be connected by another trunk route passing through different intermediate towns. Parliament also sanctioned a number of schemes for the conversion of canals into railways—schemes that were recognized at the time as being of dubious value, and which were typically promoted by canal proprietors attempting to recover the money that they had sunk into building an unwanted canal.

The capital market was unable to cope with the demand for financing all the railway schemes authorized by Parliament in 1845–46, particularly as the schemes authorized the previous year were already under construction, and were making calls on their shareholders which depleted the investors' liquidity. The result was a prolonged financial crisis, during which the agenda switched to salvaging as many railway schemes from failure as was possible. As a result, few new schemes were promoted in the period 1846–53; many of the railway Acts passed in that period related to the extension of time for the exercise of compulsory purchase, or the recapitalization of companies through the issue of additional shares. Mergers also became popular as a means of rationalizing duplicate lines.

These financial checks on the railway system delayed the completion of many lines. Half-built lines became a 'blot on the landscape', and many schemes were scaled back. Under-capitalized companies would build the most profitable sections of their lines first in order to maximize short-term revenue, and these often turned out to be the only sections that were ever built. As towns witnessed the collapse of grand long-distance schemes which would have served them, they turned their attention to building short branches to connect themselves to lines that already existed. This helped to consolidate the power of the major trunk lines—especially those serving London—as they were the most popular lines for local towns to connect with. Some railway schemes collapsed simply through a 'domino effect'; they were meant to connect with other lines which had failed, and therefore had no independent purpose of their own. Thus what should have been a well-connected network degenerated into a set of isolated branches built around the earliest trunk lines. Ambitious cross-country routes now terminated in country towns rather than by junctions with other lines, substantially reducing the connectivity of the network and thereby perpetuating the regional monopoly power of the early trunk lines.

The failure of the Mania schemes set the agenda for railway-building for the remainder of the Victorian period. By 1860 the steady growth of traffic was leading to congestion on certain parts of the railway system, and this encouraged the development of the 'Second Railway Mania' in 1861–6. The agenda was to build the lines that had not been built before and for which powers of compulsory purchase had lapsed. Old sets of plans were dusted off and updated, and resubmitted to Parliament under different names. New schemes were also hatched—in particular schemes that would liberate major towns from the tyranny of their local railway monopolist. But the regional trunk line monopolists still had considerable power—as explained below—and although they often failed to prevent the building of new lines, they were able to prevent the diversion of traffic to these lines, with the result that many were little used and became quite unprofitable.

6.6. THE CONCEPT OF COMPETITION AS APPLIED TO RAILWAYS

The government of Sir Robert Peel, in which Gladstone served at the time of the Railway Mania, was a radical and reforming government that was committed very

Table 6.3. General judgements on railway policy made explicitly by the Railway Committee of the Board of Trade in its Reports to Parliament

---

Railways will take all but short-distance passenger traffic off the roads, and all but the heaviest traffic off the canals. They will also take some traffic away from river and coastal steamers

No traffic flows are so great that they can sustain more than two or three competing railway lines

Benefits of competition are overrated. Two or three competing railway companies will soon collude or merge. In the absence of competition prices will not fall, but costs (and capital employed) will rise

Regulation of maximum fares, and the residual threat of competition from other modes, provide the best checks on railway charges

Railways that form through routes by making end-on junctions should be under common ownership to avoid a 'hold up' problem

Convenient junction layouts are required to allow connections between trains to be made with minimum inconvenience and delay. However, junctions may be prevented by natural obstacles, differences in levels, etc.

Joint stations, owned by major trunk companies which share their use, are beneficial at major junctions and in large cities

Freight flows to the nearest port, and passenger traffic to the metropolis

Local traffic and 'Omnibus traffic' does not require such well-engineered lines as trunk traffic

Trunk lines should avoid hilly terrain. Steep gradients and sharp curves will slow down traffic and require additional locomotive power. Long continuous gradients are more problematic as opposed to short undulating gradients. Tunnels can ease gradients but they increase construction costs

Safety is paramount. Crossing other lines on the level, and adding to traffic on already congested lines should be avoided if possible

---

much to the principle of free markets. Its underlying philosophy was influenced by the thinking of Adam Smith. According to Smith, the advantage of competition lay in the fact that suppliers were motivated to offer buyers the best available deal; a monopolist could afford to adopt a 'take it or leave it' attitude to his or her customers, but a competitor had to reckon with the fact that customers would switch to his or her rivals if his or her service was poor. But Peel's government was also pragmatic—and Gladstone was particularly so. While the advantages of competition in general were recognized, its limitations in the specific case of railways were appreciated too.

In the simple story expounded by advocates of competition, a supplier can operate on any scale, including a very small scale. Supply is increased by replicating suppliers, each of whom supplies only a fraction of the total market. But a railway line is a major piece of civil engineering, and once built has enormous capacity. This capacity may well exceed the entire demand in the locality that it serves. The natural way to increase supply is simply to increase capacity utilization. It is inefficient to replicate a railway line that has spare capacity. Since competition involves duplication, competition wastes resources.

In the simple story, competitors can enter and leave the industry very easily. In the UK railway industry, however, competitors needed Parliamentary authorization to enter, and established companies could oppose this. Exit was almost

Table 6.4. Specific judgements on railway policy made implicitly or explicitly by the Railway Committee of the Board of Trade, with examples

Judgement	Example (report no.)
A longer or slower route can still abstract traffic from a shorter or faster route by discounting fares; hence the shortest route is not guaranteed to be the most profitable	Manchester–Normanton–Derby–London competed successfully with Manchester–Birmingham–London, 153
Running powers can often be used to reduce monopoly power (especially bilateral arrangements between two companies)	Limerick–Tipperary, 154
A low-fare policy is financially viable and maximizes external benefits of a railway system. Guarantees on low fares can be negotiated with these companies in return for authorising branches and extensions	Dublin–Drogheda–Belfast, 119
Trunk networks will begin with construction of the most profitable sections: lines from the metropolis to junctions where routes diverge to cover the region	Dublin–west of Ireland, 156
Railway investment in Ireland, together with steam navigation, will boost exports (e.g. fat cattle) from East Coast Irish ports to West Coast mainland ports (e.g. Birkenhead)	Chester–Birkenhead Dock extension, 225; Birkenhead, Manchester and Cheshire Junction 225; Dublin–Mullingar–Athlone, 156
Dense networks are required in industrial districts to cater for 'omnibus' traffic—both freight and third-class passenger traffic. Railways can speed up the communication of orders and deliveries. They promote the division of labour, and allow districts to expand their geographical boundaries—allowing expansion without congestion	Manchester, Leeds, 61; Lancashire, 225
Lines should be placed in the ownership of companies that will work them as main lines rather than as branches	Limerick–Tipperary, 153
Other things being equal, new branches are best built by established companies, which have 'deep purses' and can operate short lines more economically	Glasgow, Barrhead, and Neilston, 120
The policies of several trunk railways are closely identified with ports in which their promoters are interested. These companies may seek to obstruct schemes that serve rival ports even though they do not directly compete for traffic between the same towns	Lancashire (225)
Railway companies seeking to develop a region should be given preference to construct desirable lines that would otherwise compete with their own (recovery of sunk costs)	LSWR: London–Guildford–Chichester–Portsmouth, 172
A company that was first in the field with a Bill should be given preference over later entrants with very similar schemes (recovery of sunk costs)	Trent Valley (over Churnet Valley Tamworth–Rugby extension), 155

Table 6.4. (Continued)

Judgement	Example (report no.)
Merchants and manufacturers may promote a railway to benefit from cheaper transport rather than profit from the speculation	Blackburn, Darwen and Bolton Railway, 226
Landowners who expect to benefit through higher rents may prefer to give land to a railway to encourage it to pass nearby, rather than ask a high price for it	South of Ireland, 154
Companies may be asked to provide security for the 'completion and efficient working of schemes' which they might otherwise abandon	GWR: Monmouth–Hereford, 155
Problems created by change of gauge are not easily resolved by mechanical transhipment of goods, mixed gauge track, etc. Existing broad gauge cannot be converted to standard gauge immediately. Problems can be minimized by suitable choice of locations for break of gauge.	Oxford, Worcester and Wolverhampton, 83–2
Atmospheric principles are mechanically sound, but operationally and financially unproven. Atmospheric lines are difficult to convert to locomotive lines as gradients are usually severe. They require double track throughout, which will be expensive. They are too inflexible to handle varied and intermittent traffic	Newcastle–Berwick, 62; Direct Portsmouth via Petersfield, 172
Amalgamation of new railways with established canals is 'a doubtful policy'	London and York and Witham Canal, 153
Bridges and viaducts across major estuaries are not viable, except some way inland	*Not viable*: Forth (Edinburgh), Tay (Dundee), Tamar (Plymouth), Severn (Bristol), Humber (Hull) *Viable*: Tyne (Newcastle), Tweed (Berwick), Severn (below Gloucester) Possible: Mersey (Runcorn) Possible but undesirable: Thames (London)
It is difficult to forecast traffic in undeveloped areas as there are few existing lines with which to make a comparison	North of Ireland, 119

impossible. The building of a railway line refashioned the landscape irreversibly; the resources committed to building the line could not be recovered by closing it down. Construction costs were sunk; only land and equipment could be put to alternative uses. But land had limited uses once a railway line had been built across it, and second-hand railway equipment could not always find a ready market.

As a result, competition in the railway industry quickly came to be understood in territorial terms. Companies sought to defend monopolies acquired through their early lead in railway construction, and fought with their neighbours over the position of the frontier. Companies behaved like emerging nation states engaged in the competitive acquisition of territory, while their managers behaved like field-marshals and generals of their armies.

Table 6.5. Acceptable compromises endorsed by the Railway Committee of the Board of Trade, with examples

Acceptable limitations	Example (report no.)
'Second best' lines are acceptable if other lines in the region have already been built in the wrong place	Plymouth–Falmouth (Cornwall Railway), 89
Parallel lines are acceptable where mountains intervene between two valleys	Blackburn, Bolton and Darwen/Manchester, Bury and Rossendale, 225
A comprehensive trunk system is acceptable even though it does not serve intermediate towns, because these can be served by branches later; the best trunk system is more important than serving all places from the outset	Caledonian (Carlisle–Carstairs–Edinburgh)/North British via Hawick, 120
Use of minor lines to build up a trunk system is acceptable provided long-distance traffic has priority	Caledonian: Carstairs–Glasgow, 120
Ferries across estuaries, and inclines over mountains, worked by stationary engines, are acceptable if the alternatives are very poor	Plymouth–Falmouth (Cornwall Railway), 89; Blackburn, Burnley, Accrington and Colne Extension, 225; Gosport–Portsmouth ferry across Portsmouth Harbour, 172
Swing bridges across rivers are acceptable if few masted boats use the river, and the alternative is a substantial deviation	Direct Northern Lincoln–Thorne–York, 153
Change of gauge is acceptable, but should occur at places with little through traffic, or at ports where transhipment must occur in any case	Oxford, Worcester and Wolverhampton, 83–2
Steep gradients can be tolerated—especially on lines where traffic may be light	*Examples* (61) Newcastle and Carlisle 1/106; Liverpool and Manchester 1/88; Edinburgh and Glasgow (Cowlairs) 1/42; Oldham–Manchester 1/27; Camden bank 1/66; Hunts Cross, Manchester 1/49
Sharp curves can be tolerated where traffic moves slowly—up to eight chains radius	Various examples, 61
Monopolies in a region are acceptable, but the region concerned should be as small as possible	Oxford, Worcester and Wolverhampton, 83–2
Duplication of stations in a town or city is acceptable if it avoids congestion due to inadequate existing facilities	Direct Northern at York, 153
Bypassing a major city is acceptable if it avoids congestion	Trent Valley avoiding Birmingham,118
Opposition from canals can be disregarded as they are vested interests which themselves once displaced other means of transport	Dublin–west of Ireland, 156

Companies could get locked in to bitter conflicts with neighbouring companies from which neither party could easily escape. Railway promoters therefore needed to think very carefully about initiating competition with another company. Unfortunately, though, it was difficult to predict what those consequences might be. If price competition broke out, with each company cutting fares in an

Table 6.6. Reasons for rejection or postponement of a railway scheme given by the Railway Committee of the Board of Trade, with examples

Reason for rejection or postponement	Example (report no.)
Two parallel lines are not normally viable. The scheme competes with a potentially better scheme	Cambridge–Huntingdon, 226; Exeter–Crediton, 89; Crediton–Barnstaple, 89; Yeovil–London, 83–1
The scheme crosses the paths of potential new lines which might be better; it may be promoted simply as a 'blocking' move	Grand Junction Railway Shrewsbury–Birmingham line, 83–2; Wymondham–East Dereham, 88
Over-optimistic traffic forecasts (lack of suitable evidence)—particularly where population density is low—warrant postonement	Diss–Beccles–Yarmouth, 88; Wells–Thetford, 88; Lynn–Swaffham, 88
Traffic, though sometimes large, may be only intermittent or seasonal	Cambridge–Bury, 226
Development of new suburbs is too speculative and may warrant postonement	Epping, 226
Where long-distance (end-to-end) traffic alone is not sufficient to warrant a line, the shortest and most direct route is not necessarily the best	Exeter–Yeovil, 83–1; Norwich–Colchester–London avoiding Ipswich, 88
The line parallels a canal whereas an alternative opens up new country instead	Lincoln–Retford–Sheffield and Chesterfield Canal, 153; London and York Boston–Lincoln loop and Witham Canal, 153
The density of the network in a lightly populated region is limited by the need for 'solvency'	London and York Boston–Lincoln loop, 153
Reliance on atmospheric principle is unwise as it is unproven economically	Newcastle–Berwick, 62; Cornwall and Devon Central, 89
Using a canal towpath for a railway line is difficult if the canal is to remain open for traffic	Dublin–Galway, 156

attempt to win all the traffic, then both companies could be ruined. One might survive by putting the other out of business before it went out of business itself, but which company would survive was difficult to know in advance. One opinion was that both companies would suffer whatever happened, which suggested that potential entrants should keep out, while another opinion was that the companies would eventually cooperate out of sheer necessity. This suggested that entry might be a good strategy provided the entrant was willing to share the market with the established company.

Competition therefore introduced a high degree of uncertainty into the railway industry. Instead of focusing the attention of railway management on the improvement of customer service, as the ideology of competition suggested that it should, it focused management attention instead on preserving local monopoly against outside attack. Customers were retained not by improving service to a level that competitors could not match, but by undermining the attempts of potential competitors to provide any service at all.

Competition was not the only source of uncertainty in the early railway industry, however. Technological uncertainty was important too (see Chapter 7). While the unexpected success of the Liverpool and Manchester Railway created considerable confidence about the potential demand for rail demand, which spurred the formation of other schemes, the promoters of these schemes knew that they were nevertheless taking considerable risks. While the demand might be considered proven, there was still considerable uncertainty about the most appropriate means of locomotive power, and also controversy about the most appropriate gauge. Furthermore, signalling and safety systems were primitive, and no one was surely how railway operation would evolve in the future.

6.7. LOCAL MONOPOLY AND THE REGULATION OF FARES

To compensate them for the considerable risks involved, the promoters expected to earn a high return if they were successful. They expected this return to come from their monopoly power. The superiority of rail over road and canal would allow a handsome price premium to be charged. From the very beginning, therefore, Parliament was faced with the issue of regulating monopoly power. Because the railways were demanding powers of compulsory purchase, there had to be public benefit—the companies could not be allowed to appropriate all the social gains for themselves. Following a precedent applied to canals, therefore, railways were restricted in the fares they could charge. Maximum rates were fixed for different classes of passenger travel, and for different types of freight. This ensured that a proportion of the benefit from railways accrued to the passengers and to the merchants who consigned their freight.

There were different fares for different classes of travel. Railways discriminated between different classes of passenger on the basis of the degree of comfort provided. On the early railways, first class was equivalent to travelling on the inside of a stage coach, second class was somewhat better than the outside of a stagecoach, and third class was the equivalent of being treated like a parcel or a piece of luggage and put in a covered wagon.

An early mistake was to stipulate maximum fares in terms of the actual mileage travelled rather than the distance as the crow flies. The method followed a precedent set on the canals. Although the method was just as unsuitable for canals as for railways, the canal system never became so extensive as the railway system because the railways arrived so soon after the canals, and so the problem was not fully appreciated.

Setting maximum fares is particularly important where the price elasticity of demand is low—that is, the number of people who wish to travel is largely invariant to the price. Most railway companies believed that demand was inelastic—especially for first class travel—and so wished to charge as high a price as possible, subject to the regulations. Where the regulated fare by a direct route was well below the maximum that the customer was willing to pay, it paid the company to send the customer via an indirect route instead—a principle well known to some taxi-drivers. This seems to have discouraged some railway companies from building cut-offs to expedite traffic on their system. While the cut off might reduce operating expenses, it could also reduce revenue.

Many commentators considered that Parliament allowed too much variation in the fares charged by different companies, with the principal error being to allow some companies to charge very high fares. James Morrison, MP, was a major champion of a low-fares policy, and under his influence the Select Committee on Railway Acts Enactments (see above) recommended a uniform low-fares policy, to be imposed by the Board of Trade. The distinguished civil engineer William Cubitt told the Committee that he

> ...should be very glad to see railroads upon a very different footing. I should like to see them exceedingly general in the country, and worked at very low and uniform fares; and I should like to see the whole of the railways throughout the kingdom worked with a common stock, and not worked by distinct Boards; that, no doubt, would be a great innovation; and I should like to see a Government Board, whose duty should be to take care that those lines were well carried, which should have great controlling legal powers.
>
> (BPP, Vol. 14, Q. 758, p. 48)

Morrison drew an analogy between railways and roads. The roads were known as the King's Highways—a term which indicated a right of access for all citizens. Freedom to travel was fundamental to social intercourse and was the basis of national society. Railways were natural monopolies because, unlike roads, different carriers could not offer competing services on the same track, because of the risk of accidents.

Morrison contrasted the low-fare policies of continental countries such as Belgium with the high-fare policy of British companies. He argued that fares should be lower in Britain because railways were cheaper to construct—due to better engineering, a more energetic work force, and cheaper iron for rails and bridges—and also cheaper to operate, because of the low price of coal and coke. He maintained that railway companies were misguided in setting high fares because passenger revenue was normally maximized by fares which were moderate. In certain cases low fares would generate even higher revenues, and even if low fares were imposed in other cases, it was unlikely that the railway company would lose much in revenue terms. The public would benefit most from low fares, and since railway companies would have little to lose, he strongly advocated a low-fare policy.

Morrison considered that competition was ineffective in reducing fares. The building of competitive lines simply doubled the amount of capital expended on the system, and did little to increase total traffic. A railway company might reduce fares in order to discourage a rival line from being built, but if this line were built, then after a short interlude of price warfare the two companies would collude or possibly amalgamate. Fares might then increase to an even higher level than originally in order to cover the cost of the double expenditure of capital.

Morrison believed that when the earliest railways were authorized the potential for future reductions in operating costs, due to greater experience, were not fully appreciated. The maximum fares the companies were allowed to charge were set too high. Later companies benefited from lower construction costs as well as low operating costs. The provisions of these early acts were repeated in later acts, and by the mid-1840s the maximum rates were far too high to curb the exercise of monopoly power. He therefore recommended that maximum fares should be set to ensure the railways did not earn more than 10 per cent return on capital. He concurred with the provisions of Gladstone's 1844 Railways Act—namely that railways which consistently earned more than 10 per cent should be bought out by the state. However, he considered that the terms laid down—namely 25 years purchase, calculated on an average of 3 years' profits—were far too generous to the companies and far too onerous for the taxpayers.

6.8. NETWORK EFFECTS AND COMPETITION

In the simple story of competition expounded above, any supplier is a potential competitor for any other supplier. In the case of a network industry, such as the railway system, however, this does not apply. A network is made up of a set of linkages and these linkages meet up with each other at hubs. Where linkages meet at a hub, one linkage may feed traffic into another linkage and take traffic from it, in which case the two linkages perform a complementary role. It is also possible, however, that one linkage may take traffic away from another linkage instead. At a simple three-way hub, for example, traffic arriving over the first linkage may be diverted from the second linkage to the third, or vice versa. In this case the second and third linkages are complementary to the first linkage but are substitutes for each other. In strategic terms, the owner of the first linkage can collaborate with either the owner of the second linkage or the owner of the third linkage, and this turns the owners of the second and third linkages into competitors.

Railway regulation in Britain was heavily based on the assumption that it was possible to distinguish between competitive and collaborative railway schemes. For example, Parliament often investigated 'competitive' schemes for new railways together, by allocating them to the same Committees. Similarly Parliament generally disapproved of mergers between companies operating competitive lines, but was willing to approve mergers between companies operating collaborative lines. In this context, lines that made end-on junctions with each other were usually deemed collaborative—such as the London and Birmingham Railway and the Grand Junction Railway that carried traffic forward from Birmingham to a junction with the Liverpool and Manchester Railway, and also the Great Western line from London to Bristol and the Bristol and Exeter line that carried London traffic forward to Exeter. Branches too were generally considered collaborative with the main lines into which they fed. On the other hand, lines that pursued alternative routes between major cities were considered competitive even though they might serve different areas en route.

In practice, however, the distinction is not absolute—instead a spectrum of possibilities is involved. Whether any pair of linkages meeting at a hub are collaborators or competitors depends on the pattern of traffic flow through the hub, which in turn reflects the destinations that are accessible from the other ends of the linkages concerned. As the network evolves, the number of destinations accessible over any given linkage tends to increase, and as the economy develops the volume of traffic destined for different places will grow as well. Hence the degree of competitiveness between any given pair of linkages at a given hub may change significantly over time. Generally speaking, the growth of the network tends to increase the degree of competition that exists between any pair of linkages since it becomes more likely that the two linkages indirectly serve similar places and therefore can accommodate the same traffic flows.

The issue is quite complex, which probably explains why neither Parliament nor the Board of Trade addressed it fully. Two linkages can only be competitors if they form part of two alternative routes. If a network affords no alternative routes then there can be no competition on it. The pure Steiner solution to network configuration, for example, as described in Chapter 3, affords no alternative routes, because if there were an alternative route between any two points then one of the routes could be eliminated by removing one of the linkages and the points would still be connected by the remaining route. A pure Steiner network therefore always involves collaboration rather than competition. The same point applies to any network with a simple 'root and branch' configuration; competition only arises once direct connections are built between locations on different branches.

On a large network linkages can be competitors or collaborators without there being any direct connection between them. In other words, substitution and complementarity between some pair of linkages can exist quite independently of whether they actually meet up at a hub. Many routes are long and therefore comprise many linkages: the East Coast and West Coast routes from London to Scotland are a case in point. On the West Coast route the linkage between Carlisle and Glasgow in the north is complementary to the linkage between London and Rugby in the south because, although they are more than 200 miles apart, they are both required to carry traffic from London to Glasgow; similarly, on the East Coast main line, the linkage from Berwick to Edinburgh is complementary to the linkage between London and Peterborough because both are required to carry traffic from London to Edinburgh. For similar reasons, the linkage from Crewe to Preston is a substitute for the linkage between Doncaster and York because the former is a crucial link in the West Coast line and the latter is a crucial link in the East Coast line. Without the former, traffic from London to Scotland would divert to the East Coast route, while in the absence of the latter it would divert to the West Coast route.

Parliament seems to have exercised reasonably good judgement in differentiating the extremes of strongly competitive routes and strongly collaborative routes, but to have failed to appreciate the very large size of the 'grey area' in between. Many dead-end branches that were considered complementary to the trunk lines they served could well have formed a part of some cross-country route that would have competed with the trunk line they joined, had they been extended. By allowing these branches to be taken over by the local main line company, opportunities for their future extension may have been foreclosed. Similarly, allowing companies operating main lines into London to extend their networks deeper into the provinces by acquiring control of provincial companies that made an end-on connection with them turned some provincial lines into mere appendages of a London-based system. As a result, opportunities to connect these regional highways with lines that entered the region from directions other than London were foreclosed. For example, by integrating the Grand Junction with the London and Birmingham, traffic from London to Liverpool received more favoured treatment in Birmingham than did traffic from Bristol that transferred from the Midland Railway. Similarly, Birmingham traffic from the Midland Railway received less favourable treatment than traffic from London when it arrived at Bristol to be forwarded along the Exeter line of the Great Western Railway. By and large, therefore, Parliament's excessively sharp distinction between competitive and collaborative lines undermined the autonomy of regional networks by allowing each potential regional network to fall into the hands of some London-based company which then routed as much traffic as possible from the region in the direction of London—including traffic that would have been more directly consigned using independent cross-country routes. This point is developed further below.

6.9. THE INTEGRATION OF OWNERSHIP AND ITS CONSEQUENCES

One of the main reasons why Parliament authorized mergers between main lines and their end-on extensions is that they anticipated that major operating economies could be achieved in this way. The operating costs of the early railways were very high, as signalling, track maintenance, and station administration were all very labour-intensive processes. In addition, locomotives needed to be changed and rested fairly frequently, so that several different locomotives might be required to complete a long single journey.

The previous discussion of competition suggests that it might have been useful to have each linkage of the system separately owned, and to have left the independent owners of the individual linkages to negotiate with each other over the terms on which their track could be used. In the early years of the railway system, however, this was not really considered to be a viable proposition and, so far as can be judged, was never actively discussed.

One reason for this is that it was considered important for the operator of the trains to be also the owner of the track. If ownership of track and trains could be neatly separated then it would be possible to integrate the ownership of trains without integrating the ownership of track. Large operating companies could run long-distance trains over multiple linkages, allowing operating economies of integration to be achieved without the anti-competitive implications of integrating the ownership of track as well. Indeed, the modern privatized UK rail system separates the ownership of track and trains, although it uses a very different arrangement from that described above. Under present arrangements, ownership of the track is monopolized by a nominally independent company (which is effectively state-controlled) while independent operators compete (to a very limited extent) in running the trains.

When the earliest railways were authorized, provisions were made for carriers to arrange their own transport over the 'iron road', using their own locomotives if necessary. This was already common practice on other modes of inland transport—not only public roads and turnpikes, but canals as well. It was soon evident, however, that serious confusion could arise if different trains were operated by different people, because of the difficulty in switching conflicting traffic to alternative lines. The high speeds involved, coupled with limited braking power, meant that confusion could easily result in serious accidents.

It was also recognized at a very early stage that substantial economies could be achieved by carrying passengers and freight in trains that consolidated different types of traffic. Unlike the roads, where even today each person typically uses their own car, railways were best served by the specialized provision of motive power. Rather than employ a single large vehicle, like a bus, the railway employed a set of vehicles—carriages and wagons—hauled by a single locomotive.

Although the trains could, in principle, be run by independent carriers, the problem of timetabling the trains to avoid conflicting traffic movements and making efficient use of the locomotives argued in favour of centralized timetabling. It therefore became the practice for passenger trains to run at publicly advertised times and for independently organized trains (such as special excursions) to become the exception rather than the rule. Wherever the volume of traffic warranted it, goods traffic and passenger traffic were separated into different trains. Most of the goods trains ran at scheduled times but, unlike the passenger trains, their schedules were not normally advertised except for the carriage of perishable goods such as milk or fish. Mineral traffic and general merchandise was normally moved in slow heavy freight trains, and passing loops were later provided to facilitate overtaking by express passenger trains.

As early as the mid-1830s it was generally agreed that the management of tracks and trains should be integrated. This did not rule out the subcontracting of train operations to independent companies, provided that these companies followed appropriate regulations, and worked to a centrally determined timetable, as on the railway system of today. Indeed, in the Victorian period a number of companies leased the operation of their lines to independent contractors, such as Thomas Brassey, the railway builder, on a short-term basis. Furthermore, many companies that owned short branch lines leased their operation to the company that owned the main line with which they connected. In this latter case the operating company usually took most of the key decisions; the owners of the branch took a passive role in which they received an agreed proportion of the net receipts from branch line traffic. With the exception of contractors' lines, therefore, the Victorian railway system may be understood as a system in which a small number of operating companies competed against each other using tracks that they either owned themselves or leased on a long-term basis from smaller companies.

An important feature of the major operating companies was that they normally owned at least one very long trunk line. As previously explained, many of the early railway schemes involved establishing connections between major urban centres, and for this purpose the entire length of track between these centres became owned by the same company. This was a natural consequence of the concern of the proprietors to gain access to the traffic at either end of the line. In theory, a number of different companies could have been formed to build independent sections of line that would then be joined up with each other end-to-end to form an inter-urban line of communication. The obvious difficulty with this is that the companies would then be left to negotiate with each other over how to split the revenue from the through traffic, and since the through traffic was the largest—and most valuable—portion of the traffic, the scope for argument was considerable. The logical way to resolve this difficulty was for the separate companies to merge. But if they were going to merge later, then they might as well merge to begin with—so that a single integrated plan could be submitted to Parliament at the outset.

Although the integration of end-on lines seemed relatively innocuous at the time, it had unforeseen negative consequences. There is an important difference between the way that competition works at the level of individual linkages and the way that it works between integrated companies that control multiple linkages. The owner of a single linkage has no control over the traffic that is fed into it from other linkages, but the owner of a trunk line can control the traffic that flows from one linkage onto the next if he or she owns both the linkages concerned. This means that the owner of a long trunk line can control the traffic that originates along the line by determining the point at which it subsequently leaves it. In terms of railway company policy, it means that the owner of a trunk line can influence the decisions of passengers or shippers who join the line at one of its stations by restricting their options with regard to the route that is taken to their destination. Where it pays the railway to charge the maximum permitted fare, and the fare is based on distance, as described above, it pays the trunk line company to carry passengers and freight as far as possible over its own tracks even if this increases the total length of the journey.

As the density of the network increased with the building of additional lines, so the number of competitive threats to major trunk lines increased. Between any pair of stations more and more alternative routes became available. But although intermediate towns on major trunk lines might emerge as local hubs, control of these hubs made it possible for the main line companies to impede connections with rival lines. In this context, a rival line was any line owned by an independent company that had the potential to provide an alternative route to destinations that the main line company claimed to serve.

The main line companies therefore artificially restricted customer choice by influencing the routes that customers could take. Any customer going to their nearest station would find that the options for transferring to the lines of other companies at intermediate points were limited. The company would not refuse to allow the customer to travel, but they might refuse to sell a through ticket. They might also point out that connections at the hub where they intended to leave the company's network were notoriously unreliable. Indeed, express trains might not even stop at the junctions concerned, thereby lengthening the duration of the journey, even though the distance might be shorter.

In fact, the owner of a long-distance trunk line could impede connections to rival lines before they were even built. If an independent company planned to intersect their trunk line, the trunk line owner could object simply on the grounds that its property rights were being infringed. More specifically, the trunk line owner had *locus standi* before Parliament in opposing any railway Bill that involved a line that crossed its own. It could argue before Parliament that it would be better that it built the intersecting line itself, as it could then ensure good connections with the trunk line. In other words, it could use its power to disrupt connections to argue that it should be allowed to build the line itself in place of the other company. The fact that Parliament was willing to entertain such arguments indicates that, although Parliament was willing to sanction interference with property rights in the interests of building railways, it was not inclined to interfere with a railway company's right to disrupt the interchange of traffic with independent lines if it wished to do so.

When applying the theory of competition to railway networks, therefore, it is important to bear in mind that railways were often promoted, not as single linkages, but as packages of linkages. Passengers needed to construct a customized package of linkages in order to accomplish their journeys. As the density of the network increased, the number of potential packages from which a customer could choose increased significantly, but the companies became increasingly adept at restricting the customer's effective choice. At each local station where a passenger might join the network the company would have some particular route that it wished the customer to take—generally the route that maximized the distance that the passenger travelled over the company's own lines. The company would use its control over fares and timetables, and its ability to delay other companies' trains, to impede the journey of a passenger who took a less profitable route. Although this antisocial behaviour was widely recognized, no action was taken by Parliament to enforce the customer's freedom of choice. Although Parliament often authorized competing lines in order to appease local interests, it failed to protect these new lines by giving them effective access to traffic originating with established rivals elsewhere on the system.

6.10. COMPETITION BY INVASION

It might be expected that the power of established companies to disrupt potential rivals would be sufficient to discourage promoters of new lines, but this was not in fact the case. The main reason was dissatisfaction in the towns, as explained above. The business elites of many towns were dissatisfied with the high fares and freight charges demanded by their local main line company. Although these charges were limited by statute, it was common knowledge that fares and rates were often lower in towns served by two independent companies than in towns served by just one company—especially when these companies offered alternative routes to the same destination. Grievances were particularly strong in towns that were served only by branches, since service was often poor as well. Competition between towns meant that it was the comparison that irked them—that rival towns had both lower fares and better service.

Once a main line company appreciated that the promotion of new lines was inevitable, it had to decide how to respond. It could oppose a new line, and threaten to disrupt its traffic, as noted above, or it could offer to build the line itself. This offer could be genuine or it could be bogus—so that if the ploy succeeded, and a rival scheme was defeated, the line would not in fact be built.

There were certainly instances of new independent lines that were built and then starved of traffic because the hubs at which they hoped to obtain traffic did not work properly. There were also instances of bogus schemes being authorized by Parliament and never built. But promoters soon 'got wise' to these situations, as did Parliament. Promoters realized that a successful independent line needed to drive right into the major traffic-generating centres in the area that it intended to serve—it could not access these centres through a hub on the local main line because the main line company would disrupt its operation.

Promoters also realized that they needed access to traffic-generating centres outside their region too, and the easiest way to obtain this was to form an alliance with a main line company elsewhere. In this way main line companies in one region became involved in promoting invading lines into other companies' regions.

When a local main line company faced an invasion led by a main line company from another region that had sufficient resources to build a rival network, it quickly realized that the disruption threat no longer had much force since the invader would avoid the use of the established company's hubs. An alternative defensive strategy was available, however: to threaten a counter-attack by forming an alliance with local interests in the invader's region.

In the meantime, however, Parliament had resolved to discourage the promotion of bogus schemes by compelling companies to build lines that they had been authorized to construct (unless they were able to procure a further act to abandon them). Hence a 'tit for tat' invasion line would have to be built if it was authorized; bluffing was no longer a viable option.

Notwithstanding the risks involved, however, many main line companies committed themselves to invasions—some unilateral and some on a 'tit for tat' basis. To spread the costs of these invasions, other companies from outside the target region might be encouraged to join a consortium for this purpose (as noted in Chapter 5). This strategy seems to have been prompted by two special considerations. The first was that demand for rail travel was increasing steadily, and so additional lines could well generate additional traffic—in particular, holiday traffic. Although duplication of existing routes was wasteful, there was a prospect of sufficient traffic in some regions to warrant duplicate provision; it might not be highly profitable, but it would at least break even.

The second consideration was that invasion of another region was a step towards becoming a national rather than a regional company (see Chapter 7). If other main line companies were expanding into new regions, then an elite group of companies with nationwide networks could emerge, and so each company had to decide whether it wished to belong to this elite or not. A national company would be able to offer a 'one stop shop' for railway travel needs, and passengers travelling by this company would be spared the frustrations of trying to make connections between the rival companies' trains. As a result, passengers might be willing to go out of their way to begin and end their journey on a national company's network, even though there might be nearer stations operated by regional or local companies. The logic of this approach is explored more fully in Appendix 7.

Although in retrospect these national ambitions seem somewhat fanciful, evidence suggests that at the time shareholders were often impressed by this form of 'strategic thinking'. Expansion-minded company chairmen like Edward Watkin were very adept at justifying their expansion plans by futuristic visions that appealed to shareholders. Indeed, in the late Victorian period many railway companies acquired their own shipping lines, and even some overseas railway operations, in order to provide a 'one stop' multi-modal transport service on an international scale. These ventures were not on the whole a financial success, however. In practice only one company—the Midland—attained a viable degree of national coverage, and this was only achieved through partnership with other railway companies.

6.11. MERGER POLICY

Things might have turned out very differently if railway companies had been free to merge with whomever they liked. For many railway managers, merger of competing interests was the natural way out of their competitive dilemmas. As early as 1840 the Midland Counties Railway and the Birmingham and Derby Junction Railway had become enmeshed in competition for traffic from Yorkshire to London. Both companies connected Derby with the London and Birmingham Railway. Passengers from Leeds and Sheffield arrived at Derby by the North Midland Railway. The Midland Counties' junction with the London and Birmingham Railway at Birmingham was bypassed by the Derby Junction's line from Whitacre to Hampton-in-Arden, which joined the Birmingham line further south.

Parliament was generally sceptical of the benefits of mergers, however. It was originally thought that competition on railways could be secured by allowing different operators to offer competing services along the same line of rails. But as early as 1839 the Select Committee on the State of Communication by Railways had recognized that this was a mistake. The safety of passengers, it said, required 'one system of management, under one superintending authority', even if the authority 'should thereby acquire an entire monopoly of the means of communication'.

The Railway Committee of the Board of Trade, in its report on proposed amalgamations five years later, was more nuanced, however. It suggested that amalgamations were quite suitable for short lines of railways, such as 'independent links and branches' and 'unprofitable lines' (BPP, 1845, Cmd. 279 p. 2). Experience had shown that short lines were often uneconomic because the fixed costs of maintaining engines in steam were high relative to the amount of traffic to be carried. When carrying coal, for example, it was advantageous to have a single locomotive collect the coal trucks from the mines and take the coal train to its destination, rather than oblige a local railway to collect the coal and then hand over the working of the train to a trunk line instead. Amalgamation with a larger railway could therefore benefit a local line: customers would gain from lower charges and better service made possible by lower overall cost of operation.

Amalgamation might also be useful where several independent companies operated a single through line. A company owning a single section of the line might put up prices to extract monopoly rents over its own portion of the line:

...attempts have been made by Companies holding one portion of a great line of communication, to extract an undue charge, by compelling passengers, who may have arrived at their terminus in second or third class carriages, either to wait or to proceed in carriages of a more expensive class. Even first class passengers also have been often subjected to delay and inconvenience... (p. 3)

The Railway Committee agreed with the Select Committee, though, that amalgamation could reinforce monopoly power. Established railway companies in a district could combine to erect a barrier to entry by pooling their resources to contest proposals to build additional lines. Experience suggested that rationalization following amalgamation could result in the closure of useful sections of line, as when York and North Midland Railway closed down a section of the Leeds and Selby Railway because it competed with its own (longer) line into Leeds.

Erecting barriers to entry was seen to be a possible motive behind the proposed amalgamation of three railways serving Liverpool: the Grand Junction Railway (to Birmingham), the Liverpool and Manchester Railway, and the North Union Railway (to Wigan and Preston). Although amalgamation might lead to greater efficiency in the working of the Liverpool terminus shared by these companies, the Committee felt that a more powerful opposition to new railways in Lancashire and Cheshire could well impede the development of recently established ports at Birkenhead and Fleetwood. Similarly, the lease of the Sheffield and Manchester Railway to the Midland Railway and Manchester and Birmingham Railway was deemed objectionable because the Sheffield and Manchester Railway could, in conjunction with one of the proposed lines from London to York, provide an alternative route from London to Manchester, which the Manchester and Birmingham should not be encouraged to block.

Judged by its recommendations in other specific cases, the Board believed that ports such as Birkenhead and Hull should be served by independent local

Table 6.7. Major railway Bills for England, Wales, and Scotland presented to Parliament in the session 1844–5

Project and promoter	Type	Remark	No. track	Miles	Gp	BoT Ref.	BoT Rec.	Parl SC	Act	Open	Cl'd
Central Kent: London–Maidstone–Canterbury–Deal	NL		NS	101	A	23	N	U	N		
London Chatham and the North Kent	NL	A	2	58	A	23	N	N	N		
London Chatham and Chilham (Croydon Railway)	NL	A	NS	61	A	23	N	N	N		
South Eastern: North Kent: Hungerford Bridge–Chilham	NL		2	55	A	23	Y	D	N		
London and Ashford (Croydon Railway)	NL	A	NS	56	A	23	N	D	N		
South Eastern: Hungerford Bridge to Tonbridge and Paddock Wood	NL		2	46	A	23	Y	Cd	N		
South Eastern: Tonbridge to Tunbridge Wells	BR		NS	6	A	23	Y	Y	Y 167	1846	
South Eastern: Tunbridge Wells to Hastings	BR		NS	27	A	23	N	W	N		
Rye Tenterden and Headcorn	NL		2	17	A	23	N	N	N		
South Eastern: Ashford to Hastings	BR		NS	26	A	23	Y	W	N		
London–Gravesend via North Woolwich Ferry	NL		NS	16	A	23	Not Cd	N	N		
Brighton, Lewes and Hastings: Keymer branch	BR		NS	9	A	226	Y	Y	Y 102	1846	
Brighton, Lewes and Hastings: Rye and Ashford branch	BR		2	33	A	292	N	Y	Y 200	1851	
South Eastern: Maidstone and Rochester	NL		NS	11	A	23	Y	P	N		
South Eastern: Minster to Deal and Walmer, and Margate deviation	BR		NS	13	A	23	Y	Y	Y 197	1847	
Kentish Coast: Herne Bay to Dover with branches to Ramsgate and Deal	NL		2	29	A	226	N	D	N		
Gravesend and Rochester (Thames and Medway Canal)	XT		1	0	A			Y	Y 168	1847	
London Chatham and Gravesend	NL	A	NS	30	A	23	N	N	N		
London and Croydon: Orpington branch	BR	A	NS	8	A	23	N	N	N		
London and Croydon: enlargement	XT	A		0	A			Y	Y 196		
London and Maidstone	NL	A	NS	38	A	23	N	U	N		

(continued)

Table 6.7. (Continued)

Project and promoter	Type	Remark	No. track	Miles	Gp	BoT Ref.	BoT Rec.	Parl SC	Act	Open	Cl'd
South Eastern: Headcorn and Rye	BR		NS	16	A	23	N	U	N		
South Eastern: London and Greenwich Railway widening	XT		2	0	A			Y	Y 186		
Leeds and West Riding Junction (Manchester and Leeds)	NL		2	47	B	61	Y	Y	N		
West Yorkshire											
Huddersfield and Manchester Railway and Canal,	NL		2	34	B	61	N	N	N	1849	
with branch to Delph	NL		2	22	B	225	N	Y	Y 100	1849	
Manchester and Leeds: Todmorden—Burnley branch	BR		2	8	B	61	Y	Y	Y 54	1848	
Manchester and Leeds: Heywood branch extension to Bury	XT		2	5	B	61	Y	Y	Y 54	1849	
Manchester and Leeds: Oldham Extension	XT			1	B	61	Y	Y	Y 54	1848	
Leeds and Thirsk	NL		2	46	B	173	P	Y	Y 104	1848	1967(P) 1970(F)
Harrogate and Ripon Junction (Great North of England)	NL		2	20	B	173	P	Y	N		
York and North Midland: Church Fenton–Harrogate branch	BR		2	18	B	173	P	Y	Y 84		
Leeds Dewsbury and Manchester	NL		2	18	B	173	N	Y	Y 36		
Barnsley Junction: Penistone–Barnsley	NL		2	10	C	61	Y	N	N		
Huddersfield and Sheffield Junction: Huddersfield–Penistone	NL		2	15	C	225	N	Y	Y 39	1850	
Leeds and Bradford extension: Shipley to Colne	XT		2	29	D	61	Y	Y	Y 38/181	1848	
Manchester Bury and Rossendale: Blackburn and Burnley Accrington and Colne Extensions	XT		2	24	D	225	Y	Y	Y 35	1849	
Blackburn Darwen and Bolton	NL		2	14	D	225	Y	Y	Y 44	1848	
Northumberland (North British)	NL	A	NS	86	E	62	N	N	N		
Newcastle and Berwick	NL		2	32	E	62	Y	Y	Y 163	1848	

Table 6.7. (Continued)

Project and promoter	Type	Remark	No. track	Miles	Gp	BoT Ref.	BoT Rec.	Parl SC	Act	Open	Cl'd
Newcastle and Darlington and Brandling Junction: extensions at Darlington, Pelaw and Monkwearmouth	T, XT		2	6	E	173	Y	Y	Y 92	1849	
Newcastle-upon-Tyne and North Shields: Tynemouth extension and branch to Quay at Newcastle	XT		2	1	E	226	Y	Y	Y 47	1847	
Oxford Worcester and Wolverhampton (GWR)	NL	BG	2	97	F	83–2	N	Y	Y 184	1853	
Oxford and Rugby (GWR)	NL	BG	2	50	F	83–2	N	Y	Y 188	1852	
Oxford and Didcot	NL		NS	9	F			U	N		
London Worcester Rugby and Oxford Railway: Tring–Banbury–Worcester–Dudley with branches from Bicester to Oxford and Banbury to Rugby (LBR)	NL		2	145	F	83–2	Y	N	N		
London Worcester Rugby and Oxford Railway: Dudley to Wolverhampton (LBR)	XT		2	7	F	83–2	Y	N	N		
London Worcester Rugby and Oxford Railway: Dudley and Sedgeley (LBR)	BR		NS	4	F	83–2	Y	N	N		
Birmingham and Gloucester Railway: Worcester branch and deviation					F	83–2	W'drawn	N	N		
Birmingham and Gloucester Railway: Wolverhampton extension	NL		2	36	F	83–2	W'drawn	W	N		
Bristol and Gloucester and Birmingham and Gloucester					F			W	N		
London Worcester and South Staffordshire	BR				F			N	N		
Grand Junction: Dudley branch	NL		NS	5	F			W	N		
Grand Junction: Shrewsbury and Stafford	NL		2	28	F	83–2	N	W	N		
Grand Junction: Shrewsbury and Wolverhampton branch	NL		2	30	F	83–2	N	W	N		
Shrewsbury Wolverhampton Dudley and Birmingham	NL		2	93	F	83–2	Y	W	N		

(continued)

Table 6.7. (Continued)

Project and promoter	Type	Remark	No. track	Miles	Gp	BoT Ref.	BoT Rec.	Parl SC	Act	Open	Cl'd
Bristol and Exeter: Durston–Yeovil branch (GWR)	BR	BG	NS	28	G	83–1	Y	Y	Y 155	1853	
London and South Western Railway: Salisbury–Yeovil extension	NL		2	42	G	83–1	N	U	N		
London and South Western Railway: Hook Pit deviation (Eastleigh cut-off)				4	G	83–1	N	U	N		
London and South Western Railway: Basingstoke–Newbury–Didcot or Swindon	NL		2	61	G	83–1	N	U	N		
Wilts Somerset and Weymouth (GWR): Chippenham–Westbury–Dorchester–Weymouth	BG		2	129	G	83–1	Y	Y	Y 53	1857	
Southampton and Dorchester (GWR—transferred to LSWR)	NL		1	59	G	83–1	Y	Y	Y 93	1847	
Berks and Hants Railway (GWR): Reading–Newbury–Hungerford and Reading–Basingstoke branches	BR	BG	2	40	G	83–1	Y	Y	Y 40	1847	
Salisbury Dorchester and Weymouth (LSWR)	NL		2	55		83–1	N	N	N		
Salisbury and Dorsetshire (LSWR): Poole branch	NL				G	NC	N	U	N		
Harwich Railway and Pier (Eastern Counties): Braithwaite's line	NL		2	15	H	174	Y	W	N		
Harwich: Hoskin's line (independent)	NL		2	17	H	174	N	W	N		
Eastern Union: Ipswich and Harwich (Manningtree–Harwich)	BR		2	11	H	174	A	W	N		
Harwich and Eastern Counties Junction: Mosse's line Colchester–Harwich (independent)	NL		2	15	H	174	N	W	N		
Colchester Port and Junction	JN		2	6	H	174	P	W	N		
Lynn and Ely, with a branch to Wisbech	NL		2	27	I	226	Y	Y	Y 55	1847	
Ely and Bedford	NL		2	43	I			Y	N		
Eastern Union: Ipswich and Norwich Extension	NL		2	46	K	88	Y	W	Y 94		
Eastern Union: Colchester–Ipswich: Additional capital	NL										

Table 6.7. (Continued)

Project and promoter	Type	Remark	No. track	Miles	Gp	BoT Ref.	BoT Rec.	Parl SC	Act	Open	Cl'd
Diss and Colchester Junction	NL		2	55	K	88	N	SO	N		
Diss and Colchester Junction: Stowmarket–Bury St. Edmunds branch	NL		2	55	K	88	N	SO	N		
Diss and Colchester Junction: Reedham branch	BR		2	36	K	88	P	SO	N		
Diss and Colchester Junction: Loddon branch	BR		2	36	K	88			N		
Norwich and Brandon: Wymondham–Dereham branch	BR		2	27	K	88	P	Y	Y 154	1846	
Norwich and Brandon: Diss branch	BR		2	27	K	88	N	Y	N		
Norwich and Brandon: Thetford deviation					K	88	Y	Y	Y 154	1846	
Norwich and Brandon: Extension into Norwich	XT		2	0		88	Y	Y	Y 41		
Lynn and Dereham: Lynn–Swaffham	NL		2	28	K	88	P	Y	Y 124	1848	
London and Norwich Direct: Elsenham–Bury St. Edmunds–Thetford	NL		2	45	K	88	N	N	N		
Chelmsford and Bury						88	Discus'd	Cd	N		
Eastern Counties: Colchester and Bury St Edmunds extension	NL		2	32	K	88	N	W	N		
Lowestoft Railway and Harbour: Reedham–Lowestoft (Norwich and Brandon)	NL		NS	15	K	88	Y	Y	Y 45	1847	
Diss Beccles and Yarmouth	NL		2	34	K	88	P	W	N		
Direct East Dereham and Norwich	NL		2	22	K	88	P	SO	N		
Eastern Counties: Cambridge and Bury St Edmunds extension via Newmarket	NL		2	25	K	226	N	N	N		
Wells and Thetford	NL		2	42	K	88	N	W	N		
Norwich and Yarmouth: Reedham–Loddon branch					K	88	Y	Y	N		
London and Portsmouth, with branches to Shoreham, Fareham, and Reigate	NL		2	103	L	172	N	U	N		
Guildford Chichester and Portsmouth, with Fareham branch (LSWR)	NL		2	52	L	172	Y	Y	N		

(continued)

Table 6.7. (Continued)

Project and promoter	Type	Remark	No. track	Miles	Gp	BoT Ref.	BoT Rec.	Parl SC	Act	Open	Cl'd
Brighton and Chichester: Portsmouth extension and branch to Fareham	XT		1	23	L	172	N	Y	Y 199	1847	
Epsom and Dorking	XT	A	NS	8	L	117	P	W	N		
London and Brighton: Redhill and Dorking branch	BR		NS	7	L	117	P	SO	N		
South Eastern: Reigate to Dorking	BR		NS	7	L	117	P	W	N		
London and Croydon: Dorking Branch	BR	A???	NS	16	L	117	P		N		
Horsham Railway (London and Brighton)	BR		2	8	L	172	P C	Y	Y 86/185		
Guildford Junction					L			Y	N		
Direct London and Portsmouth via Guildford and Petersfield, with branch to Chichester	NL	A	NS	76	L	172	N	Y	N		
North Devon: Crediton–Barnstaple	NL		NS	42	M	89	P	U	N		
Exeter and Crediton	NL	BG	2	5	M	89	P	Y	Y 88	1851	
Torquay and Newton Abbot	NL	BG	1	6		89	P		N		
South Devon: Tavistock and other branches	BR	BG, A	2	18	N	226	N	P	N		
Launceston and South Devon: Tavistock–Launceston	NL	BG, A	NS	12	N	226	N	P	N		
Cornwall and Devon Central: Exeter–Falmouth	NL		2	100	N	89	N	U	N		
Great Western and Cornwall Junction: Exeter–Falmouth	NL		2	98		89	N		N		
Cornwall: Plymouth–Falmouth (coastal)	NL	BG	1	65	N	89	Y	Y	N		
West Cornwall: Truro–Penzance	NL		NS	22	N	89	Y	P	N		
St. Ives Junction	BR		2	3	N	89	Y	W	N		
Trent Valley: Rugby–Tamworth–Stafford	NL		2	72	O	118	Y	Y	Y 112	1847	
Manchester and Birmingham: Heaton Norris–Guide Bridge	BE			10	O	225	Y	Y	Y 108		
Manchester and Birmingham: Macclesfield Branch	XT			2	O	225	Y	Y	Y 108		
Trent Valley: Alrewas branch	NL		2	72	O	118	P		N		
Trent Valley: Stafford–Stoke branch	NL		2	72	O	118	P		N		

Table 6.7. (Continued)

Project and promoter	Type	Remark	No. track	Miles	Gp	BoT Ref.	BoT Rec.	Parl SC	Act	Open	Cl'd
Churnet Valley: Macclesfield–Leek–Uttoxeter–Tamworth with branch from Stoke to Leek	NL		2	73	O	118	Y	SO	N		
Grand Junction: Potteries branch	BR		NS	12	O	225	P	Y	N		
Tamworth and Rugby (Churnet Valley)	NL		2	26	O	118	N	U	N		
South Wales Railway: Standish (Gloucester)—Fishguard with branches to Pembroke, Monmouth and Forest of Dean (GWR)	NL	BG	NS	211	P	155	Y	Y	Y 190	1856	
Monmouth and Hereford: Hereford–Gloucester with branches to Monmouth and Forest of Dean (GWR)	NL	BG	NS	44	P	155	Y	Y	Y 191	1855	
Monmouth Railway	NL		NS	28	P			U	N		
Hereford and Gloucester	NL		2	37					N		
Gloucester and Dean Forest	NL		NS	12	P	155	P	SO	N		
Newport and Pontypool	NL		NS	11	P	155	Y	Y	Y 169	1852	
Taff Vale Railway	NL				P			SO	N		
Aberdare Railway	NL		NS	8	P	226	Y	Y	Y 159	1846	
Shrewsbury Oswestry and Chester Junction	NL		2	23	Q	225	Y	Y	Y 42	1848	
Cheshire and Shropshire Junction	NL		2	48	Q			U	N		
Bedford London and Birmingham	BR		NS	16	T	153	Y	Y	Y 43	1846	
Midland Railway: Syston and Peterborough, Dunstable	NL		2	47	T	153	Y	Y	Y 56	1848	
Dunstable London and Birmingham: Leighton Buzzard–Dunstable LBR	BR		1	7	T	226	Y	Y	Y 37	1848	
Hull and Gainsborough	NL		2	29	U	153	N	SO	N		
Great Grimsby and Sheffield Junction	NL		2	52	U	153	Y	Y	Y 50	1849	
Midland Railway: Nottingham and Lincoln	NL		2	33	V	153	Y	Y	Y 49	1846	
Newark and Sheffield	NL		2	32	V	153	Y	N	N		
Manchester Sheffield and Midland Junction Railway: Chesterfield–Sheffield MR	JN		2	12	V	153	Y	N	N		

(continued)

Table 6.7. (Continued)

Project and promoter	Type	Remark	No. track	Miles	Gp	BoT Ref.	BoT Rec.	Parl SC	Act	Open	Cl'd
Goole and Snaith Railway (Aire and Calder Canal)	NL		NS	5	W	153	N	U	N		
Goole Doncaster and Sheffield and Manchester Junction	NL		2	41	W	153	N	P	N		
Wakefield Pontefract and Goole	NL		2	30	W	153	Y	Y	Y 172	1848	
York and North Midland Railway: Goole branch	BR		2	12	W	153	N	N	N		
Manchester Barnsley and Goole Railway	NL				W	153	N	U	N		
London and York (independent)	NL		NS	327	X	153	N	Y	N		
Lincoln and York and Leeds Direct (independent)	NL		2	89	X	153	Y	W	N		
Cambridge and Lincoln	NL		2	83	X	153	Y	N	N		
Direct Northern: London–Lincoln	NL		2	185	X	153	N	SO	N		
Direct Northern: Lincoln–York	NL		2	185	X	153	Y	SO	N		
Eastern Counties: Cambridge and Huntingdon	NL		NS	17	X	153	N	Y	Y 201	1847	
Eastern Counties: Brandon and Peterborough Extension					X	153/226	Y	Y	N		
Eastern Counties: Deviation of Ely–Whittlesea route away from Chatteris to March						153/226			Y 110	1846	
Eastern Counties: Finsbury extension from Shoreditch	XT		2	0	X	226	Y	W	N		
Eastern Counties: Ely and Lincoln extension	NL		2	86	X	153	N	W	N		
Rotherham Bawtry and Gainsborough Junction	NL		2	33	X	153	N	W	N		
Tottenham and Farringdon Street Junction extension	XT		2	5	X	153	Y	N	N		
Eastern Counties: Hertford and Biggleswade branch	NL		NS	24	X	153	Y	NT	N		
Midland Railway: Swinton–Doncaster	NL		2	49	X	153	Y	NT	N		
Midland Railway: Doncaster–Lincoln	NL		2	49	X	153	N	NT	N		
Midland Railway: Lincoln and Ely	NL				X	153	N	NT	N		
Sheffield and Lincolnshire Junction	NL		2	52	X	153	N	NT	N		
York and North Midland: Doncaster extension	NL		2	17	X	153	N	NT	N		

Table 6.7. (Continued)

Project and promoter	Type	Remark	No. track	Miles	Gp	BoT Ref.	BoT Rec.	Parl SC	Act	Open	Cl'd
Ely and Bedford	NL		2	43		153	P		N		
Midland Railway: Darfield-Worsborough branch	BR		2	5	Y	226	Y	SO	N		
Midland Railway: Darfield–Elsecar branch	BR		2	3	Y	226	Y		N		
Midland Railway: Chevet to Horbury branch	BR		2	3	Y	226	Y		N		
Midland Railway: Oakenshaw–Wakefield branch	BR		2	1	Y	226	Csdl		N		
Midland Railway: Ambergate–Crich branch	BR		2	2	Y	226	Y		N		
Sheffield and Rotherham: Consolidation with the Midland Railway and branch to the Sheffield and Manchester Railway	BR		NS	0	Y	226	Y	Y	Y 90	1846	
Taw Vale Railway and Dock					CC X X			Y	Y 107	1848	
Caledonian Railway: Carlisle–Carstairs–Edinburgh/Motherwell/Castle Cary with branch to Dumfries	NL		2	135	D D	120	Y	Y	Y 162	1848	
Glasgow Dumfries and Carlisle	NL		2	91	D D	120	N	N	N		
Clydesdale Junction	NL		2	15	D D	120	Y	Y	Y 160	1849	
Edinburgh and Glasgow: Stirling branch	BR		2	23	D D	120	N	Y	?	1848	
Scottish Central: Castle Cary–Perth	NL		2	47	D D	120	Y	Y	Y 161	1848	
Dundee and Perth: south line	NL		2	20	EE	120	Y	U	N		
Dundee and Perth: north line	NL		2	20	EE	120	Y	Y	Y 157	1847	
Scottish Midland Junction: Perth–Forfar via Strathmore	NL		2	33	EE	120	Y	Y	Y 170	1848	
Aberdeen Railway: Friockheim–Aberdeen	NL		2	58	EE	120	Y	Y	Y 153	1850	
Edinburgh and Northern No.1	NL		1	45	FF	120	Y	W	N	1848	
Edinburgh and Northern No.2: Burntisland—Perth	NL		1	45	FF	120	Y	Y	Y 158	1848	
Edinburgh and Hawick	NL		1	45	FF	120	Y	Y	Y 164	1849	
North British: Edinburgh and Dalkeith improvement and branch to Musselborough	BR		2	8	FF	120		Y	Y 82	1847	
Glasgow Junction: from the Edinburgh and Glasgow Railway to North Quay	JN		2	3	G G	120	Y	Y	Y 182	1849	

(continued)

Table 6.7. (Continued)

Project and promoter	Type	Remark	No. track	Miles	Gp	BoT Ref.	BoT Rec.	Parl SC	Act	Open	Cl'd
Glasgow Barrhead and Neilston Direct	NL		2	8	GG	120	Y	Y	Y 196	1855	
Greenock branch					GG			U	N		
Glasgow and Ayr: Barrhead and Neilston branch											
Glasgow and Ayr: Cumnock branch	BR		2	34	GG	120	N	Y	Y 95	1850	
Glasgow Harbour Union	JN		2	3	GG	120	N	SO	N		
Glasgow Dumbarton and Loch Lomond	NL		2	20	GG	120	Y	U	N		
Glasgow Garnkirk and Coatbridge: Improvement					GG			Y	Y 31		
Edinburgh and Glasgow: Monkland and Kirkintilloch improvement					GG	120	Y	Y	Y 46	1847	
Edinburgh and Glasgow: Campsie branch	BR					120	Y		Y 91	1848	
Pollock and Govan	JN		2	0					N		
Blackburn and Preston: Alteration	JN		2	3	HH	225	Y	Y	Y 103	1846	
North Union: branch to Victoria Quays, Preston on River Ribble	BR		NS	0	HH	226	Y	Y	Y 116	1846	
Preston and Wyre: Lytham and Blackpool branches	BR		1	14	HH	225	Y	Y	Y 125	1846	
Lancaster and Carlisle: Branch and deviations	BR		2	0	II	225	Y	Y	Y 83	1846	
Cockermouth and Workington	NL		1	8	II	225	Y	Y	Y 120	1847	
Whitehaven and Furness Junction: Whitehaven–Dalton-in-Furness	NL		1	31	II	225	Y	Y	Y 100	1850	
Kendal and Windermere	NL		1	10	KK	225	Y	Y	Y 32	1847	
Liverpool Ormskirk and Preston	NL		2	39	KK	225	P	SO	N		
Liverpool and Bury: Liverpool–Wigan–Bolton	NL		2	40	KK	225	Y	Y	Y 166	1848	
Liverpool and Manchester: City Extensions	XT		2	0	KK	225	Y	Y	Y 166	1847	
Liverpool and Manchester: branches	BR		2	0	KK	225	Y	Y	N?		
Southport and Euxton						225	P	N	N		
London and South Western: No. 1: extensions at Nine Elms	XT		2	2	LL	117	Y	N	Y 165	1848	
London and South Western: No. 2	NL		NS	14	LL			Y	N		

Table 6.7. (Continued)

Project and promoter	Type	Remark	No. track	Miles	Gp	BoT Ref.	BoT Rec.	Parl SC	Act	Open	CP'd
Richmond and West End Junction Railway: Richmond–Falconbridge	NL		2	6	LL	117	Y	Y	Y 121	1846	
Staines and Richmond	XT		2	10	LL	117	Y	SO	N		
London and Brighton: Croydon–Wandsworth branch	BR		2	6	LL	117	N	N	N		
London and South Western: Epsom branch	BR		NS	5	LL	117	N	W	N		
Grosvenor Railway (independent)	NL		2	12	M M	117	N	U	N		
Great Western: Uxbridge and Staines	BR		2	8	M M	117	N	U	N		
South London and Windsor (independent)	NL		NS	31	M M	117	N	U	N		
South Eastern: extension and widening of Greenwich Railway	XT		2	0	M M	117	Y		Y 80		
Metropolitan Central Junction (independent)	JN		2	9		117	N		N		
West London: Thames extension towards Battersea Bridge	XT		NS	1	M	226	Y	Y	N?		
West London: Knightsbridge extension	XT		NS	1	M	226	N	U	N?		
Epping Railway: Stepney–Epping (London and Blackwall) No. 1	NL		2	15	N N	226	P	SO	N?		
Epping Railway: Stepney–Epping (London and Blackwall) No. 2	NL		2	15	N N	226	P	Y	N?		
London and Gravesend via North Woolwich	NL				N N	226	N	Y	N		
Hull and Selby: Bridlington branch			2	31	O O	173	Y	Y	Y 51	1846	
York and Scarborough: deviation entering York					O O	226	Y	Y	Y 34	1845	
York and North Midland: Seamer–Bridlington branch	BR		NS	19	O O	173	N	Y	Y 58	1847	
Whitby and Pickering: deviations and sale to York and North Midland				0	O	173/279	Y	Y	Y 57		
Great North of England Clarence and Hartlepool Junction: branches to Newcastle and Darlington Junction and Clarence Railway	JN		NS	0	PP	226	N	Y	Y 118	1846	

(continued)

Table 6.7. (Continued)

Project and promoter	Type	Remark	No. track	Miles	Gp	BoT Ref.	BoT Rec.	Parl SC	Act	Open	Cl'd
Sunderland Durham and Auckland Union	XT		2	12	PP	173	Y	U	N		
Wear Valley	NL		2	11	PP	173	Y	Y	Y 152	1847	
Middlesborough and Redcar	NL		1	7	PP	173	Y	Y	Y 127	1846	
Great North of England and Richmond	BR		2	9	QQ	61	Y	Y	Y 102	1846	
Manchester and Leeds: Heywood and Oldham extension	XT		2	5	QQ	61	Y	Y	N?		
Manchester and Birmingham: Guides Bridge Branch from Stockport to Sheffield and Manchester Railway	JN		2	5	QQ	225	Y	Y	Y 108	1849	
Manchester and Buxton	NL		NS	16	QQ				N		
Ashton Stalybridge Bridge and Liverpool Junction: Ardwick extension	JN		2	1	QQ	225	Y	Y	Y 109	1848	
Ashton Stalybridge and Liverpool Junction: Guide Bridge extension	JN		2	1	QQ	225	N	Y	Y 109	1846	
Birkenhead Manchester and Cheshire Junction	NL		NS	57	RR	225	Y	Y	N		
Chester Manchester and Liverpool Junction: Chester–Preston Brook	NL		2	13	RR	225	N	Y	N		
Preston Brook and Runcorn Junction	NL		2	5	RR	225	P	Y	N		
Grand Junction: Huyton branch	BR		NS	9	RR	225	A	Y	N		
Chester and Birkenhead: Dock extension from Grange Lane to Bridge End	XT		2	1	RR	225	Y	Y	Y 99		
Manchester South Junction and Altrincham	NL		2	9	RR	225	Y	Y	Y 111	1849	
Coventry Bedworth and Nuneaton	NL		2	6	SS	226	Y	N	N		
Erewash Valley Railway: Long Eaton to junction with Mansfield and Pinxton Railway	NL		NS	25	SS	226	Y	Y	Y 189	1850	
Greenwich Colliery					TT			W	N		
St Helens and Runcorn Gap Railway and Sankey Brook Navigation					TT	117	Y	Y	Y 117		
Manchester and Leeds No.1: additional capital					TT	171	Y	Y	Y 171		

Table 6.7. (Continued)

Project and promoter	Type	Remark	No. track	Miles	Gp	BoT Ref.	BoT Rec.	Parl SC	Act	Open	Cl'd
Sheffield Ashton-under-Lyne and Manchester					TT				N		
Manchester Bury and Rossendale: amendment to land purchase and name change					TT			W	Y 101		
Manchester Leeds and Hull Associated Railways					TT			W	N		
Bristol and Gloucester No. 2					TT			W	N		
Manchester and Leeds No. 2					ZZ			Y	N?		
Amalgamation of Liverpool and Manchester and Grand Junction Railway (subsequently including Bolton and Leigh, Kenyon and Leigh Junction)					ZZ	279	N	Y	Y 198		
Lease of Sheffield Ashton-under-Lyne and Manchester to Midland and Manchester and Birmingham						279	N		N		
Amalgamation of Manchester and Leeds with Hull and Selby and Manchester Bolton and Bury						279	N		N		
Amalgamation of Chester and Holyhead with Chester and Birkenhead						279	N		N		
Amalgamation of Birmingham and Gloucester and Bristol and Gloucester and lease to Midland						279	Y	Y	Y		
Amalgamation of London and Birmingham and Trent Valley						279	Y	SO	?		
Amalgamation of Sheffield and Rotherham and Midland						279	Y	Y	?		
Amalgamation of Newcastle and North Shields and Newcastle and Berwick						279	Y	Y	?		
Chester and Holyhead: crossing of Menai Strait	XT		2	4		292	A		Y 33	1851	
Chester and Holyhead: Mold Branch	BR		NS	9		292	Cd		N?		
North Wales Railway: Porthdynllaen and Bangor	NL		NS	28		292	Y		Y 106	Not built	
Bangor and Caernarvon	NL		2	9					N		
Eastern Counties: Dartford and Romford Railway and Steam Ferry	NL		NS	9		226	N		N		

(continued)

Table 6.7. (Continued)

Project and promoter	Type	Remark	No. track	Miles	Gp	BoT Ref.	BoT Rec.	Parl SC	Act	Open	Cl'd
Eastern Counties and Thames Junction Railway to North Woolwich	XT		1	5		226	N		Y 85	1847	
Bridgewater Navigation and Railway	BR		2	10					N		
Stourbridge and Birmingham	NL		2	13		83–2			N		
Spital and Tweedmouth	NL		2	3					N		
Eastern Union: Ipswich–Bury St. Edmunds	NL		2	26					Y 97		
Hartlepool Clarence and Auckland Junction	JN		2	3		173			N		

Notes: Type of line: New Line (NL), Branch (BR), Junction (JN), Extension (XT).

Remark on special features: Broad (7 ft.) gauge (BG), Atmospheric (AM), Other novel technology (NT), Built along canal (CN).

Number of tracks: numeral, or not specified (NS).

Mileage: Number of miles of route on deposited plans (where applicable), rounded down to nearest whole number.

Group: Letters identifying the way the proposal was grouped with others for consideration by parliamentary committee.

Board of Trade reference: Paper number in British Parliamentary Papers for 1845.

Board of Trade advice: No objection (Y); Not recommended (N); Postponement recommended (P), Considered, noted or discussed, but no recommendation made (Cd), Recommended conditionally on other lines being approved/not approved (YC), Recommended in part only (Y pt).

Outcome of Parliamentary Committee: Approved (Y), Rejected (N), Thrown out on Standing Orders (SO), Withdrawn by company (W), Unsupported (U), Dropped (D), Postponed (P), Considered, but no recommendation made (Cd), No time to decide on a recommendation (NT)

Act: Yes or No, with Cmd. No. of act where passed

Open: Opening date of the main section of the line; many lines opened in stages, and for goods traffic and passenger traffic at different dates; the year selected is indicative of whether there were substantial delays in opening the line for major traffic flows.

Closed: The date that the line was closed in whole or in part.

companies which connected those ports to the network at places were traffic could be conveniently interchanged. They were opposed to any single trunk railway gaining a monopoly of access to a particular port—presumably because that company could then divert traffic away from other ports, and away from other lines which might offer shorter routes to the destination.

In any case, the Board believed that many amalgamation proposals, even when apparently reasonable, were premature. Companies might favour an alliance, first with one partner, and then another, as the threats and opportunities generated by the expansion of the railway system changed. 'The present unsettled state of the Railway system, when almost every day brings forward some proposal for a new Railway, renders it peculiarly undesirable that permanent amalgamations should be precipitately allowed...' (p. 4). Where amalgamations need to be deferred, alternative contractual arrangements, such as 'mileage arrangements' and 'arrangements for the supply of locomotive power' could prove efficient in economizing on cost (p. 5).

The Railway Committee therefore recommended that amalgamations should normally be approved only when they assisted in creating one great line communication under single management. This included end-on junctions between main lines and associated dead-end branches. As noted earlier, such mergers were condoned partly because their cost, in terms of stifling competition from cut-off lines, was not fully appreciated at the time.

Opposition to mergers between large companies was reiterated by the Cardwell Committee in 1853, and it remained the official position until the end of the century, when the policy was somewhat relaxed. Although this position sounds quite reasonable, the case is not quite so straightforward as it seems. Each large company tended to dominate a particular area of the country, and so if two companies serving different areas were to merge there might be little effect on the degree of competition in each area. Furthermore, a merger could generate operating economies in the provision of central facilities, such as engineering workshops, and might even improve the quality of cross-country services by standardizing operating practices in different regions.

The main reason why mergers between large companies were outlawed is that in practice every regional company was in competition with a neighbouring company on the border of its region. Where London-based companies were concerned, the region they dominated was effectively defined by an arc radiating out from London, and so they had two competitors—one on either side. Thus the Great Western (GWR) faced competition from London and North Western (LNWR) to the north and the London and South Western (LSWR) to the south, and so on. (The only exception concerned the railways on either side of the Thames, and even here there was stiff competition for other reasons: the Great Eastern faced competition from the London Tilbury and Southend, and the South Eastern faced competition from the London Chatham and Dover.)

It was not only intermediate towns located on a border that would suffer loss of competition as a result of a merger; big cities were liable to lose out too. Many neighbouring companies provided alternative routes between large cities. Thus the GWR and the LNWR both served Liverpool, although the GWR did so by the Birkenhead Ferry–while the GWR and the LSWR both served Exeter and Plymouth. Manchester was served by three major companies: the LNWR to the west, the Great Central (via Sheffield) to the east, and in between them the Midland via Derby. The big cities represent a powerful Parliamentary interest, and there was no way that they would throw away the benefits of competition for the sake of a monopoly.

Although these considerations did not rule out mergers between companies serving completely different parts of the country and having no borders between them, no mergers of this nature ever seem to have been proposed. Economies of scale in the provision of workshops and other central services would have been the major motive for these mergers, and the fact that they were never proposed suggests that these economies were not regarded, in practice, as a major consideration—they were certainly not considered large enough to outweigh the cost of integrating two completely separate systems using the same management team.

Had inter-regional mergers been allowed, it is likely that many of the unprofitable cross-country lines constructed in the 1860s would never have been built. Throughout the Victorian period, railway companies appreciated the potential benefits of monopoly in eliminating the wasteful duplication generated by invasion lines. Trust between competing companies was very low, and most railway managers believed that only the unification of ownership could create mutual confidence between them. No company would place their confidence in an agreement with a rival. If it was informal then it could be denied at will, and if it was purely personal then it could become void when the individuals who negotiated it moved on. Even when Parliament underwrote the agreement, as with statutory running powers, enforcement could be expensive. As a result, railway companies could not rely on non-invasion agreements, and so, in the absence of credible assurances from rivals, many of the threatened invasion lines were actually built.

Once a merger movement had got underway, it would have been likely to have culminated in the emergence of a single national company. Every time two neighbouring companies merged to stifle competition along their border in order to prevent the construction of invasion lines, the merged company would have acquired a new neighbour which might itself be the product of a merger. The same incentive would then exist to eliminate the new border through a further merger, until no borders were left because one company controlled the whole network.

This analysis suggests that with freedom of merger the integrated railway system formed on the nationalization of the railways in 1948 would have emerged spontaneously about 80 years earlier through private incentives. These incentives would, however, have created a nationwide private monopoly with formidable economic power. Unlike the railway system in 1948, which faced stiff competition from roads (and soon afterwards from air) a railway monopoly of the 1860s would have faced very little inter-modal competition. Although its fares would have been capped (through the obligations it had inherited from its constituent companies), its quality of service might have been very poor.

The monopoly system would have had certain advantages, however. The monopolist would not have wasted large amounts of capital on a network of cross-country routes that attracted little traffic. It would have built some cross-country lines, however, because it would have had an incentive to shorten the distances on major cross-country routes. This incentive would be strongest on those routes that promised the greatest growth in traffic from lower fares; to unlock this potential benefit, however, it would have been necessary for Parliament to change the basis on which fares were regulated, to prevent the monopolist from increasing charges by consigning traffic over an indirect route. With this change, it is likely that the cross-country routes constructed by the monopolist would have been similar to the cross-country routes in the counterfactual system, and therefore more efficient than the competitively constructed routes that made up the actual system.

6.12. WIDER POLICY OPTIONS

There are several ways in which the Victorians could have achieved a better railway system. The most obvious solution was nationalization. As already noted, this option was created in 1844, although its implementation was deferred for 21 years. The advantages and disadvantages of nationalization in general have been tirelessly debated, and no attempt will be made to consider all the issues here. In the specific context of Victorian railways, however, nationalization had much to recommend it. If the Board of Trade had determined the routes using the principles they developed at the time of the Railway Mania then the system would have generated greater network externalities than did the actual system. Additional social benefits would also have been generated from a low-fares policy of the type favoured by William Gladstone and James Morrison—a policy that a nationalized system could easily implement but a private system could not.

There is little evidence to support the criticism that under nationalization the structure of the system would have been unduly influenced by political and military considerations. The actual system was influenced by political considerations anyway, in so far as communication between London and Scotland, and London and the Irish coast ports was concerned, with mail contracts being used to subsidize trunk lines along these routes. The Admiralty insisted on maintaining river estuaries as natural harbours, and thereby prevented the building of railway bridges that would have been useful for civilian traffic, but there is no evidence that it would have gone even further with a nationalized system.

An alternative to nationalization would have been complete fragmentation, with each linkage having a separate owner. This arrangement would have eliminated the bias in the selection of routes which worked in favour of those routes owned by dominant integrated companies such as the GWR and the LNWR. In particular, it would have eliminated the bias towards routeing cross-country traffic via London. The disadvantage is obvious, however; the costs of coordinating the promotion of complementary linkages would have been enormous, and this would in turn have discouraged railway promotion. It would have been very risky for anyone to promote an individual linkage if they had no idea whether complementary linkages would also be promoted and also whether these linkages, if promoted, would actually be built on time. Furthermore, rigorous standards would have had to be laid down by the Board of Trade as regulator to ensure full inter-operability.

One way of overcoming these problems would have been to allow projects to be promoted as multi-linkage projects on condition that the constituent linkages were subsequently sold off. This would have addressed the needs of local towns to get themselves connected to the network, while reducing the power of any company, once its line was built, to distort the building of subsequent lines. Once again, however, rigorous regulation would have been required—this time to prevent collusion between the owners of different linkages involved in handling the same type of traffic.

Another problem with the fragmentation solution is that complex bargaining issues would arise between the owners of the various linkages that converged on any given hub. One solution to this problem would have been to place the ownership of hubs in the hands of local towns which would then arbitrate between the parties involved. This would have had the practical advantage of giving townspeople a say in the management of their local hub. A solution of this kind was actually implemented in a number of towns, by the town council providing the site for a joint station on advantageous terms. The range of regulations required to make fragmentation work efficiently is summarized in Table 6.8.

Between the two extremes of nationalization and fragmentation lie a whole range of institutional possibilities. These include state regulation of a private monopoly, and municipalization based on the public ownership of local linkages. The most realistic of these intermediate alternatives is that the Board of Trade continued to exercise the advisory role that it played in 1844–5. This is effectively the scenario that lies behind the counterfactual presented in this book. To make this arrangement effective, however, the Board of Trade would have had to strengthen its powers to regulate hubs in order to protect the interests of cut-off schemes and other competitive lines. A low-fares policy would have had to be implemented, with fares based on distance as the crow flies rather than distance travelled. This collection of measures constitutes a policy that may be termed 'regulated inter-operability'. Successful implementation of this policy would have required Parliament to accept Board of Trade advice on a recurrent basis.

While nationalization represents the simplest and most direct method of addressing the coordination problems faced by the Victorian railway system, full and immediate nationalization was not a politically feasible option at the time of the Railway Mania. By the time the issue was revisited in 1865, it was really too late to materially influence the structure of the railway system. The first Railway Mania had come and gone, leaving a legacy that was difficult to change,

Table 6.8. Measures that the Board of Trade could have proposed to remove perverse incentives on the rail system

Policy	Rationale	Implementation
Municipal part-ownership of stations in major towns. Ownership through a separate municipal station enterprise. Includes both passenger and goods stations.	Rationalize the provision of stations. Promote the role of hubs for the interchange of traffic. Invest in local facilites (hotels, refreshment rooms, etc.) Integrated approach to local land use and access.	Encourage the extension of municipal ownership to local railway facilities, for example, through the formation of joint station committees in response to local pressure
Rail regulator is to identify sets of alternative routes between major destinations and, where necessary, require companies to cooperate on multi-company routes which compete with their own wholly owned routes. Regulate connections, speed, and frequency	Prevent companies actively disrupting parts of the network to suppress competiton between alternative routes, especially between major centres.	The regulator should provide indicative planning by advising Parliament on which railway schemes should be approved, and what conditions should be imposed on the way in which they are operated
Rail regulator to ensure that where alternative routes are available, an integrated service is offered	Rival companies should not time their departures simultaneously on rival routes, but space them out.	Rail regulator to approve timetables
Base maximum rates on distance 'as the crow flies' over land rather than distance actually travelled	Reduce the incentive for established companies to oppose new schemes offering shorter routes by restricting their ability to profit from operating circuitous routes	Rail regulator to fine-tune fares policy in order to encourage cooperation while maintaining competitive checks where they are useful
Signalling services to be supplied by a state-owned company. Company needs technical advisory board to keep it up to date with new developments. Brakes and other safety equipment to be standardized. State regulator to set standards	Keep signalling decisions impartial in order to enforce running powers effectively. Standardize signals to facilitate through running by train crews. Standardize equipment to avoid misunderstandings between neighbouring signalmen using different systems. Standardize equipment to reduce procurement costs.	Create a system of railway standards, encompassing both the design and operation of equipment. Where appropriate, standardize equipment design internationally in order to reduce produrement costs

and the Second Railway Mania of 1861–66 was already underway. Railway profits were high, and this increased the cost to the exchequer of purchasing the private companies, given the generous terms specified in the 1844 Act. By this time the most that nationalization could have achieved was greater inter-operability, and wider use of the system encouraged by lower fares.

The issue of nationalization did not go away, however. As the economy began to stagnate from the 1870s onwards, traders increasing blamed the railways for high freight charges, which they claimed were a handicap to exports. Public opinion began to shift in favour of viewing the railways as a public service. Considered in this light, the UK system seemed to perform badly compared to some of its continental neighbours (Crafts, Leunig, and Mulatu, 2008). Statistical indicators confirmed the impression of poor performance, although there was considerable debate over how far other countries were meaningful comparators given the need to adjust for size of country, terrain, and population density. UK railway companies believed that they were handicapped by high business rates, and by passenger duties (which were progressively repealed), while other commentators believed that UK companies were abnormally burdened with debt because of the costs they had incurred in compensating landowners at the time they were built.

As inter-modal competition intensified—first with trams, and then with tube lines, buses, and cars—so the railway companies' financial position deteriorated. Strikes added to their problems as trade unions bargained for higher wages, particularly for the skilled grades. These problems were aggravated by the intensive use of the railways during wartime, which wore out much of their equipment. After World War 1 the railways were grouped into the Big Four companies, and the government introduced a system for licensing road lorries in order to protect the carriage of long-distance freight traffic by rail. After World War 2 the Big Four companies were in turn merged into the state-owned British Railways. The railways had finally been nationalized—though not out of any specific desire to improve their performance. Nationalization provided state funds for re-equipment and modernization, and safeguarded jobs for railwaymen returning from the war.

Fragmentation would also have been politically impossible at the time of the Railway Mania. In a modern context fragmentation appears as a pure 'free market' solution to the railway coordination problem, and might well be acceptable to modern politicians of a neoconservative persuasion. The Victorians were pragmatists, however, and believed in free enterprise, not on purely ideological grounds, but because it represented the tried and tested 'British way' of doing things. Shareholders would have objected vehemently to the forced divesture of linkages built by integrated companies. They would have been sceptical of the ability of conflicting private interests to negotiate the kind of contracts required to coordinate a fragmented system. They would have been particularly sceptical of the chances of enforcing such contracts, given the slow and cumbersome nature of the Victorian legal system.

Given the political impossibility of both the nationalization option and the fragmentation option, the regulated inter-operability option appears as the most plausible practical alternative to the actual system. Had this system been introduced at the time of the Railway Mania, it would have been possible to realize many of the potential benefits afforded by the counterfactual system. Regulated inter-operability was the best alternative available to the Victorians, and it remains a cause for profound regret that collusion between local Parliamentary interests effectively blocked it when it had already got as far as implementation on a trial basis.

6.13. OVERALL EVALUATION OF POLICY

The UK railway system as a whole was not very well regulated. The need for regulation was widely recognized, but its implementation proved controversial. In 1844 a Railway Committee of the Board of Trade was set up to advise Parliament on new railway schemes, but after a year of operation Parliament declined to accept any further advice. Thereafter the Board of Trade was mainly concerned with collecting statistics and regulating safety.

The Board of Trade's Railway Committee recognized the political necessity of working within the framework of private railway promotion, which was based on precedents concerning eighteenth-century turnpikes and canals. This system was well adapted to evaluating the social costs and benefits of stand-alone schemes, but was poorly adapted to taking account of network externalities between different schemes.

The Board of Trade wanted Parliament to approve railway schemes sparingly and selectively, with reference to an overarching requirement to construct an integrated national system composed of regional sub-systems which were adapted to the needs of particular localities. To achieve this objective, the Board recognized that a number of judgements needed to be made about how the railway system was likely to operate in future. Some of these judgements were of a technological nature and some of a commercial nature. On the technological side, the Board favoured the standard gauge over the broad gauge, and was sceptical of radical innovations such as the atmospheric system of propulsion. On technological issues its judgements appear to have been very sound.

On economic issues the Board's judgement was also generally good, although it appears to have underestimated the future growth of traffic on the railway system. The kind of network it planned was rather more sparse than the counterfactual network, and much more sparse than the network that was actually constructed. In defence of the Board, however, it did not rule out future extensions of the system; its main concern was simply that Parliament should not approve so many schemes in any one year that the capital market and the construction industry became overstretched—which is, of course, exactly what happened in 1845 once Parliament resolved to ignore the Board's advice.

The main mistake made by the Board lay in its failure to anticipate the devious strategies employed by established companies to frustrate rival schemes. The Board favoured schemes promoted by established companies over schemes promoted by independent companies on the grounds, not only that established companies were more experienced, but that integrated ownership would facilitate good connections. Parliament was aware of this apparent bias, and attempted to correct for it—for example, by encouraging the expansion of the broad-gauge GWR as a competitive check on what it perceived to be the growing monopoly power of the standard-gauge companies such as the London and Birmingham.

Unfortunately, however, Parliament merely succeeded in turning the GWR into an even greater monopolist than its rival.

As noted elsewhere in this book, Parliament was dominated by local interests where railway promotion was concerned. This 'localism' was justified by appeal to the ideology of competition. The Board of Trade was rightly sceptical of the benefits of competition to the railway system, but this attitude only increased Parliament's suspicions of the Board. The Board's encouragement of integrated ownership by established companies gave London-based companies increasing power over regional systems—power which they later used to impede the promotion of independent cross-country lines. Given the pressure from the towns for additional lines, established companies undertook to construct these lines themselves by the invasion of rival territory. Because the dominant company in each territory was able to retain control of its major hubs, the invaders were obliged to construct their lines inefficiently—often replicating the established company's lines in order to gain access to the key traffic-generating centres.

An important lesson from this is that competition can be bad for network industries unless the owners and operators of individual linkages are obliged to cooperate fully with customers who wish to combine the services of one part of the network with the services of another. The tendency for a company to obstruct a customer's use of a rival portion of the network is strongest when a few dominant firms, each operating an integrated network, aim to offer self-contained system-wide services which are inferior to 'pick and mix' combinations put together by individual customers. The tendency to disrupt is lowest when either ownership is so fragmented that no operator can conceivably offer an integrated service or when one operator controls the entire network.

Another lesson is that railways represent a distinctive type of network industry. Railways are unusual (though not unique) in that they require substantial infrastructure, not only at terminals but also for linkages. Customers wish to combine the use of these linkages in a variety of different ways. Every journey involves a unique pairing of the origin and destination. Furthermore, the customer cares about the route that they follow. Where a network has redundancy—that is, it is configured as a web rather than a tree—there is a choice of routes, and when the network is dense many alternative routes may be available. The reliance on linkage infrastructure and the consequent complexity of hub operation provides ample opportunity for operators to selectively impede various routes. As a result, competition between operators reduces rather than enhances competition between routes. When the selection of route is important to the customer, therefore, competition can reduce rather than enhance customer choice. By contrast, if customers do not need to 'pick and mix' then competition between independent networks is a more viable option; although there may still be wasteful duplication, customer service is not so seriously impaired.

Because of the somewhat exceptional characteristics of the railway system, the limitations of competition on railways do not have direct analogues in all other network industries. Nevertheless there is sufficient similarity to suggest that artificial impediments to 'picking and mixing' may be more common in network industries than is often supposed. Because competition encourages the creation of such impediments, strengthening competition may not always have the beneficial consequences that simple ideologically driven arguments suggest.

7

Business Strategies and their Effects

7.1. INTRODUCTION

This chapter examines the behaviour of the railway companies in detail, and elaborates on a number of points that have been made in previous chapters. It provides a systematic analysis of the factors that influenced company behaviour. These factors include the technological uncertainties of the time, and the regulatory regime, as described in the previous chapter. Whereas the previous chapter presented regulatory issues from the regulator's point of view, this chapter examines them from the companies' perspective.

The impact of economic conditions on railway promotion are discussed; in particular, conditions affecting the demand for rail travel and the supply of the resources required to provide it—finance from banks and private shareholders, manual labour for construction, skilled labour to operate locomotives and signals, and so on.

This chapter considers how far various factors contributed to the underperformance of the actual system. It also considers whether shortcomings in the railway system affected some areas of the economy more seriously than others. It is suggested that the countryside lost out from the railway system more than did the major cities. Numerous railway lines were driven into the major cities from various directions, providing the people who lived and worked there with good connections. Rural areas, however, were typically provided with a collection of dead-end branches, which often linked up with the rest of the system at isolated junctions rather than substantive hubs. Inland areas were often traversed by main lines, but as the expresses did not stop, connections were still often poor. Aristocratic landlords often financed local lines, but their expectations of a significant improvement in the rural economy were usually disappointed, and they sold out to the major companies at a loss.

Even in the cities there were problems: proliferation of termini inhibited the interchange of traffic, so that people who commuted into one terminal might have to transfer to another terminal to continue their journey. The railways also had a negative environmental impact that could have been reduced if the major routes had linked up with each other on the outskirts of the city before they reached the centre. On the whole, though, the cities attracted a very large share of railway investment: certainly one that was commensurate with their relative size, but probably one that was even larger because of the wasteful duplication of lines. Rural areas, by contrast, attracted relatively little capital; the major companies themselves invested very little, except when they feared that their local monopoly was threatened by invasion, although much of the deficiency was compensated for by local interests. But because of fundamental weaknesses in network structures in rural areas, purely local initiatives achieved very little.

Sections 7.2–7.4 examine the cultural context in which railway promoters operated—in particular the visions that inspired them, their business morality, and their concepts of business strategy. It emphasizes the growing influence of anonymous absentee private shareholders in the determination of railway company policy. Sections 7.5 and 7.6 examine the way that the companies acquired resources—in particular land and capital. The strategies they pursued to attract and retain traffic are discussed in Sections 7.7–7.13. The social implications of these business strategies are examined in Sections 7.14–7.19.

It is suggested that railway companies did not hesitate to resort to antisocial business strategies when it suited them to do so. Although railway employment was generally seen as secure, for example, the railway companies were not always seen as good employers. Although the companies invested heavily in advertising and promotion, this was mainly for competitive purposes, and was recognized as such. On the whole, despite the technological superiority of railways over other forms of transport, the railway industry had a weak social and political image. The companies never fully convinced the public that railways were operated in the public interest.

7.2. ENTREPRENEURIAL VISION IN THE PROMOTION OF RAILWAYS

Building a railway line was an entrepreneurial activity: it involved innovation, risk-taking, and alertness to opportunity. A lot of information needed to be synthesized—not just on the economy, but on technology too—and good judgement was required in order to make the right decisions.

The builders of the first inter-urban trunk lines required a high degree of entrepreneurship, as there were no precise precedents for what they were setting out to achieve. The level of uncertainty—both technological and economic—was very high, as Table 7.1 makes clear. Once the concept of the inter-urban railway had been proved, however, it became somewhat easier for the followers.

The strategies adopted for the building and operation of a railway line necessarily reflected a vision of what the railway would be like when it was completed. Different visions led to different strategies. Some of the early writers on railways, such as Thomas Gray and William James, visualized a national railway network from the outset (Paine 1961). But they were not sufficiently pragmatic when it came to the implementation of their schemes. Gray's proposals did not involve high-speed inter-urban travel—the key success factor in the early system—while James did not survey the lines he proposed with sufficient accuracy.

Table 7.1. Technological and economic uncertainties impinging on the development of early railways

Category	Issue	Judgement
Power	Reliability of steam locomotive	Underestimated
	Speed of steam locomotive	Underestimated
	Maximum feasible gradients	Underestimated
	Dangers of passenger travel	Overestimated
	Effectiveness of rope-hauled inclines (gravity or steam) (seen as superior to flights of locks)	Overestimated
	Effectiveness of atmospheric principle	Overestimated
Promotion	Cost of professional fees—especially legal fees	Underestimated
	Cost of land purchase	Underestimated
Construction	Geological difficulties	Underestimated
	Weather problems in construction	Underestimated
	Time and cost to complete construction	Underestimated
Operation	Operating expenditure: purchase and maintenance of rolling stock, and the growth of expense with the growth of traffic	Underestimated
	Inconvenience to passengers changing trains	Underestimated
	Inconvenience of trans-shipping freight	Underestimated
	Inconvenience of break of gauge	Underestimated
	Advantages of shared facilities—for example, joint stations	Underestimated
	Inconvenience of terminal operation	Underestimated
	Expense and inconvenience of dead-end branch line operation	Underestimated
	Importance of proximity of stations to major cities	Underestimated
Traffic demand	Long-term potential of popular travel	Underestimated
	Long-term growth of coal traffic	Underestimated
	Willingness of high-status passengers to 'mix with social inferiors' by using third-class accommodation	Underestimated
Competition	Strength of canal competition for heavy low-value goods	Overestimated

Other railway visionaries focused more on the regional than the national level. Following his work on the Liverpool and Manchester and the Manchester and Leeds, George Stephenson developed an interest in the area between Derby and York, where the railway promoter George Hudson was very active. An integrated system of trunk line communication was established, with hubs at Derby, Rotherham, Normanton (near Wakefield), and York, and this became the foundation for the Midland Railway. George's son, Robert, also developed a number of regional schemes which involved not only trunk lines, such as the London and Birmingham, but also rural schemes linked into them, such as the Buckinghamshire Railway.

Although the technologies used by the Stephensons appeared very radical at the time, they were, in practice, a succession of relatively incremental advances which, when combined, had a radical effect. Much of the technology was taken from colliery railways and then improved, using locomotives with multi-tubular boilers and rails made of wrought iron and later steel. The gradual abandonment of inclined planes was made in response to the steadily increasing power of the steam locomotive.

By contrast, Brunel's approach was overtly radical. Brunel preferred to work from first principles, using his own ideas, rather than by improving on the work of others. Brunel believed in speed and luxury. In common with other engineers at the time, he perceived friction as the main constraint on speed, and it was from this principle that he deduced the need for a broad gauge (see Chapter 4). The wheels of a railway locomotive transfer friction from the rim of the wheel to the axle-box of the locomotive, and so the total amount of friction overcome in the course of a journey is proportional to the number of times the axle rotates in its box; for a given dimension of axle this is proportional to the size of the wheel. The bigger the wheel, the lower the friction, and the greater the speed. But the bigger the wheel, the higher the centre of gravity, and the greater the instability; the train should therefore be slung between the wheels, Brunel argued, and this required a broad gauge. Unfortunately this theoretical approach proved misleading, because improved lubrication soon ameliorated the friction problem. Thereafter the ingenious Brunel invented other arguments to justify his broad gauge, such as the advantage of the large boiler diameter and the long inside cylinders used on broad gauge locomotives.

Brunel also believed in technological competition as a spur to innovation. He favoured a national railway system comprising regional networks built around trunk lines emanating from the metropolis. Each region would compete to adopt the most advanced technology, and might consequently have its own gauge. The natural hub was London, where each network would have its own terminal. Connections between different gauges outside the metropolis should focus on one particular point, such as Birmingham, where specialized transfer facilities would be used to ease the problems created by break of gauge.

Brunel's vision was not a commercial success, and he was heavily criticized by the shareholders in some of his schemes. The vision of most investors in early railways was much more parochial than that of the engineers. It has already been noted that some early railway schemes were visualized as complements to the canal system, while some later schemes were visualized as direct replacements for obsolete canals. Other railways were promoted as adjuncts to shipping networks—linking coalfields and industrial districts to a port, or providing a land-bridge that linked ports on opposite coasts, or on opposite sides of a peninsular. The most influential vision, however, was without doubt the one that was fired by the success of the Liverpool and Manchester—namely the inter-urban trunk line. The grandest railway schemes became those that linked London to major provincial centres. The promoters of these schemes were generally successful in building profitable main lines into London, served by a range of provincial feeders that converged into the trunk portion of the line at hubs such as Swindon, Rugby, and Peterborough. These hubs were jealously guarded by the big companies to prevent rival companies from abstracting traffic at these points, although none of them was completely successful in this respect.

The grand vision of the inter-urban network, organized on regional lines, with London as its national hub, was complemented by more parochial visions. The networks of rural lines visualized by Robert Stephenson and others were slow to develop, and many of the grand cross-country schemes proposed at the time of the Railway Mania failed. This led to a narrowing of vision, in which the ambition of towns in agricultural areas became simply to get themselves connected to the nearest trunk line. Rural ambitions revived at the time of the Second Railway Mania of 1861–66, when a number of new cross-country lines were built.

In the 1870s light railways were proposed as a means of connecting rural communities to the national network. Some visionaries even believed that their tracks could be made portable, with sidings being laid into fields each autumn to carry away the harvest. Light railways could be authorized by a Board of Commissioners, which saved promoters the costs of obtaining an Act, but many of the schemes built under the first Act were actually urban tramways rather than rural lines. Only after further legislation did a spate of rural proposals appear, although many of the schemes failed to get off the ground for financial reasons. Many of the rural light railways that were built around the turn of the twentieth century had a short working life, and closed due to competition from lorries, buses, and cars in the inter-war period.

7.3. STAKEHOLDERS AND SHAREHOLDERS

When discussing the business strategies of railway companies it is important to recognize that the stakeholders whom the railway companies claimed to represent changed significantly over time. At the time of their formation, early railway companies typically claimed to be inclusive, and to represent all the major local interests of the territory through which they would pass. To give credibility to this claim, a Provisional Committee would be formed on which various local interest groups would be represented (see below). The principal stakeholder interests are listed in Table 7.2.

The members of the first Board of Directors would typically be drawn from the membership of the Provisional Committee, but with an emphasis on people with practical business experience—merchants and bankers in particular. Major aristocratic landowners might also insist on having nominees on the Board. This Board would reflect private commercial interests more heavily than the Provisional Committee, with local civic and municipal interests in particular being under-represented.

Once the company had been formed and shares had been issued, however, power would switch to the Shareholders' Meetings. These meetings had the

Table 7.2. Stakeholder groups in railway projects

Type	Key examples	Ambitions
Traffic generators	Merchant based in a commercial centre Manufacturer in industrial centre Mine-owner Port-owner Estate-owner (agriculture, forestry, etc.) Property speculator (land-owner in spa, seaside resort, potential commuter area, etc.) Other railways seeking feeders or distributors for their traffic	Low freight charges
Suppliers	Construction contractors Property developers interested in selling land for railway terminals, hotels, etc. Professions seeking a market for their services: engineers, solicitors, bankers Suppliers of locomotives, rails, and other equipment	High prices for the supplier's output
Government	Post office requiring carriage of mails Army requiring carriage of troops	National social and political benefits
Local community	Mayors and councilors	Influence company policy to maximize external local benefits
Investors	Aristocrats, MPs Shareholders seeking an income higher than what is available from government bonds: widows, clergy, retired pensioners, etc. Financial speculators and stock-jobbers	Large dividends and capital gains (increased share price)

power to nominate (or re-nominate) Directors, and also to call the Directors to account—if necessary, by initiating a Shareholders Committee of Investigation which, if it reported adversely, might call for the resignation of certain Directors. This was a useful way of disciplining Directors who pursued their private vested interests at the expense of the company as a whole.

The consequence was that Directors who actively supported the shareholder interest were likely to survive longer in office—and thereby make secure the financial perks (such as attendance fees and expenses) which might come their way. Furthermore, as the century progressed, a higher proportion of schemes were overtly backed by established companies, and so the preeminence of private interest became more explicit.

Once the railway system had begun to mature and the risks perceived in railway investment had been reduced, railway shares became popular investments for gentry, clergy, and widows, and other members of the middle classes seeking a steady income or pension. First a national market and then an international market in railway shares developed, which meant that, so far as the governance of railway companies was concerned, it was no longer local shareholder interests that were dominant but shareholder interests in general. Shareholders who knew little about the local circumstances under which their railway investments were operated were more likely to place their confidence in companies whose Directors had a national rather than a purely local reputation. Thus the national celebrity came to the fore as a champion of the shareholder interest. In the case of some celebrities—such as George Hudson—the transition occurred at an early stage, although Hudson, despite being a national figure, remained strongly associated with the city of York and its business community. Thirty years later, however, Sir Edward Watkin emerged as a truly national celebrity representing the interests of shareholders in the London capital market as a whole.

As this chapter will show, these changes were reflected in the changing strategies of the companies concerned, and in the rhetoric they used and the imagery they employed. As they made the transition from local companies promoted in the public interest to national companies operated for private interest, they began to emphasize their roles as national players while continuing to claim that they served the public interest as well as a private one. Although some leading companies such as the North Eastern, North Staffordshire, and the Cambrian retained a strong regional identity, the Boards of these companies were by no means immune from the pressure to deliver shareholder dividends and capital growth.

7.4. TERRITORIAL COMPETITION AS THE BASIS OF RAILWAY STRATEGY

When modern management writers talk of business strategy they are usually referring to product or process innovation, advertising, cost reduction, and similar topics. While these issues were certainly important to Victorian railways, strategy was a far broader concept than these applications would suggest. Strategy was understood by railway managers in territorial terms: the scope of a main line railway company was defined principally by the territory that it controlled. This territory also determined the type of traffic that it handled. Product quality was important, but most railway companies offered similar services and, where they competed, offered similar fares.

Territory was secured through investment in infrastructure, and the amount invested was huge—not only by the standards of the time but by today's standards too. In the UK today Network Rail spends on average about £5 billion annually on the railway track—and that is just on maintenance and minor enhancements. Moreover, today's system is significantly smaller than the Victorian one. The Victorians built their railways from scratch, and the costs incurred were sunk— disused railway lines had no alternative uses of significant value.

The territorial ambitions of the early railway companies is evident in their choice of names. The Great Western Railway is a classic case in point. Originally promoted as a line from London to Bristol, its change of name indicated a change of strategy—towards monopolizing the entire west of the country. This example was quickly followed by other companies. Thus the South Eastern Railway, linking London to Dover by a junction with the London and Brighton Railway at Redhill, implicitly claimed a monopoly over the whole of Kent—a claim that was bitterly disputed by its great rival, the London Chatham and Dover Railway, right up to 1899 when the operations of the two companies were combined.

Naming a railway after a region rather than the towns and cities it joined had implications for the towns and cities in the region that it served. This was 'good news' for some towns and 'bad news' for others. The London and Southampton found its name a handicap when it proposed to build a branch from Basingstoke to Bath and Bristol because the proud residents of those cities did not want to be on a branch off a main line to another city, and the merchants of Bristol in particular did not want to be served by a railway company dedicated to the promotion of a rival Atlantic port. Later on, when the company proposed a branch to Portsmouth from its main line at Eastleigh the proud citizens of the naval base declined to be served by the 'Southampton' company. By changing its name to the London and South Western the company hoped to alleviate these concerns, and it was in this new guise that it finally succeeded in reaching not only Portsmouth but also Exeter and Plymouth.

Renaming a railway after a region could be bad news, however, for the towns and cities after which it was originally named. Had the citizens of Bristol been more alert, for example, they might have realized that a railway named the Great Western might not be so focused on serving Bristol as they had imagined it to be. It seems that Brunel was intent on serving other towns and cities from an early stage, and that this may have laid behind his support for the change of name. As suggested in Chapter 4, it is possible that Brunel selected a northern route for the Bristol main line in order to provide an option to expand into the West Midlands and Wales. The term 'Great Western' may not have been a compliment to Bristol, as its citizens thought, but rather an indication of Brunel's intention to develop rival Atlantic ports in Wales, such as Neyland and (unsuccessfully) Porthdynlleyn.

7.5. ACQUISITION OF LAND

As noted in Chapter 2, a great deal of Victorian enterprise involved the promotion of infrastructure projects. These projects typically had two stages: construction and operation. The construction phase of a railway project involved not only the building of the line and the stations but also laying the track, purchasing of locomotives, carriages and wagons, and installing a water supply; while operations included the timetabling of trains, hiring of staff and rostering of train crews, the pricing and sale of tickets, and making arrangements for the collection and delivery of freight and parcels.

In the construction phase the major activities were the acquisition of land and the building of the track-bed. Land needed to be acquired through compulsory purchase. Without the power of compulsory purchase landowners could hold the company to ransom. A landowner could hold out until all the other plots had been purchased and then demand an exorbitant sum for the last remaining piece of land required to complete the line. If all the landowners understood the situation in this way then they would all hold out unless the company offered them an exorbitant price to begin with. If the company had many options so far as the route was concerned then it could play off different groups of landowners against each other, but within each group of landowners the problem would still remain. An early mineral line, the Stanhope and Tyne, had been built without powers of compulsory purchase and was effectively bankrupted by the exorbitant demands of landowners when it came to build the final portion of its line to the banks of the River Tyne. Renting land (or using a short-lived 'way-leave') was not an option because once the lease expired the rental could be raised. The only exception concerned short lines where all the land was owned by the same person; in such cases the railway could be built as a private venture without compulsory purchase—for example, Lord Londonderry's Railway in County Durham. To obtain powers of compulsory purchase, a special Act of Parliament was required, as explained earlier.

Land was expensive, and purchasing enough line to build a railway was normally beyond the means of any single person—including an aristocrat. Even a business partnership involving a small number of individuals (a common form of organization in Victorian Britain) would be financially stretched. The solution was to form a joint stock company with the power to issue shares. Furthermore, in order to secure a wide market for these shares, limited liability had to be provided. Ordinary members of the public did not have the confidence to purchase shares in companies over which they could not exert direct control unless their liability for losses was limited to the price that they had paid for their shares. Until the company law reforms of the mid-Victorian period, however, joint stock businesses with limited liability had to be authorized individually by Parliament. Thus the key to railway promotion was to obtain an Act of Parliament. This not only authorized the compulsory purchase of land, but also permitted the sale of shares to finance it.

7.6. RAISING FINANCE

As explained in the previous chapter, Parliament was very strict about the conditions that a railway project had to fulfil before an Act was granted. The company had to deposit a large-scale Plan of the route, and a Book of Reference which detailed the ownership and use of all the land lying near to the line. The Bill submitted to Parliament (on which the Act would be based) had to explain, in the preamble to its main clauses, why a railway was needed. The Bill would also stipulate the amount of capital to be raised. The capital involved a mixture of equities and debentures; because of the high risks associated with a railway project, the equity capital was normally three times the size of the debenture capital. The total amount of capital to be raised was based upon an estimate of the cost involved in building and equipping the railway, and purchasing the land. The Standing Orders governing the submission of Bills were based on those that had been applied to canals, but as new problems began to arise in connection with railways, so the standing orders were tightened up and extended, so that by the time of the Railway Mania compliance had become quite onerous. One of the most important requirements was that half the shares had been taken up and that deposits had been paid on them (Williams 1948–49).

Technically speaking, however, there were no shares to be taken up until the Act had been passed, because there was no company to issue them. Until the Act was obtained, the company was under the control of a Provisional Committee, which acted as a 'shadow' board of Directors. This board collected promises to purchase shares (if and when they were issued), and the promises were made in such a way that they were legally binding. (After the Railway Mania had collapsed, however, controversy arose as to the meaning of these promises, and the courts ruled that while some of these promises were binding, others were not, depending on how the company had expressed the invitation to subscribe to the shares.) In return, the prospective shareholder received scrip—a receipt for their allotment of shares and for the 10 per cent deposit they had paid on it. Crucially, scrip could be resold—it was a liquid asset. The price paid for allotted shares was based on their nominal value, and the scrip was, in modern parlance, an 'option'—it was the right to acquire a share at a future date at a fixed price by paying the balance of its nominal value.

In boom conditions, such as the Railway Mania, shares would trade at above their nominal value, and so once an Act was passed scrip could appreciate dramatically in value. Holders of scrip could make an enormous capital gain with a relatively small outlay. The system was a forerunner of modern options trading, and it is therefore not surprising, with the benefit of hindsight, that it encouraged massive speculation.

Options could only be exercised if the Act was successful, however. If it was not, then the deposit would be returned, once professional fees had been deducted—though in practice the professional fees were often so high that no money was in fact returned. It should also be noted that shares could quickly turn from assets into liabilities when confidence collapsed. Railway companies called up the balance on their shares as and when they needed it, so that the proportion of shares paid up increased as the construction of the line progressed. But in some cases it became evident even before the line had been completed that the company was unlikely to be profitable, and that investors paying calls were simply 'throwing good money after bad'. Impoverished investors who could not dispose of their shares fast enough faced bankruptcy.

7.7. THE PROVISIONAL COMMITTEE

The Provisional Committee would normally be formed as the result of resolutions passed at a public meeting (usually held at an inn or local assembly rooms). The promoters would convene a meeting, appoint a prestigious, and nominally independent chairman, such as a local squire or justice of the peace, and line up speakers to express a favourable opinion. If the meeting went well, the motions would be passed and the promoters and their allies would be elected to the committee. The Provisional Committee would then draft a prospectus, which would be published in local newspapers and, from the 1840s onwards, in specialist journals for railway investors.

Meetings could be unpredictable, however. Local gentry might resent the interference with their estates, or fear the social consequences of increasing the mobility of poorer people. They might also have interests in local turnpikes or canals which would be adversely affected by the railway. Promoters of a rival railway might infiltrate the meeting, making disparaging remarks about the scheme, and turning the meeting into a platform for their own proposals instead. A successful promoter would anticipate such difficulties, meeting them with forceful arguments or, in the case of outsiders, with other forms of force—such as ejection from the premises.

The Provisional Committee would draw upon a range of different skills. There would be local merchants, manufacturers, and agriculturalists, who would provide informed estimates of future patterns of traffic. They would be aware of the strengths and weaknesses of alternative modes of transport in the area, and so would be able to help to make the case for a railway in place of a road or a canal. Local landowners would be represented too. The acquisition of land was simplified considerably when a major landowner offered a substantial tract of land to the railway at a reasonable price—and was willing to accept payment in shares rather than cash. Local councillors or aldermen were also useful members, particularly if the town council could supply facilities such as a convenient site for a terminus (see below). A local Member of Parliament was an invaluable member of the committee, because he could advise on how to smooth the passage of the bill through Parliament. He could lobby other MPs, encouraging them to support the Bill or, if they could not support it because of conflicting interests, at least not to oppose it. In particular, he could make deals of the kind: 'I won't oppose your Bill if you don't oppose mine'.

The Provisional Committee would be supported by a local solicitor and a local bank. As well as providing professional services, the solicitors and bankers would endeavour to place shares with their clients. The committee would also distribute shares to stock-jobbers who would sell them on to the public at large. In some cases solicitors and bankers would also be on the Provisional Committee. In the early years of railway promotion conflicts of interest were quite common, and were considered to some extent to be a normal feature of business life. Where a small local scheme was concerned, almost every member of the committee might have some sort of vested interest—either in consigning traffic over the railway or in supplying services to it. Once railways became operational, however, and new shareholders bought into the company, toleration of vested interests diminished. It became quite common for ordinary shareholders to instigate committees of inquiry which led to the resignation of directors who had failed to handle conflicting interests properly.

7.8. SELECTION OF THE ROUTE

In order to prepare the Plan and the Book of Reference, strategic decisions had to be taken about the location of the termini and the route between them—in particular, which intermediate towns were to be served. Such decisions were clearly the responsibility of the Board, but where the Board was inexperienced they would rely heavily on external advice. They often turned to the civil engineer. It was the engineer's responsibility to optimize the route within the parameters set by the Board, but an eminent engineer with previous experience of railway projects might well have a say about the route as a whole. In some cases there might be local controversy over the best route to be followed, and the engineer would be called upon to provide an independent and objective assessment of the alternatives. An astute engineer would be aware of the local economic and political considerations influencing the Board and would bear these in mind when making his recommendation.

A highly reputable engineer might be hired simply as a consultant. He would ride out on horseback to take a general view of the countryside, and after sketching out the route would delegate other issues to a resident engineer, in some cases assisted by a local surveyor. The most important of these issues was to get the levels right—in other words, to choose a route with appropriate gradients; not so severe as to impede the operation of the railway, nor so flat that considerable expense was incurred with bridges and tunnels, embankments, and cuttings. Curvature of the track was also important—there was no point in engineering a line for speed by having level gradients if the trains then had to slow down for bends. The Board would indicate whether they wanted an expensive high-speed trunk line that was straight and levels or a cheap secondary line that was steeper and more curved, and the engineer would deliver his plans accordingly.

Choosing levels also had an economic dimension. If the amount of soil removed from cuttings equalled the amount of soil required for embankments, then embankments could be built out of the soil removed from the cuttings, and no surplus soil would remain that had to be tipped onto waste land. On the other hand, allowing the levels to be dictated by soil requirements could result in a line that was too high or too low for traffic requirements. Most railways started and finished close to sea level in major towns, and ascended to a summit somewhere in the middle. If the termini were too high then access to the town would be poor, while if the railway were built low down then expensive tunnelling might be required through hilly country *en route.*

The cost of land also had to be factored into the choice of route. Land in the centre of a city was expensive, and so many early railways terminated some way out. As a railway terminal needed quite a lot of land, cheap sites were very desirable. Swampy land near the cattle market, gasworks, workhouse, and lunatic asylum was quite popular; people would not notice the additional smoke and smells coming from the railway, and the people who lived nearby were too poor to make much of a fuss if they did (see Chapter 2). In addition, the railway could generate business from taking cattle to and from the market and bringing in supplies of coal to the gas works. Other popular locations provided inter-modal links—for example, close to river quays, canal basins, and turnpike gates.

Negotiating with major landowners was a job for the engineer, although the process of purchase was handled by the company's solicitors. Brunel had a great reputation for his ability to charm influential opponents of the railway—after he had been to interview them they often not only withdrew their objections to the railway but also took shares in it.

A consulting engineer would be retained by a fee but might also be expected to purchase some shares in the railway as a token of goodwill, and to give him a financial stake in its success. The resident engineer might be an associate of the consulting engineer, or a local engineer appointed by the company. The engineers were not necessarily railway specialists. In the early stages of railway building there were not enough schemes to create full-time work for a specialized body of people; even later, the 'boom and bust' cycles of railway construction meant that engineers switched into railway construction at the time of a boom and switched out again later. Many leading Victorian engineers proved themselves competent in several different fields of engineering, and could use a reputation gained in one field to good effect in another.

The Institution of Civil Engineers (ICE) was the established professional association in the field, but not everyone who called themselves a civil engineer, or who practised as a railway engineer, was a member. The ICE was controlled by an earlier generation of road builders, bridge builders, and canal builders. Indeed, George Stephenson, the 'Father of the Railways, was excluded from membership—a snub which galvanized Stephenson's supporters into founding the Institution of Mechanical Engineers, which although ostensibly concerned with a different field of engineering was initially a rival institution.

7.9. DIRECT LINES AND EXTENDED BRANCHES

The builders of early trunk lines quickly realized that although they might claim a monopoly of a particular route, they were always vulnerable to competition from the subsequent construction of alternative routes. Parliament indicated at an early stage that companies might well be confronted by competition from new companies entering their region, and companies therefore sought to invest in 'barriers to entry' to deter these entrants.

As noted earlier, an important strategy for deterring competition was to build the shortest and fastest route between the major towns at either end. There was a strong belief by railway promoters that if competition were to develop later then the company with the shortest and fastest route would capture most of the traffic. One reason was that if two rival companies matched each other's fares then customers, being indifferent to the fares, would opt for the fastest route. This would normally be the most direct route. Provided that fares were not so low that a company would make a loss on marginal traffic, the company that won the most traffic would be the most profitable one.

The early trunk lines often bypassed towns of considerable size. Thus the Liverpool and Manchester Railway bypassed Warrington to the south and both Wigan and St. Helens to the north; the London and Birmingham bypassed Aylesbury and Northampton, the Birmingham and Gloucester bypassed Worcester and Kidderminster, while Brunel's Great Western bypassed several country towns, including Wallingford, Wantage, and Faringdon (see Chapter 4). It used to be said that this was because the townspeople were short-sighted and objected to the railway, but closer examination of the evidence has failed to provide much support for this view. The overriding impression is that the companies were obsessed with building the shortest and fastest line between the major centres at either end of the line.

One reason for bypassing intermediate towns was that the promoters, who were typically merchants and financiers based at either end of the line, feared that intermediate centres might be favoured by the railway at the expense of their own towns. Thus Worcester, which was left off the Birmingham to Gloucester main line, was a threat to Gloucester as a rival port for Birmingham traffic. In general, however, the most important reason seems to be that the promoters feared that if they took an indirect route then a competitor would build a rival direct route instead.

The obvious disadvantage of a direct route was that it failed to serve some of the major intermediate towns. These towns would be served by branches instead. In the early stages of railway development, much of the concern of towns focused on being connected to the railway network, and there was only minor concern over whether a town was served by a branch or a main line. It quickly became evident, however, that branches were a poor substitute for a main line, especially where passenger traffic was concerned. A long wait at a country junction was not a good way to start or finish a journey.

Once a trunk line company had secured a monopoly—albeit a temporary one—it was in its interests to extend the area that it monopolized. Many trunk line monopolies therefore set out to dominate an entire region of the country and not just the traffic between the major towns at either end of their line. The London and Southampton, as noted above, had an ambition to serve the entire south-west, rather than just the South Coast; it quickly changed its name to the London and South Western and eventually reached Exeter and Plymouth. Thus a trunk line that began simply as a connection between two towns finished up becoming the highway for an entire region instead.

One way in which a trunk line operator could increase the area they dominated was to extend their branch lines further than the intermediate towns they by-passed. By building long branches at right angles to their main line they maximized the width of the territory they served. The London and Birmingham, for example, extended its short branch to Northampton as far as Peterborough, in order to reinforce its claim to serve the whole of the South and East Midlands. A few years later, at the time of the Railway Mania, the Midland Railway built a similar line further north, from Leicester to Peterborough, in an unsuccessful attempt to forestall a competing line. At the same time, the Great Western set about building a branch from Chippenham through Trowbridge to the South Coast at Weymouth, to forestall the London and South Western's plans to build a rival link from Exeter to London (see Chapter 4).

Many of these lines were of limited use to the towns they served, as they connected to places that people did not particularly wish to visit, and only connected them to places they did wish to visit by an indirect route. But the promoters of these lines hoped that if and when rival lines were promoted later, their prior occupation of the territory would give them grounds for opposing the new schemes. If their objections failed, and the new lines were built, they would use their control of points of intersection along the branch line to make it difficult for people who lived along their branch line to change to the new line once it was built.

7.10. PARLIAMENTARY ADVOCACY

Many railway schemes foundered in Parliament, as explained in the earlier chapters. Opposition to schemes could come from several quarters (see Table 7.3). The engineer was a key witness before the Parliamentary Committee that examined a Bill. The robustness of his evidence was crucial. The traditional British approach of adversarial cross-examination reached new heights—or new depths of depravity, depending on one's point of view—in the scrutiny of railway Bills. If a Bill was opposed by influential interests—in particular, a well-established rival railway—then the engineer could expect to have a tough time. The opposition would hire the best barristers that money could buy, and much of their effort would go, not into marshalling support for their own schemes, but into demolishing the cases for rival schemes.

Parliamentary advocacy was big business, and some companies spent a high proportion of their parliamentary expenditure merely in opposing other com-panies' Bills. Parliament became so concerned about the problem that it instigated

Table 7.3. Interested parties liable to oppose railways

Type	Key examples	Ambition
Direct competitors	Other railway companies seeking to serve the same territory or already operating a competing line Canal proprietors Turnpike trustees, coach operators, and local carriers	Stop the project or force it to be scaled down
Local interests	Property-owners or occupiers; aristocrats with landscaped gardens, representatives of local people who will need to be rehoused, etc.	Reduction of nuisance and heavy financial compensation
National interests	Admiralty	Protection of access to harbours, etc.

an enquiry into the subject, from which the statistics in Figures 7.1 and 7.2 are derived. Figure 7.1 shows that while most companies did not spend money on opposing Bills, about 25 per cent of companies channelled more than 20 per cent of their Parliamentary expenses purely into opposing other companies' Bills. Table 7.2 shows that these companies were also the biggest spenders on Parliamentary activity—they were the established regional monopolists who were doing their best to prevent invasions by rival companies.

Various tactics could be deployed where opposition was concerned. One approach may be termed the 'death by a thousand cuts'. The idea was to persuade the Committee members that the plans had not been properly prepared. Inaccuracies in the description of property would be alleged—for example, that a cattleshed had been wrongly described as a barn, that a field described as pasture

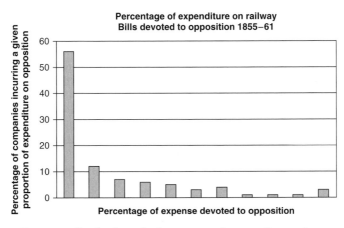

Figure 7.1. Frequency distribution of railway companies according to the percentage of Parliamentary expenditure devoted purely to opposition

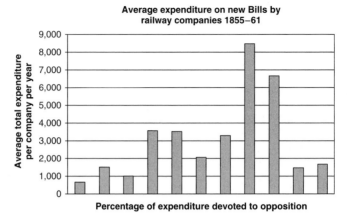

Figure 7.2. Average expenditure on new Bills by companies categorized according to the percentage of Parliamentary expenditure devoted purely to opposition

was actually used as a market garden, and so on. Property ownership was often uncertain, and the engineer had to be careful to list all possible owners of a piece of land, which in turn would require him, or his assistant, to speak with all the parties claiming to own or occupy each plot. Another source of quibbles concerned the shareholders who had placed their deposits; for example, it might be alleged that while they were able to pay the deposit, they were too poor be able to pay the balance later.

More damaging allegations related to problems with the levels. Everyone knew that getting the levels correct was difficult; surveys of arable fields normally had to be carried out after farmers had gathered in the autumn harvest, and since the plans had to be submitted by the end of November, there was very little time to complete the job. Different surveyors might be responsible for different portions of the route, and so mistakes could easily occur where adjoining portions met. Opponents would therefore scrutinize each other's levels in order to find weaknesses they could expose in front of the Committee.

Another approach was to destroy the reputation of the engineer. Some inconsistency might be alleged between his approach to the current scheme and his approach to previous schemes in which he had been involved. As railway technology was continually evolving, it was perfectly reasonable for engineers to change their mind on matters such as gradients and curvature, but this could always be portrayed as indecision or incompetence instead.

It could also be suggested that the line was built purely for private profit and not for public interest. Since it was public benefit that warranted the intrusion of the railway onto private property, demonstrating a public interest was an important part of proving the preamble to the Bill. It might therefore be suggested to the engineer that his choice of route reflected a disregard for local interests and an exclusive concern for one kind of traffic over all the others. Although this was not strictly the engineer's domain, everyone know that the engineer was the crucial source of expertise, and so there was much more to be gained by scoring a point against him on this subject than by scoring a point against an ordinary witness of less repute.

The cost of hiring barristers could be reduced if opponents were bought off before the Committee hearing began. A successful promoter would know just how much it was worth paying someone to withdraw their opposition before the Committee met. This would leave the barristers to deal just with those opponents who were demanding too high a price. Landowners were often bought off in this way. Indeed, where landowners appeared as opponents of a Bill, the barrister conducting the cross-examination might suggest to the landowner that he had recently improved his property merely to extract more compensation from the railway company; he might then add that the landowner would actually profit from the coming of the railway through an increase in his rents, and that he therefore had no legitimate grounds for opposing the railway at all.

If all opposition could be bought off then a Bill could expect a much smoother passage through Parliament, because unopposed Bills received favoured treatment in Parliamentary procedure. A local scheme in a relatively poor area might well be unopposed, because no rival company would consider the area commercially attractive; in addition, social pressure within a paternalistic local elite might encourage factions to bury their differences and present a united front.

A large scheme designed to serve a prosperous area could almost certainly count on opposition, however. Parliament was reluctant to make a straight choice between such schemes and therefore often encouraged the parties to merge their plans. By making clear their disapproval of conflicting schemes, Parliament was sometimes able to effect rationalization through merger. But when two protagonists continued their opposition through successive Parliamentary sessions, Parliament was inclined to cave in and approve both schemes. In the short run, therefore, the effect of rivalry was to delay schemes, but in the long run its effects was to allow duplication where promoters refused to merge.

Successful promoters required a mixture of aggressive and defensive skills. They needed a repertoire of aggressive tactics for buying off opponents and for defeating those who persisted in their opposition. They also needed defensive tactics to immunize their own schemes to aggressive cross-examination. It was also advantageous to have a capacity for cooperation, because this was sometimes the simplest strategy for gaining Parliamentary approval. For example, the merger of competing schemes into the Great Northern Railway was successful in overcoming objections to the East Coast main line from rival railways that remained outside the merger.

7.11. PARLIAMENTARY STRATEGY: BOGUS SCHEMES

The analysis so far has assumed that the promoters of the railway genuinely wished to build a railway that they believed would be socially beneficial and also privately profitable. At the time of the Railway Mania, however, contemporary commentators were convinced that many schemes were not promoted with the intention of ever being built.

Stock-jobbers' lines. One allegation was that schemes were put together by stock-jobbers who simply wanted to sell scrip or shares—selfish people whose only interest lay in the commissions they received from the railway companies for placing their shares, or from the capital gains they made while holding the stock themselves. It must be remembered, however, that these allegations were made mostly in the immediate aftermath of the Railway Mania when many families had been ruined by speculation, and where scapegoats were actively being sought out. It is difficult to identify from among schemes that actually reached Parliament a distinctive set of schemes that appear to be so bad that they were evidently not designed to be built. Most critics do not mention any schemes by name, but rather claim that the schemes with the most extravagant titles are the strongest suspects. But grandiose titles for railway companies were not unusual at the time. Both the Grand Junction and the Great Western had been operating for some time, and it is not surprising that this style attracted imitators. It is possible, however, that a systematic study of schemes that were advertised in the press but never actually submitted plans to Parliament would reveal a number of schemes of this type.

Solicitors' lines. A more plausible allegation is that railway companies were promoted in order to boost the fee incomes of solicitors and engineers. London-based solicitors are particularly suspect because one or two London firms un-doubtedly promoted a very large number of railway schemes at the time of the Mania, and it is seems doubtful that the people involved could have lavished a great deal of individual attention on them. Furthermore, the members of the Provisional Committees often seem to have had little direct connection with the provincial territories to be served by the railways, but rather to have had interests in the City of London instead. On the other hand, several of these schemes were actually built, and achieved satisfactory levels of profit. However, the solicitors and engineers also did well out of the schemes that failed, because they kept much of the shareholders' deposit money and used it to reimburse their professional fees. Because these services were in such great demand at the time of the Mania, their fees were very high.

Blackmailers' lines. It was alleged that some railway schemes were promoted simply as a device for blackmailing the promoters of *bona fide* schemes. The lines had nuisance value to other schemes, even though they were not well thought out in terms of how they would be constructed, and were promoted solely so that others would buy them off. Once again, however, it is difficult to identify specific schemes of this nature. While some promoters certainly withdrew their schemes—perhaps because of a financial settlement—the schemes themselves were often perfectly reasonable ones, and the result was simply to rationalize the schemes that were finally considered by Parliament by eliminating wasteful duplication.

A variant of the blackmailer's line was the *tit-for-tat* line. In this case the pay-off was not pecuniary, but rather the withdrawal of a rival scheme. When a dominant company in some territory was threatened with invasion by a company that dominated some other territory then it might threaten a counter-invasion which it would offer to withdraw if the invader withdrew its own scheme. In the early years of the railway system, this ploy worked reasonably well, but by the 1860s many independent lines were being promoted, and established companies began to realize that invasion was unstoppable. Companies therefore began to invade each other irrespective of any threats of reprisal because they had to forestall the independents, and because they knew that sooner or later they would themselves be invaded whether or not they had made a deal with another company.

Distraction lines. The most significant form of bogus line—and by the far the best documented—is the distraction line. The aim of the distraction line is purely to block other lines. Unlike a blackmailer's line, the aim is not to withdraw the scheme in return for a suitable reward, but to get the scheme adopted in place of a rival scheme. Having blocked the rival scheme, there may be little incentive to actually build the line. In this case the territory that was to be served by the rival line would be left with no railway at all—or, more precisely, residents would be obliged to use the nearest railway, however inconvenient, which was the railway operated by the company that promoted the bogus scheme.

Distraction lines were typically promoted by local monopolists as a means of keeping invaders out of their territory. The promoter of the distraction line would advertise it as a means of incorporating into its network towns that it did not already serve and that would otherwise be served by the rival line. It would be commended to Parliament as the preferable line because it connected with the existing network in the region. The Great Western Railway was adept at this manoeuvre; it argued that only broad gauge lines should be built in areas already served by the broad gauge, because standard gauge invaders would not be able to interchange traffic with the established broad gauge network. Although this argument appears spurious in the light of the general difficulties created by its non-standard gauge, its argument often won the day in a Parliamentary Committee.

A distraction line would normally be promoted immediately that a rival scheme appeared, so that it could be considered in the same session of Parliament. Time was of the essence, for if the scheme did not appear until the following year the rival schemes might already have been authorized. In some cases, though, a company could attempt to 'buy time' by opposing the rival scheme in the first year and then putting up its own scheme the following year.

7.12. RAILWAY BATTLES

If Parliamentary strategy failed, and an unwelcome rival railway scheme was authorized, a company could always fall back on a strategy of obstruction. This could involve interfering with the construction of the rival's line—for example, by luring away construction workers with offers of higher wages—or by head-hunting key managerial staff. Landowners could be offered financial support to take the rival company to arbitration over the price of land, and so on. Although such strategies were alleged to have been used, it is difficult to know how common they were in practice.

There is very good evidence, however, for the strategy of physically obstructing the operation of newly opened lines. Table 7.4 reports well-publicized examples, most of which involve an established company resisting a new company trying to make a junction with its lines. These instances underline the fact that railway companies did not always welcome junctions, on the grounds that they introduced feeder traffic, but rather opposed them on the grounds that they might obstruct traffic, or introduce an undesirable element of competition that could lead to a reduction of fares. Some of these cases involved physical violence between groups of employees. Some took place at stations in front of passengers, while in other cases passengers were imprisoned in trains that had been immobilized through dangerous manoeuvres such as the removal of rails.

Table 7.4. Railway battles

Date	Place	Company	Company
1849	Carlisle	Lancaster and Carlisle	Maryport and Carlisle
1849	Chester	Shrewsbury and Chester	London and North Western
1849	Clifton Junction, Salford	East Lancashire	Lancashire and Yorkshire
1849	Methley Junction, near Leeds	Great Northern	Manchester Sheffield and Lincolnshire
1850	Blackburn	East Lancashire	Lancashire and Yorkshire
1851	Wolverhampton	Shrewsbury and Birmingham	London and North Western
1851	Hastings	London Brighton and South Coast Railway	South Eastern Railway
1852	Nottingham	Great Northern	Midland
1854	East Croydon	London Brighton and South Coast Railway	South Eastern Railway
1856	Manchester	London and North Western	Manchester Sheffield and Lincolnshire
1858	Havant, near Portsmouth	London Brighton and South Coast Railway	London and South Western Railway

Source: Body, Geoffrey (1994) *Great Railway Battles: Dramatic Conflicts of the Early Railway Years*, Wadenhoe, Peterborough: Silver Link.

It should be noticed, however, that the reported instances all took place in a 10-year period, 1849–58. This was the period when many of the Mania lines were approaching completion and when the long-established companies were therefore facing potential competition from a wave of newly opened lines. After 1858 standards of behaviour appear to have improved, but the general strategy of obstructing the interchange of traffic did not. Other devices, such as creating congestion at junctions by blocking express passenger trains with slow-moving goods trains, timetabling trains to miss connections, and failing to maintain connections when arrivals were delayed, were all deployed.

Railway managers appear to have considered such behaviour to be an inevitable consequence of competition. They tended to argue that only merger could provide them with an incentive to interchange traffic with another route; cooperative agreements were of little value because rival companies could not be trusted. Since the established companies were often keen to take over their new competitors, in order to strengthen their monopoly power, the blame, they suggested, lay with Parliament for blocking mergers.

7.13. THE RAILWAY CONTRACTOR

Assembling the workforce to carry out construction was a crucial role. Railways were built by gangs of able-bodied 'navvies'—itinerant labourers who had previously built the canals. The gangs were employed by private contractors, some of whom had a reputation in their own right—for example, Thomas Brassey and Frederick Morton Peto. The engineers would divide up the line into sections of several miles each, and let contracts for each by competitive tender. Contracting was a very risky activity. Bad weather, serious accidents, and shortage of materials could all create problems. Enormous profits could be made if everything went well, but many contractors eventually went bankrupt. This was not only annoying to the company, for the resulting delay in opening for traffic could have serious financial consequences, but also for the local residents, who were left with a large empty building site nearby until activity resumed.

Working conditions were often poor, even where reputable contractors were involved. Conditions could be particularly harsh in remote areas (such as the Woodhead Tunnel through the Pennines) where local amenities were nonexistent. Workers often remained loyal to the better employers, however, and followed them round the country as one contract came to an end and another began. Conversely, it was in the contractor's interests to maintain continuity of employment for the better workers, although given the fluctuations in railway building, this was difficult to achieve. Some contractors therefore played an active part in railway promotion, helping to maintain employment through a recession. Contractors did not confine promotion activity to depressions, though. By taking an active role in the management of a project, a contractor could avoid the competitive discipline of the tendering process and award themselves a contract at a monopoly price. This was only possible, however, if their fellow directors were purely passive, or were organizing their own little scams, or could be bribed.

Many early railway promoters failed to provide adequate rolling stock for their operations. They became so obsessed with opening their line on time that they lost sight of the need for carriages and wagons to convey the traffic. Since rolling stock was one of the last items to be purchased, cost over-runs on construction often took their toll on carrying capacity. This created the ironic situation that just when the railway was finally ready to start generating revenue, the revenue was constrained by a shortage of vehicles. As the railway system developed, second-hand markets and rental markets developed to mitigate this problem. Another problem was that many civil engineers had a limited understanding of locomotive power. The Stephensons—father and son—were unusual in having a grasp of both. Even Brunel turned out to be a disaster where locomotion was concerned—he was forced to rely on the expertise of a 21-year-old colleague, Daniel Gooch, to provide broad-gauge express locomotives for the Great Western Railway. Across the network as a whole, the problem was solved by separating the civil and mechanical engineering sides of railway operation, and in particular by creating a special post of locomotive superintendent responsible for the specification and design of motive power.

7.14. RAILWAY OPERATIONS

Many of the early railway promoters thought that they were purchasing a regional or local monopoly. Their strategy was to exploit this monopoly position to the full, by charging the maximum permitted fares. Most companies offered three classes of travel, and in addition from 1844 they were obliged to run Parliamentary trains, which served all the stations on a line at a basic third-class fare. The companies then became worried that passengers might trade down to a lower class of travel. It was widely alleged that some companies made second-class coaches deliberately uncomfortable relative to first-class coaches, and third-class coaches even more uncomfortable relative to second-class coaches, merely to sustain the premium they levied on the superior class of travel. Some expresses conveyed only first- and second-class passengers, and every opportunity was taken to charge for extras (luggage, dogs, etc.) or for superior service. Some companies set out to segregate the different classes of traveller as much as possible, not only by providing different waiting rooms at stations but also by extending different levels of courtesy to different classes of passenger, in the hope that a person's class of travel would become a social signal of their gentility.

Parliamentary trains were often scheduled to run at inconvenient times—such as the early morning, and a similar principle of inconveniencing the customer was occasionally employed on the special 'workmen's trains' that were introduced later on the government's initiative.

The Board of Trade repeatedly referred to deficiencies in the quality of service on the railway system in its annual reports throughout the 1870s and 1880s. The companies were unpopular with manufacturers and wholesalers because of the high level of freight rates. Cross-country freight journeys often involved more than one company. At hubs where traffic was exchanged, each company would have its own goods yard, so local 'trip' workings were required to move wagons from one yard to another. These added considerably to the costs of moving freight. In addition, the trip working delayed consignments and, by causing congestion at the hubs, delayed passenger trains too.

Passengers had their own set of grievances. This was a period when railway passenger traffic was expanding, with a significant growth in the amount of third-class travel. At some busy stations the platforms were so narrow that passengers were in danger of being accidentally pushed onto the track. Punctuality on many lines seemed to be getting worse (see Figure 7.3). Surveys reveal that in the early 1890s more than half the expresses arriving at London termini were more than 10 minutes late. The crack expresses were often late because the long distances they covered meant that minor delays were cumulative. The companies were so keen to advertise high speed that there was no slack in the timetable to allow lost time to be made up. The expresses in turn created delays for other traffic as trains had to be shunted off the main line to allow the express to pass. Waiting for a train on a chilly station platform with few amenities was a normal part of life. Travellers would have to count themselves lucky that they were sufficiently affluent to be able to afford the fares.

In response to these problems, many companies embarked on significant improvements in the 1890s—doubling single tracks, quadrupling double tracks, building more flyovers to avoid conflicting traffic movements, and rebuilding stations to provide more spacious accommodation. Much of the surviving station architecture on today's network dates from this time. But these improvements only managed to keep pace with rising expectations. The railways were being viewed more and more, not as private enterprises, but as dysfunctional constituents of a public transport system. In terms of passengers, railways were expected to cater for the masses and not just for the elite. To some extent they already did this—but mainly through excursion traffic rather than scheduled services. While travel was becoming cheaper, regular travel at ordinary third-class fares was still beyond the reach of many workers and their families.

In terms of mass transit, quality of service remained poor. It was not just a question of congestion and delay: long journeys of any kind were often difficult for passengers to make. The number of hubs where it was convenient to change for an onward portion of a journey remained relatively small. Changing at major centres like London, Manchester, Leeds, and Glasgow would normally involve change of station as well as change of train. The most important hubs were often at places that few people would really wish to visit, such as Crewe, Eastleigh, and Ashford. Furthermore, these hubs were mainly operated by a single company, so that the choice of company was limited for the travellers who needed to avail themselves of such a hub (see Chapter 3). Many journeys would begin and end

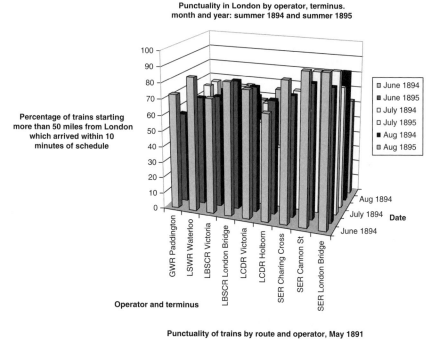

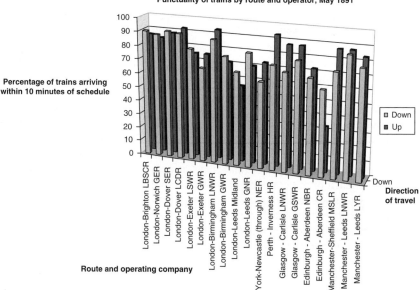

Figure 7.3. Punctuality of long-distance trains arriving in London, 1894–5

with a change of train, in addition to a change *en route*. This was because many country towns were on dead-end branch lines, having been bypassed by the nearest trunk line. They were served by country junctions, most of which still had few amenities; missing a connection at a country junction could leave the traveller with a long and uncomfortable wait.

7.15. ATTITUDES TO EMPLOYEES

The exploitation of monopoly power against customers was coupled, in some cases, with a cheap labour policy towards the lower grades of employee. Companies were aware that jobs such as station master, engine driver, and signalman were very responsible, and special efforts were made to attract and retain suitable staff, especially when they had to work night shifts, or to live in remote rural areas. Compensation packages included not only wages and salaries but also subsidized accommodation and cheap travel, and prospects for promotion were good while the railway system was expanding.

In some of the major railway towns—in particular those where large workshops were located—companies adopted a paternalistic attitude towards their employees. Some companies provided workers' villages—for example, at Swindon and Derby—and others provided parks as well—for example, at Crewe. Steps were taken to discourage visits to public houses by providing alternative social amenities, such as workers' institutes. There was a substantial element of self-interest in provision of these special facilities, as skilled artisans could be difficult to attract to railway towns; it was important to retain the best apprentices and to encourage them to spend their leisure time on activities related to their work.

There were many other jobs, however, such as porter and shunter, that were not considered to require special qualities, and in urban areas there was no shortage of people willing to take on such work. Some jobs, such as cleaning out cattle wagons, were distinctly unpleasant, while others, such as night-time shunting, were inherently dangerous, but little was done until the end of the Victorian period to make life healthier or safer for the ordinary employees.

Safety problems affected passengers and member of the general public too, as explained below. Any departure from routine created a potential safety hazard; thus special excursion trains were particularly liable to accidents. Other problems were endemic; thus poor fencing meant that farm animals often strayed onto the track, and farm workers had to put themselves at risk by going onto the track to retrieve them.

7.16. RAILWAYS AND THE RURAL ECONOMY

Given that so many of the early railways were promoted by merchants and industrialists, it is hardly surprising that large towns and cities were major beneficiaries of the railway system. While the cities would have benefited even more from a rational system like the counterfactual one, they were certainly much better off than they would have been without the railway. The railway improved business communication by making it easier for businessmen from different cities to meet face to face. It became easier to market goods nationally and to organize firms on a national basis. National banks and national newspapers began to supersede their regional equivalents.

The picture in rural areas was more mixed, however. Some rural areas were transformed by the growth of mining. The extension of the railway system made it far easier than before to carry away the minerals from a mine. While the old-fashioned mineral railway carried products downhill from the mine to the nearest river or port, the Victorian railway system could carry mineral traffic long distances over land; thus haematite ore from Cumbria, for example, was used in the steel furnaces of the north-east.

Mining areas did not necessarily receive a good passenger service, however. Miners were expected to live next to the mine at which they worked, and to remove themselves and their families if they went to work at another mine; commuting to work was not encouraged. Where miners' trains were run they were generally for miners only, and were not usually advertised in national timetables. Special trains might be run on market days, however, for the benefit of miners' wives going shopping.

Where rural areas remained agricultural, the railway often had little impact, however. Many aristocratic landlords had great expectations that the value of their estates would be enhanced by access to the railway. Coal and fertilizer would be brought in at lower farm-gate prices and produce carried away at higher prices. The landlords often failed to appreciate, however, that other agricultural districts would also benefit from cheaper coal and fertilizer, and that competition between different districts would put downward pressure on agricultural prices.

Although the demand for agricultural produce was increasing due to population growth in the towns, an increasing proportion of this demand was being met by food imports. The railways played a prominent role in the distribution of these imports. This was particularly evident in the live cattle trade. Cattle were reared in Ireland, shipped to Birkenhead and other ports, and then transported in train-loads to London. The London and North Western and the Great Western competed for this trade, and because of economies of train-load operation, railway rates were very low. As a result, it was cheaper to move cattle to London from Birkenhead than it was to move it from a town in the Midlands that was on the same route and less than half the distance away. The individual farmer consigning wagon-load traffic could not compete with the wholesale importers consigning train-load traffic.

Import competition became even more serious in agricultural areas after the development of refrigeration. This stimulated international trade in meat and in dairy products such as butter and cheese. It allowed distant settler economies such as New Zealand to take a growing share of the British market for such products. Once again, the railways played a prominent role in distributing food products from the ports to the cities.

The most prosperous agricultural areas tended to be those that specialized in particular products. Fresh milk and vegetables were increasingly recognized as important components of a healthy diet. Prior to the advent of the railways, urban consumer demands had been met by farms immediately surrounding towns and cities, but the railways were able to transport these products from greater distances. Regions with good pasture—such as Devon and Somerset—and good soils—such as East Anglia—were in a strong position to develop specialized farming to exploit these new opportunities.

A major factor inhibiting rural development was that many neighbouring country towns were not connected up to each other. They were often at the end of dead-end branches, and so to reach another town it was necessary to make two changes on the main line. Once on the main line, however, the passenger might have a choice of several local towns to visit. On the other hand, neighbouring towns could be on branches from different main lines that passed to either side of the area concerned. If these lines were operated by rival companies then connections between them might be poor; even where the same company operated both lines, connections would often be timed to favour travellers to London at the expense of travellers to other local towns.

Although cross-country routes connected local towns in some areas, trains were often infrequent and slow; if they connected with main line trains at distant junctions then punctuality could be poor as well. Furthermore, some connecting lines were built simply to fill up space as a deterrent to invaders, and served no other useful purpose. As a consequence the railway system failed to realize its network potential in many rural areas. This was not because the density of lines was low, but rather because the hubs were weak. As a result, residents of neighbouring towns often remained cut off from each other and had to continue to use the roads for local communication. Different towns could not afford to specialize in certain functions because residents of other towns could not reach them easily. The towns retained their local character, but at the expense of having a narrow range of shops and other facilities. It was not until the arrival of the bus and the car that rural towns began to interact significantly as a components of an integrated rural economy.

7.17. WHY DID THE RAILWAYS MISS THE COUNTRY TOWNS?

The poor performance of the railways in meeting rural needs was reflected in the poor financial performance of many rural lines. Why then did the railways provide such poor service if they could have generated greater revenue by providing better service? Why were towns left off main lines, and why were rural stations often so badly sited with respect to the towns they claimed to serve?

The most straightforward explanation is that railways were interested in serving rural areas only when they lay on a direct line between urban areas that they planned to connect. The urban areas represented the economic future as centres of commerce and industry, while the country towns represented the legacy of the past. Railways were meant to last for decades—even centuries—and many people confidently expected that during this time the cities would continue to grow and the country towns to decline. The 1830s and 1840s were times of major rural hardship, with the Enclosure movement having reduced the demand for male labour, and the decline of proto-industries such as straw-hat and glove making reducing domestic employment for women and children. Country markets were in decline as agricultural produce was increasingly consigned direct to urban markets from the farm gate.

As noted above, main line companies were keen to build direct lines between the major cities in order to deter rivals from building competing lines. Diverting lines through towns could also increase costs; the lines would be longer and land would be more expensive near the intermediate towns. It was difficult for a landowner to hold a railway company to ransom over the sale of land if the company had a free choice of its route, but if the railway was committed to serving specific intermediate towns then its route options were more limited and the chance of being held to ransom by a landowner were correspondingly greater. In addition, some country towns were initially unsympathetic to railways, although they soon changed their attitudes when the economic cost of rejecting a railway line became clear from the fate of similar towns.

The early main line companies perceived themselves as building the Victorian equivalent of motorways, with railheads (the analogues of motorway junctions) being located where turnpikes and canals crossed the route. In this respect they may have been too futuristic, as many towns subsequently revealed a strong desire for a branch of their own.

Although branch lines could be built to lighter standards than main lines, and were therefore cheaper to construct, they were often costly to operate because one or two locomotives had to be kept in steam all day to provide connecting services, even though they were used for only a small amount of time. Had the main line companies correctly anticipated the cost of branch line operation they might have preferred to route the main line through the town after all. In many cases, however, the main line companies only operated the branch on behalf of a nominally independent local company, and it was this local company, and its local shareholders, who bore the brunt of the economic loss.

Even when towns were served by the railway, the station was often badly sited from the passenger's point of view. The siting was often better from the freight point of view, however, being close to a canal basin, gasworks (for coal deliveries), or cattle market (see above). Furthermore, land was cheaper on the edge of the town, and objections from residents would be fewer too. In some cases, however, the bad siting of the station simply reflected the fact that there was no real intention of serving the town at all. Where the 'motorway principle' was applied, a railhead might be named after the nearest town even though it was some distance away. Passengers who arrived at stations of this description could be in for a nasty shock unless they had arranged in advance to be met at the station. The railway catered for wealthy passengers who could provide their own transport to and from the station rather than middle-income passengers who wished to use the trains for shopping, or to commute to the local town. Bad experiences of country stations did nothing to encourage ordinary people to move to rural areas or to set up businesses there.

7.18. PROMOTING THE RAILWAY IMAGE

During the 1880s it became increasingly clear to railway managements that public attitudes to the railway were changing. As noted above, passengers were increasingly thinking in terms of the railways as providers of a public service, while merchants and manufacturers were increasingly demanding lower freight charges and more reliable service. Government was increasingly willing to intervene on behalf of the national interest, restricting the companies' commercial freedom and prescribing safety measures that they had to adopt. At the same time, advances in printing and publicity techniques made it possible for the railways to communicate more effectively with their customers—on both the passenger and freight side—and possibly, through public opinion, to influence government too.

Railways therefore became increasingly conscious of public relations. They had improvements to track and stations to publicize. The larger companies increasingly operated networks with a national scope—when connecting services provided by allied companies were included. Shipping connections with Ireland and continental Europe could also be emphasized—not to mention ferries to the Channel Islands and the Isle of Man. Furthermore, a network of hotels embracing major cities, ports, and resorts allowed the larger companies to offer an integrated travel service inclusive of accommodation.

Railways had been image-conscious right from the start, and these new developments merely intensified existing attitudes. It was noted earlier that at the time of the Railway Mania many companies chose grandiose names. This reflected, in part, the ambitious scope of their projects, and the fact that they were seeking finance from investors in the London capital market. More modest schemes often emphasized their local roots instead. Many of the earliest schemes were locally financed, and chose to emphasize their local credentials by linking the names of the towns they connected in their titles.

New lines were often promoted by business communities in the towns at either end of the route, as noted above. Townspeople were encouraged to believe that the line would terminate permanently in their town, so that local facilities would be much in demand as passengers and freight transferred from rail to road or canal. In practice, once absentee shareholders became involved, the company would tend to develop wider ambitions in which the interests of the original towns played a subordinate role. Extensions were often planned, often named after the town to which the extension was to be made, and financed mainly by the residents of that town. As companies increasingly sought regional dominance, that too was reflected in an appropriate change of name.

Visual identity was important too. Almost all railway companies had crests or other heraldic devices, which often 'twinned' the coats of arms of connecting towns. Ambitious schemes might include three or four separate coats of arms. A monogram based on the company acronym was another favourite motif. Colourful liveries were chosen for passenger trains, with locomotives and carriage liveries being carefully matched. Locomotives were often painted in one colour and then lined out in two or more other colours. Polished brass was often favoured for handles, rails, and locomotive chimneys and domes. Less attention was paid to freight trains, which typically comprised a variety of different types of wagon owned by different companies, or by collieries and other private businesses. Coordinated colour schemes were out of the question, and so freight locomotives were often painted plain black.

The most notable feature of early railways was the unprecedented speed of travel they provided, and speed remained one of the main 'selling points' of the railway. Exploits based on high-speed running had the added advantage of being newsworthy. Comfort and reliability were important too. The Midland was the first company to introduce luxury Pullman cars from the USA; it also abolished second-class travel, and upgraded third-class provision to the old second-class levels. The Midland always felt itself handicapped in winning north–south traffic because its route was not so fast as the East Coast and West Coast main lines, and this was in part an effort to redress the balance. Its initiatives were so successful that other companies felt compelled to follow suit.

Passenger safety was another important consideration, but one to which the railways paid only limited attention. Their main response was to play down the frequency of accidents rather than to take measures to reduce them. Accidents were surprisingly common by today's standards. While train crashes were the most spectacular phenomenon, accidents at stations and level crossings were a regular occurrence. The companies bemoaned the high cost of safety systems, such as interlocking signals, continuous brakes, and improvements in on-board heating and lighting systems. Passengers took the risks sufficiently seriously to take out insurance before a long journey, and it was only pressure from the Board of Trade that induced the more recalcitrant companies to address safety issues.

Railway travel was popular with women, both for visiting relatives and for taking holidays in fashionable spas and resorts. Contemporary paintings and photographs suggest that they often travelled alone, or accompanied by their young children. They were afforded their own waiting rooms and toilets, but special compartments were not always provided. Although attacks on solitary women occurred from time to time, the frequency was not so great as to discourage women from travelling. Railway companies were very concerned about smoking, however, both as a safety hazard and as a nuisance to other passengers in the same compartment, and segregation of smokers was often imposed.

A notable feature of railway travel is that the passenger is intimately involved in day-to-day operations: waiting on platforms, riding in trains, and so on. A lot of what goes on is seen by the passenger. Railways sought to capitalize on passenger interest by publishing postcards featuring railway scenes, distributing leaflets pointing out line-side attractions, and turning station masters into local celebrities. For obvious reasons, first class passengers were specially targeted. There was a substantial premium paid by first-class travellers that was not normally reflected in the speed of service, except in the early days when expresses were sometime reserved for premium passengers. Some companies tried to emphasis the social exclusivity of first-class travel, but this did not always succeed, as even the social elite showed a penchant for economy where railways were concerned, even if it involved close proximity to the 'lower orders'. Nevertheless, many stations featured waiting rooms reserved for the use of first-class passengers.

While railways could—and did—make extravagant claims for themselves, they needed to gain credibility for these claims. Station architecture became an important means of achieving this. Two distinct approaches can be detected in railway architecture. The first emphasizes the greatness of railway and its contribution to civilization. This approach is exemplified by some of the London terminals, whose styles allude to the early empires of Greece, Rome, and Egypt, and by other constructions such as Robert Stephenson's Menai Bridge. The second approach emphasizes the railway as an integral part of the local community. It is reflected in the design of country stations, which often echo the local architectural style and make selective use of local materials. Few companies adopted a uniform house style for station buildings, but concentrated rather on designing buildings that were appropriate to their location.

When the major companies later attempted to cultivate a national image, they sought ways of differentiating themselves from other 'national' players. They adopted slogans such as 'The Royal Line', 'The Holiday Line', and began to describe their major destinations in exotic terms. The quality of the scenery 'through the window' was often emphasized—particularly by the companies with the slower routes. Technological improvements helped to reinforce this aggressive image-building. Corridor trains allowed passengers to take exercise, and facilitated the introduction of restaurant cars—a welcome alternative to the scrum that previously ensued at station refreshment rooms. Corridor trains also reduced the pressure on station toilets, while shorter station stops meant faster journey times.

7.19. CORPORATE SOCIAL RESPONSIBILITY OF VICTORIAN RAILWAY COMPANIES

The concept of personal responsibility was very familiar to Victorians, especially through the religious instruction they received as children. A 'stakeholder view' of society underpinned much of the social and political agitation that was common throughout the Victorian period—especially regarding the extension of the franchise and trade union bargaining rights. Cooperatives rose to prominence in retailing, while municipal ownership of utilities became increasingly common after 1870. The social and political elite was generally agreed that the British had a particular genius for private enterprise, but they also recognized that economic prosperity was based on social and political stability which could only be sustained by recognizing the claims of various stakeholder groups. In general, however, it was considered much more important to make government representative of the people than to make the individual firm representative of the people, as a comprehensive application of the stakeholder principle would suggest.

While railway image-building was generally successful in bringing innovations in speed and comfort to the attention of the travelling public, and by turning first-class railway travel into an aesthetic experience, it was not sufficient to convince the public that railway companies were socially responsible. Press coverage and Parliamentary debates both confirm that public criticism of the social responsibility of railway companies was common throughout the Victorian period, and if anything intensified towards the end.

Although many of the companies adopted paternalistic attitudes towards their staff, this was very much in line with general Victorian practice. They made an effort to integrate into local communities—using vernacular architecture for station buildings and encouraging the station master to take an interest in local affairs. They made charitable contributions too (see Figure 7.4); the principal beneficiaries were hospitals and other medical charities—especially those that cared for injured workers—together with schools and churches. Although railway companies were often requested to subscribe to good causes of a more general nature, it seems that they usually declined to do so. Their justification appears to have been that the directors of the company did not have a mandate to give away the shareholder's funds in this way. While railway companies recognized their wider social responsibilities, therefore, the resources they devoted to fulfilling these responsibilities were limited, and most of them were directed to charities whose activities directly benefited the company.

It is instructive to note that the civil and mechanical engineers—most notably George Stephenson—have always been the cultural heroes of the British railway system (MacLeod 2007), from the inception of railways down to the present day. By contrast, the railway promoters have either been anonymous, or the subject of criticism—and even vilification in the case of George Hudson. The most obvious explanation lies not in the personal achievements or misdemeanours of these specific individuals, but rather their iconic status as representatives of two social and professional classes—the engineers being practical social benefactors, and the railway promoters as representatives of an increasingly parasitic propertied class.

Although this distinction is overdrawn—many engineers profited from fees obtained from aborted schemes, while early investors in local lines took on considerable risks in support of community-based investments—there is undoubtedly a grain of truth in it. Railway managers were well aware of the

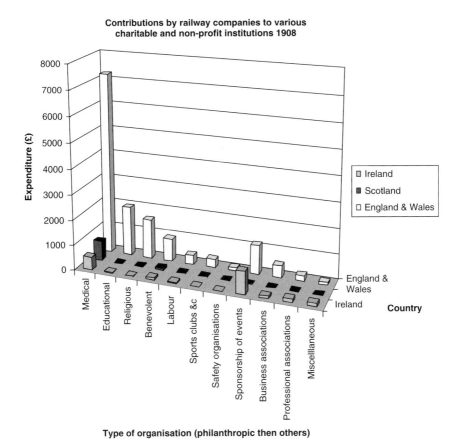

Figure 7.4. Charitable contributions of railway companies classified by type of charity

deficiencies in the regulation of the railway system, but instead of compensating for these in a socially responsible manner they chose instead to pursue private advantage on behalf of their shareholders. Railway customers suffered from the antisocial competitive tactics adopted by the companies, and in the long run the economy suffered too. The business strategies of the railway companies are intelligible only in terms of shareholder self-interest; companies managed in a socially responsible way would have behaved very differently and treated their customers much better.

8

Conclusions

8.1. INTRODUCTION

The Victorian railway was a major experiment in using private enterprise to construct and operate a national transport network. The railway system developed within a distinctive institutional context in which government sought to foster competition whilst securing private profit for socially beneficial schemes. Railway companies' need for joint stock status and powers of compulsory purchase gave government considerable influence over railway investment decisions.

As early as the mid-1830s, the railway system was widely recognized as superior to turnpike roads and canals so far as long-distance traffic was concerned. The railways were part of a steam revolution which was affecting other industries too—including mining, manufacturing, and shipping. Steam railways could connect steam-powered manufacturing at one end of the line with steam shipping at the other—just as the pioneering Liverpool and Manchester Railway had done. Railways facilitated the formation of a steam-based international inter-modal transport system, with inter-modal hubs at major ports. Railways could act as feeders to these ports, or as land-bridges between them.

Steam facilitated speed, and speed attracted passenger traffic as well as freight. The potential of speed encouraged the construction of long-distance inter-urban main lines—lines very different from the very first horse-drawn mineral railways. It was not long before some inter-urban railway lines earned as much revenue from passengers as they did from freight—in contrast to the major canals, where passenger fly-boat traffic was relatively small.

Railways were as superior to canals for the transport of passengers, parcels and light freight as canals had been superior to roads for the carriage of heavy freight. Railway investors therefore believed that they could obtain monopoly profits that would equal the profits made by the early investors in canals. Furthermore, the legal mechanism for promoting a railway was basically the same as for a canal.

It turned out, however, that railways were not to be the 'new canals'—at least not as envisaged at the time. To begin with, vertical integration of track and trains quickly emerged as the preferred method of railway organization. On the canals, the boats were usually independently owned, but on the railway independent ownership of trains created congestion and was a safety hazard. Railway companies soon insisted on operating the trains themselves (or franchising an exclusive operator to do it for them).

Competition was also more intense on the railway system than on the canal system, partly because advances in civil engineering made railways easier and quicker to construct. The early trunk line railways soon found that their 'territory' (as they saw it) was being invaded by rival firms. They therefore attempted to consolidate their initial lead by buying up other companies in their area. Each region of the country soon came to be dominated by one particular company. Many of these dominant companies linked London to one of the provincial capitals. They took over feeder lines—both local branches from intermediate country junctions and longer lines reaching out from the provincial centre into more remote (often coastal) areas. These large integrated companies then competed with each other, fighting over their boundaries and sometimes organizing full-scale invasions of one another's territories.

8.2. THE EFFICIENCY OF THE NETWORK

Opinions about the performance of this network have differed. There has also been confusion. Some historical writers have suggested both that the railway system was a success, because the density of lines, relative to area and population, was relatively high, and also that it was a failure because part of this density was accounted for by the duplication of lines. This book has set out to assess whether the network, as finally configured, was wasteful or not.

For this purpose a counterfactual network has been constructed using a small set of heuristic principles. The object of the exercise has been to derive an alternative network that would have met the traffic requirements of the time with minimum route mileage. The traffic requirements have been expressed in terms of performance indicators, which measure the average length of journeys between various pairs of towns. These indicators are constructed for different types of traffic that flow between different types of towns. Length is measured using two metrics—distance and journey time. Distance comparisons are surprisingly difficult to make, because it is not always clear whether certain linkages on the actual system were designed to be used by certain types of traffic or not. Implementation of the time metric is focused specifically on passenger traffic. The exercise requires a counterfactual timetable which can be compared with the actual timetable (Bradshaw's Guide being used for this purpose). Although the construction of the counterfactual timetable is a laborious exercise, the construction of an indicator is relatively straightforward once this has been done. It is also required that each route has a capacity equal to the volume of traffic it needs to carry; this is reflected in the gradients and curvature of the line.

The comparison shows that the actual network is very inferior to the counterfactual network. This finding is robust because the counterfactual equals or exceeds the performance of the actual system in the time dimension for every category of traffic; the conclusion is therefore immune to the criticism that certain types of traffic have been weighted more heavily than they should have been, since the weights have no effect on the final result. It is possible, however, to argue that some of these categories should have been disaggregated and that, if this had been done, sub-categories would emerge for which the counterfactual is inferior. It could then be argued that the traffic in these sub-categories is more important than any other type of traffic on the system. Given the copious information supplied in the appendices, it is open to any reader to perform such an exercise if they wish; it seems unlikely, however, that it will materially alter the result.

8.3. ADVERSARIAL COMPETITION ON THE RAILWAY SYSTEM

The result of this comparison raises the question as to how a competitive system operating in the world's most successful economy of the time could possibly incur so much waste. The answer lies in the competitive process. Victorian Britons believed that they had a genius for free enterprise, and that competition was a natural and healthy part of the free enterprise system. Competition can take many forms, however, and only some of these forms benefit the public. In particular, if competitors expend more effort on raising their rivals' costs and impeding access to their services than they do on improving the quality of their own services then customers may well lose out. This is precisely what seems to have happened on the actual system.

The popular image of competition between railway companies in the nineteenth century is dominated by high-profile events such as the Railway Race to the North of 1894–5, and the race between the Great Western Railway (GWR) and the London and South Western Railway (LSWR) to bring trans-Atlantic passengers and mails from Plymouth to London. These images of speeding trains, hauled by gleaming express engines in colourful company liveries, are exactly the picture of competition that the railway companies strove to create. They were essentially publicity stunts, involving short uneconomic trains, compromises on safety, and inconvenience to other traffic.

The timing of these races can be explained by shifts in competitive advantage caused by the completion of new lines. The Railway Race to the north was between two alliances: the East Coast alliance of the Great Northern, North Eastern and the North British companies, and the West Coast alliance comprising the London and North Western and the Caledonian companies. The East Coast alliance was taking advantage of the newly opened Forth Bridge, which avoided the use of a ferry, or a detour via Perth, between Edinburgh and Aberdeen. In the case of the Plymouth traffic, the LSWR was exploiting its recently opened North Devon line between Exeter and Plymouth via Okehampton.

But there is a deeper significance to these stunts, which concern the performance of crack expresses used by only a tiny proportion of the population—the wealthy business and aristocratic elites. High-speed expresses were not indicative of a high level of performance across the system as a whole. Railway provision for mass public transport was relatively poor. In rural areas in particular, railway lines made little contribution to worker mobility or to stimulating competition between neighbouring market towns.

Furthermore, competition was by no means so prevalent as these stunts might suggest. The Railway Race to the North took place on routes of over 500 miles. Throughout the network, competition tended to be stronger on long-distance routes than on short-distance routes because there were more viable alternative routes between distant towns than between nearby towns. Thus the long-distance traveller could, in principle, benefit more from competition than the short-distance traveller. Most journeys on the British railway system were short (and still are); thus the typical traveller had little alternative but to use the route provided by their nearest station. (Ironically, it is the car that has helped most to stimulate competition between routes on the modern railway system, as it allows passengers to drive from home to different stations on alternative routes.)

Even more misleading is the notion suggested by these races that competition on the railway network was generally a good thing. The racing analogy suggests that competition was stimulating the railway companies to give of their best, and that without the spur of competition they would generally have performed much worse. This idea is broadly consistent with the common view that competition leads to an improvement in customer service. Competing firms vie for the customer's patronage, and in doing so offer the customer a better deal than they could expect from a monopolist.

In practice, however, competition on the railway system often worked very differently, and had adverse consequences for the customer. There is an element of natural monopoly in any railway system that arises simply from the fact that each potential passenger has a nearest station and the next station may be some distance away. Thus so far as the passenger is concerned, the company that owns the nearest station has a degree of monopoly power. Indeed, if the second-nearest station is on the same line as the first then it is likely that the same company will own the other station too. Furthermore, the company may own many of the lines in the region, in which case the chance of finding a convenient station owned by a rival company in some parts of the country is remote.

Railway companies understood right from the very beginning that monopoly power held the key to profitability. When the early trunk lines were built, the companies that built them sought to extend their monopoly to the entire region surrounding the line, by building branches, establishing railheads at intersections with canals and turnpikes, and so on. So far as companies serving London were concerned, they sought a monopoly over the entire region of the country with which they made connection, and to maximize this area they built feeder lines (or bought them up). So far as railway operations were concerned, it made sense to integrate lines that made end-on connections with each other in order to facilitate through running. But as a consequence, the country became partitioned into a set of independent radial territories with London as a hub. This had a number of unfortunate implications.

The first was that companies were reluctant to allow customers who joined their network at their local station to leave the network again by changing to some other company's lines at the nearest convenient hub. Wherever possible, they believed, the customer should go the 'full distance' over the network on which they began their journey. Where cross-country journeys were concerned, this involved the passenger travelling up to London and changing there—however indirect the resultant route might be. Although the railways would have carried more traffic if they had given passengers access to a wider range of routes, few individual companies saw any private advantage in permitting this. They were more concerned with the loss of revenue from existing customers than the additional revenue they might get from new ones.

Railway companies understood the value of hubs perfectly well, but they wished to exploit them as a private resource. Access to the hub was a perk to be offered to the loyal customer who changed onto another of the company's routes—hubs were not there for the benefit of disloyal customers who wished to switch to a rival route.

The inconvenience of cross-country travel was widely recognized, and the issue was addressed by a number of schemes. The first major cross-country schemes appeared at the time of the Railway Mania, and met with little success, but some of the later schemes promoted during the Second Railway Mania of 1861–6 were actually built. Even so, these schemes faced opposition from the established regional companies. The established companies perceived the newcomers as invaders of their territory. They opposed the schemes in Parliament, but this tactic often failed, and so instead they began to promote similar schemes of their own. The companies were only committed to these lines for 'defensive' reasons, however, as they regarded the lines as to some extent competitive with their own existing lines. Having defeated the invader, therefore, they did not always bother to build the lines they had promised to build, until Parliament insisted that they did so.

Although invasion lines might win Parliamentary approval, the invaders did not usually get access to the hubs of the established companies, and so they could not easily tap in to local traffic. This made their lines unprofitable. To get access to local traffic they had to build their own network of local lines, effectively duplicating the network of the established company. Even if they could get access to a local hub, they might be reluctant to use it, for fear that the rival company would disrupt the operation of the hub once the new line was opened. In the meantime, the established company might promote additional local lines of its own, merely to 'fill up the gaps' in the area it claimed to serve, so that it could oppose the building of the invader's feeder lines more effectively.

The difficulty of gaining access to traffic at a hub controlled by a rival company meant that companies seeking access to traffic had to drive their lines right into the heart of the traffic-generating area they wished to serve. This need for independent access to traffic led to widespread duplication of lines. Although the phenomenon of duplication is well-known, the link between duplication and the private control of traffic hubs that encouraged it has not been sufficiently emphasized before.

Duplication affected all sort of areas—not only big cities but also mining areas, industrial districts, and major ports. In the context of London, the need for independent access was felt so strongly that companies such as the Midland and the Great Central felt compelled to build their own trunk lines into the metropolis—the Midland in the 1860s and the Great Central as late as the 1890s.

As so many lines radiated from London, it was inevitable that trunk lines came into competition with their neighbours. Manchester, for example, was served at one time or another by four different routes from London. The London and North Western reached Manchester by a branch from the West Coast main line at Crewe, the Midland reached Manchester via its hub at Derby, on the main line from Manchester to Leeds, the Great Central reached Manchester via Nottingham and Sheffield, whilst the Great Northern reached Manchester via Sheffield and Retford, using a branch from the East Coast main line. There were even further permutations involving Stafford and Stoke-on-Trent. One of the key considerations when travelling to the metropolis was the convenience of the London terminal; the North Western's terminus at Euston, for example, was better sited than the Great Northern's terminus at Kings Cross. Companies with termini on the outskirts of London had a strong incentive to push their termini further into the heart of the city. Faced with opposition from residents and conservationists, 'slum clearance' became an important justification for these 'improvement' schemes.

Another way for a company to improve its competitive position was to offer passengers a choice of termini. This was particularly important to companies operating south of London, serving the growing professional commuter belt. Instead of constructing a rationalized system, however, each company built its own links, proliferating termini as a result.

Companies found it difficult to share the use of terminals—not only in London, but in every major city. Railway managers were concerned that if they shared a terminal with a rival then a 'platform auction' would develop with each company having to cut its fares to match the fares being quoted by their rival. They preferred to operate their own terminal where they were in full control of operations. Their exclusive city terminus became a marketing outlet, and it often had impressive architecture to match.

With so many lines converging on London, and cross-country connections being so poor, it might be expected that connections in London would be good, but this was not in fact the case. As in most other major cities, passengers had to make their own way between terminals. This could be a major problem—particularly if they had luggage. Roads were congested with slow-moving horse-traffic, and buses, trams, and taxis could all be slow as well. It was not until the advent of underground railways that connections in London became easier, and even then the traveller had to cope initially with heavy smoke and long flights of stairs.

8.4. POLICY RESPONSES

As the nineteenth century drew to a close, the weaknesses of the railways system became increasingly obvious. Manufacturers and wholesalers portrayed the system as a handicap to British competitiveness in export markets. Unfavourable comparisons were drawn with the railways in other countries—particularly continental European competitors such as France and Belgium, although the relevance of these comparisons was hotly disputed by the companies.

In fact, these observations were nothing new. Similar concerns about the British railway system had been expressed as early as the 1840s and 1850s, but, although noted at the time, they were not acted upon. Had these concerns been addressed at the time they first appeared, decisive action could have been taken. But from 1860 onwards it was really too late to do much about the problem. Railway lines were already being duplicated, hubs were performing inefficiently, and those hubs that were performing well were generally used by just a single company.

A missed opportunity occurred at the time of the Railway Mania, 1844–5. The Railway Mania is often blamed for some of the subsequent problems of the railway system, but usually for the wrong reasons. Shortly after the collapse of 1846 a number of influential books appeared explaining how numerous individuals had lost money through the promotion of fraudulent schemes. Most subsequent historical writing on the Mania has drawn heavily on these sources, and ascribed to them a degree of objectivity that they do not deserve.

A close examination of these so-called fraudulent schemes suggests that many of them had a sound economic logic. These schemes often correspond to linkages in the counterfactual railway system constructed for the purposes of this study, and would therefore have formed part of an efficient national railway network, had such a network been built. Some of the grandiose names of these schemes are scoffed at, as though, with the benefit of hindsight, they were often put together simply to fleece the gullible investor. But, once again, a close examination of these schemes suggests that their names were often quite appropriate, simply because they featured the names of the principal traffic-generating centres they proposed to serve, or identified the region concerned. Whilst it is true that epithets such as 'Grand' and 'Great' were quite common, it should be noted that such appellations were also widely used by established and highly reputable companies.

Further examination shows that variants of many of these schemes were subsequently built later in the century by other promoters using different names. It is hard to see how a scheme can be obviously fraudulent when promoted in 1844, and yet be regarded as a perfectly sensible scheme when built under a different name twenty years later.

It is certainly true that a lot of people lost a lot of money in the Railway Mania. It is also true that many schemes failed and that when they failed the engineers and lawyers usually got their fees and the shareholders got nothing. It is also true that many people were foolish to speculate in railway 'scrip' and that professional stock-jobbers almost certainly took advantage of their gullibility. But the suggestion that a significant number of railways were promoted merely to give the stock-jobbers some shares to sell remains unproven.

Railway Mania schemes did not fail because Parliament refused to approve them. Quite the contrary, in fact: many railway schemes failed because Parliament approved so many of them. Whilst a reasonable number of schemes were approved in 1845, a quite excessive number of schemes were approved in 1846. The excess is obvious given that the successful 1845 schemes were already in the process of making calls on their shareholders and letting construction contracts. It also seems fairly clear that Parliament knew that there was a looming problem. Several of the railway acts that were passed in 1846 refer explicitly to rival schemes which have also been authorized, and contain special clauses designed to avoid the building of almost identical lines. In addition, there are numerous Acts that authorize the building of lines that would cater for similar traffic even if they did not pass through exactly the same towns.

The huge number of railways authorized by Parliament in 1846 contributed directly to the ensuing financial crisis. (It was not the only factor, however; changes in tariffs, the Irish famine, and the collapse of Peel's government were also involved.) The burden of finance to be raised proved insuperable, and interest rates, which had been low for some time, suddenly began to rise. In addition, railway shareholders began to realize that the monopoly profits they had hoped to earn had been undermined by the prospective competition unleashed by the duplication of lines. Shares in both new and established companies fell in value, although it was the shares of the new companies that suffered most.

The railways that survived this financial stringency were generally those that served specific towns that had wealthy residents and good traffic prospects. Conversely, the railways that suffered most were those whose role was to link up other lines rather than to generate traffic of their own. In some cases the problem was that the schemes to which they proposed to link themselves collapsed, and in other cases that the company was considered to be too dependent on others for its traffic. In many cases the more ambitious schemes were simply cut back to fulfil more local objectives; in this way cross-country lines finished up as short dead-end branches from an existing main line.

Why then did Parliament authorize so many schemes? The answer seems to be that MPs had become heavily involved in railway promotion—not necessarily in any undesirable way, but simply as members of Provisional Committees promoting schemes that were seen as beneficial to their constituents. They needed to get railways authorized in order to keep their jobs. Whilst the merchants on the Provisional Committee would be pledging to consign their traffic over the railway, and the bankers would be promising to raise funds, the MP's job was to guide the railway Bill through Parliament and to deliver the Act required. In the wake of the great Reform Bill 1832, and the troubled political atmosphere of the time, MPs were deemed accountable to their constituents, and those MPs who did not think this way risked losing their seats. National political parties were not so strong as they are today, and the constituents held the 'whip' hand.

MPs faced a difficulty, however—namely that they reviewed each other's proposals in Parliamentary Committees. It was therefore necessary to broker a deal with other MPs in order to be sure of getting a Bill approved. The obvious deal was not to oppose another MP's Bill if they did not oppose your own. Everyone could help everyone else by simply approving as many Bills as possible. Although wasteful duplication of lines would occur, and the capital market might even collapse, MPs would get to keep their seats.

There was another more serious difficulty, however. There was a group of Parliamentarians—including William Gladstone, Earl Dalhousie, and James Morrison—who believed that the railway system should be constructed in response to national rather than local interest. These people were generally agreed to be very knowledgeable on the subject of railways. They were acutely aware of the divergence between private interest and public interest in railway policy. Their view of the public interest included the interests of the great mass of workmen and their families, and not just the social elite. They were notable for thinking ahead towards a railway system based on the principles of public transport, carrying large volumes of traffic at low fares. Although aware of the benefits of private enterprise, they did not rule out public ownership for industries such as railways in which they believed that competition was likely to fail. They believed that the right of a railway to interfere with private property, in the interests of merchants and industrialists, could only be defended if the railway, once built, served the interests of workmen and the public as a whole.

These Parliamentarians believed that there was a set of rational principles which could be applied to the railway system. These principles are similar in some respects to the principles used to devise the counterfactual system in this study, although there is no formal connection between them. The similarity is sufficiently striking, however, to suggest that these individuals could have derived a blue-print not unlike the counterfactual had they resolved to do so. Indeed, there is good evidence that they actually did so.

Gladstone established a Railway Committee at the Board of Trade with a mandate to advise Parliament on railway schemes. The Railway Committee produced a succession of impressive reports on schemes that had either been submitted to Parliament, or were in preparation and were about to be submitted. These schemes were generally evaluated on a regional basis, although thematic issues such as amalgamations between companies were also addressed. Each report on a region set out how the general principles applied to the region and outlined specific requirements that the railway network should meet. Some of these reports were remarkably insightful—especially the report on the cotton textile districts of Lancashire, which anticipated the analysis of industrial districts presented by the economist Alfred Marshall some fifty years later.

In the Parliamentary session 1844–5, the recommendations of the Railway Committee were broadly accepted by Parliament, which suggests that the members of Parliamentary Committees on railway Bills broadly agreed with the Railway Committee. Indeed, the records show that there were remarkably few issues on which there was any disagreement—the main exception being the standardization of railway gauges. As a result of following the Railway Committee's advice, a high proportion of Bills were rejected, and many schemes were postponed on the grounds that better ones were likely to be submitted the following year. The consequence of this outcome was a large number of disappointed constituents who felt that they had been let down by their MPs. MPs therefore resolved not to take any more advice from the Railway Committee in future, and as a result its mandate was lost. Sir Robert Peel's government was too weak, because of its unpopularity on other issues, to insist that MPs continue to take unwelcome advice.

8.5. COMPETITION BETWEEN TOWNS

Why were MPs so anxious to attract railways to their towns? It has often been asserted that towns did not want the railway to come near them. This was broadly true up to about 1840. Of course, it is necessary to distinguish between the large cities and ports, which were generally well-disposed to railways from the outset, and the smaller country market towns, which were very suspicious of railways to begin with.

Some people regarded the steam locomotive as a monstrous being—a snorting mechanical horse—although the popular actress Fanny Kemble thought a steam locomotive to be rather sweet when she rode on one with George Stephenson. The noise made by steam locomotives would frighten horses, it was said, as well as creating smoke and other nuisances for local residents. Railway travel would be dangerous—people would suffocate in tunnels, trains would accelerate out of control on inclines, and so on. Passengers were in danger too: William Huskisson was killed by the Rocket locomotive on the opening day of the Liverpool and Manchester Railway as he strolled along the track. They could also be uncomfortable: Brunel complained about the rough ride on the Liverpool and Manchester line—a problem he planned to cure with his broad gauge.

But it turned out that despite the risks and the inconvenience there was an unsatisfied demand for railway travel. Romantics might extol the virtues of the stage-coach, and inn-keepers and coachmen demand protection for their livelihoods, but when a railway line was built, the public deserted the stage-coach almost overnight. Coachmen and local carriers were reduced to running feeder services to the nearest station. Where a railway line bypassed a traditional coaching town, the economic consequences could be devastating: inns and shops closed, property values declined, and local banks went bankrupt. Economic reality overpowered any romantic attachment to what was rapidly becoming a bygone age.

For many towns, therefore, getting on to the railway network was a matter of economic survival. To become a railway hub was ideal, to be on a main line would do, and even to be on a branch was better than nothing.

There were, of course, different factions in the towns, and some towns were more cohesive than others. Merchants were generally in favour of a railway, and so too were property developers. There were many property speculators in Victorian Britain, and there was considerable competition to identify properties that would appreciate in value from the coming of the railways. In some cases land could be sold for use by the railway company itself—perhaps as the site for a local station—whilst in other cases the property would simply appreciate in value because of its proximity to the railway.

Opposition to the railway often came from aristocrats and other owners of large estates—particularly those who had devoted time and money to landscaping their grounds and creating 'pleasure parks'. Opposition usually rested on loss of visual amenity, however, and could be addressed by putting the railway into a tunnel or removing it further from the house. Many aristocrats took their local obligations seriously, and were reluctant to block a railway scheme completely when local people were in favour of it; they just demanded financial compensation instead.

Large estates could benefit economically from the railway, which could bring in cheap coal and fertilizer and carry away agricultural products—especially high-value items such as milk and fresh vegetables. Some landowners took a leading role in promoting local railways, which gave them the financial clout to protect their personal interests in the process.

Access to a railway could give a town a lead over other market towns. Towns were always in competition with their neighbours to attract local trade. The right to hold a market was one of the most ancient rights of the towns, and was jealously guarded. Business must be enticed away from neighbouring markets, the citizens believed, and a railway was one means of doing this. Towns were not primarily interested in railway communication with other local towns, for this would only make competition between them more intense. They were interested instead in communication with major cities and other traffic-generating centres, which for many English towns meant good communication with London. To have a better link to London than did a neighbouring town was an advantage well worth fighting for.

The natural person to lead this fight for this advantage was, of course, the local MP—someone who not only had contacts in London, but who also had a personal need for the railway to make his journey up to London easier. It is easy to see, therefore, why once the economic benefits of railway communication were evident, MPs had a very strong incentive to get a railway to their town as quickly as possible.

8.6. COOPERATION

Given the emphasis on competition above, it is reasonable to ask how the existence of cooperation between railway companies is to be explained. Many railway companies owned joint lines and shared the use of joint stations. How could they compete so strongly when they were cooperating too?

The short answer is that most of the cooperation was an illusion. Take the case of Bristol Temple Meads station, for example, which was shared by two great enemies: the Great Western and the Midland. The agreement to share the station was made when the Midland's line was actually owned by a local company that was considered to be an ally of the Great Western. But the Great Western then decided to take a tough line with its ally over the price at which it would buy its line, and the ally found that it could get a better deal with the Midland. The Midland then inherited the right to use Temple Meads, to the annoyance of the Great Western.

A related point is that cooperation was often brokered by third parties. A number of towns with cohesive elites decided to promote themselves as railway hubs. These were towns that, by and large, considered themselves to have had a glorious past but not to have much of a future—for example, Chester, Shrewsbury, and York—and so they embraced the future by becoming a railway hub. Typically they offered a prime site to the railway companies on condition that they built a joint station. Interestingly, though, once the joint station had been built, the companies tended to close ranks and keep out later railways arriving in the town if they could.

A longer answer to the question is that cooperation was a useful instrument of competition—in particular, joint lines helped to spread the costs of invading other companies' territories. Companies were quite adept at cooperating with a company on one front whilst competing with them on another. There was little loyalty in most cooperative arrangements. They were made because the partners saw immediate advantage in them, and were often dissolved when circumstances changed. Some partnerships seem to have emerged because of genuine trust between the managers of different companies, but these arrangements often dissolved when the personnel changed.

When it came to fixing fares, most companies were very fearful of any kind of price war. Tacit collusion tended to prevail in pricing, the most common arrangement being that every company would match the lowest available fare. This arrangement discouraged price competition, since any price cut would immediately be matched by other companies. It meant that passengers would take their decisions on the basis of factors other than price. Companies therefore agreed amongst themselves to compete on quality of service instead. There were many dimensions to quality of service—journey speed, frequency of service, convenient access to and from the station, catering facilities, comfort, and so on. In the 1870s, a company's accident record was a pertinent consideration too.

It seems fairly clear that the intensity of competition was the factor that limited cooperation, because on non-competitive issues the companies cooperated very closely. The Railway Clearing House performed a valuable role for the industry from its foundation in 1842, whilst the Railway Companies Association lobbied actively on matters of common concern such as passenger duty and the level of local rates.

This calculated approach to cooperation is consistent with what can be discerned of railway companies' attitudes on other issues. Railway companies were happy to cooperate for the benefit of customers when it suited them to do so. In the Railway Races to the North, for example, the companies in the two competing alliances did not stint in offering the best possible service to their customers in terms of speed. On the other hand, though, comfort may have left something to be desired as the trains rattled along as fast as the locomotives could go. By contrast, cross-country passengers who switched to lines that they were not supposed to use could be deliberately inconvenienced by being forced to wait at isolated country junctions after having missed their connections. In the early days of competition, passengers were obliged to witness violence between the employees of rival companies, and were actually put in danger when rails were removed to obstruct the movement of rival companies' trains.

8.7. FINAL THOUGHTS

In recent years many people have lamented what they perceive as the decline of the British railway system. The root of the problem is often attributed to the Beeching cuts of the 1960s, which eliminated many dead-end branches and some duplicate main lines. Privatization in 1994 is also said to have made matters even worse. What is certain, however, is that the problems of the British railway network did not begin as late as this. The network today is largely a legacy of the Victorian system. It was certainly much larger in 1914 than it is today, but even then it was not as good as it should have been given the route mileage of track.

The British railway system was never designed to be operated as a national network. This is reflected, amongst other things, in the fact that when the railways were rationalized in the 1970s, a lot of new connecting spurs had to be built. This was because entire duplicate lines had been built because connections could not be made at the obvious places—namely the natural hubs on the system. When the duplicate lines were eliminated, the missing connections had to be put in so that the hubs could begin to perform the role that they should have performed many years earlier.

If the Victorians had not built so many dead-end branches, there would not have been so many of them for Beeching to close down. If the advice of the Railway Committee of the Board of Trade had been followed in 1845, many of these branches might in fact have been through routes. Furthermore, some of the secondary single-track cross-country lines Beeching closed might have been built as high-speed inter-urban lines instead. But they could only have been built this way if their promoters had enjoyed access to major hubs along their route, which they did not have.

A statutory obligation to facilitate interchange of traffic at natural hubs was never introduced, and this allowed established companies to prevent later lines from fulfilling their true potential. These lines were often starved of traffic at the outset, and so it is no wonder that they were amongst the first to be closed. Conversely, the early trunk lines, which selected the most direct routes between the greatest urban centres, still survive to this day. Unfortunately, however, they still bypass the same towns that they bypassed when they were built. The only difference is that now there are no longer any branches to connect the towns to the main lines.

Connectivity on the Victorian network became so poor that thousands of miles of additional track were built in order to make good the operational deficiencies created by a few miles of missing connections around natural hubs. Towns and cities that serve as important hubs on the counterfactual system were often mere traffic-generators on the actual system, comprising independent terminals of rival companies linked, if at all, by spurs suitable only for local freight traffic. The wasteful proliferation of terminals is evident in London today; it is only the tube connections that make the inconvenience tolerable. Such waste was clearly fore-seen at the time of the Railway Mania, but Parliament lacked the will to address the issue; as a result, short-term local interest triumphed over long-term national interest.

Bibliography

This bibliography lists all the major sources used in this study. Not all of the sources are explicitly referenced in the text. Many of the studies refer to local and regional lines, and contain details of proposed railways along the route of the line as well as the lines actually built. These studies were useful in interpreting information contained in the deposited plans, and were used extensively in constructing the profiles of the actual and counterfactual networks; they also informed the discussion of regional subsystems in Chapter 4 and joint lines in Chapter 5. Documenting each fact about each local railway, as mentioned in these two chapters, would have produced an enormous number of footnotes.

The bibliography is organized by topic. Readers who wish to identify the source for any particular fact can easily do so using the classification system. Company histories and histories of individual lines have been listed separately, and the histories of individual lines have been classified on a geographical basis. The geographical units have been chosen by reference to the coverage of the literature and do not correspond exactly to the regional categories employed in the main text. Histories of the major companies whose lines spanned several regions have been listed separately, but the histories of purely regional companies have been included in the geographical listings.

There is a huge literature on railways, much of it written by enthusiasts, and most of it well researched (although there is some uncritical use of secondary literature). No attempt has been made to record all of this work; items that deal mainly with locomotives, carriages, and wagons have been omitted, and items that are mainly photographic have been included only if the photographs and their captions inform the discussion in this book. In this connection, it should be noted that photographs can be extremely informative where railways are concerned, particularly where the length of passenger trains, and the variety of goods carried on freight trains can be assessed, and the place and date of the photograph are known. Sources that address the image and reputation of railways have been included, because they affect the manner in which railways were promoted and regulated, but literature on other issues has generally been omitted.

There are many fascinating and obscure items of contemporary literature that shed light on the Victorian railway system. Excellent collections of such material can be found in the Science Museum Library, the London School of Economics Library, the Library of the Institution of Civil Engineers, and libraries of deposit, such as the British Library and the Bodleian Library, Oxford. These books have not be listed unless they have a direct bearing on a specific issue; however, where these books have been reprinted since 1945, and are consequently available in local studies libraries and second-hand bookshops, they have been included out of interest.

Railway archive guides, bibliographies, and reference

Boase, Frederic (1965) *Modern English Biography: Persons who have Died between the Years 1851–1900*, London: Frank Cass.

Bond, Maurice F. (1959) Materials for transport history amongst the record of Parliament, *Journal of Transport History*, 4(1), 37–52.

—— (1971) *Guide to the Records of Parliament*, London: HMSO.

Casson, Janet (2007) *A Study of Women Landowners and Lessees in the Nineteenth Century and an Analysis of the Usage of their Landholdings as revealed by the Books of Reference produced by the Railway Companies*, Oxford: MSc dissertation, Oxford University.

Clifford, Frederick (1885–7) *A History of Private Bill Legislation*, 2 vols, London: Butterworths.

Clinker, C.R. (1984) *Railway History in Acts of Parliament*, Weston-super-Mare: Avon Anglia.

Clwyd Record Office (1991) *Handlist of the Denbigh Quarter Sessions Records, Vol II* (ed. A.G. Veysey), Hawarden: CRO.

Cotterell, S. (ed.) (1969) *Bibliography and Priced Catalogue of Early Railway Books*, 1893, Reprint ed., Newton Abbot: David & Charles.

Davey, Roger (2003) *East Sussex Parliamentary Deposited Plans, 1799–1970: Schemes for Railways, Canals, Harbours, Roads, Tramways, Piers and Public Utilities: Sussex Maps III*, Lewes: Sussex Record Society (Volume 87).

Dorset Archives Service (1997) *Railway Records in the Dorset Record Office*, Dorchester: Dorset County Council.

Given-Wilson, Christopher (2005) *The Parliament Rolls of Medieval England*, Leicester: Scholarly Digital Editions.

Hampshire Archivists' Group (1973) *Transport in Hampshire and the Isle of Wight: A Guide to the Records*, Winchester: Hampshire County Council.

Haskell, Daniel C. (1955) *A Tentative Check-list of Early European Railway Literature, 1831–1848*, Boston, MA: Baker Library, Harvard Graduate School of Business Administration.

Hawkings, David T. (1995) *Railway Ancestors: A Guide to the Staff Records of the Railway Companies of England and Wales, 1822–1947*, Stroud: Alan Sutton for the Public Record Office.

House of Lords (2000) *Companion to the Standing Orders and Guide to the Proceedings of the House of Lords*, London: Stationery Office.

North Yorkshire County Record Office (1997) *List of North Yorkshire and North Riding Plans of Railway Lines and Buildings*, Northallerton: NYCRO.

Ottley, George (ed.) (1965–1998) *A Bibliography of British Railway History* (3 vols, separately published, including a second supplement by G. Boyes, M. Searle, and D. Steggles for the Railway & Canal Historical Society), London: Allen & Unwin/HMSO and York: National Railway Museum.

Oxfordshire County Council (1983) *A Handlist of Plans, Sections and Books of Reference for the Proposed Railways in Oxfordshire, 1825–1936*, Oxford: OCC.

Railway Clearing House (1969) *Railway Junction Diagrams, 1915*, reprint, Newton Abbot: David & Charles.

Richards, Tom (2002) *Was your Grandfather a Railwayman? A Directory of Railway Archive Sources for Family Historians*, 4th ed. Bury: FFHS Publications.

Riden, Philip (compiler) (2000) *Catalogue of Plans of Proposed Canals, Turnpike Roads, Railways and other Public Works deposited with the Clerks of the Peace for Northamptonshire,* the County Borough of Northamptonshire and the Soke of the Peterborough, 1792–1960, in the Northamptonshire Record Office, Northampton: NRO.

Steer, Francis W. (ed.) (1968) *A Catalogue of Sussex Estate Maps, West Sussex Inclosure Maps, West Sussex Deposited Plans, Miscellaneous and Printed Sussex Maps*, [Sussex Maps II], Lewes: Sussex Record Society (Volume 66).

Stenton, Michael (ed.) (1976) *Who's Who of British Members of Parliament, Volume I, 1832–1885: A Biographical Dictionary of the House of Commons*, Hassocks, Sussex: Harvester Press.

Wardle, D.B. (1955) Sources for the history of railways at the Public Record Office, *Journal of Transport History*, **2**, 214–34.

Williams, O. Cyprian (1948–9) The Historical Development of Private Bill Procedure and Standing Orders in the House of Commons, 2 vols, London: HMSO.

General

Acworth, William (1891) *The Railways and the Traders*, London: John Murray.

—— (1904) *The Elements of Railway Economics*, Oxford: Clarendon Press.

Addyman, John and Victoria Haworth (2005) *Robert Stephenson: Railway Engineer*, Stretford, Manchester: North Eastern Railway Association.

Aldcroft, Derek H. (1964) The entrepreneur and the British economy, 1870–1914, *Economic History Review*, 17, 113–34.

Alderman, Geoffrey (1973) *The Railway Interest*, Leicester: Leicester University Press.

Ambler, R.W. (ed.) (1999) *The History and Practice of Britain's Railways: A New Research Agenda*, Aldershot: Ashgate.

Andersson-Skog, Lena and Olle Krantz (eds.) (1999) *Institutions in the Transport and Communications Industries: State and Private Actors in the Making of Institutional Patterns, 1850–1990*, Canton, MA: Science History Publications.

Arnold, A.J. and S. McCartney (2004) *George Hudson: The Rise and Fall of the Railway King: A Study in Victorian Entrepreneurship*, London: Hambledon & London.

Ashton, Thomas S. and Joseph Sykes (1929) *The Coal Industry of the Eighteenth Century*, Manchester: Manchester University Press.

Bagwell, Philip (1963) *The Railwaymen*, London: Allen & Unwin.

—— (1968) *The Railway Clearing House in the British Economy, 1842–1922*, London: Allen & Unwin.

—— and Peter Lyth (2002) *Transport in Britain: From Canal Lock to Gridlock*, London: Hambledon & London.

Bailey, Brian (1995) *George Hudson: The Rise and Fall of the Railway King*, Stroud: Alan Sutton.

Bailey, Michael R. (ed.) (2003) *Robert Stephenson: The Eminent Engineer*, Aldershot: Ashgate.

Bannister, David, Roberta Capello, and Peter Nijkamp (eds.) (1995) *European Transport and Communications Networks: Policy Evolution and Change*, Chichester: Wiley.

Barnett, A.L. (1992) *The Light Railway King of the North*, Mold: Railway & Canal Historical Society.

Bassett, Herbert H. (ed.) (1913) *Bradshaw's Railway Manual, Shareholders' Guide and Official Directory*, London: Henry Blacklock.

Baumol, William J. (1994) *Entrepreneurship, Management and the Structure of Pay-offs*, Cambridge, MA: MIT Press.

Baumol, William J. (2002) *The Free-market Innovation Machine*, Princeton, NJ: Princeton University Press.

Beaumont, Robert (2002) *The Railway King: A Biography of George Hudson*, London: Review.

Body, Geoffrey (1994) *Great Railway Battles: Dramatic Conflicts of the Early Railway Years*, Wadenhoe, Peterborough: Silver Link.

Bosley, Peter (1990) *Light Railways in England & Wales*, Manchester: Manchester University Press.

Broadberry, Stephen (1997) *The Productivity Race: British Manufacturing in International Perspective, 1850–1990*, Cambridge: Cambridge University Press.

—— (2006) *Market Services and the Productivity Race, 1850–2000*, Cambridge: Cambridge University Press.

Broadbridge, Seymour (1970) *Studies in Railway Expansion and the Capital Market in England, 1825–1873*, London: Frank Cass.

Brunel, Isambard K. (1843) *Letterbooks*, University of Bristol Special Collections, DM1306.

Burton, Anthony and John Scott-Morgan (1985) *Britain's Light Railways*, Ashbourne: Moorland.

Butt, John (1981) Achievement and Prospect: Transport history in the 1970s and 1980s, *Journal of Transport History*, 3rd series, 2(1), 1–24.

Buxton, Neill K. (1978) *Economic Development of the British Coal Industry from the Industrial Revolution to the Present Day*. London: Batsford.

Cain, P.J. (1973) Traders versus Railways: The genesis of the Railway and Canal Traffic Act of 1894, *Journal of Transport History*, New series, 2(2), 65–84.

—— and A.G. Hopkins (2002) *British Imperialism 1688–2000*, 2nd ed., London: Longman.

Calzada, Joan and Tommaso Valetti (2008) Network competition and entry deterrence, *Economic Journal*, 118 (4) 1223–44.

Casserly, H.C. (1968) *Britain's Joint Lines*. Shepperton: Ian Allan.

Casson, Mark (1982) *The Entrepreneur: An Economic Theory*, Oxford: Martin Robertson.

—— (2000) *Enterprise and Leadership*, Cheltenham: Edward Elgar.

—— Bernard Yeung, Anuradha Basu, and Bernard Yeung (eds.) (2006) *Oxford Handbook of Entrepreneurship*, Oxford: Oxford University Press.

Chalklin, Christopher W. (1998) *English Counties and Public Building, 1650–1830*, London: Hambledon Press.

Chandler, Alfred D., Jr. (1965) *Railroads: The Nation's First Big Business*.

—— (1990) *Scale and Scope: The Dynamics of Victorian Capitalism*, Cambridge, MA: Harvard University Press.

Channon, Geoffrey (1981) A.D. Chandler's 'visible hand' in transport history: A review article, *Journal of Transport History*, 3rd series, 2(1), 53–64.

—— (2001) Railways in Britain and the United States, 1830–1940, Aldershot: Ashgate.

—— (ed.) (1996) *Railways, Vol. I*, Aldershot: Scolar Press.

Church, Roy A. (1975) *The Great Victorian Boom, 1850–1873*, London: Macmillan.

—— (1986) *History of the British Coal Industry, Vol. 3: 1830–1913, Victorian Pre-eminence*, Oxford: Clarendon Press.

Clapham, John H. (1926–38) *An Economic History of Modern Britain*, 3 vols., Cambridge: Cambridge University Press.

Cleveland-Stevens, Edward (1915) *English Railways: Their Development and their Relation to the State*, London: Routledge.

Cobb, Michael H. (2008) *An Historical Atlas of the Railways of Great Britain*, 2nd ed., Shepperton: Ian Allan.

Corley, Tony A.B. (1994) Britain's overseas investments in 1914 revisited, *Business History*, 36, 71–88.

Crafts, Nicholas F.R. (1985) *British Industrial Growth during the Industrial Revolution*, Oxford: Oxford University Press.

—— Timothy Leunig, and Abay Mulatu (2008) Were British railway companies well managed in the early twentieth century? *Economic History Review*, 61 (4), 842–66.

Darby, H.C. (ed.) (1976) *A New Historical Geography of England before 1600*. Cambridge: Cambridge University Press.

Davidson, Edward (1868) *The Railways of India*, London: E & F.N. Spon.

Deane, Phyllis (1979) *The First Industrial Nation*, Cambridge: Cambridge University Press.

Dendy Marshall, C.F. (1938) *A History of British Railways down to the Year 1830*, London: Oxford University Press.

Dumett, Raymond E. (2008) *Mining Tycoons in the Age of Empire, 1870–1945*, Aldershot: Ashgate.

Evans, A.K.B. and J.V. Gough (eds.) (2003) *The Impact of the Railway on Society in Britain: Essays in Honour of Jack Simmons*, Aldershot: Ashgate.

Evans, D. Morier (1968) *Facts, Failures and Frauds: Revelations Financial, Mercantile, Criminal* (reprint), Newton Abbot: David & Charles.

Farr, Michael (n.d.) *Thomas Edmondson and His Tickets*, Andover: The author.

Fishlow, Albert (1965) *American Railroads and the Transformation of the Ante-Bellum Economy*, Cambridge, MA: Harvard University Press.

Flyvberg, Bent, Nils Bruzalius, and Werner Rothengatter (2003) *Megaprojects and Risk: The Anatomy of Ambition*, Cambridge: Cambridge University Press.

Fogel, Robert W. (1964) *Railroads and Economic Growth: Essays in Econometric History*, Baltimore: Johns Hopkins University Press.

Francis, John (1851) A History of the English Railway: Its Social Relations and Revelations, 1820–1845, Reprinted 1968, New York: Augustus M. Kelley.

Godley, Andrew (2001) Jewish Immigrant Entrepreneurship in New York and London, 1880–1914, London: Palgrave.

Gomez-Ibanez, Jose A. (2003) *Regulating Infrastructure: Monopoly, Contracts and Discretion*, Cambridge MA: Harvard University Press.

Gooch, Daniel (1972) *Memoirs and Diary* (ed. R.B. Wilson), Newton Abbot: David & Charles.

Gourvish, Terence R. (1972) Mark Huish and the London & North Western Railway: A Study of Management, Leicester: Leicester University Press.

—— (1980) *Railways and the British Economy, 1830–1914*, London: Macmillan.

Gourvish, Terry (1993) What kind of railway history did we get? Forty years of research, *Journal of Transport History*, 3rd series 14(2), 111–25.

—— (ed.) (1996) *Railways, Vol. II*, Aldershot: Scolar Press.

Haggett, Peter and Richard J. Chorley (1969) *Network Analysis in Geography*, London: Edward Arnold.

Hardin, Garrett (1968) The tragedy of the commons, *Science*, 162, No. 3859, 1243–8.

Harrison, David (2004) *The Bridges of Medieval England: Transport and Society 400–1800*, Oxford: Oxford University Press.

Hatcher, John (1993) *The History of the British Coal Industry, Volume 1: Before 1700: Towards the Age of Coal*, Oxford: Clarendon Press.

Hawke, Gary (1970) *Railways and Economic Growth in England & Wales, 1840–1870*, Oxford: Clarendon Press.

Hildenbrand, Stefan and Anthony Tromba (1996) *The Parsimonious Universe: Shape and Form in the Natural World*, New York: Copernicus.

Hills, R.L. and D. Patrick (1982) *Beyer Peacock: Locomotive Builders to the World*, reprinted 1998, Venture Publications.

Hirst, Francis W. (1931) *Gladstone as Financier and Economist*, London: Ernest Benn.

Hodgkins, David (2001) *The Second Railway King: The Life and Times of Sir Edward Watkin, 1819–1901*, Whitchurch, Cardiff: Merton Priory Press.

Holtgrefe, A.A.I. (1975) *An Optimizing Medium-Term Model for the Netherlands Railways*, Rotterdam: Rotterdam University Press.

Hwang, F.K., D.S. Richards, and P. Winter (1992) *The Steiner Tree Problem*, Amsterdam: North Holland.

Hyde, Francis E. (1934) *Mr. Gladstone at the Board of Trade*, London: Cobden-Sanderson.

Irving, R.J. (1984) The capitalisation of Britain's railways, *Journal of Transport History*, 3rd series, 5(1), 1–24.

Ivanov, Alaxandr O. and Alexei A. Tuzhilin (1994) *Minimal Networks: The Steiner Problem and its Generalisation*, Boca Raton: CRC Press.

Jackman, W.T. (1962) *The Development of Transportation in Modern England*, New ed., London: Frank Cass.

Jeaffreson, J.C. (1864) *The Life of Robert Stephenson, FRS*, 2 vols, London: Longman.

[Joint lines; problem of] The problem of joint lines: Fruitful field for railway economies, *Modern Transport*, 19 September, p. 3.

[Joint lines; problem of] Dendy-Marshall, C.F., Letter to *Modern Transport*, 26 September, 1931.

Jones, Geoffrey G. (2000) *From Merchants to Multinationals*, Oxford: Oxford University Press.

—— (ed.) (1998) *The Multinational Traders*, London: Routledge.

Jones, Ian (2001) Railway franchising: is it sufficient? On-rail competition in the privatised passenger rail industry, in C. Robinson (ed.) *Regulating Utilities: New Issues, New Solutions*, Cheltenham: Edward Elgar, 120–41.

Jowett, Alan (1989) *Jowett's Railway Atlas of Great Britain and Ireland from Pre-Grouping to the Present Day*, London: Guild Publishing.

Judd, Gerrit P. (1955) *Members of Parliament, 1734–1832*, New Haven, CT: Yale University Press.

Kellett, John R. (1964) Urban and transport history from legal records: An example from Glasgow solicitors' papers, *Journal of Transport History*, 6(4), 222–40.

—— (1969) *The Impact of Railways on Victorian Cities*, London: Routledge & Kegan Paul.

Kerr, Ian J. (1997) *Building the Railways of the Raj, 1850–1900*, Delhi: Oxford University Press.

Kihlstrom, R.E. and J.J. Laffont (1979) A general equilibrium entrepreneurial theory of firm formation based on risk aversion, *Journal of Political Economy*, 87, 719–48.

Kingsford, P.W. (1970) *Victorian Railwaymen: The Emergence and Growth of Railway Labour, 1830–1870*, London: Frank Cass.

Kirzner, Israel M. (1973) *Competition and Entrepreneurship*, Chicago: University of Chicago Press.

—— (1979) *Perception, Opportunity and Profit*, Chicago: University of Chicago Press.

Klein, Michael (1998) Network Industries, in D. Helm and T. Jenkinson (eds.), *Competition in Regulated Industries*, Oxford: Oxford University Press.

Knight, Frank H. (1921) *Risk Uncertainty and Profit*, Boston: Houghton Mifflin.

Knoop, Douglas (1913) *Outlines of Railway Economics*, London: Macmillan.

Kostal, Rande W. (1994) *Law and English Railway Capitalism, 1825–1875*, Oxford: Clarendon Press.

Lambert, Richard S. (1934) *The Railway King, 1800–1871: A study of George Hudson and the Business Morals of his Times*, London: Allen & Unwin.

Lardner, Dionysius (1968) *Railway Economy: A Treatise on the New Art of Transport*, reprint of 1850 ed., Newton Abbot: David & Charles.

Lee, Charles E. (1937) *The Evolution of Railways*, London: Railway Gazette.

Lee, Der-Horng (ed.) (2004) *Urban and Regional Transportation Modelling: Essays in honour of David Boyce*, Cheltenham: Edward Elgar.

Leigh, Christopher (1987) *The Aerofilms Book of Britain's Railways from the Air*, Shepperton: Ian Allan.

—— and Aerofilms (1990) *The Second Book of Britain's Railways from the Air*, Shepperton: Ian Allan.

Leunig, Tim (2001) New answers to old questions: explaining the slow adoption of ring spinning in Lancashire, 1880–1913, *Journal of Economic History*, 61(2), 439–66.

Leunig, Timothy (2006) Time is money: A re-assessment of the social savings from Victorian British railways, *Journal of Economic History*, 66(3), 635–73.

Lewin, Henry G. (1936) *The Railway Mania and its Aftermath, 1845–52* (ed. C.R. Clinker), Newton Abbot: David & Charles.

Lewis, M.J.T. (1970) *Early Wooden Railways*, London: Routledge.

Lowe, John C. and S. Moryadas (1975) *The Geography of Movement*, Boston: Houghton Mifflin.

Matthew, H.C.G. (2004) Gladstone, William Ewart (1809–1898), *Oxford Dictionary of National Biography*, Oxford, article 10787.

MacLeod, Christine (2007) *Heroes of Invention: Technology, Liberalism and British Identity, 1750–1914*, Cambridge: Cambridge University Press.

McCloskey, Donald N. (ed.) (1971) *Essays on a Mature Economy: Britain after 1840*, Princeton, NJ: Princeton University Press.

McKenna, Frank (1980) *The Railway Workers, 1840–1970*, London: Faber & Faber.

Mellor, Roy E.H. (1994) *Railways in Britain: An Historical Geographical Perspective*, Aberdeen: Department of Geography, University of Aberdeen.

Miller, Robert C.B. (2003) *Railways.com: Parallels between the Early British Railways and the ICT Revolution*, London: Institute of Economic Affairs.

Milligan, Edward H. (1992) *Quakers and Railways*, York: Sessions Book Trust.

Milward, Robert (1991) Emergence of gas and water monopolies in nineteenth-century Britain: contested markets and public control, in James Foreman-Peck (ed.) *New Perspectives on the Late Victorian Economy*, Cambridge: Cambridge University Press, 96–124.

—— (2005) *Private and Public Enterprise in Europe: Energy, Telecommunications and Transport, 1830–1990*, Cambridge: Cambridge University Press.

Mitchell, Brian R. (1984) *Economic Development of the British Coal Industry*, Cambridge: Cambridge University Press.

Mitchener, Kris J. and Marc Weidenmeier (2008) Trade and Empire, *Economic Journal*, 118, 1805–34.

Mokyr, Joel (2004) *The Gifts of Athena: Historical Origins of the Knowledge Economy*, Princeton, NJ: Princeton University Press.

Munby, D.L. (1978) *Inland Transport Statistics: Great Britain, 1900–1970, Vol. 1* (ed. A.H. Watson) Oxford: Clarendon Press.

Nash, Christopher, Mark Wardman, Kenneth Buton, and Peter Nijkamp (eds.) (2002) *Railways*, Cheltenham: Edward Elgar.

Nef, John U. (1932) *The Rise of the British Coal Industry*, 2 vols., London: Routledge.

Nicholson, J. Shield (1909) *Project of Empire*, London: Macmillan.

Nock, O.S. (1957) *Branch Lines*, London: Batsford.

O'Brien, Patrick (1977) *The New Economic History of Railways*, London: Croom Helm.

O'Brien, Patrick (ed.) (1983) *Railways and the Economic Development of Western Europe, 1830–1914*, London: Macmillan.

O'Dell, A.C. (1956) *Railways and Geography*, London: Hutchinson.

Oeynhausen, C. von and H. von Dechen (1971) *Railways in England 1826 and 1827* (ed. Charles E. Lee and K.R. Gilbert, trans. E.A. Forward), Cambridge: W. Heffer & Sons for the Newcomen Society.

Officer, Lawrence H. (2005) The Annual Real and Nominal GDP for the United Kingdom, 1086–2005, Economic History Services: http://eh.net/hmit/ukgdp.

Olson, Mancur (1982) *The Rise and Decline of Nations*, New Haven, CT: Yale University Press.

Paget-Thompson, Edward (1990) *The Railway Carriers: The History of Wordie & Co., Carriers, Hauliers and Store Keepers*, Lavenham: Terence Dalton.

Parris, Henry (1965) *Government and the Railways in Nineteenth Century Britain*, London: Routledge.

Pattmore, J. Alan (ed.) *Forgotten Railways*, 10 vols., 1975–84, Newton Abbot: David & Charles.

Payne, Peter L. (1988) *British Entrepreneurship in the Nineteenth Century*, 2nd ed., London: Macmillan.

Peacock, A.J. and Joy, David (1971) *George Hudson of York*, Clapham: Dalesman.

Pearson, Robin and David Richardson (2001) Business networking in the Industrial Revolution, *Economic History Review*, 54, 657–79.

Peeters, Leon W.P. (2003) *Cyclic Railway Timetable Optimisation*, Rotterdam: Erasmus University.

Philbin, J. Holladay (1965) *Parliamentary Representation, 1832: England and Wales*, New Haven, CT: Yale University Press.

Pole, Felix J.C. (1968) *Felix Pole: His Book*, New ed. Bracknell: Town & Country Press.

Pollard, Sidney (1997) *Marginal Europe: The Contribution of Marginal Lands since the Middle Ages*, Oxford: Clarendon Press.

Pollins, Harold (1957) Railway contractors and the finance of railway development in Britain, *Journal of Transport History*, 3, 41–51, 103–10, reprinted in revised form in M.C. Reed (ed.) *Railways in the Victorian Economy: Studies in Finance and Economic Growth*, 1969, Newton Abbot: David & Charles, 212–28.

Popplewell, Lawrence (1985) *Branch Lines, Links and Local Communities*, Bournemouth: Melledgen Press.

—— (1986) *Against the Grain: The Manchester & Southampton Railway Dream*, Bournemouth: Melledgen Press.

—— (1988) *Contractors' Lines*, Bournemouth: Melledgen Press.

—— (1994) *Port-poaching and Pressure-point Railways*, Bournemouth: Melledgen Press.

Pratt, Edwin A. (1912) *A History of Inland Transport and Communication*, London: Kegan Paul, Trench, Trubner.

Prest, John (2004) Peel, Sir Robert, Second Baronet (1788–1850), *Oxford Dictionary of National Biography*, article 21764.

Promel, H.J. and A. Steger (2002) *The Steiner Tree Problem: A Tour through Graphs, Algorithms and Complexity*, Wiesbaden: Vieweg & Teubner.

Ransome, P.J.G. (1990) *The Victorian Railway and How it Evolved*, London: Heinemann.

Reed, M.C. (ed.) (1969) *Railways and the Victorian Economy: Studies in Finance and Economic Growth*, Newton Abbot: David & Charles.

—— (1975) *Investment in Railways in Britain, 1820–1844*, Oxford: Oxford University Press.

Robbins, Michael (1962) *The Railway Age*, London: Routledge & Kegan Paul.

Robbins, Michael (1991) The progress of transport history, *Journal of Transport History*, 3rd series, 12(1), 74–87.

Robinson, Roger (1977) *Ways to Move: The Geography of Networks and Accessibility*, Cambridge: Cambridge University Press.

Rolt, L.T.C. (1957) *Isambard Kingdom Brunel: A Biography*, London: Longman.

Rose, Mary B. (1993) Beyond Buddenbrooks: The management of family business succession, in Jonathan Brown and Mary B. Rose (eds.) *Entrepreneurship Networks and Modern Business*, Manchester: Manchester University Press.

Roth, Rolf and Marie-Noelle Polino (eds.) (2003) *The City and the Railway in Europe*, Aldershot: Ashgate.

—— and Gunther Dinhobl (eds.) (2008) *Across Borders: Financing the World's railways in the Nineteenth and Twentieth Centuries*, Aldershot: Ashgate.

Saul, S.B. (1969) *The Myth of the Great Depression, 1873–1896*, London: Macmillan.

Schumpeter, Joseph A. (1939) *Business Cycles*, New York: McGraw-Hill.

Scott-Morgan, John (1997) *The Light Railway Era, 1896–1996*, Penryn: Atlantic.

Searle, Geoffrey R. (1998) *Morality and the Market in Victorian Britain*, Oxford: Clarendon Press.

Shenkar, Oded and Jeffrey Reuer (eds.) (2005) *Handbook of Strategic Alliances*, Thousand Oaks, CA: Sage.

Simmons, Jack (1978) *The Railway in England & Wales, Volume 1: The System and its Working*, Leicester: Leicester University Press.

—— (1986) *The Railway in Town and Country, 1830–1914*, Newton Abbot: David & Charles.

—— (1991) *The Victorian Railway*, London: Thames & Hudson.

—— (1994) *The Express Train and Other Railway Studies*, Nairn: Thomas & Lochar.

—— and Gordon Biddle (eds.) (1997), *Oxford Companion to British Railway History; From 1603 to the 1990s*, Oxford: Oxford University Press.

Simnett, W.E. (1923) *Railway Amalgamation in Great Britain*, London: Railway Gazette.

Simon, Herbert A. (1983) *Reason in Human Affairs*, Oxford: Blackwell.

Smiles, Samuel (1862) *Lives of the Engineers*, London: John Murray.

—— John Charles Rees, and Edward Hyde (1858) *Statement in Support of the Proposed London Bridge and Charing Cross Railway; submitted for the Consideration of the Directors of the South Eastern Railway*, London.

Smith, Martin (1994) *Britain's Light Railways*, Shepperton: Ian Allan.

Thomas, David St. John and J. Alan Pattmore (eds.) (1960–95) *A Regional History of the Railways of Great Britain*, 16 vols., Newton Abbot: David & Charles.

Tsuji, Masatsugu, Sanford V. Berg, and Michael G. Pollitt (eds.) (2000) *Private Initiatives in Infrastructure: Priorities, Incentives and Performance*, Chiba: Institute of Developing Economies.

Turnock, David (1998) *An Historical Geography of Railways in Great Britain and Ireland*, Aldershot: Ashgate.

Wiener, Martin (1981) *English Culture and the Decline of the Industrial Spirit*, Cambridge: Cambridge University Press.

Wilkins, Mira (1986) The Free-standing company, 1870–1914: An important type of British foreign direct investment, *Economic History Review*, 2nd series, 41, 259–82.

—— (1989) *The History of Foreign Investment in the Unites States to 1914*, Cambridge, Mass: Harvard University Press.

—— and Harm Schroter (eds.) (1998) *The Free-Standing Company in the World Economy, 1830–1996*, Oxford: Oxford University Press.

Williams, Frederick S. (1852) *Our Iron Roads: Their History, Construction and Social Influences*, London: Ingram Cooke, reprinted 1991, Old Woking: Gresham Books.

Winter, James (1999) *Secure from Rash Assault: Sustaining the Victorian Environment*, Berkeley, CA: University of California Press.

Major companies

Addyman, John (ed.) (n.d.) *The North Eastern Railway, 1854–1923*, British Railway Journal, Special Issue, Didcot: Wild Swan.

Allen, Cecil J. (1961) *The Great Eastern Railway*, 3rd ed., Shepperton: Ian Allan.

—— (1964) *The North Eastern Railway*, Shepperton: Ian Allan.

Barclay-Harvey, Malcolm (1949) *A History of the Great North of Scotland Railway*, The author.

Barnes, E.G. (1966a) *Rise of the Midland Railway, 1844–1874*, London: Allen & Unwin.

—— (1966b) *The Midland Main Line, 1975–1922*, London: Allen & Unwin.

Bell, R. (1951) *Twenty-five Years of the North Eastern Railway, 1898–1922*, London: Railway Gazette.

Christiansen, Rex (1997) *Portrait of the North Staffordshire Railway*, Shepperton: Ian Allan.

—— and R.W. Miller (1971) *The North Staffordshire Railway*, Newton Abbot: David & Charles.

—— and —— (1967–68) *The Cambrian Railways*, 2 vols., Newton Abbot: David & Charles.

Clinker, C.R. (1961) *London & North Western Railway: A Chronology of Opening and Closing Dates of Lines and Stations*, Dawlish: David & Charles.

Cook, R.A. and Ken Hoole (1991) *North Eastern Railway: Historical Maps*, 2nd ed., Mold: Railway & Canal Historical Society.

Davey, C.R. (1984) *Reflections of the Furness Railway*, Barrow-in-Furness: Lakeland Heritage Books.

Dendy Marshall, C.F. (1963) *History of the Southern Railway* (rev. ed. by R.W. Kidner), Shepperton: Ian Allan.

Dow, George (1959–65) *Great Central*, 3 vols., Shepperton: Ian Allan.

Ellis, C. Hamilton (1955a) *The Midland Railway*, 2nd ed., London: Ian Allan.

—— (1955b) *The North British Railway*, London: Ian Allan.

—— (1956) *The North British Railway*, London: Ian Allan.

—— (1960) *The South Western Railway*, London: Allen & Unwin.

Faulkner, J.N. and R.A. Williams (1988) *The LSWR in the Twentieth Century*, Newton Abbot: David & Charles.

Gasquoine, C.P. (1973) *The Story of the Cambrian: A Biography of a Railway*, 2nd impression, Llandybie: Christopher Davies.

Gibson, Cyril (n.d.) *Bristol's Merchants and the Great Western Railway*, Bristol: Historical Association.

Gough, John (1989) *The Midland Railway: A Chronology*, Mold: Railway & Canal Historical Society.

Gray, Adrian (1984) *The London, Chatham & Dover Railway*, Rainham: Meresborough Books.

—— (1990) *South Eastern Railway*, Midhurst: Middleton Press.

—— (1998) *South Eastern & Chatham Railways: A Marriage of Convenience*, Midhurst: Middleton Press.

Gren, Andre (2003) *The Foundation of Brunel's Great Western Railway*, Kettering: Silver Link.

Grinling, Charles (1966) *The History of the Great Northern Railway, 1845–1922* (new ed. with supplementary chapters by H.V. Borley & C. Hamilton Ellis), London: Allen & Unwin.

Highet, Campbell (1965) *The Glasgow & South Western Railway*, Lingfield: Oakwood.

Hinchcliffe, B. (ed.) (1980) *The Hull & Barnsley Railway, Vol. 2*, Sheffield: Turntable.

Hoole, Ken (ed.) (1972) *The Hull & Barnsley Railway, Vol. 1*, Newton Abbot: David & Charles.

Hughes, Geoffrey (1992) The Board of Directors of the London & North Eastern Railway, *Journal of Transport History*, 3rd series, 13(2), 163–79.

Irving, R.J. (1976) *The North Eastern Railway Company, 1870–1914: An Economic History*, Leicester: Leicester University Press.

Jeuda, Basil (1996) *'The Knotty': An Illustrated Survey of the North Staffordshire Railway*, Lydney: Lightmoor Press.

Macdermott, E.T. (1927–31) *History of the Great Western Railway*, 3 vols., London: GWR.

Marshall, John (1969–72) *The Lancashire & Yorkshire Railway*, 3 vols., Newton Abbot: David & Charles.

National Railway Museum and Science Museum (1979) *North London Railway: A Pictorial Record*, London: HMSO.

Nock, O.S. (1951) *The Great Western Railway: An Appreciation*, Cambridge: W. Heffer & Sons.

—— (1958) *The Great Northern Railway*, Shepperton: Ian Allan.

—— (1961) *The South Eastern & Chatham*, London: Ian Allan.

—— (1964) *The Caledonian Railway*, 2nd ed., London: Ian Allan.

—— (1965*a*) *The Highland Railway*, London: Ian Allan.

—— (1965*b*) *The London & South Western Railway*, London: Ian Allan.

—— (1968) *North Western: A Saga of the Premier Line of Great Britain: 1846–1922*, Shepperton: Ian Allan.

—— (1969) *The Lancashire & Yorkshire Railway: A Concise History*, Shepperton: Ian Allan.

Norman, K.J. (1994) *The Furness Railway*, Peterborough: Silver Link.

Quayle, Howard (2000) *Furness Railway: A View from the Past*, Shepperton: Ian Allan.

Reed, M.C. (1970) The origins of the Grand Junction Railway, 1829–33, *Transport History*, 3(3), 304–24.

—— (1996) *The London & North Western Railway: A History*, Penryn: Atlantic.

Richards, Peter and William Simpson (2004) *A History of the London & Birmingham Railway, Vol. 1: Euston to Bletchley*, Witney: Lamplight.

Rush, R.W. (1973) *The Furness Railway 1843–1923*, Tarrant Hinton: Oakwood.

—— (1987) *The Furness Railway Locomotives and Rolling Stock*, 2nd ed. Oxford: Oakwood.

Scott, W.J. (1972) *The Great Great Western* (new ed. with an introduction by K. Miller), East Ardsley: EP Publishing.

Sekon, G.A. (1989) *The London & South Western Railway: Half a Century of Railway Progress to 1896* (reprint), Weston-super-Mare: Avon-Anglia.

Simmons, Jack (ed.) (1971) *The Birth of the Great Western Railway: Extracts from the Diary and Correspondence of George Henry Gibbs*, Bath: Adams & Dart.

Sinclair, Neil T. (2005) *Highland Railway: People and Places*, Derby: Breedon Books.

Stephenson Locomotive Society (1972) *'Little and Good': The Great North of Scotland Railway*, Newton Hall: SLS.

Thomas, John (1969) *The North British Railway*, Vol. 1, Newton Abbot: David & Charles.

Tomlinson, William W. (1967) *The North Eastern Railway: Its Rise and Development* (New ed. by K. Hoole) Newton Abbot: David & Charles.

Turner, J. Howard (1977–79) *The London, Brighton & South Coast Railway*, 3 vols., London: Batsford.

Vallance, H.A. (1985) *The Highland Railway* (4th ed. with additional material by C.R. Clinker and A.J. Lambert), Newton Abbot: David & Charles.

—— (1989) *The Great North of Scotland Railway* (rev. ed. By GNSR Association), Newton Abbot: David & Charles.

Waters, Laurence (1999) *The Great Western Broad Gauge*, Shepperton: Ian Allan.

Webster, Norman W. (1972) *Britain's First Trunk Line: The Grand Junction Railway*, Bath: Adams & Dart.

Williams, Frederick S. (1968) *The Midland Railway: Its Rise and Progress*, 5th ed. reprint with new introduction by C.R. Clinker), Newton Abbot: David & Charles.

Williams, Roy (1988) *The Midland Railway: A New History*, Newton Abbot: David & Charles.

Williams, R.A. (1968–73) *The London & South Western Railway*, 2 vols., Newton Abbot: David & Charles.

Wrottesley, John (1979) *The Great Northern Railway*, 2 vols., London: Batsford.

Geographical regions

Kent

Catt, A.R. (1970) *The East Kent Railway*, Lingfield: Oakwood.

Course, Edwin (1976) *The Railways of Southern England: Independent and Light Railways*, London: Batsford.

—— (n.d.) *The Bexleyheath Line*, Tisbury: Oakwood.

Finch, M. Lawson and S.R. Garrett (2003) *The East Kent Railway*, 2 vols, Usk: Oakwood.

Garrett, Stephen (1987) *The Kent & East Sussex Railway*, 2nd ed., Oxford: Oakwood.

Gould, David (n.d.) *Three Bridges to Tunbridge Wells*, Tisbury: Oakwood.

Gould, David (1999) *The Westerham Valley Railway*, 2nd ed., Usk: Oakwood.

Harding, Peter A. (1982) *The Hawkhurst Branch Line*, Knaphill: The author.

—— (1984) *The Sheppey Light Railway*, Knaphill: The author.

Hart, Brian (1987) *The Hythe & Sandgate Railway*, Didcot: Wild Swan.

—— (1989) *The Hundred of Hoo Railway*, Didcot: Wild Swan.

—— (1991) *The Canterbury & Whitstable Railway*, Didcot: Wild Swan.

—— (1992) *The Sheppey Light Railway*, Didcot: Wild Swan.

—— (2000) *The Hawkhurst Branch*, Didcot: Wild Swan.

—— (2002) *Folkestone's Railways*, Didcot: Wild Swan.

Judge, C. (ed.) (1995) *The Rye and Camber Tramway*, Oxford: Oakwood.

Kidner, R.W. (1972) *The Oxted Line*, Tisbury: Oakwood.

Maxted, I. (1970) *The Canterbury & Whitstable Railway*, Lingfield: Oakwood.

Oppitz, Leslie (1988) *Kent Railways Remembered*, Newbury: Countryside Books.

Pallant, N. (1984) *The Gravesend West Branch*, Shaftesbury: Oakwood.

Taylor, M. Minter (1986) *The Davington Light Railway*, Oxford: Oakwood.

Turner, Gordon (1984) *Ashford: The Coming of the Railway*, Maidstone: Christine Swift Bookshop.

White, H.P. (ed.) *Railways South East: The Album*, Harrow Weald: Capital Transport.

Woodman, Trevor (1982) *The Railways to Hayes*, Hayes: Hayes (Kent) Village Association.

Hampshire, Dorset, and Isle of Wight

Baker, Michael (1987) *The Waterloo to Weymouth Line*, Wellingborough: Patrick Stephens.

Caddy, C.L. (n.d.) *The Weymouth Quay Tramway*, Radipole: Dorset Transport Circle.

Chandler, Nick and Robin Vetcher (1989) *Centenary of the Freshwater Railway, 1899–1989*, Mattingley, IoW: Centenary Trust.

Cooper, B.K. (1981) *Rail Centres: Brighton*, Shepperton: Ian Allan.

Course, Edwin (1973) *The Southampton and Netley Railway*, Southampton: City of Southampton.

Cox, J.G. (1975) *Castleman's Corkscrew: The Southampton & Dorchester Railway, 1844–1848*, Southampton: City of Southampton.

Dean, Martin, Kevin Robertson, and Roger Simmonds (1998) *The Basingstoke & Alton Light Railway*, Crowcombe: Crusader Press.

Fairman, J.R. (1984) *Netley Hospital and its Railways*, Southampton: Kingfisher Railway Productions.

—— (2002) *The Fawley Branch*, Usk: Oakwood.

Glenn, David Fereday (1983) *Rail Routes in Hampshire & East Dorset*, Shepperton: Ian Allan.

Griffith, Edward (1970) *The Basingstoke & Alton Light Railway, 1901–1936*, Farnham: The author.

Harding, Peter A. (1992) *The Longparish Branch Line*, Knaphill: The author.

Jackson, Brian L. (1989) *The Abbotsbury Branch*, Didcot: Wild Swan.

—— (1999–2000) *The Isle of Portland Railways*, 3 vols, Usk: Oakwood.

—— (2003) *Yeovil: 150 Years of Railways*, Usk: Oakwood.

—— (2007) *Castleman's Corkscrew including the Railways of Bournemouth and Associated Lines: Volume One: The Nineteenth Century*, Usk: Oakwood.

Jackson, B.L. and M.J. Tatterhall (1998) *The Bridport Railway*, Usk: Oakwood.

Karau, Paul, Michael Parsons and Kevin Robertson (1981) *The Didcot, Newbury & Southampton Railway*, Upper Bucklebury: Wild Swan.

Kidner, R.W. (1983) *The Waterloo–Southampton Line*, Tisbury: Oakwood.

—— (1988) *The Railways of Purbeck*, Oxford: Oakwood.

Lucking, J.H. (1968) *Railways of Dorset*, London: Railway Correspondence & Travel Society and Dorchester: Dorset Natural History & Archaeological Society.

Maggs, Colin G. (1996) *Branch Lines of Dorset*, Stroud: Budding Books.

Maycock, R.J. and R. Silsbury (1999) *The Isle of Wight Railway*, Usk: Oakwood.

—— and —— (2001) *The Isle of Wight Central Railway*, Usk.

—— and —— (2003) *The Freshwater, Yarmouth & Newport Railway*, Usk: Oakwood.

Moody, Bert (1997) *Southampton's Railways*, New ed., Penryn: Atlantic.

Paye, Peter (1979) *The Lymington Branch*, Tarrant Hinton: Oakwood.

—— (1992) *The Ventnor West Branch*, Didcot: Wild Swan.

Phillips, Derek (2000) *From Salisbury to Exeter: The Branch Lines*, Shepperton: Oxford Publishing.

Popplewell, Lawrence (1974) *Bournemouth Railway History: An Exposure of Victorian Engineering Fraud*, Sherborne: Dorset Publishing.

—— (1978) *Railway Competition in Central Southern England*, Ferndown: Melledgen Press.

—— (1989) *Coastal Shields to Blue Water: Railways and the Channel*, Bouremouth: Melledgen Press.

Popplewell, Lawrence (1995) *American Dreams from Slippery Cove: Brean Down and the Somerset & Dorset Railway,* Bouremouth: Melledgen Press.

Robertson, Kevin (1985) *The Southsea Railway,* Southampton: Kingfisher Railway Productions.

—— (1986) *The Railways of Gosport, including the Stokes Bay and Lee-on-the-Solent Branches,* Southampton: Kingfisher Railway Productions.

—— and Roger Simmonds (1988) *The Railways of Winchester,* Sheffield: Platform 5.

Robbins, Michael (1953) *The Isle of Wight Railways,* South Godstone: Oakwood.

Simmonds, Roger and Kevin Robertson (1988) *The Bishops Waltham Branch,* Didcot: Wild Swan.

Smith, Martin (1997) *Railways of the Isle of Portland,* Clophill: Irwell Press.

Stone, Colin (1999) *Rails to Poole Harbour,* Usk: Oakwood.

Stone, R.A. (1983) *The Meon Valley Railway,* Southampton: Kingfisher Railway Productions.

Wakeford, Iain (1973) *Woking 150: The History of Woking and its Railway,* Old Woking: Mayford & Woking District History Society.

Young, J.A. (1984) *The Ringwood, Christchurch & Bournemouth Railway,* Bournemouth: Bournemouth Local Studies Publications.

East Anglia (Norfolk, Suffolk, Cambridgeshire, Huntingdonshire, Essex)

Adderson, Richard (1981) *Steam around Norwich,* Norwich and King's Lynn: Becknell Books.

Beckett, G. (1981) *Steam around Norfolk,* Norwich and King's Lynn: Becknell Books.

Bonavia, Michael R. (1995) *The Cambridge Line,* Shepperton: Ian Allan.

Brodribb, John (1994) *Railways of Norwich,* Shepperton: Ian Allen Publishing.

Clark, Ronald H. (1967) *A Short History of the Midland and Great Northern Joint Railway,* Norwich: Goose and Son.

Comfort, N.A. (1986) *The Mid-Suffolk Light Railway,* new ed. Oxford: Oakwood.

Cooper, John M. (1982) *The East Suffolk Railway,* Tisbury: Oakwood.

Cross, Dennis (1993) *Suffolk's Railways: A Portrait in Old Picture Postcards,* Seaford: S.B. Publications.

Edwards, J.K. (1965) Communications and the Economic Development of Norwich, 1750–1850, *Journal of Transport History,* 7(2), 96–108.

Fellows, Reginald B. (1976a) *Railways to Cambridge Actual and Proposed,* rep. Cambridge: The Oleander Press.

—— (1976b) *London to Cambridge by Train—1845–1938,* rep. Cambridge: The Oleander Press.

Frost, K.A. (1995) The Railways of Yarmouth, *Back Track,* 9(5), 260–4, 9(6), 292–5.

Jenkins, A. Barrett (compiler) (1987) *Memories of the Southwold Railway,* 8th ed. Southwold: L and S. Rexton.

Jenkins, Stanley C. (1987) *The Lynn and Hunstanton Railway and the West Norfolk Branch,* Oxford: Oakwood.

—— (1988) *The Wells-Next-The-Sea Branch via Wymondham and Dereham,* Oxford: Oakwood.

—— (1989) *The Cromer Branch,* Oxford: Oakwood.

—— (1991) *The Melton Constable to Cromer Branch,* Oxford: Oakwood.

—— (1993) *The Lynn and Dereham Railway: The King's Lynn to Norwich Line,* Oxford: Oakwood.

Kay, Peter (1996–7) *The London, Tilbury & Southend Railway,* 2 vols., Teignmouth: The author.

Lombardelli, C.P. (1979) *Branch Lines to Braintree,* Colne: Stour Valley Railway Preservation Society.

Moffat, Hugh (1987) *East Anglia's Railways : Peter Bruff and the Eastern Union Railway,* Lavenham: Terence Dalton Ltd.

Oppitz, Leslie (2005) *Lost Railways of East Anglia,* Newbury: Countryside Books.

Paye. Peter (1976) *The Elsenham and Thaxted Light Railway,* Tarrant Hinton: Oakwood.

—— (1980) *The Mellis and Eye Railway,* Tarrant Hinton: Oakwood.

—— (1981) *The Saffron Walden Branch,* Oxford: Oxford Publishing.

—— (1982) *The Ely and St. Ives Railway,* Tisbury: Oakwood.

—— (1984) *The Thaxted Branch,* Poole: Oxford Publishing.

—— (1985) *The Tollesbury Branch,* Poole: Oxford Publishing.

—— (1988) *The Mildenhall Branch,* Didcot: Wild Swan.

—— (1995) *The Wivenhoe & Brightlingsea Railway,* Romford: Ian Henry.

—— (1997) *The Brightlingsea Branch,* Bishops Stortford: John Masters.

—— (2005) *The Snape Branch,* Usk: Oakwood.

—— (2006) *The Hadleigh Branch,* Usk: Oakwood.

—— (2008) *The Framlingham Branch,* Usk: Oakwood.

Phillips, Charles (1984) *The Shenfield to Southend Line,* Shaftesbury: Oakwood.

Portway, Christopher (1983) *The Colne Valley Railway: A pictorial survey including station plans depicting the Colne Valley Railway past and present,* Foxton: Apex Publications.

Quayle, H.I. and Bradbury, G.T. (1978) *The Felixstowe Railway,* Tarrant Hinton: Oakwood.

Rhodes, John (1986) *Branch Lines to Ramsey,* Oxford: Oakwood.

Slack, John (2001) *The Arrival of the Midland Railway at Kimbolton, Cambridgeshire in 1866,* St. Neots: The author.

Swindale, Dennis L. (1981) *Branch Line to Southminster,* Colne: The author and The Stour Valley Railway Preservation Society.

Turner, Peter (1978) *By Rail to Mildenhall: The Story of the Cambridge to Mildenhall Railway,* Mildenhall: Mildenhall Museum Publications.

Whitehead, R.A. and Simpson, F.D. (1987) *The Colne Valley and Halstead Railway, 2nd ed.* Oxford: Oakwood.

Wrottesley, A.J. (1970) *The Midland and Great Northern Joint Railway,* Newton Abbot: David and Charles.

Lincolnshire

Anderson, Paul (1992) *Railways of Lincolnshire,* Oldham: Irwell Press.

Cartwright, Adam and Stephen Walker (1987) *Boston: A Railway Town (Part One—To 1922),* Boston: KMS Books.

Cossey, Frank (1983) *Grantham and Railways,* Grantham: BG Publications.

Dow, George (1984) *Alford & Sutton Tramway, 2nd ed.,* Audlem: The author.

Goode, C.T. (1984) *Midland Railway: Derby–Lincoln,* Anlaby: The author.

Goode, C.V.T. (1985) *The Railways of North Lincolnshire,* Anlaby: The author.

Henthorn, Frank (ed.) (1975) *Letters and Papers concerning the Establishment of the Trent, Ancholme and Grimsby Railway, 1860–1862,* Lincoln: Lincoln Record society (Volume 70).

Jordan, Arthur and Elizabeth Jordan (1996) *Stamford All Change! How the Railway came to Stamford,* Stamford: Amphion Press.

Judge, C.W. (1994) *The Axholme Joint Railway*, Oxford: Headington.

King, Paul K. and David R. Hewins (1998) *Scenes from the Past: 5. The Railways around Grimsby, Cleethorpes, Immingham and North-East Lincolnshire*, Stockport: Foxline.

Longbone, Bryan (1996) *Steam and Steel: An Illustrated History of Scunthorpe's Railways*, Caernarfon: Irwell Press.

Ludlam, A.J. (1985) *The Spilsby to Firsby Railway*, Oxford: Oakwood.

—— (1986) *The Horncastle & Woodhall Junction Railway*, Oxford: Oakwood.

—— (1987*a*) *The Louth, Mablethorpe & Willoughby Loop*, Oxford: Oakwood.

—— (1987*b*) *The Louth to Bardney Branch*, Oxford: Oakwood.

—— (1991) *The East Lincolnshire Railway*, Oxford: Oakwood.

—— (1995) *The Lincolnshire Loop Line (GNR) and the River Witham*, Oxford: Oakwood.

—— (1996) *Railways to New Holland and the Humber Ferries*, Oxford: Oakwood.

—— (1997) *Railways to Skegness, including Kirkstead to Little Steeping*, Oxford: Oakwood.

Rhodes, John (1988) *Great Northern Branch Lines to Stamford*, Boston: KMS Books.

Ruddock, J.G. and R.E. Pearson (1985) *The Railway History of Lincoln*, 2nd ed. Lincoln: J. Ruddock.

Squires, Stewart E. (1988) *The Lost Railways of Lincolnshire*, Ware: Castlemead Publications.

—— (1996) *The Lincoln to Grantham Line via Honington*, Oxford: Oakwood Press.

—— (1998) *Lincolnshire Railways*, Lincoln: Lincolnshire Books.

Walker, Stephen (1987) *Firsby to Wainfleet & Skegness*, Boston: KMS Books.

East Midlands (Derbyshire, Nottinghamshire, Leicestershire, and part of Northamptonshire)

Anderson, Paul and Jack Cupit (2000) *An Illustrated History of Mansfield's Railways*, Clophill: Irwell Press.

Banks, Chris (1994) *The Birmingham to Leicester Line*, Sparkford: Oxford Publishing.

Billson, Peter (1996) *Derby and the Midland Railway*, Derby: Breedon Books.

Clinker, C.R. (1960) *The Railways of Northamptonshire (including the Soke of Peterborough) 1800–1960: A List of Authorising Acts of Parliament, Opening and Closing Dates*, Rugby: The author.

—— (1977) *The Leicester & Swannington Railway*, Bristol: Avon-Anglia.

—— (1982) *The Birmingham & Derby Junction Railway*, Weston-super-Mare: Avon Anglia.

—— and P.S. Stevenson (eds.) (1989) *The Midland Counties Railway*, Mold: Railway & Canal Historical Society.

Cupit, J. and W. Taylor (1988) *The Lancashire, Derbyshire & East Coast Railway*, Oxford: Oakwood.

Fisher, Jeffrey N. (1990) *The Rishworth Branch*, Oxford: Oakwood.

Forster, A. and W. Taylor (1991) *Scenes from the Past: 1. Railways in and around Nottingham*, Stockport: Foxline.

Franks, D.L. (1975) *The Ashby & Nuneaton Joint Railway, together with the Charwood Forest Railway*, Sheffield: Turntable.

Hatley, Victor A. (1966) Northampton hoodwinked? How a main line of railway missed the town a second time, *Journal of Transport History*, 7(3), 160–72.

Helsey, M. (n.d.) *A History of the Charnwood Forest Railway*, reprint, Loughborough: David Dover.

Higginson, Mark (ed.) *The Midland Counties Railway, 1839–1989*: A Pictorial Survey, Ripley: Midland Railway Trust.

Hudson, William (1990) *Through Limestone Hills: The Peak Line-Ambergate to Chinley*, rep. Sparkford: Oxford Publishing.

Hurst, Geoffrey (1987) *The Midland Railway Around Nottinghamshire, Vol. 1*, Worksop: Milestone Publications.

—— (1993) *LNWR Branch Lines of West Leicestershire and East Warwickshire*, Worksop: Milepost Publications.

Irons, Ruth and Stanley C. Jenkins (1999) *Woodford Halse: A Railway Community*, Usk: Oakwood.

Jenkins, Stanley C. (1990) *The Northampton & Banbury Junction Railway*, Oxford: Oakwood.

Nicholson, Christopher P. and Barnes, Peter (1975) *Railways in the Peak District*, 2nd ed. Clapham: Dalesman.

Plant, K.P. (1987) *The Ashover Light Railway*, rev. ed., Oxford: Oakwood.

Railway Correspondence & Travel Society (East Midland Branch) (1969) *The Railways of Nottingham*, Nottingham: RCTS.

Radford, Brian (1986) *Rail Centres: Derby*, Shepperton: Ian Allan.

Rhodes, John (1976) *The Nene Valley Railway: Blisworth–Northampton–Peterborough*, Sheffield: Turntable.

—— (1984) *The Kettering–Huntingdon Line*, Tisbury: Oakwood.

Rimmer, David (1989) *The Peak Forest Tramway, including the Peak Forest Canal*, 3rd ed., Oxford: Oakwood.

Sprenger, Howard (1987) *The Wirksworth Branch*, Oxford: Oakwood.

Stretton, John (1988) *An Illustrated History of Leicester's Railways*, Clophill: Irwell Press.

Twells, H.N. (1984) *Railways in Burton and the Trent Valley through 145 Years*, Burton-on-Trent: Trent Valley Publications.

—— (1985) *A Pictorial Record of the Leicester and Burton Branch Railway*, Stapenhill: Trent Valley Publications.

—— (1997) *Railways in and around Burton-on-Trent*, Grasscroft: Challenger Publications.

Vanns, Michael A. (1993) *Rail Centres: Nottingham*, Shepperton: Ian Allan.

—— (1999) *The Railways of Newark-on-Trent*, Usk: Oakwood.

Waring, Roger (1994) *The Stonebridge Railway: A Portrait of a Midland Branch Line*, Studley: Brewin Books.

Waszak, Peter (1984) *Rail Centres: Peterborough*, Shepperton: Ian Allan.

Williams, Cliff (1984) *Driving the Clay Cross Tunnel: Navvies on the Derby/Leeds Railway*, Cromford: Scarthin Books.

Wilson, J.P. (n.d.) *The Development of Nottingham's Railways*, Nottingham: Nottingham Civic Society.

Sussex

Clark, Paul (1976) *The Railways of Devil's Dyke*, Sheffield: Turntable.

—— (1979) *The Chichester & Midhurst Railway*, Sheffield: Turntable.

Elliott, A.C. (n.d.) *The Cuckoo Line*, Didcot: Wild Swan.

Gage, William, Michael Harris and Anthony Sullivan (1997) *Going off the Rails: The Country Railway in West Sussex*, Chichester: West Sussex Record Office.

Gray, Adrian (1975) *The Railways of Mid-Sussex*, Tarrant Hinton: Oakwood.

Griffith, Edward (1968) *The Hundred of Manhood and Selsey Tramway*, New ed., Farnham: The author.

Harding, Peter A. (1983) *The New Romney Branch Line*, Knaphill: The author.

Harding, Peter A. (1985) *The Rye & Camber Tramway*, Knaphill: The author.

—— (2002) *The Bexhill West Branch Line*, Knaphill: The author.

Hodd, H.R. (1975) *The Horsham–Guildford Direct Railway*, Tarrant Hinton: Oakwood.

Jordan, S. (1989) *The Bognor Branch Line*: Oxford: Oakwood.

Kidner, R.W. (n.d.) *The Newhaven & Seaford Branch*, Tarrant Hinton: Oakwood.

Marx, Klaus (2000) *An Illustrated History of the Lewes & East Grinstead Railway*, Shepperton: Oxford Publishing.

Paye, Peter (1979) *The Hayling Railway*, Tarrant Hinton: Oakwood.

Vaughan, John (2004) *Branches and Byways: Sussex and Hampshire*, Hersham: Oxford Publishing.

Surrey

Course, Edwin (ed.) (1987) *Minutes of the Board of Directors of the Reading, Guildford and Reigate Railway Company*, Guildford: Surrey Record Society (Volume 33).

Gould, David (2003) *The Croydon, Oxted & East Grinstead Railway*, Usk: Oakwood.

Jackson, Alan A. (1988) *Dorking's Railways*, Dorking: Dorking Local History Group.

—— (1999) *The Railway in Surrey*, Penryn: Atlantic.

Kirkby, J.R.W. (1983) *The Banstead & Epsom Downs Railway*, Tisbury: Oakwood.

Sherwood, Tim (1991) *The Railways of Richmond-upon-Thames*, Wokingham: Forge Books.

Skinner, M.W.G. (1985) *Croydon's Railways*, Southampton: Kingfisher Railway Productions.

Spence, Jeoffry (1986) *The Caterham Railway: the Story of a Feud—and its Aftermath*, 2nd ed., Oxford: Oakwood.

Bedfordshire, Buckinghamshire, Hertfordshire, and part of Northamptonshire

Blakey, Michael (1983) *The Story of Bedfordshire Railways*, Ampthill, Beds: Teaching Media Resource Service.

Cockman, Frederick G. (1971) *The Railways of Buckinghamshire*, Aylesbury: Centre for Buckinghamshire Studies, unpublished typescript.

—— (1972) The railway era in Buckinghamshire, *Records of Buckinghamshire*, XIX(2), 156–68.

—— (1974) *The Railway Age in Bedfordshire*, Bedford: Bedfordshire Historical Record Society.

—— (1983) *The Railways of Hertfordshire, with a Full Account of those which were Proposed but not Built*, 2nd ed., Stevenage: Hertfordshire Publications.

Dent, David (1993) *150 Years of the Hertford and Ware Railway*, Ware: Rockingham Press.

Foxell, Clive (1998) *Chesham Branch Album*, Chesham: The author.

Giles, John, Ruth Jeavons, Mike Martin, Dolly Smith, and Roy Smith (1995) *Wheathampstead Railway Recollections*, Wheathampstead: Wheathampstead Local History Group.

Gladwyn, Thomas W., Peter W. Neville, and Douglas E. White (1986) *Welwyn's Railways: A History of the Great Northern Line from 1850 to 1986*, Ware: Castlemead Publications.

Goode, C.T. (1983) *The Railways of Uxbridge*, Anlaby: The author.

Goslin, Geoffrey (1994) *The London Extension of the Midland Railway: St. Pancras to Bedford*, Cernarfon: Irwell Press.

Goudie, F.W. and Stuckey, Douglas (1990) *West of Watford: Watford Metropolitan and the L.M.S. Croxley Green and Rickmansworth branches*, Bracknell: Forge Books.

Gough, John (1984) *The Northampton & Harborough Line*, Oakham: Railway & Canal Historical Society.

Grigg, A.E. (1980) *Town of Trains: Bletchley and the Oxbridge Line*, Buckingham: Barracuda Books.

Healy, John M.C. (1996) *History of the Chiltern Line*, rev. ed. London: Greenwich Editions,

Jenkins, Stanley C. (1978) *The Great Western & Great Central Joint Railway*, Tarrant Hinton: Oakwood,

—— (1990) *The Watford to St. Albans Branch*, Oxford: Oakwood,

Jones, Ken (1974) *The Wotton Tramway (Brill Branch)*, Lingfield: Oakwood,

Karau, Paul and Turner, Chris (n.d.) *The Marlow Branch*, Didcot: Wild Swan Publications Ltd.

Paye, Peter (1981) *The Bishop's Stortford. Dunmow & Braintree Branch*, Oxford: Oxford Publishing.

Simpson, William (1981) *Oxford to Cambridge Railway, Volume One: Oxford to Bletchley*, Oxford: Oxford Publishing Company.

—— (1985) *The Brill Tramway: Including the Railway from Aylesbury to Verney Junction*, Poole: Oxford Publishing Co.

—— (1989) *The Aylesbury Railway: The First Branch Line*, Cheddington–Aylesbury, Yeovil: Haynes Publishing Group.

—— (1994) *The Banbury to Verney Junction Branch*, New ed., Witney: Lamplight.

—— (1995) *The Wolverton to Newport Pagnell Branch*, Witney: Lamplight.

—— (1998) *The Dunstable Branch*, Witney: Lamplight.

West, William (1988) *The Moving Force: The Men of Wolverton*, Buckingham: Barracuda Books.

Woodward, Sue and Geoff Woodward (1994) *The Hatfield, Luton & Dunstable Railway (and on to Leighton Buzzard)*, Oxford: Oakwood.

—— and —— (1996) *The Harpenden to Hemel Hempstead Railway (The Nickey Line)*, Oxford: Oakwood.

Young, John N. (1977) *Great Northern Suburban*, Newton Abbot: David & Charles.

Berkshire, Oxfordshire, and Wiltshire

Allen, Peter (1999) *Cherwell Valley Railway*, Stroud: Tempus.

Barrett, David, Brian Bridgeman and Denis Bird (1981) *A M&SWJR Album, Vol 1: 1872–1899*, Swindon: Redbrick.

Bray, Nigel S.M. (1984) *The Devizes Branch: A Wiltshire Railway Remembered*, Chippenham: Picton.

—— (1998) *The Cirencester Branch*, Usk: Oakwood.

Fenton, D.M. (1977) *The Malmesbury Railway*, Tarrant Hinton: Oakwood.

Gardner, Jack (1996) *Brunel's Didcot: Great Western Railway to Great Western Society*, Cheltenham: Runpast Publishing.

Harding, Peter A. (1991) *The Bulford Branch Line*, Knaphill: the author.

Hepple, James R. (1974) Abingdon and the GWR: Or why the Oxford line missed the town, *Journal of Transport History*, 2(3), 155–66.

Higgins, S.H. Pearce (2002) *The Wantage Tramway*, Brora: Adam Gordon.

Holden, J.S. (1974) *The Watlington Branch*, Oxford: Oxford Publishing.

Hutson, M. (1994) *The Staines, Wokingham & Woking Railway, Typescript for publication in the South Western Circular, 1995/6*, Reading: Berkshire Record Office.

Jenkins, Stanley C. (1987) *The Woodstock Branch*, Didcot: Wild Swan.

Karau, Paul (1982) *An Illustrated History of The Henley-on-Thames Branch,* Upper Bucklebury: Wild Swan.

—— and Turner, Chris (1982) *An Illustrated History of The Wallingford Branch,* Upper
Bucklebury: Wild Swan.

Lingard, Richard (1973) *The Woodstock Branch,* Oxford: Oxford Publishing.

Lingham, Brian (1992) *The Railway comes to Didcot: A History of the Town, 1839–1918,*
Stroud: Alan Sutton.

Maggs, Colin G. (1967) *The Midland & South Western Junction Railway,* Newton Abbot:
David & Charles.

—— (1981) *Railways of the Cotswolds,* Cheltenham: Peter Nicholson.

—— (1982) *The Bath to Weymouth Line,* Tisbury: Oakwood.

—— (1983) *Rail Centres: Swindon,* Shepperton: Ian Allan.

Pearse, Marion and John Pearse (2002) *Twyford's Railway Heritage,* Twyford: Twyford &
Ruscombe Local History Society.

Phillips, Daphne (ed.) (1975) *How the Great Western came to Berkshire: A Railway History,
1833–1882,* Reading: Reading Libraries.

Price, M.R.C. (1964) *The Lambourn Valley Railway,* Lingfield: Oakwood.

Russell, J.H. (1984) *The Banbury and Cheltenham Railway 1887–1962,* rep. Poole: Oxford
Publishing Co.

Sands, T.B. (1971) *The Didcot, Newbury & Southampton Railway,* Lingfield: Oakwood.

—— (1990) *The Midland & South Western Junction Railway* (rev. by S.C. Jenkins), Oxford:
Oxford Publishing.

Simpson, William (1997–2001) *A History of the Railways of Oxfordshire,* 2 vols. Witney:
Lamplight.

Trinder, B.S. (ed.) *A Victorian M.P. and his Constituents: The Correspondence of H.W.
Tancred, 1841–1859,* Banbury: Banbury Historical Society (Volume 8).

Wells, Matthew (1973) *One Hundred Years of the Marlow Donkey,* Marlow: The Marlow/
Maidenhead Railway Passengers' Association.

—— (n.d.) First Stop Maidenhead, Maidenhead: The author.

Waters, Laurence (1986) *Rail Centres: Oxford,* Shepperton: Ian Allan.

—— (1990) *Rail Centres: Reading,* Shepperton: Ian Allan.

West Midlands and Welsh Borders (Shropshire, Warwickshire, and Worcestershire)

Beck, Keith M. (1986) *The Great Western North of Wolverhampton,* London: Ian Allan.

Boynton, John (1993) *"Rails Across the City" The Story of the Birmingham Cross City Line:
Lichfield-Birmingham-Redditch, Kidderminster: Mid England Books.*

—— (1995) *Rails Through the Hills, Birmingham-Stourbridge-Worcester-Malvern-Here-
ford: From "Old Worse and Worse" to the Jewellery Line,* Kidderminster: Mid England
Books.

—— (1996) *Rails Around Walsall Yesterday and Today: The Lines to Birmingham, Dudley,
Lichfield, Rugeley, Sutton Park and Wolverhampton, featuring Bescot and Ryecroft,* Kidderminster: Mid England Books.

—— (1997) *A Century of Railways around Birmingham and the West Midlands: Volume
One 1900–1947,* Kidderminster: Mid England Books.

—— (2002) *The Oxford Worcester and Wolverhampton Railway,* Kidderminster: Mid
England Books.

Butcher, Clive (1998) *The Railways of Stourbridge,* Usk: Oakwood.

Casserley, H.C. (1990) *The Lickey Incline,* Oxford: Oakwood.

Clinker, C.R. (1954) *Railways of the West Midlands, A Chronology: 1808–1954*, London: Stephenson Locomotive Society.

Collins, Paul (1990) *Rail Centres: Wolverhampton*, Shepperton: Ian Allan.

—— (1992) *Britain's Rail Super Centres: Birmingham*, Shepperton: Ian Allan.

Denton, John Horsley (1986) *Shrewsbury Railway Station: A Brief History*, Welshpool: The author.

Foster, Richard (1990) *Birmingham New Street: The Story of a Great Station including Curzon Street*, 3 vols., Didcot: Wild Swan.

Gale, W.K.V. (1975) *A History of the Pensnett Railway*, Cambridge: Goose & Son.

Geens, Barrie 1985) *The Severn Valley Railway at Arley*, Upper Bucklebury: Wild Swan.

Goode, C.T. (1978) *The North Warwickshire Railway*, Tarrant Hinton: Oakwood.

Griffith, Edward (1977) *The Bishop's Castle Railway, 1865–1935*, Farnham: The author.

Hale, Michael (1995) *The Oxford, Worcester & Wolverhampton Railway through the Black Country*, Woodsetton: The author.

—— (1997) *Brunel's Broad Gauge in the Black Country*, Woodsetton: The author.

—— (2000) *Traffic and Transport in Nineteenth Century Kingswinford*, Woodsetton: The author.

—— and Ned Williams (1974) *By Rail to Halesowen: A History of the GWR branch from Dudley to Halesowen via Old Hill, and the Halesowen Railway to Northfield*, Dudley: Michael Hale and Uralia Press.

Harrison, Derek (1978) *Salute to Snow Hill*, Edgbaston: Barbryn.

—— (1986) *Birmingham Snow Hill: A First Class Return*, Gloucester: Peter Watts Publishing.

Hughes, Mervyn (1964) Telford, Parnell and the Great Irish Road, *Journal of Transport History*, 6(4), 199–209.

Jones, Ken (1998) *The Wenlock Branch: Wellington to Craven Arms*, Usk: Oakwood.

Leach, Robin D. (1985) *Kenilworth's Railway Age*, Kenilworth: Odibourne Press.

Maggs, Colin G. (1994) *Branch Lines of Warwickshire*, Stroud: Alan Sutton.

Marshall, John (1989) *The Severn Valley Railway*, Newton Abbot: David & Charles.

Morriss, Richard K. (1983) *Railways of Shropshire: A Brief History*, Shrewsbury: Shropshire Libraries.

—— (1986) *Rail Centres: Shrewsbury*, Shepperton: Ian Allan.

Pixton, Robert (2004) *Oxford Worcester and Wolverhampton, Portrait of a Famous Route: Part Two: Worcester to Wolverhampton*, Cheltenham: Runpast Publishing.

Price, M.R.C. (1995) *The Cleobury Mortimer & Ditton Priors Light Railway*, 3rd ed. Oxford: Oakwood.

Shropshire Railway Society (1982) *Shropshire Railways Revisited*, Shrewsbury: Shropshire Libraries.

Smith, D.J. (1970) *The Severn Valley Railway*, 2nd ed. Bracknell: Town and Country Press Ltd.

Smith, Donald J. (1984) *New Street Remembered: The Story of Birmingham's New Street Railway Station 1854–1967*, Birmingham: Barbryn Press.

—— and Harrison, Derek (1995) *The Harborne Express*, Studley: Brewin Books.

Smith, W. and K. Beddoes (1980) *The Cleobury Mortimer and Ditton Priors Light Railway*, Oxford: The Oxford Publishing Company.

Smith, William H. (1998) *The Bromyard Branch from Worcester to Leominster*, Kidderminster: Kidderminster Railway Museum.

Turner, Keith (1991) *The Lost Railways of Birmingham*, Birmingham: Brewin Books.

—— and S.L. Turner (1974) *The Kinver Light Railway*, Lingfield: Oakwood.

Whitehouse, P.B. (1984) *Pre-Grouping in the West Midlands*, Poole: Oxford Publishing.

Williams, J. Ned (1969) *By Rail to Wombourn*, Dudley: Uralia.

Yate, Robert (2003) *The Shropshire Union Railway: Stafford to Shrewsbury including the Coalport Branch*, Usk: Oakwood.

Gloucestershire

Baker, Audie (1994) *An Illustrated History of the Stratford on Avon to Cheltenham Railway*, Oldham: Irwell Press.

Bick, David (1987) *The Gloucester & Cheltenham Tramroad and the Leckhampton Quarry Lines*, Oxford: Oakwood.

Boynton, John (1994) *'Shakespeare's Railways': The Lines Around Stratford-upon-Avon: Then and Now*, Kidderminster: Mid England Books.

Essery, R.J. (2002) *An Illustrated History of the Ashchurch to Barnt Green Line—The Evesham Route*, Oxford: Oxford Publishing Company.

Goode, C.T. (1998) *The Birmingham & Gloucester Loop*, Anlaby: The author.

Harris, Peter (1986) *Bristol's 'Railway Mania'*, Bristol: Historical Association, Bristol Branch.

Jenkins, Stanley C. (1985) *The Fairford Branch*, Oxford: Oakwood.

—— and R.S. Carpenter (1997) *The Shipton-on-Stour Branch*, Didcot: Wild Swan Publications.

Jordan, Arthur (1982) *The Stratford-upon-Avon and Midland Junction Railway: The Shakespeare Route*, Oxford: Oxford Publishing Company.

Long, P.J. and W.V. Awdry (1987) *The Birmingham and Gloucester Railway*, Gloucester: Alan Sutton.

Maggs, Colin G. (1975) *The Bristol Port Railway & Pier*, Tarrant Hinton: Oakwood.

—— (1986) *The Birmingham–Gloucester Line*, Cheltenham: Line One Publishing Ltd.

—— (1992) *The Mangotsfield to Bath Branch*, Oxford: Oakwood.

—— (2000) *The Nailsworth to Stroud Branch*, Usk: Oakwood.

—— (2002) *The Yate to Thornbury Branch*, Usk: Oakwood.

Norris, John (1985) *The Bristol & South Wales Union Railway*, Oakham: Railway & Canal Historical Society.

Simpson, Helen (1997) *The Day the Trains Came: The Herefordshire Railways: the people who built them and who rejoiced when they arrived*, Leominster: Gracewing Fowler Wright Books.

Smith, Peter (1981) *The Dursley Branch*, Tisbury: Oakwood.

Wood, Gordon (2003) *Railways of Hereford: A Study of the Historical Development and Operation of Railways in the City*, Kidderminster: Kidderminster Railway Museum.

Somerset

Athill, Robin (1985) *The Somerset & Dorset Railway*, 2nd ed., Newton Abbot: David & Charles.

Clinker, C.R. (1980) *The West Somerset Railway*, Dulverton: Exmoor Press.

Harrison, J.D. (1990) *The Bridgewater Railway*, Oxford: Oakwood.

Maggs, Colin G. (1986) *Highbridge in its Heyday*, Oxford: Oakwood.

—— (1986) *Rail Centres: Bristol*, 2nd ed. Shepperton: Ian Allan.

—— (1990) *The Weston, Clevedon & Portishead Light Railway*, Oxford: Oakwood.

—— (1998) *The Minehead Branch and the West Somerset Railway*, Usk: Oakwood.

—— (2004) *The Wrington Vale Light Railway*, Usk: Oakwood.

Oakley, M. (1986) *Railways in Avon*, Weston-super-Mare: Avon Anglia.

Sellick, R.J. (1976) *The Old Mineral Line*, Dulverton: The Exmoor Press.

Vincent, Mike (1983) *Reflections on the Portishead Branch*, Oxford: Oxford Publishing.

Devon

Beck, Keith and John Copsey (n.d.) *The Great Western in South Devon*, Didcot: Wild Swan.

Catchpole, L.T. (1998) *The Lynton & Barnstaple Railway, 1895–1935*, Usk: Oakwood.

Crombleholme, Roger, Douglas Stuckey, and C.F.D. Whetmath (1964) *The Culm Valley Light Railway*, Teddington: Branch Line Books and Stoke-on-Trent: West Country Publications.

Gregory, R.H. (1982) *The South Devon Railway*, Tisbury: Oakwood.

Harris, Helen (2001) *Devon's Railways*, Launceston: Bossiney Books.

Jenkins, Stanley C. (1993) *The Bideford, Westward Ho! & Appledore Railway*, Oxford: Oakwood.

—— and L.J. Pomeroy (1989) *The Moretonhampstead & South Devon Railway*, Oxford: Oakwood.

Kingdom, Anthony R. (1995) *The Totnes to Ashburton Railway (and the Totnes Quay Line)*, Newton Abbot: Ark.

Maggs, Colin G. (1978) *The Barnstaple & Ilfracombe Railway*, Tarrant Hinton: Oakwood.

—— (1980) *Railways to Exmouth*, Tarrant Hinton: Oakwood.

—— (1985) *Rail Centres: Exeter*, Shepperton: Ian Allan.

—— (1997) *The Exeter & Exmouth Railway*, Usk: Oakwood.

—— (n.d.) *The Taunton to Barnstaple Line: Devon & Somerset Railway*, Tisbury: Oakwood.

—— (2006) *The Culm Valley Light Railway: Tiverton Junction to Hemyock*, Usk: Oakwood.

—— and Peter Paye (1979) *The Sidmouth, Seaton and Lyme Regis Branches*, Tarrant Hinton: Oakwood.

Pomroy, L.W. (1984) *The Teign Valley Line*, Oxford: Oxford Publishing.

Potts, C.R. (1986) *The Brixham Branch*, Oxford: Oakwood.

Simmons, Jack (1959) South Western versus Great Western: Railway competition in Devon and Cornwall, *Journal of Transport History*, 4(1), 13–36.

Whetmath, C.F.D. and Douglas Stuckey (1963) *The North Devon & Cornwall Junction Light Railway: Halwill to Torrington*, Lingfield: Oakwood.

Cornwall

Anthony, G.H. (1968) *The Hayle, West Cornwall and Helston Railways*, Lingfield: Oakwood.

—— (1971) *The Tavistock, Launceston and Princetown Railways*, Lingfield: Oakwood.

—— (1997) *The Launceston Branch* (rev. by Stanley C. Jenkins) Oxford: Oakwood.

Barton, D.B. (1966) *The Redruth & Chasewater Railway*, 182401915, rev. ed., Truro: D. Bradford Barton.

Cheeseman, A.J. (1967) *The Plymouth, Devonport & South Western Junction Railway*, Lingfield: Oakwood.

Clinker, C.R. (1963) *The Railways of Cornwall, 1809–1963: A List of Authorising Acts of Parliament, Opening and Closing Dates*, Dawlish: David & Charles.

Crombleholme, Roger, Douglas Stuckey, & C.F.D. Whetmath (1967) *Callington Railways: Bere Alston–Calstock–Callington*, Teddington: Branch Line Society and Bracknell: West Country Handbooks.

Drew, John Henry (1986) *Rail and Sail to Pentewan* (ed. M.J.T. Lewis) Truro: Twelveheads Press.

Fairclough, A. (1970) *The Story of Cornwall's Railways*, Truro: Tor Mark Press.

Fryer, Stephen (1997) *The Building of the Plymouth, Devonport & South Western Junction Railway*, Plymouth: The author.

Hall, R.M.S. (1987) *The Lee Moor Tramway*, Oxford: Oakwood.

Jenkins, Stanley C. (1992) *The Helston Branch Railway*, Oxford: Oakwood.

—— and R.C. Langley (2002) *The West Cornwall Railway: Truro to Penzance*, Usk: Oakwood.

Kendall, H.G. (1968) *The Plymouth & Dartmoor Railway*, Lingfield: Oakwood.

Kingdom, Anthony R. (1991) *The Yelverton to Princetown Railway*, Newton Abbot: Ark.

—— (1996) *The Plymouth to Turnchapel Railway (and the Cattewater Goods Line)*, Newton Abbot: Ark.

—— (2001) *The Plymouth, Tavistock & Launceston Railway*, Newton Abbot: Ark.

Popplewell, Lawrence (1977) *The Railways, Canal and Mines of Looe and Liskeard*, Tarrant Hinton: Oakwood.

Shepherd, Eric R. (1997) *The Plymouth & Dartmoor Railway and the Lee Moor Tramway*, Newton Abbot: Ark.

Vaughan, John (2008) *Rails to Newquay–Railways–Tramways–Town–Transport*, Usk: Oakwood.

Whetmath, C.F.D. (1967) *The Bodmin & Wadebridge Railway*, 2nd ed., Teddington: Branch Line Handbooks and Bracknell: West Country Publications.

Williams, Ken and Dermot Reynolds (1997) *The Kingsbridge Branch: The Primrose Line*, 2nd ed., Oxford: Oakwood.

Woodfin, R.J. (1960) *The Centenary of the Cornwall Railway*, The author.

North East (County Durham, Northumberland)

Abley, R.S. (1975) *The Byers Green Branch of the Clarence Railway*, Durham: Durham County Local History Society.

Addyman, John and William Fawcett (1999) *The High-Level Bridge and Newcastle Central Station: 150 Years across the Tyne*, Newcastle: High Level Bridge and Central Station 150 Committee.

Betteney, Alan (1993) *The Castle Eden Branch of the North Eastern Railway*, Hartlepool: The author.

Corkin, Robert (1977) *Shildon: Cradle of the Railways*, Newcastle: Frank Graham.

Davies, Christopher (1991) Northallerton, *Back Track*, 5(5), 196–203.

Groundwater, Kenneth (1998) *Newcastle's Railways: A View from the Past*, Shepperton: Ian Allan.

Hartley, K.E. (1991) *The Easingwold Railway* (rev. by R.N. Redman) Oxford: Oakwood.

Hoole, K. (1986) *Rail Centres: Newcastle*, Shepperton: Ian Allan.

—— (1984) *North-Eastern Branch Lines, Past & Present*, Poole: Oxford Publishing.

—— (1985*a*) *North-Eastern Branch Line Termini*, Poole: Oxford Publishing.

—— (1985*b*) *Railway Stations of the North East*, Newton Abbot: David & Charles.

—— (1987) *The North Eastern Electrics*, Oxford: Oakwood.

Jenkins, Stanley C. (2001) *The Alston Branch*, Usk: Oakwood.

Kirby, Maurice W. (1993) *The Origins of Railway Enterprise: The Stockton & Darlington Railway, 1821–1863*, Cambridge: Cambridge University Press.

MacLean, John S. (1948) *The Newcastle & Carlisle Railway*, Newton Abbot: David & Charles.

Maitland, Alan (n.d.) *Durham City and the Railway Age*, Durham: Durham County Local History Society.

Manns, Ernest (2000) *Carrying Coals to Dunston: Coal and the Railway*, Usk: Oakwood.

Moorsom, Norman (compiler) (1975) *The Stockton & Darlington Railway: The Foundation of Middlesborough*, Middlesborough.

Northumberland Record Office (1969) *Northumberland Railways from 1700*, North Gosford: NRO.

Rounthwaite, T.E. (1965) *The Railways of Weardale*, London: Railway Correspondence & Travel Society.

Semmens, Peter W. (1975) *Exploring the Stockton & Darlington Railway*, Newcastle: Frank Graham.

Sewell, G.W.M. (1992) *The North British Railway in Northumberland*, Braunton: Merlin.

Sinclair, Neil T. (1985) *Railways of Sunderland*, Gateshead: Tyne & Wear County Council Museums.

Wall, John (2001) *First in the World: The Stockton & Darlington Railway*, Stroud: Sutton Publishing.

Warn, C.R. (1976) *Main Line Railways of Northumberland*, Newcastle: Frank Graham.

—— (1978) *Rural Branch Lines of Northumberland*, 2nd ed., Newcastle: Frank Graham.

—— (n.d.) *Rails between Wear and Tyne*, Newcastle: Frank Graham.

Whittle, G. (1971) *The Railways of Consett and North-west Durham*, Newton Abbot: David & Charles.

—— (1979) *The Newcastle & Carlisle Railway*, Newton Abbot: David & Charles.

Whitworth, Alan (1998) *Esk Valley Railway: A Travellers' Guide*, Barnsley: Wharncliffe.

Wright, Alan (1988) *The North Sunderland Railway*, Oxford: Oakwood.

Scotland

Bruce, W. Scott (1980) *The Railways of Fife*, Perth: Melven Press.

Byrom, Bernard (2004) *The Railways of Upper Strathearn: Crieff–Balquhidder*, Usk: Oakwood.

Clark, A.J.C. (2001) *Caley to the Coast, or Rothesay by Wemyss Bay*, Usk: Oakwood.

Corstorphine, James K. (n.d.) *East of Thornton Junction: The Story of the Fife Coast Line*, Leven: The author.

Dawson, Ian K. (n.d.) *The Findhorn Railway*, Tisbury: Oakwood.

Ferguson, Niall (1995) *The Dundee & Newtyle Railway, including the Alyth and Blairgowrie Branches*, Usk: Oakwood.

—— (2000) *The Arbroath & Forfar Railway, the Dundee Direct Line, and the Kirriemuir Branch*, Usk: Oakwood.

Fryer, C.E.J. (1989) *The Callander & Oban Railway*, Oxford: Oakwood.

—— (1991) *The Portpatrick & Wigtownshire Railways*, Oxford: Oakwood.

—— (1994) *The Girvan & Portpatrick Junction Railway*, Oxford: Oakwood.

Hajducki, Andrew M. (1992) *The North Berwick and Gullane Branch Lines*, Oxford: Oakwood.

—— (1994) *The Haddington, Macmerry and Gifford Branch Lines*, Oxford: Oakwood.

—— and Alan Simpson (1996) *The Lauder Light Railway*, Oxford: Oakwood.

Hajducki, Andrew, Jodeluk, Michael, and Simpson, Alan (2008) *The St Andrews Railway*: Usk: Oakwood.

Hurst, Jeff (1999) *The Glencorse Branch*, Usk: Oakwood.

Jackson, Richard (2001) *Royal Deeside's Railway: Aberdeen to Ballater*, rev. rep. Guildtown: The Great North of Scotland Railway Association.

Jenkins, Stanley C. (1991) *The Rothbury Branch*, Oxford: Oakwood.

Kirkpatrick, Ian (1996) *The Railways of Dundee*, Oxford: Oakwood.

—— (1998) *The Scottish Central Railway: Perth to Stirling*, Usk: Oakwood.

—— (2000) *The Cairn Valley Light Railway: Moniave to Dumfries*, Usk: Oakwood.

Maclean, A.A. (2006) *The Edinburgh Suburban and South Side Junction Railway*, Usk: Oakwood.

Marshall, Peter (2001) *Burntisland: Fife's Railway Port*, Usk: Oakwood.

—— (2005) *Peebles Railways*, Usk: Oakwood.

Martin, Donald (1981) *The Garnkirk and Glasgow Railway*, Glasgow: Strathkelvin District Libraries and Museums.

McConnell, David (1997) *Rails to Kyle of Lochalsh: The Story of the Dingwall & Skye Railway, including the Strathpeffer Branch*, Oxford: Oakwood.

Mullay, A.J. (1991) *Rail Centres: Edinburgh*, Shepperton: Ian Allan.

Robertson, C.J.A. (1983) *The Origins of the Scottish Railway System, 1722–1844*, Edinburgh: John Donald.

Sangster, Alan H. (ed.) (1983) *The Story and Tales of the Buchan Line*, Oxford: Oxford Publishing.

Shaw, Donald (1989) *The Balerno Branch and the Caley in Edinburgh*, Oxford: Oakwood.

Sinclair, Neil T. (1998) *The Highland Main Line*, Penryn: Atlantic Publishers.

Smith, David L. (1969) *The Little Railways of South West Scotland*, Newton Abbot: David & Charles.

Smith, W.A.C. and Paul Anderson (1997) *An Illustrated History of Tayside's Railways: Dundee and Perth*, Clophill: Irwell Press.

Tatlow, Peter (1985) *Highland Railway Miscellany: A Pictorial Record of the Company's Activities in the Public Eye and behind the Scenes*, Poole: Oxford Publishing Company.

Thomas, John (1972) *Mountain, Moor and Loch on the Route of the West Highland Railway (1895)*, reprint, Newton Abbot: David and Charles.

—— (1990*a*) *The Skye Railway* (rev. ed. by John Farrington), Newton Abbot: David & Charles.

—— (1990*b*) *The Callander & Oban Railway* (rev. by John Farrington), Newton Abbot: David & Charles.

Thorne, H.D. (1976) *Rails to Portpatrick*, Prescot: T. Stephenson and Sons.

London

Atkinson, J.B. (1972) *The West London Joint Railways*, Shepperton: Ian Allan.

Baker, C. (1960) *The Metropolitan Railway*, Lingfield: Oakwood.

Borley, H.V. and Kidner, R.W. (n.d.) *The West London Railway and the W.L.E.R.*, Lingfield: Oakwood.

Body, Geoffrey (n.d.) *The Blackwall and Millwall Extension Railways*, Weston-super-Mare: Avon-AngliA Publications.

Connor, J.E. (1984) *Stepney's Own Railway: A History of the London and Blackwall System*, Colchester: Connor and Butler.

Faulkner, J.N. (1991) *Rail Centres: Clapham Junction*, Shepperton: Ian Allan.

Goode, C.T. (1984) *To the Crystal Palace*, Bracknell: Forge Books.

Goudie, Frank, Robert Barker and Douglas Stuckey (1996) *Railways of Wembley*, Wokingham: Forge Books.

Goslin, Geoff (2002) *London's Elevated Electric Railway: The LBSCR Suburban Overhead Electrification 1909–1929*, Colchester: Connor and Butler.

Gray, Adrian (1977) *The London to Brighton Line 1841–1977*, Tarrant Hinton: Oakwood.

Jackson, Alan A. (1986) *London's Metropolitan Railway*, Newton Abbot: David & Charles.

Klapper, Charles (1976) *London's Lost Railways*, London: Routledge & Kegan Paul.

Lake, G.H. (1945) *The Railways of Tottenham: A Detailed Description and Historical Survey of their Development*, London: Greenlake Publications Ltd.

Lane, C.B. (1860) *Railway Communication in London and the Thames Embankment*, London: James Ridgway.

Lee, Charles E. (1988) *The Metropolitan District Railway*, Oxford: Oakwood.

Line 112 Group (1970) *The Railway to Walthamstow and Chingford*, London: Walthamstow Antiquarian Society.

Peacock, Thomas B. (1978) *Great Western London Suburban Services*, Tarrant Hinton: Oakwood.

Pond, C.C. (1982) *The Walthamstow and Chingford Railway*, London: Walthamstow Antiquarian Society.

Robbins, Michael (1974 rev.) *The North London Railway*, Tarrant Hinton: Oakwood.

Scott, Peter G. (1987) *The London & Birmingham Railway through Harrow, 1837–1987*, Harrow: London Borough of Harrow.

—— (1981) *The Harrow & Stanmore Railway*, 2nd ed., Greenhill: Harvest Productions.

Simpson, William (2003–4) *A History of the Metropolitan Railway*, 2 vols. Witney: Lamplight.

Taylor, Sheila (ed.) (2001) *The Moving Metropolis: A History of London's Transport since 1800*, London: Laurence King for London Transport Museum.

Thomas, R.H.G. (1972) *London's First Railway: The London & Greenwich*, London: Batsford.

Wilmot, George (1973 2nd rev. ed.) *The Railway in Finchley: A study in suburban development*, London: Libraries and Arts Committee of the Barnet London Borough Council.

Yorkshire

Appleby, Ken (1993) *Britain's Rail Super Centres: York*, Shepperton: Ian Allan.

Bairstow, J. (1979) *Railways of Keighley*, Clapham: Dalesman.

Bairstow, Martin (1982) *The Great Northern Railway in West Yorkshire*, Skipton: Wyvern Publications.

Barnett, A.L. (1984) *The Railways of the South Yorkshire Coalfield from 1880*, Leicester: The Railway Correspondence and Travel Society.

Barrie, D.S.M. (ed.) (1978 3rd rev. ed.) *The Derwent Valley Railway*, Tarrant Hinton: Oakwood.

Batty, Stephen R. (1989*a*) *Rail Centres: Leeds/Bradford*, Shepperton: Ian Allan.

—— (1989*b*) *Rail Centres: Sheffield*, 2nd impression, Shepperton: Ian Allan.

—— (1991) *Rail Centres: Doncaster*, Shepperton: Ian Allan.

Baughan, Peter E. (1966) *North of Leeds: the Leeds–Settle–Carlisle Line and its Branches*, Hatch End: Roundhouse Books.

Belcher, Henry (1977 rep.) *A Tour of the Whitby and Pickering Railway in 1836 with notes and introduction by John Cranfield*, Pinner: Cranfield and Bonfiel Books Yorkshire.

Binns, Donald (1988) *Railways in the Northern Dales: Railways around Skipton*, Skipton: Wyvern.

Boyes, Grahame (1973) *The Heck Bridge and Wentbridge Railway*, Leeds: Turntable.

Burton, Warwick (1997) *The Malton & Pickering Junction Railway*, Halifax: Martin Bairstow.

Croft, D.J. (1972) *The Nidd Valley Railway*, Lingfield: Oakwood.

Earnshaw, Alan (1990) The Huddersfield and Sheffield Junction Railway, *Back Track*, 4(2), 61–99.

—— (1993) *Pennine Branch Lines*, Shepperton: Ian Allan.

Edwards, Brian (1985) *Totley and the Tunnel*, Sheffield: Shape Design Shop.

Elliott, B.J. (2002 2nd ed.) *The South Yorkshire Joint Railway and the Coalfield*, Usk: Oakwood.

Fisher, J.N. (1997) *The Huddersfield and Kirkburton Branch*, Usk, Oakwood.

Franks, D.L. (1973) *East and West Yorkshire Union Railways*, Leeds: Turntable Enterprises.

—— (1979) *Swinton and Knottingley Railway*, Clapham: The Dalesman Pub. Co.

Goodchild, John (2002) *Wakefield's First Railway and its Collieries 1798 to 1880*, Wakefield: Wakefield Historical Publications.

Goode, C.T. (1976) *The Goole and Selby Railway*, Tarrant Hinton: Oakwood.

—— (1986) *The Dearne Valley Railway*, Anlaby: The author.

—— (1991) *The Railways of Castleford: Normanton and Methley*, Anlaby: The author.

Hoole, K. (1983) *Rail Centres: York*, Shepperton: Ian Allan.

Hoole, K. (1976) *The Railways of York*, Clapham: Dalesman.

Jenkins, Stanley C. (2002) *The Wensleydale Branch: A New History*, 2nd ed. Usk: Oakwood.

Lane, Barry C. (1998) *The Holmfirth Branch*, 2nd ed., Nottingham: Lancashire and Yorkshire Railway Society.

Macmahon, K.A. (1974) *The Beginnings of the East Yorkshire Railways*, rev. ed. by Baron F. Duckham, York: East Yorkshire Local History Society.

MacTurk, G.G. (1970) *A History of the Hull Railways*, rev. ed. by Ken Hoole Knaresborough: Nidd Valley Narrow Gauge Railways Ltd.

Middleton Railway Trust (2004) *A History of the Middleton Railway, Leeds*, 8th ed., Leeds, MRT.

Moore, R.F. (1973) *Paddy Waddell's Railway*, Whitby: Whitby Literary and Philosophical Society in conjunction with The N. Yorks. Moors Railway.

Murray, Hugh (1984) *Servants of Business: Portraits in the Board and Committee Rooms at York*, York: British Rail, North Eastern Region.

Nicholson, M. and W.B. Yeadon (1993) *An Illustrated History of Hull's Railways*, Grasscroft: Irwell Press.

Parkes, G.D. (1959) *The Hull and Barnsley Railway*, 3rd ed. Lingfield: Oakwood.

Pixton, Robert and John Hooper (1998) *Great Provincial Stations: Leeds Termini*, Nottingham: Challenger.

Potter, G.W.J. (1969) *A History of the Whitby and Pickering Railway*, 2nd ed., reprinted with a new introduction by K. Hoole and postscript by G.D. Calvert, Wakefield: S.R. Publishers.

Price, Peter (1989) *Lost Railways of Holderness: The Hull Withernsea and Hull Hornsea Lines*, Beverley: Hutton Press.

Reading, S.J. (1976) *The Derwent Valley Railway: A Progressive Yorkshire Railway*, 2nd ed. Tarrant Hinton: Oakwood.

Rogers, James (1986) *Railways of Harrogate & District*, Starbeck: The author.

Rule, Christopher (2005) *South Milford and the Railways*, London: Selia.

Speakman, Colin (1969) *Transport in Yorkshire*, Clapham: Dalesman.

Stocks, William B. (1960) *Pennine Journey: Being the History of the Railways, Tramways and Canals in Huddersfield and District*, Huddersfield: The Advertiser Press Ltd.

Unwin, Robert (1981) The transport systems of the Vale of York, 1660–1775, *Journal of Transport History*, 3rd series, 2(2), 17–37.

Waring, Roy (1989) *The Leeds New Line: The Heaton Lodge and Wortley Railway*, Oxford: Oakwood.

Whitaker, Alan and Cryer, Bob (1984) *The Queensbury Lines: A Pictorial Centenary Edition*, Lancaster: Dalesman Pub. Co.

Wilson, Andrew (2001) *Hellifield & its Railways*, Stroud: Tempus.

Yeadon, W.B. (1995) *More Illustrated History of the Railways of Hull*, Oldham: Challenger.

Lancashire and Cumbria

Bairstow, Martin (1983) *The Manchester & Leeds Railway: The Calder Valley Line*, Skipton: Wyvern.

—— (1984) *The Leeds, Huddersfield & Manchester Railway: The Standedge Line*, Pudsey: The author.

Bairstow, Martin (1993) *The East Lancashire Railway*, Halifax: The author.

Bardsley, J.R. (1982) *The Railways of Bolton 1824–1959*, 2nd ed. Bolton: The author.

Biddle, Gordon (1989) *The Railways around Preston: An Historical Review*, Romiley: Foxline.

Binns, Donald (1982a) *The Scenic Settle & Carlisle Railway*, Skipton: Wyvern.

—— (1982b) *The 'Little' North Western Railway*, Skipton: Wyvern.

Booth, Henry (1969) *An Account of the Liverpool & Manchester Railway* (reprinted with an introduction by Charles E. Lee), London: Frank Cass.

Bowtell, Harold D. (1999–2000) *Rails through Lakeland: An Illustrated History of the Workington–Cockermouth–Keswick–Penrith Railway, 1847–1972*, New ed., 2 vols., Kettering: Silver Link.

Brumhead, Derek (1990) Railways of New Mills and district: their development and impact, 1840–1902, *Transactions of the Lancashire and Cheshire Antiquarian Society*, **86**, 52–86.

Carlson, Robert E. (1969) *The Liverpool & Manchester Railway Project, 1821–1831*, New York: Augustus M. Kelley.

Coates, N.G. and P. Harrison (1992) *The Colne Branch*, Sandal: Lancashire & Yorkshire Railway Society.

Cotterall, J.E. (1982) *The West Lancashire Railway*, with additional notes by R.W. Rush Tisbury: Oakwood.

Davies, W.J.K. (1981) *The Ravenglass & Eskdale Railway*, 2nd ed., Newton Abbot: David & Charles.

Donaghy, Thomas J. (1972) *Liverpool & Manchester Railway Operations, 1831–1845*, Newton Abbot: David & Charles.

Edgar, Stuart and Sinton, John M. (1980) *The Solway Junction*, Oxford: Oakwood.

Ferneyhough, Frank (1980) *Liverpool & Manchester Railway, 1830–1980*, London: Robert Hale.

Gahan, John W. (1983) *Steel Wheels to Deeside: The Wirral Railway past and present*, Birkenhead: Countyvise Ltd. and Weston-super-Mare: AvonAngliA Publications.

—— (1985) *Seaport to Seaside: Lines to Southport and Ormskirk—13 Decades of Trains and Travel*, Birkenhead: Countyvise Ltd. and Weston-super-Mare: AvonAnglia.

Gilpin, Leslie R. (n.d.) *Grange-over-sands: A Resort and its Railway*, Wolverhampton: Cumbrian Railways Association.

Goode, C.T. (1986) *The Railways of Manchester*, Anlaby: The author.

Greville, M.D. (1973) *Chronology of the Railways of Lancashire: Dates of incorporation, opening and amalgamation, etc. of all lines in the county*, Caterham: Railway and Canal Historical Society.

Hall, Stanley (1995) *Rail Centres: Manchester,* Shepperton: Ian Allan.

Harrison, William (1967) *History of the Manchester Railways (1882)*, 2nd ed. Manchester: The Lancashire and Cheshire Antiquarian Society.

Hulme, Charles (1991) *Rails of Manchester: A Short History of the City's Rail Network,* Manchester: John Rylands University Library of Manchester.

Jenkinson, David (1973) *Rails in the Fells: A Railway Case study,* Seaton: Peco.

Johnson, E.M. (1989) *Railways in and around the Manchester Suburbs: A Selective Pictorial Review,* Romiley: Foxline.

Joy, David (1967) *Main Line Over Shap: The Story of the Lancaster-Carlisle Railway,* Clapham: Dalesman.

—— (1968) *Cumbrian CoastRailways,* Clapham: Dalesman.

Mather, F.C. (1971) The battle of the Manchester railway junctions, *Transport History,* 4(2), 144–65.

McLoughlin, Barry (1999) *A Nostalgic look at the Railways of Blackpool and the Fylde: Britain's Premier Resort,* 2nd ed. Kettering: Silver Link Publishing Co.

Mellentin, Julian (1980) *Kendal and Windermere Railway,* Clapham: Dalesman Books.

Mitchell W.R and Joy, David (1976) *Settle-Carlisle Railway: A Centenary Edition* (4th ed.) Clapham: Dalesman.

Parker, Norman (1972) *The Preston and Longridge Railway,* Lingfield: Oakwood.

Quayle, H.I. and Jenkins, Stanley C. (1977) *Lakeside and Haverthwaite Railway,* Clapham: Dalesman.

Roberts, B. (1974) *Railways and Mineral Tramways of Rossendale,* Lingfield: Oakwood.

Robinson, Peter W. (1986) *Rail Centres: Carlisle,* Shepperton: Ian Allan.

Rush, R.W. (1983) *The East Lancashire Railway,* Tisbury: Oakwood.

—— and Price, M.R.C. (1985) *The Garstang and Knott End Railway,* 2nd ed. Oxford: Oakwood.

Simmons, Jack (1947) *The Maryport and Carlisle Railway,* Chislehurst: Oakwood.

Singleton, David (1975) *Liverpool and Manchester Railway: A Mile by Mile Guide to the World's First "Modern" Railway,* Clapham: Dalesman.

Smith, Lynton J. (1977) The impact of the Liverpool and Manchester Railway on a South Lancashire township: Newton-le-Willows, 1821–1851, *Transactions of the Historic Society of Lancashire and Cheshire,* **129**, 109–23.

Smith, Richard (n.d.) *The Kendal & Windermere Railway,* Barrow-in-Furness: Cumbrian Railways Association.

Tattersall, W.D. (1973) *The Bolton, Blackburn, Clitheroe and West Yorkshire Railway,* Lingfield: Oakwood.

Taylor, Stuart (1994) *The Railways of Colne, Lancashire,* Romiley: Foxline.

Thomas, R.H.G. (1980) *The Liverpool & Manchester Railway,* London: B.T. Batsford.

Tolson, J.M. (1983) *The St Helens Railway its Rivals and Successors,* Tisbury: Oakwood.

Wells, J. (1993) *An Illustrated History of Rochdale's Railways,* Grasscroft: Irwell Press.

—— and E.F. Bentley (n.d.) *East Lancashire Lines: Bury to Heywood and Rawtenstall,* Romiley: Foxline.

Westall, David (1988) *The Holcombe Brook Branch,* Keighley: Lancashire and Yorkshire Railway Society.

Western, Robert G. (1971) *The Lowgill Branch: A Lost Route to Scotland,* Lingfield: Oakwood.

—— (1990) *The Ingleton Branch: A Lost Route to Scotland,* Oxford: Oakwood.

—— (1997) *The Eden Valley Railway,* Oxford: Oakwood.

—— (2001) *The Cockermouth, Keswick and Penrith Railway,* Usk: Oakwood.

Wilby, C. Richard (1983) *Railways around East Lancashire*, Skipton: Wyvern.
Wilson, Andrew (2001) *Hellifield and its Railways,* Stroud: Tempus Publishing.

South Wales

Barrie, D.S. (1962) *The Barry Railway,* Lingfield: Oakwood.
—— (1973) *The Rhymney Railway,* Lingfield: Oakwood.
—— (1991) *The Brecon & Merthyr Railway* (rev ed. by R.W. Kidner), Oxford: Oakwood.
Chapman, Colin (1984) *The Cowbridge Railway,* Poole: Oxford Publishing.
—— (1996) *The Llantrisant Branch of the Taff Vale Railway,* Oxford: Oakwood.
—— (1997) *The Llantrisant Branch of the Taff Vale Railway,* Oxford: Oakwood.
—— (1998) *The Vale of Glamorgan Railway,* Usk: Oakwood.
—— (2000) *The Ely Valley Railway: Llantrisant–Penygraig,* Usk: Oakwood.
Evans, E.A. (1994) *The Viaducts: An Account of the Railways of Quakers Yard,* Nelson: The author.
Hutton, John (1988) *Taff Vale Miscellany,* Sparkford: Oxford Publishing.
—— (2002) *The Newport Docks & Railway Company,* New ed., Kettering: Silver Link.
—— (2004) *The Rhymney Railway,* 2 vols., Kettering: Silver Link.
Jones, Gwyn Briwnant and Denis Dunstone (1999) *The Origins of the LMS in South Wales,* Llandysul: Gomer Press.
—— and —— (1999) *The Vale of Neath Line: Neath to Pontypool Road,* 2nd ed., Llandysul: Gomer Press.
—— and —— (2000) *The Railways of Wales c. 1900,* Llandysul: Gomer Press.
Mountford, Eric and N. Sprinks (1993) *Taff Vale Lines to Penarth,* Oxford: Oakwood.
Mountford, Eric R. and R.W. Kidner (n.d.) *The Aberdare Railway,* Oxford: Oakwood.
Page, James (1989) *Rails in the Valleys,* reprint, London: Guild Publishing.
Parry, V.J. (1970) *Brecon & Merthyr Railway.*
Price, M.R.C. (1997) *The Gwendraeth Valley Railway: Kidwelly to Mynydd-y-Garreg.*
Tasker, W.W. (1986) *The Merthyr, Tredegar & Abergavenny Railway and Branches,* Poole: Oxford Publishing.
—— (1992) *Railways in the Sirhowy Valley,* Oxford: Oakwood.
Waters, Laurence (1995) *Railways of Cardiff,* Shepperton: Ian Allan.

Forest of Dean and Mid-Wales

Beddoes, Keith and William H. Smith (1995) *The Tenbury and Bewdley Railway,* Didcot: Wild Swan.
Boyd, James I.C. (1965) *Narrow Gauge Railways in Mid-Wales,* Lingfield: Oakwood.
Clinker, C.R. (1960) *The Hay Railway,* Dawlish: David & Charles.
Cook, R.A. and C.R. Clinker (1984) *Early Railways between Abergavenny & Hereford,* Oakham: Railway & Canal Historical Society.
de Courtais, Nicholas (1992) *The New Radnor Branch,* Didcot: Wild Swan.
Doughty, A. (1997) *The Central Wales Line: An Illustrated History of the Shrewsbury to Swansea Railway,* Sparkford: Oxford Publishing.
Green, C.C. (1986) *An Illustrated History of the Vale of Rheidol Light Railway,* Didcot: Wild Swan.
Glover, Mark and Celia Glover (1994) *The Ross & Monmouth Railway* (rev. by Celia Glover) Studley: Brewin Books.
Handley, Brian M. (1988) *The Wye Valley Railway,* Oxford: Oakwood.
—— and R. Dingwall (1998) *The Wye Valley Railway and the Coleford Branch,* Usk: Oakwood.

Hughes, Stephen (1990) *The Brecon Forest Tramroads*, Aberystwyth: Royal Commission on Ancient & Historical Monuments in Wales.

Jenkins, Stanley C. (2002) *The Ross, Monmouth and Pontypool Line*, Usk: Oakwood.

Jones, G. Briwnant (1994) *Great Western Corris*, Llandysul: Gomer.

Kidner, R.W. (1990) *The Mid-Wales Railway*, Oxford: Oakwood.

Morgan, John Scott (2003) *Bishop's Castle: Portrait of a Country Railway*, reprinted, Bishop's Castle: Bishop's Castle Railway Society.

Morris, R.J. (1997) *The Forest of Dean Tramroad: The Bullo Pill to Churchway Tramroad via Soudley and Cinderford, 1807–1854*, Coleford: Rock House.

Mowat, Charles Loch (1964) *The Golden Valley Railway*, Cardiff: University of Wales Press.

Paar, H.W. (1971) *The Great Western Railway in Dean*, 2nd ed., Newton Abbot: David & Charles.

—— (1973) *The Severn & Wye Railway*, 2nd ed., Newton Abbot: David & Charles.

Pope, Ian, Robert How, and Paul Karau (1983–5) *Illustrated History of the Severn & Wye Railway*, 2 vols., Upper Bucklebury: Wild Swan.

—— and Paul Karau (1992–7) *The Forest of Dean Branch*, 2 vols., Didcot: Wild Swan.

Price, M.R.C. (1995) *The Lampeter, Aberayron & New Quay Light Railway*, Oxford: Oakwood.

Pritchard, Arthur J. (1962) *Historical Notes on the Railways of S.E. Monmouthshire*, Lingfield: Oakwood.

Rattenbury, Gordon and Ray Cook (1996) *The Hay and Kington Railways*, Mold: Railway & Canal Historical Society.

Shirehampton, W.J.P. (1959) *Monmouth's Railways: A Historical Survey*, Monmouth: The Monmouth District Field Club & Antiquarian Society.

Sinclair, J.B. and R.W.D. Fenn (1991) *The Facility of Locomotion: The Kington Railways*, Kington: Mid-Border Books.

Smith, Martin (1995) *Portrait of the Central Wales Line*, Shepperton: Ian Allan.

Smith, Peter (1983) *An Historical Survey of the Forest of Dean Railways*, Poole: Oxford Publishing.

Smith, William. H. (1993) *The Golden Valley Railway*, Didcot: Wild Swan.

Turner, Keith and Susan Turner (1982) *The Shropshire and Montgomeryshire Light Railway*, Newton Abbot: David and Charles.

West Wales

Gabb, Gerald (1987) *The Life and Times of the Swansea & Mumbles Railway*, Cowbridge: D. Brown & Sons.

Holden, J.S. (1979) *The Manchester & Milford Railway*, Tarrant Hinton: Oakwood.

Jermy, R.C. (1986) *The Railways of Porthgain and Abereiddi*, Oxford: Oakwood.

Lee, Charles E. (1942) *The First Passenger Railway: The Oystermouth or Swansea & Mumbles Line*, London: Railway Publishing.

—— (1954) *The Swansea & Mumbles Railway*, South Godstone: Oakwood.

Morris, J.P. (1969) *The North Pembroke & Fishguard Railway*, Tarrant Hinton: Oakwood.

Morris, J.P. (1976) *The Pembroke & Tenby Railway*, Haverfordwest: Laidlaw-Burgess.

Padfield, Roger and Barrie Burgess (1974) *The Teifi Valley Railway*, Haverfordwest: Laidlaw-Burgess.

Price, M.R.C. (1964) *The Saundersfoot Railway*, Lingfield: Oakwood.

—— (1986) *The Pembroke & Tenby Railway*, Lingfield: Oakwood.

—— (1991) *The Whitland & Cardigan Railway*, 2nd ed., Lingfield: Oakwood.

—— (1992) *The Llanelly & Mynydd Mawr Railway*, Lingfield: Oakwood.

North Wales

Baughan, Peter E. (1972) *The Chester & Holyhead Railway, Vol. 1: The Main Line up to 1880*, Newton Abbot: David & Charles.

Boyd, James I.C. (1975) *Festiniog Railway*, Tarrant Hinton: Oakwood.

—— (1981–9) *Narrow Gauge Railways in Caernarvonshire*, 5 vols. Tarrant Hinton: Oakwood.

—— (1988) *The Tal-y-Llyn Railway*, Didcot: Wild Swan.

—— (1991) *The Wrexham, Mold & Connah's Quay Railway, including the Buckley Railway*, Oxford: Oakwood.

Carpenter, Roger (1990) *The Criggion Branch of the Shropshire and Montgomeryshire Light Railway*, Didcot: Wild Swan.

Christiansen, Rex (2001) *Chester and North Wales Border Railways: A View from the Past*, Hersham: Ian Allan.

Corris Railway Society (1988) *A Return to Corris: The Continuing Story of the Corris Railway*, Weston-super-Mare: Avon-Anglia.

Cozens, Lewis (1972) *The Mawddwy, Van and Kerry Railways* (rev. by R.W. Kidner), Lingfield: Oakwood.

Davies, David Llewelyn (1991) *The Glyn Valley Tramway* (rev. by R.W. Kidner), Oxford: Oakwood.

Dean, R.J. (1968) *Historical Notes for a Tour of Flintshire Railways, including Tramroads*, Railway and Canal Historical Society, North West Group.

Dunn, J.M. (1968) *The Chester & Holyhead Railway*, Lingfield: Oakwood.

Elis-Williams, M. (1984) *Packet to Ireland Porthdinllaen's Challenge to Holyhead*, Caernarfon: Gwynedd Archives Service.

Ganley, Colin (1991) The railway under the lake, *Back Track*, 5(4), 186–9.

—— (1994) The Llanfyllin Railway—the story of a border branch line, *Back Track*, 8(3), 186–9.

Goodall, Stephen P. (1992) *The Vale of Clwyd Railway: Rhyl to Denbigh*, The author.

Jenkins, Stanley C. and John M. Strange (2004) *The Wrexham & Ellesmere Railway*, Usk: Oakwood.

Johnson, Peter (2002) *An Illustrated History of the Welsh Highland Railway*, Hersham: Oxford Publishing.

Jones, G. Briwnant (1990) *Railway through Talerddig: The Story of the Newtown and Machynlleth and Associated Railways in the Dyfi Valley*, Llandysul: Gomer.

Jones, Ivor Wynne and Gordon Hatherill (1977) *Llechwedd and Other Ffestiniog Railways*, Blaenau Ffestiniog: Quarry Tours.

Lee, Charles E. (1970) *The Welsh Highland Railway*, Newton Abbot: David and Charles and The Welsh Highland Light Railway.

Lewis, M.J.T. (1965) *How Ffestiniog got its Railway*, Caterham: Railway & Canal Historical Society.

Lloyd, Michael (1990) *The Tanat Valley Light Railway*, Didcot: Wild Swan.

Milner, W.J. (1984) *The Glyn Valley Tramway*, Poole: Oxford Publishing.

Rear, William (2003) *From Chester to Holyhead: The Branch Lines*, Hersham: Oxford Publishing.

Thomas, J.R. (1995) *The Tramways and Railways to Holywell*, Bagillt: The author.

Thompson, Trefor (1978) *The Prestatyn and Dyserth Railway*, North Clwyd: North Clwyd Railway Association.

Wade, E.A. (1997) *The Plynlimon and Hafan Tramway,* Truro: Twelveheads Press.

Wren, Wilfred J. (1979) *The Tanat Valley Railway,* Tarrant Hinton: Oakwood.

Cheshire and North Staffordshire

Baker, Allan C. (1979) *The Cheadle Railway,* Tarrant Hinton: Oakwood.

—— (1986) *The Potteries Loop Line: An Illustrated History,* Burton-on-Trent: Trent Valley Publications.

Christiansen, Rex (1993) *Rail Centres: Crewe,* Shepperton: Ian Allan.

Clark, P.L. (1981) *Staffordshire Railways,* reprinted from the Victoria History of the County of Stafford, Stafford: County Library.

Dixon, Frank (1994) *The Manchester South Junction and Altrincham Railway,* 2nd ed. Oxford: Oakwood.

Drummond, Diane K. (1995) *Crewe: Railway Town, Company and People, 1840–1914,* Aldershot: Scolar Press.

Dyckhoff, Nigel (1999) *Portrait of the Cheshire Lines Committee,* Shepperton: Ian Allan.

Gahan, John W. (1983) *The Line Beneath the Liners: A Hundred years of Mersey Railway sights and sounds,* Birkenhead: Countyvise Ltd. and Weston-super-Mare: AvonAngliA Publications.

Goode, C.T. (1985) *Trentham-The Hall, Gardens and Branch Railway,* Anlaby, The author.

—— (1990) *The Ashbourne to Buxton Railway,* Anlaby: The author.

Greville, M.D. (1954) *Chronological List of the Railways of Cheshire, 1837–1939,* Transactions of the Historic Society of Lancashire and Cheshire, Vol. 106, 1954. pp. 135–44.

Griffiths, R. Prys (1947) *The CheshireLines Railway,* South Godstone: Oaxwood.

Hewitt, H.J. (1972) *The Building of Railways in Cheshire Down to 1860,* Didsbury: E.J. Morten (Publishers).

Highet, Campbell (1961) *The Wirral Railway,* Lingfield: Oakwood.

Jermy, R.C (1981) *The Storeton Tramway,* Birkenhead: Countyvise Ltd. and Weston-super-Mare: AvonAngliA Publications.

Jeuda, Basil (1980) *The Leek, Caldon and Waterhouses Railway,* Cheadle: North Staffordshire Railway Company.

—— (1983) *The Macclesfield, Bollington & Marple Railway: The Great Central & North Staffordshire Joint Railway,* Chester, Cheshire County Council.

—— (1984) *Railways of the Macclesfield District,* Skipton: Wyvern.

—— (1986) *Memories of the North Staffordshire Railway,* Chester: Cheshire Libraries.

—— (1999) *The Churnet Valley Railway,* Lydney: Lightmoor Press.

Jones, P. (1981) *The Stafford and Uttoxeter Railway,* Tisbury: Oakwood.

Jones, Norman and Michael Bentley (n.d.) *Railways of the High Peak: Whaley Bridge to Friden,* Romilay: Foxline.

Keys, R. and the North Staffordshire Railway Society (1974) *The Churnet Valley Railway,* Buxton: Moorland Publishing.

—— and Porter, L. (1972) *The Manifold Valley and its Light Railway,* Leek: Moorland Publishing.

Lee, Peter (1988) *The Trent Valley Railway (Rugby–Stafford, 1847–1966): A Pictorial Record,* Winshill: Trent Valley Publications.

Lester, C.R. (1983) *The Stoke to Market Drayton Line and Associated Canals and Mineral Branches,* Tisbury: Oakwood.

Maund, T.B. (2000) *The Birkenhead Railway (LMS & GW Joint),* Sawtry: Railway Correspondence & Travel Society.

Merseyside Railway History Group (1982) *The Hooton to West Kirby Branch Line and the Wirral Way,* Birkenhead: Central Library.

—— (2002) *Railway Stations of Wirral,* reprint, Prenton: Ian & Marilyn Boumphrey.

Miller, R.W. (1999) *The Winsford and Over Branch,* Usk: Oakwood.

Parkin, G.W. (n.d.) *The Mersey Railway,* Lingfield: Oakwood.

Talbot, Edward (n.d.) *Railways in and around Stafford,* Romiley: Foxline.

Yate, Bob (2005) *By Great Western to Crewe: The Story of the Wellington to Nantwich and Crew Line,* Usk: Oakwood.

Engineers

Addyman, John and Victoria Haworth (2005) *Robert Stephenson: Railway Engineer,* Willerby, Hull: North Eastern Railway Association and Newcastle-upon-Tyne: Robert Stephenson trust.

Awdry, Christopher (1993) *Over the Summit: How Britain's Railways crossed the High Hills,* Peterborough: Silver Link.

Bailey, Michael R. (ed.) (2003) *Robert Stephenson: The Eminent Engineer,* Aldershot: Ashgate.

Beckett, Derrick (1984) *Stephenson's Britain,* Newton Abbot: David & Charles.

Biddle, Gordon (1990) *The Railway Surveyors: The Story of Railway Property Management, 1800–1990,* London: Ian Allan.

Brindle, Stephen (2005) *Brunel: The Man who built the World,* London: Weidenfeld & Nicolson.

Brooke, David (1983) *The Railway Navvy,* Newton Abbot: David & Charles.

—— (ed.) (2000) *The Diary of William Mackenzie: The first international Railway Contractor,* London: Institution of Civil Engineers.

Brookes, Edward C. (1996) *Sir Samuel Morton Peto Bt., 1809–1889,* Bury St. Edmunds: Bury Clerical Society.

Brunel, Isambard (2004) *The Life of Isambard Kingdon Brunel, Civil Engineer,* reprint of 1870 ed., Brora: Adam Gordon.

Bryan, Timothy (1999) *Brunel: The Great Engineer,* Shepperton: Ian Allan.

Chacksfield, J.E. (2007) *F.W. Webb: In the Right Place at the Right Time,* Usk: Oakwood.

Chrimes, Michael (ed.) (1997) *The Civil Engineering of Canals and Railways before 1850,* Aldershot: Ashgate.

—— Mary K. Murphy, and George Ribeill (compilers) (1994) *Mackenzie—Giant of the Railways,* London: Institution of Civil Engineers.

Clark, E.F. (1983) *George Parker Bidder: The Calculating Boy,* Bedford: KSL Publications.

Coleman, Terry (1965) *The Navvies,* London: Hutchinson.

Conder, F.R. (1983) *The Men who Built Railways: A Reprint of 'Personal Recollections of English Engineers'* (ed. J. Simmons) London: Thomas Telford.

Cowles, Roger (1989) *The Making of the Severn Railway Tunnel,* Gloucester: Alan Sutton.

Cross-Rudkin, P.S.M., Chrimes, Michael M., and Michael R. Bailey (eds.) (2008) *A Biographical Dictionary of Civil Engineers in Great Britain and Ireland, Vol 2, !830–1890,* London: Thomas Telford.

Gooderson, P.J. (1970) Railway construction in mid-nineteenth century North Lancashire: A study based on the diary of James Stelfox, 1855–70, *Transactions of the Historic Society of Lancashire and Cheshire,* **122,** 137–52.

Helps, Arthur (1972) *Life and Labours of Mr. Brassey, 1805–1870,* London: Bell & Daldy.

Joby, R.S. (1983) *The Railway Builders: Lives and Works of the Victorian Railway Contractors*, Newton Abbot: David & Charles.

Kentley, Eric, Angie Hudson, and James Peto (compilers) (2000) *Isambard Kingdom Brunel: Recent Works*, London: Design Museum.

Leery, G.G. (1949) *Henry Robertson: Pioneer of Railways into Wales*, Oswestry: Woodalls.

Marshall, John (1978) *A Biographical Dictionary of Railway Engineers*, Newton Abbot: David & Charles.

Middlemas, Robert Keith (1963) *The Master Builders: Thomas Brassey; Sir John Aird; Lord Cowdray; Sir John Norton-Griffiths*, London: Hutchinson.

Morgan, Brian (1971) Civil *Engineering: Railways, London:* Longman.

Murray, Anthony (1988) *The Forth Railway Bridge: A Celebration*, New ed. Edinburgh: Mainstream.

National Library of Wales (1996) Notes in the Henry Robertson archive, compiled by Stephen Benham, deposited 1949.

Paine, E.M.S. (1961) *The Two James's and the Two Stephensons; Or the Earliest History of Passenger Transit on Railways*, Dawlish: David & Charles (reprint of 1861 ed.).

Paul, J. Ann (2003) *Three Thousand Strangers: Navvy Life on the Kettering to Manton Railway*, Kettering: Silver Link.

Platt, Alan (1987) *The Life and Times of Daniel Gooch*, Gloucester: Alan Sutton.

Pollins, Harold (1957) Railway contractors and the finance of railway development in Britain—I, *Journal of Transport History*, 3(1), 41–51.

Popplewell, Lawrence (1982–89) *A Gazetteer of the Railway Contractors and Engineers*, 8 vols., Ferndown/Bournemouth: Melledgen Press.

Prebble, John (1956) *The High Girders: The Story of the Tay Bridge Disaster*, London: Secker & Warburg.

Pugsley, Alfred (ed.) (1976) *The Works of Isambard Kingdom Brunel: An Engineering Appreciation*, London: Institution of Civil Engineers & Bristol: University of Bristol.

Rapley, John (2003) *The Britannia and Other Tubular Bridges*, Stroud: Tempus.

Rolt, L.T.C. (1957) *Isambard Kingdon Brunel: A Biography*, London: Longman.

—— (1960) *George and Robert Stephenson: The Railway Revolution*, London: Longman.

Rosenberg, Nathan and Walter G. Vincenti (1978) *The Britannia Bridge: The Generation and Diffusion of Knowledge*, Cambridge, MA: MIT Press.

Sopwith, Robert (1994) *Thomas Sopwith, Surveyor: An Exercise in Self-Help*, Bishop Auckland: Pentland Press.

Skeat, W.O. (1973) *George Stephenson: The Engineer & his Letters*, London: Institution of Mechanical Engineers.

Smiles, Samuel (1857) *Life of George Stephenson: Railway Engineer*, London: John Murray.

Vaughan, Adrian (1991) *Isambard Kingdom Brunel: Engineering Knight-Errant*, London: John Murray.

Walker, Charles (1969) *Thomas Brassey: Railway Builder*, London: Frederick Muller.

Warren, J.G.H. (1970) *A Century of Locomotive Building by Robert Stephenson & Co.* 1823–1923 (reprinted with a new intro by W.A. Tuplin), Newton Abbot: David & Charles.

Watson, Garth (1988) *The Civils: The Story of the Institution of Civil Engineers*, London: Thomas Telford.

Webster, N.W. (1970) *Joseph Locke: Railway Revolutionary*, London: George Allen & Unwin.

Wilson, Robert Burdett (ed.) (1972) *Sir Daniel Gooch: Memoirs & Diary*, Newton Abbot: David & Charles.

Architecture

Anderson, V.R. and Fox, G.K. (1985) *Midland Railway Architecture: A Pictorial Record of Midland Railway Stations,* Poole: Oxford Publishing Co.

Anon (1981) *All Stations: A Journey Through 150 Years of Railway History,* London: Thames and Hudson.

Ashley, Peter (2001) *Whistle Stops: Railway Architecture,* London: Everyman Publishers.

Betjeman, John (1972) *London's Historic Railway Stations,* Photographed by John Gay, London: John Murray.

Biddle, Gordon (1973) *Victorian Stations: Railway Stations in England and Wales 1830–1923,* Newton Abbot: David & Charles.

—— (1986) *Great Railway Stations of Britain: Their Architecture, Growth and Development,* Newton Abbot: David and Charles.

—— (2003) *Britain's Historic Railway Buildings: An Oxford Gazetteer of Structures and Sites,* Oxford: Oxford University Press.

Body, Geoffrey (1990) *Railway Stations of Britain: A guide to 75 important centres,* Wellingborough: Patrick Stephens Ltd.

Brindle, Steven (2004) *Paddington Station: Its History and Architecture,* Swindon: English Heritage.

Brodribb, John (1988) *LNER Country Stations,* London: Ian Allen.

Bryan, Tim (1997) *Railway Heritage, Paddington: Great Western Gateway: A portrait of the 'aristocrat' of London's railway termini,* rep. Kettering: Silver Link Publishing Ltd.

Cole, David (1958) Mocatta's stations for the Brighton railway, *Journal of Transport History,* 3(3), 149–57.

Croughton, Godfrey, R.W. Kidner, and Alan Young (1982) *Private and Untimelabled Railway Stations: Halts and Stopping Places,* Tisbury: Oakwood.

Ellaway, K.J. (1994) *The Great British Railway Station: Euston,* Oldham: Irwell Press.

Ellis, Norman (1989) *West Yorkshire Railway Stations* (ed. Peter Tuffrey), Doncaster: Bond Publications.

Fitzgerald, R.S. (1980) *Liverpool Road Station, Manchester: An Historical and Architectural Survey,* Manchester: Manchester University Press for the Royal Commision on Historical Monuments and Greater Manchester Council.

Hawkins, Chris (1990) *The Great British Railway Station: Kings Cross,* Pinner: Irwell Press.

Hoare, John (1979) *Sussex Railway Architecture: An Historical Survey,* Hassocks: The Harvester Press.

Hooper, John (1995) *Manchester London Road: An Illustrated Historical Survey of a Great Provincial Station,* Grasscroft: Challenger Publications.

Hunter, Michael and Thorne, Robert (eds.) (1990) *Change at King's Cross From 1800 to the Present,* London: Historical Publications Ltd.

Jackson, Alan A. (1969) *LondonTermini,* Newton Abbot: David & Charles.

Johnston, Colin and Hume, John R. (1979) *Glasgow Stations,* Newton Abbot: David and Charles.

Leigh, Chris (1981–84) *GWR Country Stations,* 2 vols., Shepperton: Ian Allan.

London Midland & Scottish Railway (1938) *Old Euston: An Account of the Beginning of the London and Birmingham Railway and the Building of Euston Station,* London: Country Life.

Makepeace, Chris (ed.) (n.d.) *Oldest in the World: The Story of Liverpool Road Station Manchester,* rep. Manchester: Liverpool Road Station Society and Manchester Region Industrial Archaeological Society.

Meeks, Carroll L.V. (1957) *The Railway Station: An Architectural History*, London: Architectural Press.

Minett, M.J. (1965) The railway stations of George Townsend Andrews, *Journal of Transport History*, 7(1), 44–53.

Rankin, Stuart (1978/9) *A Huge Palace of Business*, York: British Rail Eastern Region.

Reed, Colin (1992) *Gateway to the West: A History of the Riverside Station Liverpool MD and HB-LNWR*, Potters Bar: London and North Western Railway Society.

Richards, Jeffrey and John M. MacKenzie (1986) *The Railway Station: A Social History*, Oxford: Oxford University Press.

Sheeran, George (1994) *Railway Buildings of West Yorkshire 1812–1920*, Keele: Ryburn.

Simmons, Jack (2003) *St. Pancras Station* (rev. ed. by Robert Thorne), Chichester: Historical Publications.

Thorne, Robert (1978) *Liverpool Street Station*, London: Academy Editions.

Tutton, Michael (1999) *Paddington Station 1833–1854: A Study of the Procurement of Land for, and Construction of, the First London Terminus of the Great Western Railway*, Mold: Railway and Canal Historical Society.

Vaughan, Adrian (1988) *GWR Junction Stations*, Shepperton: Ian Allen.

Design, publicity, and art

Barnicote, John (1972) *Posters: A Concise History*, London: Thames and Hudson.

Beck, Keith and Nigel Harris (1987) *GWR Reflections: A Collection of Photographs from the Hulton Picture Library*, Wadenhoe, Northants: Silver Link.

Bray, Maurice I. (1986) *Railway Picture Postcards*, Ashbourne, Derbyshire: Moorland.

Bury, T.T. (1831) *Coloured Views of the Liverpool and Manchester Railway*, London: R. Ackerman, New ed. with An Historical Introduction by George Ottley, Oldham: Hugh Broadbent, 1976.

Carter, Ernest F. (1979) *Britain's Railway Liveries: Colours, Crests and Linings 1825–1948*, 3rd ed., London: Harold Starke Ltd.

Coghlan, Francis (1970) *The Iron Road Book and Railway Comanion from London to Birmingham, Manchester and Liverpool*, reprint of 1838 ed., London: E&W Books.

Cole, Beverley and Richard Durack (1990) *Happy as a Sand-Boy: Early Railway Posters*, London: HMSO for the National Railway Museum.

—— and Richard Durack (1992) *Railway Posters 1923–1947*, London: Laurence King for the National Railway Museum.

Delgado, Alan (1977) *The Annual Outing and Other Excursions*, London: Allen and Unwin Ltd.

Drake, James (1974) *Drake's Road Book of the Grand Junction Railway (1838)*, reprint, Harington: Moorland.

Dow, George (1973) *Railway Heraldry and Other Insignia*, Newton Abbot: David & Charles.

Ellis, C. Hamilton (1977) *Railway Art*, London: Ash & Grant.

Hammerton, J.A. (ed.) (n.d.) *Mr Punch's Railway Book*, London: The Educational Book Co. Ltd.

Haresnape, Brian (1968) *Design for Steam, 1830–1960*, Shepperton: Ian Allan.

Jordan, Arthur and Jordan, Elisabeth, *Away for the Day: The Railway Excursion in Britain, 1830 to the present day* (1991) Kettering: Silver link Publishing Ltd.

Kennedy, Ian and Treuherz, Julian (2008) *The Railway: Art in the Age of Steam*, New Haven and London: Yale University Press.

Lambert, Anthony J. (1984) *Nineteenth Century Railway History through The Illustrated London News,* Newton Abbot: David and Charles.

Measom, George (1970) *The Official Illustrated Guide to the South-Eastern Railway and its Branches: including the North Kent and Greenwich Lines,* rep. London: E. and W. Books (Publishers) Ltd.

—— (1983) *The Illustrated Guide to the Great Western Railway 1852,* rep. Berkshire: Berkshire County Library and Countryside Books.

Rees, Gareth (1980) *Early Railway Prints: A Social History of the Railways from 1825 to 1850,* Oxford: Phaidon.

Schivelbusch, Wolfgang (1986) *The Railway Journey: The Industrialization of Time and Space in the 19th Century,* new ed. Leamington Spa: Berg.

Sellwood Arthur and Sellwood Mary (1979) *The Victorian Railway Murders,* Newton Abbot: David and Charles.

Shackleton, J.T. (1976) *The Golden Age of the Railway Poster,* Secaucus, New Jersey: Chartwell Books Inc.

Smith, David Norman (1988) *The Railway and Its Passengers: A Social History,* Newton Abbot: David & Charles.

Smullen, Ivor (1968) *Taken for a Ride: A Distressing Account of the Misfortunes and Misbehaviour of the early British Railway Traveller,* London: Herbert Jenkins.

Spence, Jeoffrey (1975) *Victorian & Edwardian Railways from Old Photographs,* London: B.T. Batsford.

Tourist, A. (1980) *The Railway Companion Describing an Excursion along the Liverpool Line,* Manchester: Liverpool Road Station Society.

Wigg, Julia (1996) *Bon Voyage! Travel Posters of the Edwardian Era,* London: HMSO for the Public Record Office.

Wilson, Roger Burdett (1987) *Go Great Western: A History of GWR Publicity,* 2nd ed., revised by Colin Judge, Newton Abbot: David & Charles.

APPENDIX 1

Deposited Plans

Introduction

Deposited plans have been little used by railway historians, although their importance in recording the 'might have beens' of railway history has been widely recognized (Simmons and Biddle). There are several reasons for this neglect.

- There are approximately 8,000 plans, and so it is difficult for the researcher to know where to start. Because the present study has been grounded in economic theory, the information requirements were clearly specified at the outset. It was therefore possible to develop a systematic sequential approach, which indicated which plans should be consulted first.
- The main deposits are distributed around county record offices which, although convenient for local historians, creates a difficulty for those conducting a national study. A substantial budget is required to cover the travel and subsistence involved in a national study.
- Until the 1960s, many holdings of deposited plans were not properly catalogued, and were poorly conserved. Without a catalogue, researchers were obliged to rummage through the storerooms, although, unless they had good local connections, they would usually be barred from consulting the documents altogether.
- It is only since 2000 that the Access to Archives programme has placed many catalogues of plans online, thereby allowing researchers to plan their search strategies in advance of a visit to a record office.
- The plans are often large and unwieldy, and so time-consuming to consult.
- Although the House of Lords Record Library has comprehensive holdings, documents have to be ordered in advance, and it has limited space available.

Despite recent advances in cataloguing, computerization, and conservation, most plans remain little used. This is evident from the state in which the documents are produced, and in some cases from the difficulty experienced by assistants in locating the relevant boxes or shelves. This suggests that it is the overwhelming amount of material which has proved the major deterrent to a scholarly investigation of deposited plans. Most writers who have drawn attention to the importance of the plans have referred mainly to their pleasure of browsing through them. Most systematic work has been confined to cataloguing. For particular counties, such as Northamptonshire, scholars have produced excellent catalogues of plans, while in other cases, such as Buckinghamshire, enthusiasts have produced manuscript notes on them. In other cases, county archivists and their staff have shown considerable enthusiasm for the plans, as in Dorset and Oxfordshire. In Warwickshire, the noted historian C. R. Clinker organized a Workers Educational Association class to catalogue plans; his exercise comes very close to the work carried out for the present study.

Three main items were deposited by railway promoters: a Plan, a Section, and a Book of Reference. In some record offices these are filed together, while in others they are separated. Most record offices only allow a reader to consult one plan at a time, and restrict the number of documents ordered up at any one time to between three and six. This means that where plans have been separated from sections, two items have to be ordered up for every scheme.

Additional items were also deposited in many cases. The most useful is a 1-in. Ordnance Survey map (or its equivalent), showing the route in red ink. A summary of the Bill is sometimes available too, indicating which companies were interested in subscribing to the project, or in working the railway after it was built.

It is hoped that some readers may be interested in investigating deposited plans for themselves. The wide scope of the present study means that only a limited amount of time has been devoted to the study of each plan, and there are almost certainly many interesting features of individual plans which have been overlooked.

Outline History of Legislation Regarding the Deposit of Railway Plans

The use of statutory powers to implement public undertakings has a long history. In the early fourteenth-century there were petitions to the monarch to levy tolls for the construction and maintenance of bridges (there may be even earlier precedents, but the official records do not reveal them). The monarch subsequently devolved the consideration of such petitions to Parliament. A chronology of the major administrative developments, as recorded in the Parliamentary Rolls, is presented in Table A1.1.

On 7 June 1792 Parliament introduced new standing orders governing private Bills involving the compulsory purchase of land. At the time, these Bills mainly concerned projects for draining and improving land, building bridges, and making turnpikes, river navigations, and canals (Riden 2000, on which much of this section is based). The change in standing orders was an attempt to streamline the consideration of private Bills in response to the large number of Bills submitted during the Canal Mania of that year.

Promoters were required to deposit a Plan and a Book of Reference with the clerk of the peace or town clerk of each quarter sessions borough affected by a scheme. In addition, notices had to be published in the London Gazette and local newspapers.

Two Select Committees on private Bill procedure reported in 1837, in response to the first Railway Mania, which occurred that year (for more details see Clifford 1885–7 and Williams 1949). The scale of the deposited Plan was set at no less than 4 in. to the mile, and the Plan was to show the limit of deviation either side of the intended route. The Plan must record distances, give the radii of the sharper curves, and indicate tunnelling and the diversion of roads and footpaths. Analogous stipulations were made regarding the Sections which accompanied the Plan.

By 1851 a comprehensive code had evolved which stipulated (from 1846) that a map of the route on a 1-in. scale Ordnance Survey map should also be included. Water and gas undertakings were included from 1847, street tramways from 1870, electricity networks from 1882, tramroads running on reserved track alongside roads from 1889, and light railways from 1896.

Sources of Confusion in the Interpretation of Deposited Railway Plans

Plans were normally deposited on 30 November of the year before the Bill was to be enacted. While the title page of most early plans gives the year of deposit, many later plans give the year of the parliamentary session instead. This has led to numerous errors in cataloguing: the same plans deposited in different counties may carry different dates in

Table A1.1. The evolution of Parliamentary Acts to authorize investment in infrastructure

Date	Title/reference	Provisions
1301	30 Edward I	The burgesses of Huntingdon are authorized to improve the paving of their streets through a toll on horses and vehicles
1302	30 Edward I	Bridges at Walton-en-le-Dale over the Rivers Derwent and Ribble to be repaired using income from pontage
1391	15 Richard II	A new stone bridge, built at Rochester to replace a wooden structure, is to be maintained by wardens who are to be treated as members of a corporation. Sir Robert Knowles and Sir John Cobham built the new bridge as an act of charity, but do not have the resources to keep it in repair in perpetuity. The people of Kent who were responsible for the upkeep of the original bridge become responsible for the upkeep of the new one.
1421	9 Henry V c. 11	Roads and bridges at Culham, between Abingdon and Dorchester, Oxon, are to be improved in order to prevent obstruction from flooding by the River Thames
1439	18 Henry VI	Kingston-upon-Hull and Plymouth are incorporated as municipalities. Both were important ports that were vulnerable to foreign attack. Plymouth is incorporated by statute; the town is to be fortified with crenelated walls, partly financed by anchorage dues and tolls on imports and exports, levied on foreign vessels.
1442	20 Henry VI	Rebuilding of Turnbrigg bridge over a tributary of the River Humber at Snaith, Yorkshire, is to be financed by tolls on river traffic for the raising of a drawbridge
1541	33 Henry VIII c. 35	Renewal of conduits for the supply of water to Gloucester
1556	8 Elizabeth c. 22	Reclamation of Plumstead Marsh by John Baptista Castilian, groom of the Chamber, and associates
1585	27 Elizabeth c. 10	Leet from Dartmoor to be constructed to feed fresh water to Plymouth (promoted by Sir Francis Drake)
1606	3 James I c. 18	Water from Hertfordshire springs to be brought down a trench to London. Powers transferred to Hugh Middleton, a goldsmith, who established the New River Company for this purpose
1607	4 James I c. 11	First Inclosure Act, for manors, lordships and parishes in Herefordshire, notable for its extreme caution regarding adverse effects on the local community
1607	4 James I c. 13	Early Act for the draining of the Fens, at the Ring of Waldersea and Coldham

(*continued*)

Table A1.1. (Continued)

Date	Title/reference	Provisions
1662	14 Carolus II c. 2	Street paving becomes the responsibility of a municipality rather than individual householders. in response to a rapid growth of housing in London and Westminster, Commissioners are appointed to improve and widen streets, license hackney carriages, and install new sewers
1666	18 and 19 Carolus II c. 8	An Act to regulate the rebuilding of London after the Great Fire
1693	1 George I	'Two Pennies Scot's Act' for Edinburgh authorizes a tax on beer to pay for renewal of water pipes and for harbour improvements at Leith
1695	7 and 8 William III c. 9	Earliest turnpike provision. Improvement of the road from London to Harwich, Essex, to be financed partly by the collection of tolls at gates between Brentwood and Ingatestone
1757	31 George II, c. 22 (Private Act)	First Act authorizing a railway line: the Middleton Railway, at Leeds, is a mineral line dedicated to the use of specific collieries
1762	2 George III, c. 11 (Private Act)	Bridgewater Canal Act passed after long Parliamentary contest with the Mersey and Irwell Navigation, breaking the latter's monopoly of freight traffic between Manchester and Liverpool
1766	6 George III, c. 96, 97	Canal Acts authorize a link between the Rivers Trent, Mersey, and Severn. They are promoted by the Duke of Bridgewater, Josiah Wedgewood, and other landowners and manufacturers
1776	16 George III c. 32	Railways proposed as links between canals. The Trent and Mersey Navigation is authorized to make a railway between Froghall and Caldon, Staffs. Only the use of horses is envisaged
1799	39 George III c. 69	After a major Parliamentary contest the Corporation of London and the West India merchants are jointly authorized to construct the West India Docks in the Isle of Dogs, East London. Further expansion of London Docks follows shortly afterwards
1801	41 George III c. 33	The world's first public railway is authorized. The Surrey Iron Railway is authorized to run from Wandsworth, on the South Bank of the River Thames, to Croydon, South of London, with a branch to Carshalton. It is for general use, on payment of a toll, by carriers providing their own vehicles and horse power. Expected traffic was coal, corn, and general merchandise to the metropolis
1805	45 George III c. 117	The first attempt at a Thames Tunnel is authorized, from Wapping to Rotherhithe. Engineering problems caused the suspension of works, but powers were revived in 1824 and work continued under Marc Brunel, and his son Isambard.

Table A1.1. (Continued)

Date	Title/reference	Provisions
		Opening finally in 1843, it was a commercial failure and was purchased by the East London Railway in 1865. It is now part of the London Underground system
1810	50 George III c. 124	An early attempt at a Severn Tunnel, near Newnham. Seriously under-capitalized, the scheme failed. Traffic congestion induced the Great Western Railway to revive the idea for a tunnel in 1872. Powers were taken to abandon the work in case of engineering difficulties, and came near to being exercised, but the tunnel was finally opened in 1886. Its expense was such that the company was authorized to charge for 12 miles travel even though the route (including the approaches) was only 8 miles long
1810	50 George III c. 163	The Gas Light and Coke Company is formed to make 'inflammable air for the lighting of the streets of the metropolis' and for procuring various by-products from coal. Its powers for building gas works and laying pipes under the streets could only be exercised once £100,000 had been subscribed; no dividend could be paid out of capital; and penalties were incurred if the price of gas lighting exceeded the price of lighting by oil
1823	4 George IV c. 33	Stockton and Darlington Railway Act anticipates the carriage of passengers by railway—but mainly in their own vehicles. Provisions for level crossings indicate that flanges were assumed to be on the rails, rather than on the wheels, as actually constructed
1826	7 George VI c. 49	Liverpool and Manchester Railway Act authorizes the first inter-urban main line, with an option of using steam locomotives, except within the town of Liverpool.
1862	25 and 26 Victoria c. 93	First modern Act for the embankment of the River Thames, between Westminster Bridge and Blackfriars Bridge, under the auspices of the Metropolitan Board of Works (established in 1855)
1863	26 and 27 Victoria c. 45	Programme of new roads in London initiated by the Metropolitan Board of Works, beginning with Queen Victoria Street, linking Blackfriars to Mansion House, including several new streets around Charing Cross
1868	31 and 32 Victoria c. 98, 167	Two tramway schemes are authorized: in Liverpool, and from the Somerset and Dorset Railway at Glastonbury to Street
1871	34 and 35 Victoria c. 121	The London Hydraulic Pressure Company is authorized to supply hydraulic power for cranes, dock gates, machinery, and fire-fighting through a network of under-street pipes

(continued)

Table A1.1. (Continued)

Date	Title/reference	Provisions
1874	37 and 38 Victoria c. 103	The South Eastern and Chatham Railway and the London Chatham and Dover Railway are jointly authorized to spend £20,000 each on trial borings for a Channel Tunnel from near Folkestone to near Calais
1879	42 and 43 Victoria c. 213	First authority for a municipality to provide electric lighting for streets, public buildings, and private premises, conferred separately on Liverpool, Leicester, Darwen, and Blackpool
1884	47 and 48 Victoria c. 199	Birmingham Compressed Air Company is authorized to lay pipes 'for distributing motive power...to manufactories, furnaces and works, and the supply of air for ventilating, refrigerating or blowing furnaces...'

Sources: Clifford (1885–7); Darby (1976); Harrison (2004); Given-Wilson (2005).

the catalogues, although the difference is only one year. It is therefore sometimes difficult to identify from the catalogues alone whether or not two sets of plans are identical. Confusion is particularly likely when an unsuccessful scheme was resubmitted the following year.

A further difficulty arises because some promoters of schemes covering several county boroughs deposited in each county only those parts of their Plan relevant to that county, whereas other promoters deposited their entire Plan in each county. It is therefore possible that two sets of plans in different county record offices with similar titles and dates may differ. If, however, the first set of plans consulted turns out to include details relating to other counties then it may be inferred that the plans deposited elsewhere are identical, whereas if the coverage is only partial, it may be inferred that the plans in other offices concern different parts of the scheme.

From about 1860 onwards the railway system was progressively consolidated through minor projects involving the enlargement of stations, the doubling or quadrupling of track, the elimination of level-crossings, the widening of bridges, and so on. The major companies began to group these minor schemes into composite Bills, but while some companies, such as the London and South Western Railway, typically deposited their entire Plan with each relevant county, other companies, such as a London and North Western Railway, usually deposited only the local part of their Plan with each county, while companies such as the Great Western Railway followed no consistent policy at all. It is therefore sufficient for a researcher to consult the plans of the London and South Western Railway only once, but necessary to study every set of plans deposited by the London and North Western Railway, since each county's records typically relate to different projects.

Classification of Deposited Plans

In most record offices the railway plans are part of a single sequence relating to public undertakings, but in a few cases the railway plans have been separated out. The plans as a whole were classified according to the scheme described in Table 2.1 of Chapter 2. Ambiguities can arise when a railway scheme is combined with other schemes, for example,

Table A1.2. Classification of railway plans

Code	Description
N	New company
NL	New line
XT	Extension of existing line
DV	Deviation in route
MP	Widening or other improvement
ST	New or enlarged station
L	Purchase of additional land not otherwise specified

a railway serves a harbour or canal basin, or the scheme involves the building of new roads, or the diversion of existing ones. All schemes involving any significant length of railway were allocated to the railway category.

While some plans relate to wholly new undertakings, other plans relate to refinements of these undertakings. To distinguish major original proposals from minor incremental ones, all railway plans were classified in the manner described in Table A1.2. The availability of plans is summarized in Table A1.3.

Table A1.3. Deposited plans of railway schemes in county and city record offices in England and Wales, 1792–1914

County	Document reference	Publications/ comments	Percentage sampled
Anglesey	Railways: WCD 29–50		0
Bedfordshire	Railways: PDR/1/ 1–30/13	Cockman (1974), Blakey (1983)	20
Berkshire	All schemes: Q/ Rum/1–273	Berkshire Record Office, *Sources for Railway History*, pamphlet, n.d.	100
Breconshire	Powis Archives, Llandrindod Wells All schemes: B/Q/ RP/1–200		10
Buckinghamshire	Railways: P/uC 1–225	Cockman (1971, 1972)	100
Caernarvonshire	Gwynedd Arch- ives, Caernarfon Office, Railways: Plans R/1–139		0
Cambridgeshire	Cambridge Office All schemes: Q/ Rum/1–152		10
Cardiganshire	Few survive: see Ceredigion Arch- ives, Aberystwyth CC/C/s; DB/5; ACC451		0

(*continued*)

Table A1.3. (Continued)

County	Document reference	Publications/comments	Percentage sampled
Carmarthenshire	Railways: RW1–224		
Cheshire	All schemes: QDP/1–866		10
Cleveland	Teeside Archives, Middlesbrough Railways: U/CR/11–29		100
Cornwall	Railways: QSPDR/1/1–27/3	Fairclough (1970)	10
Cumberland	Cumbria Record Office, Carlisle, Railways: QRZ/1–174		20
Denbighshire	Railways: QSD/DR/1–312	Clwyd Record Office (1991)	10
Derbyshire	Railways: Q/RP2/1–309		10
Devon	Exeter Office All schemes: QS/DP/1–674		10
Dorset	Railways: QDP (M):R3/1–126	Dorset Archives Service (1997), Lucking (1968, 1982)	30
Durham	All schemes: Q/D/P/1–524		100
East Riding of Yorkshire	Beverley Office All schemes: QDP/1–336		10
East Sussex	Lewes Office All schemes: QDP/1–735	Davey (2003)	10
Essex	All schemes: Q/RUM2/1–358		10
Flintshire	Railways: QS/DR/1–253		10
Glamorganshire	All schemes: Q/D/P/1–835		10
Gloucestershire	All schemes: Q/Rum/1–728		10
Hampshire (excluding Isle of Wight)	All schemes: DP/1–698		100
Herefordshire	Railways: Q/RW/R1-R93; Q/RW/T1-T15; AL88/1–84		100
Hertfordshire	Railways R/1–744		10
Huntingdonshire	Cambridgeshire Record Office, Huntingdon Railways: RP/1–133		10

Table A1.3. (Continued)

County	Document reference	Publications/comments	Percentage sampled
Kent	Centre for Kentish Studies, Maidstone All schemes: Q/R/Um/82–1189		10
Lancashire	Railways PDR/1–244		10
Leicestershire	Railways: QS/73/1–371		10
Lincolnshire	Kesteven, Railways: KP/6/1–240 Lindsey, All schemes: Lind/Dep/Plans/1/1–292	Sources relating to Railways at Lincolnshire Archives (n.d.)	10
Merionethshire	Gwynedd Archives, Dolgellau Office Railways: Z/CD/40–166		0
Middlesex	London Metropolitan Archive All schemes: MR/UP/1–?; MR/UP/NS/1–368		70
Monmouthshire	Welsh Archives Council, Gwent Office		10
Montgomeryshire	Powys Archives, Llandrindod Wells Railways: M/Q/RP/1–94	Microfilmed	0
Norfolk	All schemes: C/Scf1/1–515		50
Northamptonshire	Main series All schemes: QS/1–279	Riden (2000)	50
North Riding of Yorkshire	Northallerton Office All schemes: QDP/1–351	Microfilmed	50
Northumberland	All schemes: QRUP/1–265		10
Nottinghamshire	Railways: DP/R/1–240	Illustrated analytical catalogue	10
Oxfordshire	Railways: PD2/1–145	Oxfordshire County Council (1983)	100
Pembrokeshire	All schemes: QRZ/6–278		10
Radnorshire	Powys Archives, Llandrindod Wells R/QS/3591–3667	Microfilmed	0
Shropshire	All schemes: DP302–714		10

(continued)

Table A1.3. (Continued)

County	Document reference	Publications/comments	Percentage sampled
Somerset	All schemes: Q/RUp/1–593		10
Staffordshire	Stafford Office All schemes: Q/Rum/		10
Suffolk	Railways: B/150/2/5.1–239		10
Surrey	All schemes: QS6/8/1–1489		50
Warwickshire	All schemes: QS/111/1–598	Clinker (1954)	100
West Riding of Yorkshire	Wakefield office Railways: QE/20/1/1810/1–1914/19		20
Westmoreland	Cumbria Record Office, Kendal All schemes: WQ/R/DP/1–92		100
West Sussex	Chichester office All schemes: QDP/W/1–248, 352	Publication	100
Wiltshire	All schemes: A1/371/1MS-170MS	Set of detailed maps of railway projects in Wiltshire	20
Worcestershire	All schemes: 161/1–365; 209.161/366–508		100
City	**Document reference**	**Publications/comments**	
Bristol	All schemes: 07790/1–96		100
Hull	All schemes: CQP/1–114		100
London	The City of London and its environs are covered by Middlesex and Westminster plans, which are consolidated in the Middlesex series at the London Metropolitan Archive—see above		80
Newcastle	Tyne and Wear Archives All schemes: D/NCP/4/1–213		100

Note: The following major cities hold no significant collections of deposited plans of railways: Birmingham, Leeds, Liverpool, and Manchester.

Parliamentary Procedure for Private Bills
and the Evolution of Standing Orders

A debate on a private bill is conducted under the same rules of order as regulate any other debate, but the Standing Orders (SOs) governing the progress of a private bill through Parliament are very different from those of a public bill.

> The mysteries of private bill legislation are confined to the committee rooms, and even more, in the House of Commons, to the Private Bill office, the rooms of the Chairman of Ways and Means, the Deputy Chairman and the Speakers' Counsel, to the chambers of counsel who practice at the parliamentary Bar and to the offices of the parliamentary agents. (Williams 1948, p. 1)

SOs for private bills have evolved from the procedures governing the consideration of petitions to the monarch, as explained above. The key steps in this evolution are set out in Table A1.4. Many changes in SOs were made in response to the growth in the number of railway bills during the nineteenth century, although many of the SOs relating to railways were swept away as obsolete in a radical review of 1945. Railway schemes are today dealt with differently: either through standard planning procedures or hybrid bills. As a result, the basic role of SOs is to provide 'transparency' in the process by which private individuals and companies acquire from the state powers over others (notably for compulsory purchase). Promoters of a bill must demonstrate before an examiner that they have informed all those likely to be adversely affected by their proposal, and indicate whether or not they have obtained their assent to the proposal. They must submit their proposal in sufficient time for Parliament to be able to give it due consideration. They must also supply sufficient collateral information, in the form of plans, estimates of cost, etc. to allow Parliament to exercise proper judgement. Where a bill does not comply with these requirements, discretion can sometimes be exercised if the promoters agree to amend their proposal. Precedent is normally an important consideration where discretion is allowed.

Table A1.4. Key dates in the evolution of Standing Orders governing the deposit of plans relating to Bills for railways and other infrastructure projects

Date	Event
1685	Private bills can be brought in only by first making a petition. (The petition will normally identify a problem which can only be resolved by the petitioners invoking special powers.)
1699	Early rules for the passage of private bills through Parliament are made, including a three-day interval between successive readings of a bill (presumably to prevent a bill from being rushed through before opponents were aware of it)
1716	Bills for highways, and the funding of works through tolls or duties, are to be examined before being considered by the House of Commons
1752	Committees are to ensure that all future turnpike Acts require sureties from treasurers, and that commissioners involved in active management of turnpikes have adequate personal wealth
1774	The House of Commons appoints a Committee which leads to the formulation of SOs for Bills relating to turnpike roads, canals, and river navigations, and to inclosing, draining, or improving lands, fens or commons. The SOs related to notices, consents, estimates of expense, and payments of the sums subscribed.

(continued)

Table A1.4. (Continued)

Date	Event
1789	In response to the increasing number of canal Bills, new SOs are made governing the notice that promoters must give to Quarter Sessions.
1791	SOs are made relating to notices of urban improvement schemes
1792	At the beginning of the Canal Mania, promoters are required to publish notices in the *London Gazette* and local newspapers, listing the parishes through which a canal passes. A map or plan, together with a Book of Reference, is to be deposited on or before 30 November with the Clerk of the Peace or Town Clerk of an English borough, or the Principal Sheriff Clerk in Scotland.
1794	Further measures regarding canals, aqueducts and river navigations require, *inter alia*, that a duplicate Plan and Book of Reference is to be deposited with the House of Commons.
1799	Most of the 1794 provisions regarding canals are extended to 'railways or dram roads'
1806–7	Revised SOs governing the deposit of maps and plans, and applications to owners of land, are introduced with respect to turnpike roads
1810–11	A Select Committee is appointed, which recommends the establishment of a Private Bill Office. The SOs are revised and extended, so that Sections as well as plans have to be deposited. Duplicates of Plans, Sections, Books of Reference, and other requisite documents must be deposited both locally and nationally.
1812–14	The scale of Plans is to be in the range 3–5 in. to the mile, instead of 1 in. to the mile as previously. Extracts of Plans must be submitted to Parish officials, detailing the land and buildings in the Parish that will be affected by the project.
1836–7	Two Select Committees revise SOs, producing one set for all private Bills and another specifically for railway Bills. The scale is to be not less than 4 in. to the mile. The Plan must show all land to be taken, together with the limits of permitted deviation from the proposed route. Enlargements are required under certain circumstances. One of the duplicate copies deposited locally is to be kept sealed until sent for by either House of Parliament. The date of deposit was moved forward to 1 March.
1842	The date of deposit is put back to the original date of 30 November.
1845	A set of duplicate Plans is to be deposited with the Board of Trade.
1846	A 1-in. map (Ordnance Survey map, where available) is to be deposited along with the detailed Plans, to indicate the general orientation of the route.
1847	SOs are extended to cover water and gas undertakings. The times of day at which deposits can be reduced slightly.
1851	A comprehensive set of SOs is published which effectively completes the procedural system.
1865	At the suggestion of the civil engineer T. E. Harrison, Plans and Sections must show existing lines with which a junction is made for 800 yards to either side of the junction.
1870	Extension of SOs to street tramways.
1884	Duplicate tramway Plans must also be deposited with the Board of Trade.
1889	Extension of SOs to tramways running on reserved tracks.
1896	Extension to railways promoted under the Light Railways Act, 1896.
1900	Plans relating to electricity schemes must be deposited with the Board of Trade.

Sources: Biddle (1990), Bond (1971), Clifford (1885–7), and Williams (1948–49). The format is adapted from Riden (2000), who summarizes the above sources, and gives additional details.

Parliament has an obligation to consider bills carefully. It is important to allocate each bill to an appropriate committee whose members are impartial (i.e. have no vested interest in the outcome). The committee must be aware of general requirements—for example, regarding level crossings, bridges, and road diversions that are involved in the construction of a railway—and ensure that bills comply with them. General issues of Parliamentary process must also be addressed, concerning the interaction between committees and the chambers (how the recommendations of committees are presented) and the interaction between the chambers themselves (whether a bill commences in the Commons and the Lords, and how it moves between the two). Both the House of Commons and the House of Lords must read a bill three times before it can become law, as with any other piece of legislation. SOs are broadly similar in the Commons and the Lords, and it is generally agreed that a bill's chances of success do not materially depend on which House it is introduced to first. In each session roughly equal numbers of bills are allocated to each House.

Bills that are unopposed are given an easier passage through Parliament than opposed ones. SOs regulate both, but address in particular detail the presentation of evidence in connection with opposed bills. This includes resolving issues of *locus standi*—which parties have sufficient interest in a bill to have a right to be heard, and which do not. Opposed bills may become 'unopposed' if the promoters succeed in buying off opposition early in the Parliamentary process, and thereby expedite their progress.

The first reading of a bill is a formality, but the second reading can trigger a debate if a member of the House raises an objection. If an objector successfully moves a motion to delay the bill then it is effectively lost.

The main examination of a bill takes place in a committee which sits between the second and third readings of the bill. The committee first considers the preamble to the bill, which sets out the benefits of the project and makes the general case for it. If the preamble is proved, the committee proceeds to consider individual clauses and to propose changes. If the changes are radical they may damage the bill so much that the promoters decide to withdraw it. A bill that raises wider issues of public policy may be referred to a select committee—in some cases a joint committee of both Houses—during its second reading. The committee will resolve each issue where members disagree with a vote. Bills which survive the committee stage are read a third time (in their modified form) and, if not delayed by a motion of the House, proceed to the other House, where the procedure is repeated all over again. Once the third reading has been completed successfully in the other House, the bill is ready to receive the Royal Assent. If the other House amends the bill then the originating House will consider the amendments, although disagreements between the two Houses are rare where private bills are concerned. The resultant Act (classified as 'Local and Personal') takes effect from the date of assent.

While SOs have the force of public law, the practice of advocacy in committee rests largely on common practice within the legal profession. Williams (1948, p. 10) quotes Sir Cecil Carr: 'Where two or three lawyers are gathered together, they will introduce their accustomed procedure, the opening speech, the examination in chief, cross-examination and re-examination of witnesses, and the occasional protests that something is not evidence...'. Some criticisms of Parliamentary procedure on private bills focus more upon the slowness and expense of the legal proceedings rather than the system of SOs within which the practice is embedded. However, the fact that bills are considered separately and sequentially by the two Houses adds to both the cost and the time required for the procedure, as does the practice of having three readings as well as a committee of investigation in each House. Furthermore, the framing of some of the SOs creates plenty of opportunity for strategic behaviour by promoters and their opponents, and to this extent the SOs encourage game-playing by counsel appearing before a committee.

Extracting Information from the Deposited Plans, Illustrated with Case Studies

The information extracted from the deposited plans for the purposes of this study is summarized in Table A1.5. The easiest way to describe how information is extracted from the plans is by means of case studies, and so three case studies, of increasing degrees of complexity, are presented below.

The main information was extracted from the Plans. Books of Reference were not

Table A1.5. Principal information that can be recorded from deposited plans

Item	Source	Comment
Name of project	Plan, Sections, and Book of Reference	The same project may have different names on different documents, and changes of name were common when plans were resubmitted in a following year
Name of engineer	Plan and Sections	Many projects had several engineers. Very occasionally the address of the engineer's practice is given
Name of solicitor	Book of Reference; occasionally the Plan also	There is often a London solicitor and one or more local solicitors. The solicitors are often partnerships; their addresses are usually given.
Name of Parliamentary Agent	Book of Reference	Not always given
Date of submission	Plan, and sometimes the Sections and Book of Reference	Usually the last day of November, but other dates can also be found (in particular, the last day of February).
Reference	Catalogue, and tag on documents	Since deposits were made in all counties through which a railway passed, most schemes have multiple references
Mileage	Sections, and usually plans too	Many schemes consist of multiple lines connected together, so there may be several mileages to record. Mileage on the plan is usually given at the end of each section of line. See the text for a fuller discussion of this issue.
Maximum gradient (i.e. steepest section of route)	Sections only	To determine the maximum gradient it is necessary that the sections are complete. In practice the sections are often less complete than the plans.
Length of tunnels	Sections, and sometimes Plan	In a few cases lengths are not given where tunnels are indicated, and so only the number of tunnels can be recorded
Number of viaducts	Sections	It is often difficult to distinguish between a large bridge and a viaduct. It is, however, possible to distinguish between a really high viaduct and the 'arches' often used in urban areas.

Table A1.5. (Continued)

Item	Source	Comment
Route: parishes	Plan and Books of Reference (occasionally Sections too)	Because some country parishes are so large, the parish provides little information about the exact route. Some catalogues of deposited plans already record parish information extracted from the plans.
Route: identifying points (large houses, farms, woods, hamlets, etc.)	Plan (*plus* the OS map, where available)	This information is the most useful for recording in written form the route of the railway. Some plans name key properties, but many do not. The precise properties through which the line would pass can be identified by comparing the plans with the Book of Reference, but this is a lengthy process. Where the plans do not name properties, the simplest way of recording the route is from the OS map. A magnifying glass is very useful for this purpose, since the print on early OS maps is very small.
Route: layout of junctions	Plan	The direction in which the lines face at a junction can usually be discerned from the plans, although some early plans show lines meeting at right-angles—possibly because the promoters envisaged exchanging traffic with the aid of turntables.

systematically consulted, although where they were supplied together with the Plan, information on the solicitors and Parliamentary Agents was extracted. For a detailed discussion of how to extract and summarize information on landownership from a Book of Reference see Casson, J. (2007)

The first case study (described in Table A1.6) relates to the proposed Cleveland Extension Mineral Railway, which connects the seaside town of Saltburn with the existing Esk Valley line to Grosmont and Whitby (see Figure A1.1). It is a fairly simple local scheme. It is a minor variation of an unsuccessful scheme of a previous year, revised so that the new line joins the existing Esk Valley line east of the original planned junction. It was never built, although a connection serving a similar purpose was later constructed on a different alignment.

The second project (described in Table A1.7) relates to a typical scheme of the Second Railway Mania of 1863–6: the Bedford Northampton and Leamington Railway. It involves an east–west cross-country link. It was designed as a two-part scheme, with an eastern and western section linked by a portion of the Daventry Railway, which had already been authorized (see Figure A1.2). It was never built, although a line from Bedford to Northampton was subsequently constructed. The Daventry Railway was extended to Leamington. An east–west link from Bedfordshire to Warwickshire was eventually completed by

Table A1.6. Case study 1: Cleveland Extension Mineral Railway

Date of deposit; Reference	1872; North Riding QDP/184
Title	Cleveland Extension Mineral Railway
Engineer	R. Francis Reed
Solicitor	James B. Batten, 32, Great George Street, Westminster
Parliamentary agent	Wyatt, Hoskins and Hooker, 28, Parliament Street, Westminster
Length; Ruling gradient	11 miles 1 furlongs; 1/40
Engineering features	Tunnel 343 yards; Viaduct
Route	East Pasture, Skelton, junction with the North Eastern Railway (NER) Saltburn Extension Railway from Saltburn to Skinningrove, facing North East—cross NER, Cleveland Branch, from Morton Grange to Skinningrove, with trailing spur from West–South Lane House–Liverton Moor–Lealholm Hall–Oak Bridge Holm, near Galisdale Iron Works, junction with NER North Yorkshire and Cleveland Branch [the Esk Valley line] north-west of Glaisdale station, facing south-east

the East and West Junction Railway, but it did not start at Bedford and did not run through Northampton, and was not a financial success.

The third project (described in Table A1.8) is an ambitious scheme designed to develop a new residential district and improve the flow of traffic on the approaches to London: the London Chatham and Dover Railway Metropolitan Extensions. The main line from

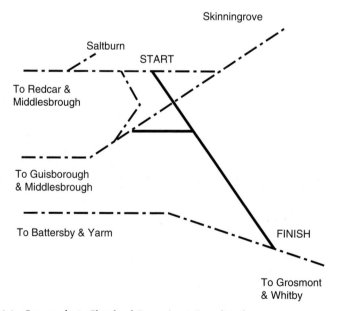

Figure A1.1. Case study 1: Cleveland Extension Mineral Railway

Table A1.7. Case study 2: Bedford Northampton and Leamington Railway

Date of deposit; Reference	1864; Buckinghamshire P/uC 10
Title	Bedford Northampton and Leamington Railway
Engineer	Sir Charles Fox and Son
Solicitor	Druce and Co., 53, Victoria Street, Westminster
	Durnford & Co., 39, Parliament Street, Westminster
Parliamentary agent	Not specified
Length; Ruling gradient	Route 1: 27 miles 3 furlongs; 1/90
	Route 2: 18 miles 0 furlongs; 1/90
Engineering features	Route 1: Viaduct
	Route 2: None
Route	Route 1: *Bedford to near Northampton.* Bedford, terminus due west of Midland Railway (MR) station—trailing junction with spur to MR line from Leicester to Hitchin, north of station, facing south–Olney–Hardingstone–cross Northampton and Peterborough Railway with spur to south-west–Northampton, All Saints, triangular junction with short spur to terminus to north–Harpole Mill–Flore Mill, cross London and North Western Railway (LNWR) main line from London to Rugby—Dodford, junction with authorized line of Daventry Railway, trailing in from junction with LNWR main line to south-east, facing west to Daventry.
	Route 2. *Daventry to Leamington.* Daventry, junction with authorized Daventry Railway, south-east of its proposed terminus, facing east–Braunston–Southam–Radford Semele, run close to and south of Rugby and Leamington Railway–T-junction with spurs to Rugby and Leamington Railway, east of LNWR station, facing north-west, and to Great Western Railway (GWR) line from Banbury to Leamington, east of GWR station, facing west.

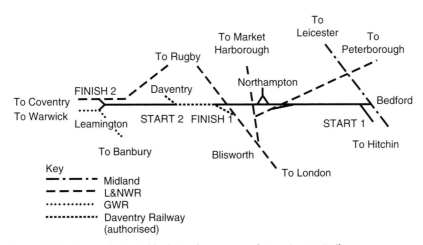

Figure A1.2. Case study 2: Bedford Northampton and Leamington Railway

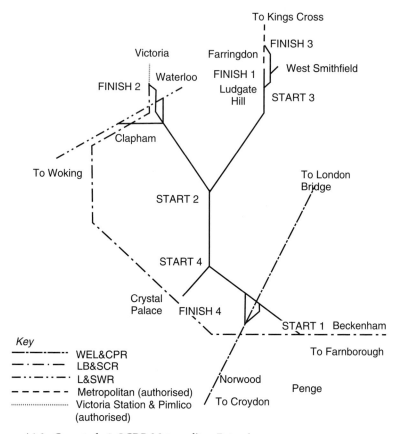

Figure A1.3. Case study 3: LCDR Metropolitan Extensions

Beckenham to Ludgate Hill (Route 1), and Victoria branch (Route 2), were both built after a major Parliamentary contest. A variant of the Metropolitan branch (Route 3) was built later by the Metropolitan Railway. Crystal Palace (Route 4) was eventually served by a longer branch from Nunhead.

Table A1.8. Case study 3: LCDR Metropolitan Extensions

Date of deposit; Reference	1859; Middlesex MR/UP 550
Title	London Chatham and Dover Railway: Metropolitan Extensions
Engineer	Joseph Cubitt, Frederick T. Turner
Solicitor	Freshfields and Newman
Parliamentary agent	Not specified
Length; ruling gradient	Route 1: 8 miles 5 furlongs; 1/101
	Route 2: 2 miles 6 furlongs; 1/60
	Route 3: 0 miles 2 furlongs; 1/40
	Route 4: 1 mile 0 furlong; 1/20
Engineering features	Route 1: Tunnel 1,600 yards
	Route 2: Viaducts
	Route 3: Viaducts
	Route 4: None
Route	Route 1: *Main line from Penge to Ludgate Hill* [Railways 1 and 2]. NE of Penge station, Beckenham, junction with West End of London and Crystal Palace Railway (WELCPR), Extension to Farnborough, Kent, facing East to Beckenham [Junction] station—cross London Brighton and South Coast Railway (LBSCR) main line from London Bridge to Croydon, with two trailing spurs forming a flying junction under the main line (with the western spur partly under an existing flyover junction), facing south–Alleyns Head Inn, Camberwell, trailing junction with branch to Crystal Palace (Route 4) from south-west–Half Moon Public House, Herne Hill, Camberwell, junction with Victoria branch (Route 2) to north-west–Coldharbour Lane, Denmark Hill, Lambeth, trailing junction with spur to Victoria Branch (third side of triangular junction, 6 furlongs long) from east–run west of Camberwell Road and Walworth Road to Elephant and Castle—Gravel Lane, Southwark–cross River Thames adjacent to east side of Blackfriars Bridge–Ludgate Hill, junction with Metropolitan Branch (Route 3) to north-west–Terminus at Bear Alley, Farringdon [near the present City Thameslink station]
	Route 2: *Victoria Branch.* [Railway 3] Half Moon Public House, Herne Hill, junction with main line (Route 1) facing south–Manor Rise, Stockwell, trailing junction with spur from main line facing East–Stewarts Lane, Clapham, cross London and South Western Railway main line from Waterloo to Woking, with spurs to north-east and south-west—run parallel and to east of WELCPR line from Crystal Palace to Battersea—junction with Victoria Station and Pimlico Railway at the north end of the WELCPR station at Victoria Road, Battersea, facing north to Victoria station.
	Route 3: *Metropolitan Branch*: Ludgate Hill, junction with main line (Route 1), facing south–Skinner Street, Holborn, junction with short spur (1 furlong) to terminus at West Smithfield to east— junction with authorized Metropolitan Railway from Farringdon to Kings Cross, facing north
	Route 4: *Crystal Palace Branch* (Route 4): Alleyns Head Inn, Camberwell, junction with main line (Route 1), facing north–Crystal Palace, terminus to north-east of the Palace [the WELCPR station is on the other side of the Palace, to the south-west]

Notes on the Local and Personal Acts tabulated in Chapter 2

The table was compiled by allocating every Local and Personal Act to 1 of 16 categories. The classification was developed using a pilot exercise which examined 1 year in every 10 throughout the period, beginning with 1800. This classification is broadly consistent with the classification used since 1870 for the official Annual Index to the Local and Personal Acts. There are differences of detail, however, because of the objectives of the exercise are different in the two cases. Furthermore, the official classification does not deal adequately with projects such as turnpike roads, which had become obsolete by 1870.

It would have been possible to use an even finer classification of projects involving extra categories, but the number in each category would on average have been much smaller and the influence of random variations correspondingly greater.

The object of the table is to measure the intensity of entrepreneurial activity in the promotion of different kinds of major infrastructure project. In the context of railways, the objective is to generate a summary measure of railway entrepreneurship which can be compared with entrepreneurship in other areas of activity. Unlike the official Index, all Acts promoted by railway companies are therefore ascribed to railways, even though they may involve allied activities such as steamship services or construction of quays. It seemed somewhat artificial to separate out strategically important railway projects promoted by railway companies just because they did not involve the laying of rails.

Many Acts naturally fall into one particular category, but some do not. Many tramway schemes, for example, are linked to the extension of borough boundaries. The focus on infrastructure meant that in such cases the infrastructure component was given precedence over the administrative aspect, and such schemes were reported solely as tramway schemes. Only if several different types of infrastructure were involved would the schemes be classified as town improvement instead. If the tramway schemes were part of a larger plan to pave the streets and improve their lighting, then the Act would be classified as 'town improvement' instead.

In some cases an Act clearly specifies two or more separate fields; for example, a Confirmation of Gas and Water Orders. In such cases the convention was adopted that only the first-named field was recorded. Contrary to the Official index, no attempt was made to report the same Act under different headings in order to reflect the diversity of activities involved. A major advantage of avoiding the duplication of entries, and consequent double-counting of Acts, is that the sum of the number of Acts in each category in any year is always equal to the total number of Acts passed in that year.

One way of fudging this issue is to place such ambiguous cases into the 'Other' category. However, a special effort was made to keep this residual category as small as possible. The category is more heterogeneous than the others, as it contains a mixture of Acts which have little to do with major infrastructure schemes. It includes Acts that deal with legal issues or disputes relating to financial institutions, manufacturing enterprises and charities; to lotteries and fisheries; and also includes general local government measures that deal with several different counties or towns.

All Local and Personal Acts are included in the table. It would have been possible to exclude certain types of Act as either irrelevant or misleading. Thus railway Acts are included even if they involve no new construction; for example, they authorize a merger, or a deviation in a previously authorized line. Acts for the abandonment of railway schemes are also included, even though they record the failure of a scheme. These Acts are indicative of measures taken to manage risks in the railway industry. However, where railway purchases of canals are concerned, the schemes are imputed to the canal sector on the grounds that they are more significant as an exit strategy for canal proprietors than as an entry strategy for railway promoters.

A consequence of this approach is that as the stock of railway schemes accumulates, a flow of derivative projects develops, concerned with amendments to or extensions of existing schemes. This means, for example, that the statistics probably overstate the level of entrepreneurial activity in the years following a boom, as Acts will continue to be passed in the absence of any proposals for new construction purely to deal with the problems arising from over-optimistic expectations at the time of the boom.

In general, it was deemed prudent to include all projects in the database unconditionally, rather than to vet the projects for suitability beforehand; this means that issues of interpretation arise in the context of the examination of unexplained residual variation in the data, rather than through the screening of the data at the outset.

It would have been possible to disaggregate the statistics in the geographical dimension, by reporting separate counts for England, Wales, Scotland, and Ireland. This has been carried out as a separate exercise, however, as it results in very small numbers for certain types of project in certain countries—for example, tramway projects in Wales and Ireland. The patterns are nevertheless instructive: for example, in Wales and Ireland long-distance railway projects got off to a much slower start than in England and Scotland. Overseas railway projects are also included in the statistics, but their numbers are not large. The projects enter the dataset mainly because they involved financial problems which Parliament was called upon to resolve.

Despite best intentions, it is unavoidable that over a period of 120 years the nature of the projects in any category will change to some degree. Underground railways, for example, became increasingly common after 1860; most trams were horse-drawn prior to 1890, but thereafter electric traction became more common; while until 1830 a road scheme normally involved the construction of a turnpike, but from 1910 onwards it was more likely to involve a 'rail-less traction' scheme—that is, a trolleybus.

As a given type of project matures, so its promotion becomes more routine. In addition, minor projects for extension and modification of existing schemes proliferate. As a result, there are administrative advantages which group several incremental minor schemes into a single Act (although if one scheme is particularly controversial, the promoters may seek a separate Act in order to prevent problems in Parliament delaying the more straightfor-ward schemes). Thus by the 1890s most leading railway companies grouped all their minor schemes for enlarging stations, diverting footpaths, and replacing level crossings into a single comprehensive annual Act. This does not seriously distort the data, however, because the entrepreneurial content of all these tiny schemes is probably equivalent to one large scheme of the kind that the company promoted in earlier years.

The routinization of project promotion gathered momentum from the 1860s onwards. For certain types of project, administrative Orders replaced Acts, and Acts were used simply to confirm the legality of the Orders. The framework was set, and precedents created, by the General Pier and Harbours Act, 1861, the Elementary Education Act, 1870, the Tramways Act, 1870, and the Public Health Act, 1875.

For some categories of project, the use of these procedures may have produced misleading statistical results. For example, by the time that electricity schemes got underway in the 1890s, the promotion of local utilities had been streamlined. In addition, many local authorities promoted such schemes as municipal enterprises. Thus right from the outset, several Orders for electricity schemes in different towns and cities were often authorized using a single Act. Thus the data may understate the extent to which electricity schemes competed with gas schemes towards the end of the period. Tramway schemes were also grouped in a similar way, but not to the same extent. Nevertheless, it is quite possible that the data also understate the extent to which tramway projects competed against railway projects at this time.

It should be emphasized that a significant proportion of the Acts described here were never implemented in full. There could be difficulties raising the capital, and the scheme might have to be scaled back to fit the funds available. In some cases a scheme would take so long to implement that a further Act would have to be obtained to extend the time allowed for the compulsory purchase of land. The Acts do not, therefore, indicate the actual amount of investment undertaken, but only the intentions of the promoters.

It is also important to emphasize that the data relate to the number of schemes and not to their value. The nominal value of each scheme, as visualized by the promoters, can be determined from the financial provisions of the Act. Where capital reconstructions are involved, however, the real as opposed to the nominal value of the scheme can only be assessed from a knowledge of the share price. Thus valuing all the projects in the dataset is a formidable task which has not been attempted here. The main justification for concentrating on the number rather than the value of the projects is that the cost of promotion to the entrepreneur, in terms of the commitment of time, is largely independent on the value of the scheme, so that the number of projects promoted, rather than their nominal value, is the most appropriate measure of the intensity of entrepreneurial activity.

Steiner Geometry

The Steiner problem and its solution are not so well known as might be expected. There are a number of versions of the problem; this appendix is concerned only with the simplest version of the problem in which three points in an ordinary plane are to be connected up at minimum total distance, and a hub, if required, can be located anywhere in the plane. The problem can be analysed using a variety of mathematical methods: the approach here is geometrical—reflecting the mathematical origins of the problem in the eighteenth century.

One of the clearest and most popular expositions of the subject is Hildebrandt and Tromba (1996); more advanced treatments can be found in Hwang, Richards, and Winter (1992), Ivanov and Tuzhilin (1994), and Promel and Steger (1992).

The solution presented below is analogous to the geometrical illustrations used in economics to illustrate trade-offs. In the present case the trade-off involves reducing the distance between two points without increasing too much the distance to the third point.

Consider three points, A, B, and C, which are to be connected at shortest total distance (see Figure A3.1). A key question is whether any two points, say A and B, will be connected through the third point, C, or through a separate specialized hub, H. The problem is trivial if the three points lie on the same straight line. It is therefore assumed that they do not, in which case they form the vertices of a triangle ABC instead. The sides of the triangle represent straight-line connections between the three points.

If the triangle ABC contains an angle greater than or equal to 120 degrees at one of its vertices then overall distance is minimized when the vertex at which that angle is found is the intermediate point on the route between the other two locations. Otherwise overall distance is minimized by using a specialized hub, H, located in the interior of the triangle. When the specialized hub is optimally located, the three routes converging on it meet each other at angles of 120 degrees. This result can be used to identify the precise location of the hub. The logic of the situation can be explored by either algebraic or purely geometric means.

The proof employs the following four geometrical properties:

1. Points on the circumference of a circle are equidistant from its centre.
2. Points on the perimeter of an ellipse are equidistant from the focal points of the ellipse, in the sense that the sum of the distances from a given point, P, on the perimeter to each of the two focal points is the same for every point P. This means, for example, that an ellipse with focal points at A and B maps out all points which have the same combined distance to A and to B.
3. A tangent to a circle at any given point, P, meets the radius from the centre to P at a right-angle.
4. A tangent to an ellipse at any given point, P, makes the same angle with each of the lines joining P to the focal points. In other words, for any point P, a line to P from one of the focal points is reflected in the perimeter back to the other focal point with an angle of incidence at P that is equal to the angle of reflection.

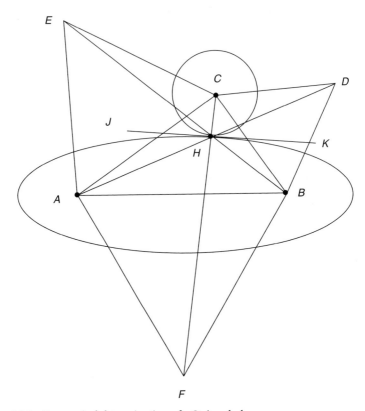

Figure A3.1. Geometrical determination of a Steiner hub

Suppose to begin with that all the angles in *ABC* are less than 120 degrees. If a specialized hub *H* minimizes the total route distance between *A*, *B*, and *C* then, for any given distances from *A* to *H* and *B* to *H*, the distance from *C* to *H* must be a minimum. Similarly, for any given distances from *B* to *H* and *C* to *H*, the distance from *A* to *H* must be a minimum, and for any given distances from *A* to *H* and *C* to *H* the distance from *B* to *H* must be a minimum.

Consider now the first of these requirements. For any given distances from *A* to *H* and *B* to *H*, the distance from *C* to *H* is a minimum if and only if the circumference of a circle centred at *C*, and passing through *H*, is tangent at *H* to an ellipse with focal points at *A* and *B*. The proof relies on propositions 1 and 2 above. If, instead of being tangent to each other, the circle and ellipse intersected at *H*, then it would be possible to achieve a shorter connection between *A*, *B*, and *C* by moving *H* along the circle to a point of tangency with another (smaller) ellipse or, conversely, moving *H* along the ellipse to a point of tangency with another (smaller) circle. Thus tangency is a necessary condition for optimality.

Furthermore, from properties 3 and 4 we can deduce that the line from *C* to *H* makes equal angles with the lines from *A* to *H* and from *B* to *H*. The line from *C*, being the radius of a circle, makes an angle of 90 degrees with the tangent *JK* at *H*, while because of the 'reflection' property of an ellipse, the lines from A and B make equal angles with this same tangent. Thus the angle between the lines from A and C is equal to 90 degrees plus the angle between the tangent and line from A, while the angle between the lines from B and C is equal to 90 degrees plus the angle between the tangent and the line from B, which is the same as the angle between the tangent and the line from A. Hence the angles at H between A and C and B and C are the same.

Similar reasoning shows that for any given distance from B to H and C to H, the distance from A to H is a minimum if and only if the circumference of a circle centred at A is tangent to an ellipse with focal points at B and C. This implies that at H the angle between the lines from A and B, and from A and C, must be equal. Combining these two sets of results shows that the angles at H between all three lines must be the same. Since there are 360 degrees in a circle, this means that the angles between the lines A and B, A and C, and B and C are all 120 degrees.

This is a very powerful result, but it is rather cumbersome to use it to calculate the precise location of the hub H. Fortunately there is a simple technique for locating the hub. Three equilateral triangles are constructed, each using one of the three sides of the triangle ABC as a base. These triangles are shown in the figure as ABF, ACE, and BCD. Straight lines AD, BE, and CF are then drawn from the vertices of the triangle ABC to the furthest vertex of the opposite equilateral triangle. The intersection of these lines, H, is the Steiner hub. Since the intersection of any two lines uniquely determines a point, it is sufficient to construct just two of the equilateral triangles in order to determine the location of the hub.

The Counterfactual Network: Description of Routes

Introduction

This appendix describes the basic counterfactual network. There is an associated book of maps which plots the routes on a scale of 2.4 in. to the mile. Photocopies are available from the author (m.c.casson@henley.reading.ac.uk). The routes are described below by means of tables; they are specified in sufficient detail to allow precise measures of distances to be made, and the major towns along the routes to be clearly identified.

The specification of a railway network is extremely complex, and considerable care has therefore been given to the best way to present the relevant information. This appendix employs a tabular method. If every section of every route were itemized separately then the table would be extremely long. To condense the information, and facilitate its interpretation, long-distance through routes have been constructed by connecting consecutive links in the network. With the exception of two 'orbital' routes, and other lines designated as 'loops', these through routes pursue a particular orientation (e.g. east–west) throughout their length.

In most cases a through route is suitable for a timetabled passenger service, running from end to end. In a few cases, however, the route would be more useful if different services operated along different portions of the line, with trains joining and leaving the route at appropriate points.

Each route is characterized in two ways: by the quality of the infrastructure, which determines the volume of traffic that can be carried and the speed that can be sustained, and by the role of the route within the context of the network as a whole. These two dimensions are summarized in Tables A4.1 and A4.2 below.

Table A4.1 summarizes the four-way classification of infrastructure quality, outlined in the main text. It ranges from trunk routes, through primary routes and secondary routes, to local routes. Trunk routes are straight and level, with a high minimum radius of curvature, and low ruling gradients while, at the other extreme, local routes may have high curvatures and steep gradients. Trunk routes consist of double track (or more), while local routes will typically be single track with passing loops every few miles.

Table A4.1. Quality of infrastructure

Code	Type	Speed	Traffic
T	Trunk	High	Heavy
P	Primary	High	Moderate
S	Secondary	Moderate	Moderate
L	Local	Low	Low

Table A4.2. Role in the network

Code	Type	Description
R	Radial	Radiates from London
G	Inter-regional	Links different regions, avoiding London
F	Feeder	Feeds traffic into a major urban centre or major route
U	Urban loop	Loop into city centre from bypass
C	Coastal loop	Loop through coastal towns
N	Inland loop	Loop through inland towns
O	Orbital	Circular loop around either a city or a region; may not be completely closed
B	Branch	Line to dead-end terminus that is not part of other routes above
K	Link	Linkage that does not correspond to any of the types above

Three columns are used to tabulate the network in Table A4.3. The first shows a code that identifies the route. This has three parts. The first is a letter identifying the minimum quality of the infrastructure along the route, derived from Table A4.1; the second is another letter which identifies the role of the route within the network as a whole, and is derived from Table A4.2; while the third is a number that identifies the specific route.

The second column of Table A4.3 summarizes the route, and in some cases gives it a name—for example, the 'North Wales coastal loop'. Only the key locations needed to identify the route are shown in this column. Locations shown in italic are served only by connections. Locations connected by trunk lines are shown in bold.

The details of the route are presented in the third column. Hubs at which connections can be made are shown in bold, and the connections are shown in italics within brackets after the name of the hub. Distances in miles between adjacent centres are shown between the dashes. The smaller towns and villages which are incidentally served along a route are indicated only on the maps mentioned above.

Table A4.3. Listing of routes

Ref	Origin–destination	Route
	Long radial routes: Trunk throughout	*Very long-distance primary routes radiating from London carrying heavy traffic at high speed*
TR1	**London–Exeter–Plymouth** [226.8 m]	**London** (NW)–2.0–Hammersmith–3.3–**Brentford** (BTF) (*Twickenham, Ealing,* London Suburban Circle)–4.5–{**Feltham** (ST) (*Twickenham*)}–4.8–**Staines** (ST) (*Ash–Southampton, Addlestone, Uxbridge,* London Outer Orbital)–2.0–Egham–5.5–Ascot–8.0–**Wokingham** (RG) (*Ash–Guildford*)–6.6–**Reading** (RG) (*Pangbourne–Oxford, Henley–Cookham, Maidenhead* loop)–5.3–{**Theale** (RG) (*Pangbourne–Wallingford*)}–2.6–**Aldermaston** (AM) (*Basingstoke*)–6.0–Thatcham–3.0–**Newbury** (NB) (*Whitchurch–Southampton*)–9.3–**Hungerford** (NB) (*Ramsbury–Swindon, Marlborough* loop)–14.4–Pewsey–2.4–**Manningford Bruce** (DZ) (*Amesbury–Idmiston–Salisbury*)–8.4–**Devizes** (DZ) (*Melksham* loop)–10.3–**Trowbridge** (TB) (*Limpley Stoke–Bath–Bristol, Warminster, Melksham* loop)–8.5–**Frome** (BT)

(continued)

Table A4.3. (Continued)

Ref	Origin–destination	Route
		(*Warminster*)–11.3–**Bruton** (BT) (*Wincanton–Yeovil, Shepton Mallet–Wells*)–4.0–Castle Cary–8.3–Somerton–5.0–**Langport** (LG) (*Bridgewater, Glastonbury–Wells, Yeovil*)–8.4–{**Wrantage** (TA) (*Ilminster–Chard Junction*)}–5.2–**Taunton** (TA) (*Minehead*)–6.0–Wellington–13.0–**Tiverton** (EX) (*Bampton, Barnstaple* loop)–14.0–**Exeter** (EX) (*Shilstone–Barnstaple, Ottery St. Mary, Yeovil, Axminster* loop, *Harpsford, Exmouth* loop)–6.0–**Great Matridge** (EX) (*Moretonhampstead*)–9.6–**Heathfield** (EX) (*Newton Abbot, Torquay* loop)–5.8–Ashburton–8.8–**South Brent** (PM) (*Halwell, Torquay* loop)–2.5–Bittaford–2.0–Ivybridge–10.0–**Plymouth** (PM) (*Liskeard–Penzance, Tavistock–Lydford–Launceston*)
TR2	*London–Reading–Gloucester–Cardiff–Carmarthen* [197.5 m]	*London* (NW)–**Reading** (RG) (*Aldermaston–Newbury, Henley–Cookham, Maidenhead* loop)–5.8–{**Pangbourne** (WL) (*Theale–Basingstoke*)}–9.0–**Wallingford** (WL) (*Watlington–Aylesbury*)–8.4–**Radley** (OX) (*Abingdon, Wantage* loop)–3.6–**Oxford** (OX) (*Kidlington–Banbury, Thame–Aylesbury*)–10.8–**Witney** (OX) (*Bampton–Lechlade, Wootton Bassett* loop)–7.3–Burford–10.0–**Northleach** (NL) (*Cirencester, Stow-on-the-Wold–Stratford-on-Avon, Fosse Way* loop)–11.5–**Cheltenham** (NL) (*Coombe Hill–Tewkesbury*)–8.5–**Gloucester** (GL) (*Newent–Aberystwyth, Coombe Hill–Tewkesbury, Stonehouse (Glos.)–Bristol*)–11.3–**Newnham** (GL) (*Cinderford–Coleford, Forest of Dean* loop)–8.0–**Lydney** (NP) (*Coleford, Forest of Dean* loop)–9.0–Chepstow–4.0–Portskewett (Pilning ferry)–14.0–**Newport** (NP) (*Little Mill–Abergavenny*)–11.3–**Cardiff** (CF) (*Tongwynlais, Aberdare* loop, *Barry* loop)–10.0–Llantrisant–8.3–**Bridgend** (BG) (*Tondu–Maesteg, Barry* loop)–5.3–**Pyle** (BG) (*Porthcawl*)–7.4–Aberavon–4.5–**Neath** (NB) (*Swansea* loop, *Pont Nedd Fechan, Aberdare* loop)–5.3–{**Ynystawe** (YN) (*Pontardawe–Gurnos, Morriston–Swansea*)}–6.0–**Pontarddulais** (PD) (*Gorseinon*)–3.2–{**Treneddyn** (PD) (*Ammanford–Llandeilo*)}–3.6–Cross Hands–4.9–{**Llanddarog** (CM) (*Llandeilo*)}–6.5–**Carmarthen** (CM) (*Narberth–Haverfordwest, Llanelly–Gorseinon, Swansea* loop, *Llangeler–Cardigan, Pembroke* loop)
TR3	**London–Stoke–Carlisle–Glasgow** [403.3 m]	**London** (NW)–4.4–**Wembley** (WW) (*Edgware–Ponders End, Ealing–Brentford,* London Suburban Circle)–2.8–Harrow–6.0–**Watford** (WT) (*Rickmansworth, St. Albans,* London Outer Orbital)–7.5–**Boxmoor** (TG) (*Hemel Hempstead–St. Albans*)–3.3–Berkhampstead–6.6–{**Tring** (**Marsworth**)} (TG) (*Aylesbury–Brackley–Banbury*)–7.3–**Leighton Buzzard** (LB) (*Flitwick–Bedford, Aylesbury, Winslow–Buckingham, St. Albans, Dunstable* loop)–12.5–Newport Pagnell–6.3–{**Ravenstone** (NH) (*Olney–Bedford*)}–8.0–**Northampton** (NH) (*Wellingborough, Towcester,* Nene Valley link)–8.4–{**Whilton** (NH) (*Daventry–Leamington*)}–7.2–{**Crick** (NH) (*Coventry–Birmingham, Lutterworth–*

Table A4.3. (Continued)

Ref	Origin–destination	Route
		Leicester)}–18.5–**Nuneaton** (NN) (*Hinkley–Leicester, Coles-hill–Birmingham, Bedworth–Coventry–Leamington*)–5.4–Atherstone–7.6–Tamworth–7.8–**Lichfield** (LF) (*Burton-on-Trent, Sutton Coldfield, Walsall, Cannock*)–8.0–Rugeley–2.5–{**Colwich** (LF) (*Stafford* loop)}–11.3–**Stone** (SK) (*Stafford* loop)–8.5–**Stoke-on-Trent** (SK) (*Leek, Draycott–Derby*)–4.8–Tunstall–3.0–**Kidsgrove** (SK) (*Macclesfield–Stockport–Manchester, Nantwich–Chester–Holyhead, Biddulph*)–6.6–Sandbach–4.7–**Middlewich** (NW) (*Winsford*)–6.0–**North-wich** (NW) (*Sutton Weaver–Runcorn, Mobberley–Stock-port*)–10.3–**Warrington** (WR) (*Huyton–Liverpool, St. Helens–Southport, Hollins Green–Manchester, Widnes, Mer-sey* loop)–7.5–Ashton-in-Makerfield–4.4–**Wigan** (WG) (*Ormskirk–Southport, Lostock–Bolton, Tyldesley–Manches-ter*)–8.0–**Chorley** (CU) (*Ormskirk–Liverpool, Bolton–Man-chester, Blackburn*)–3.2–Leyland–3.3–**Preston** (PR) (*Blackburn, Kirkham,* Fylde loop)–11.0–**Garstang** (LC) (*Poulton, Fylde* loop)–10.5–**Lancaster** (LC) (*Morecambe–Heysham*)–7.8–Hornby–7.2–**Kirkby Lonsdale** (KL) (*Milnthorpe,* Furness loop)–8.5–**Sedbergh Junction** (SS) (*Sedbergh–Hawes–Leyburn, Kirkby Stephen* loop)–3.5–{**Beck Foot** (SS) (*Milnthorpe, Kendal* loop)}–5.5–Tebay–8.3–Shap–10.0–**Penrith** (PN) (*Keswick, Workington, Sedbergh, Kirkby Stephen* loop)–18.3–**Carlisle** (CL) (*Hexham–Swalwell–New-castle, Wigton–Bromfield–Workington,* Furness loop)–6.0–{**Todhills** (CL) (*Langholm*)}–4.0–Gretna–6.5–{**Creca** (CL) (*Annan–Dumfries*)}–9.6–Lockerbie–2.4–{**Millhousebridge** (SY) (*Dumfries*)}–12.0–Moffat (*Beattock*)–17.5–Abington–9.0–**Symington** (SY) (*Biggar–Edinburgh*)–5.8–{**Pettinain** (SY) (*Hyndford Bridge, Lanark* loop)}–8.4–{**Carluke** (WS) (*Lanark* loop)}–4.0–**Wishaw** (WS) (*Shotts–Edinburgh, Stonehouse* (*Lanark*)–*Strathaven*)–4.0–**Motherwell** (MW) (*Coatbridge–Stirling, Hamilton* loop)–4.0–{**Uddingston** (GG) (*Hamilton* loop)}–7.8–**Glasgow** (GG) (*Dumbarton–Inverness, Kirkintilloch–Castlecary–Stirling, Coatbridge–Air-drie, Clarkston, Lugton–Ayr, Paisley–Greenock, Clyde* loop)
TR4	London–Cambridge–Nor-wich–Great Yarmouth [144.9 m]	**London** (NE)–8.1–**Ponders End** (PO) (*Enfield–Wembley, Chingford–Buckhurst Hill,* London Suburban Circle)–3.6–Cheshunt–7.0–{**St. Margarets** (WE) (*Harlow,* London Outer Orbital)}–2.8–**Ware** (WE) (*Hertford–St. Albans,* London Outer Orbital)–4.8–Watton-at-Stone–5.8–**Stevenage** (HC) (*Hitchin–Peterborough*)–6.3–**Baldock** (SE) (*Hitchin, Wel-wyn–St. Albans*)–8.8–Royston–13.0–**Cambridge** (CB) (*St. Ives–Huntingdon, Linton–Haverhill*)–8.6–{**Swaffham Bulbeck** (CB) (*Soham–Ely*)}–4.6–**Newmarket** (CB) (*Bury St. Edmunds*)–8.8–Mildenhall–11.8–**Thetford** (TF) (*Bran-don–Downham Market–Wisbech, Bury St. Edmunds*)–7.2–{**Roudham** (TF) (*East Dereham, Diss*)}–7.2–Attleborough–7.8–Wymondham–9.5–**Norwich** (NR) (*Swanton Abbot–*

Table A4.3. (Continued)

Ref	Origin–destination	Route
		Cromer, Bungay–Lowestoft)–6.2–Brundall–13.0–Great Yarmouth (*Lowestoft–Ilketshall–Ipswich*)
	Short radial routes: Trunk throughout	
TR5	*London–Dover* [77.8 m]	**London** (S Central)–4.3–**Lewisham** (LN) (*Croydon, Woolwich,* London Suburban Circle)–12.5–**Dartford** CT) (*Bromley–Croydon, Woolwich–Lewisham,* Surrey Docks loop)–6.8–Gravesend–6.8–**Strood** (CT) (*Wallend*)–1.3–**Chatham** (CT) (*Burham–Maidstone–Ashford*)–10.8–**Sittingbourne** (CT) (*Sheerness*)–8.0–**Faversham** (CT) (*Ramsgate–Sandwich*)–9.8–**Canterbury** (CY) (*Ashford, Wingham–Sandwich*)–14.5–{**Whitfield** (DV) (*Folkestone–Hythe, Deal–Sandwich*)}–3.0–Dover
TR6	*London–Horsham–Brighton* [63.4 m]	**London** (S Central)–3.0–**Clapham** (LN) (*Croydon, Carshalton, Lewisham, London* (*SW*), London Inner Circle)–5.0–Wimbledon–6.0–{**Ewell** (EP) (*Carshalton–Croydon,* London Suburban Circle)}–1.5–**Epsom** (EP) (*Surbiton,* London Suburban Circle)–4.8–**Leatherhead** (LQ) (*East Horsley–Guildford, Cobham–Addlestone,* London Outer Orbital)–4.8–**Dorking** (DK) (*Horsley–Guildford, Godstone,* London Outer Orbital)–14.3–**Horsham** (HS) (*Pulborough–Chichester, Cranleigh–Guildford, East Grinstead, Cuckfield–Lewes*)–7.2–Partridge Green–6.7–Bramber–3.6–**Shoreham** (BN) (*Worthing*)–6.5–**Brighton** (BN) (*Lewes*)
TR7	*London–Staines Southampton–Poole* [93.6 m]	*London* (NW)–**Staines** (ST) (*Wokingham–Reading, Addlestone–Guildford, Uxbridge,* London Outer Orbital)–7.2–{**Chobham** (ST) (*Woking–Guildford*)}–8.9–**Ash** (AS) (*Wokingham–Reading, Guildford, Basingstoke*)–5.3–Farnham–4.0–**Bentley** (AS) (*Petersfield–Havant–Portsmouth*)–6.0–Alton–10.5–Alresford–7.5–**Winchester** (WN) (*Sutton Scotney–Whitchurch* [*Hants*])–3.6–{**Shawford** (WN) (*Romsey–Salisbury*)}–4.2–{**North Stoneham** (SH) (*Southampton* loop, *Fareham–Portsmouth*)}–3.6–{**Millbrook** (SH) (*Romsey, Southampton* loop)}–6.5–Lyndhurst–4.1–**Brockenhurst** (SH) (*Lymington* loop)–11.7–**Christchurch** (PL) (*Lymington* loop, *Ringwood–Alderbury–Salisbury*)–6.5–Bournemouth–4.0–**Poole** (PL) (*Wareham–Weymouth, Wimborne–Blandford*)
TR8	*London–Ipswich* [72.8 m]	**London** (NE)–3.6–West Ham–2.4–**Barking** (BK) (*Dagenham–Upminster, Beckton, Buckhurst Hill,* London Suburban Circle)–5.5–Romford–7.5–**Brentwood** (BW) (*Basildon–Southend, Chipping Ongar–Harlow,* London Outer Orbital)–5.3–Ingatestone–6.5–**Chelmsford** (CD) (*Maldon–Southminster, Braintree–Halstead–Bury St. Edmunds*)–8.4–Witham–6.7–**Coggeshall** (**Broad Green**) (CR) (*Earls Colne–Halstead*)–7.9–**Colchester** (CR) (*Clacton-on-Sea*)–8.5–**Manningtree** (CR) (*Harwich*)–10.5–**Ipswich** (IP) (*Saxmundham–Great Yarmouth, Stowmarket–Bury St. Edmunds, Hadleigh–Sudbury, Felixstowe*)

Table A4.3. (Continued)

Ref	Origin–destination	Route
	Trunk feeders to radial trunk lines	*These lines carry heavy traffic at high speed, which feeds into longer-distance trunk lines*
TF1	London–Northampton–**Crick**–**Birmingham**–**Wolverhampton** [49.9 m]	*London* (NW)–*Northampton*–{**Crick** (NH) (*Nuneaton, Lutterworth–Leicester*)}–5.4–Rugby–11.8–**Coventry** (CV) (*Kenilworth–Warwick, Bedworth–Nuneaton*)–10.6–{**Coleshill** (BM) (*Nuneaton*)}–8.6–**Birmingham** (BM) (*Walsall, Redditch, Sutton Coldfield–Lichfield, Solihull–Warwick*)–3.6–**Handsworth** (BM) (*Stourbridge*)–4.6–**Wednesbury** (WY) (*Dudley–Stourbridge, Walsall*)–5.3–**Wolverhampton** (WH) (*Shifnal–Shrewsbury, Penkridge–Stafford, Wimborne–Kidderminster*)
TF2	**Liverpool**–**Chorley**–*Glasgow* [26.1 m]	**Liverpool** (LV) (*Huyton–Warrington, Formby–Southport, Widnes–Warrington, Mersey* loop, Birkenhead ferry)–5.2–Aintree–2.8–Maghull–4.5–**Ormskirk** (OM) (*Southport, Digmoor–Wigan*)–2.5–Burscough–3.5–Parbold–7.6–**Chorley** (CU) (*Wigan, Lostock–Bolton, Preston–Glasgow, Blackburn*)
TF3	*London*–**Symington**–**Edinburgh** [32.9 m]	*London* (NW)–**Symington** (SY) (*Pettinain–Glasgow*)–4.0–**Biggar** (SY) (*Peebles*)–19.9–**Penicuik** (ED) (*Peebles*)–9.0–**Edinburgh** (ED) (*Longniddry–Dunbar*)
TF4	London–**Motherwell**–**Aberdeen** [148.1 m]	*London* (NW)–**Motherwell** (MW) (*Uddingston–Glasgow*)–5.9–**Coatbridge** (CG) (*Airdrie, Glasgow*)–9.2–{**Castlecary** (CC) (*Falkirk–Edinburgh, Kirkintilloch–Glasgow*)}–3.4–**Denny** (SL) (*Falkirk–Edinburgh*)–7.9–**Stirling** (SL) (Alloa, *Fife Coast* loop)–6.0–**Dunblane** (SL) (*Doune–Crianlarich*)–15.0–**Auchterarder** (PH) (*Crieff*)–13.3–**Perth** (PH) (*Cargill, Forfar* loop, *Lathrisk, Fife Coast* loop)–21.3–**Dundee** (DD) (*Forfar*, Tayport ferry)–17.8–Arbroath–11.8–**Montrose** (AB) (*Brechin, Forfar* loop)–13.3–Inverbervie–9.2–Stonehaven–14.0–**Aberdeen** (AB) (*Dyce–Inverness, Ballater*)
TF5	London–Northampton–**Leicester**–**Leeds**–**Newcastle** [217.8 m]	*London* (NW)–{**Crick** (NH) (*Nuneaton, Coventry–Birmingham*)}–7.8–Lutterworth–14.0–**Leicester** (LE) (*Desford–Nuneaton, Market Harborough–Wellingborough, Kettering* loop)–6.6–Mountsorrel–4.6–**Loughborough** (LE) (*Shepshed–Derby*)–6.0 {**Gotham** (LE) (*Ruddington–Nottingham*)}–9.4–**Ilkeston** (IK) (*Derby, Nottingham*)–10.2–Alfreton–10.8–**Chesterfield** (CHF) (*Bakewell*)–4.0–**Staveley** (CHF) (*Shirebrook–Nottingham, Mansfield* loop)–12.1–{(**Beighton** (BET) (*Sheffield* loop, *Worksop–Lincoln*)}–6.0–**Rotherham** (MX) (*Sheffield* loop)–5.3–**Mexborough** (MX) (*Doncaster–Thorne*)–8.7–**Cudworth** (MX) (*Barnsley–Penistone*)–9.3–**Wakefield** (WK) (*Dewsbury, Pontefract–Knottingley*)–3.5–{**East Ardsley** (LS) (*Dewsbury*)}–5.3–**Leeds** (LS) (*Rawdon–Skipton, Castleford–Knottingley, Pudsey,* West Yorkshire loop)–12.3–**Wetherby** (WB) (*York, Selby, Pool–Otley–Burley, Wharfedale* loop)–7.3–**Knaresborough** (WB) (*Harrogate*)–10.0–**Ripon** (RP) (*Thirsk–Northallerton*)–6.0–{**West Tanfield** (RP) (*Constable Burton–Leyburn*)}–6.8–Bedale–6.5–**Catterick** (CK) (*Richmond, Northallerton, Constable Burton–Leyburn*)–5.0–{**Middleton Tyas** (CK)

(continued)

Table A4.3. (Continued)

Ref	Origin–destination	Route
		(*Winston–Barnard Castle*)}–7.3–**Darlington** (DL) (*Barnard Castle–Middleton-in-Teesdale, Eaglescliffe–Middlesborough*)–6.4–**Newton Aycliffe** (NA) (*Bishop Auckland–Stanhope, Stockton*)–6.0–**Spennymoor** (DH) (*Bishop Auckland–West Auckland–Barnard Castle*)–6.0–**Durham** (DH) (*Pittington–Houghton-le-Spring–Sunderland, Consett* (*Leadgate*), *Shotley Bridge* loop)–6.3–**Chester-le-Street** (CS) (*Beamish–Consett* (*Leadgate*), *Penshaw–Sunderland*)–8.3–**Newcastle** (NE) (*Morpeth–Glasgow, Moulton–Sunderland, Tynemouth, Blyth* loop, *Swalwell–Carlisle, Byker* loop)
	Inter-regional trunk lines	
TG1	**Liverpool–Manchester–Hull** [127.9 m]	**Liverpool** (LV) (*Ormskirk, Formby–Southport, Widnes, Mersey* loop)–6.6–**Huyton** (LV) (*St. Helens–Wigan*)–10.6–**Warrington** (WR) (*Northwich–London, Wigan, St. Helens, Sutton Weaver–Chester, Widnes, Mersey* loop)–7.1–{**Hollins Green** (WR) (*Altrincham–Wilmslow*)}–6.6–{**Stretford** (MN) (*Altrincham–Knutsford*)}–3.6–**Manchester** (MN) (*Stockport, Bury, Worsley–Bolton, Middleton–Rochdale, Oldham, Altrincham*)–6.7–Ashton-under-Lyne–2.5–**Stalybridge** (STY) (*Hyde–Stockport, Glossop*)–4.6–**Grasscroft** (STY) (*Oldham*)–12.6–**Huddersfield** (HF) (*Holmfirth*)–2.5–**Deighton** (HF) (*Penistone–Sheffield, Brighouse–Halifax*)–2.8–**Mirfield** (DW) (*Brighouse*)–3.3–**Dewsbury** (DW) (*Batley, East Ardsley–Leeds*)–2.0–Ossett–3.4–**Wakefield** (WK) (*Cudworth, East Ardsley*)–8.4–Pontefract–2.1–**Knottingley** (KN) (*Kirk Smeaton–Doncaster, Castleford–Leeds*)–11.0–**Snaith** (SN) (*Selby, Thorne–Grimsby*)–6.3–**Goole** (BC) (*Thorne*)–4.3–**Balkholme** (BC) (*Selby, Market Weighton*)–10.0–Brough (E. Riding)–6.0–Hessle (Barton-on-Humber ferry)–4.9–**Hull** (HL) (*Beverley–Scarborough, Withernsea*)
TG2	*Manchester–***Stalybridge–Sheffield** [37.1 m]	*Manchester–***Stalybridge** (STY) (*Stockport, Grasscroft–Huddersfield*)–2.7–Mottram-in-Longdendale–2.4–**Hadfield** (STY) (*Glossop*)–10.0–Dunsford Bridge–6.0–**Penistone** (PC) (*Deighton–Huddersfield, Barnsley–Cudworth*)–4.0–Stocksbridge–12.0–**Sheffield** (SF) (*Rotherham, Beighton–Chesterfield*)
TG3	**Glasgow–Edinburgh** [49.6 m]	**Glasgow** (GG) (*Uddingston–London, Dumbarton–Crianlarich–Inverness, Coatbridge–Airdrie, Clarkston, Lugton–Ayr, Paisley–Greenock, Clyde* loop, *Bishopton, Renfrew* loop)–3.2–Bishopbriggs–3.9–Kirkintilloch–4.6–Kilsyth–4.8–{**Castlecary** (CC) (*Coatbridge–Motherwell*)}–7.3–**Falkirk** (ED) (*Denny–Stirling*)–7.3–Bo'ness–8.5–South Queensferry (Inverkeithing ferry)–10.0–**Edinburgh** (ED) (*Longniddry–Dunbar, Falkirk–Stirling, Penicuik–Biggar, Dalkeith–Melrose, Shotts–Wishaw*)
TG4	**Newcastle–Biggar**–*Glasgow* [127.1 m]	**Newcastle** (NE) (*Chester-le-Street–Durham, Monkton–Sunderland, Swalwell–Carlisle, Wallsend–Tynemouth, Blyth* loop, *Byker* koop)–14.5–**Morpeth** (MP) (*Newbiggin, Blyth* loop)–18.8–Alnwick–17.5–Wooler–14.0–**Coldstream** (CE) (*Swinton–Berwick-upon-Tweed, Dunbar* loop)–8.8–Kelso–7.6–

Table A4.3. (Continued)

Ref	Origin–destination	Route
		Maxton (ML) (*Ancrum–Hawick*)–2.6–St. Boswells–6.0–**Melrose** (ML) (*Galashiels–Edinburgh*)–2.5–**Lindean** (ML) (*Selkirk*)–12.0–Innerleithen–6.3–**Peebles** (PE) (*Penicuik–Edinburgh*)–16.5–**Biggar** (SY) (*West Linton–Edinburgh*)–*Symington–Glasgow*
	Trunk links	
TK1	*Dover*–Chatham–Otford–Guildford–***Reading*** [57.5 m]	*Dover–Sittingbourne*–**Chatham** (CT) (*Strood–London*)–4.8–**Burham** (MD) (*Maidstone*)–2.2–New Hythe–2.4–**West Malling** (MD) (*Maidstone*)–5.3–**Ightham** (OT) (*Hadlow–Tunbridge Wells*)–4.9–**Otford** (OT) (*Sevenoaks, Orpington–Bromley*)–2.6–Chipstead–3.9–Westerham–3.6–Oxted–3.0–**Godstone** (GD) (*Croydon–London, East Grinstead–Eastbourne, Hever–Tunbridge Wells*)–7.1–Reigate–6.3–**Dorking** (DK) (*Horsham, Leatherhead*)–5.0–{**East Horsley** (DK) (*Leatherhead*)}–6.4–**Guildford** (GF) (*Woking–Chobham, Horsham, Godalming–Witley*)–*Ash–Wokingham–Reading*
TK2	**Southampton cut-off:** *Winchester*–Shawford–Romsey–***Salisbury*** [7.5 m]	*Winchester*–**Shawford** (*North Stoneham–Southampton*)–4.7–Ampfield–2.8–**Romsey** (*Millbrook*)–*Salisbury*
TK3	**Trowbridge cut-off:** *Salisbury*–Warminster–Frome–***Taunton*** [7.0 m]	*Salisbury*–**Warminster** (*Trowbridge*)–7.0–**Frome** (*Trowbridge*)–*Bruton–Taunton*
TK4	*Gloucester*–Oxford–Aylesbury–***Cambridge*** [22.4 m]	*Gloucester*–**Oxford** (OX) (*Kidlington–Banbury, Radley–Abingdon*)–13.5–**Thame** (OX) (*Princes Risborough–High Wycombe*)–8.9–**Aylesbury** (AY) (*Tring–London, Buckingham, North Lee–Amersham*)–*Leighton Buzzard–Bedford–Cambridge*
TK5	Gloucester cut-off: *London*–**Cheltenham–Coombe Hill**–*Tewkesbury* [5.6 m]	*London–Oxford*–**Cheltenham** (GL) (*Gloucester*)–5.6–{**Coombe Hill** (GL) (*Gloucester*)}–*Tewkesbury*
TK6	*Holyhead*–Chester–Warrington–***Carlisle*** [19.7 m]	*Holyhead–Bangor*–**Chester** (CH) (*Wrexham, Broxton–Stoke-on-Trent, Hooton–Birkenhead*)–10.8–Frodsham–2.0–**Sutton Weaver** (WR) (*Runcorn, Northwich*)–6.9–**Warrington** (WR) (*Wigan, Hollins Green–Manchester, Huyton–Liverpool, St. Helens, Widnes, Mersey* loop)
TK7	*Stirling*–Denny–Falkirk–***Edinburgh*** 5.0 m	Stirling–**Denny** (CC) (*Castlecary–Glasgow*)–5.0–**Falkirk** (CC) (*Castlecary–Glasgow*)–*Edinburgh*
TK8	Newcastle–*Melrose–Edinburgh* [33.3 m]	*Newcastle–Coldstream*–**Melrose** (MR) (*Lindean–Peebles*)–2.5–Galashiels–23.8–Dalkeith–7.0–**Edinburgh** (ED) (*Falkirk–Stirling, Longniddry–Dunbar, etc.*)
TK9	*Newcastle*–Wetherby–Balkholme–***Hull*** [29.8 m]	*Newcastle*–**Wetherby** (WB) (*Knaresborough–Ripon–Newcastle, York, Pool–Otley–Burley, Wharfedale* loop)–6.4–Tadcaster–10.8–**Selby** (SN) (*York, Snaith*)–9.8–Howden–2.8–**Balkholme** (SN) (*Goole*)–*Hull*
TK10	*Mexborough–Goole* [27.3 m]	**Mexborough** (MX) (*Rotherham–Sheffield, Cudworth–Leeds*)–8.3–**Doncaster** (DC) (*Carcroft–Knottingley, Bawtry–Ranby–Lincoln*)–11.0–**Thorne** (SN) (*Snaith–Selby, Gunness–Brigg–Grimsby, Epworth–Gainsborough–Lincoln*)–8.0–**Goole** (SN) (*Snaith–Knottingley*)–*Balkholme–Hull*

(*continued*)

Table A4.3. (Continued)

Ref	Origin–destination	Route
	Trunk loops into urban centres	
TU1	*Southampton loop* [7.0 m]	{**North Stoneham** (SH) (*Shawford–Winchester, Botley–Fareham, Millbrook*)}–3.5–Southampton–3.5–{**Millbrook** (SH) (*Brockenhurst–Poole, Romsey, North Stoneham*)}
TU2	*Birmingham loop* [25.4 m + (3.6 m)]	**Stourbridge** (SP) (*Kidderminster, Dudley*)–4.3–**Old Hill** (BM) (*Halesowen*)–5.0–**Handsworth** (BM) (*Wednesbury–Wolverhampton*)–(3.6, TF1)–**Birmingham** (BM) (*Walsall, Coleshill, Solihull–Warwick, Redditch*)–7.1–Sutton Coldfield–9.0–**Lichfield** (LF) (*Burton-on-Trent, Colwich–Stoke, Tamworth–Nuneaton, Walsall, Cannock, Dudley*)
TU3	*Nottingham loop* [15.9 m]	Loughborough–{**Gotham** (LE) (*Ilkeston*)}–3.8–Ruddington–4.6–**Nottingham** (NG) (*Lowdham–Newark, Harby–Grantham, Mansfield–Staveley*)–7.5–**Ilkeston** (IK) (*Chesterfield, Derby, Gotham–Loughborough*)
TU4	*Stafford loop* [6.7 m + (7.3 m)]	Lichfield–Rugeley–{**Colwich** (SD) (*Stone*)}–6.7–**Stafford** (SD) (*Penkridge–Wolverhampton, Newport* (Salop)–*Shrewsbury*)–(7.3, PG4)–**Stone** (SD) (*Stoke-on-Trent, Colwich, Eccleshall–Newport* [Staffs])
TU5	*Sheffield loop* [9.4 m]	{**Beighton** (SF) (*Staveley–London, Worksop–Lincoln, Rotherham*)}–5.2–**Sheffield** (SF) (*Penistone–Manchester*)–4.2–**Rotherham** (SF) (*Mexborough–Leeds, Beighton*)
TU6	*Manchester Loop:* Stoke-on-Trent–*Stockport–Manchester–Chorley* [57.3 m]	Stoke-on-Trent–Tunstall–**Kidsgove** (SK) (*Nantwich–Chester, Middlewich–Warrington*)–6.0–Congleton–8.4–**Macclesfield** (SK) (*Wilmslow*)–3.6–Bollington–8.4–**Stockport** (TP) (*Hyde–Stalybridge–Leeds, Buxton–Bakewell, Wilmslow–Northwich*)–7.5–**Manchester** (MN) (*Whitefield–Bury, Stalybridge, Rochdale, Oldham, Stretford–Warrington*)–2.5–Salford–3.9–**Worsley** (MN) (*Tyldesley–Wigan*)–2.8–Farnworth–3.2–**Bolton** (BL) (*Bury*)–4.0–{**Lostock** (BL) (*Aspull–Wigan*)}–1.8–Horwich–5.2–**Chorley** (PR) (*Preston–Glasgow, Ormskirk–Liverpool, Wigan–Warrington, Blackburn*)
	Inter-regional primary routes, some with a trunk portion	*Long cross-country routes, carrying moderate levels of traffic at high speed throughout, some with trunk portions carrying high levels of traffic*
PG1	Dover–**Brighton–Salisbury–Trowbridge–Bath–Bristol** [30.3 m + (10.1 m)] 79.4 m + (3.0 m)	Dover–(3.0, TR5)–**Whitfield** (DV) (*Canterbury, Deal–Sandwich*)–6.5–Folkestone–4.0–Hythe–3.8 {**Lympne** (DV) (*Ashford*)}–3.0–Dymchurch–6.8–Lydd–7.5–**Rye** (HT) (*Tenterden–Ashford*)–12.5–**Hastings** (HT) (*Hurst Green–Tunbridge Wells*)–4.8–Bexhill–6.5–**Pevensey** (EB) (*Eastbourne loop*)–4.5–**Polegate** (EB) (*Eastbourne loop, Uckfield–East Grinstead*)–11.2–**Lewes** (LW) (*Uckfield, Seaford, Horsham*)–8.3–[**Brighton** (BN)–(6.5, TR6)–**Shoreham** (BN) (*Horsham*)–5.0–Worthing–3.0–**Goring-by-Sea** (BN) (*Littlehampton, Bognor loop*)–7.0–**Arundel** (AD) (*Pulborough–Horsham, Littlehampton*)–10.3–**Chichester** (HV) (*Littlehampton, Bognor loop*)–10.0–**Havant** (HV) (*Petersfield–Bentley–Farnham*)–2.8–**Cosham** (HV) (*Portsmouth*)–5.0–**Fareham** (SH) (*Gosport*)–3.7–**Botley** (SH) (*Bishops Waltham–Petersfield*)–7.3–**North Stoneham** (SH) (*Shawford–*

Table A4.3. (Continued)

Ref	Origin–destination	Route
		Winchester, Southampton loop)–(3.6, TR7)–**Millbrook** (SH) (*Wareham–Dorchester*)–5.5–**Romsey** (RO) (*Shawford*)–4.3–{**Mottisfont** (RO) (*Stockbridge–Andover*)}–9.6–{**Alderbury** (SB) (*Downton–Christchurch*)}–3.9–**Salisbury** (SB) (*Amesbury*)–3.4–**Wilton** (SB) (*Shaftesbury–Milborne Port–Yeovil*)–15.9–**Warminster** (SB) (*Frome–Taunton*)–8.5–**Trowbridge** (TB) (*Melksham, Devizes, Frome*)–3.0–Bradford-on-Avon–3.0–**Limpley Stoke** (BH) (*Radstock–Shepton Mallet*)–7.3–**Bath** (BH) (*Corsham–Chippenham*)–11.8–**Bristol** (BR) (*Nailsea–Bridgwater, Filton–Gloucester*)]
PG2	*Brighton–Horsham–Guild-ford–Reading–Oxford–Lea-mington–Nuneaton* [41.8 m + (33.4 m)] 66.3 m	*Brighton–Shoreham–*[**Horsham** (HS) (*Pulborough–Arundel, East Grinstead*)–10.5–Cranleigh–8.8–**Guildford** (GF) (*Woking–Chobham–London, East Horsley–Leatherhead, Godalming–Witley*)–7.8–**Ash** (AS) (*Farnham–Bentley–Southampton, Basingstoke, Chobham–Staines*)–4.6–Frimley–5.1–Sandhurst–5.0–**Wokingham** (RG) (*Egham–Staines*)–(6.6, TR1)–**Reading** (RG) (*Theale–Newbury, Cookham, Henley* loop)–(5.8, TR2)–**Pangbourne** (RG) (*Theale–Aldermaston–Basingstoke*)–(9.0, TR2)–**Wallingford** (RG) (*Watlington–Princes Risborough–Aylesbury*)–(8.4, TR2)–**Radley** (OX) (*Abingdon, Wantage* loop)–(3.6, TR2)–**Oxford** (OX) (*Witney–Cheltenham, Thame–Aylesbury*)]–5.2–**Kidlington** (OX) (*Bicester–Buckingham, Chipping Norton–Moreton-in-Marsh*)–4.5–Tackley–3.8–Hopcrofts Holt–4.4–Deddington–3.0–Adderbury–3.7–**Banbury** (BB) (*Chipping Norton, Brackley*)–15.0–**Southam** (LM) (*Daventry–Whilton–Northampton*)–7.5–**Leamington** (LM) (*Warwick–Birmingham*)–5.0–Kenilworth–5.0–**Coventry** (CV) (*Crick–Northampton, Coleshill–Birmingham*)–6.2–Bedworth–3.0–**Nuneaton** (NN) (*Hinckley–Leicester, Tamworth–Lichfield, Coleshill–Birmingham, Crick–Northampton*)
PG3	*Southampton–Winchester–Newbury–Thame–Bedford–*Peterborough–Spalding–Grimsby [97.4 m + (11.6 m)] 130.4 m	*Southampton–Shawford–*[**Winchester** (WN) (*Alresford–Bentley–Farnham*)–7.5–Sutton Scotney–5.1–**Whitchurch** (HC) (*Overton–Basingstoke, Andover*)–3.7–Lichfield–9.6–**Newbury** (RG) (*Hungerford*)–3.0–Thatcham–6.0–**Aldermaston** (RG) (*Basingstoke*)–(2.6, TR1)–**Theale** (RG) (*Reading*)–3.9–**Pangbourne** (RG) (*Reading*)–(9.0, TR2)–**Wallingford** (RG) (*Radley–Oxford*)–6.6–Watlington–5.3–Chinnor–2.7–**Princes Risborough** (AY) (*High Wycombe–Loudwater–Uxbridge, Thame*)–4.0–**North Lee** (AY) (*Amersham–Rickmansworth*)–4.0–**Aylesbury** (AY) (*Winslow–Buckingham, Tring, Thame–Oxford*)–10.0–**Leighton Buzzard** (LB) (*Ravenstone–Northampton, Tring*)–11.4–Flitwick–2.0–Ampthill–8.6–**Bedford** (BD) (*Olney–Ravenstone–Northampton*)–4.0–{**Willington (Beds.)** (BD) (*Sandy–Cambridge*)}]–1.8–{**Tempsford** (BD) (*Sandy*)}–4.4–St. Neots (Beds.)–8.5–**Huntingdon** (HN) (*St. Ives–Cambridge, Warboys–Chatteris*)–19.5–**Peterborough** (PB) (*Whittlesey–March, Oundle–Irthlingborough–Wellingborough*)–4.0–{**Werrington** (PB) (*Stamford–Manton–Leicester, Bourne–*

Table A4.3. (Continued)

Ref	Origin–destination	Route
		Grantham)}–6.5–Crowland–8.0–**Spalding** (SG) (*Holbeach–Wisbech, Bourne*)–6.0–**Gosberton** (SG) (*Donington–Sleaford, Holbeach*)–3.6–Wigtoft–6.4–Boston–21.3–Skegness–6.2–Chapel St. Leonards–7.2–**Alford** (AL) (*Mablethorpe, Horncastle–Metheringham*)–11.0–**Louth** (LH) (*Market Rasen*)–14.0–Cleethorpes–2.0–**Grimsby** (GR) (*Caistor–Thorne*)
PG4	Taunton–Bristol–Gloucester–Stoke-on-Trent–Leeds–Wetherby–York–Scarborough [175.0 m + (86.2 m)] 55.6 m	[**Taunton** (TA) (*Tiverton–Plymouth, Minehead*)–9.8–**Bridgewater** (WM) (*Langport–Yeovil*)–6.9–**Highbridge** (WM) (*Weston-super-Mare* loop)–7.2 {**Loxton** (WM) (*Weston-super-Mare, Cheddar–Wells*)}–12.6–**Nailsea** (WM) (*Weston-super-Mare* loop, *Portishead*)–8.6–**Bristol** (BR) (*Bath–Limpley Stoke–Trowbridge*)–4.6–**Filton** (BR) (*Avonmouth, Pilning, Chipping Sodbury*)–7.6–Thornbury–10.3–**Cam** (GL) (*Dursley*)–5.3–**Stonehouse (Glos.)** (GL) (*Stroud–Cherington–Cirencester*)–10.0–**Gloucester** (GL) (*Cheltenham–Oxford, Newnham–Lydney–Cardiff, Newent–Hereford*)–7.0–{**Coombe Hill** (GL) (*Cheltenham*)}–4.0–Tewkesbury (Gl) (*Evesham–Stratford-on-Avon*)–6.0–**Upton-on-Severn** (GL) (*Welland–Great Malvern* loop)–4.5–{**Pirton** (WC) (*Pershore–Evesham*)}–5.0–**Worcester** (WC) (*Great Malvern–Welland–Ross-on-Wye, Droitwich–Bromsgrove, Knightwick–Tenbury Wells*)–11.8–**Stourport** (SP) (*Bridgnorth–Coalport–Shrewsbury, Stockton-on-Teme–Tenbury Wells, Bromsgrove*)–4.0–**Kidderminster** (SP) (*Stourbridge–Birmingham*)–10.0–Wombourne–4.6–**Wolverhampton** (WH) (*Shifnal–Shrewsbury, Walsall, Wednesbury*)–9.3–**Penkridge** (WH) (*Cannock*)–4.6–**Stafford** (SD) (*Colwich–Lichfield, Newport* [*Salop*])–7.3–**Stone** (SD) (*Colwich–Lichfield, Eccleshall–Newport* [*Staffs*])–(8.6, TR3)–**Stoke-on-Trent** (SK) (*Draycott–Derby, Leek*)–(4.8, TR3)–Tunstall–(3.0, TR3)–**Kidsgrove** (SK) (*Middlewich–Warrington, Nantwich–Chester, Biddulph*)–(6.0, TU6)–Congleton–(8.4, TU6)–Macclesfield (SK) (*Wilmslow*)–(3.6, TU6)–Bollington–(8.4, TU6)–**Stockport** (TP) (*Manchester, Buxton–Bakewell, Wilmslow–Northwich*)–4.3–Hyde–4.5–**Stalybridge** (TY) (*Manchester, Hadfield–Sheffield*)–(4.6, TG1)–**Grasscroft** (HD) (*Oldham*)–(12.6, TG1)–**Huddersfield** (HD) (*Honley–Holmfirth*)–(2.5, TG1)–**Deighton** (HD) (*Penistone–Sheffield, Brighouse–Halifax*)–(2.8, TG1)–**Mirfield** (DW) (*Brighouse*)–(3.3, TG1)–**Dewsbury** (DW) (*Batley, Wakefield*)–5.2–**East Ardsley** (LS) (*Wakefield*)–(5.3, TF5)–**Leeds** (LS) (*Rawdon–Skipton, Castleford–Knottingley, Pudsey, Batley,* West Yorkshire loop)–(12.3, TF5)–**Wetherby** (WB) (*Knaresborough–Newcastle, Pool–Otley–Burley, Wharfedale* loop)]–13.0–**York** (YK) (*Selby, Market Weighton–Beverley–Hull*)–18.5–Malton–7.8–**Thornton-le-Dale** (PK) (*Pickering–Whitby*)–6.0–Snainton–4.9–West Ayton–2.0–Irton–3.4–**Scarborough** (SC) (*Beverley, Bridlington* loop)

Table A4.3. (Continued)

Ref	Origin–destination	Route
PG5	*Swansea*–Gorseinon–Leominster–**Stourport–Walsall–Nottingham–Lincoln**–Grimsby [103.2 m + (11.5 m)] 150.7 m + (3.2 m)	*Swansea*–**Gorseinon** (SW) (*Llanelly–Carmarthen*)–4.0–**Pontarddulais** (SW) (*Ynystawe–Neath*)–(3.2, TR2)–{**Treneddyn** (SW) (*Llanddarog–Carmarthen*)}–4.7–**Ammanford** (AM) (*Glanaman–Gurnos, Aberdare* loop)–7.2–**Llandeilo** (LY) (*Llanddarog–Carmarthen*)–12.0–**Llandovery** (LY) (*Sennybridge–Brecon*)–12.0–Llanwrtyd Wells–12.0–**Builth Wells** (BU) (*Llandrindod Wells–Aberystwyth*)–14.0–**Three Cocks** (HA) (*Brecon–Sennybridge*)–5.3–Hay-on-Wye–6.6–**Willersley** (HA) (*Hereford–Gloucester, Kington–Walford, Ludlow* loop)–5.5–Weobley–8.0–**Leominster** (WF) (*Bodenham–Bromyard*)–7.3–**Woofferton** (WF) (*Ludlow–Berriew*)–5.0–Tenbury Wells–9.3–**Stockton-on-Teme** (WF) (*Knightwick–Worcester, Cleobury Mortimer*)–8.5–[**Stourport** (SP) (*Bridgnorth–Coalport–Shrewsbury, Bromsgrove–Redditch, Worcester*)–(4.0, PG4)–**Kidderminster** (SP) (*Wolverhampton*)–7.5–**Stourbridge** (SP) (*Old Hill–Birmingham* loop)–6.0–Dudley–2.8–**Wednesbury** (WY) (*Wolverhampton, Handsworth–Birmingham*)–4.5–**Walsall** (WL) (*Wolverhampton, Birmingham, Cannock*)–11.0–**Lichfield** (LF) (*Colwich–Stoke, Tamworth–Nuneaton, Burntwood–Cannock, Sutton Coldfield*)–5.0–Alrewas–7.2–**Burton-on-Trent** (DB) (*Swannington–Leicester*)–5.0–**Willington (Derbys.)** (DB) (*Uttoxeter–Stoke, Melbourne–Loughborough*)–7.0–**Derby** (DB) (*Shepshed–Loughborough, Matlock–Bakewell*)–(9.6, PU2)–**Ilkeston** (IK) (*Chesterfield, Gotham–Loughborough*) (7.5, TU4)–**Nottingham** (NG) (*Gotham–Loughborough, Harby–Grantham, Shirebrook–Staveley, Mansfield* loop)–8.4–Lowdham–5.4–**Southwell** (NK) (*Mansfield*)–6.8–**Newark** (NK) (*Sleaford*)–17.0–**Lincoln** (LI) (*Torksey–Gainsborough,Metheringham–Sleaford*)]–15.0–**Market Rasen** (MR) (*Louth*)–8.5–**Caistor** (GR) (*Brigg*)–14.3–**Grimsby** (GR) (*Cleethorpes–Louth*)
PG6	Worcester–**Northampton–Bedford–Cambridge**–Ipswich–Felixstowe [37.7 m + (38.6 m)] 114.4 m	[**Worcester** (WC) (*Stourport–Kidderminster, Droitwich–Redditch Knightwick–Tenbury Wells, Ludlow* loop, *Great Malvern–Welland–Ross-on-Wye*)–(5.0, PG4)–{**Pirton** (WC) (*Upton-on-Severn–Tewkesbury*)}]–4.8–Pershore–6.0–**Evesham** (BV) (*Tewkesbury*)–7.5–**Bidford-on-Avon** (BV) (*Alcester–Redditch–Birmingham*)–8.0–**Stratford-on-Avon** (LM) (*Shipston-on-Stour–Moreton-in-Marsh, Fosse Way* loop)–9.8–**Warwick** (LM) (*Solihull–Birmingham*)–2.5–**Leamington** (LM) (*Kenilworth–Coventry*)–7.5–**Southam** (LM) (*Banbury–Oxford*)–11.0–Daventry–4.6–[{**Whilton** (NH) (*Crick–Nuneaton*)}–(8.4, TR3)–**Northampton** (NH) (*Towcester, Wellingborough*, Nene Valley link)–(8.0, TR3)–{**Ravenstone** (NH) (*Leighton Buzzard*)}–3.2–Olney–12.0–**Bedford** (BD) (*Ampthill–Leighton Buzzard*)–(4.0, PG3)–{**Willington (Beds.)** (BD) (*Tempsford–Huntingdon*)}–3.5–**Sandy** (BD) (*Biggleswade–Hitchin, Tempsford–Huntingon*)–3.4–Potton–2.4–Gamlingay–9.8–Comberton–3.4* + (1.6)–**Cambridge** (CB) (*Linton–Colchester, Royston–Baldock, St.*

(*continued*)

Table A4.3. (Continued)

Ref	Origin–destination	Route
		Ives–Huntingdon)–(8.6, TR4)–{**Swaffham Bulbeck** (CB) (*Soham–Ely*)}–(4.6, TR4)–**Newmarket** (CB) (*Thetford–Norwich, Burwell–Ely*)]–14.4–**Bury St. Edmunds** (BE) (*Sudbury–Chelmsford, Thetford*)–13.3–**Stowmarket** (IP) (*Eye–Diss*)–12.0–**Ipswich** (IP) (*Manningtree–Colchester, Saxmundham–Great Yarmouth, Hadleigh–Sudbury*)–13.0–Felixstowe
PG7	**Holyhead–Chester–Stoke-on-Trent–Nottingham–Newark–Boston** [154.5 m + (45.7 m)] 34.4 m	[Holyhead–16.0–Llangefni–6.6–**Menai Bridge** (BX) (*Benllech–Amlwch, Beaumaris*)–2.5–**Bangor** (BX) (*Caernarvon–Criccieth, North Wales* loop)–16.3–**Conway** (LD) (*Llandudno* loop, *Betwys-y-Coed*)–5.8–**Colwyn Bay** (LD) (*Llandudno* loop)–11.2–**Rhyl** (LD) (*St. Asaph–Bodfari*)–19.0–Flint–6.6–**Queensferry** (CH) (*Mold–Bodfari–Ruthin*)–5.0–**Chester** (CH) (*Sutton Weaver–Warrington, Hooton–Birkenhead, Wrexham*)–9.9–**Broxton** (CH) (*Malpas–Whitchurch*)–11.5–**Nantwich** (SK) (*Wrenbury–Whitchurch*)–10.0–Alsager–2.4–**Kidsgrove** (SK) (*Macclesfield–Manchester, Middlewich–Warrington, Biddulph*)–(3.0, TR3)–Tunstall–(4.8, TR3)–**Stoke-on-Trent** (SK) (*Stone–London, Leek*)–8.4–**Draycott** (SK) (*Cheadle*)–8.3–**Uttoxeter** (DB) (*Ashbourne*)–15.0–{**Willington (Derbys.)** (DB) (*Burton-on-Trent–Lichfield, Melbourne–Loughborough*)}—(7.0, PG5)–**Derby** (DB) (*Melbourne–Loughborough, Bakewell*)–(9.6, PU2)–**Ilkeston** (IK) (*Chesterfield, Gotham–Loughborough*)–(7.5, TU3)–**Nottingham** (NG) (*Gotham–Loughborough, Harby–Grantham, Kettering* loop, *Staveley, Mansfield* loop)–(8.4, PG5)–Lowdham–(5.4, PG5)–Southwell–(6.8, PG5)–**Newark** (NK) (*Lincoln*)]–9.6–Fulbeck–8.5–**Sleaford** (SO) (*Metheringham–Lincoln, Aunsby–Bourne*)–4.8–**Heckington** (SO) (*Spalding*)–12.0–**Boston** (*Skegness–Alford–Grimsby, Gosberton–Spalding*)
PG8	Fleetwood–Preston–Penistone–Sheffield–Lincoln–Kings Lynn–Norwich [21.2 m] 222.3 m + (4.8 m)	Fleetwood–5.3–**Poulton-le-Fylde** (PF) (*Garstang, Blackpool–Kirkham, Fylde* loop)–6.8–**Kirkham** (PR) (*Blackpool–Poulton-le-Fylde, Fylde* loop)–7.8–**Preston** (PR) (*Chorley–London, Garstang–Carlisle, Kirkham–Fleetwood*)–9.3–**Blackburn** (PR) (*Darwen, Chorley*)–5.0–**Clayton-le-Moors** (CA) (*Clitheroe, Accrington–Helmshore–Manchester*)–4.0–Padiham–3.0–**Burnley** (CA) (*Colne–Elslack–Skipton, Wharfedale* loop)–8.8–**Todmorden** (HX) (*Rochdale–Manchester*)–4.4–Hebden Bridge–5.4–**Sowerby Bridge** (HX) (*Halifax–Bradford*)–3.4–**Greetland** (HX) (*Halifax*)–4.3–**Brighouse** (HF) (*Mirfield*)–3.0–**Deighton** (HF) (*Huddersfield, Mirfield–Leeds*)–4.7–Kirkburton–3.3–Denby Dale–3.3–[**Penistone** (HF) (*Barnsley*)–(4.0, TG2)–Stocksbridge–(12.0, TG2)–**Sheffield** (SF) (*Rotherham*)–(5.2, TU5)–**Beighton** (SF) (*Staveley–Chesterfield*)]–10.0–**Worksop** (WP) (*Creswell–Shirebrook*)–4.5–**Ranby** (WP) (*Blyth–Doncaster*)–3.4–Retford–3.3–{**North Leverton** (WP) (*Gainsborough*)}–5.8–{**Torksey** (LI) (*Gainsborough*)}–4.1–Saxilby–6.4–**Lincoln**

Table A4.3. (Continued)

Ref	Origin–destination	Route
		(LI) (*Market Rasen–Grimsby, Newark*)–8.5–**Metheringham** (SO) (*Horncastle–Alford–Mablethorpe*)–10.1–**Sleaford** (SO) (*Aunsby–Bourne, Newark*)–(4.8, PG7) **Heckington** (SO) (*Boston*)–7.2–Donington–3.2–**Gosberton** (SG) (*Boston, Spalding*)–9.0–**Holbeach** (SG) (*Spalding*)–4.8–**Long Sutton** (SG) (*Wisbech–Downham Market–Thetford*)–14.0–**Kings Lynn** (KY) (*Wisbech, Hunstanton–Wells-next-the-Sea, Cromer* loop)–16.3–Swaffham–7.6–**Shipdham** (ER) (*Watton* (*Norfolk*)–*Roudham*)–5.0–**East Dereham** (ER) (*Fakenham–Wells-next-the-Sea*)–17.3–**Norwich** (NR) (*Great Yarmouth, Bungay–Ilketshall–Ipswich, Wymondham–Roudham–Thetford, Swanton Abbot, Cromer* loop)
PG9	Kirby Lonsdale–Skipton–Leeds–Knottingley–Thorne–Grimsby [83.8 m + (11.0 m)] 31.5 m + (14.3 m)	[**Kirby Lonsdale** (KL) (*Milnthorpe, Furness* loop, *Lancaster, Sedburgh Junction–Carlisle*)–7.2–Ingleton–4.6–Clapham–5.8–Giggleswick–8.0–{**Bell Busk** (SX) (*Elslack–Colne*)}–7.0–**Skipton** (SX) (*Elslack–Colne, Ilkley–Burley, Wharfedale* loop)–8.5–**Keighley** (SX) (*Haworth*)–3.8–Bingley–2.8–**Shipley** (BF) (*Bradford–Halifax*)–3.8–**Rawdon** (LS) (*Burley*)–9.0–**Leeds** (LS) (*East Ardsley–Wakefield, Wetherby, Pudsey, Batley, West Yorkshire* loop)–4.8–Rothwell–6.2–Castleford–4.8–**Knottingley** (SN) (*Wakefield, Doncaster*)–(11.0, TG1)–**Snaith** (SN) (*Selby, Goole–Hull*)]–7.5–**Thorne** (SN) (*Doncaster, Goole, Epworth–Gainsborough–Lincoln*)]–5.8–Crowle–4.8–**Gunness** (BI) (*Epworth–Gainsborough*)–3.6–Scunthorpe–8.5–**Brigg** (BI) (*Barton-on-Humber*)–8.8–**Caistor** (GR) (*Market Rasen*)–(14.3, PG5)–**Grimsby** (GR) (*Cleethorpes–Louth–Boston*)
	Primary orbital routes	
PO1	London Outer Orbital 94.7 m + (2.8 m)	*Chatham–Otford–Godstone–Dorking*–**Leatherhead** (DK) (*Epsom–London, East Horsley–Guildford*)–4.8–Cobham–4.8–**Addlestone** (ST) (*Weybridge–Surbiton*)–2.0–Chertsey–3.2–**Staines** (ST) (*Wokingham–Reading, Ash–Southampton, Feltham–London*)–8.8–**Uxbridge** (UX) (*Beaconsfield–Loudwater–High Wycombe, Ealing–London*)–7.3–**Rickmansworth** (WT) (*Amersham–Aylesbury*)–3.8–**Watford** (WT) (*Boxmoor–Tring, Wembley–London*)–7.5–**St. Albans** (SA) (*Hemel Hempstead–Boxmoor, Welwyn–Stevenage, Luton–Leighton Buzzard, Dunstable* loop)–5.8–Hatfield–7.5–Hertford–3.0–**Ware** (WE) (*Stevenage*)–(2.8, TR4)–**St. Margarets** (WE) (*Broxbourne–Ponders End*)–6.0–**Harlow** (HO) (*Bishops Stortford–Newport (Essex)–Cambridge, Buckhurst Hill–London*)–7.5–Chipping Ongar–7.2–**Brentwood** (BW) (*Basildon–Southend, Chelmsford, Romford–Barking*)–6.0–**Upminster** (UP) (*Barking*)–9.5–Tilbury (Gravesend ferry)
	Primary feeders	*Long-distance primary routes feeding in traffic to, or distributing traffic from, trunk routes, and carrying moderate levels of traffic at high speed*
PF1	Ramsgate–Faversham–*London* 31.1 m	**Ramsgate** (*Sandwich*)–5.8–Margate–16.8–Whitstable–8.5–**Faversham** (CT) (*Canterbury–Dover*)–*Sittingbourne–London*

(*continued*)

Table A4.3. (Continued)

Ref	Origin–destination	Route
PF2	Dover–Ashford–Maidstone–Otford–Lewisham–*London*: 57.0 m + (10.2 m)	Dover–**Lympne** (DV) (*Rye*)–9.9–**Ashford** (AH) (*Tenterden–Canterbury*)–12.5–**Headcorn** (MD) (*Tenterden*)–3.9–**Chart Sutton** (MD) (*Cranbrook*)–5.5–**Maidstone** (MD) (*Hadlow–Tonbridge, Burham–Chatham*)–6.0–**West Malling** (MD) (*Burham*)–(5.3, TK1)–**Ightham** (OT) (*Hadlow*)–(4.9, TK1)–**Otford** (OT) (*Sevenoaks, Oxted–Godstone*)–8.0–Orpington–6.2–**Bromley** (LN) (*Dartford, Croydon*)–5.0–**Lewisham** (LN) (*Croydon, Clapham, Dartford, Woolwich*, Surrey Docks loop)–*London* (S Central)
PF3	Hastings–Tunbridge Wells–*London* 45.8 m + (1.5 m)	**Hastings** (HT) (*Rye, Pevensey–Eastbourne*)–5.3* + (1.5)–Battle–5.4–Robertsbridge–3.0–**Hurst Green** (HT) (*Hawkhurst–Cranbrook–Maidstone*)–3.7–Ticehurst–3.8–Wadhurst–2.8–**Bells Yew Green** (*Lamberhurst–Cranbrook–Tenterden*)–3.9–**Tunbridge Wells** (TW) (*Tonbridge–Hadlow–Maidstone, Uckfield*)–8.0–**Hever** (TW) (*East Grinstead*)–2.0–Edenbridge–7.9–**Godstone** (GD) (*Reigate–Dorking, Oxted–Ightham–Maidstone, East Grinstead*)–Croydon–London
PF4	Portsmouth–Bentley–*Farnham–London* 31.1 m + (2.8 m)	Portsmouth–5.0–**Cosham** (HV) (*Fareham–Southampton*)–(2.8, PG1)–**Havant** (HV) (*Chichester–Brighton*)–12.5–**Petersfield** (PT) (*Midhurst–Pulborough, Bishops Waltham–Botley*, Weald link)–8.8–Bordon–4.8–**Bentley** (AS) (*Alton–Winchester*)–Farnham–London
PF5	Isle of Portland–Weymouth–Dorchester–Poole–*London* 38.5 m	Fortuneswell, Portland–4.8–Weymouth–4.0–**Upwey** (DR) (*Bridport–Crewkerne–Taunton*)–4.2–**Dorchester** (DR) (*Maiden Newton–Yeovil*)–11.2–Wool–5.3–**Wareham** (PL) (*Swanage*)–9.0–**Poole** (PL) (*Wimborne–Milborne Port–Yeovil*)–*Christchurch–Southampton–London*
PF6	*Weymouth*–Dorchester–Bridgewater 43.3 m	Weymouth–**Dorchester** (DR) (*Wareham–Poole*)–8.0–Maiden Newton–12.5–**Yeovil** (YV) (*Milborne Port–Bruton–London, Crewkerne–Exeter, Axminster* loop)–12.3–**Langport** (LG) (*Glastonbury–Wells, Wrantage–Taunton, Bruton*)–10.5–**Bridgewater** (WM) (*Highbridge–Bristol, Taunton*)
PF7	Penzance–Plymouth–*London* 84.8 m	St. Just–7.2–Penzance–3.0–**Ludgvan** (PZ) (*Treluswell, Helston* loop)–3.6–**Lelant** (PZ) (*St. Ives*)–7.5–Camborne–3.3–**Redruth** (RR) (*Portreath, Treluswell–Falmouth*)–8.5–**Truro** (TR) (*Newquay–Tredinnick, North Cornwall* loop, *Treluswell–Falmouth*)–13.3–St. Austell–8.8–**Lostwithiel** (BJ) (*Fowey*)–3.3–**Llanhydrock** (BJ) (*Bodmin–Wadebridge*)–9.5–**Liskeard** (BJ) (*Looe*)–12.0–Saltash–4.8–**Plymouth** (PM) (*South Brent–London, Tavistock–Shilstone–Exeter*)
PF8	Haverfordwest–Carmarthen 31.0 m	**Haverfordwest** (HW) (*Milford Haven–Pembroke–Narberth, Fishguard–Cardigan–Carmarthen, Cardigan & Tenby* loop)–10.0–**Narberth** (CM) (*Tenby–Milford Haven, Cardigan & Tenby* loop)–6.3–Whitland–5.0–St. Clears–9.7–**Carmarthen** (CM) (*Llangeler–Aberystwyth, Treneddyn–Cardiff, Llanelly–Gorseinon–Swansea*)
PF9	Aberystwyth–Llangurig–Gloucester–*London* 98.6 m + (25.9 m)	**Aberystwyth** (AW) (*Aberdovey–Barmouth*, North Wales Coast loop)–10.5–**Llanafan** (AW) (*Tregaron–Llangeler–Carmarthen*)–8.0–Cwmystwyth–10.0–**Llangurig** (LR) (*Llanidloes–*

Table A4.3. (Continued)

Ref	Origin–destination	Route
		Berriew–Shrewsbury)–9.7–Rhayader–7.6–**Llandrindod Wells** (BU) (*Presteigne*)–6.0–**Builth Wells** (BU) (*Llanwrtyd Wells– Llandeilo–Carmarthen*)–(14.0, PG5)–**Three Cocks** (HA) (*Brecon*)–(5.3, PG5)–Hay-on-Wye–(6.6, PG5)–**Willersley** (HA) (*Leominster–Worcester, Kington–Walford*)–14.5–**Hereford** (HR) (*Bodenham–Leominster, Ledbury–Bromsberrow Heath–Great Malvern, Pontrilas–Abergavenny*)–14.4–**Ross-on-Wye** (RW) (*Monmouth–Pontypool*)–8.4–**Newent** (RW) (*Bromsberrow Heath–Great Malvern*)–9.5–**Gloucester** (GL) (*Cheltenham–London, Stonehouse (Glos.)–Bristol, Coombe Hill–Tewkesbury*)
PF10	*Welshpool*–Arddlin–Shrewsbury–Wolverhampton 47.8 m	*Welshpool*–**Arddlin** (WO) (*Llanymynech–Oswestry*)–10.0–**Shrawardine** (SR) (*Oswestry*)–7.0–**Shrewsbury** (SR) (*Wem–Whitchurch*)–7.7–**Uppington** (WJ) (*Leighton–Coalport*)–3.6–Wellington (Staffs.)–3.2–**Oakengates** (WJ) (*Newport (Staffs.)–Stafford*)–4.0–**Shifnal** (WJ) (*Coalport–Bridgnorth*)–8.4–Codsall–3.9–**Wolverhampton** (WH) (*Wednesbury–Birmingham, Penkridge–Stafford, Wimborne–Kidderminster, Walsall*)
PF11	Stranraer–Creca–*Carlisle*–96.4 m	Stranraer–7.2–**Whitecrook** (SJ) (*Girvan–Ayr–Glasgow*)–17.6–**Newton Stewart** (SJ) (*Wigtown–Whithorn*)–16.3–Gatehouse of Fleet–8.0–Kirkcudbright–10.0–Castle Douglas–5.2–Dalbeattie–13.0–**Dumfries** (DF) (*Lochmaben–Millhousebridge–Glasgow, Thornhill–Mauchline–Kilmarnock*)–16.3–Annan–2.8–{**Creca** (DF) (*Lockerbie–Millhousebridge*)}–Todhills–Carlisle
PF12	Fochabers–Inverness–Glasgow–*London* 241.1 m	–**Fochabers** (FB) (*Keith–Milltown–Aberdeen, Rothes–Craigellachie–Spean Bridge, Aviemore loop, Turriff, Banff loop*)–9.0–**Elgin** (FB) (*Lossiemouth*)–12.8–Forres–10.0–Nairn–17.5–**Inverness** (IV) (*Muir of Ord–Thurso, Schlod–Carrbridge–Aviemore*)–14.6–Strone–11.9–**Invermoriston** (IV) (*Kyle of Lochalsh*)–5.5–Fort Augustus–7.5–Invergarry–15.0–**Spean Bridge** (FW) (*Aviemore–Carrbridge–Fochabers*)–9.4–Fort William–12.5–Ballachulish–11.5–Portnacroish–12.3–**Connel Ferry** (FW) (*Oban*)–16.2–Lochawe–20.8–**Crianlarich** (FW) (*Lochearnhead–Dunblane*)–16.0–Tarbet–9.8–Luss–9.3–Balloch–4.5–Dumbarton–15.0–**Glasgow** (GG) (*Uddingston–Carlisle, Kirkintilloch–Castlecary–Edinburgh, Lugton–Kilmarnock, Coatbridge–Airdrie, Clarkston, Paisley–Greenock, Clyde loop*)
PF13	York–Lincoln–Stevenage–*London* 99.7 m + (73.0 m)	**York** (YK) (*Malton–Scarborough, Wetherby, Carlton Husthwaite–Thirsk, Market Weighton–Hull*)–14.5–**Selby** (SN) (*Wetherby, Balkholme–Hull*)–7.5–**Snaith** (SN) (*Goole–Hull, Knottingley*)–(7.5, PG9)–**Thorne** (SN) (*Doncaster–Sheffield, Gunness–Brigg–Grimsby*)–9.0–**Epworth** (GB) (*Gunness–Scunthorpe*)–2.3–Haxey (East Lound)–7.2–**Gainsborough** (GB) (*North Leverton–Retford*)–7.4–**Torksey** (LI) (*North Leverton–Retford*)–(4.1, PG8)–Saxilby–(6.4, PG8)–**Lincoln** (LI) (*Newark, Market Rasen*)–(8.5, PG8)–**Metheringham** (SO) (*Horncastle–Alford*)–10.1–**Sleaford** (SO)

(*continued*)

Table A4.3. (Continued)

Ref	Origin–destination	Route
		(*Heckington–Spalding, Newark*)–4.0–**Aunsby** (SO) (*Ropsley–Grantham*)–6.0–**Aslackby** (RE) (*Ropsley–Grantham*)–7.3–**Bourne** (RE) (*Spalding*)–7.5–Market Deeping–5.0–{**Werrington** (PB) (*Spalding, Stamford–Manton–Leicester*)}–(4.0, PG3)–**Peterborough** (PB) (*Whittlesey–March, Oundle–Irthlingborough–Northampton*)–(19.5, PG3)–**Huntingdon** (HN) (*St. Ives–Cambridge, Warboys–Chatteris*)–(8.5, PG3)–St. Neots–(4.4, PG3)–**Tempsford** (BD) (*Willington (Beds.)–Bedford*)–3.2–**Sandy** (BD) (*Willington (Beds.)–Bedford, Potton–Cambridge*)–3.2–Biggleswade–10.8–**Hitchin** (SE) (*Luton, Baldock*)–4.8–**Stevenage** (SE) (*Baldock–Cambridge, Welwyn–St. Albans*)–*London*
PF14	Great Yarmouth–Ipswich–London 62.5 m	**Great Yarmouth** (YA) (*Brundall–Norwich*)–10.0–Lowestoft–9.8–Beccles–3.8–**Ilketshall** (BC) (*Bungay–Norwich*)–6.8–**Halesworth** (BC) (*Southwold*)–10.0–**Saxmundham** (IP) (*Leiston–Aldeburgh, Framlingham*)–13.3–Woodbridge–8.8–**Ipswich** (IP) (*Manningtree–London, Stowmarket–Cambridge, Hadleigh–Sudbury, Felixstowe*)
Primary coastal loops		
PC1	Teesideloop: Newcastle–Sunderland–Hartlepool–Stockton–Darlington 54.4 m + (2.0 m)	**Newcastle** (NE) (*Morpeth–Glasgow, Chester-le-Street, Swalwell–Carlisle, Tynemouth, Blyth loop, Byker loop*)–5.3* + (2.0)–**Monkton** (NE) (*South Shields*)–6.3–**Sunderland** (SU) (*Penshaw–Durham*)–5.5–Seaham–5.2–**Easington** (SQ) (*Pittington–Durham*)–8.6–Hartlepool–7.2–Billingham–3.5–**Stockton-on-Tees** (SQ) (*Middlesbrough–Saltburn, Newton Aycliffe*)–3.8–**Eaglescliffe** (SQ) (*Yarm–Crathorne–Northallerton*)–9.0–**Darlington** (DL) (*Barnard Castle–Middleton-in-Teesdale, Newton Aycliffe–Durham*)
Primary links		
PK1	*Chatham–Burham–Maidstone* 5.0 m	*Chatham*–**Burham** (MD) (*West Malling*)–5.0–**Maidstone** (MD) (*Chart Sutton–Ashford, Ightham–Dorking, Hadlow–Tunbridge Wells*)
PK2	Ringwood link: Christchurch–Alberbury–Salisbury 23.5 m	**Christchurch** (PL) (*Poole, Brockenhurst, Lymington loop*)–8.6–Ringwood–11.3–Downton (Hants)–3.6–**Alderbury** (SB) (*Mottisfont–Romsey*)–*Salisbury*
PK3	Boxmoor–Hemel Hempstead–St. Albans–Stevenage 20.0 m + (3.7 m)	**Boxmoor** (TG) (*Tring (Marsworth), Watford*)–2.3–Hemel Hempstead–5.3–**St. Albans** (SA) (*Hatfield, Watford, London Outer Orbital, Leighton Buzzard, Dunstable loop*)–3.2* + (2.0)–Wheathampstead–4.4–Welwyn–2.9–Knebworth–1.9 + (1.7)–**Stevenage** (SE) (*Hitchin–Sandy–Peterborough, Ware*)
PK4	*Aberystwyth–Llangurig–Welshpool–Oswestry–Chester–Birkenhead* 94.7 m	*Aberystwyth–Llanafan–***Llangurig** (LR) (*Newbridge–Rhayader–Gloucester*)–5.3–Llanidloes–8.8–Caersws–6.5–Newtown–9.0–**Berriew** (WO) (*Montgomery–Walford–Ludlow, Bishops Castle* link)–6.3–Welshpool–5.3–**Arddlin** (WO) (*Shrawardine–Shrewsbury*)–4.0–Llanymynech–6.6–**Oswestry** (RU) (*Ellesmere–Penley–Whitchurch, Shrawardine–Shrewsbury*)–10.0–**Ruabon** (RU) (*Llangollen–Barmouth, Overton-on-Dee–Penley–Whitchurch*)–4.6–**Wrexham** (RU) (*Hope–Buckley*)–12.3–**Chester** (CH) (*Sutton Weaver–Warrington,*

Table A4.3. (Continued)

Ref	Origin–destination	Route
		Queensferry–Rhyl–Holyhead, Broxton–Nantwich–Stoke)– 8.4–**Hooton** (CH) (*Heswall–Birkenhead*, Wirral loop)–4.1– Bebington–3.5–**Birkenhead** (BK) (*Wallasey–West Kirby– Hooton*, Wirral loop, *Liverpool* ferry)
PK5	Todmorden–Rochdale–Man-chester 21.4 m	**Todmorden** (HX) (*Burnley, Sowerby Bridge*)–2.0–Walsden– 4.5–Littleborough–4.0–**Rochdale** (RC) (*Bury, Oldham*)– 5.5–**Middleton** (MN) (*Bury, Oldham*)–5.4–**Manchester** (MN) *Stalybridge, Stockport, Stretford–Warrington, Worsley– Bolton, Whitefield–Bury*)
PK6	Wensleydale link: Catterick–Leyburn–Hawes–Sedbergh 36.9 m + (1.5 m)	**Catterick** (CK) (*Middleton Tyas–Darlington, Northallerton, Richmond, West Tanfield–Ripon*)–7.0* + (1.5)–{**Constable Burton** (CK) (*West Tanfield–Ripon*)}–3.0–Leyburn–15.8– Hawes–9.3–**Sedbergh** (SS) (*Brough, Kirkby Stephen* loop)– 1.8–**Sedbergh Junction** (SS) (*Beck Foot–Penrith, Kirky Lonsdale–Lancaster*)
PK7	*Ripon*–West Tanfield–Con-stable Burton–*Leyburn* 11.1 m	*Ripon*–{**West Tanfield** (CK) (*Catterick*)}–3.5–Masham–7.6– {**Constable Burton** (CK) (*Catterick*)}–*Leyburn*
PK8	Catterick–Northallerton 9.6 m	**Catterick** (CK) (*Middleton Tyas–Darlington, Constable Bur-ton–Leyburn, Bedale–West Tanfied–Ripon*)–9.6–**Northaller-ton** (NA) (*Thirsk, Crathorne–Stockton-on-Tees*)
PK9	Waverley link: *Carlisle*–Tod-hills–Hawick–Maxton–*Edin-burgh* 52.7 m	*Carlisle*–**Todhills** (CL) (*Creca–Glasgow*)–3.4–Longtown– 5.7–Canonbie–6.0–Langholm–13.5–Teviothead–9.7– Hawick–10.8–**Ancrum** (ML) (*Jedburgh*)–3.6–**Maxton** (ML) (*Kelso–Coldstream–Newcastle*)–*Melrose–Galashiels–Edin-burgh*
PK10	Tyne Valley link: Carlisle–Hexham–Newcastle 61.1 m + (2.0 m)	**Carlisle** (CL) (*Todhills–Glasgow, Penrith, Wigton–Bromfield– Workington*, Furness loop)–9.8–Brampton–12.5–**Haltwhis-tle** (NE) (*Alston*)–16.0–Hexham–4.0–Corbridge–7.5–Prud-hoe–7.0–**Swalwell** (NE) (*Consett* (*Leadgate*), *Shotley Bridge* loop)–4.3* (+ 2.0)–**Newcastle** (NE) (*Morpeth–Glasgow, Monkton–Sunderland, Chester-le-Street–Darlington, Wall-send–Tynemouth, Blyth* loop, *Byker* loop)
PK11	Halifax link: Shipley–Brad-ford–Halifax–Mirfield 24.4 m + (4.3 m)	**Shipley** (BF) (*Rawdon–Leeds, Keighley–Skipton*)–3.8–**Brad-ford** (BF) (*Dudley Hill*)–4.5–Thornton–4.8–Ovenden–1.5– **Halifax** (HX) (*Sowerby Bridge–Burnley*)–4.0–**Greetland** (HX) (*Sowerby Bridge–Burnley*)–(4.3, PG8)–**Brighouse** (HF) (*Deighton–Penistone*)–5.8–**Mirfield** (HF) (*Dewsbury– Wakefield, Deighton–Huddersfield*)
PK12	Halifax–Sowerby Bridge 3.6 m	**Halifax** (HX) (*Thornton–Bradford, Greetland*)–3.6–**Sowerby Bridge** (HX) (*Hebden Bridge–Burnley, Greetland*)
PK13	Derby cut-off: *Stoke-on-Trent*–Willington (Derbys.)–Melbourne–*Loughborough* 6.3 m *Not used for passenger traffic*	*Stoke-on-Trent*–**Willington (Derbys.)** (*Burton-on-Trent, Derby*)–6.3–**Melbourne** (*Derby*)–*Shepshed–Loughborough*
PK14	Bungay link: Ilketshall–Bun-gay–Norwich 18.7 m	**Ilketshall** (BC) (*Halesworth–Saxmundham–Ipswich, Beccles– Great Yarmouth*)–3.2–**Bungay** (BC) (*Harleston–Diss*)–15.5– **Norwich** (NR) (*East Dereham–Kings Lynn, Wymondham– Roudham–Thetford, Great Yarmouth, Swanton Abbot–Cro-mer*, North Norfolk loop)

(continued)

Table A4.3. (Continued)

Ref	Origin–destination	Route
	Primary loops into urban centres	
PU1	**Swansea loop** [5.5 m + (1.2 m)] 30.8 m	[**Neath** (SW) (*Pyle–Gloucester, Ynystawe*)–5.5* + (1.2)–**Swansea** (SW) (*Morriston–Ynystawe*)]–6.8–**Gorseinon** (SW) (*Pontarddulais*)–5.0–Llanelly–4.5–Burry Port–4.5–Kidwelly–10.0–**Carmarthen** (CM) (*Narberth–Haverfordwest, Llangeler–Cardigan, Llanddarog–Llandeilo*)
PU2	*Derby loop* 18.6 m + (9.6 m)	**Loughborough** (LE) (*Birstall–Leicester, Gotham–Ilkeston*)–4.1–**Shepshed** (LE) (*Swannington–Burton-on-Trent*)–7.2–**Melbourne** (*Willington* (*Derbys.*)–*Stoke-on-Trent*)–7.3–**Derby** (DB) (*Willington* (*Derbys.*)–*Burton-on-Trent, Bakewell*)–(9.6, PG5)–**Ilkeston** (IK) (*Chesterfield, Nottingham, Gotham–Loughborough*)
	Inter-regional secondary lines	*Long-distance or medium-distance lines carrying moderate amounts of traffic at moderate speed*
SG1	Weald link: Sandwich–Canterbury–Ashford–Tenterden–Tunbridge Wells–Horsham–Petersfield–Botley–*Southampton* 140.0 m + (11.9 m)	**Sandwich** (CT) (*Ramsgate–Faversham, Whitfield–Dover, Deal* loop)–5.8–Wingham–7.4–**Canterbury** (CT) (*Faversham–London, Whitfield–Dover*)–3.2–Chartham–2.4–Chilham–4.9–Wye–3.5–**Ashford** (AH) (*Headcorn–Maidstone, Lympne–Folkestone–Dover*)–2.0–Great Chart–10.0–**Tenterden** (TN) (*Rye, Headcorn*)–3.4–Rolvenden–5.4–**Cranbrook** (TN) (*Hawkhurst–Hurst Green–Hastings, Staplehurst–Chart Sutton–Maidstone*)–4.0–Goudhurst–3.7–Lamberhurst–3.4–{**Bells Yew Green** (TW) (*Wadhurst–Hurst Green–Hastings*)}–(3.9, PF3)–**Tunbridge Wells** (TW) (*Tonbridge–West Peckham–Ightham*)–(7.8, PF3)–**Hever** (TW) (*Edenbridge–Godstone*)–7.5–**East Grinstead** (EG) (*Uckfield, Godstone*)–9.0–Crawley–7.8–**Horsham** (HS) (*Brighton, Dorking, Guildford, Uckfield*)–8.0–Billingshurst–6.0–**Pulborough** (HS) (*Arundel–Littlehampton*)–5.5–Petworth–7.0–Midhurst–10.4–**Petersfield** (PT) (*Havant–Portsmouth, Bentley–Farnham*)–5.0–East Meon–5.2–Corhampton–4.2–Bishops Waltham–5.3–**Botley** (SH) (*Fareham–Portsmouth*)–North Stoneham–Southampton
SG2	Nene Valley link: *Trowbridge–Melksham–Chippenham–*Great Somerford–Swindon–Witney–Oxford–Buckingham–Northampton–Peterborough–March–*Kings Lynn* 134.5 m + (16.0 m)	*Trowbridge–Melksham–Chippenham–***Great Somerford** (CP) (*Malmesbury–Cherington–Stratford-on-Avon, Fosse Way* loop)–3.7–Brinkworth–3.6–Wootton Bassett–5.9–**Swindon** (WW) (*Cricklade–Ampney St. Peter–Cirencester, Ramsbury–Hungerford*)–7.2–Highworth–4.9–**Lechlade** (WW) (*Cirencester, Faringdon–Oxford, Wantage* loop)–7.3–Bampton–5.7–**Witney** (OX) (*Burford–Northleach*)–(10.8, TR2)–**Oxford** (OX) (*Radley–London, Thame–Aylesbury*)–(5.2, PG2)–{**Kidlington** (OX) (*Chipping Norton, Banbury*)}–8.0–Bicester–11.0–**Buckingham** (KH) (*Brackley–Banbury, Winslow–Aylesbury*)–10.0–Towcester–9.6–**Northampton** (NH) (*Whilton–Crick–Carlisle, Ravenstone–Leighton Buzzard–London*)–7.2–Earls Barton–4.0–**Wellingborough** (WL) (*Kettering–Leicester*)–4.2–**Irthlingborough** (WL) (*Higham Ferres–Rushden*)–3.8–Raunds–4.0–Thrapston–7.2–Oundle–12.3–**Peterborough** (PB) (*Werrington–Spalding, Huntingdon*)–5.1–

Table A4.3. (Continued)

Ref	Origin–destination	Route
		Whittlesey–9.8–**March** (MC) (*Chatteris–Ely, Wisbech–Kings Lynn*)
SG3	Birmingham–Leicester–Cambridge–Clacton-on-Sea 148.6 m + (41.3 m)	**Birmingham** (BM) (*Handsworth–Wolverhampton, Redditch, Warwick, Walsall, Lichfield*)–(8.4, TF1)–{**Coleshill** (BM) (*Coventry*)}–10.9–**Nuneaton** (NN) (*Crick–Northampton, Tamworth–Lichfield*)–4.8–Hinckley–3.4–Earl Shilton–4.4–**Desford** (LE) (*Swannington*)–6.0–**Leicester** (LE) (*Loughborough, Lutterworth–Crick–Northampton, Market Harborough–Kettering–Wellingborough*)–13.5* + (3.0)–**Melton Mowbray** (MM) (*Harby–Grantham*)–11.0–Oakham–3.5–**Manton** (MM) (*Uppingham*)–10.0–Stamford–9.5–{**Werrington** (PB) (*Spalding, Bourne–Grantham*)}–(4.0, PG3)–**Peterborough** (PB) (*Whittlesey–March, Oundle–Irthlingborough–Northampton*)–(19.5, PG3)–**Huntingdon** (HN) (*Tempsford–Stevenage, Warboys–Chatteris*)–5.8–St. Ives–12.8–**Cambridge** (CB) (*Swaffham Bulbeck–Newmarket–Norwich, Royston–Baldock, Sandy–Bedford, Ely–Kings Lynn*)–10.8–**Linton** (CB) (*Newport (Essex)–Bishops Stortford–Harlow*)–7.2–Haverhill–4.0–**Wixoe** (SZ) (*Long Melford–Sudbury–Ipswich*)–7.0–Sible Hedingham–4.5–**Halstead** (SU) (*Braintree, Sudbury*)–2.6–Earls Colne–4.4–**Coggeshall** (**Broad Green**) (CR) (*Chelmsford*)–(7.9, TR8)–**Colchester** (CR) (*Manningtree–Ipswich*)–4.0–Wivenhoe–4.5–Brightlingsea–6.0–Clacton-on-Sea
SG4	Cumbrian link: Darlington–Penrith–Keswick–Workington 94.8 m	**Darlington** (DL) (*Middleton Tyas–Catterick–London, Newton Aycliffe–Durham, Eaglescliffe–Stockton-on-Tees*)–5.5–Piercebridge–3.5–**Winston** (BZ) (*Middleton Tyas*)–6.0–**Barnard Castle** (BZ) (*Bishop Auckland, Middleton-in-Teesdale*)–4.9–Bowes–13.9–**Brough** (**Cumbria**) (BZ) (*Kirkby Stephen–Sedbergh*)–8.5–Appleby–13.5–**Penrith** (PN) (*Carlisle, Beck Foot–Lancaster*)–6.0–Penruddock–6.0–Scales–6.3–Keswick–2.5–Braithwaite–10.2–Cockermouth–8.0–**Workington** (WO) (*Whitehaven–Dalton-in-Furness–Ulverston, Maryport–Bromfield–Carlisle, Furness loop*)
SG5	Fochabers–Aberdeen 64.6 m	**Fochabers** (FB) (*Elgin–Inverness, Rothes–Craigellachie–Spean Bridge, Aviemore loop, Turriff, Banff loop*)–8.0–Keith–7.8–**Milltown** (TU) (*Huntly*)–12.4–**Turriff** (TU) (*Fraserburgh–Dyce, Peterhead loop, Fochabers, Banff loop*)–9.2–Fyvie–7.8–Old Meldrum–4.4–Inverurie–10.0–**Dyce** (AB) (*Ellon–Turriff, Peterhead loop*)–5.0–**Aberdeen** (AB) (*Stonehaven–Montrose–Perth, Ballater*)
	Secondary feeders	*Lines carrying moderate amounts of traffic at moderate speeds to feed it into a major hub*
SF1	Eastbourne–East Grinstead–Clapham–*London* 57.7 m + (2.5 m)	Eastbourne–5.0–**Polegate** (EB) (*Lewes, Pevensey–Bexhill–Hastings*)–3.5–Hailsham–11.3–**Uckfield** (UK) (*Lewes, Tunbridge Wells*)–11.0–Forest Row–3.5–**East Grinstead** (EG) (*Crawley–Horsham, Hever–Tunbridbge Wells*)–3.7–Lingfield–3.0* + (2.5)–**Godstone** (GD) (*Reigate–Dorking, Oxted–Ightham–Maidstone*)–9.0–**Croydon** (CN) (*Carshalton–Epsom, Lewisham, Bromley–Dartford*)–4.5–Streatham–

(*continued*)

Table A4.3. (Continued)

Ref	Origin–destination	Route
		3.2–**Clapham** (LN) (*Wimbledon–Ewell, Carshalton–Ewell, Lewisham, London (SW)*, London Inner Orbital)–London (S)
SF2	Witley–Godalming–Guild-ford–Leatherhead–*London* 13.1 m + (6.4 m)	Witley–1.5–Milford–1.8–Godalming–4.6–**Guildford** (GF) (*Woking–Chobham, Ash–Reading, Horsham*)–(6.4, TK1)–**East Horsley** (DK) (*Dorking*)–5.2–**Leatherhead** (DK) (*Dorking–Brighton*)–*Epsom–London*
SF3	Warwick–Birmingham 21.8 m	**Warwick** (LM) (*Stratford-upon-Avon–Evesham, Leamington–Banbury*)–14.0–Solihull–7.8–**Birmingham** (BM) (*Handsworth–Wolverhampton, Sutton Coldfield–Lichfield, Coleshill–Coventry, Walsall, Redditch*)
SF4	Southport–Wigan–Worsley–*Manchester* 31.5 m	**Southport** (SM) (*Formby–Liverpool, Tarleton–Preston*)–8.3–**Ormskirk** (OM) (*Maghull–Liverpool, Chorley–Preston*)–5.0–{**Digmoor** (OM) (*St. Helens*)}–3.6–Orrell–3.4–**Wigan** (WG) (*Bolton, Chorley, Warrington, St. Helens*)–2.4–Hindley–3.7–Atherton–1.6–Tyldesley–3.5–**Worsley** (MN) (*Bolton*)–*Salford–Manchester*
SF5	*Ormskirk*–Digmoor–St. Helens–Warrington 14.4 m	*Ormskirk*–{**Digmoor** (OM) (*Wigan*)}–2.5–Rainford–3.9–**St. Helens** (SI) (*Huyton–Liverpool, Wigan*)–8.0–**Warrington** (WR) (*Northwich–London, Sutton Weaver–Chester, Hollins Green–Manchester, Huyton–Liverpool, Widnes, Mersey* loop)
SF6	Clitheroe–Clayton-le-Moors–Accrington–Manchester 32.6 m	Clitheroe–3.8–Whalley–4.0–**Clayton-le-Moors** (CA) (*Blackburn–Preston, Burnley*)–2.0–Accrington–5.3–**Helmshore** (BQ) (*Rochdale, Bacup* loop)–3.0–Ramsbottom–5.0–**Bury** (BQ) (*Rochdale, Bolton*)–3.0–**Whitefield** (BQ) (*Middleton–Oldham*)–2.4–Prestwich–4.1–**Manchester** (MN) (*Stockport, Stalybridge, Middleton–Rochdale, Worsley–Bolton, Stretford–Warrington*)
SF7	*Stranraer*–Whitecrook–Girvan–Ayr–Lugton–Glasgow 89.2 m	*Stranraer*–**Whitecrook** (SJ) (*Newton Stewart–Dumfries–Carlisle*)–5.5–New Luce–12.2–Barrhill–4.8–Pinwherry–6.6–Girvan–9.0–Craigoch–4.2–Maybole–9.0–**Ayr** (*Mauchline*)–4.5–**Prestwick** (AR) (*Irvine, Troon* loop)–8.3–**Kilmarnock** (KM) (*Irvine, Mauchline–Dumfries, Strathaven–Stonehouse [Lanark]*)–5.0–Stewarton–4.8–**Lugton** (KM) (*Kilwinning, Dalry* loop)–7.2–**Barrhead** (*Clarkston, Paisley*)–8.1–**Glasgow** (GG) (*Dumbarton–Crianlarich–Inverness, Castlecary–Stirling, Uddingston–Carlisle, Coatbridge–Airdrie, Clarkston, Paisley–Greenock, Clyde* loop, *Bishopton, Renfrew* loop)
SF8	Thurso–Inverness 140.4 m	Thurso–6.4–Halkirk–8.5–Watten–8.8–Wick–7.1–Ulbster–7.2–Lybster–3.4–Latheron–18.8–Helmsdale–12.2–Brora–6.1–Golspie–10.0–Dornoch Road–6.2–Tain–13.0–Invergordon–3.5–Altness–10.3–Dingwall–6.5–**Muir of Ord** (IV) (*Cromarty*)–2.5–Beauly–9.9–**Inverness** (IV) (*Invermoriston–Fort William–Glasgow, Elgin–Aberdeen, Carrbridge–Aviemore*)
SF9	Kings Lynn–Wisbech–St. Ives–*Huntingdon–London* 41.7 m + (2.4 m)	**Kings Lynn** (KY) (*Swaffham, Long Sutton–Spalding, Hunstanton–Wells-next-the-Sea, North Norfolk* loop)–12.7–**Wisbech** (KY) (*Downham Market–Thetford, Long Sutton*)–9.8–**March** (MC) (*Whittlesey–Peterborough*)–7.0–**Chatteris** (MC) (*Ely*)–7.2–**Warboys** (HN) (*Ramsey*)–5.0 + (2.4)–

Table A4.3. (Continued)

Ref	Origin–destination	Route
		Huntingdon (HN) (*Tempsford–Stevenage–London, Peter-borough, St. Ives–Cambridge*)
SF10	Kings Lynn–Ely–Cambridge 45.1 m	**Kings Lynn** (KY) (*Wisbech, Swaffham, Long Sutton–Spalding, Hunstanton–Well-next-the-Sea,* North Norfolk loop)–11.5–**Downham Market** (KY) (*Wisbech, Thetford*)–16.8–**Ely** (EL) (*Chatteris, Soham–Swaffham Bulbeck*)–16.8–**Cambridge** (CB) (*Linton–Bishops Stortford, Swaffham Bulbeck–Newmarket, Baldock–Stevenage, St. Ives–Huntingdon*)
SF11	Long Sutton–Wisbech–Thetford–Bury St. Edmunds–Chelmsford–*London* 98.7 m	**Long Sutton** (KY) (*Holbeach–Spalding*)–3.0–Tydd St. Mary–6.3–**Wisbech** (KY) (*Kings Lynn, March*)–5.0–Outwell–6.4–**Downham Market** (KY) (*Kings Lynn–Ely*)–11.0–Feltwell–5.8–Brandon–6.0–**Thetford** (TF) (*Newmarket, Roudham–Norwich*)–11.8–**Bury St. Edmunds** (BE) (*Newmarket, Stow-market–Ipswich*)–11.0–Lavenham–5.5–**Sudbury** (SZ) (*Hadleigh–Ipswich, Long Melford–Wixoe–Haverhill*)–8.5–**Halstead** (SZ) (*Earls Colne–Coggeshall–Colchester, Sible Headingham–Wixoe*)–7.2–Braintree–7.2–**Little Waltham** (CD) (*Great Dunmow–Thaxted*)–4.0–**Chelmsford** (CD) (*Maldon, Witham–Coggeshall–Colchester*)–Brentwood–London
SF12	Southend–Brentwood–*London* 20.8 m	Southend–10.0–Pitsea–10.8–**Brentwood** (BW) (*Chelmsford, Chipping Ongar–Harlow, Upminster*)–Romford–London
	Coastal loops: *Secondary routes*	
SC1	Deal loop 19.5 m + (3.0 m)	Ramsgate (*Faversham*)–6.5–**Sandwich** (CB) (*Wingham–Canterbury*)–5.0–Deal–8.0–**Whitfield** (DV) (*Canterbury, Folkestone–Lympne–Brighton*)–(3.0, TR5)–Dover
SC2	Axminster loop 68.8 m	**Exeter** (EX) (*Great Matridge–Plymouth, Shilstone–Barnstaple, Harpford, Exmouth* loop)–12.0–**Ottery St. Mary** (OF) (*Harpford, Exmouth* loop)–5.3–Honiton–7.2–{**Whitford** (AX) (*Seaton*)}–3.6–**Axminster** (AX) (*Lyme Regis*)–5.0–**Chard Junction** (AX) (*Chard–Ilminster–Taunton*)–7.3–**Crewkerne** (CW) (*Beaminster–Upwey–Weymouth, Ilminster*)–8.8–**Yeovil** (YV) (*Dorchester, Langport*)–5.3–Sherborne–3.7–**Milborne Port** (YV) (*Sturminster Newton–Poole*)–6.0–**Wincanton** (BT) (*Shaftesbury–Wilton–Salisbury*)–4.6–**Bruton** (BT) (*Frome–London, Shepton Mallet–Weston-super-Mare*)
SC3	Barnstaple loop: Tiverton–South Molton–Barnstaple–Bideford–Crediton–Exeter 89.7 m + (2.4 m)	**Tiverton** (EX) (*Exeter, Taunton*)–7.0–Bampton–3.5–Dulverton–3.8–East Anstey–10.0–South Molton–12.2–**Barnstaple** (RN) (*Ilfracombe*)–9.0–Bideford–6.4–Great Torrington–10.4–**Hatherleigh** (EX) (*Holsworthy–Bude–Collamore Head*)–4.8–**Shilstone** (EX) (*Okehampton–Lydford–Wadebridge,* North Cornwall loop)–8.4–Bow–8.2–Crediton–6.0* + (2.4)–**Exeter** (EX) (*Tiverton–Taunton, Great Matridge–Plymouth, Ottery St. Mary–Yeovil, Axminster* loop, *Harpsford, Exmouth* loop)
SC4	Torquay loop 30.9 m	**Heathfield** (EX) (*Great Matridge–Exeter, Ashburton–South Brent–Plymouth*)–3.5–**Newton Abbot** (EX) (*Teignmouth–Dawlish Road*)–5.5–Torquay–2.5–**Paignton** (PG)

(continued)

Table A4.3. (Continued)

Ref	Origin–destination	Route
		(*Brixham*)–6.0–Totnes–5.9–**Halwell** (PG) (*Dartmouth, Kingsbridge*)–7.5–**South Brent** (PM) (*Ivybridge–Plymouth, Buckfastleigh–Heathfield–Exeter*)
SC5	Barry loop 25.3 m	**Cardiff** (CF) (*Llantrisant–Bridgend, Newport–Gloucester, Tongwynlais–Pontypridd, Aberdare* loop)–8.0–Barry–9.0–Llantwit Major–8.3–**Bridgend** (BG) (*Pyle–Neath–Carmarthen, Llantrisant–Cardiff, Tondu–Maesteg*)
SC6	Pembroke loop 97.6 m	**Carmarthen** (CM) (*Llanddarog–Swansea, Narberth–Haverfordwest*)–12.9–**Llangeler** (CM) (*Lampeter–Llanafan–Aberystwyth*)–4.8–Newcastle Emlyn–9.0–Cardigan–11.0–Newport (Cardigan)–7.1–Fishguard–10.0–Spittal–5.3–**Haverfordwest** (HW) (*Narberth–Carmarthen*)–4.0–Johnston–4.0–Milford Haven–4.6–Neyland–3.5–Pembroke–6.6–Manorbier–4.8–Tenby–3.0–Saundersfoot–7.0–**Narberth** (CM) (*Whitland–Carmarthen, Haverfordwest*)
SC7	North Wales loop: Aberystwyth–Barmouth–Portmadoc–Caernarvon–Bangor 79.5 m	**Aberystwyth** (AW) (*Llanafan–London*)–10.8–**Aberdovey** (AW) (*Machynlleth*)–4.3–Towyn–11.8–**Barmouth** (BP) (*Dolgellau–Ruabon–Chester*)–11.5–Harlech–6.3–**Penrhyndeudraeth** (CJ) (*Blaenau Ffestiniog*)–3.5–Portmadoc–5.0–**Criccieth** (CJ) (*Pwllheli*)–17.3–**Caernarvon** (BX) (*Llanberis*)–9.0–**Bangor** (BX) (*Menai Bridge–Holyhead, Conway–Chester*)
SC8	Mersey loop: Preston–Southport–Liverpool–Widnes–Warrington 56.0 m	**Preston** (PR) (*Chorley–Warrington, Garstang–Lancaster, Blackburn–Burnley, Kirkham–Blackpool*)–8.5–Tarleton–8.5–**Southport** (SM) (*Ormskirk*)–7.3–Formby–5.5–Crosby–3.8–Bootle–2.5–**Liverpool** (LP) (*Huyton–Warrington, Ormskirk, Birkenhead* ferry)–6.3–Garston–7.3–Widnes–6.3–**Warrington** (WR) (*Northwich–London, Hollins Green–Manchester, Wigan, Sutton Weaver–Chester*)
SC9	Fylde loop 27.9 m	*Preston*–**Kirkham** (PR) (*Poulton-le-Fylde–Fleetwood*)–5.3–Lytham–8.0–Blackpool–3.8–**Poulton-le-Fylde** (PF) (*Fleetwood, Kirkham*)–4.8–Great Eccleston–6.0–**Garstang** (LC) (*Lancaster, Preston*)
SC10	Furness loop 110.3 m	**Kirkby Lonsdale** (KL) (*Lancaster–London, Bell Busk–Skipton–Leeds*)–7.8–**Milnthorpe** (KL) (*Beck Foot, Kendal* loop)–13.8–Ulverston–5.0–**Dalton-in-Furness** (DA) (*Barrow-in-Furness*)–7.8–Foxfield–4.9–Millom–13.0–Ravenglass–11.0–Egremont–5.8–Whitehaven–7.3–**Workington** (WQ) (*Cockermouth–Penrith*)–5.5–Maryport–7.7–Aspatria–4.2–**Bromfield** (CL) (*Silloth*)–5.5–Wigton–11.0–**Carlisle** (CL) (*Hexham–Swalwell–Newcastle, Todhills–Glasgow, Penrith*)
SC11	Clyde loop: Glasgow–Greenock–Largs–Ardrossan–Kilmarnock 64.5 m + (2.0 m)	**Glasgow** (GG) (*Dumbarton–Inverness, Kirkintilloch–Castlecary–Stirling, Coatbridge–Airdrie, Clarkston, Barrhead–Lugton–Ayr, Uddingston–Motherwell, Renfrew* loop)–5.5 + (2.0)–**Paisley** (PA) (*Barrhead, Port Glasgow, Bridge of Weir* loop)–5.8–**Bishopton** (GK) (*Govan, Renfrew* loop)–7.2–**Port Glasgow** (GK) (*Paisley, Bridge of Weir* loop)–3.8–**Greenock** (GK) (*Gourock*)–8.0–Wemyss Bay–6.8–Largs–7.5–West Kilbride–4.5–Ardrossan–4.8–**Kilwinning** (KW) (*Lugton–Glasgow, Kilbirnie* loop)–3.3–**Irvine** (KM) (*Prestwick, Troon*

Table A4.3. (Continued)

Ref	Origin–destination	Route
		loop)–7.3–**Kilmarnock** (KM) (*Ayr, Mauchline–Dumfries, Lugton–Glasgow, Strathaven–Stonehouse (Lanark)–Wishaw*)
SC12	Troon loop 19.1 m + (3.3 m)	**Lugton** (KM) (*Barrhead–Glasgow, Kilmarnock, Kilbirnie* loop)–10.0–**Kilwinning** (KM) (*Ardrossan–Greenock, Clyde* loop, *Lugton, Kilbirnie* loop)–(3.3, LC11)–**Irvine** (KM) (*Kilmarnock, Clyde* loop)–5.8–**Troon**–3.3–**Prestwick** (AR) (*Ayr–Girvan, Kilmarnock*)
SC13	Dunbar loop: Coldstream–Dunbar–Edinburgh 75.7 m	**Coldstream** (CE) (*Kelso–Maxton–Melrose, Wooler–Morpeth–Newcastle*)–5.4–**Swinton** (CE) (*Duns*)–6.0–Fishwick–6.0–Berwick-upon-Tweed–5.8–Burnmouth–10.2–Grantshouse–12.8–Dunbar–6.2–East Linton–5.2–Haddington–5.0–**Longniddry** (ED) (*North Berwick*)–3.0–Tranent–4.3–Mussel-burgh–5.8–**Edinburgh** (ED) (*Falkirk, Penicuik–Biggar, Dalkeith–Galashiels–Melrose, Shotts–Wishaw, Granton*)
SC14	Bridlington loop: *Hull*–Beverley–Bridlington–Scarborough 49.7 m + (2.4 m)	**Hull** (HL) (*Withernsea, Hessle–Balkholme–Leeds*)–8.5–**Beverley** (HL) (*Market Weighton–York, Hornsea*)–12.3–Driffield–12.5–Bridlington–9.8–Filey–6.6* + (2.4)–**Scarborough** (SC) (*Thornton-le-Dale–Malton–York*)
SC15	Norfolk Coast loop 83.2 m	**Kings Lynn** (KY) (*Long Sutton–Spalding, Wisbech, Swaffham–East Dereham, Downham Market–Ely*)–7.8–Dersing-ham–2.8–Snettisham–5.2–Hunstanton–6.8–Brancaster–4.0–Burnham Market–5.8–**Wells-next-the-Sea** (WX) (*Fakenham–East Dereham*)–10.0–Cley-next-the-Sea–4.0–Holt–6.3–Sheringham–4.5–Cromer–9.0–North Walsham–3.0–**Swanton Abbot** (NR) (*Aylsham*)–6.0–Wroxham–8.0–**Norwich** (NR) (*Wymondham–Roudham–Thetford, Great Yarmouth, Bungay, East Dereham*)
	Inland loops: Secondary routes	
SN1	*Stockbridge loop*: Romsey–Mottisfont–Andover 13.7 m	Romsey–**Mottisfont** (RO) (*Alderbury–Salisbury*)–7.0–Stockbridge–6.7–**Andover** (HC) (*Whitchurch, Idmiston–Salisbury*)
SN2	*Blandford loop*: Poole–Blandford Forum–Milborne Port–*Yeovil* 33.1 m + (1.5 m)	**Poole** (PL) (*Christchurch, Wareham*)–4.5* + (1.5)–Wimborne–9.5–Blandford Forum–9.0–Sturminster Newton–6.3–Stalbridge–3.8–**Milborne Port** (YV) (*Wincanton–Bruton*)–*Sherborne–Yeovil*
SN3	Bridport loop: Taunton–Crewkerne–Beaminster–Bridport–Upwey–*Weymouth* 41.9 m	*Taunton*–{**Wrantage** (TA) (*Langport*)}–6.5–**Ilminster** (TA) (*Chard Junction*)–7.0–**Crewkerne** (CW) (*Yeovil, Chard Junction*)–7.0–Beaminster–6.0–Bridport–9.5–Abbotsbury–5.9–**Upwey** (DR) (*Dorchester*)–*Weymouth*
SN4	Shaftesbury loop 93.2 m + (3.4 m)	**Wincanton** (BT) (*Milborne Port–Yeovil, Bruton–Frome*)–6.8–Gillingham–5.0–Shaftesbury–4.4–Donhead St. Andrew–3.9–Tisbury–10.5–**Wilton** (SB) (*Warminster*)–(3.4, PG1)–**Salisbury** (SB) (*Alderbury–Romsey*)–6.0–**Idmiston** (SB) (*Amesbury–Manningford Bruce–Devizes*)–7.2–Grate-ley–12.4–**Andover** (HC) (*Stockbridge–Mottisfont–Romsey*)–7.5–**Whitchurch** (HC) (*Winchester, Newbury*)–3.8–Over-ton–8.0–**Basingstoke** (BS) (*Aldermaston–Reading*)–7.4–Odiham–8.8–Aldershot–1.5–**Ash** (AS) (*Guildford, Wokingham–Reading, Farnham–Bentley–Southampton*)–Chobham–Staines–London

(*continued*)

Table A4.3. (Continued)

Ref	Origin–destination	Route
SN5	Maidenhead loop: Staines–Windsor–Maidenhead–Henley–Reading 35.9 m	**Staines** (ST) (*Feltham–London* (NW), *Wokingham, Chobham–Ash, Addlestone–Leatherhead*)–6.3–**Windsor**–6.3–Maidenhead–2.0–**Cookham** (CQ) (*Loudwater–High Wycombe*)–4.0–Marlow–4.5–Medmenham–5.0–Henley-on-Thames–2.8–Shiplake–5.0–**Reading** (RG) (*Pangbourne–Wallingford–Oxford, Theale–Newbury, Basingstoke, Wokingham*)
SN6	Wantage loop: *Oxford–Abingdon–Wantage–Cirencester–Stroud–Gloucester* 59.8 m	*Oxford*–**Radley** (OX) (*Wallingford–London*)–2.4–Abingdon–8.5–Wantage–9.0–Faringdon–5.8–**Lechlade** (WW) (*Swindon–Great Somerford–Chippenham, Wootton Bassett* loop)–5.0–Fairford–4.0–**Ampney St. Peter** (CX) (*Cricklade–Swindon–Hungerford*)–5.0–**Cirencester** (CX) (*Northleach, Fosse Way* loop)–8.7–**Cherington** (CX) (*Malmesbury–Melksham, Fosse Way* loop)–4.4–Nailsworth–3.5–Stroud–3.5–**Stonehouse (Glos.)** (GL) (*Cam–Thornbury–Bristol*)–*Gloucester*
SN7	Marlborough loop: Bath–Chippenham–Hungerford 41.3 m + (2.0 m)	**Bath** (BH) (*Bristol, Limpley Stoke–Trowbridge*)–1.1* + (2.0)–Batheaston–5.9–Corsham–3.8–**Chippenham** (CP) (*Melksham, Great Somerford–Cirencester*)–5.4–Calne–6.6–Beckhampton–7.4–Marlborough–6.5–**Ramsbury** (NB) (*Swindon, Cricklade* link)–4.6–**Hungerford** (NB) (*Newbury–Reading, Manningford Bruce–Devizes*)
SN8	Melksham loop 5.4 m + (6.6 m)	**Devizes** (TB) (*Hungerford–London, Trowbridge*)–3.0* + (3.8)–**Melksham** (TB) (*Chippenham–Cherington–Cirencester, Fosse Way* loop)–2.4* + (2.8)–**Trowbridge** (TB) (*Frome–Taunton, Bradford-on-Avon–Limpley Stoke–Bath, Warminster, Devizes*)
SN9	Fosse Way loop: *Trowbridge–Melksham–Malmesbury–Cirencester–Stratford-on-Avon* 67.6 m + (8.7 m)	*Trowbridge*–**Melksham** (TB) (*Devizes*)–7.0–**Chippenham** (CP) (*Corsham–Bath, Calne–Hungerford, Marlborough* loop)–3.9–Sutton Benger–3.3–**Great Somerford** (CP) (*Swindon–Lechlade–Oxford*, Nene Valley loop)–3.8–Malmesbury–4.7–Tetbury–3.7–**Cherington** (CX) (*Nailsworth–Stroud–Stonehouse (Glos.), Wantage* loop)–(8.7, SN5)–**Cirencester** (CX) (*Ampney St. Peter–Faringdon, Wantage* loop)–10.8–**Northleach** (NL) (*Cheltenham, Burford–Witney–Oxford*)–5.6–Bourton-on-the-Water–3.6–Stow-on-the-Wold–4.7–**Moreton-in-Marsh** (MO) (*Evesham, Chipping Norton–Oxford*)–6.5–Shipston-on-Stour–10.0–**Stratford-on-Avon** (LM) (*Warwick, Bidford-on-Avon–Worcester*)
SN10	Cotswold loop: *Worcester–Evesham–Moreton-in-Marsh–Chipping Norton–Oxford* 40.3 m	*Worcester*–Pershore–**Evesham** (BV) (*Tewkesbury, Bidford-on-Avon, Stratford-on-Avon*)–5.2–Honeybourne–4.6–Chipping Campden–3.0–Blockley–3.3–**Moreton-in-Marsh** (MO) (*Shipston-on-Stour–Stratford-on-Avon, Stow-on-the-Wold–Northleach, Fosse Way* loop)–8.2–**Chipping Norton** (MO) (*Bloxham–Banbury*)–6.3–Charlbury–6.2–Woodstock–3.5–**Kidlington** (OX) (*Deddington–Banbury, Bicester–Northampton*)–*Oxford*
SN11	Buckingham loop: Chipping Norton–Banbury–Buckingham–Aylesbury–Tring–*London* 54.9 m + (2.0 m)	**Chipping Norton** (MO) (*Moreton-in-Marsh–Evesham, Kidlington–Oxford, Cotswold* loop)–10.1–Bloxham–2.5* + (2.0)–**Banbury** (BB) (*Southam–Leamington, Deddington–*

Table A4.3. (Continued)

Ref	Origin–destination	Route
		Kidlington–Oxford)–9.5–Brackley–7.8–**Buckingham** (KH) (*Bicester–Oxford, Towcester–Northampton*)–7.0–**Winslow** (KH) (*Leighton Buzzard*, Dunstable loop)–5.0–Whitchurch (Bucks)–5.0–**Aylesbury** (AY) (*Thame–Oxford, North Lee–Princes Risborough*)–8.0–**Tring** (**Marsworth**) (TG) (*Leighton Buzzard*)–*Boxmoor–London*
SN12	Aberdare loop: Newport–Hengoed–Aberdare–Hirwaun–Ammanford 61.4 m + (1.2m)	**Newport** (NP) (*Chepstow–Lydney–London, Cardiff, Pontypool*)–5.0* + (1.2)–Risca–1.2–**Cross Keys** (NP) (*Aberbeeg–Brynmawr*)–4.9–**Pontllanfraith** (LV) (*Tredegar–Dukestown*)–2.2–Hengoed (LV) (*Rhymney–Llechryd, Caerphilly–Tongwynlais–Cardiff*)–5.1–**Abercynon** (PP) (*Merthyr, Pontypridd–Cardiff*)–7.5–Aberdare–3.5–**Hirwaun** (HR) (*Merthyr*)–5.5–**Pont Nedd Fechan** (HR) (*Resolven–Neath*)–5.7–**Colbren** (GN) (*Sennybridge*)–5.5–**Gurnos** (GN) (*Pontardawe–Ynystawe–Swansea*)–7.5–Brynamman–4.8–Glanaman–3.0–**Ammanford** (AM) (*Treneddyn–Pontarddulais, Llandeilo*)
SN13	Heads of the Valleys loop: Raglan–Merthyr–Neath 47.5 m + (5.5 m)	**Raglan** (MM) (*Monmouth–Ross-on-Wye, Usk–Little Mill*)–6.0–**The Bryn** (AV) (*Little Mill–Newport*)–3.6–**Abergavenny** (AV) (*Brecon, Pontrilas–Hereford*)–6.0–Clydach–2.9–**Brynmawr** (HD) (*Blaenavon–Pontypool, Nantyglo–Aberbeeg*)–1.5–**Beaufort** (HD) (*Ebbw Vale–Aberbeeg*)–2.0–Dukestown (HD) (*Tredegar–Pontllanfraith*)–2.5–**Llechryd** (HD) (*Rhymney–Hengoed*)–2.2–**Dowlais** (MT) (*Merthyr–Abercynon*)–3.6–**Cefn-coed** (MT) (*Merthyr*)–5.9–**Hirwaun** (HR) (*Abercynon, Aberdare* loop)–(5.5, SN10)–**Pont Nedd Fechan** (HR) (*Colbren, Aberdare* loop)–6.3–Resolven–5.0–**Neath** (SW) (*Ynystawe–Pontarddulais–Carmarthen, Swansea* loop, *Pyle–Cardiff*)
SN14	Ludlow loop: Willersley–Presteigne–Ludlow–Tenbury Wells–Worcester 49.9 m + (20.1 m)	**Willersley** (HA) (*Hay-on-Wye–Three Cocks–Brecon, Leominster, Hereford*)–7.0–Kington–3.7–Walton–5.0–Presteigne–2.9–Kinsham–2.1–Lingen–2.7–Letton–1.5–**Walford** (WF) (*Knighton–Llandrindod Wells, Berriew–Welshpool, Bishops Castle* link)–3.4–Downton (Salop)–4.8–Bromfield–1.2* + (1.8)–**Ludlow** (WF) (*Much Wenlock–Leighton–Shrewsbury*)–(4.0, SK17)–**Woofferton** (WF) (*Leominster–Willersley*)–(5.0, PG5)–Tenbury Wells–(9.3, PG5)–**Stockton-on-Teme** (WF) (*Stourport–Birmingham, Cleobury Mortimer*)–8.5–**Knightwick** (WC) (*Bromyard–Bodenham–Hereford*)–7.1–**Worcester** (WC) (*Stourport–Birmingham, Pirton–Tewkesbury, Droitwich–Redditch, Great Malvern–Welland–Ross-on-Wye*)
SN15	Dunstable loop: *Watford*–St. Albans–Dunstable–Leighton Buzzard–Winslow 30.3 m + (2.8 m)	*Watford*–**St. Albans** (SA) (*Hemel Hempstead, Welwyn–Stevenage, Hatfield–Ware*, London Outer Orbital)–2.2* + (2.8)–Harpenden–5.0–**Luton** (LT) (*Hitchin–Baldock*)–5.0–Dunstable–8.0–**Leighton Buzzard** (LB) (*Newport Pagnell–Ravenstone–Northampton, Bedford, Aylesbury, Tring*)–4.1–Stewkley–6.0–**Winslow** (KH) (*Buckingham–Banbury, Bicester–Kidlington–Oxford, Aylesbury, Buckingham* loop)

(continued)

Table A4.3. (Continued)

Ref	Origin–destination	Route
SN16	Redditch loop: *Evesham*–Bidford-on-Avon–Redditch–Birmingham 26.8 m	*Evesham*–**Bidford-on-Avon** (BV) (*Stratford-upon-Avon*)–4.0–Alcester–8.3–**Redditch** (BV) (*Bromsgrove–Worcester*)–3.3–Alvechurch–4.9–Kings Norton–6.3–**Birmingham** (BM) (*Handsworth–Wolverhampton, Walsall, Sutton Coldfield–Lichfield, Coleshill–Coventry, Warwick*)
SN17	Peak District loop: Derby–Matlock–Bakewell–Buxton Stockport 55.9 m + (2.4 m)	**Derby** (DB) (*Shepshed–Loughborough, Willington (Derbys.)–Burton, Ilkeston*)–6.4* + (2.4)–Belper–9.6–Matlock–8.4–**Bakewell** (TP) (*Chesterfield*)–12.0–Buxton–4.8–Chapel-en-le-Frith–3.8–Whaley Bridge–6.2–Marple–4.7–**Stockport** (TP) (*Manchester, Hyde–Stalybridge, Macclesfield–Kidsgrove–Stoke-on-Trent, Wilmslow–Northwich*)
SN18	Mold loop: Rhyl–St. Asaph–Mold–Chester 28.8 m	**Rhyl** (LD) (*Colwyn Bay–Bangor, Queensferry–Chester*)–2.8–Rhuddlan–3.0–St. Asaph–4.0–**Bodfari** (MZ) (*Denbigh–Ruthin*)–12.0–Mold–2.7–**Buckley** (MZ) (*Hope–Wrexham*)–2.7–Hawarden–1.6–**Queensferry** (CH) (*Rhyl–Holyhead*)–Chester
SN19	Bury loop: *Liverpool*–Huyton–Wigan–Bolton–Bury–Rochdale–Oldham–Manchester 46.8 m + (4.0 m)	*Liverpool*–**Huyton** (LP) (*Warrington*)–2.0–Prescot–3.4–**St. Helens** (SI) (*Warrington, Rainford–Digmoor–Ormskirk*)–3.2–Billinge–5.2–**Wigan** (WG) (*Chorley–Preston, Digmoor–Ormskirk, Warrington, Worsley–Manchester*)–2.6–Aspull–3.0–{**Lostock** (BL) (*Horwich–Chorley*)–(4.0, TU7)}–**Bolton** (BL) (*Worsley–Manchester*)–6.0–**Bury** (BQ) (*Helmshore–Accrington, Whitefield–Manchester, Middleton–Oldham*)–3.2–Heywood–3.2–**Rochdale** (RC) (*Littleborough–Todmorden, Middleton–Manchester*)–2.0–Milnrow–2.5–Shaw–2.8–**Oldham** (OD) (*Grasscroft, Middleton–Bury*)–3.5–Failsworth–4.2–**Manchester** (MN) (*Stalybridge, Stockport, Altrincham, Stretford–Warrington, Worsley–Wigan, Whitefield–Bury, Middleton–Rochdale*)
SN20	Sanquhar loop: Dumfries–Sanquhar–Kilmarnock 60.6 m	**Dumfries** (DF) (*Annan–Creca–Carlisle, Lochmaben–Millhousebridge–Lockerbie*)–14.4–Thornhill–5.7–Enterkinfoot–7.2–Sanquhar–3.6–Kirkconnel–8.0–New Cumnock–6.1–Cumnock–6.8–**Mauchline** (KM) (*Ayr*)–8.8–**Kilmarnock** (KM) (*Lugton–Glasgow, Prestwick–Ayr, Irvine–Ardrossan, Clyde* loop, *Strathaven–Stonehouse (Lanark)–Wishaw, Shotts* loop)
SN21	Shotts loop: Kilmarnock–Edinburgh 64.4 m	**Kilmarnock** (KM) (*Ayr, Mauchline–Dumfries, Lugton–Glasgow, Irvine–Ardrossan, Clyde* loop)–9.3–Darvel–12.5–Strathaven–3.8–**Stonehouse (Lanark)** (LK) (*Lanark*)–3.7–Larkhall–4.0–**Wishaw** (WS) (*Motherwell, Carluke–London*)–6.0–Shotts–6.0–Whitburn–3.5–Bathgate–3.8–Broxburn–11.8–**Edinburgh** (ED) (*Longniddry–Dunbar, Dalkeith–Galashiels–Melrose, Penicuik–Biggar, Falkirk–Stirling, Leith–Granton*)
SN22	Lanark loop 11.1 m	**Pettinain** (LK) (*Symington–Carlisle, Carluke*)–3.3–**Hyndford Bridge** (LK) (*Douglas*)–2.5–**Lanark** (LK) (*Stonehouse (Lanark)–Kilmarnock*)–5.3–**Carluke** (LK) (*Wishaw–Glasgow, Pettinain*)

Table A4.3. (Continued)

Ref	Origin–destination	Route
SN23	Hamilton loop 6.3 m	**Motherwell** (WS) (*Wishaw–Carlisle, Coatbridge–Stirling, Uddingston–Glasgow*)–2.8–**Hamilton** (WS) (*Clarkston–Barrhead*)–3.5–**Uddingston** (GG) (*Glasgow, Motherwell*)
SN24	Kilbirnie loop 16.3 m	**Lugton** (KM) (*Barrhead–Glasgow, Kilwinning, Kilmarnock*)–4.3–Beith–3.0–Kilbirnie–5.0–Dalry–4.0–**Kilwinning** (KM) (*Irvine–Ayr, Ardrossan–Greenock, Clyde* loop)
SN25	Bridge of Weir loop: *Motherwell*–Hamilton–East Kilbride–Paisley–Port Glasgow 35.3 m	*Motherwell*–**Hamilton** (WS) (*Uddingston*)–5.5–East Kilbride–5.3–**Clarkston** (RH) (*Pollokshaws–Glasgow*)–5.2–**Barrhead** (RH) (*Lugton, Glasgow*)–3.9–**Paisley** (PA) (*Bishopton–Greenock, Glasgow*)–4.5–Johnstone–3.4–Bridge of Weir–3.6–Kilmalcolm–3.9–**Port Glasgow** (GK) (*Bishopton–Paisley, Greenock,* Renfrew loop)
SN26	Forfar loop: Perth–Forfar–Brechin–Montrose 57.0 m + (1.2 m)	**Perth** (PH) (*Auchterarder–Stirling, Dundee, Lathrisk–Kirkcaldy, Fife Coast* loop)–10.0–**Cargill** (PH) (*Dunkeld–Ballinluig–Pitlochry*)–5.2–Coupar Angus–4.3–Blairgowrie–5.5–Alyth–9.8–Kirriemuir–5.6–**Forfar** (FF) (*Dundee*)–10.2–Brechin–6.4* + (1.2)–**Montrose** (AB) ((*Inverbervie–Aberdeen, Arbroath–Dundee–Perth*)
SN27	Aviemore loop: *Fort William*–Spean Bridge–Aviemore–Grantown-on-Spey–Fochabers 103.1 m	**Spean Bridge** (FW) (*Fort William, Invergarry–Invermoriston–Inverness*)–14.0–Moy–22.2–Newtonmore–15.3–Aviemore–7.2–**Carrbridge** (CI) (*Inverness*)–9.1–Grantown-on-Spey–9.0–Advie–6.6–Knockando–6.0–Aberlour–2.0–**Craigellachie** (FB) (*Dufftown*)–3.2–Rothes–8.5–**Fochabers** (FB) (*Elgin–Inverness, Keith–Milltown–Aberdeen, Buckie–Turriff, Banff* loop)
SN28	Thirsk loop: Ripon–Thirsk–Northallerton–Eaglescliffe–*Stockton-on-Tees* 36.8 m	**Ripon** (RP) (*Knaresborough–Wetherby, West Tanfield–Leyburn*)–11.0–**Thirsk** (TH) (*Carlton Husthwaite–York*)–9.0–**Northallerton** (NA) (*Catterick–Richmond*)–10.6–{**Crathorne** (SQ) (*Stokesley–Whitby*)–3.7–Yarm–2.5–**Eaglescliffe** (SQ) (*Darlington, Stockton-on-Tees–Middlesbrough*)
SN29	Harrogate loop: Pool–Knaresborough 11.5 m	**Pool** (IL) (*Otley–Burley-in-Wharfedale, Wetherby*)–8.0–Harrogate–3.5–**Knaresborough** (WB) (*Wetherby, Ripon*)
SN30	Wharfedale loop: Burnley–Skipton–Wetherby 53.0 m	**Burnley** (CA) (*Clayton-le-Moors–Preston*)–4.0–Nelson–2.7–Colne–5.0–Barnoldswick–4.6–**Elslack** (SX) (*Bell Busk–Kirkby Lonsdale*)–4.0–Skipton (SX) (*Bell Busk, Keighley–Leeds*)–8.0–Addingham–3.0–Ilkley–4.3–**Burley** (IL) (*Rawdon–Leeds*)–2.5–Otley–3.0–**Pool** (IL) (*Harrogate–Knaresborough*)–11.9–**Wetherby** (WB) (*York, Knaresborough–Ripon, Leeds, Tadcaster–Selby*)
SN31	Bawtry loop: *Leeds*–Knottingley–Bawtry–Shirebrook–*Nottingham* 42.2 m + (4.5 m)	*Leeds*–Castleford–**Knottingley** (SN) (*Snaith–Hull, Pontefract–Wakefield*)–5.2–Kirk Smeaton–4.9–Carcroft–5.1–**Doncaster** (DC) (*Mexborough–Sheffield, Thorne–Scunthorpe*)–8.0–Bawtry–4.5–Blyth–4.5–**Ranby** (WP) (*Retford–Lincoln*)–(4.5, PG8)–**Worksop** (WP) (*Beighton–Sheffield*)–5.1–Creswell–4.9–**Shirebrook** (MA) (*Staveley–Chesterfield*)–*Mansfield–Nottingham*
SN32	Mansfield loop: *Chesterfield*–Staveley–Mansfield–Nottingham 29.8 m	*Chesterfield*–**Staveley** (SV) (*Beighton–Sheffield*)–3.8–Bolsover–3.7–**Shirebrook** (MA) (*Creswell–Worksop*)–4.3–**Mansfield** (MA) (*Southwell–Newark*)–5.9–Kirkby-in-Ashfield–5.9–Hucknall–6.2–**Nottingham** (NG) (*Gotham–Loughborough,*

(*continued*)

Table A4.3. (Continued)

Ref	Origin–destination	Route
		Lowdham–Newark–Lincoln, Ilkeston–Derby, Harby–Grantham)
SN33	Grantham loop: Nottingham–Grantham–Aslackby–*Peterborough* 36.0 m	**Nottingham** (NG) (*Ilkeston–Derby, Gotham–Loughborough, Mansfield, Southwell–Newark–Lincoln*)–2.0–West Bridgeford–4.7–Cotgrave–7.4–**Harby** (NG) (*Melton Mowbray*)–5.0–Belvoir–6.9–Grantham–5.0–**Ropsley** (NG) (*Aunsby–Sleaford*)–5.0–**Aslackby** (RE) (*Aunsby–Sleaford*)–Bourne–Peterborough
SN34	Kettering loop: *Northampton–*Wellingborough–Kettering–Leicester 38.1 m	Northampton–**Wellingborough** (WL) (*Irthlingborough–Thrapston–Peterborough*)–7.8–**Kettering** (WL) (*Uppingham–Manton*)–12.5–Market Harborough–17.8–**Leicester** (LE) (*Loughborough, Lutterworth–London, Desford–Nuneaton, Melton Mowbray*)
SN35	Waveney Valley loop: Wells-next-the-Sea–East Dereham–Diss–Bungay–*Great Yarmouth* 66.1 m + (5.0 m)	**Wells-next-the-Sea** (WX) (*Burnham Market–King Lynn, Cley-next-the-Sea–Swanton Abbott–Norwich*)–4.5–Walsingham–4.8–Fakenham–12.0–**East Dereham** (ER) (*Norwich*)–(5.0, PG8)–**Shipdham** (ER) (*Swaffham–Kings Lynn*)–5.0–Watton (Norfolk)–8.8–**Roudham** (TF) (*Thetford–London, Attleborough–Norwich*)–7.5–South Lopham–5.2–**Diss** (DS) (*Eye–Stowmarket*)–9.5–Harleston–8.8–**Bungay** (BC) (*Norwich*)–Ilketshall–Beccles–Great Yarmouth
SN36	Bishops Stortford loop: London–Harlow–Bishops Stortford–Saffron Walden–*Cambridge* 47.6 m	**London** (NE)–4.5–Walthamstow–4.5–**Buckhurst Hill** (LN) (*Chingford–Ponders End, Chigwell–Barking*, London Suburban Circle)–2.5–Loughton–3.8–Epping–6.0–**Harlow** (HO) (*St. Margarets–Ware, Chipping Ongar–Brentwood*)–7.3–Bishops Stortford–9.5–**Newport** (NQ) (*Thaxted–Little Waltham–Chelmsford, Buntingford–Baldock*)–3.5–Saffron Walden–6.0–**Linton** (CB) (*Haverhill*)–Cambridge
SN37	Upminster loop 8.8 m + (6.0 m)	**Barking** (LN) (*London (NE), Romford–Brentwood, Chigwell–Ponder End*, London Suburban Circle)–4.4–Dagenham–4.4–**Upminster** (UP) (*Tilbury*)–(6.0, PO1)–**Brentwood** (BW) (*Chelmsford, Romford–Barking, Chipping Ongar–Harlow, Southend*)
	Secondary links	
SK1	Rye–Tenterden–Headcorn–*Maidstone* 17.3 m	**Rye** (HT) (*Lydd–Lympne, Hastings*)–4.8–Wittersham–4.5–**Tenterden** (TN) (*Rolvenden–Cranbrook–Tunbridge Wells*)–4.0–Biddesden–4.0–Headcorn (MD) (*Ashford*)–Maidstone
SK2	Staplehurst link: *Hastings–*Hurst Green–Chart Sutton–*Maidstone* 17.1 m	Hastings–**Hurst Green** (HT) (*Bells Yew Green–Tunbridge Wells*)–3.6–Hawkhurst–4.0–**Cranbrook** (RD) (*Tenterden, Bells Yew Green–Tunbridge Wells*)–1.5–Sissinghurst–4.0–Staplehurst–4.0–**Chart Sutton** (MD) (*Headcorn–Ashford*)–Maidstone
SK3	Seaford–Lewes–Tunbridge Wells–Maidstone 51.0 m	Seaford–3.0–Newhaven–6.3–**Lewes** (LW) (*Brighton, Polegate–Hastings, Cuckfield–Horsham*)–8.0–Uckfield (*East Grinstead, Hailsham–Polegate*)–8.5–Rotherfield–4.7–Frant–2.8–**Tunbridge Wells** (TW) (*Hever–East Grinstead, Bells Yew Green–Hurst Green*)–4.8–Tonbridge–3.3–**Hadlow** (TW) (*Ightham*)–9.6–**Maidstone** (MD) (*Burham–Chatham–London, Chart Sutton–Ashford–Dover*)

Table A4.3. (Continued)

Ref	Origin–destination	Route
SK4	Wivelsfield link: Lewes–Horsham 23.5 m	Lewes (LW) (*Seaford, Brighton, Polegate–Hastings, Uckfield*)–9.5–Wivelsfield–4.0–Cuckfield–10.0–Horsham (HS) (*Dorking, Shoreham–Brighton, Pulborough–Littlehampton, Crawley–East Grinstead*)
SK5	Littlehampton–Arundel–Horsham–*East Grinstead* 12.6 m + (14.0 m)	**Littlehampton** (LH) (*Goring-by-Sea–Worthing, Chichester, Bognor* loop)–3.8–**Arundel** (AD) (*Chichester, Goring-by-Sea*)–8.8–**Pulborough** (HS) (*Midhurst–Petersfield*)–(6.0, SG1)–Billingshurst–(8.0, SG1)–**Horsham** (HS) (*Crawley–East Grinstead, Dorking–London, Guildford, Shoreham–Brighton, Cuckfield–Lewes*)
SK6	Woking link: Guildford–Chobham) 9.8 m	**Guildford** (GF) (*Ash, East Horsley–Dorking, Horsham, Witley*)–6.3–Woking–3.5–**Chobham** (ST) (*Ash, Staines*)
SK7	Tadley link: Basingstoke–Aldermaston 11.5 m	**Basingstoke** (AS) (*Whitchurch, Ash*)–7.0–Tadley–4.5–**Aldermaston** (AY) (*Newbury, Theale–Reading*)
SK8	Amersham link: Rickmansworth–North Lee–Aylesbury 20.0 m	**Rickmansworth** (WT) (*Watford, Uxbridge*)–7.5–**Amersham** (WT) (*Chesham*)–5.0–Great Missenden–4.5–Wendover–3.0–**North Lee** (AY) (*Princes Risborough*)–Aylesbury
SK9	Bourne End link: Cookham–Loudwater 4.0 m	**Cookham** (CQ) (*Staines, Henley-on-Thames–Reading, Maidenhead* loop)–2.0–Bourne End–2.0–**Loudwater** (CQ) (*High Wycombe–North Lee–Aylesbury, Beaconsfield–Uxbridge*)
SK10	Princes Risborough–Thame 7.5 m	**Princes Risborough** (AY) (*North Lee–Aylesbury, Watlington–Wallingford, High Wycombe–Loudwater*)–7.5–**Thame** (OX) (*Oxford, Aylesbury*)
SK11	Chiltern link: Thame–Princes Risborough–High Wycombe–London 41.4 m	**Thame** (OX) (*Oxford, Aylesbury*)–7.0–**Princes Risborough** (AY) (*North Lee–Aylesbury, Chinnor–Wallingford*)–9.3–High Wycombe–2.5–**Loudwater** (CQ) (*Cookham*)–2.8–Beaconsfield–8.4–**Uxbridge** (UX) (*Staines, Rickmansworth*, London Outer Orbital)–8.6–**Ealing** (LN) (*Wembley, Brentford–Twickenham*, London Suburban Circle)–2.8–**London** (NW)
SK12	Ermine Way link: Hungerford–Swindon–Cricklade–Ampney St. Peter–Cirencester 32.8 m	**Hungerford** (NB) (*Newbury, Manningford Bruce–Devizes*)–4.6–**Ramsbury** (NB) (*Marlborough–Chyippenham*)–2.9–Aldbourne–9.0–Chiseldon–4.0–Wroughton–1.4–**Swindon** (WW) (*Lechlade–Witney, Great Somerford–Chippenham, Wootton Bassett* loop)–7.0–Cricklade–3.9–**Ampney St. Peter** (CX) (*Fairford–Lechlade, Wantage* loop)–Cirencester
SK13	Amesbury link: *Salisbury*–Idmiston–Manningford Bruce–*Devizes* 16.4 m	*Salisbury*–**Idmiston** (SB) (*Andover–Longparish–Basingstoke*)–3.9–Amesbury–2.0–Durrington–7.6–Upavon–2.9–**Manningford Bruce** (NB) (*Pewsey–Hungerford*)–Devizes
SK14	Worcester–Great Malvern–Ross-on-Wye–Monmouth–Little Mill–*Newport* 53.7 m + (8.4 m)	**Worcester** (WC) (*Stourport–Birmingham, Knightwick–Tenbury Wells, Bromsgrove–Redditch*)–7.5–Great Malvern–3.9–**Welland** (NT) (*Upton-on-Severn, Great Malvern* loop)–7.4–**Bromsberrow Heath** (NT) (*Ledbury*)–5.0–**Newent** (NT) (*Ross-on-Wye, Gloucester*)–(8.4, PF6)–**Ross-on-Wye** (RW) (*Newent–Gloucester, Hereford*)–11.4–**Monmouth** (MU) (*Coleford*)–8.5–**Raglan** (MU) (*The Bryn–Abergavenny*)–5.5–Usk–4.5–**Little Mill** (NP) (*Abergavenny–Brecon–Three Cocks*)–Pontypool–Newport

(continued)

Table A4.3. (Continued)

Ref	Origin–destination	Route
SK15	Newport–Brecon 37.2 m + (3.6 m)	**Newport** (NP) (*Chepstow–Lydney–London, Cardiff*)–3.6–Llantarnam–4.8–**Pontypool** (NP) (*Blaenavon–Brynmawr*)–3.0–**Little Mill** (NP) (*Usk–Monmouth–Ross-on-Wye*)–4.4–**The Bryn** (AV) (*Raglan*)–(3.6, SN11)–Abergavenny (AV) (*Hereford*)–7.0–Crickhowell–8.2–Talybont-on-Usk–6.2–**Brecon** (BQ) (*Three Cocks–Willersley–Leominster, Senny-bridge–Llandovery*)
SK16	Taff Vale link: Dowlais–Merthyr–Abercynon 26.5 m	**Dowlais** (MT) (*Cefn-coed, Llechryd–Abergavenny*)–2.6–**Merthyr** (MT) (*Cefn–coed*)–8.3–**Abercynon** (PP) (*Neath, Hengoed–Newport, Aberdare loop*)–3.8–**Pontypridd** (PP) (*Porth–Treherbert*)–6.5–**Tongwynlais** (CF) (*Caerphilly–Hen-goed–Rhymney*)–5.3–**Cardiff** (CF) (*Newport–Gloucester, Bridgend–Neath, Barry loop*)
SK17	Merthyr link 1.8 m	**Cefn-coed** (MT) (*Hirwaun, Dowlais*)–1.8–**Merthyr** (MT) (*Abercynon–Pontypridd, Dowlais*)
SK18	*Carmarthen*–Llanddarog–Llandeilo–Llandovery–Brecon 44.3 m + (12.0 m)	**Carmarthen–Llanddarog** (CM) (*Treneddyn–Neath*)–9.9–**Llandeilo** (LY) (*Ammanford*)–(12.0, PG5)–**Llandovery** (LY) (*Llanwrtyd Wells–Builth Wells*)–6.0–Halfway–7.4–**Senny-bridge** (BQ) (*Colbren–Swansea*)–8.5–**Brecon** (BQ) (*Crick-howell–Abergavenny*)–12.5–**Three Cocks** (HA) (*Builth Wells, Hay-on-Wye–Willersley–Hereford*)
SK19	*Brecon*–Sennybridge–Pontar-dawe–Swansea 30.9 m + (5.5 m)	*Brecon*–**Sennybridge** (BQ) (*Llandeilo*)–3.6–Cray–10.1–**Colbren** (GN) (*Pont Nedd Fechan–Hirwaun–Merthyr*)–(5.5, SN10-)–**Gurnos** (GN) (*Brynamman–Ammanford*)–7.0–Pontardawe–4.0–{**Ynystawe** (SW) (*Neath–Pontarddulais*)}–2.2–Morriston–4.0–**Swansea** (SW) (*Gorseinon–Carmarthen, Neath*)
SK20	Welsh Borders link: *Newport*–*The Bryn*–Abergavenny–Hereford–Leominster–Ludlow–Much Wenlock–Uppington–*Shrewsbury* 66.8 m + (7.3 m)	*Newport–The Bryn*–**Abergavenny** (AV) (*Brynmawr–Merthyr, Brecon*)–11.5–Pontrilas–12.0–**Hereford** (HR) (*Ross-on-Wye, Willersley–Brecon, Ledbury–Bromsberrow Heath–Newent,*)–7.5–**Bodenham** (HR) (*Bromyard–Knightwick–Worcester*)–6.0–**Leominster** (*Willersley–Brecon*)–(7.3, PG5)–**Woofferton** (WF) (*Tenbury Wells–Stockton-on-Teme–Stourport*)–4.0–**Ludlow** (WF) (*Walford–Presteigne*)–10.8–Holdgate–8.7–Much Wenlock–3.5–**Leighton** (WJ) (*Buildwas–Coalport–Shifnal*)–2.8–**Uppington** (WJ) (*Wellington–Oakengates–Wolverhampton*)–*Shrewsbury*
SK21	Bromyard link: *Hereford*–Bodenham–Bromyard–Knightwick–*Worcester* 16.4 m	*Hereford*–**Bodenham** (HR) (*Leominster–Ludlow*, Welsh Bor-ders link)–5.6–Pencombe–4.3–Bromyard–3.2–Linley Green–3.3–**Knightwick** (WC) (*Stockton-on-Teme, Tenbury Wells*)–*Worcester*
SK22	Tewkesbury–Evesham 13.0 m	**Tewkesbury** (GL) (*Coombe Hill–Gloucester, Upton-on-Sev-ern–Worcester*)–13.0–**Evesham** (BV) (*Bidford-on-Avon–Lea-mington, Pirton–Pershore–Worcester*)
SK23	Bridgnorth link: Stourport–Bewdley–Bridgnorth–Leighton–*Shrewsbury* 30.2 m	**Stourport** (SP) (*Worcester, Bromsgrove, Kidderminster–Bir-mingham, Stockton-on-Teme–Ludlow*)–3.5–Bewdley–6.6–Highley–6.4–Bridgnorth–7.4–**Coalport** (WJ) (*Shifnal*)–1.8–Ironbridge–2.5–Buildwas–2.0–**Leighton** (WJ) (*Much Wen-lock–Ludlow*)–Uppington–Shrewsbury

Table A4.3. (Continued)

Ref	Origin–destination	Route
SK24	Coalport–Shifnal 4.9 m	**Coalport** (WJ) (*Bridgnorth–Stourport, Leighton–Shrewsbury*)–1.0–Madeley–3.9–**Shifnal** (WJ) (*Oakengates–Wellington, Wolverhampton*)
SK25	Llangollen link: Barmouth–Ruabon–Whitchurch–Stafford 108.5 m	**Barmouth** (BP) (*Penrhyndeudraeth–Porthmadoc, Aberdovey–Aberystwyth*, North Wales Coast loop)–8.5–Dolgellau–13.5–Llanuwchllyn–5.5–Bala–12.3–Corwen–10.0–Llangollen–6.8–**Ruabon** (RU) (*Wrexham–Chester, Oswestry–Shrewsbury*)–5.0–Overton-on-Dee–3.4–**Penley** (WI) (*Ellesmere–Oswestry*)–9.0–**Whitchurch** (WI) (*Prees–Wem–Shrewsbury, Nantwich, Malpas–Broxton–Chester*)–10.0–Market Drayton–11.7–**Newport (Salop)** (SD) (*Stone–Stoke-on-Trent, Oakengates–Wellington*)–6.0–Gnosall–6.8–**Stafford** (SD) (*Colwich–Lichfield–London, Stone, Penkridge–Wolverhampton*)
SK26	*Shrewsbury*–Shrawardine–Oswestry–*Chester* 11.4 m	*Shrewsbury*–**Shrawardine** (SR) (*Arddlin–Welshpool*)–11.4–**Oswestry** (OS) (*Ellesmere–Penley–Whitchurch, Arddlin–Welshpool*)–*Ruabon–Chester*
SK27	*Shrewsbury*–Oakengates–Stone–*Stoke-on-Trent* 21.0 m	*Shrewsbury*–**Oakengates** (WJ) (*Shifnal–Wolverhampton*)–6.2–**Newport (Salop)** (SD) (*Gnossal–Stafford, Market Drayton–Whitchurch*)–8.6–Eccleshall–6.2–**Stone** (SD) (*Colwich–Lichfield, Stafford*)–*Stoke-on-Trent*
SK28	Shrewsbury–Whitchurch–Broxton–*Chester* 33.6 m	**Shrewsbury** (SR) (*Uppington–Wolverhampton, Shrawardine–Welshpool–Aberystwyth*)–6.0–Hadnall–6.2–Wem–4.8–Prees–5.5–**Whitchurch (Salop)** (WI) (*Penley–Ruabon, Market Drayton–Newport [Staffs]*)–6.0–Malpas–5.1–**Broxton** (CH) (*Nantwich–Stoke-on-Trent*)–*Chester*
SK29	Oswestry–Whitchurch–Nantwich 22.0 m + (9.0 m)	**Oswestry** (RU) (*Llandrinio–Welshpool, Ruabon–Chester*)–8.3–Ellesmere–2.8–**Penley** (WI) (*Overton-on-Dee–Ruabon, Llangollen* link)–(9.0, SK21)–**Whitchurch (Salop)** (WI) (*Broxton–Chester, Millenheath–Market Drayton–Newport [Staffs.]*)–5.8–Wrenbury–5.1–**Nantwich** (SK) (*Broxton–Chester, Kidsgrove–Stoke-on-Trent*)
SK30	Preston cut-off: Blackburn–Chorley 9.8 m	**Blackburn** (PR) (*Clayton-le-Moors–Burnley, Preston, Darwen*)–4.9–Hoghton–4.9–**Chorley** (PR) (*Ormskirk–Liverpool, Wigan–Warrington, Lostock–Bolton, Preston*)
SK31	Bakewell–Chesterfield 11.9 m	**Bakewell** (TP) (*Buxton–Stockport, Matlock–Derby*)–3.2–Baslow–8.7–**Chesterfield** (SV) (*Staveley–Sheffield, Alfreton–Ilkeston*)
SK32	Barnsley link: Penistone–Cudworth 9.2 m	**Penistone** (PS) (*Hadfield–Manchester, Deighton–Huddersfield, Sheffield*)–4.3–Dodworth–2.6–Barnsley–2.3–**Cudworth** (MX) (*Mexborough–Sheffield, Wakefield*)
SK33	*Bury*–Whitefield–Oldham–Grasscroft–*Huddersfield* 13.0 m	*Bury*–**Whitefield** (BQ) (*Prestwich–Manchester*)–3.5–**Middleton** (MN) (*Rochdale, Manchester*)–4.5–**Oldham** (OD) (*Milnrow–Rochdale, Manchester*)–2.8–Lees–2.2–**Grasscroft** (HF) (*Stalybridge*)–*Huddersfield*
SK34	Kirkby Stephen link 19.0 m	**Sedbergh** (SS) (*Sedbergh Junction, Hawes–Leyburn–Constable Burton–Ripon*)–14.4–Kirkby Stephen–4.6–**Brough (Cumbria)** (BZ) (*Barnard Castle–Darlington, Appleby–Penrith*)

(*continued*)

Table A4.3. (Continued)

Ref	Origin–destination	Route
SK35	Dumfries link 11.5 m	**Dumfries** (DF) (*Newton Stewart–Stranraer, Annan–Creca–Carlisle*)–9.2–Lochmaben–2.3–{**Millhousebridge** (DF) (*Moffat (Beattock)–Symington–Glasgow, Lockerbie–Creca–Carlisle*)}
SK306	Mauchline–Ayr 12.1 m	**Mauchline** (KM) (*Cumnock–Dumfries, Kilmarnock*)–7.0–Mossblown–5.1–**Ayr** (AR) (*Girvan–Whitecrook–Stranraer, Prestwick–Irvine*)
SK37	Stonehouse link: Stonehouse–Lanark 8.9 m	**Stonehouse** (*Darvel–Kilmarnock, Wishaw*)–2.8–Draffan–6.1–**Lanark** (LK) (*Hyndford Bridge–Pettinain–Symington, Carluke*)
SK38	Dunblane–Crianlarich 42.2 m	**Dunblane** (SL) (*Stirling, Auchterarder–Perth*)–3.6–Doune–8.0–**Callander** (SL) (*Aberfoyle*)–13.8–Lochearnhead–16.8–**Crianlarich** (FW) (*Connel Ferry–Fort William, Tarbet–Dumbarton–Glasgow*)
SK39	Carrbridge–Inverness 29.7 m	**Carrbridge** (CI) (*Aviemore–Spean Bridge, Grantown-on-Spey–Craigellachie–Fochabers*)–4.5–Schlod–9.0–Moy–4.5–Craggie–11.7–**Inverness** (IV) (*Thurso, Invermoriston–Fort William, Nairn–Elgin–Fochabers*)
SK40	Houghton-le-Spring link: Durham–Sunderland 11.4 m	**Durham** (DH) (*Spennymoor, Chester-le-Street, Consett* [*Leadgate*])–4.0–**Pittington** (DH) (*Easington*)–3.6–Houghton-le-Spring–3.8–**Penshaw** (SU) (*Chester-le-Street*)–**Sunderland** (SU) (*Monkton–Newcastle, Easington–Hartlepool*)
SK41	Haswell link: Durham–Pittington–Easington 6.0 m	*Durham*–**Pittington** (DH) (*Houghton-le-Spring–Penshaw*)–3.0–Haswell–3.0–**Easington** (SQ) (*Sunderland, Hartlepool–Stockton-on-Tees*)
SK42	Staindrop link: Barnard Castle–Spennymoor–*Newcastle* 20.1 m	**Barnard Castle** (BZ) (*Brough (Cumbria)–Penrith, Winston–Darlington, Middleton-in-Teesdale*)–6.6–Staindrop–5.4–West Auckland–3.3–**Bishop Auckland** (BA) (*Stanhope, Newton Aycliffe–Stockton-on-Tees*)–4.8–**Spennymoor** (BA) (*Newton Aycliffe–Darlington*)–*Durham–Newcastle*
SK43	Darlington cut-off: Middleton Tyas–Winston 9.0 m. No passenger service	**Middleton Tyas** (CK) (*Catterick–Ripon, Darlington*)–9.0–**Winston** (BZ) (*Barnard Castle, Darlington*)
SK44	Easingwold link: York–Thirsk 24.7 m	**York** (YK) (*Wetherby, Selby, Beverley–Hull, Malton–Thornton-le-Dale–Scarborough*)–12.5–Easingwold–5.2–**Carlton Husthwaite** (NA) (*Helmsley–Pickering*)–7.0–**Thirsk** (NA) (*Northallerton, Ripon*)
SK45	Skipton cut-off: Elslack–Bell Busk 3.6 m *No passenger service*	**Elslack** (SX) (*Barnoldswick–Colne–Burnley*)–3.6–**Bell Busk** (SX) (*Giggleswick–Kirkby Lonsdale, Skipton*)
SK46	Guiseley link: Burley-in-Wharfedale–Rawdon 6.0 m	**Burley-in-Wharfedale** (IL) (*Ilkley–Skipton, Otley–Pool–Wetherby*)–3.5–Guiseley–2.5–**Rawdon** (*Leeds, Shipley–Keighley*)
SK47	Pocklington link: York–Market Weighton–Beverley 32.0 m	**York** (YK) (*Wetherby, Carlton Husthwaite–Northallerton, Malton–Scarborough, Selby*)–14.3–Pocklington–7.5–**Market Weighton** (HL) (*Balkholme–Goole*)–10.2–**Beverley** (HL) (*Hornsea, Driffield–Scarborough, Bridlington* loop)
SK48	Holme link: Market Weighton–Balkholme 12.3 m	**Market Weighton** (HL) (*Pocklington–York, Beverley*)–5.0–Holme-upon-Spalding-Moor–7.3–**Balkholme** (HL) (*Hull, Selby, Goole–Thorne*)
SK49	Market Rasen–Louth 15.5 m	**Market Rasen** (MR) (*Lincoln, Caistor–Brigg*)–15.5–**Louth** (AL) (*Grimsby, Alford–Skegness–Boston*)

Table A4.3. (Continued)

Ref	Origin–destination	Route
SK50	*Nottingham*–Harby–Melton Mowbray 8.7 m	*Nottingham*–**Harby** (NG) (*Grantham*)–5.2–Scalby–3.5–**Melton Mowbray** (MM) (*Birstall–Leicester, Oakham–Manton–Peterborough*)
SK51	Swannington–Shepshed 5.4 m	**Swannington** (WV) (*Burton-on-Trent, Desford–Leicester*)–5.4–**Shepshed** (LE) (*Loughborough, Melbourne–Derby*)
SK52	Ropsley link: *Grantham*–Ropsley–Aunsby–*Sleaford* 5.0 m	*Nottingham–Grantham*–**Ropsley** (NG) (*Aslackby–Bourne*)–5.0–**Aunsby** (SO) (*Aslackby–Bourne*)–*Sleaford*
SK53	Uppingham link: Oakham–Manton–Kettering–*Northampton* 19.4 m	**Manton** (MM) (*Stamford–Werrington–Peterborough, Oakham–Leicester*)–3.1. Uppingham–6.3–Rockingham–10.0–**Kettering** (WL) (*Market Harborough–Leicester*)–*Wellingborough–Northampton*
SK54	Bourne–Spalding–Holbeach 17.9 m	**Bourne** (RE) (*Grantham, Werrington*)–3.8–Twenty–6.4–**Spalding** (SG) (*Gosberton–Boston, Crowland–Werrington–Peterborough*)–3.8–Moulton–1.6–Whaplode–2.3–**Holbeach** (SG) (*Long Sutton–Kings Lynn, Gosberton–Sleaford*)
SK55	Burton-on-Trent–Desford 23.8 m	**Burton-on-Trent** (DB) (*Willington (Derbys.)–Derby, Lichfield–Birmingham*)–5.1–Swadlincote–4.5–Ashby-de-la-Zouch–3.6–**Swannington** (WV) (*Shepshed–Loughborough*)–1.6–Snibston–9.0–**Desford** (LE) (*Leicester, Hinckley–Nuneaton*)
SK56	Stour Valley link: Wixoe–Sudbury–Hadleigh–Ipswich 32.5 m	**Wixoe** (SZ) (*Haverhill, Halstead*)–3.5–Clare–3.0–Cavendish–4.0–Long Melford–2.9–**Sudbury** (SZ) (*Halstead–Braintree, Lavenham–Bury St. Edmunds*)–10.6–Hadleigh–8.5–**Ipswich** (IP) (*Manningtree–London, Stowmarket–Cambridge, Saxmundham–Great Yarmouth*)
	Major dead-end branches: secondary routes	*Dead-end branches not forming termini of other routes, carrying moderate traffic at moderate speeds*
SB1	Gosport–Fareham 5.5 m	Gosport–5.5–**Fareham** (SH) (*Botley–North Stoneham–Southampton, Cosham–Brighton*)
SB2	Pilning–Filton 6.0 m	Pilning (Portskewett ferry)–6.0–**Filton** (BR) (*Bristol, Cam-Stonehouse–Gloucester, Chipping Sodbury, Avonmouth*)
SB3	Treherbert–Pontypridd–*Cardiff* 12.0 m	Treherbert–2.5–Treorchy–6.0–Porth–3.5–**Pontypridd** (PP) (*Abercynon–Neath, Aberdare* loop)–*Cardiff*
SB4	Pwllheli–Criccieth 9.3 m	Pwllheli–9.3–**Criccieth** (CJ) (*Porthmadoc–Penrhyndeudraeth–Barmouth, Caernarvon–Bangor*, North Wales Coast loop)
SB5	Ruthin–Bodfari 11.5 m	Ruthin–7.5–Denbigh–4.0–**Bodfari** (MZ) (*Mold–Buckley–Chester, St. Asaph–Rhyl*)
SB6	Darwen–Blackburn 5.0 m	Darwen–5.0–**Blackburn** (PR) (*Preston, Chorley, Clayton-le-Moors–Burnley*)
SB7	Heysham–Morecambe–Lancaster 6.8 m	Heysham–3.3–Morecambe–3.5–**Lancaster** (LC) (*Garstang–London, Kirkby Lonsdale*)
SB8	Barrow in Furness–Dalton-in-Furness 5.0 m	Barrow in Furness–5.0–**Dalton-in-Furness** (DA) (*Millom–Workington, Ulverston–Milnthorpe*, Tyne-Wensleydale Circular)
SB9	Gourock–Greenock 3.3 m	Gourock–3.3–**Greenock** (GK) (*Paisley–Glasgow, Largs–Ardrossan–Kilwinning, Clyde* loop)
SB10	Oban–Connel Ferry 5.5 m	Oban–5.5–**Connel Ferry** (FW) (*Lochawe–Crianlarich–Glasgow, Portnacroish–Spean Bridge–Inverness*)

(*continued*)

Table A4.3. (Continued)

Ref	Origin–destination	Route
SB11	Pitlochry–Cargill 22.0 m	Pitlochry–4.5–**Ballinluig** (PH) (*Aberfeldy*)–8.3–Dunkeld–9.2–**Cargill** (PH) (*Perth, Coupar Angus–Montrose, Forfar loop*)
SB12	Duns–Swinton 5.0 m	Duns–5.0–**Swinton** (CE) (*Coldstream, Berwick-upon-Tweed*)
SB13	South Shields–Monkton 3.8 m	South Shields–2.8–Jarrow–1.0–**Monkton** (NE) (*Newcastle, Sunderland*, Tyne & Wensleydale Circular)
SB14	Middleton-in-Teesdale–Barnard Castle 9.2 m	Middleton-in-Teesdale–5.2–Romaldkirk–4.0–**Barnard Castle** (BZ) (*Winston–Darlington, Bishop Auckland, Brough* [*Cumbria*])
SB15	Felixstowe–Ipswich: 12.5 m	Felixstowe–12.5–**Ipswich** (IP) (*Manningtree–London, Stowmarket–Bury St. Edmunds, Saxmundham–Great Yarmouth*)
SB16	Harwich–Manningtree 11.5 m	Harwich–11.5–**Manningtree** (CR) (*Colchester–London, Ipswich*)
	Secondary urban loops	
SU1	Eastbourne loop 5.1 m + (5.0 m)	**Pevensey** (EB) (*Bexhill–Hastings, Polegate*)–5.1–Eastbourne–(5.0, SF1)–**Polegate** (EB) (*Lewes, Hailsham–Uckfield*)
SU2	Weston-super-Mare loop 23.2 m	**Highbridge** (WM) (*Bridgewater–Taunton, Loxton–Nailsea*)–1.6–Burnham-on-Sea–8.0–**Weston-super-Mare** (WM) (*Loxton–Cheddar–Wells*)–9.6–Clevedon–4.0–**Nailsea** (WM) (*Bristol, Loxton–Highbridge*)
SU3	*Llandudno loop* 8.7 m + (1.8 m)	**Colwyn Bay** (LD) (*Rhyl–Chester*)–2.4–Penrhyn Bay–2.8–Llandudno–2.0–Deganwy–1.5* + (1.8)–**Conway** (LD) (*Bangor–Holyhead, Betwys-y-Coed*)
SU4	Kendal loop 15.7 m	*Kirkby Lonsdale*–**Milnthorpe** (KL) (*Ulverston–Dalton-in-Furness*)–7.5–Kendal–2.9–Meal Bank–5.3–**Beck Foot** (SS) (*Tebay–Penrith, Sedbergh Junction–Kirkby Lonsdale*)
	Coastal loops: Local routes	
LC1	*Surrey Docks loop* 15.0 m	**Dartford** (CT) (*Strood–Dover, Lewisham*)–3.6–Erith–6.1–Woolwich–3.3–Deptford–2.0–**Lewisham** (*London* (S Central), *Clapham, Gravesend–Strood–Dover, Croydon, Bromley–Otford*)
LC2	Bognor loop 19.5 m	**Goring-by-Sea** (BN) (*Worthing–Brighton, Arundel*)–5.5–**Littlehampton** (LH) (*Arundel–Horsham*)–7.0–Bognor Regis–7.0–**Chichester** (HV) (*Havant–Southampton, Arundel*)
LC3	Lymington loop 14.3 m + (3.5 m)	**Brockenhurst** (SH) (*Lyndhurst–Millbrook–Southampton, Christchurch*)–4.8–Lymington–3.5–Milford–3.5–Barton–2.5* + (3.5)–**Christchurch** (PL) (*Poole, Ringwood–Alderbury–Salisbury*)
LC4	Exmouth loop 23.2 m	**Exeter** (EX) (*Great Matridge–Plymouth, Shilstone–Barnstaple, Tiverton–Taunton, Ottery St. Mary*)–4.3–Topsham–5.3–Exmouth–4.5–Budleigh Salterton–5.8–**Harpford** (OS) (*Sidmouth*)–3.3–**Ottery St. Mary** (OS) (*Honiton–Whitford–Yeovil, Exeter*)
LC5	North Cornwall loop: *Exeter–Shilstone–Okehampton–Wadebridge–Newquay–Truro* 87.4 m	*Exeter–Crediton–***Shilstone** (EX) (*Hatherleigh, Barnstaple*)–4.1–Okehampton–10.2–**Lydford** (LA) (*Tavistock–Plymouth*)–2.5–Coryton–8.8–Launceston–12.1–**Collamore Head** (LA) (*Bude*)–9.3–Camelford–10.8–**Wadebridge** (WD) (*Bodmin–Llanhydrock*)–4.8–**Tredinnick** (WD) (*Padstow*)–

Table A4.3. (Continued)

Ref	Origin–destination	Route
		5.1–St. Columb Major–7.3–Newquay–5.4–Goonhavern–7.0–**Truro** (TR) (*Redruth–Penzance, St. Austell–Lostwithiel, Treluswell–Falmouth, Helston* loop)
LC6	Bude loop: Hatherleigh–Bude–Collamore Head 33.7 m	**Hatherleigh** (RN) (*Bideford–Barnstaple, Shilstone–Crediton–Exeter*)–14.6–Holsworthy–9.1–Bude–10.0–**Collamore Head** (LA) (*Launceston–Lydford, Wadebridge, North Cornwall* loop)
LC7	Helston loop: Truro–Helston–Ludgvan–*Penzance* 28.7 m	**Truro** (TR) (*St. Austell–Lostwithiel, Redruth–Penzance*)–7.0–**Treluswell** (TR) (*Falmouth*)–7.5–Wendron–2.8–Helston–3.6–Breage–6.4–Marazion–1.4–**Ludgvan** (PZ) (*Lelant–Truro*)–*Penzance–St. Just*
LC8	Lampeter loop: *Aberystwyth*–Llanafan–Lampeter–Llangeler–*Carmarthen* 37.5 m	Aberystwyth–**Llanafan** (AW) (*Cwmystwyth–Llangurig*)–10.0–Tregaron–11.0–Lampeter–16.5–**Llangeler** (LQ) (*Newcastle Emlyn–Fishguard–Haverfordwest, Cardigan & Tenby* loop)–*Carmarthen*
LC9	Wirral loop: Hooton–Heswall 24.7 m	**Hooton** (CH) (*Birkenhead, Chester*)–4.5–Neston–1.0–Parkgate–3.0–Heswall–5.2–West Kirby–7.4–Wallasey–3.6–**Birkenhead** (BK) (*Hooton–Chester,* Liverpool ferry)
LC10	Renfrew loop: Glasgow–Bishopton 9.9 m + (2.0 m)	**Glasgow** (GG) (*Dumbarton–Inverness, Kirkintilloch–Castlecary–Stirling, Coatbridge–Airdrie, Clarkston, Barrhead–Lugton–Ayr, Paisley, Milngavie, Uddingston–Motherwell*)–1.4* + (2.0)–Govan–3.2–Renfrew–5.3–**Bishopton** (GK) (*Port Glasgow–Greenock, Paisley*)
LC11	Banff loop: Fochabers–Banff–Turriff 35.9 m	**Fochabers** (FB) (*Elgin–Inverness, Keith–Turriff, Rothes–Craigellachie–Grantown-on-Spey, Aviemore* loop)–7.0–Buckie–3.4–Findochty–3.9–Cullen–5.0–Portsoy–6.8–Banff–9.8–**Turriff** (TU) (*Milltown–Keith–Fochabers, Fyvie–Dyce–Aberdeen, Fraserburgh, Peterhead* loop)
LC12	Peterhead loop: Turriff–Fraserburgh–Peterhead–Dyce–*Aberdeen* 53.7 m	**Turriff** (TU) (*Milltown–Fochabers–Inverness, Fyvie–Dyce*)–3.7–Cuminestown–13.0–Fraserburgh–3.6–Rathven–10.4–Peterhead–5.8–Cruden Bay–7.2–Ellon–10.0–**Dyce** (AB) (*Inverurie–Turriff*)–*Aberdeen*
LC13	Fife Coast loop 113.4 m + (1.8 m)	**Perth** (PH) (*Dundee–Montrose, Auchterarder–Stirling, Cargill, Forfar* loop)–11.3–Newburgh–5.0–Auchtermuchty–3.2–**Lathrisk** (CU) (*Markinch–Balgonie*)–2.0–Ladybank–5.4–Cupar–4.5–**Dairsie** (CU) (*Tayport*)–4.8–St. Andrews–9.3–Crail–5.3–Anstruther–2.9–St. Monans–10.3–Leven–4.1–**Balgonie** (KK) (*Markinch–Lathrisk*)–5.0–**Kirkaldy** (KK) (*Dunfermline, Cardenden* loop)–6.0–Burntisland–8.8–Inverkeithing (*Queensferry* ferry)–3.2–**Dunfermline** (DM) (*Kirkcaldy, Cowdenbeath–Kinross–Auchtermuchty*)–6.0–Culross–3.8–Kincardine–6.2–**Alloa** (SL) (*Dollar*)–6.3* + (1.8)–**Stirling** (SL) (*Denny–Glasgow, Dunblane–Perth*)
LC14	Blyth loop: Newcastle–Tynemouth–Blyth–Morpeth 28.2 m	**Newcastle** (NE) (*Swalwell–Carlisle, Chester-le-Street–London, Morpeth–Glasgow, Monkton–Sunderland, Byker* loop)–3.8–**Wallsend** (NE) (*Byker* loop)–4.3–North Shields–1.0–Tynemouth–3.3–Whitley Bay–7.0–Blyth–4.0–Bedlington–4.8–**Morpeth** (MP) (*Alnwick–Glasgow, Newcastle, Newbiggin*)

(continued)

Table A4.3. (Continued)

Ref	Origin–destination	Route
LC15	Byker loop 4.3 m	**Newcastle** (NE) (*Swalwell–Carlisle, Chester-le-Street–London, Morpeth–Glasgow, Monkton–Sunderland, Tynemouth–Morpeth, Blyth* loop)–2.0–Byker–1.1–Walker–1.2–**Wallsend** (NE) (*Newcastle, Tynemouth–Morpeth*)
LC16	Middlesbrough loop 30.4 m	**Stockton-on-Tees** (SQ) (*Newton Aycliffe–Bishop Auckland, Hartlepool–Easington–Sunderland, Eaglescliffe–Darlington, Tyne & Wensleydale Circular*)–4.5–Middlesbrough–8.5–Redcar–4.5–Saltburn–1.5–Skelton–3.5–Guisborough–5.3–Great Ayton–2.6–**Stokeseley** (SQ) (*Crathorne–Northallerton, Grosmont–Whitby*)
LC17	North Yorkshire Moors loop: *Malton–Stokeseley–Yarm* 45.1 m	*Malton*–**Thornton-le-Dale** (PK) (*Scarborough*)–2.5–**Pickering** (PK) (*Helmsley–Easingwold, Ampleforth* link)–17.3–**Grosmont** (PK) (*Whitby*)–7.9–Castleton–11.9–**Stokesley** (SQ) (*Guisborough–Stockton, Middlesbrough* loop)–5.5–**Crathorne** (SQ) (*Northallerton, Tyne & Wensleydale* Circular)–*Yarm–Stockton-on-Tees*
	Inland loops: *Local routes*	
LN1	Cheddar loop: Bruton–Wells–Cheddar–Weston-super-Mare 30.6 m + (2.0 m)	**Bruton** (BT) (*Frome–London, Wincanton–Poole, Castle Cary–Langport–Taunton*)–3.8–Evercreech–3.8–**Shepton Mallet** (WZ) (*Radstock–Limpley Stoke–Bath*)–4.8–**Wells** (WZ) (*Glastonbury–Langport*)–8.4–Cheddar–5.8–**Loxton** (WM) (*Highbridge–Taunton, Nailsea–Bristol*)–4.0* + (2.0)–**Weston-super-Mare** (WM) (*Highbridge–Taunton, Clevedon–Nailsea–Bristol*)
LN2	Glastonbury loop: *Taunton–Langport–Glastonbury–Wells–Radstock–Bath* 33.1 m + (4.8 m)	*Taunton*–**Langport** (LG) (*Taunton, Yeovil, Bridgewater, Bruton*)–7.6–Street–2.2–Glastonbury–6.0–**Wells** (WZ) (*Cheddar–Loxton–Weston-super-Mare*)–(4.8, LN1)–**Shepton Mallet** (WZ) (*Bruton*)–8.0–Midsomer Norton–2.0–Radstock–7.3–**Limpley Stoke** (BH) (*Trowbridge*)–*Bath*
LN3	Richmond loop: Feltham–Twickenham–Richmond–London 10.8 m	**Feltham** (ST) (*Staines, Brentford–London* [NW])–3.6–**Twickenham** (LN) (*Kingston, Ealing*)–2.0–Richmond–1.8–Mortlake–1.0–Barnes–2.4–**London** (W Central)
LN4	Esher loop: Addlestone–Wimbledon 15.3 m	**Addlestone** (ST) (*Chertsey–Staines, Leatherhead*)–1.5–Weybridge–2.4–Walton–2.4–Esher–3.6–**Surbiton** (LN) (*Epsom, Kingston–Twickenham*, London Suburban Circle)–5.0–**Wimbledon** (LN) (*Ewell–Epsom*)–Clapham–London (S Central)
LN5	Forest of Dean loop: Newnham–Cinderford–Coleford–Lydney 19.3 m	**Newnham** (CO) (*Gloucester, Lydney*)–3.3–Cinderford–1.8–Nailbridge–7.2–**Coleford** (CO) (*Monmouth*)–7.0–**Lydney** (CO) (*Chepstow–Newport* (Mon.), *Newnham–Gloucester*)
LN6	Ledbury loop: Hereford–Bromsberrow Heath 17.6 m	**Hereford** (HR) (*Willersley–Hay-on-Wye, Ross-on-Wye, Pontrilas–Abergavenny, Bodenham–Leominster*)–7.3–Tarrington–6.3–Ledbury–4.0–**Bromsberrow Heath** (NT) (*Ross-on-Wye, Welland–Great Malvern*)
LN7	Great Malvern loop 3.7 m + (11.3 m)	**Upton-on-Severn** (GL) (*Tewkesbury–Cheltenham, Pirton–Worcester*)–3.7–**Welland** (WZ) (*Bromsberrow Heath–Ross-on-Wye*)–(3.9, SK11)–Great Malvern–(7.5, SK11)–**Worcester** (WC) (*Stourport–Birmingham, Knightwick–Tenbury Wells, Bronsgove–Redditch*)

Table A4.3. (Continued)

Ref	Origin–destination	Route
LN8	Bromsgrove loop: Worcester–Bromsgrove–Redditch 20.5 m	**Worcester** (WC) (*Pirton–Tewkesbury, Stourport–Kiddermin-ster, Knightwick–Tenbury Wells, Ludlow* loop, *Great Malvern–Welland–Ross-on-Wye*)–7.0–Droitwich–6.5–Bromsgrove–7.0–**Redditch** (BV) (*Kings Norton–Birmingham, Alcester–Bidford-on-Avon–Evesham*)
LN9	Walsall loop 16.5 m	**Birmingham** (BM) (*Coleshill–Coventry, Sutton Coldfield–Lichfield, Solihull–Warwick, Redditch, Handsworth*)–9.5–**Walsall** (WA) (*Wednesbury–Dudley, Wolverhampton, Lich-field, Cannock*)–7.0–**Wolverhampton** (WH) (*Wednesbury, Shifnal–Shrewsbury, Penkridge–Stafford, Wombourne–Kid-derminster*)
LN10	Cannock loop 13.2 m	**Walsall** (WA) (*Birmingham, Wolverhampton, Wednesbury–Dudley, Lichfield*)–7.9–**Cannock** (LF) (*Lichfield*)–5.3–**Penk-ridge** (*Stafford, Wolverhampton*)
LN11	Knutsford loop: Chester–Sut-ton Weaver–Northwich–Altrincham–Manchester 29.0 m	*Chester–Frodsham–***Sutton Weaver** (CH) (*Runcorn*)–5.6–Weaverham–3.3–**Northwich** (NW) (*Middlewich–Stoke-on-Trent, Warrington*)–7.3–Knutsford–3.0–**Mobberley** (MB) (*Wilmslow–Stockport*)–4.6–**Altrincham** (MB) (*Hollins Green–Warrington*)–3.4–Sale–1.8–**Stretford** (MN) (*Hollins Green–Warrington*)–**Manchester** (MN) (*Middleton–Roch-dale, Stalybridge, Stockport, Worsley–Bolton, Whitefield–Bury, Oldham*)
LN12	Wilmslow loop 12.6 m + (2.0 m)	**Macclesfield** (SK) (*Kidsgrove–Stoke-on-Trent, Stockport*)–3.1–Prestbury–4.0–**Wilmslow** (MB) (*Mobberley–Altrinc-ham*)–4.0–Bramhall–1.5* + (2.0)–**Stockport** (TP) (*Bux-ton–Bakewell, Manchester, Macclesfield–Kidsgrove, Hyde–Stalybridge*)
LN13	Bacup loop: Rochdale–Bacup–Helmshore 13.6 m	**Rochdale** (RC) (*Littleborough–Todmorden, Oldham, Bury, Middleton–Manchester*)–3.6–Whitworth–1.6–Shawforth–2.4–Bacup–4.2–Rawtenstall–1.8–**Helmshore** (BQ) (*Bury–Manchester, Accrington–Clayton-le-Moors–Clitheroe*)
LN14	Cardenden loop 9.0 m	**Cowdenbeath** (DM) (*Dunfermline, Kinross–Auchter-muchty*)–1.8–Lochgelly–2.4–Cardenden–4.8–**Kirkcaldy** (KK) (*Balgonie, Inverkeithing–Dunfermline*, Fife loop)
LN15	Shotley Bridge loop: Dur-ham–Consett (Leadgate)–Swalwell–*Newcastle* 24.4 m	**Durham** (DH) (*Spennymoor–Darlington, Chester-le-Street–Newcastle*)–7.6–Lanchester–4.6–**Consett (Leadgate)** (LJ) (*Annfield–Chester-le-Street*)–2.2–Shotley Bridge–6.5–Row-lands Gill–3.5–**Swalwell** (NE) (*Hexham–Haltwhistle–Car-lisle)–Newcastle*
LN16	Ely loop 12.2 m	**Ely** (EL) (*Cambridge, Downham Market, Chatteris*)–6.0–Soham–4.2–Burwell–2.0–{**Swaffham Bulbeck** (CB) (*New-market*)}–*Cambridge*
LN17	Upminster loop 8.8 m + (6.0 m)	**Barking** (LN) (*London (NE), Romford–Brentwood, Chigwell–Ponder End*, London Suburban Circle)–4.4–Dagenham–4.4–**Upminster** (UP) (*Tilbury*)–(6.0, PO1)–**Brentwood** (BW) (*Chelmsford, Romford–Barking, Chipping Ongar–Harlow, Southend*)

(continued)

Table A4.3. (Continued)

Ref	Origin–destination	Route
	Local orbital	
LO1	**London Terminal Circle** 21.8 m	**London** (NE) (*Barking–Ipswich, Ponders End–Cambridge, Buckhurst Hill–Harlow*)–4.0–**London** (N Central) (*Barnet*)–5.3–**London** (NW) (*Wembley–Glasgow, Ealing–Uxbridge, Brentford–Plymouth*)–2.5–**London** (W Central) (*Barnes–Twickenham*)–4.5–**Clapham** (LN) (*Wimbledon–Ewell–Brighton, Mitcham–Carshalton, Croydon–Tunbridge Wells, London South Central*)–5.5–**Lewisham** (LN) (*Dartford–Dover, Croydon, Woolwich, London South Central, Woolwich, Surrey Docks loop*)
LO2	London Suburban Circle 74.4 m + (1.5 m)	**Dartford** (CT) (*Strood, Lewisham, Surrey Docks loop*)–7.3–Bexley–3.0–**Bromley** (LN) (*Lewisham, Otford*)–6.3–**Croydon** (CN) (*Mitcham–Clapham, Godstone–East Grinstead*)–3.2–**Carshalton** (EP) (*Streatham–Clapham*)–4.0–**Ewell** (EP) (*Wimbledon–Clapham*)–(1.5, TR6)–**Epsom** (EP) (*Leatherhead*)–4.8–**Surbiton** (LN) (*Addlestone, Wimbledon, Esher loop*)–1.0–Kingston–2.7–**Twickenham** (LN) (*Richmond–Barnes–London* [W Central])–3.6–**Brentford** (LN) (*London* (NW), *Feltham–Staines*)–2.3–**Ealing** (LN) (*Uxbridge–Princes Risborough, London* [NW])–4.0–**Wembley** (LN) (*Watford, London* [NW])–4.0–Edgware–2.5–Arkley–3.5–Barnet–5.0–Enfield–2.6–**Ponders End** (LN) (*Broxbourne–Ware, London* [NE])–1.9–Chingford–1.6–**Buckhurst Hill** (LN) (*Epping–Harlow, London* [NE])–1.9–Chigwell–6.9–**Barking** (LN) (*Romford, Upminster, London* [NE])–2.3–Beckton
LO3	West Yorkshire loop 26.1 m	**Leeds** (LS) (*Wetherby, Rawdon–Shipley, Castleford–Knottingley, East Ardsley–Wakefield*)–5.3–Pudsey–3.0–**Dudley Hill** (BF) (*Bradford*)–2.7–Oakenshaw–2.6–Cleckheaton–1.4–Liversedge–1.3–Heckmondwike–1.9–**Batley** (DW) (*Dewsbury*)–2.6–Morley–2.9–Beeston–2.4–Leeds
	Local links	
LK1	Hadlow–Ightham 5.8 m	**Hadlow** (TW) (*Tonbridge–Tunbridge Wells, Maidstone*)–5.8–**Ightham** (OT) (*Otford–Godstone, West Malling–Maidstone*)
LK2	Penge link: Croydon–Lewisham 8.0 m	**Croydon** (CN) (*Godstone, Carshalton–Epsom, Clapham, Bromley*)–4.0–Penge–4.0–**Lewisham** (LN) (*London* (S Central), *Clapham, Dartford, Surrey Docks loop*)
LK3	Mitcham link: Carshalton–Clapham 7.9 m	**Carshalton** (EP) (*Ewell–Epsom, Croydon*)–3.0–Mitcham–2.6–Tooting–2.3–**Clapham** (LN) (*London* (S Central, *Croydon, Lewisham, Wimbledon–Epsom*)
LK4	Richmond-on-Thames link: Twickenham–London (W Central) 9.2 m	**Twickenham** (LN) (*Brentford, Kingston–Surbiton*, London Suburban Circle)–2.0–Richmond-on-Thames–2.0–Kew–1.5–Mortlake–1.2–Barnes–2.5–**London** (W Central)
LK5	Finchley link: Barnet–London 11.0 m	**Barnet** (LN) (*Edgware–Wembley, Enfield–Ponders End*)–4.0–Finchley–2.0–Golders Green–5.0–**London** (N Central)
LK6	Chard link: Ilminster–Chard Junction 7.5 m	*Taunton*–**Ilminster** (TA) (*Crewkerne*)–5.0–Chard–2.5–**Chard Junction** (AX) (*Crewkerne–Yeovil, Axminster*)
LK7	Tavistock link 22.0 m	**Plymouth** (PM) (*South Brent–London, Liskeard–Penzance*)–8.3–Yelverton–6.3–Tavistock–7.4–**Lydford** (LA) (*Launceston, Okehampton–Shilstone–Exeter*)

Table A4.3. (Continued)

Ref	Origin–destination	Route
LK8	Bodmin link: Wadebridge–Llanhydrock 10.0 m	**Wadebridge** (WD) (*Tredinnick–Newquay–Truro, Collamore Head–Exeter,* North Cornwall loop)–7.2–Bodmin–2.8–**Llanhydrock** (BJ) (*Liskeard–Plymouth, Lostwithiel–Penzance*)
LK9	Monmouth–Coleford 5.0 m	**Monmouth** (MU) (*Ross-on-Wye, Raglan–Little Mill*)–5.0–**Coleford** (CO) (*Lydney, Cinderford–Newnham,* Forest of Dean loop)
LK10	Blaenavon link: Brynmawr–Pontypool 13.1 m	**Brynmawr** (HV) (*Beaufort–Merthyr, Abergavenny*)–5.5–Blaenavon–7.6–**Pontypool** (NP) (*Newport, Little Mill–Abergavenny*)
LK11	Brynmawr–Aberbeeg–Cross Keys–*Newport* 15.4 m	**Brynmawr** (HD) (*Beaufort–Merthyr, Abergavenny*)–2.3–Nantyglo–4.0–Abertillery–1.8–**Aberbeeg** (NP) (*Ebbw Vale*)–3.8–Newbridge–3.5–**Cross Keys** (NP) (*Pontllanfraith–Tredegar*)–*Newport*
LK12	Beaufort–Ebbw Vale–Aberbeeg–*Newport* 7.8 m	**Beaufort** (HV) (*Dukestown–Merthyr, Brynmawr–Abergavenny*)–1.8–Ebbw Vale–6.0–**Aberbeeg** (NP) (*Abertillery–Brynmawr*)–*Cross Keys–Newport*
LK173	Sirhowy link: Dukestown–Tredegar Pontllanfraith–*Newport* 11.9 m	**Dukestown** (HV) (*Llechryd–Merthyr, Beaufort–Abergavenny*)–1.6–Tredegar–8.3–Blackwood–2.0–**Pontlllanfraith** (NP) (*Hengoed*)–*Newport*
LK14	Rhymney Link: Llechryd–Hengoed–*Cardiff* 20.9 m	**Llechryd** (HV) (*Dowlais–Merthyr, Dukestown–The Bryn*)–1.6–Rhymney–7.0–Bargoed–3.3–**Hengoed** (HG) (*Abercynon, Pontllanfraith, Aberdare* loop)–5.2–Caerphilly–3.8–**Tongwynlais** (CF) (*Pontypridd, Aberdare* loop)–*Cardiff*
LK15	Llandrindod Wells–Presteigne–*Ludlow* 26.7 m + (1.6 m)	**Llandrindod Wells** (BU) (*Rhayader–Llangurig, Builth Wells*)–6.3* + (1.6)–Dolau–6.0–Llangunllo–7.6–Knighton–5.5–Brampton Bryan–1.3–**Walford** (WF) (*Presteigne–Willersley, Berriew*)–*Ludlow*
LK16	Bishops Castle link: Ludlow–Walford Bishops Castle–Berriew–*Welshpool* 26.8 m	Ludlow–**Walford** (WF) (*Knighton–Llandrindod Wells, Presteigne–Willersley*)–5.6–Clunbury–3.5–Lydbury North–3.8–Bishops Castle–1.8–Lydham–9.5–Montgomery–2.6–**Berriew** (WO) (*Welshpool–Arddlin–Shrewsbury, Newtown–Llangurig–Aberystwyth*)
LK17	Cannock–Lichfield 8.9 m	**Cannock** (LF) (*Penkridge, Walsall*)–4.8–Burntwood–4.1–**Lichfield** (LF) (*Colwich–Stafford, Tamworth–Nuneaton, Burton-on-Trent–Derby, Sutton Coldfield, Walsall*)
LK18	Hope link: Buckley–Wrexham 11.9 m	**Buckley** (MZ) (*Mold–Bodfari–Ruthin, Queensferry–Chester*)–5.2–Hope–6.7–**Wrexham** (RU) (*Ruabon–Shrewsbury, Chester*)
LK19	Warrington–Wilmslow–Macclesfield 9.8 m + (11.7 m)	*Warrington–***Hollins Green**) (WA) (*Stretford–Manchester*)–5.2–**Altrincham** (MB) (*Stretford–Manchester*)–(4.6, LN11)–**Mobberley** (MB) (*Knutsford–Northwich*)–4.6–**Wilmslow** (MB) (*Macclesfield*)–(4.0, LN12)–Prestbury–(3.1, LN12)–**Macclesfield** (SK) (*Kidsgrove–Stoke-on-Trent, Stockport*)
LK20	Pollokshaws link 4.6 m + (2.0 m)	**Clarkston** (RH) (*East Kilbride–Hamilton–Motherwell, Barrhead, Bridge of Weir* loop)–2.3–Rutherglen–2.3* + (2.0)–**Glasgow** (GG) (GG) (*Dumbarton–Inverness, Kirkintilloch–Castlecary–Stirling, Coatbridge–Airdrie, Uddingston–Motherwell, Lugton–Ayr, Paisley–Greenock, Clyde* loop)

(continued)

Table A4.3. (Continued)

Ref	Origin–destination	Route
LK21	Forfar–Dundee 14.9 m	**Forfar** (FF) (*Kirriemuir–Cargill–Perth, Brechin–Montrose*)–4.4–Inverarity–10.5–**Dundee** (DD) (*Perth, Arbroath–Montrose*, Tayport ferry)
LK22	Dunfermline–Auchtermuchty–*Perth* 23.8 m	**Dunfermline** (DM) (*Inverkeithing–Kircaldy, Culross–Alloa*, Fife Coast loop)–5.5–**Cowdenbeath** (DM) (*Kirkcaldy, Cardenden* loop)–7.8–Kinross–10.5–**Auchtermuchty** (CU) (*Lathrisk–St. Andrews*, Fife Coast loop)–*Newburgh–Perth*
LK23	Lathrisk–Balgonie 8.1 m	**Lathrisk** (CU) (*Auchtermuchty–Perth, Cupar–Dairsie–St. Andrews, Fife Coast* loop)–5.1–Markinch–3.0–**Balgonie** (KK) (*Kirkcaldy, Leven–Dairsie–Cupar, Fife Coast* loop)
LK24	Peebles–Penicuik–*Edinburgh* 13.6 m	**Peebles** (PE) (*Innerleithen–Lindean–Melrose, Biggar*)–10.3–Leadburn–3.3–**Penicuik** (ED) (*West Linton–Biggar*)–*Edinburgh*
LK25	Beamish link: Sunderland–Penshaw–Chester-le-Street–Consett (Leadgate) 14.1 m	*Sunderland*–**Penshaw** (SU) (*Houghton-le-Spring–Pittington–Durham*)–5.3–**Chester-le-Street** (CS) (*Durham–London, Newcastle*)–3.2–Beamish–2.6–Stanley–3.0–**Consett (Leadgate)** (LJ) (*Lanchester–Durham, Shotley Bridge–Swalwell*)
LK26	Bishop Auckland–Newton Aycliffe–Stockton-on-Tees 16.4 m	**Bishop Auckland** (BA) (*Spennymoor–Durham, West Auckland–Barnard Castke, Stanhope*)–1.8–Coundon Grange–3.6–**Newton Aycliffe** (BA) (*Darlington, Spennymoor–Durham*)–7.5–Redmarshall–3.5–**Stockton-on-Tees** (SQ) (*Eaglescliffe–Yarm–Northallerton, Hartlepool–Easington–Sunderland, Middlesbrough* loop)
LK27	Ampleforth link: Pickering–Carlton Husthwaite–*Thirsk* 25.1 m	**Pickering** (PK) (*Thornton-le-Dale–Scarborough, Grosmont–Whitby*)–7.0–Kirkbymoorside–6.3–Helmsley–3.9–Oswaldkirk–3.1–Ampleforth–3.3–Coxwold–1.5–**Carlton Husthwaite** (NA) (*Easingwold–York*)–*Thirsk*
LK28	Batley link: Batley–Dewsbury 2.3 m	**Batley** (DW) (*Cleckheaton–Dudley Hill, Morley–Leeds*)–2.3–**Dewsbury** (DW) (*Ossett–Wakefield, Mirfield–Huddersfield*)
LK29	Bradford link: Bradford–Dudley Hill 2.0 m	**Bradford** (BF) (*Thornton–Halifax, Shipley–Skipton*)–2.0–**Dudley Hill** (BF) (*Pudsey–Leeds, Batley*, West Yorkshire loop)
LK30	*Scunthorpe*–Gunness–Epworth–*Gainsborough* 6.6 m	*Scunthorpe*–{**Gunness** (BI) (*Crowle–Thorne*)}–6.6–**Epworth** (GA) (*Thorne*)–*Gainsborough*
LK31	Gainsborough–North Leverton–*Retford* 6.7 m	**Gainsborough** (GA) (*Epworth–Scunthorpe, Torksey–Lincoln*)–6.7–{**North Leverton** (WP) (*Torksey–Lincoln*)}–Retford
LK32	Horncastle link: Alford–Metheringham 34.9 m	**Alford** (AL) (*Louth–Grimsby, Skegness–Boston, Mablethorpe*)–8.2–Spilsby–10.0–Horncastle–6.5–Woodhall Spa–10.2–**Metheringham** (SO) (*Lincoln, Sleaford*)
LK33	Mansfield–Southwell 13.4 m	**Mansfield** (MA) (*Shirebrook–Staveley*)–5.8–Blidworth–7.6–**Southwell** (NK) (*Newark, Lowdham–Nottingham*)
LK34	Buntingford link: Luton–Hitchin–Baldock–Buntingford–Newport (Essex)–Thaxted–Little waltham–*Chelmsford* 58.1 m	**Luton** (LT) (*Leighton Buzzard, St. Albans*, Dunstable loop)–5.6–Great Offley–3.4–**Hitchin** (SE) (*Stevenage, Sandy–Huntingdon*)–4.0–Letchworth–1.8–**Baldock** (SE) (*Royston–Cambridge, Stevenage*)–8.9–Buntingford–12.0–**Newport (Essex)** (NQ) (*Saffron Walden–Linton–Cambridge, Bishops Stortford–London*)–7.7–Thaxted–6.7–Great Dunmow–8.0–{**Little Waltham** (CD) (*Braintree*)}–Chelmsford

Table A4.3. (Continued)

Ref	Origin–destination	Route
LK35	Eye link: Diss–Stowmarket 16.9 m	**Diss** (DS) (*Roudham–Thetford, Harleston–Bungay–Norwich*)–4.9–Eye–12.0–**Stowmarket** (IP) (*Ipswich, Bury St. Edmunds*)
	Minor dead-end branches: local routes	*Dead-end branches not forming termini of other routes, carrying light traffic at relatively low speeds*
LB1	Sheerness–Sittingbourne 8.3 m	Sheerness–8.3–**Sittingbourne** (CT) (*Chatham, Faversham–Dover*)
LB2	Wallend–Strood 12.5 m	Wallend–8.0–Hoo–4.5–**Strood** (CT) (*Gravesend, Chatham*)
LB3	Sevenoaks–Otford 3.0 m	Sevenoaks–3.0–**Otford** (OT) (*Orpington–Bromley–London, Oxted–Godstone, Ightham–Maidstone*)
LB4	Chesham–Amersham 2.6 m	Chesham–2.6–**Amersham** (WT) (*North Lee–Aylesbury, Rickmansworth*)
LB5	Swanage–Wareham 9.6 m	Swanage–4.8–Corfe Castle–4.8–**Wareham** (PL) (*Poole–London, Dorchester*)
LB6	Lyme Regis–Axminster 6.0 m	Lyme Regis–6.0–**Axminster** (AX) (Chard Junction–Yeovil, Whitford–Honiton, *Axminster* loop)
LB7	Seaton–Whitford 4.5 m	Seaton–4.5–**Whitford** (AX) (*Honiton–Ottery St. Mary, Axminster*)
LB8	Sidmouth–Harpford 3.0 m	Sidmouth–3.0–**Harpford** (OS) (*Ottery St. Mary, Budleigh Salterton–Exeter, Exmouth* loop)
LB9	Moretonhampstead–Great Matridge–*Exeter* 11.9 m	Moretonhampstead–3.2–Easton (for Chagford)–7.0–Dunsford–1.7–**Great Matridge** (EX) *Heathfield–Plymouth*)–*Exeter*
LB10	Dawlish Road–Newton Abbot 7.2 m	Dawlish Road (Holcombe)–1.8–Teignmouth–5.4–**Newton Abbot** (EX) (*Great Matridge–Exeter, Ashburton–South Brent–Plymouth*)
LB11	Brixham–Paignton 5.3 m	Brixham–1.8–Churston–3.5–**Paignton** (PG) (*Torquay–Heathfield–Exeter, Totnes–Halwell–South Brent*)
LB12	Dartmouth–Halwell 7.3 m	Dartmouth–7.3–**Halwell** (PG) (*Totnes–Paignton, South Brent–Plymouth*)
LB13	Kingsbridge–Halwell 8.0 m	Kingsbridge–8.0–**Halwell** (PG) (*Totnes–Paignton, South Brent–Plymouth*)
LB14	Ilfracombe–Barnstaple 12.3 m	Ilfracombe–7.3–Braunston–5.0–**Barnstaple** (RN) (*Bideford–Shilstone–Crediton–Exeter, South Molton*)
LB15	Looe–Liskeard 8.0 m	Looe–8.0–**Liskeard** (PM) (*Plymouth, Llanhydrock–Penzance*)
LB16	Fowey–Lostwithiel 5.6 m	Fowey–5.6–**Lostwithiel** (BJ) (*St. Austell–Truro, Llanhydrock–Plymouth*)
LB17	Falmouth–Portreath (double branch *plus* link) 15.3 m	Falmouth–2.8–Penrhyn–1.6–**Treluswell** (TR) (*Truro, Longrock–Penzance, Helston* loop)–3.5–Gwennap–3.2–**Redruth** (RR) (*Camborne–Lelant–Penzance, Truro*)–4.2–Portreath
LB18	St. Ives–Lelant 3.3 m	St. Ives–3.3–**Lelant** (RR) (*Camborne–Redruth, Longrock–Penzance*)
LB19	Padstow–Tredinnick 4.9 m	Padstow–4.9–**Tredinnick** (*Wadebridge, Newquay–Truro*)
LB20	Minehead–Taunton 23.5 m	Minehead–7.5–Watchet–16.0–**Taunton** (TA) (*Wrantage–Langport–London, Tiverton–Exeter, Bridgewater–Bristol*)
LB21	Portishead–Nailsea 4.8 m	Portishead–4.8–**Nailsea** (WM) (*Bristol, Loxton–Highbridge, Weston-super Mare* loop)

(*continued*)

Table A4.3. (Continued)

Ref	Origin–destination	Route
LB22	Avonmouth–Filton–Chipping Sodbury (double branch) 15.1 m	Avonmouth–3.2–Henbury–2.4–**Filton** (BR) (*Bristol, Thornbury–Cam–Gloucester, Pilning*)–8.2–Yate–1.3–Chipping Sodbury
LB23	Dursley–Cam 2.5 m	Dursley–2.5–**Cam** (GL) (*Stonehouse (Glos.)–Gloucester, Thornbury–Filton–Bristol*)
LB24	Maerdy–Porth 6.9 m	Maerdy–2.0–Ferndale–4.9–**Porth** (PP) (*Pontypridd, Treherbert*)
LB25	Porthcawl–Pyle 4.3 m	Porthcawl–4.3–**Pyle** (BG) (*Bridgend, Neath*)
LB26	Maesteg–Bridgend 9.6 m	Maesteg–6.1–**Tondu** (BG) (*Blaengarw, Nant-y-moel*)–3.5–**Bridgend** (BG) (*Llantrisant–Cardiff, Pyle–Neath, Llantwit Major, Barry loop*)
LB27	Blaengarw–Tondu 6.5 m	Blaengarw–1.0–Pontycymer–5.5–**Tondu** (BG) (*Bridgend, Maesteg, Nant-y-moel*)
LB28	Nant-y-moel–Tondu 8.0 m	Nant-y-moel–1.8–Ogmore Vale–2.5–Blackmill–3.7–**Tondu** (BG) (*Bridgend, Maesteg, Blaengarw*)
LB29	Cleobury Mortimer–Stockton-on-Teme 7.0 m	Cleobury Mortimer–7.0–**Stockton-on-Teme** (WF) (*Knightwick–Worcester, Great Witley–Stourport-on-Severn, Tenbury Wells–Woofferton–Ludlow*)
LB30	Halesowen–Old Hill 2.5 m	Halesowen–2.5–**Old Hill** (BM) (*Stourbridge–Kidderminster, Handsworth–Birmingham*)
LB31	Machynlleth–Aberdovey 10.3 m	Machynlleth–10.3–**Aberdovey** (AW) (*Aberystwyth, Barmouth*, North Wales Coast loop)
LB32	Blaenau Ffestiniog–Penrhyndeudraeth 10.3 m	Blaenau Ffestiniog–10.3–**Penrhyndeudraeth** (CJ) (*Porthmadoc–Criccieth–Pwllheli, Barmouth*, North Wales Coast loop)
LB33	Llanberis–Caernarvon 8.0 m	Llanberis–8.0–**Caernarvon** (BX) (*Bangor, Criccieth*, North Wales Coast loop)
LB34	Amlwch–Benllech–Menai Bridge 17.3 m	Amlwch–9.0–Benllech–8.3–**Menai Bridge** (BX) (*Bangor, Llangefni–Holyhead*)
LB35	Beaumaris–Menai Bridge 6.0 m	Beaumaris–6.0–**Menai Bridge** (BX) (*Bangor, Llangefni–Holyhead*)
LB36	Betwys-y-Coed–Conway 16.1 m	Betwys-y-Coed–3.8–Llanwrst–7.3–Tal-y-Cafn–5.0–**Conway** (LD) (*Rhyl–Chester, Bangor–Holyhead*)
LB37	Biddulph–Kidsgrove 5.2 m	Biddulph–3.6–Newchapel–1.6–**Kidsgrove** (SK) (*Stoke-on-Trent, Congleton–Macclesfield, Middlewich–Warrington, Nantwich–Chester*)
LB398	Winsford–Middlewich 3.6 m	Winsford–3.6–**Middlewich** (NW) (*Northwich–Warrington, Kidsgrove–Stoke-on-Trent*)
LB39	Runcorn–Sutton Weaver 2.4 m	Runcorn–2.4–**Sutton Weaver** (CH) (*Frodsham–Chester, Warrington, Northwich*)
LB40	Glossop–Hadfield 1.8 m	Glossop–1.8–**Hadfield** (TY) (*Stalybridge, Penistone–Sheffield*)
LB41	Alston–Haltwhistle 15.0 m	Alston–4.7–Slaggyford–4.8–Lambley–5.5–**Haltwhistle** (CL) (*Carlisle, Swalwell–Newcastle*)
LB42	Silloth–Bromfield 6.6 m	Silloth–6.6–**Bromfield** (CL) (*Wigton–Carlisle, Aspatria–Workington*)
LB43	Whithorn–Newton Stewart 16.6 m	Whithorn–9.7–Wigtown–6.9–**Newton Stewart** (*Castle Douglas–Dumfries, Whitecrook–Stranraer*)
LB44	Douglas–Hyndford Bridge–Lanark 9.6 m	Douglas–9.6–**Hyndford Bridge** (LK) (*Pettinain–Symington–Carlisle*)–Lanark

Table A4.3. (Continued)

Ref	Origin–destination	Route
LB45	Airdrie–Coatbridge–Glasgow 12.0 m	Airdrie–2.3–**Coatbridge** (CG) (*Castlecary–Stirling, Motherwell–Carlisle*)–9.7–**Glasgow** (GG) (*Uddingston–Carlisle, Dumbarton–Crianlarich–Fort William, Castlecary–Falkirk, Lugton–Kilmarnock, Clarkston, Milngavie, Paisley–Greenock,* Clyde loop, *Bishopton, Renfrew* loop)
LB46	Milngavie–Glasgow 6.8 m	Milngavie–3.5–Maryhill–3.3–**Glasgow** (GG) (*Uddingston–Carlisle, Dumbarton–Crianlarich–Fort William, Castlecary–Falkirk, Lugton–Kilmarnock, Coatbridge–Airdrie, Clarkston, Paisley–Greenock,* Clyde loop, *Bishopton, Renfrew* loop)
LB47	Aberfoyle–Callander 8.9 m	Aberfoyle–4.6–Port of Mentieth–4.3–**Callander** (SL) (*Dunblane–Stirling, Crianlarich–Fort William*)
LB48	Kyle of Lochalsh–Invermoriston 51.5 m	Kyle of Lochalsh–8.0–Ardelve–7.3–Shiel Bridge–20.3–Bun Loyne–6.9–Torgyle–9.0–**Invermoriston** (IV) (*Inverness, Fort Augustus–Spean Bridge–Fort William*)
LB49	Cromarty–Muir of Ord 20.3 m	Cromarty–7.0–White Bog–1.7–Rosemarkie–1.0–Fortrose–10.6–**Muir of Ord** (IV) (Beauly–Inverness, Thurso)
LB50	Lossiemouth–Elgin 5.5 m	Lossiemouth–5.5–**Elgin** (FB) (*Forres–Inverness, Fochabers–Aberdeen*)
LB51	Dufftown–Craigellachie 5.2 m	Dufftown–5.2–**Craigellachie** (FB) (*Aberlour–Fochabers, Grantown-on-Spey–Carrbridge–Spean Bridge*)
LB52	Huntly–Milltown 6.2 m	Huntly–6.2–**Milltown** (TU) (*Keith–Fochabers–Inverness, Turriff–Aberdeen*)
LB53	Ballater–Aberdeen 41.3 m	Ballater–11.3–Aboyne–13.0–Banchory–17.0–**Aberdeen** (AB) (*Dyce–Inverness, Stonehaven–Montrose–London*)
LB54	Aberfeldy–Ballinluig 9.5 m	Aberfeldy–5.2–Grandtully–4.3–**Ballinluig** (PH) (*Dunkeld–Cargill, Pitlochry*)
LB55	Crieff–Auchterarder 8.2 m	Crieff–8.2–**Auchterarder** (*Perth, Dunblane–Stirling*)
LB56	Tayport–Dairsie 9.0 m	Tayport (Dundee ferry)–2.0–Newport-on-Tay–7.0–**Dairsie** (CU) (*Cupar–Lathrisk–Perth, St. Andrews–Balgonie–Kirkaldy, Fife Coast* loop)
LB57	Dollar–Alloa 6.4 m	Dollar–2.9–Tillicoultry–3.5–**Alloa** (SL) (*Stirling, Kincardine–Dunfermline, Fife Coast* loop)
LB58	Granton–Leith–Edinburgh 4.7 m	Granton–2.4–Leith–2.3–**Edinburgh** (ED) (*Penicuik–Biggar, Dalkeith–Galashiels–Melrose, Falkirk, Shotts–Wishaw, Longniddry–Dunbar*)
LB59	North Berwick–Longniddry 10.1 m	North Berwick–4.3–Gullane–5.8–**Longniddry** (ED) (*Edinburgh, Dunbar*)
LB60	Jedburgh–Ancrum 2.6 m	Jedburgh–2.6–**Ancrum** (ML) (*Maxton–Melrose, Hawick*)
LB61	Selkirk–Lindean 2.3 m	Selkirk–2.3–**Lindean** (ML) (*Melrose–Newcastle, Innerleithen–Biggar–Glasgow*)
LB62	Newbiggin-by-Sea–Morpeth 7.8 m	Newbiggin-by-Sea–2.5–Ashington–5.3–**Morpeth** (MP) (*Newcastle, Alnwick–Coldstream–Glasgow*)
LB63	Stanhope–Bishop Auckland 16.8 m	Stanhope–6.0–Wolsingham–6.8–Crook Road (Howden-le-Wear)–4.0–**Bishop Auckland** (BA) (*Newton Aycliffe–Stockton-on-Tees, Spennymoor–Durham, West Auckland–Barnard Castle*)–1.8–Coundon Grange–3.6–**Newton Aycliffe** (BA) (*Darlington, Spennymoor–Durham*)–7.5–Redmarshall–3.5–**Stockton-on-Tees** (SQ) (*Eaglescliffe–Yarm–Northallerton, Hartlepool–Sunderland, Middlesbrough* loop)

(continued)

Table A4.3. (Continued)

Ref	Origin–destination	Route
LB64	Richmond–Catterick 5.3 m	Richmond–5.3–**Catterick** (CK) (*Darlington, Constable Burton–Leyburn, Bedale–Ripon, Northallerton*)
LB65	Whitby–Grosmont 6.5 m	Whitby–6.5–**Grosmont** (PK) (*Pickering–Malton, Stokesley–Crathorne–Stockton-on-Tees*)
LB66	Hornsea–Beverley 13.0 m	Hornsea–13.0–**Beverley** (HL) (*Hull, Market Weighton–York, Driffield–Scarborough, Bridlington* loop)
LB67	Withernsea–Hull 21.4 m	Withernsea–4.0–Patrington–10.8–Hedon–6.6–**Hull** (HL) (*Hessle–Balkholme–Leeds, Beverley*)
LB68	Haworth–Keighley 5.0 m	Haworth–5.0–**Keighley** (SX) (*Skipton, Shipley–Leeds*)
LB69	Holmfirth–Huddersfield 6.6 m	Holmfirth–3.0–**Honley** (HF) (*Meltham*)–3.6–**Huddersfield** (HF) (*Deighton–Mirfield, Grasscroft–Manchester*)
LB70	Meltham–Honley 3.0 m	Meltham–3.0–**Honley** (HF) (*Huddersfield, Holmfirth*)
LB71	Barton-on-Humber–Brigg 11.0 m	Barton-on-Humber (Hessle ferry)–11.0–**Brigg** (BI) (*Caistor–Grimsby, Scunthorpe–Gunness–Thorne*)
LB72	Mablethorpe–Alford 8.5 m	Mablethorpe–2.4–Sutton-on-Sea–6.1–**Alford** (AL) (*Louth–Grimsby, Skegness–Boston–Wigtoft–Spalding, Metheringham, Horncastle* loop)
LB73	Leek–Stoke-on-Trent 10.8 m	Leek–5.6–Endon–5.2–**Stoke-on-Trent** (SK) (*Stone–London, Kidsgrove–Warrington, Draycott–Uttoxeter*)
LB74	Cheadle–Draycott 2.8 m	Cheadle–2.8–**Draycott** (SK) (*Stoke-on-Trent, Uttoxeter–Derby*)
LB75	Ashbourne–Uttoxeter 11.0 m	Ashbourne–7.2–Rocester–3.8–**Uttoxeter** (SK) (*Draycott–Stoke-on-Trent, Willington* (*Derbys.*)–*Derby*)
LB76	Rushden–Irthlingborough 3.0 m	Rushden–1.6–Higham Ferres–1.4–**Irthlingborough** (WL) (*Wellingborough–Northampton, Raunds–Peterborough*)
LB77	Ramsey–Warboys 3.6 m	Ramsey–3.6–**Warboys** (HN) (*Huntingdon, Chatteris*)
LB78	Aylsham–Swanton Abbott 4.9 m	Aylsham–4.9–**Swanton Abbott** (NR) (*Norwich, Cromer–Wells-next-the-Sea*)
LB79	Southwold–Halesworth 8.6 m	Southwold–8.6–**Halesworth** (BC) (*Saxmundhom–Ipswich, Ilketshall–Norwich*)
LB80	Aldeburgh–Saxmundham–Framlingham (double branch) 15.1 m	Aldeburgh–4.7–Leiston–3.9–**Saxmundham** (IP) (*Ipswich, Halesworth–Norwich*)–6.5–Framlingham
LB81	Burnham-on-Crouch–Maldon–Chelmsford–*London* 21.8 m	Burnham-on-Crouch–2.5–Southminster–4.8–Maylandsea–4.6–Maldon–4.6–Danbury–3.6–Great Baddow–1.7–**Chelmsford** (CD) (*Witham–Coggeshall (Broad Green)–Colcheste, Little Witham–Braintree)–Brentwood–London*
	Isle of Wight system	
LB82	Ryde–Totland 22.1 m	**Ryde** (RD) (*Brading–Shanklin*)–7.3–**Newport** (NO) (*Cowes, Whiteley Bank*)–11.5–Yarmouth–3.3–Totland
LB83	Ryde–Ventnor 15.2 m	**Ryde** (RD) (*Newport*)–4.0–**Brading** (RD) (*Bembridge*)–4.8–Shanklin–2.4–**Whiteley Bank** (WU) (*Newport*)–4.0–Ventnor
LB84	Cowes–Whiteley Bank–*Ventnor* 11.8 m	Cowes–4.8–**Newport** (NO) (*Ryde, Yarmouth–Totland*)–7.0–**Whiteley Bank** (WU) (*Shanklin–Brading–Ryde*)–Ventnor
LB85	Bembridge–Brading 3.8 m	Bembridge–3.8–**Brading** (RD) (*Ryde, Shanklin–Whiteley Bank–Ventnor*)

Table A4.4. Overall route mileage of the counterfactual network analysed by type of route and quality of infrastructure

Type	Trunk	Primary	Secondary	Local	Total
Radial (R)	1,280.1				1,280.1
Feeder (F)	474.8	1,008.7	607.0		2,090.5
Inter-regional (G)	1,086.6	885.0	582.5		2,554.1
Orbital (O)		94.7	46.9	122.3	263.9
Urban bypass (U)	121.7	49.4	52.7		223.8
Coastal loop (C)		54.4	897.7	604.9	1,557.0
Inland loop (N)			1,558.5	290.2	1,848.7
Link (K)	214.8	388.8	1,207.7	500.5	2,320.5
Dead-end branch (B)			133.9	792.2	926.1
Total	3,178.0	2,481.0	5,086.9	2,310.1	13,056.0

Routes may join or divide at rural junctions at which it is unlikely that trains would ever wish to stop. Where clarity demands it, these junctions are identified by placing the names of the junctions within curly brackets to show that they are not places at which connections can be made. In most cases, however, the precise location of these junctions has been suppressed in order to avoid unnecessary complication. Where two routes join at a rural junction, the distance attributed to one of the routes must be reduced to avoid 'double-counting' the overall length of the network. A distance imputed in this way is indicated by an asterisk. When estimating journey times from the recorded distances it is important to remember that in such cases the actual distance travelled by a train along the route will exceed the distance shown in the table.

Two routes occasionally overlap for a portion of the journey because they both use the same link between adjacent centres. The distance of the linkage is imputed to only one of the routes. For the other route, the distance is shown in curved brackets to indicate that it should not be included in any estimate of the total length of the network.

The quality of the infrastructure may vary along some long-distance routes. Where the route passes through areas of high population density, or acts as a link between two trunk routes that it intersects, a higher quality of infrastructure may be required. In such cases the higher-quality portions of the route are shown within square brackets in the third column of the table.

Within each category, the routes are listed in a clockwise order, beginning with routes in the south-east, on the south bank of the River Thames, and ending with routes on the north bank of the River Thames. Along any given radius, routes closer to London are listed before routes more distant from London. The implementation of these principles is modified when two routes that would otherwise appear at different places in the sequence are strongly interdependent; in such cases they are listed together.

The total mileage of each route is listed in the middle column of the table. A distinction is drawn between gross mileage and net mileage. Gross mileage is the total distance that would be travelled by a train along a route. The net mileage is the addition to the total route mileage of the system effected by the route. The difference between the two is accounted for by the mileage that has already been imputed to some other route. The distance between a rural junction and the neighbouring station mentioned in the table is an example of such duplicate mileage.

The total route mileage of the counterfactual network is calculated by summing the relevant mileages from the middle column of Table A4.3. Table A4.4 shows mileage figures classified by the quality of infrastructure (as specified in Table A4.1) and its role by the network (as specified in Table A4.2).

The total route mileage is only 13,056, which is only two-thirds of the actual size of the network in 1914.

APPENDIX 5
Analysis of Hubs

The Definition of a Hub

A major advantage of the counterfactual system lies in its efficient pattern of hubs. To demonstrate this rigorously, however, it is necessary to define the meaning of a hub. For the purpose of this analysis a hub is defined as the point at which three or more lines meet and where traffic can be conveniently interchanged.

The focus on passenger traffic is retained in the analysis of hubs. The interchange of passengers, who can make their own way between stations or between platforms, is simpler than the interchange of goods, which involves transhipment of consignments or the shunting of wagons in freight yards, and possibly the operation of local 'transfer freight trains' between yards as well.

The definition rules out as a hub any point where only two lines meet, irrespective of the amount of traffic originating or arriving there. Thus an intermediate station at which there is no junction cannot be a hub however much traffic it generates. On the counterfactual system, for example, Birkenhead, Grimsby, Hartlepool, Llanelli, and Pembroke are all ports that generate significant amounts of traffic, but they are not hubs, because they are simply intermediate points on a coastal loop line. A similar point applies to major resorts like Blackpool, Bournemouth, Newquay, and Scarborough. Neither can a station at which one or two dead-end branches terminate be a hub. Thus large coastal centres on dead-end spurs, such as Portsmouth, are not hubs.

Not all three-way junctions are hubs, either. This is because there may be a more convenient location nearby for the interchange of traffic. If all three-way junctions were hubs then there would be an enormous number of hubs, with many having little potential for interchange. Through trains that called at every one of these hubs would have a very large number of stops to make, and journeys would consequently be very slow.

Composite Hubs

In many cases a constellation of neighbouring three-way junctions constitutes a convenient interchange; this may be termed a 'composite hub'. There is a main station, usually at the most important junction, and a range of stations at the other junctions; these are known as the 'satellite hubs'. Many of the hubs identified in our analysis are composite hubs, and some have a substantial number of satellites. A hub with no satellites is known as a 'simple hub'. The preponderance of composite hubs reduces the number of hubs that are used to describe the network and effects a significant economy in the analysis.

The most important junction in a composite hub is the one that handles the most interchange traffic. Typically the satellite junctions feed traffic into and out of this hub. If a satellite handles a large amount of interchange traffic that is not funnelled through the major hub then it is more appropriate to distinguish it as a separate hub in its own right.

Consider the lines of the counterfactual centred on Bidford-on-Avon, for example. The major traffic flows are to and from Evesham, to the south-west, and so Bidford is the natural point at which passengers on trains from Evesham to Birmingham change for Leamington, and passengers from Evesham to Leamington change for Birmingham. However, passengers from Bromsgrove to Birmingham will prefer to change at Redditch, while passengers from Moreton-in-Marsh to Leamington will prefer to change at Stratford-on-Avon. Thus Redditch and Stratford function as satellite hubs to Bidford, at which more modest levels of traffic are interchanged. Most of the traffic through Redditch and Stratford is on its way to or from Evesham, but not of all of it goes that way.

A common configuration of three-way junctions arises where two routes cross at an acute angle. At Wells, Somerset, for example, a line running north-east from Taunton and Langport to Radstcok and Bath intersects a line running south-west from Cheddar to Bruton. The lines from Langport and Cheddar converge at Wells, share the tracks between Wells and Shepton Mallet, and then diverge. Passengers could change from one route to another at either Wells or Shepton Mallet. Since Wells is the more important town, however, and the number of passengers from the Langport line who wish to change at Wells is likely to exceed the number of passengers who want to change from the Bruton line to the Radstock line, it is most appropriate to designate Wells as the composite hub and Shepton Mallet as its satellite. If Shepton Mallet were the more important town, and there was more traffic from Bruton to Radstock than there was from Langport to Cheddar then it would be appropriate to designate Shepton Mallet as the major hub instead. Likewise, if Wells and Shepton Mallet were equally important sources of traffic, and interchange from Langport to Cheddar and from Bruton to Radstock were equally great then it would be appropriate to identify Wells and Shepton Mallet as independent simple hubs.

Table A5.1. Hubs on the counterfactual system

Code	Hub	T	B	Satellite hubs	Analogues
AB	Aberdeen	5	1	Dyce (3), Montrose (3)	Aberdeen
AD	Arundel	4			Ford
AH	Ashford	4			Ashford
AL	Alford	5	1	Louth (3)	Firsby, Louth
AM	Aldermaston	4			Reading
AR	Ayr	4		Prestwick (3)	Ayr
AS	Ash	7		Bentley (3)	Farnham
AV	Abergavenny	10		Brynmawr (4), Beaufort (3), Dukestown (3), Llechryd (3), The Bryn (3)	Abergavenny
AW	Aberystwyth	4	1	Llanafan (3), Aberdovey (3)	Aberystwyth
AX	Axminster	5	2	Chard Junction (3), Whitford (3)	Sidmouth Junction
AY	Aylesbury	8		Princes Risborough (4), North Lee (3), Loudwater (3)	Aylesbury
BA	Bishop Auckland	4			Bishop Auckland
BAK	Bakewell	3			Chinley
BAR	Barnstaple	3	1		Barnstaple
BAS	Basingstoke	3			Basingstoke
BB	Banbury	4			Banbury
BC	Balkholme	5		Goole (3)	Goole
BD	Bedford	4		Willington (Beds.) (3)	Bedford

Table A5.1. (Continued)

Code	Hub	T	B	Satellite hubs	Analogues
BDG	Brading (IoW)	3			Sandown (IoW)
BE	Bury St. Edmunds	4			Bury St. Edmunds
BET	Beighton	4			Killamarsh
BF	Bradford	5		Halifax (3), Dudley Hill (3)	Low Moor, Laisterdyke
BG	Bridgend	7	4	Tondu (4), Pyle (3)	Bridgend
BGH	Brighouse	4		Greetland (3)	Mirfield, Greetland
BH	Buckhurst Hill	4			
BHD	Barrhead	6		Lugton (4)	Lugton, Giffen
BI	Brigg	5		Gunness (3), Caistor (3)	Barnetby, Ulceby
BJ	Barnard Castle	5	1	Winston	Barnard Castle
BK	Barking	4			Barking, Stratford
BKH	Buckingham	5		Winslow (3)	Verney Junction
BL	Bolton	4		Lostock (3)	Bolton, Blackrod
BM	Birmingham	9	1	Handsworth (3), Coleshill (3), Old Hill (3)	Birmingham, Whitacre
BMY	Bromley	4			Bromley
BN	Brighton	4		Shoreham (3), Goring-by-Sea (3)	Brighton
BNE	Bourne	4		Aslackby (3)	Bourne
BO	Boston	3			Boston
BP	Barmouth	3			Barmouth
BQ	Brecon	4		Sennybridge (3)	Talyllyn Junction
BR	Bristol	10	4	Filton (5), Nailsea (4), Bath (3), Limpley Stoke (3)	Bristol, Bath, Yatton, Patchway
BRW	Bridgwater	6		Loxton (4), Highbridge (3)	Bridgewater, Highbridge
BS	Bury	6		Helmshore (3), Whitefield (3)	Bury
BT	Bruton	5		Frome (3)	Frome
BTF	Brentford	4			Kew Bridge
BU	Builth Wells	4		Llandrindod Wells (3)	Builth Road
BV	Bidford-on-Avon	6		Evesham (4), Stratford-on-Avon (3), Redditch (3)	Evesham, Stratford-on-Avon, Broom Junction
BVL	Beverley	5	1	Market Weighton (3)	Market Weighton
BW	Brentwood	5	1		Shenfield
BX	Bangor	6		Menai Bridge (4), Caernarvon (3)	Bangor
BY	Burley-in-Wharfedale	4		Pool (3)	Otley, Menston
BZ	Brough (Cumbria)	3			Kirkby Stephen
CA	Clayton-le-Moors	8	2	Blackburn (4), Burnley (3), Elslack (3)	Blackburn, Accrington, Rose Grove
CB	Cambridge	10		Linton (3), Swaffham Bulbeck (3), Newmarket (3), Wixoe (3)	Cambridge, Fordham
CC	Castlecary	4			Larbert
CD	Chelmsford	5		Little Waltham (3)	Romford, Witham
CE	Coldstream	4		Swinton (3)	Tweedmouth
CF	Cardiff	5		Tongwynlais (3)	Cardiff

(continued)

Table A5.1. (Continued)

Code	Hub	T	B	Satellite hubs	Analogues
CG	Coatbridge	4			Coatbridge
CH	Chester	10		Sutton Weaver (4), Queensferry (3), Hooton (3), Broxton (3)	Chester
CHF	Chesterfield	4		Staveley (3)	Chesterfield
CI	Carrbridge	3			Aviemore
CJ	Criccieth	4		Penrhyndeudraeth (3)	Portmadoc
CK	Catterick	6	1	Middleton Tyas (3)	
CL	Carlisle	8	1	Todhills (3), Creca (3), Bromfield (3), Haltwhistle (3)	Carlisle, Gretna, Longtown, Haltwhistle, Abbeyholme
CLP	Clapham	6			Clapham Junction, London Waterloo, Wandsworth Road, Peckham Rye, Herne Hill
CM	Carmarthen	7		Narberth (3), Llanddarog (3), Llangeler (3)	Carmarthen, Whitland
CN	Croydon	5			East Croydon, West Croydon, Norwood Junction
CO	Conway	4		Newnham, Lydney	Llandudno Junction
CP	Chippenham	6		Melksham (3), Great Somerford (3)	Chippenham
CR	Colchester	5	2	Manningtree (3), Coggeshall (Broad Green) (3)	Colchester, Halstead
CRL	Crianlarich	4	1	Connel Ferry (3)	Crianlarich
CS	Chester-le-Street	4			Durham
CT	Chatham	9	1	Dartford (4), Sittingbourne (3), Faversham (3), Strood (3), Burham (3)	Gravesend, Sittingbourne
CU	Chorley	5			Preston
CV	Coventry	4			Coventry
CW	Crewkerne	4			Yeovil
CX	Cirencester	5		Cherington (3), Ampney St. Peter (3)	Swindon
CY	Canterbury	5		Sandwich (3)	Canterbury
CZ	Cranbrook	4			
DA	Dalton-in-Furness	3			Dalton-in-Furness
DB	Derby	8		Willington (Derbys) (4), Burton-on-Trent (3), Uttoxeter (3)	Derby, Burton-on-Trent, Egginton, Uttoxeter
DC	Doncaster	4			Doncaster
DD	Dundee	3			Dundee
DF	Dumfries	4		Newton Stewart (3)	Dumfries
DH	Durham	6		Spennymoor (3), Pittington (3)	Durham
DK	Dorking	4			Redhill
DL	Darlington	4			Darlington
DM	Dunfermline	4		Cowdenbeath (3)	Dunfermline
DN	Downham Market	4			Kings Lynn

Table A5.1. (Continued)

Code	Hub	T	B	Satellite hubs	Analogues
DR	Dorchester	4	1	Upwey (3)	Weymouth
DS	Diss	3			Tivetshall
DV	Dover	5	1	Whitfield (4), Lympne (3)	Dover
DW	Dewsbury	6		Mirfield (3), Batley (3)	Dewsbury, Thornhill, Horbury and Ossett
DZ	Devizes	4		Manningford Bruce (3)	Savernake
ED	Edinburgh	8		Falkirk (3), Penicuik (3), Longniddry (3)	Edinburgh, Portobello, Dalmeny
EG	East Grinstead	4			East Grinstead
EL	Ealing	4			Ealing, South Acton, Gunnersbury
EP	Epsom	5		Ewell (3), Carshalton (3)	Epsom, Sutton, Mitcham Junction
ER	East Dereham	4		Shipdham (3)	East Dereham
EX	Exeter	7		Tiverton (3), Great Matridge (3), Heathfield (3)	Exeter, Tiverton, Newton Abbot
EY	Ely	4			Ely
FB	Fochabers	6		Elgin (3), Craigellachie (3)	Elgin
FF	Forfar	3			Forfar
GB	Gainsborough	4		Epworth (3)	Gainsborough
GD	Godstone	5			Redhill, Oxted
GF	Guildford	6	1	East Horsley (3)	East Horsley
GG	Glasgow	10	1	Uddingston (3)	Glasgow
GK	Greenock	5		Port Glasgow (3), Bishopton (3)	Paisley
GL	Gloucester	8	1	Stonehouse (Glos.) (3), Cam (3), Newnham (3)	Gloucester
GN	Gurnos	4		Colbren (3)	Neath
GT	Grantham	3			Grantham, Honington
HA	Hay-on-Wye	5		Willersley (4), Three Cocks (3)	Talyllyn Junction, Titley
HB	Halstead	4			Colchester
HC	Hitchin	6		Stevenage (4), Baldock (4)	Hitchin
HE	Hengoed	4			Caerphilly
HF	Huddersfield	6		Deighton (4), Honley (3)	Huddersfield
HH	Hatherleigh	4		Shilstone (3)	Exeter
HI	Hirwaun	4		Pont Nedd Fechan (3)	Neath
HL	Hull	3	1		Hull
HM	Hamilton	4		Clarkston (3)	Hamilton
HN	Huntingdon	7		Warboys (3), Chatteris (3), Tempsford (3)	Huntingdon, St. Ives
HO	Harlow	4			Broxbourne
HR	Hereford	6		Bodenham (3)	Hereford
HS	Horsham	7		Pulborough (3)	Christs Hospital
HT	Hastings	6		Rye (3), Hurst Green (3), Pevensey (3)	Hastings, Robertsbridge
HV	Havant	5	1	Chichester (3), Cosham (3)	Havant, Chichester

(*continued*)

Table A5.1. (Continued)

Code	Hub	T	B	Satellite hubs	Analogues
HW	Haverfordwest	3			
IK	Ilkeston	4			Trent, Trowell, Codnor Park, Daybrook
IP	Ipswich	8	3	Saxmundham (4), Stowmarket (3)	Ipswich
IT	Ilketshall	5	1	Bungay (3), Halesworth (3)	Beccles
IV	Inverness	6	2	Muir of Ord (3), Invermoriston (3)	Inverness, Dingwall
KK	Kirkaldy	4		Balgonie (3)	Thornton Junction
KL	Kirkby Lonsdale	6		Milnthorpe (3), Bell Busk (3)	Carnforth
KM	Kilmarnock	5		Stonehouse (Lanark) (3)	Kilmarnock
KN	Knottingley	4			Pontefract
KW	Kilwinning	5		Irvine (3)	Kilwinning
KY	Kings Lynn	5			Kings Lynn
LA	Launceston	4		Lydford (3), Collamore Head (3)	Launceston
LB	Leighton Buzzard	7		Luton (3)	Bletchley
LC	Lancaster	4	1	Garstang (3)	Lancaster
LD	Loudwater	4			Princes Risborough
LE	Leicester	10		Loughborough (3), Shepshed (3), Desford (3), Gotham (3), Melbourne (3)	Leicester
LF	Lichfield	8		Cannock (3), Colwich (3)	Lichfield, Rugeley
LG	Langport	5			Taunton
LH	Littlehampton	3			
LI	Lincoln	7		Torksey (3), Metheringham (3), Market Rasen (3)	Lincoln, Woodhall Junction
LJ	Consett (Leadgate)	3			Blackhill
LK	Lanark	4	1	Hyndford Bridge (3)	Carluke
LL	Lechlade	4			
LM	Leamington	5		Warwick (3), Southam (3)	Leamington, Fenny Compton
LN	Lewisham	6			New Cross, New Cross Gate, Catford Bridge
LNC	London (North Central)	3			Dalston Junction
LNE	London (North East)	4			London Kings Cross, London Liverpool Street, London Fenchurch Street, Finsbury Park
LNN	London (North West)	5			London Paddington, Willesden Junction, Kentish Town, West Hampstead
LNW	London (West Central)	3			Kensington (Addison Road, Earls Court, West Brompton

Table A5.1. (Continued)

Code	Hub	T	B	Satellite hubs	Analogues
LO	Lostwithiel	5	2	Llanhydrock (3), Liskeard (3)	Bodmin Road, Par
LQ	Leatherhead	4			Epsom
LR	Llangurig	3			Welshpool
LS	Leeds	8		Rawdon (3), East Ardsley (3)	Leeds, Lofthouse
LT	Lathrisk	5	1	Auchtermuchty (3), Dairsie (3)	Ladybank, Leuchars
LV	Liverpool	5		Huyton (3)	Liverpool, Ditton Junction, Halewood
LW	Lewes	5	1		Lewes
LX	Loxton	4			Yatton, Highbridge
LY	Llandovery	4		Llandeilo (3)	Llandeilo
MA	Macclesfield	3			Macclesfield
MB	Mobberley	5		Altrincham (3), Wilmslow (3)	
MC	March	4		Chatteris (3)	March
MD	Maidstone	6		Chart Sutton (3), Headcorn (3)	Maidstone
MF	Mansfield	4		Shirebrook (3)	Mansfield, Langwith Junction
MH	Mauchline	3			Mauchline
MI	Middleton	4			Manchester
ML	Melrose	6	2	Maxton (3), Ancrum (3), Lindean (3)	St. Boswells, Galashiels
MM	Melton Mowbray	4		Manton (3)	Melton Mowbray
MN	Manchester	9		Stretford (3), Worsley (3)	Manchester
MO	Moreton-in-Marsh	5		Chipping Norton (3)	Lingham
MP	Morpeth	5	1	Wallsend (3)	Morpeth, Newsham, Tynemouth
MT	Merthyr Tydfil	3		Cefn-coed (3), Dowlais (3)	Merthyr Tydfil, Dowlais
MU	Monmouth	5		Raglan (3), Coleford (3)	Monmouth
MW	Motherwell	4			Motherwell
MX	Mexborough	5		Cudworth (3), Rother-ham (3)	Rotherham, Swinton, Barnsley
MZ	Mold	4		Bodfari (3), Buckley (3)	Hope
NA	Newton Aycliffe	4			Ferryhill
NB	Newbury	4		Hungerford (3)	Newbury
ND	Neath	4			Neath
NE	Newcastle	8		Monkton (3), Swalwell (3)	Newcastle
NG	Nottingham	6		Harby (3)	Nottingham, Radcliffe
NH	Northampton	11	1	Crick (4), Ravenstone (3), Whilton (3), Wellingbor-ough (3), Irthlingborough (3), Kettering (3)	Northampton, Rugby, Roade
NK	Newark	4		Southwell (3)	Newark
NL	Northleach	5		Cheltenham (3)	Cheltenham
NN	Nuneaton	5			Nuneaton
NO	Newport (IoW)	5		Whiteley Bank (3)	Newport (IoW)

(*continued*)

Table A5.1. (Continued)

Code	Hub	T	B	Satellite hubs	Analogues
NP	Newport (Mon.)	9		Pontypool (3), Little Mill (3), Lydney (3), Cross Keys (3), Pontllanfraith (3), Aberbeeg (3)	Newport (Mon.), Pontypool, Lydney
NQ	Newport (Essex)	4			Broxbourne
NR	Norwich	6	1	Swanton Abbot (3)	Norwich, North Walsham
NS	Newport (Staffs)	4			
NT	Newent	5		Ross-on-Wye (3), Bromsberrow Heath (3)	Worcester
NW	Northwich	5		Middlewich (3)	Northwich
OD	Oldham	4			Oldham
OM	Ormskirk	5		Digmoor (3)	Ormskirk
OS	Ottery St. Mary	4		Harpsford (3)	Sidmouth Junction
OT	Otford	5		Ightham (3), West Malling (3)	Swanley
OX	Oxford	9		Kidlington (4), Radley (3), Witney (3), Thame (3)	Oxford
OW	Oswestry	4			Oswestry
PA	Paisley	4			Paisley, Elderslie
PB	Peterborough	6		Werrington (4)	Peterborough
PC	Penistone	4			Penistone
PD	Pontarddulais	5		Treneddyn (3), Ammanford (3)	Pontarddulais
PE	Peebles	3			Peebles
PF	Poulton-le-Fylde	4	1		Preston
PG	Paignton	6	4	Halwell (4), Newton Abbot (3)	Newton Abbot
PH	Perth	7	3	Aucheterarder (3), Cargill (3), Ballinluig (3)	Perth, Coupar Angus
PJ	Polegate	4			Polegate
PK	Pickering	5		Thornton-le-Dale (3), Grosmont (3)	Malton
PL	Poole	6	1	Christchurch (4), Swanage (3)	Bournemouth, Hamworthy, Broadstone
PM	Plymouth	5	2	Liskeard (3), South Brent (3)	Plymouth
PN	Penrith	4			Penrith
PO	Ponders End	5		Cockfosters (3)	Tottenham Hale, South Tottenham, Seven Sisters, Lower Edmonton
PP	Pontypridd	6	2	Abercynon (4), Porth (3)	Pontypridd, Quakers Yard
PR	Preston	6		Kirkham (3)	Preston
PT	Petersfield	4			Havant
PZ	Penzance	4	2	Ludgvan (3), Lelant (3)	Penzance
RC	Rochdale	5			Rochdale
RG	Reading	5		Wokingham (3)	Reading
RL	Rhyl	4		Colwyn Bay (3)	Rhyl
RM	Romsey	4		Mottisfont (3)	Romsey
RP	Ripon	4		West Tanfield (3)	Starbeck

Table A5.1. (Continued)

Code	Hub	T	B	Satellite hubs	Analogues
RR	Redruth	4			
RU	Ruabon	5		Wrexham (3)	Wrexham
SA	St. Albans	5			St. Albans, Hatfield, Harpenden
SB	Salisbury	7		Wilton (3), Warminster (3), Alderbury (3), Idmiston (3)	Salisbury
SD	Stafford	4			Stafford
SE	Selby	4			Selby
SF	Sheffield	3			Sheffield
SG	Spalding	6		Gosberton (4), Holbeach (3), Long Sutton (3)	Spalding
SH	Southampton	7	1	North Stoneham (4), Millbrook (4), Brockenhurst (3), Botley (3), Fareham (3)	Southampton, Fareham
SHP	Shipley	4		Keighley (3)	Shipley
SI	St. Helens	4			St. Helens
SJ	Stranraer	3		Whitecrook (3)	Stranraer
SK	Stoke-on-Trent	11	3	Kidsgrove (5), Stone (4), Nantwich (3), Draycott (3)	Stoke-on-Trent, Crewe, Sandbach
SL	Stirling	7	1	Denny (3), Alloa (3), Dunblane (3), Callander (3)	Stirling, Larbert, Alloa
SM	Southport	3			Southport
SN	Snaith	4			Hull
SND	Sandy	4			Sandy
SO	Sleaford	6		Heckington (3), Aunsby (3)	Sleaford
SP	Stourport	7		Kidderminster (3), Stour-bridge (3), Coalport (3)	Stourbridge Junction, Bewdley
SPB	Spean Bridge	3			
SQ	Stockton-on-Tees	8		Eaglescliffe (3), Crathorne (3), Stokesley (3), Easington (3)	Stockton-on-Tees, Middlesbrough, Eaglescliffe
SR	Shrewsbury	7		Shrawardine (3), Uppington (3), Leighton (3), Oakengates (3)	Shrewsbury, Wellington, Buildwas
SS	Sedbergh	6		Sedbergh Junction (3), Beck Foot (3), Constable Burton (3)	Tebay, Oxenholme
ST	Staines	10		Feltham (3), Chobham (3), Addlestone (3), Cookham (3)	Staines, Virginia Water, Woking, Slough
STP	Stockport	5			Stockport
STT	Stockton-on-Teme	4	1		Leominster
STY	Stalybridge	6		Hadfield (3), Grasscroft (3)	Stalybridge, Guide Bridge, Godley
SU	Sunderland	4		Penshaw (3)	Sunderland, Penshaw

(*continued*)

Table A5.1. (Continued)

Code	Hub	T	B	Satellite hubs	Analogues
SUB	Surbiton	4			Wimbledon
SV	Swannington	3			Coalville
SW	Swansea	4		Gorseinon (3)	Swansea
SWD	Swindon	4			Swindon
SX	Skipton	4			Skipton, Hellifield
SY	Symington	6		Biggar (3), Pettinain (3), Millhousebridge (3)	Carstairs, Lockerbie
SZ	Sudbury	4			Colchester
TA	Taunton	7	1	Wrantage (3), Ilminster (3)	Taunton
TB	Trowbridge	5			Westbury
TC	Twickenham	4			Richmond
TE	Thorne	5			Doncaster, Stainforth
TF	Thetford	6		Roudham (4)	Thetford
TG	Tring	4		Boxmoor (3)	
TH	Thirsk	5		Northallerton (3), Carlton Husthwaite (3)	Thirsk, Northallerton
TK	Tewkesbury	5		Coombe Hill (3), Upton-on-Severn (3)	Ashchurch
TM	Todmorden	4		Sowerby Bridge (3)	Todmorden, Sowerby Bridge
TN	Tenterden	4			
TR	Truro	6	1	Treluswell (4)	Truro
TU	Turriff	5	1	Milltown (3)	Keith, Tillynaught
TW	Tunbridge Wells	7		Hadlow (3), Hever (3), Bells Yew Green (3), Hurst Green (3)	Tunbridge Wells, Tonbridge, Eridge
UK	Uckfield	4			
UP	Upminster	3	1		Upminster
UX	Uxbridge	4			West Drayton
WA	Walsall	5			Walsall
WB	Wetherby	6		Knaresborough (3)	Church Fenton, Starbeck
WC	Worcester	8		Pirton (3), Knightwick (3), Welland (3)	Worcester
WD	Wadebridge	4		Tredinnick (3)	Wadebridge
WE	Ware	4		St. Margarets (3)	Hertford, Broxbourne
WF	Woofferton	7		Walford (4), Ludlow (3), Leominster (3)	Leominster
WG	Wigan	6			Wigan
WH	Wolver-hampton	7		Penkridge (3), Shifnal (3)	Wolverhampton
WI	Whitchurch (Salop)	6		Penley (3)	Whitchurch (Salop)
WJ	Whitchurch (Hants)	5		Andover (3)	Whitchurch (Hants)
WK	Wakefield	4			Wakefield
WL	Wallingford	4		Pangbourne (3)	Didcot
WM	Weston-super-Mare	3			Weston-super-Mare, Yatton
WN	Winchester	4		Shawford (3)	Eastleigh
WO	Welshpool	4		Arddlin (3), Berriew (3)	Welshpool
WP	Worksop	5		Ranby (3), North Leverton (3)	Shireoaks

Table A5.1. (Continued)

Code	Hub	T	B	Satellite hubs	Analogues
WQ	Workington	3			Workington
WR	Warrington	8		Hollins Green (3)	Warrington, Earlstown, Glazebrook
WS	Wishaw	5		Carluke (3)	Wishaw, Carluke, New-mains
WT	Watford	7		Amersham (4), Rick-mansworth (3)	Watford Junction
WU	Wisbech	4			Wisbech
WV	Wimbledon	3			Wimbledon
WW	Wembley	4			Harrow, South Ruislip
WX	Wells-next –the-Sea	3			Melton Constable
WY	Wednesbury	4			Dudley, Dudley Port
WZ	Wells (Somerset)	4		Shepton Mallet (3)	Frome, Glastonbury
YK	York	5			York
YN	Ynystawe	4			
YV	Yeovil	6		Milborne Port (3), Win-canton (3)	Yeovil

When summarizing the properties of a composite hub, the focus is on the number of lines entering and leaving the hub as a whole—that is, the number of lines crossing the boundary and not the number of lines that lie within it. Thus both Bidford-on-Avon and Wells are four-way hubs. However, the number of lines entering or leaving a satellite hub includes both internal and external lines; thus all three of the satellite hubs discussed above are three-way hubs, since although only two of the lines leaving each satellite cross the boundary of the composite hub, the third line (to the major hub), although internal, is crucial to the role of the satellite within the hub as a whole.

Not all four-way hubs are composite, of course. A good example of a simple four-way hub is Lechlade. Lying at the intersection of a line from Swindon to Witney and a line from Cirencester to Abingdon, Lechlade provides connections from any one of the four towns to any other without any need for satellite hubs.

The logic of the composite hub is that the primary role of each satellite is to feed traffic into the major hub, and providing its own connections is a secondary role. From this perspective the distance between the major hub and its satellite is irrelevant. A consequence of this is that composite hubs may be spatially quite dispersed, with long distances between the major hub and some of its satellites. This is quite unlikely in well-populated areas. Both Somerset and the Avon Valley in Warwickshire, though rural, are reasonably populous and so the composite hubs at Bidford and Wells are reasonably compact. But in more remote areas, such as the northern Pennines, hubs may be quite dispersed. This is illustrated by the hub at Sedbergh, on a trans-Pennine route through Wensleydale, which runs east to Constable Burton, where it divides into lines for Darlington to the north and Ripon to the south. Constable Burton, on the opposite side of the Pennines, is much closer to the hubs at Darlington and Ripon than it is to Sedbergh. But its primary role is to consolidate trans-Pennine traffic to and from Sedbergh. Traffic between Darlington and Ripon will go direct through Catterick rather than deviate to the west through Constable Burton. It is therefore inappropriate to consolidate Constable Burton with either Darlington or Ripon. It is also inappropriate to identify it as an independent hub since it is a small village that generates little traffic of its own, and the even the nearest town, Leyburn, is not a major traffic-generating centre in the same league as Darlington or Ripon. Sedbergh, on the other hand, is a major junction on the West Coast main line where lines to Brough and Kendal (via Beck Foot) diverge.

In other cases, however, distance leads to independence as regards traffic flow. Boston in Lincolnshire, for example, is a relatively isolated three-way hub. As a small hub, it might seem appropriate to consolidate it with the five-way hub at Alford (to the north), or the six-way hubs at Sleaford (to the east) or Spalding (to the south). Sleaford and Spalding have a direct trunk connection that bypasses Boston, however, and so it is inappropriate to consolidate it with either of them. Boston collects traffic from London (via Spalding) and the Midlands (via Sleaford) and consigns it to Grimsby via Alford. Thus if consolidation is to be effected then Alford is the logical choice for a composite hub. But much of the traffic handled at Alford has nothing to do with Boston; it is traffic between Mablethorpe and Lincoln. More importantly, a lot of traffic is generated locally at the port at Boston, and most of this is consigned south and east rather than north through Alford. Apart from Grimsby through traffic, therefore, Boston and Alford are relatively independent, and it is therefore appropriate to analyse them as independent hubs, even though the total number of hubs identified is increased as a result.

Bypasses

A useful way of thinking about a hub is as a 'pinch point' at which traffic on different routes is all channelled through the same point. Such a pinch point can easily become congested, however, and as a result it may be bypassed. The question then arises as to whether the three-way junctions at which the bypass begins and ends should be consolidated into a composite hub centred on the town or city that is bypassed. Bypasses are quite common in the counterfactual system. Indeed, it is a characteristic of any robust well-connected system that any point on the system can be easily bypassed. Bypasses expedite long-distance express traffic and can also act as diversionary routes. Thus the treatment of bypasses is an important issue in the analysis of hubs.

Although the principle of simplification suggests that bypasses should be internalized within the boundaries of a composite hub, economic logic suggests the exact reverse. In a composite hub the primary role of the satellites is to channel traffic into the major hubs and not away from it—as a bypass does. What this means in practice is that if an express bypasses a hub then passengers cannot make connections because the train does not stop. If the train were to stop then it would stop at one of the satellites—or even at both satellites at either end of the bypass. Not only would this defeat the object of speeding up the train, but also it would involve stopping the train at a small place affording limited onward connections rather than at the major centre affording many onward connections. If passengers took a connecting train from the satellite to the major hub then those requiring onward connections would have to change twice rather than just the once at the major hub. The use of bypasses is such an important feature of a network that it cannot be subsumed as an activity internal to a hub. Thus in analysing hubs the points at which bypasses begin and end are identified as independent hubs in their own right.

Hubs on the Actual System

Company-specific Hubs

So far the concept of a hub has been illustrated by reference to the counterfactual system. This is because hubs are much easier to identify on the counterfactual system than on the actual system. This in turn reflects the fact that the counterfactual system has been devised using a formal algorithm whereas the actual system has not. There is no doubt, as explained elsewhere, that Victorian railway engineers and policymakers understood the value of networks and the important role that hubs play within them. But in practice each railway company tended to apply the hub concept to its own system, by developing company-specific hubs like Crewe on the London and North Western Railway, Derby on the Midland Railway, and York on the North Eastern Railway. Other towns and cities evolved into hubs because they were served by competing lines and therefore provided opportunities for traffic to switch from one company's system to another—an opportunity which the companies often strove to deny. As a result, there are a number of difficult issues that must be confronted when applying the hub concept to the actual system.

Multiple Stations

In the counterfactual each town is served by a single main station. The exception is London, which has five central stations located on an inner orbital line. By contrast, on the actual system towns and cities often have separate stations belonging to different companies. The question then arises as to whether a town where different lines converge on different stations qualifies as a hub, and if so, whether each station separately is to be considered as a hub, or the set of stations as a whole.

The simplest way to preserve comparability between the actual and counterfactual systems is to focus on location, and to adopt the convention that any town or city on which routes converge is a potential hub, irrespective of how many stations are involved. A multiplicity of stations is then interpreted as a structural weakness of the hub.

Lines that are Not Regularly Used

Comparing the networks of lines owned by the companies with the networks of services operated over them shows that many lines were not used. More precisely, they were not used for passenger traffic—which is the basis of the comparison made in this study. Thus many places that would have functioned as hubs if all the lines had been used did not in practice function as hubs at all.

Many of these unused lines were constructed for strategic reasons to gain access to another company's network, and were not used because the other company prevented the use of their network. The lines were often short spurs built where two lines crossed each other or ran parallel to each other. In some cases the lines were built in anticipation of running powers that were never obtained, and in other cases they became redundant because running powers proved to be unenforceable, so that traffic was routed some other way instead. In other cases the lines were used for freight traffic only, because a passenger service was considered to be unremunerative.

In analysing the actual network the focus has been placed on centres that actually functioned as hubs, which means that the lines included in the study are those that were actually operated rather than all of those that were built. Thus the hubs identified on the actual system are fewer than would otherwise appear. Since one of our main findings is that the actual system involved a wasteful proliferation of hubs, this ensures that the finding cannot be explained simply by the inclusion of purely 'hypothetical' hubs.

Intersections that are Not Hubs

On the actual system railways sometimes crossed each other in open countryside, with no physical connection between them. In most cases the lines went over or under each other, but in a few cases the crossing was 'on the flat'. So far as connections are concerned however, the situation was the same, although a flat crossing obviously raised additional issue regarding conflicting traffic movements and safety considerations.

It seems unrealistic to describe mere crossings as hubs—particularly where there were no stations nearby. Where the crossings occurred near towns or villages, stations would normally be provided, but they were often some distance apart. With no connecting spurs, all the 'connecting' had to be done by passengers making their own way between the stations by taxi, bus, or on foot.

A defining characteristic of a hub is that interchange must be convenient, and this implies that some facility for interchange must be provided. A minimum requirement used in this study is that there must be stations in appropriate locations and at least one junction. In other words, a mere crossing place is not a hub; it is only when the crossing is combined with some stations and a junction that it becomes a hub. This junction may link the intersecting lines, or may simply branch off from one of these lines in some other direction.

The requirement of at least one junction rules out places like Tamworth, where the Midland main line from Derby to Birmingham crossed over the London and North Western main line from London to Crewe. Although there was a connecting spur linking Derby to Crewe, it was never used for passenger traffic. A potentially more useful spur, linking Derby to London, was never built because it was against the Midland's interests to do so. However, the two stations—high level and low level—were built on top of each other to facilitate passenger interchange. This seems to have been a concession to local passengers from Burton-on-Trent, rather than a serious attempt to improve the connectivity of the main line railway system, however. Thus the failure of Tamworth to qualify as a hub is plausible given that the Midland Railway was opposed to its use for this purpose.

The issue of crossings that are not hubs does not arise on the counterfactual, as one of the characteristics of an efficient network is that lines do not normally cross unless there is a need to interchange traffic between them. The only exception is where a high-speed bypass around a large town or city intersects the route of a local line into the city centre, so that it is efficient to concentrate all connections between the local branch and the rest of the system at the central hub.

Reversals

Reversal of the direction of travel complicates the operation of a hub. Reversing a train is more complicated than running it straight through, and reversing the direction of travel when joining a connecting train can be disconcerting for a passenger. On the counterfactual system most trains and most passengers maintain the same direction of travel throughout their journey and normally leave a hub in the same direction they entered it. They normally do not change direction by more than 90 degrees.

On the actual system, however, quite a number of reversals occur. This is because there are quite a lot of dead-ends on the actual system. In particular, passengers travel into a terminal station in one direction and leave it in the opposite direction. There are a number of important centres which are served mainly by a set of terminal stations, so that if passengers do not continue their journey by changing stations then they continue by reversing out of the station at which they have arrived. The question then arises as to whether locations with such inconvenient arrangement can be properly designated as hubs. Consistent application of general principles suggests that such places can indeed be regarded as hubs.

Continuity of direction of travel is not a defining characteristic of a hub. Furthermore, the geography of certain locations favours the use of terminals at which reversals occur. An obvious case is coastal hubs such as Cromer and Yarmouth, where the object is to deliver passengers as close as possible to the beach. Another example concerns large cities. When driving a railway into the heart of a city where the price of land is high and the nuisance created by the railway is very great, a dead-end line to a city-centre terminus may be far less costly than pushing a through line into the area. The operational inconvenience is more than compensated for by the saving of capital cost. The inefficiency in this case results from driving the railway into the heart of the city to begin with, instead of improving urban public transport to link the station better to the city. This drive was one of consequences of the competition between railway companies. Direct access by rail to the city centre was seen as important in promoting suburban living for office-workers and other commuters. Competition to develop different areas of the commuter belt led to termini being pushed ever further into cities. Once the terminals had been constructed for the benefit of commuters, it was considered logical to use them for express services too—a tendency reinforced by the duplication of trunk lines, which made the location of the city centre terminus an important factor in the choice of route by inter-city business travellers. Thus increasing numbers of people travelled into the city in order to connect with expresses there—whether they left from the terminal they entered or from another terminal else-where. It would be misleading to analyse the role of hubs in the actual system without recognizing that in practice many passengers reversed direction of travel.

Scope of the Comparison

As the counterfactual does not address the provision of tube transport in London or other major cities, the network analysis of the actual system excludes hubs on the London Underground system. More specifically, it excludes the hubs, such as Oxford Circus—which are used by the 'tube' railways, but includes hubs, such as West Brompton and Ealing—that were used by some of the present underground lines when they were still an integral part of the 'overground' system, before the modern London Transport Under-ground system had been formed.

The hubs on the actual system are listed in Table A5.2. The hubs are ordered geograph-ically. For each hub the total number of lines converging is indicated (T), together with the number of these lines which are dead-end branches (B), the number of different companies involved (C), and the number of town-centre stations involved (S). The satellite hubs are also identified, together with analogous hub(s) on the counterfactual system.

There are a number of prominent intersections which have not been identified as hubs because their interchange potential is weak. These are listed in Table A5.3, classified according to their configurations.

The comparison is made for the year 1914. One consequence of this is that some of the proliferation of termini on the actual system is understated, as some rationalization of termini had already been effected by that date. Thus end-on terminals had been converted

Table A5.2. Hubs on the actual system

Hub	T	B	C	S	Satellite hubs	Analogues
East Anglia						
Southend	5	1	2	2	Pitsea, Grays	
Romford	6	3	2	1	Shenfield, Wickford, Woodham Ferres	Brentford
Witham	5	2	1	1	Kelvedon	Chelmsford
Colchester	10	5	1	2	Marks Tey, Chappel, Long Melford, Wivenhoe, Thorpe-le-Soken, Manningtree, Bentley	Colchester, Halstead, Sudbury
Ipswich	9	5	1	1	Haughley, Westerfield, Wickham Market, Sax-mundham, Mellis	Ipswich
Bury St. Edmunds	5		1	1	Kennet	Bury St. Edmunds
Beccles	6	1	1	1	Halesworth, Aldeby	Ilketshall
Yarmouth	6		2(3)	3	St. Olaves	
Lowestoft	4		2(3)	1	Somerleyton	
Wymondham	4		1	1		
Tivetshall	4		1	1	Forncett	
Thetford	4		1	1	Roudham	Thetford
Fordham	4		1	1		Cambridge
East Dereham	4	1	1	1	County School	East Dereham
Melton Constable	4		1	1		Wells-next-the-Sea
Norwich	9		2	3	Whittingham, Brundall, Reedham, Wroxham, Haddiscoe (Low Level)	Norwich
North Walsham	5		2	2		Norwich
Cromer	3		3(3)	2		
Kings Lynn	10	3	2(3)	1	Sutton Bridge, South Lynn, Heacham, Swaff-ham, Magdalen Road, Denver	Kings Lynn
March	5		2(2)	1		March
Wisbech	5	1	2(3)	2		Wisbech
St. Ives	5	1	2(2)	1	Somersham	Huntingdon
Ely	6		1	1		Ely
Cambridge	10		2	1	Bartlow, Shelford, Haverhill	Cambridge
Humberside and Lincolnshire						
Grimsby	3		2	1		
Barnetby	5	1	1	1	Scunthorpe	Brigg
Ulceby	3	1	1	1		Brigg
Gainsborough	5		3(5)	2	Haxey	Gainsborough
Louth	4		1	1		Alford
Firsby	6	2	1	1	Willoughby	Alford
Lincoln	8		4(4)	2	Saxilby	Lincoln
Woodhall Junction	5	1	1	1	Bardney	Lincoln
Boston	4		1	1		Boston
Sleaford	5		2	1		Sleaford

Table A5.2. (Continued)

Hub	T	B	C	S	Satellite hubs	Analogues
Honington	4		1	1		Grantham
Spalding	6		3(3)	1		Spalding
Tyne and Wear						
Newcastle	15		1	1		Newcastle
Hexham	4		2	1		
Haltwhistle	4	2	1	1	Brampton	Carlisle
Morpeth	8	3	2	1	Scotsgap, Chevington, Alnmouth, Chathill	Morpeth
Newsham	5	2	1	1	Bedlington, Hartley	Morpeth
Tynemouth	4		1	1	Monkseaton, Percy Main	Morpeth
Tyne Dock	3		1	1		
Sunderland	8		1	1	Murton, East Boldon, Pittington, Wellfield, Millfield	Sunderland
Penshaw	4		1	1		Sunderland
Blackhill	4		1	1		Consett (Leadgate)
Durham	7	1	1	2		Durham
Darlington	6	1	1	2		Croft Spa
Northallerton	5		1	1		Thirsk
Bishop Auckland	7		1	1	Wear Valley Junction, Shildon	Bishop Auckland
Barnard Castle	4		1	1		Barnard Castle
Kirkby Stephen	5		2	2		Brough
Ferryhill	7		1	1	Sherburn House	Newton Aycliffe
Stillington	5		1	1	Carlton	
Leamside	4		1	1	Penshaw	
Hart	5	1	1	1	Castle Eden	Stockton-on-Tees
Stockton-on-Tees	6	1	1	1	Billingham	Stockton-on-Tees
Middlesbrough	9	3	1	1	Thornaby, Nunthorpe, Hutton Gate, Cargo Fleet, Marske	Stockton-on-Tees
Eaglescliffe	5		1	1	Picton	Stockton-on-Tees
Battersby	3		1	1		
North Yorkshire and Humberside						
York	8	1	2	2	Alne	York
Thirsk	5		1	1	Pilmoor	Thirsk
Starbeck	10		1	1	Melmerby, Spofforth, Knaresborough, Harrogate, Weeton	Wetherby, Ripon
Church Fenton	7		1	1		Wetherby
Whitby	7		1	2	Grosmont, Brotton, Pickering	
Seamer	6		1	1	Seamer, Driffield	
Hull	11	3	2	2	Beverley, Staddlethorpe, Calton, Kirk Smeaton, Wilmington	Hull
Malton	5		1	1	Rillington	Pickering
Market Weighton	4		1	1		Beverley

Table A5.2. (Continued)

Hub	T	B	C	S	Satellite hubs	Analogues
Trent and Ouse						
Doncaster	9		5	1	Mexborough, Arksey	Doncaster, Thorne
Selby	8	1	1	1		Selby
Goole	6	1	3(2)	1	Reedness	Balkholme
Stainforth	4		1	1		Thorne
Retford	5		2	2		
Shireoaks	4		1	1		Worksop
Newark	6		2	2	Rolleston Junction	Newark
Tuxford	5		2	2	Edwinstowe	
Grantham	7		1	1	Essendine, Barkston, Bot-tesford	Grantham
Bourne	4		2(2)			Bourne
Peterborough	7		5(4)	2		Peterborough
Wansford	4	1	2	1		
Huntingdon	5		3(3)	2		Huntingdon
Aire and Calder						
Leeds	15		4	3	Calverley, Farnley, Meth-ley, Garforth, Beeston, Bramley, Arthington, Cross Gates, Micklefield	Leeds
Lofthouse	6		1	1	Ardsley	Leeds
Shipley	6	2	2	2	Keighley	Shipley
Castleford	6		1	1		
Pontefract	6		3(3)	2	Knottingley	Knottingley
Moorthorpe	4		2(4)	1	Hemsworth	
South Elmsall	4		2(4)	1		
Wakefield	13		2	2	Horbury, Osset, Sandal	Wakefield
Menston	4		1	1	Guiseley	Burley-in-Wharfedale
Otley	4		2(2)	1		Burley-in-Wharfedale
Skipton	7	2	1	1	Earby	Skipton
Hellifield	7		2	1	Clapham, Wennington, Hawes Junction	Skipton
Todmorden	3		1	1		Todmorden
Sowerby Bridge	4		1	1		Todmorden
Laisterdyke	6		1	1		Bradford
Low Moor	6		2	1	Wyke, Bowling Junction	Bradford
Halifax	4		2	2		Bradford
Queensbury	4	2	2(2)	1	Holmfield	Bradford
Dudley Hill	6		1	1	Drighlington	Bradford
Greetland	4		1	1		Brighouse
Mirfield	6		3	1		Brighouse
Dewsbury	7	1	3	3	Batley	Dewsbury
Thornhill	5		2	1		Dewsbury
Horbury and Ossett	4		1	1		Dewsbury
Huddersfield	10	3	2	2		Huddersfield
Normanton	4		3	1		

Table A5.2. (Continued)

Hub	T	B	C	S	Satellite hubs	Analogues
North Midlands						
Sheffield	9		2	2	Dore, Woodhouse, Brightside	Sheffield
Rotherham	5		2	2		Mexborough
Swinton	5		2	2		Mexborough
Barnsley	6		3	2		Mexborough
Killamarsh	5		2	2		Beighton
Penistone	4		2	1		Penistone
Chesterfield	9		2	3	Barrow Hill, Staveley, Clay Cross	Chesterfield
Ambergate	5		1	1	Millers Dale	Derby
Langwith	7		3	2	Elmton	Mansfield
Kirkby-in-Ashfield	8		3	2	Mansfield	Mansfield
Pleasley	5		2	2		
Trowell	6	1	1	1		Ilkeston
Daybrook	8	2	1	1	Ilkeston, Carlton, Kimberley	Ilkeston
Codnor Park	7	1	2	2	Butterley, Westhouses, Pye Bridge, Ripley	Ilkeston
Trent	6		1	1	Weston-on-Trent	Ilkeston
Derby	10	1	2	2	Duffield, Swarkestone, Peartree	Derby
Egginton	4		2	1		Derby
Burton-on-Trent	7		1	1	Repton, Gresley, Barton, Rolleston-on-Dove	Derby
Uttoxeter	6		2	1	Rocester, Tutbury	Derby
Nottingham	11		3	3	Radford, Bingham, Netherfield	Nottingham
Radcliffe	4		1	1		Nottingham
South and East Midlands						
Leicester	10		4	4	Lowesby, Syston, Wigston	Leicester
Melton Mowbray	11		3	2	Saxby, John O'Gaunt, Hallaton, Manton, Harby, Redmire	Melton Mowbray
Market Harborough	6		3	2		
Seaton	5		1	1	Rockingham	
Bedford	7		3	2		Bedford
Sandy	4		1	2		Sandy
Kettering	4		1	1		Northampton
Wellingborough	5	1	2	2		Northampton
Northampton	6		2	3		Northampton
Rugby	9		3	2		Northampton
Roade	7	1	2	1	Blisworth, Wolverton, Weedon	Northampton
Nuneaton	8		3(2)	2	Shackerstone, Donnisthorpe	Nuneaton
Coventry	4		1	1		Coventry
Leamington	7		2	2	Kenilworth, Hatton	Leamington
Fenny Compton	5		2	2	Byfield	Leamington

Table A5.2. (Continued)

Hub	T	B	C	S	Satellite hubs	Analogues
Towcester	4		1	1		
Woodford and Hinton	5		2	1	Calvert	
Bletchley	6	1	1	1	Leighton Buzzard, Cheddington	Leighton Buzzard
Cumbria and The Lakes						
Carlisle	9	1	6	1	Drumburgh, Wigton	Carlisle
Gretna	4		3	1		Carlisle
Longtown	4		1	1	Riddings	Carlisle
Abbeyholme	4		2	1		Carlisle
Haltwhistle	4		2	1	Brampton Junction	Carlisle
Aspatria	6		2	1	Dearham	
Workington	7	1	4(4)	2	Camerton, Brigham	Workington
Whitehaven	7		4(3)	1	Moor Row, Ullock, Corkicle, Parton	
Distington	5		2(3)	1		
Ravenglass	4	1	1	1	Sellafield	
Dalton-in-Furness	7	3	1	1	Ulverston, Arnside, Foxfield	Dalton-in-Furness
Barrow-in-Furness	3	1	1	1		
Penrith	4		2	1		Penrith
Tebay	4		2	1	Low Gill	Sedbergh
Oxenholme	4		2	1		Sedbergh
Carnforth	5	1	2	1	Hest Bank	
Lancaster	7	4	2	2		Lancaster
Morecambe	4	1	2	2		
North-west						
Preston	12	6	3	1	Kirkham, Poulton-le-Fylde, Garstang, Euxton	Preston, Poulton-le-Fylde
Blackburn	7		2	1	Bamber Bridge	Clayton-le-Moors
Accrington	3		1	1		Clayton-le-Moors
Rose Grove	4		1	1		Clayton-le-Moors
Southport	7		2(4)	3	Burscough Bridge	Southport
Wigan	13		3	3	Board Head, Hindley, Rainsford	Wigan
Chorley	4		2(2)	1		Chorley
Bolton	8		2	2		Bolton
Blackrod	4	1	1			Bolton
Warrington	11		3(5)	1	Broadheath, Sankey	Warrington
Earlstown	7	1	1	1	Newton-le-Willows, St. Helens Junction, Kenyon Junction, Pennington	Warrington
Glazebrook	5		1(3)	1	Lowton St. Marys	Warrington
St. Helens	6		2	2		St. Helens
Ditton Junction	5		1	1		Liverpool
Halewood	5	3	1(3)	1	Hough Green, West Derby	Liverpool
Liverpool	9		4(6)	3		Liverpool
Birkenhead	6		4(7)	3	Hooton, Ince	

Table A5.2. (Continued)

Hub	T	B	C	S	Satellite hubs	Analogues
Bidston	6	3	3	1	Burton Point	
Frodsham	4		2(2)	1	Helsby	Chester
Northwich	6	1	2(4)	1	Cuddington, Mouldsworth, Altrincham	Northwich
Ormskirk	6		1	1	Aintree, Burscough Junction	Ormskirk
Manchester	23		4(5)	4	Chorlton-cum-Hardy, Timperley, Droylsden, Eccles, Miles Platting, Worsley, Ashburys, Long-sight, Gorton, Heaton Mersey, Middleton Junction, Daisy Hill	Manchester, Middleton
Bury	7	1	1	2	Ramsbottom	Bury
Rochdale	5	1	1	1	Castleton	Rochdale
Oldham	6	1	3(3)	2	Werneth, Royton	Oldham
Stalybridge	5		3	1		Stalybridge
Guide Bridge	7		4(3)	2	Fairfield	Stalybridge
Godley	4		2(3)	1	Dinting	Stalybridge
Woodley	4		2(3)	1		
Romiley	6	1	2(3)	1	New Mills Central	
Stockport	12		2(4)	2	Baguley, Cheadle Hulme, Heaton Norris	Stockport
Macclesfield	4		3(3)	2		
Chinley	4		2(2)	1	Bugsworth	Bakewell
Buxton	4		2	1		
Crewe	7		3	1	Nantwich	Stoke-on-Trent
Stoke-on-Trent	14	3	1	1	Stone, Cresswell, Long-port, Kidsgrove	Stoke-on-Trent
Sandbach	5		2	1	Wilmslow	Stoke-on-Trent
Leek	4	1	1	1	Cheddleton Junction	
Stafford	6		3	1	Norton Bridge	Stafford
North Wales and Welsh Borders						
Bangor	9	7	2	1	Caernarvon, Gaerwen, Holland Arms, Dinas, Tryfan	Bangor
Llandudno Junction	4	2	1	1		Conway
Rhyl	5	2	1	1		Rhyl
Corwen	6	1	2	1	Bala Junction, Denbigh	
Portmadoc	5	3	4	3	Afon Wen	Criccieth
Barmouth	3		1	1		Barmouth
Machynlleth	6	3	3	1	Dovey Junction, Cemmaes Road, Towyn	
Aberystwyth	3	1	2	2		Aberystwyth
Welshpool	5		3(4)	2	Moat Lane, Buttington	Welshpool
Llanymyncech	4	1	2	2		
Chester	9		4(5)	2	Waverton, Saughall	Chester

(*continued*)

Table A5.2. (Continued)

Hub	T	B	C	S	Satellite hubs	Analogues
Hope	5		2	2	Hawarden Bridge	Mold
Wrexham	12	5	3(5)	3	Ruabon, Gobowen, Chirk, Legacy	Wrexham
Oswestry	4	1	2	1	Llynclys	Oswestry
Whitchurch (Salop)	5		2	1	Ellesmere	Whitchurch
Shrewsbury	9	2	4(3)	2	Hanwood, Kinnerley Junction	Shrewsbury
Wellington	7	1	4(3)	1	Hadley, Market Drayton	
Buildwas	5		1	1	Lightmoor Junction	Shrewsbury
Craven Arms	5		4(3)	1		
Llandeilo	3		2(2)	1		Llandovery
Leominster	6	2	3(3)	1	Woofferton, Cleobury Mortimer	Woofferton
Hereford	6		3(3)	1	Ross-on-Wye	Hereford
Titley	4	2	1	1		
West Midlands						
Birmingham	18	1	3	3	Monumnent Lane, Old Hill, Handsworth, Handsworth Wood, Swan Village, Tyseley, Winson Green	Birmingham
Aston	5		1	1	Perry Barr	
Bescot	4		1	1	Great Barr	
Walsall	8		2	1	Wednesbury	Walsall
Dudley Port	6		2	1	Tipton	Wednesbury
Dudley	4		2	2	Netherton	
Wolverhampton	9		3	2	Priestfield, Darlaston, Shifnal	Wolverhampton
Sutton Coldfield	6		2	2		
Castle Bromwich	4		1	1		
Lichfield	5		1	2		Lichfield
Rugeley	4		2	1	Colwich	Lichfield
Hampton-in-Arden	5		2	1	Stechford	
Whitacre	4		1	1		
Kings Norton	6		2(2)	1	Longridge, Barnt Green, Bromsgrove	
South Wales and Forest of Dean						
Whitland	7	6	1	1	Clynderwen, Clarbeston Road, Johnston	Carmarthen
Carmarthen	8	3	2	1	Pencade, Lampeter, Llanelli	Carmarthen
Swansea	9	3	6	5	Gowerton, Pontardawe	Swansea
Neath	9	2	4	3	Hirwaun, Llandore	Neath
Pontarddulais	4		2	2	Pantyffynon	Pontarddulais
Cymmer	6		3	3		
Bridgend	4		2	1		Bridgend
Tondu	6	3	1	1	Brynmenyn, Black Mill	Bridgend

Table A5.2. (Continued)

Hub	T	B	C	S	Satellite hubs	Analogues
Pyle	4		1	1		Bridgend
Port Talbot	5		3	3	Aberavon	
Llantrisant	5	1	2	2		
Cadoxton	5	1	2	1	Barry	
Cardiff	8		5	3	Cogan	Cardiff
Pontypridd	12	4	4	2	Abercynon, Porth, Treforest	Pontypridd
Quakers Yard	5	1	3(3)	2		Pontypridd
Caerphilly	7	1	4	1	Ystrad Mynach, Bargoed	Hengoed
Nelson and Llancaiach	5		4(3)	1		
Merthyr	5		4(5)	1	Pontsarn	Merthyr
Dowlais	5		3(4)	4		Merthyr
Talyllyn Junction	7	4	4	1	Three Cocks, Hay-on-Wye, Eardisley, Colbren, Pontsticill	Brecon, Hay-on-Wye
Brynmawr	7	1	3(3)	1	Beaufort, Nantybwch, Rhymney Bridge	Abergavenny
Abergavenny	4		2	3	Pontrilas	Abergavenny
Newport	12	2	3	1	Chepstow, Machen, Severn Tunnel Junction, Pengam, Risca, Aberbeeg, Llantarnam	Newport
Pontypool	6	1	1	3	Upper Pontnewydd, Little Mill	Newport
Lydney	4		2(2)	2		Newport
Monmouth	5	1	2(2)	2	Lydbrook Junction	Monmouth
Cinderford	5	2	2	2	Drybrook Road, Parkend	
Somerset and Severn						
Bristol	9	1	2	1	Filton	Bristol
Bath	5		2(3)	2	Bathampton	Bristol
Patchway	4		1	1	Pilning	Bristol
Yatton	6	1	1	1	Congresbury, Puxton	Bristol, Loxton
Weston-super-Mare	3	1	2	2		Weston-super-Mare
Clevedon	3	2	2	2		
Mangotsfield	5	2	1	1	Fish Ponds, Yate	
Avonmouth	5	1	2(2)	1	Sea Mills	
Bradford-on-Avon	5		1	1	Limpley Stoke, Holt Junction	
Chippenham	4	1	1	1		
Frome	7		1	1	Wells, Witham, Hallatrow, Castle Cary	Bruton, Wells
Glastonbury	4	2	1(2)	1	Edington Junction	Wells
Westbury	5		1	1	Trowbridge	Trowbridge
Gloucester	12	4	4(2)	2	Stonehouse, Durbridge, Grange Court, Newnham, Coaley Junction, Berkeley Road	Gloucester
Cheltenham	6	1	4(3)	3	Andoversford	Northleach
Ashchurch	5		1	1	Wadborough	Tewkesbury

(continued)

Table A5.2. (Continued)

Hub	T	B	C	S	Satellite hubs	Analogues
Worcester	9		2	2	Droitwich, Henwick, Norton, Great Malvern, Ledbury, Hartlebury	Worcester
Bewdley	4		1	1		Stourport
Stourbridge Junction	5	1	1	1	Kidderminster	Stourport
Broom Junction	4		3	1	Alcester	Bidford-on-Avon
Evesham	5		2	2	Honeyboutne	Bidford-on-Avon
Stratford-on-Avon	9		2	2	Bearley, Henley-in-Arden, Long Marston, Claverdon	Bidford-on-Avon
Kingham	5	1	1	1	Moreton-in-Marsh	Moreton-in-Marsh
Banbury	7		4	2	King Sutton, Farthinghoe	Banbury
Oxford	8	1	2	2	Kidlington, Yarnton, Radley	Oxford
Thames and Chilterns						
Swindon	10	4	2	2	Wootton Bassett, Dauntsey, Kemble	Swindon, Cirencester
Didcot	6	2	1	1	Uffington, Wantage Road	Wallingford
Savernake	6	1	2	2	Patney	Devizes
Newbury	5	1	1	1		Newbury
Reading	7	1	3	2	Cholsey, Wokingham	Reading
Princes Risborough	8	1	3(2)	1	High Wycombe, Bourne End, Haddenham	Aylesbury
Aylesbury	6	1	4(4)	2	Quainton Road	Aylesbury
Verney Junction	4		2(3)	1		
South West						
Penzance	4	2	1	1		Penzance
Truro	4	2	1	1	Chacewater	Truro
Par	4	1	1	1	St. Blazey	Lostwithiel
Bodmin Road	5	3	1	1	Lostwithiel, Liskeard	Lostwithiel
Plymouth	8	4	2	3	Brent, Totnes	Plymouth
Tavistock	6	2	2	2	Lydford, Bere Alston, Yelverton	
Launceston	3		2	2		Launceston
Barnstaple	6	2	3	3	Dulverton	Barnstaple
Exeter	11	2	2	2	Yeoford, Okehampton, Halwill, Stoke Canon	Exeter
Tiverton Junction	4	1	1	1		Exeter
Newton Abbot	6	3	1	1	Heathfield, Churston	Exeter, Paignton
Wadebridge	3	2	1	1		Wadebridge
Taunton	7	1	1	1	Norton Fitzwarren, Durston, Athelny	Taunton, Langport
Bridgwater	3		2(3)	2		Bridgwater
Highbridge	5	1	2(3)	1	Bleadon	Bridgwater, Loxton
Wessex and Isle of Wight						
Sidmouth Junction	5	2	1	1	Tipton St. Johns, Seaton Junction	Axminster, Ottery St. Mary

Table A5.2. (Continued)

Hub	T	B	C	S	Satellite hubs	Analogues
Yeovil	7	1	2	3	Chard Junction, Axminster	Yeovil, Axminster
Templecombe	5	2(2)	1	1	Evercreech Junction	
Salisbury	5		2	2		
Weymouth	5	3	2	3	Melcombe Regis, Upwey, Dorchester, Maiden Newton	Dorchester
Hamworthy	4	1	1	1	Wareham	Poole
Broadstone	5		2(2)	1	Wimborne, West Moors	Poole
Bournemouth	4	1	2(2)	2	Christchurch, Poole	Poole
Southampton	7	1	1	2	Redbridge, Brockenhurst, St. Denys, Ringwood	Southampton
Fareham	9	5	2(2)	1	Botley, Cosham, Fort Brockhurst	Southampton
Romsey	5		1	1	Fullerton	Romsey
Eastleigh	6		2	1	Shawford, Winchester	Winchester
Andover	6	2	2	1	Ludgershall, Grateley	Whitchurch (Hants)
Whitchurch (Hants)	5		2	2	Hurstbourne	Whitchurch (Hants)
Basingstoke	5		2	1		Basingstoke
Sandown (IoW)	4	3	2	1	Brading	Brading
Newport (IoW)	5	4	2	1	Merstone	Newport (IoW)
Fratton	5	3	1(2)	1	Hilsea	
Havant	6	2	3(2)	1	Farlington, Petersfield	Havant
Chichester	4	1	2	2		Havant
Guildford	9		3	1	Wanborough, Ash, Effingham	Guildford
Farnham	8	1	1	1	Bentley, Aldershot, Ash Vale, Alton	Ash
Christs Hospital	7		1	1	Horsham, Pulborough, Midhurst	Horsham
Ford	5	2	1	1	Barnham	Arundel
Kent and Sussex						
Brighton	6	2	1	1	Shoreham	Brighton
Lewes	6	1	1	1		Lewes
Haywards Heath	4		1	1	Wivelsfield	
Redhill	6		2	1	Three Bridges	Godstone, Dorking
Oxted	5		3(2)	1	Hurst Green, Selsdon Road	Godstone
East Grinstead	5		1	1	Horstead Keynes	East Grinstead
Eridge	4		1	1	Tunbridge Wells	Tunbridge Wells
Tunbridge Wells	5		2	2	Groombridge	Tunbridge Wells
Tonbridge	9	1	1	1	Paddock Wood, Headcorn, Sevenoaks, Edenbridge	Tunbriddge Wells
Hastings	4	1	2	1	Pevensey	Hastings
Robertsbridge	4	1	2	1	Crowhurst	Hastings
Polegate	4	1	1	1		Polegate
Dover	4		1	1	Folkestone	Dover
Canterbury	7	1	1	2	Minster	Canterbury

(*continued*)

Table A5.2. (Continued)

Hub	T	B	C	S	Satellite hubs	Analogues
Ashford	8		1	1	Sandling, Appledore, Lydd	Ashford
Orpington	4	1	1	1	Petts Wood, Dunton Green	
Swanley	6		1	1	St. Mary Cray, Otford, Farningham Road	Otford
Gravesend	8	1	1	2	Hoo, Strood, Dartford, Charlton	Chatham
Sittingbourne	6	2	1	1	Rochester, Faversham	Chatham
Maidstone	5		1	2	Kemsing	Maidstone
London Central						
Fenchurch Street	6	3	2	1	Stepney, Burdett Road, Bow Road, West India Docks	London (NE)
Liverpool Street	8	2	2(6)	1	Bishopsgate, Bethnal Green, Deptford Road, Hackney Downs, Clapton	London (NE)
Dalston Junction	4	2	1	1	Canonbury	London (NE)
Kings Cross	4		3	2	Farringdon	London (NE)
Finsbury Park	7	2	1	1	Highgate, Hornsea, Finchley	London (NE)
Willesden Junction	7	1	3(4)	1	Chalk Farm, Queens Park	Willesden
Kentish Town	3	1	1	1		London (NW)
West Hampstead	5		2(3)	2	Gospel Oak, Neasden	London (NW)
Paddington	4		2	1		London (NW)
Waterloo	4	2	2	2	Queens Road	Clapham
Wandsworth Road	6	1	2	1	Brixton	Clapham
Peckham Rye	8	1	2	1	Nunhead, Denmark Hill, Old Kent Road	Clapham
Herne Hill	4		1	1		Clapham
Clapham Junction	12		4(5)	1	Balham, Wandsworth Town, Barnes	Clapham
London Bridge	7		2	1	Southwark Park, South Bermondsey	
Ludgate Hill	7	1	2	1	Snow Hill, Loughborough Junction	
New Cross	10	1	2(6)	1	St. Johns, Lewisham, Hither Green, Chisel-hurst, Grove Park, Blackheath	Lewisham
New Cross Gate	5		2(6)	1		Lewisham
Catford Bridge	6	2	2	1	Ladywell, New Beckenham, Elmers End, Woodside	Lewisham
London E and NE						
Upminster	4		2	1		Upminster
Barking	6	1	3(3)	1	Woodgrange Park, Bromley-by-Bow	Barking
Stratford	12	4	2	1	Leytonstone, Woodford, Forest Gate, Ilford	Barking

Table A5.2. (Continued)

Hub	T	B	C	S	Satellite hubs	Analogues
Victoria Park	5	1	1	1	Bow Road	
Canning Town	6	5	1	1	Custom House, Stratford Market	
Hitchin	5		2	1	Stevenage	Hitchin
Hatfield	5	1	1	1		St. Albans
Harpenden	5	1	2	2		St. Albans
Broxbourne	8	2	1	1	St. Margarets, Cheshunt, Elsenham, Audley End, Bishops Stortford	Ware, Harlow
Hertford	4		2	2		Ware
Seven Sisters	4	1	1	1		Ponders End
Lower Edmonton	4		1	1		Ponders End
Tottenham Hale	5	1	2	1		Ponders End
South Tottenham	5	1	3(3)	1	Junction Road	Ponders End
London West						
Watford Junction	5	3	1	1		Watford
Harrow	5	3	1	1	Carpenders Park	Wembley
South Ruislip	5	1	2(2)	1	Greenford	Wembley
South Acton	5	1	3(5)	1		Ealing
Gunnersbury	4		2	1		Ealing
Ealing	6		2	1	West Ealing	Ealing
Kew Bridge	5		1	1	Hounslow	Brentford
Ravenscourt Park	5		2	1	Grove Road	
Kensington (Addison Road)	5		4(5)	1	St. Quintin Park	London (NW)
Earls Court	4		1	1		
West Brompton	6	2	2(5)	1	Battersea	
West Drayton	5	3	1	1	Southall	Uxbridge
Slough	5	2	1	1	Maidenhead, Twyford	Staines
London S and SW						
Virginia Water	6		1	1	Ascot, Frimley, Addlestone	Staines
Staines	5		2	2	Feltham	Staines
Woking	6		1	1	Byfleet, Brookwood	Staines
Richmond	6	1	2	1	Twickenham, Strawberry Hill, Whitton	Twickenham
Wimbledon	13	2	3	1	Raynes Park, New Malden, Surbiton, Weybridge, Merton Park, East Putney	Wimbledon, Surbiton
Epsom	4		3(2)	2	Leatherhead	Epsom
Sutton	4		1	1		Epsom
Mitcham Junction	5		1	1		Epsom
East Croydon	6	2	2(2)	1	South Croydon, Purley	Croydon
West Croydon	4		1	1		Croydon
Norwood Junction	7		1	1		Croydon
Selhurst	5		1	1		
Crystal Palace	6		2	2		

(*continued*)

Table A5.2. (Continued)

Hub	T	B	C	S	Satellite hubs	Analogues
Tulse Hill	7		2	1		
Bromley	8		2	2	Shortlands, Beckenham Junction, Bickley	Bromley
Highlands and Grampians						
Wick	4	2	1	1	Georgmas, The Mound	
Spean Bridge	3	2	2	1		
Dingwall	5	2	1	1		Inverness
Inverness	4	1	1	1	Muir Of Ord	Inverness
Crianlarich	6	3	2	2	Connel Ferry, Killin Junction	
Forres	4	1	1	1	Gollanfield Junction	
Elgin	7	2	2	2	Alves, Craigellachie	Fochabers
Aviemore	4		2	1	Boat of Garten	Carrbridge
Keith	6	1	2	2	Grange, Orbliston	Turriff
Tillynaught	5	1	2	1	Knock, Portessie	Turriff
Aberdeen	11	7	2	1	Dyce, Ellon, Maud, Inveramsay, Kintore, Cairnie Junction, Inverurie, Craigo	Aberdeen
Bridge of Dun	5	2	1	1	Glasterlaw	Aberdeen
Montrose	4	1	2	2		Aberdeen
Brechin	3	1	1	1		
Forfar	6	1	1	1	Guthrie	Forfar
Arbroath	5	1	3(2)	1	Friockheim, Elliot Junction	
Dundee	8	1	3(2)	3	Inchture, St. Fort	Dundee
Fife and Midlothian						
Perth	11	3	3	1	Strathord, Stanley, Bridge of Earn, Newburgh, Tibbermuir	Perth
Coupar Angus	5	2	1	1		Perth
Balquhidder	4		1	1	Crieff	
Leuchars	4		1	1		Lathrisk
Ladybank	5	1	1	1	Markinch	Lathrisk
Thornton	5	1	1	1		Kirkcaldy
Kinross	4		1	1	Mawcarse	
Dunfermline	6	1	1	2		Dunfermline
Alloa	5	1	1	1	Cambus	Stirling
Stirling	6		2	1	Dunblane, Crieff Junction	Stirling
Larbert	7	2	2	1		Stirling, Castlecary
Buchlyvie	4	2	1	1	Balfron	
Manuel	6	1	1	1	Polmont, Philipstoun	
Camelon	5	2	2	1	Falkirk (Grahamston)	Edinburgh
Edinburgh	15	7	2	2	Saughton	Edinburgh
Dalmeny	5		1	1	Inverkeithing	Edinburgh
Portobello	20	14	1	1	New Hailes, Ormiston, Longniddry, Drem, Millerhill, Eskbank, Hawthornden, Fountainhall, Leadburn	Edinburgh

Table A5.2. (Continued)

Hub	T	B	C	S	Satellite hubs	Analogues
Bathgate	4		1	2		
Clydeside						
Glasgow	29	6	4(3)	3	Stobcross, Gartcosh, Lenzie, Kirkintilloch, West Pollokshaws, Partick, Great Western Road, Bridgeton Cross, Bell Grove, Ibrox, Rutherglen, Shettleston	Glasgow
Carmyle	5		1	1		Glasgow
Paisley	8	2	3(2)	2	Port Glasgow	Paisley
Elderslie	5		1	1		Paisley
Maryhill	7		2	2	Possil Park	
Westerton	4	1	1	1		
Dumbarton	6	2	3(2)	1	Dalmuir, Dalreoch, Craigendoran	
Gartcosh	4	1	1	1	Robroyston	
Lugton	5	1	2(2)	2		Barrhead
Giffen	4	1	1	1		Barrhead
Newton	8	1	1	1	Uddingston, Blantyre	Barrhead
Coatbridge	10	2	2	3	Moss End, Gartsherrie, Blackstone	
Holytown	5		1	1		
Newmains	4		1	1		Wishaw
Carluke	4		1	1	Cleghorn	Wishaw
Wishaw	5	1	1	2		Wishaw
Dalry	4		1	1		
Kilwinning	6	3	2	2		Kilwinning
Irvine	5	1	2	2	Bogside	Kilwinning
Kilmarnock	6		2(2)	1	Crosshouse, Hurlford	Kilmarnock
Ayr	7	1	1	1	Barassie, Annbank	Ayr
Mauchline	5	1	1	1	Auchinleck	Mauchline
Strathaven	4		1	1	High Blantyre	
Hamilton	11	3	2	2	Bothwell, Ferniegair, Brocketsbrae, Stonehouse	Hamilton
Douglas West	3		1	1		
Galloway and Borders						
Stranraer	3	1	2(2)	2	Dunragit	Stranraer
Dumfries	7	3	3(2)	1	Castle Douglas, Newton Stewart	Dumfries
Lockerbie	5	1	1	1	Beattock, Kirtlebridge	Symington
Annan	4		2	2		
Peebles	3		2	2		Peebles
Galashiels	4	1	1	1		Melrose
St. Boswells	6	1	1	1	Roxburgh, Riccarton Junction	Melrose
Tweedmouth	6	1	2	1	Burnmouth, Coldstream, Reston	Coldstream

Table A5.3. Rail crossings and multiple termini

Town or city	Railway companies	Comment
2 × 2 crossings with interchange arrangements—not listed as hubs		
Tamworth	MR-LNWR	High level–low level
Builth Road	Cambrian-LNWR	
Radstock	GWR-SDJR	
Whittington	GWR-Cambrian	High level–low level
Haddiscoe	GER-GER	High level–low level
2 × 2 crossings with same name and no interchange arrangements—not listed as hubs		
Fakenham	GER-MGNR	
Appleby	MR-NER	
Dorking	LBSCR-SECR	
Edenbridge	LBSCR-SECR	
Leytonstone	GER-MR/LTS	
Murrow	GNR/GER-MGNR	
Bicester	GWR-LNWR	
Mill Hill	MR-GNR	
Wotton	GCR/MetR-GCR	
Shepton Mallet	SDJR-GWR	
Helmdon	GCR-SMJR	
Brackley	GCR-LNWR	
Braunston	GCR-LNWR	
Thrapston	MR-LNWR	
Reepham	GER-MGNR	
Madeley (Staffs)	LNWR-NSR	
Hawarden	LNWR-GCR	
Crumlin	GWR-GWR	High-level/low-level but separate
Farnborough	LSWR-SECR	
North Camp	LSWR-SECR	
Somerford	GWR-GWR	
Brockley	LBSCR-SECR	
Neston	LNWR/GWR-GCR	
Tibshelf	MR-GCR	
Bolsover	MR-GCR	
Helsby	LNWR/GWR-CLC	
Hartford	LNWR-CLC	
Middlewood	NSR/GCR-LNWR	Upper/lower
Aintree	LYR-CLC	
Levenshulme	LNWR-CLC	
Golborne	LNWR-GCR	
Crowle	LYR/NER-GCR	
Drax	HBR-NER	
Howden	HBR-NER	
Midford	SDJR-GWR	
Bellshill	NBR-CR	
Platt Bridge	LNWR-GCR	
Atherton	LNWR-LYR	
Walkden	LNWR-LYR	
Tipton	LNWR-GWR	
Maesteg	GWR-Port Talbot	

Table A5.3. (Continued)

Town or city	Railway companies	Comment
2 × 2 crossings with different names and no interchange arrangements—not listed as hubs		
Cole-Bruton	SDJR-GWR	
Little Bytham-Castle Bytham	GNR-MGNR	
Heck-Hensall	GNR-LYR	
Ingestre-Neston	GNR-NSR	
Ash Vale-North Camp	LSWR-LSWR	
Briton Ferry Road-Jersey Marine	GWR-Rhondda and Swansea Bay	
Parallel lines with no interchange arrangements—not listed as hubs		
Garth	Port Talbot-GWR	
Bargoed	Rhymney-GWR	
Aylsham	GER-MGNR	
New Mills	GCR/MR-LNWR	
Chapel-en-le Frith	MR-LNWR	
Clown	GCR-MR	
Cresswell	GCR-MR	
Woodhouse	GCR-MR	
Willenhall	MR-LNWR	
Chapeltown	GCR-MR	
Ecclesfield	GCR-MR	
Widnes	LNWR-CLC	
Luton	MR-GNR	
Wembley	LNWR-GCR	
Streatham	LBSCR-LBSCR	
Midsomer Norton	GWR-SDJR	
Royston	MR-GCR	
Wath	MR-GCR	
Swinton	MR-GCR	
Kilnhurst	MR-GCR	
Parkgate	MR-GCR	
Woodhouse	MR-GCR	
Eckington	MR-GCR	
Eastwood	MR-GCR	
Lutterworth	MR-GCR	
Ingrow	MR-GNR	
Netherfield	MR-GNR	
Sutton-in-Ashfield	GCR-GNR	
Bulwell (× 3)	MR-GCR-GNR	
Hucknall (× 3)	MR-GCR-GNR	
Linby (× 3)	MR-GCR-GNR	
Newstead (× 3)	MR-GCR-GNR	
Bowling	CR-NBR	
Kilpatrick	CR-NBR	
Dalmuir	CR-NBR	
Clydebank	CR-NBR	
Yoker	CR-NBR	
Parkhead	CR-NBR	
Broomhouse	CR-NBR	

(continued)

Table A5.3. (Continued)

Town or city	Railway companies	Comment
Uddingston	CR-NBR	
Pollokshaws	GSWR/CR-CR	
Lynedoch	GSWR-CR	
Greenock	GSWR-CR	
Port Glasgow	GSWR-CR	
Stevenston	GSWR-CR	
Saltcoats	GSWR-CR	
Ardrossan	GSWR-CR	
Bogside	GSWR-CR	
Tavistock	GWR-LSWR	
Penrhiwceiber	Taff Vale-GWR	
Mountain Ash	Taff Vale-GWR	
Aberdare	Taff Vale-GWR	
Pontnewydd	GWR-GWR	
Pontllanfraith	LNWR-GWR	
Hanwood	GWR-Shropshire and Montgomeryshire	
Madeley (Salop)	GWR-LNWR	
Bonnybridge(× 3)	CR/NBR-CR-NBR	
Cleckheaton	LNWR-LYR	
Heckmondwike	LNWR-LYR	
Liversedge	LNWR-LYR	
St. Budeaux	LSWR-GWR	
Treforest	Taff Vale-Barry	
Briton Ferry	GWR-Rhondda and Swansea Bay	
Morriston	GWR-MR	
Two termini—not listed as hubs		
Uxbridge	GWR-GWR	
Ramsgate	SECR-SECR	
Leith (× 4)	NBR-NBR-NBR-CR	
Blackpool	LNWR/LYR-LNWR/LYR	
Coleford	GWR/MR-GWR	
Bodmin	GWR-LSWR	Separate but with a connection creating a double terminus at GWR station
Portishead	GWR-WLPR	Close
Ramsey	GNR-GER	Separate
Winsford	LNWR-CLC	Separate
Blaenavon	GWR-LNWR	Separate
Ebbw Vale	GWR-LNWR	Separate
Shared termini—not listed as hubs		
Bacup	LYR-LYR	
Eastbourne	LBSCR-LBSCR	
Portsmouth	LBSCR-LSWR	
Fowey	GWR-GWR	
Wells-next-the-Sea	GER-GER	
Newquay	GWR-GWR	
Maldon	GER-GER	Triangle
Lanark	CR-CR	Triangle

Table A5.3. (Continued)

Town or city	Railway companies	Comment
4-way crossings comprising a through line and a separate double-terminus—not listed as hubs		
St. Albans	MR(through)/LNWR-GNR(terminus)	
Ilkeston	GNR(through)/MR-MR (terminus)	
3-way crossing comprising a through line and a separate terminus—not listed as hubs		
Rickmansworth	GCR/MetR(2)-LNWR(1)	
Coalport	GWR(2)-LNWR(1)	
Cirencester	MSWJR(2)-GWR(1)	
Enfield	GNR(2)-GER(1)	
Brentford	LSWR(2)-GWR(1)	
Marlborough	MSJWR(2)-GWR(1)	
Bothwell	NBR(2)-CR(1)	
Airdrie	NBR(2)-CR(1)	
Renfrew	CR/GSWR(2)-GSWR(1)	
Birstall	LNWR(2)-LNWR(1)	
Pinxton	MR(2)-GNR(1)	
Oldbury	LNWR(2)-GWR(1)	
Aberthaw	Barry(2)-Taff Vale(1)	
Alexandra Palace	GNR(2)-GNR(1)	

into through stations—e.g. at Bristol and York—and surplus dead-end terminals had been converted to goods depots, as at Bricklayers Arms, London, and Carlisle. Much of this early rationalization was effected as a result of mergers between the companies concerned, although pressure from urban authorities to create a grand joint station was a factor in some cases.

Excerpts from the Counterfactual Timetable

The derivation of a railway timetable is a major task, but it is much easier to achieve for the counterfactual network than for the actual UK network. This is because the counterfactual network is designed to achieve a high degree of connectivity using a relatively parsimonious set of linkages. The emphasis is on through lines rather than dead-end branches, as through lines not only provide cut-offs for less direct long-distance routes but also allow traffic to leave intermediate towns in two directions rather than just one. The timetable can therefore be drawn up by scheduling trains running over a small number of long-distance routes rather than over a proliferation of minor branches.

Timetabling has been further simplified by imposing an equal-interval service (Peeters 2003), with a normal frequency of two hours (which implies a higher local frequency where several long-distance routes share the same tracks).

There is a fundamental problem, however, that any timetabler must confront, but which is particularly acute on a well-connected network. It is normally impossible to schedule a long-distance through train so that it connects conveniently with other long-distance through trains on every route that it intersects. For if intersecting trains are to be scheduled so that they all make convenient connections with trains on a particular route, then these connecting trains cannot also be scheduled to connect with each other at other places—namely hubs on either side of the route. There are only a few degrees of freedom to play with—namely the relative timing of the trains on the various routes—but many more constraints, arising from the need for good connections at all the various hubs. Requiring that all trains connect conveniently with each other therefore leads to an over-determined system to which there is no solution.

Various remedies are possible: trains can be held at hubs to await the next available connection before they depart, but this not only delays through passengers but also leads to congestion at hubs because of the number of waiting trains that may build up. The frequency of service can be increased, so that 'another train will be along shortly' even if an earlier connection is missed. This increases operating costs, however, although it has the advantage that passengers do not necessarily need to study the timetable before they commence their journey—they can just 'turn up and go'.

Two main solutions are used in this study. The first is to reduce the number of required connections by introducing a system of priorities. In the present context, connections between trunk routes are prioritized. Not all trunk line connections are prioritized, however, but only those that involve substantial traffic. If, for example, a hub affords the shortest trunk line connection between two major centres then the connection will be prioritized, whereas if the same connection can be made more conveniently using some other hub then it will not. The timetabling of trains over the rest of the network is subordinated to these requirements. Thus regional subsystems are timetabled so that local traffic feeds in conveniently to trunk line trains at the major regional hubs.

The second solution involves timetabling trains in opposite directions along a route so that they meet at convenient points. There is only one degree of freedom available, however—the timing of trains passing through the network in one direction can be fixed relative to the timing of all the trains going in the other direction, but timings cannot be altered independently on different routes because this would destroy connections.

The timetable used in this study was constructed on the principle that long-distance connections would not be made in central London but at hubs elsewhere—including satellite hubs around London itself. A system of regional connectivity was therefore established to begin with, and London traffic was then fitted in with this. Connectivity was prioritized by establishing a grand circuit of the core of the country. This route skirts all the main peripheral areas, passing through hubs at which traffic to or from the peripheral areas feeds into the core system. It begins at Dover, runs along the South Coast to Southampton, turns north to Bristol and Gloucester, and then divides. The right-hand fork serves Newcastle via Birmingham, while the left-hand fork serves Glasgow via Stoke-on-Trent and Carlisle. At Stoke-on-Trent north-bound traffic from Cambridge via Nottingham feeds in from the east. As this line runs along the inland boundaries of peripheral areas, it picks up and deposits traffic for each area. Thus a north-bound train collects traffic from South Wales at Gloucester and deposits traffic for North Wales at Stoke-on-Trent. It then picks up more north-bound traffic from Wales at Warrington, including traffic from Swansea via Chester. These connections are not intended for travel within the region—thus there are other more direct links between North and South Wales—but rather to feed trunk line traffic from various parts of the country into the region concerned through convenient regional hubs.

Trains along this main circuit are scheduled to cross at Gloucester. They stop at Gloucester for a short time to allow connections to be made with trains from London to South Wales, which also cross at Gloucester. The crossing at Gloucester is also convenient because it is compatible with similar crossings at other hubs on the system. Trains are also held at other hubs for short periods in order to optimize connections; in addition, trains are sometimes held for a short time at intermediate stations on cross-country lines in order to ensure convenient connections at either end.

Optimizing the timetable with respect to connections can create difficulties with the utilization of rolling stock, as a train may arrive at a terminus just as a train in the opposite direction is ready to depart, so that the incoming locomotive and coaches have to wait for nearly two hours before they can commence their return journey. The timetable has been designed to eliminate serious waste of this kind, but control of such waste has not been taken as a high priority. A common example of this problem involves a dead-end branch line whose services connect with main line trains that pass through the hub in opposite directions about an hour apart. If the branch line train takes more than an hour for a return trip, then two trains are required to provide connections with main line trains in both directions. On the actual system, economy was usually achieved by providing connections only to London, but on the counterfactual the more expensive alternative has sometimes been adopted of providing two trains instead.

The full timetable is available from the author (m.c.casson@henley.reading.ac.uk). An example of how the timetable works for a small region of the country is presented in Table A6.1.

Table A6.1. Excerpt from the timetable: Hampshire and Dorset
T1 London–Winchester–Southampton–Poole–Weymouth–Fortuneswell (TR7/PF5)
Winchester–Romsey (TK2)
Wareham–Swanage (LB3)

		A	B	C		C	B	A
London(NW)	dep	5.54		7.02	arr	11.08		12.16
Staines		6.16		7.24		10.46		11.54
Chobham		6.27		7.35		10.35		11.43
Ash		6.41		7.49		10.21		11.29
Farnham		6.49		7.57		10.13		11.21
Bentley	arr	6.55		8.03	dep	10.07		11.15
	dep	7.00		8.03	arr	10.07		11.10
Alton		7.09		8.12		9.58		11.01
Winchester		7.36		8.39		9.31		10.34
Southampton	arr	7.53		8.56	dep	9.14		10.17
	dep	XXX		8.57	arr	9.13		XXX
Lyndhurst				9.12		8.58		
Brockenhurst				9.19		8.51		
Christchurch			8.28	9.37		8.33	9.42	
Bournemouth			8.37	9.46		8.24	9.33	
Poole			8.44	9.53		8.17	9.26	
Wareham		D		10.07		8.03		D
Dorchester		9.23		10.32		7.38		8.47
Upwey		9.30		10.39		7.31		8.40
Weymouth		9.36		10.45		7.25		8.34
Fortuneswell	arr	9.44		10.53	dep	7.17		8.26
Winchester	dep	8.44			arr	9.26		
Romsey	arr	9.01			dep	9.09		
Wareham	dep	10.12			arr	9.58		
Swanage	arr	10.41			dep	9.29		

Note: A: London–Portsmouth; change at Bentley for train to Southampton; B: London–Fortuneswell; C: Brockenhurst–Lymington–Poole; D: Yeovil–Fortuneswell.
For other trains between London, Staines, and Chobham see the London–Staines–Reading summary table and the notes thereto.

T2 Stockbridge loop: Romsey–Andover–Whitchurch (SN1)

Romsey	dep	9.11			arr			10.59
Mottisfont		9.17						10.53
Stockbridge		9.31						10.39
Andover		9.45		10.52			9.18	10.25
Whitchurch	arr	10.00		11.07	dep		9.03	10.10

T3 Basingstoke–Aldermaston (SK7)

Basingstoke	dep		10.32		arr	11.38
Tadley			10.46			11.24
Aldermaston	arr		10.55		dep	11.15
Reading	arr		11.14		dep	10.56

T4 Shaftesbury loop: Yeovil–Salisbury–Andover–Basingstoke–Ash–London (SN4)

		A	*B*		*B*	*A*
Yeovil	*dep*	12.41		*arr*		15.29
Milborne Port		12.55				15.15
Wincanton		13.04				15.06
Shaftesbury		13.28				14.42
Salisbury	*arr*	14.11		*dep*		13.59
	dep	14.16	15.38	*arr*	12.32	13.54
Idmiston		14.28	15.50		12.20	13.42
Andover		14.52				13.18
Whitchurch (Hants)		15.07				13.03
Overton		15.15				12.55
Basingstoke		15.31				12.39
Odiham		15.46				12.24
Ash		16.07				12.03
Chobham		16.18				11.52
Staines	*arr*	16.32		*dep*		11.38
	dep	16.35		*arr*		11.35
London	*arr*	16.57		*dep*		11.13

Note: A: Taunton–Salisbury–London (NW); B: Salisbury–Amesbury–Devizes.

T5 Amesbury link: Salisbury–Idmiston–Manningford Bruce–Devizes (SK13)

		A	*B*		*B*	*A*
Salisbury	*dep*	9.38	10.16	*arr*	9.54	10.32
Idmiston	*arr*	9.50	10.28	*dep*	9.42	10.20
	dep	9.50	10.33	*arr*	9.37	10.20
Amesbury		9.58	10.41		9.29	10.12
Manningford Bruce		10.23				9.47
Devizes	*arr*	10.36		*dep*		9.34

Note: A: Salisbury–Devizes; B: Yeovil–London; change at Idmiston for Amesbury connection.
For other trains between Manningford Bruce and Devizes see the London (NW)–Penzance table.

T6 Ringwood link: Christchurch–Salisbury (PK2)

Christchurch	*dep*	8.46	9.42	*arr*	8.28	9.24
Ringwood		8.59	9.55		8.15	9.11
Downton	*arr*	9.16	10.12	*dep*	7.58	8.54
	dep	9.16	10.32	*arr*	7.38	8.54
Alderbury		9.22	10.38		7.32	8.48
Salisbury	*arr*	9.28	10.44	*dep*	7.26	8.42

For other trains between Alderbury and Salisbury see the Dover–Bristol timetable.

T7 Lymington loop: Brockenhurst–Christchurch–Poole (LC3)

Southampton	*dep*	8.57	*arr*	11.13
Brockenhurst	*dep*	9.24	*arr*	10.46
Lymington	*arr*	9.39	*dep*	10.31
	dep	9.54	*arr*	10.16
Christchurch		10.28		9.42
Poole	*arr*	10.44	*dep*	9.26

Note: For other trains between Christchurch and Poole see the London (NW)–Fortunes-well timetable (T1).

A Formal Model of Victorian Railway Regulation

Methodology

This appendix presents a formal model of regulation in network industries which explains how, under certain circumstances, competition can generate excess capacity. The model is used to explain how excess capacity developed in the Victorian railway system; it is sufficiently general, however, to be applied to other industries too.

According to the model, each private operator attempts to build their own self-contained network. As rival networks expand, the network with the highest density of terminals obtains the greatest market share. Competition for market share stimulates over-capacity. Network size stabilizes where the returns from higher density are just offset by the financial burden of excess capacity. If increasing returns to the scale of the network are modest then this point may be reached before profits have fallen to a break-even level, but if returns are high then erosion of profits will directly check growth.

In principle, standard theories of regulation should explain this pattern of behaviour, but in practice they do not. Most theories of regulation are prescriptive; they deduce what an efficient regulator would do, but do not explain how companies will respond to inefficient regulation.

The model is quite orthodox from an economic perspective, in so far as it involves strategic interactions between rational economic agents. In contrast to many economic models, however, which derive their hypotheses from wholly unrealistic assumptions, the assumptions of the present model are quite realistic. In particular, the government, as the regulator of the industry, bases its policies on a highly imperfect view of the industry. The model does not, therefore, predict that regulation will be optimal, but rather predicts how the industry responds to sub-optimal regulation.

Networks generate economies of scale. Both demand and supply may have a role in this. On the demand side, economies of scale arise when customers value connectivity. When a new customer is added to a network, existing customers may derive additional value because they are connected to a larger number of other people. This positive externality increases in value the greater the number of existing users of the network, thereby generating economies of scale. On the supply side, economies of scale arise when the network utilizes indivisible assets. These are assets, often located at terminals and hubs, which have the capacity to serve very large numbers of customers. Each additional customer reduces the average cost per user and thereby generates an economy of scale.

Early economic literature on networks emphasized the instability of competition under economies of scale. Competition will drive down prices to marginal costs. Since marginal costs are lower than average costs under economies of scale, this forces firms to run at a loss, and so the system can only be kept going by subsidies.

Recent economic literature has emphasized the virtues of regulated competition, in which competition keeps down price while allowing private owners and operators to break even. Competition is seen as indispensable in checking cost inflation and promoting customer-focus. The regulator is modelled as a 'principal' who establishes an incentive structure to which the suppliers—or 'agents'—respond. The suppliers have private information about costs and demand which the regulator does not have. The regulator aims to establish a regime in which the suppliers are encouraged to use their privileged information to offer the best value-for-money to customers.

These models tend to assume that the privileged information held by the suppliers is correct, and that the regulator fully understands the strategic options available to the suppliers and the factors that will govern their choices between them. These assumptions are very strong, and limit the relevance of the theory for historical analysis. As indicated above, these models are developed primarily for prescriptive rather than descriptive purposes.

On some networks competition is confined to operational activities that deliver the service to the customer, while a regulated monopoly owns and controls the infrastructure. If the economies of scale reside in the infrastructure then competition between such operators may well be viable. In practice, however, rival networks of infrastructure have been quite common, particularly in the railway sector, and have survived in private hands for longer than theory would suggest.

The entrepreneurs who first establish these private networks often make significant profits. News about these profits stimulates competitive entry by other network operators. In the early stages first-movers retain profits to invest, both to exploit short-term demand and to deter entry in the longer run. Network systems of this type often finish up with excess capacity, however, as attempts at entry deterrence fail. Profit expectations are disappointed, but the firms manage to survive through collusion.

Policymakers sometimes condone this competitive solution. They believe that competition is a spur to innovation and, in particular, to improvements in customer service. Indeed, policymakers may block attempts by rival firms to merge, even though this might serve to reduce costs by rationalizing capacity. This was the situation in the Victorian railway system. Such a regulatory stance can perpetuate a low-profit equilibrium of excess capacity in a mature network industry.

This appendix presents a simple model in which network externalities exploited by private firms lead to an equilibrium characterized by low profit and excess capacity. The focus of the model is on demand externalities driven by consumers' desires for connectivity. This focus is motivated by a view that demand-side externalities are the main factors that figure in the strategic thinking of the owners and managers of the firms, and are therefore the principal determinant of industry behaviour. Supply-side externalities can be easily introduced into the model (using fixed costs) but they have been omitted in the interests of clarity.

A Classification of Networks

There are many different types of network—both physical and social. Within the class of physical networks there are also many types, as indicated in Table A7.1. The table identifies five main characteristics by which physical networks differ—these are listed in the headings of the right-hand columns in the table. Differences between networks are important, because the nature of competition varies according to the type of network involved. The model presented below is based upon one particular type of network—exemplified by a railway network. Although the principles are perfectly general, the specific results derived below reflect the particular type of network on which the model is based.

As noted in Chapter 2, the Victorians invested heavily in network infrastructure. They inherited a unique mix of networks—roads and bridges, turnpikes, river navigations,

Table A7.1. A simple classification of network industries

Type of network industry	Date	Direction of traffic flow	Diversity of traffic	Typical network configuration	Linkage infrastructure	Geographical scope of network
Utilities						
Water	C19	Distribution	Low	Branch	Yes	Local
Gas	C19	Distribution	Low	Branch	Yes	Local and national
Electricity	C20	Distribution	Low	Branch	Yes	Local and national
Drainage	C17	Collection	Low	Root	Yes	Local
Sewage	C19	Collection	Low	Root	Yes	Local
Transport and communication						
Road bridges	C14	Two-way	High	Web	Yes	National
Turnpikes	C18	Two-way	High	Web	Yes	National
River navigations	C17	Two-way	High	Branch	Yes	National
Canals	C18	Two-way	High	Web	Yes	National
Railways	C19	Two-way	High	Web	Yes	National
Steam ships	C19	Two-way	High	Web	No	National and international
Air	C20	Two-way	High	Web	No	National and international
Remote communication						
Electric telegraph	C19	Two-way	High	Web	Yes	National and international
Telephone (landlines)	C20	Two-way	High	Web	Yes	National and international
Radio and TV broadcasting	C20	Distribution	High	Diffusion	No	National and international
Radio/satellite telecoms	C21	Two-way	High	Web	Some	National and international

fenland drainage, and narrow canals. They passed on a legacy comprising a different, and even broader mix—new systems of transport and communication, such as railways, telegraphs, steamships, and ship canals, together with urban-centred utilities such as gas, water, and sewage. They also enhanced some of the networks that they had inherited from the past, for example, roads, although others fell into disrepair, for example, narrow canals. The Edwardians developed electricity and telephone networks, while their successors pioneered radio, TV, and airlines.

Some networks carry traffic in only one direction; thus sewage and drainage systems collect waste or overflow from feeder systems and discharge it in bulk into the sea. Conversely, gas, water, and electricity systems distribute resources from centralized plants and storage facilities (gas works, reservoirs, power stations, etc.) to a multitude of businesses and households. Two-way traffic is the norm in transport and communications, however. Two-way flow changes the user's perception of a network quite profoundly.

Where a one-way flow is concerned, the user simply wants to be connected to the network itself, for example, by a water tap in the kitchen, a power point in each room, and a drain for the toilet; whereas with two-way flow the user wants the network to connect him to other people and other players. Access to the network is simply the first stage of a two-way process: the second, and more important stage, is to use the network to communicate with another person, or to travel to a distant destination. With one-way traffic, the issue is simply 'Can I get access?', while with two-way flow there is also the issue 'Once I have access, how many different people and places can I get in contact with?'

One-way networks typically have a root and branch structure. In collection networks the roots feed traffic into the trunk, where it is consolidated, while in distribution networks traffic from the trunk is split up between the branches using break-bulk operations. Two-way traffic is normally handled using webs. To economize on the number of linkages, webs typically employ hubs at which traffic is concentrated and sorted before forwarding.

One-way networks typically handle homogeneous traffic, while two-way networks typically handle a wide diversity of traffic. Not only is a wide variety of traffic handled but also each consignment has a distinctive origin and destination. The coordination of traffic flow along a two-way network is a complex operation: not only is it necessary to separate the flows going in opposite directions but also each consignment must be routed along the appropriate channel out of each hub.

Land-based networks typically use dedicated infrastructure to channel traffic: utilities typically use underground pipes (although telephones and electricity sometimes use posts and pylons instead), while transport systems use various types of highway: road, river, canal, and rail. The movement of traffic along one-way land-based networks is typically controlled by gravity (in sewage and drainage systems), pressure (gas), or voltage (electricity); in two-way land-based systems, traffic is normally carried in powered vehicles (horse-power for carts and barges, sail, and steam for ships, etc.) A distinctive feature of railways is the organization of vehicles into trains with an independent head-end power unit (the locomotive).

Sea- and air-based networks use only terminal infrastructure, such as ports, as the vehicles support themselves through buoyancy or lift. This affords a major economy, as channel infrastructure is very expensive. Infrastructure is particularly expensive in the case of main line railways. Being engineered to move heavy loads at high speed with minimal use of energy, railways must be straight and level; when built over undulating country, cuttings, embankments, tunnels, and bridges are required. The technological supremacy of rail during the Victorian era made it important not to under-invest on account of the capital cost. On the other hand, the very high capital cost made it important not to over-invest, and thereby divert scarce resources from better uses.

Networks may be local, national, or international. Before the development of national grids in the twentieth century, utilities were primarily local. By contrast, shipping networks have always been international, and this characteristic was reinforced by Victorian free trade and imperialism. Canal and turnpike networks were national by 1800, but rail systems remained local until 1830. Prior to 1830, rail networks usually handled local one-way traffic from mine to port, channelled along a root and branch network, but as regional and (from 1845) national networks developed, so two-way traffic routed through webs became dominant.

Parliament regulated railway construction from the outset, but often took a local view of the interests involved. Pressure to take a national view grew strongly after 1840, but it was not until the 1880s that Parliament confronted the issue of optimizing the performance of a national network of two-way traffic flow, and even then many of the issues were fudged.

Outline of the Model

This section presents a non-technical summary of the model. In the basic version there are just two railway networks, each of which is privately owned and self-contained. Each network aims to provide a nation-wide service by operating a range of stations distributed over the country. Although their routes intersect, there are no connections between them. Each network employs hubs, but these handle only traffic between different parts of the same network.

In line with the rest of the book, the focus is on passenger traffic. Passengers make trips from the places where they live to a variety of different places that they wish to visit—for example, places where their family, friends, and business acquaintances live. Each person's journeys start at the *same* place, but finish at *different* places. Different people *live* at *different* places, but everyone wants to *visit* the *same* range of places. All passengers make the same number of trips each period.

Firms compete on quality of service rather than on price; they tacitly collude by setting fares equal to the maximum fare imposed by the government regulator. In the model quality of service depends solely on network size, as explained below.

When a person lives nearer to a station on one network than on the other, they incur a cost premium when using the more distant station; this is known as an *access cost.* Similarly, when a destination is nearer to a station on one network than on the other, a passenger arriving at the more distant station incurs a *delivery cost.* Access costs are the same for any point of origin, and delivery costs are the same for any destination. It is also assumed, to begin with, that access costs are the same for everyone, however near or far they live from their local station, but this assumption is relaxed later on.

There is a third component of cost: the cost of familiarization. Because networks are complex, and timetables are difficult to master, an individual incurs a cost whenever they use a particular network for the first time. Once they have learned to use the network, however, they can continue to use it for other trips without incurring any additional cost. So far as the passenger is concerned, therefore, the cost of familiarization represents a fixed cost of using a network. It is independent of the number of trips per period, but is incurred each period in which a trip is made.

Because timetables change each period, familiarization must start over again at the beginning of each new period. If a person makes the same number of trips per period in successive periods then the familiarization cost becomes, in effect, a recurrent fixed cost of using the network. It is assumed that the cost of familiarization is the same for everyone. The size of the cost has a crucial impact on behaviour. When the familiarization cost is low people can afford to use both networks—selecting whichever is the most convenient for a given trip—but when it is high, they can only afford to use one network.

Suppose to begin with that there is no familiarization cost. The model shows that if the access cost exceeds the delivery cost then rational travellers will always use the station nearest to where they live, since any saving in the delivery cost achieved by using a more distant station is outweighed by the access cost. Thus each passenger uses only one network—the one with the station that is closest to where he or she lives. The larger the network, the higher its spatial density of stations, and the more likely it is that any individual's nearest station lies on the network concerned. When everyone uses their local station, therefore, traffic on each network is proportional to the number of stations provided.

If, on the other hand, access cost is lower than delivery cost then the rational traveller will choose the network that delivers them closest to their destination. Individuals will use both networks, selecting one or the other according to the destination of their trip. The larger the network, the greater the probability that it operates the nearest station to a given destination, and therefore the larger its share of the traffic. Once again, the division of traffic between the networks is proportional to the size of the network, but now all individuals use both networks, rather than just a single one.

Suppose now that the familiarization cost is positive. Using two networks requires the individual to familiarize themselves with both of them, and so the total cost of familiarization may be high. If an individual travels only infrequently, it may be cheaper overall to use just a single network. When the access cost exceeds the delivery cost, the familiarization cost simply reinforces the tendency to use their local station, but when the delivery cost exceeds the access cost it may induce them to switch to the other network altogether. This will apply if the cost of familiarization is high and the other network is larger than their local one.

There is a critical size that the smaller network must attain in order to survive under these conditions. If the net saving in delivery costs afforded by using both networks is less than the additional cost of familiarization involved then passengers will use only the larger network, and abandon the smaller network altogether. The net saving in delivery cost is equal to the excess of the delivery cost over the access cost, scaled up by the number of trips made by the passenger per period.

The results are summarized in Table A7.2. This table shows how the three elements of cost interact to determine how people behave. Collective behaviour generates three possible types of outcome so far as the network is concerned, and these are summarized in Table A7.3. Basically, when either access cost exceeds delivery cost or the cost of familiarization is low, the rival networks share the traffic in proportion to network size, but when delivery cost exceeds access cost and the cost of familiarization is high then the 'winner takes all'—the larger network carries all the traffic.

In this latter case there is a 'tipping point': if a network operates 49 per cent of the stations it will have no traffic, while if it operates 51 per cent of the stations then it will command 100 per cent of the traffic. The only way that both networks can survive under these conditions is that they have an equal number of stations and share the traffic equally. This is not a stable outcome, however, because if one network builds a single extra station then it can gain all the traffic rather than just half of it. There is therefore an enormous

Table A7.2. Impact of the three elements of cost on network behaviour when all individuals face the same access cost

Delivery cost exceeds access cost	Familiarization cost is zero	Familiarization cost is large and positive
No	Each passenger always uses their local station. Market share is proportional to the size of the network	Each passenger always uses their local station: market share is proportional to the size of the network
Yes	Each passenger uses whichever local station will deliver them closest to their destination. Market share is proportional to the size of the network	Each passenger uses the nearest station that belongs to the larger network. The larger network takes all the traffic

Table A7.3. Network outcomes associated with the previous scenarios

Customer loyalty	Rival networks share traffic	'Winner takes all': the larger network carries all the traffic
Each customer is loyal to a single network	Access cost exceeds delivery cost. Each customer uses their local station	Delivery cost exceeds access cost and familiarization cost is high. Each customer uses the larger network, even if it does not serve their nearest station
Each customer uses both networks	Delivery cost exceeds access costs. The cost of familiarization is zero. Each customer uses whatever network that delivers them closest to their destination	

incentive to expand the network incrementally. For this reason stability will be achieved only when one of the rival networks runs out of profit. If they have different costs, then the high-cost network will stop expanding first and the low-cost network will take all the traffic. If they have similar costs, then expansion will come to a stop when they both run out of profit. At this point both networks will be of equal size and they will therefore share the market equally.

The formal model considers the more general case in which access costs vary across passengers. Some passengers face high access costs because they live much closer to a station on one network than on another, while others have negligible access costs because they live equidistant from the nearest stations on each network. This general model contains the simple model discussed above as a special case, except that the general model assumes throughout that the two networks have identical costs.

In this general model passengers switch strategies at a range of network sizes instead of at a single critical size. As the size of the larger network increases, passengers with low access costs are the first to abandon using both networks and to switch to exclusive use of the larger one. As the relative size of the larger network continues to increase, so other passengers with higher access costs make the switch as well. Unlike the simple model, where market share responds to network size either proportionately (when passengers use both networks) or discretely (when all passengers switch to the larger network), the general model includes an intermediate case in which the market share of a network responds continuously but disproportionately to its size.

As a network increases in relative size from a zero base, it remains stuck initially with zero market share. Once it attains a critical relative size it begins to acquire market share at a constant rate. By the time it has grown to the point where its rival's relative size has been reduced to the same critical level, it is ready to acquire all of the market. The higher the ratio of delivery cost to access cost, and the higher the familiarization cost, the higher the rate at which relative network size is converted into market share at an intermediate relative size.

Equilibrium is achieved when the networks share the market equally (this generalizes the previous result for the simple model with identical network costs). The higher the rate at which size is converted into market share, the larger the absolute size of the networks in equilibrium, and the smaller their profits. When the rate of conversion is two, profit is just eliminated at the absolute network size where the incentive for further expansion disappears. Above this rate, network size is constrained to the same level by the break-even condition. Below this rate, equilibrium is attained with smaller networks that make positive profits.

The observed impact of regulation on the Victorian railway network is consistent with the special case of the model outlined above in which delivery cost exceeds access cost, the cost of familiarization is believed to be high, and the rate of conversion of relative network size into market share is greater than or equal to two.

Practical application of the model is constrained by the fact that more than two railway networks were involved in competition for national traffic. However, generalization of the model is relatively straightforward, as explained below. The basic insight, that firms compete for market share by attempting to increase the relative sizes of their networks, also applies to the more general case.

Application is also complicated by the fact that access costs, delivery costs, and familiarization costs may have changed over the lifetime of the system. This complication can be turned to advantage, however, by noting the implication that different patterns of behaviour may have emerged at different times because of different structures of cost. Prior to the Railway Mania, it may be argued that access costs were considered just as important, if not more important, than delivery costs, but that as the density of the system increased after the Mania, with the completion of new lines, so access became less of an issue. Once access became relatively easy, passengers became more concerned about how they completed their journey. This tendency would be exacerbated by the fact that increasing numbers of people were likely to have been taking advantage of the railway to travel to parts of the country that were unfamiliar to them. So far as familiarization costs are concerned, it might be thought that these would decrease as passengers got used to the railway system. However, after the spread of cheap fares and popular second-class travel in the 1870s, many more people began to use the railway system for the first time. Thus while there may have been a core of regular travellers who were familiar with the system, there may have been an increasing proportion of novice travellers. Furthermore, the proliferation of routes increased the number of timetabling permutations, and possibly increased the cognitive costs of planning and executing railway journeys. On balance, therefore, it is quite plausible to suppose that familiarization costs remained high right through the nineteenth century, and indeed for much later.

The railway companies responded to these conditions by attempting to convert their regional systems into national systems. These attempts gathered momentum in the 1860s and 1870s—just around the time when the previous discussion suggests that there was a particularly strong incentive to such behaviour. With restrictions on mergers, and weak enforcement of running powers, companies resorted to over-investment in order to attain the critical relative size needed to defend their market share on the national system. Invading other companies' territory through alliances with rival firms proved to be a popular strategy. It satisfied the regulator because, on balance, it appeared to strengthen rather than weaken competition, and it satisfied the companies as it helped to spread the cost of new investment. Customers believed that they gained from greater competition, even though price collusion was usually sustained. In fact, however, they would have been better off if the regulator had reduced prices and enforced inter-operability between rival networks in order to reduce system-wide operating costs. The economy as a whole would have benefited too, as less capital would have been wasted on over-investment in the railway system.

Specification of the Formal Model

The national railway system consists of two independently owned networks, each comprising a set of stations linked together by a set of routes. Let n_j be the number of stations operated by firm j ($j = 1, 2$). The total number of stations is

$$n = n_1 + n_2 \tag{1}$$

All variables are non-negative unless otherwise stated. By convention, network 1 is the smaller in terms of the number of stations, $n_1 \leq n_2$. It is assumed that the total number of stations is very large, and that the number of stations operated by each firm is also large, even though it may be relatively small compared to the network total. For many purposes it is the relative rather than the absolute size of a network that is important, where the relative size, s_j, is measured by

$$s_j = n_j/n \tag{2}$$

There are no connections between the two networks; thus any journey must terminate at a station on the same network as the station at which the journey began. Where connections are technically possible, it is the policy of each firm not to permit the traveller to transfer at an intermediate point and complete their journey on the rival's network.

There is a fixed population, z, distributed evenly over the territory of the nation state. Each station has a natural catchment area comprising all the people who are closer to that station than to any other. The boundary of each area separates it from the adjoining catchment areas of neighbouring stations. The stations are spaced out so that each station has the same number of people, z/n, residing in its natural catchment area.

Each person has the same demand for travel, namely a fixed number of trips per period, q. It is possible that the number of trips a person wishes to make depends upon the size of population, as with a larger population there are more people to visit. The model presented here assumes however, that a larger population simply gives people a greater choice of whom to visit without inducing them to visit more people in total.

Each person makes return trips from the place at which they reside; no one-way or circular trips are made. Each trip is valued by the traveller at v, irrespective of the destination involved. A rational traveller will always make a trip provided that the total cost he incurs is less than or equal to v.

Each person has a list of contacts, comprising people that he or she may wish to visit. The location of each person's contacts is evenly distributed across the different catchment areas. Persons select the individual they wish to visit next at random from their contacts list. Having selected their contact, visitors determine their travel plan; this involves selecting the origin station and the destination station. These stations may not be the local stations serving the catchment areas because these two areas may not beserved by the same network.

Any trip between any two points can be made by either network, provided that the traveller always uses the nearest available stations to start and end their journey on their chosen network. However, costs are incurred when the traveller uses a network whose station is not the nearest station for the purposes of their trip.

Travellers must be familiar with the networks they use in order to plan their journeys efficiently. A fixed cost of familiarization, f, is incurred each period whenever a given network is used. The cost is independent of the number of trips actually made, and is the same for everyone. It is a recurrent cost because travellers need to refresh their memories and update their knowledge of network timetables in each successive period.

A rail journey is typically the middle part of an inter-modal journey. An outward journey begins with a transfer from home to the station and ends with a transfer from the station to the final destination, and conversely for the return journey. Transfers may involve walking, using a private conveyance (e.g. horse and buggy), a hired conveyance (e.g. a taxi), or public transport (e.g. bus or tram).

Because of the way that trips are organized, each individual always starts their trips from the same location, but rarely visits the same destination twice. Origin and destination stations therefore have distinctive roles in network usage. An access cost, a, is incurred each time a traveller starts a trip from a station outside the catchment area in which they live. A delivery cost of b per trip is incurred whenever a traveller's final destination lies outside the catchment area of the station at which their journey terminates.

Different travellers incur different access costs. Travellers residing very near to their local station, and hence near to the centre of its natural catchment area, incur a higher access cost than those located near the boundary of the catchment area and therefore nearer, on average, to an alternative station on the rival network. Within each catchment area, the access cost is uniformly distributed across the local resident population. Its maximum value is A and its minimum value 0. Since all travellers visit a range of different destinations, the average delivery cost is the same for everyone.

As the total number of stations, n, varies, the catchment areas shrink in terms of both territory and population. For simplicity, 'lock in' is ignored; as the network expands or contracts, stations are relocated in order to maintain catchment areas of equal size. The smaller the average size of a catchment area, the shorter the average distance a traveller has to go to reach either their local station or the nearest station on the other network. If stations are laid out in two dimensions across a territory of given size, then the average distance to a station will decline in proportion to the square root of n. For mathematical convenience, however, it is useful to suppose that the average distance actually declines in proportion to n itself. To capture the benefits of increased density, therefore, it is assumed that, in addition to access and delivery costs, each traveller incurs a distance penalty per trip d/n, where d is a parameter measuring the role of network density in reducing the traveller's overall cost per trip.

There are economies of scale in the operation of stations, as each station can handle an unlimited amount of traffic. The cost per period of maintaining and operating a station is r; this includes the cost of financing the capital expenditure, maintaining the building and staffing the station. Train operation involves a mixture of constant and increasing returns. There are constant returns to train operation, because the length of trains and/or their frequency needs to be increased in direct proportion to the total number of trips made; on the other hand, there are economies of scale in the length of a trip; the cost of each trip is w, irrespective of its length. Both companies use the same technologies and operating practices, and therefore incur identical costs.

Fares are regulated by the government. The government sets a maximum fare, P, per trip, and the companies tacitly collude by charging the maximum. The regulated fare is sufficiently high that the companies can make an operating surplus, but sufficiently low that low travellers make all the trips that they wish to make:

$$w < P \le v - a - b - (d/n) - (f/q) \tag{3}$$

Each railway company maximizes its expected profits, π_j. Let m_j be firm j's market share. Revenue and cost are

$$R_j = Pqzm_j \tag{4}$$

$$C_j = wqzm_j - rn_j \tag{5}$$

and thus profit is

$$\pi_j = R_j - C_j = (P - w)qzm_j - rn_j \tag{6}$$

With prices fixed, each firm's competitive strategy focuses on optimizing the size of its network, as measured by the number of its stations, n_j. Each firm's market share, m_j, depends upon its relative size, as measured by s_j. The total size of the system, as measured by the total number of stations, n, is determined by the interplay of the rival strategies. Each firm decides the number of stations to operate based on expectations of the number of stations established by its rival, N_j.

Solution of the Model

The solution involves three main stages.

- Express the market share m_j in terms of relative size, s_j. This is the most substantive step; once it has been completed, the model can be reformulated as a fairly standard model of duopolistic rivalry, albeit with some unusual features.
- Solve the duopoly model to determine the number of stations on each network, the total size of the system, and the profitability of the firms.
- Compare the outcome with the ideal social outcome.

The first stage is the main subject of this section.

Consider a traveller residing in the catchment area of a local station belonging to network j. He has q trips to make, but he has not yet selected his specific destinations.

- If he uses his local station for every trip (strategy 1) he avoids the access cost a altogether. He can expect to be delivered direct to the catchment area of his chosen destination a proportion s_j of the time.[1] This means that he incurs the delivery cost b a proportion $1 - s_j$ of the time. He also incurs the cost f of familiarizing himself with network j. The resultant expected total cost is shown in the right-hand column of the first line of Table A7.4.
- If the traveller incurs a cost a then he can use the nearest station belonging to the rival network (strategy 2) and expect to be delivered direct to the catchment area a proportion $1 - s_j$ of the time. This means that he incurs the delivery cost b only a proportion s_j of the time. The resultant cost is shown in the second line of Table A7.4.
- If he is willing to incur the cost of familiarizing himself with both networks, rather than just one, then he can choose to be delivered direct to every destination by selecting his departure station according to his destination (strategy 3), He incurs a cost a every time he uses the rival network, but avoids delivery costs altogether. He uses the other network a proportion $1 - s_j$ of the time. The expected cost of strategy 3 is shown in the third row of the table.

---

[1] Because people do not use the network to visit their immediate neighbours, the proportion is actually $(s_j n - 1)/(n - 1)$, but for large n this approximates to s_j.

Table A7.4. Expected costs of a traveller's alternative strategies

Traveller's strategy	Expected cost
1. Use only local station	$f + b(1 - s_j)q$
2. Use only station on other network	$f + (a + bs_j)q$
3. Use either station	$2f + a(1 - s_j)q$

Comparing the first two rows of the table shows that the traveller will always use the local station (strategy 1) rather than always use the nearest rival station (strategy 2) when relative size s_j exceeds a critical level $s_{j1}{}^*$:

$$s_j \geq s_{j1}{}^* = \begin{matrix} (1 - (a/b))/2 & a \leq b \\ 0 & a > b \end{matrix} \qquad (7)$$

If $a > b$ then the traveller will always use their local station since the saving in moving to the other station, b, is less than the cost, a, of getting there. Since relative size cannot be negative, $s_{j1}{}^* = 0$ in this case.

Comparing the first and third rows of the table shows that the traveller will always use the local station (strategy 1) rather than use either station (strategy 3) when

$$s_j \geq s_{j2}{}^* = \begin{matrix} 1 - (f/(b-a)q) & a \leq b \\ 0 & a > b \end{matrix} \qquad (8)$$

This implies that a small network can retain the exclusive custom of passengers when familiarization costs are high, the number of trips made is low, and delivery costs exceed access costs by only a small margin. These conditions ensure that the advantage to the traveller of switching to a larger network when a destination is not directly served by the smaller network is relatively small compared to the cost of familiarization with the larger network.

Comparing the second and third rows of the table shows that traveller will always use the nearest rival station (strategy 2) rather than use either station (strategy 3) when

$$s_j \geq s_{j3}{}^* = f/(a+b)q \qquad (9)$$

This result is only relevant when $a < b$ for otherwise strategy 1 dominates both strategies 2 and 3. It implies that a small network can survive in competition with a larger network by sharing customers with it when the cost of familiarization is low, trips are frequent, and costs of access and delivery are high. High access and delivery costs encourage travellers to seek out the cheapest route for each trip, while the combination of high frequency and low familiarization cost means that the aggregate savings on the trips will outweigh the cost of becoming familiar with the smaller network.

It follows that there are two main reasons why a local station may be used. It may be used as part of strategy to use the station exclusively (strategy 1) or as part of a strategy to use it only when it affords direct access to the chosen destination (strategy 3); it is never used under strategy 2.

To simplify the subsequent analysis, it is assumed that only strategies 1 and 2 are economic: strategy 3 is not viable because the cost of familiarization is so high that it is not worth the traveller's interest to use both networks in the same period, even under the most favourable conditions in which the traveller lives on the border between the catchment areas of two networks of equal size. The necessary and sufficient condition is that the cost of familiarization is more than one half the delivery cost incurred by finishing every journey at a distant station:

$$f > bq/2 \qquad (10)$$

With strategy 3 eliminated, the remaining choice is between strategies 1 and 2. Residents only use the local station when the saving in access costs equals or exceeds the saving in delivery costs that could be achieved by using a larger network accessible from a more distant station. Residents living on the border of the catchment area, and especially those adjacent to an area with a station on the rival network, have the strongest incentive to switch to the rival network. Substituting $a = 0$ into inequality (8) shows that they will switch to the rival network whenever the local network's relative size is less than one half, that is, the network is smaller than its rival. The last people to switch out will be those who live adjacent to the local station; substituting $a = A$ into (8) shows that they will switch out only when relative size falls to $(1 - (A/b))/2$.

The converse of this is that when the network served by the local station is large, it will start to attract people from neighbouring catchment areas. People living near the boundaries of the other network's catchment areas will start to switch in to it as soon as the network becomes larger than its rival, and by the time it has attained a relative size $A/2b$ it will have taken all the traffic from the other network.

The expected cost schedules are illustrated graphically in Figure A7.1. The figure illustrates a case in which inequality (10) is satisfied, and in which a rational traveller

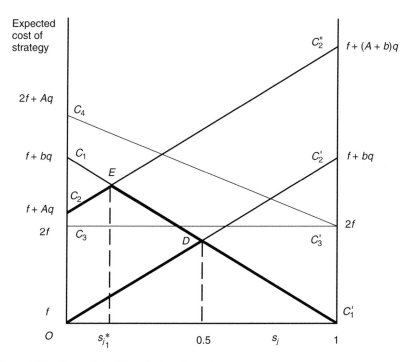

Figure A7.1. Cost-minimizing choice of travel strategy

therefore uses only a single network. The relative size of network j, s_j, is measured along the horizontal axis, which is of unit length. The figure illustrates how the relative attractiveness of different strategies varies with the relative size of network

- The expected cost of strategy 1 is indicated by the downward sloping straight line C_1C_1'.
- The expected cost of strategy 2 depends upon how close the traveller lives to the border with the catchment area of the rival network's closest station, as this determines the relevant value of a. If he lives on the border ($a = 0$) then the schedule is OC_2', while if he lives adjacent to his local station ($a = A$) then it is C_2C_2''. The schedule C_2C_2'' is parallel to the schedule OC_2', but a distance A above it. The schedule OC_2' intersects the schedule C_1C_1' at the point D, which corresponds to the mid-point on the horizontal axis where the two networks are of equal size.
- The expected cost of strategy 3 also depends upon where the traveller resides. If he lives on the border then the schedule is the horizontal line C_3C_3', whereas if he lives adjacent to the station then it is the downward-sloping line C_4C_3'.

The rational traveller minimizes expected cost by operating on an envelope formed by the lowest of the three cost schedules. For a traveller located centrally at their local station, the minimum cost envelope is illustrated by the piecewise linear schedule shown in bold C_2EDC_1'. The schedule shows that the traveller uses strategy 2 when relative network size is small, and so does not use their local station at all, but switches to strategy 1 at the critical size $s_{j1}*$. The switch point is indicated by the point E, at the intersection of the schedules C_1C_1' and C_2C_2'. For a traveller located at the border of their local catchment area, the minimum cost envelope is ODC_1'. This traveller switches from strategy 2 to strategy 1 at the point D, where C_1C_1' and OC_2' intersect.

Because the cost of access, a, is uniformly distributed across the residents of a catchment area, the critical relative sizes at which travellers switch are distributed uniformly along the segment ED. Projecting the switch points onto the horizontal axis shows that they are uniformaly distributed between $s_{j1}*$ and 0.5. This indicates that as the relative size of the network increases people switch into it at a constant rate. It follows that market share of the jth network is governed by relative network size in the following way:

$$m_j = \begin{matrix} 0 \\ h(s_j - s_{j1}*) \\ 1 \end{matrix} \qquad \begin{matrix} 0 < s_j < s_{j1}* \\ s_{j1}* < s_j < 1 - s_{j1}* \\ 1 - s_{j1}* < s_j < 1 \end{matrix} \qquad (11)$$

where

$$h = \begin{matrix} 1/(1 - 2s_{j1}*) = b/A \\ 1 \end{matrix} \qquad \begin{matrix} A \le b \\ A > b \end{matrix} \qquad (12)$$

The variable h measures the sensitivity of market share to the relative size of the network, and is of fundamental importance to the results that follow. When $h = 1$ density effects dominate network competition. Each traveller always uses their local station, and so the firm that achieves the greater spatial density attains *pro rata* a correspondingly greater market share.

Once delivery costs exceed access costs, every additional increase in delivery costs increases the value of h. Rising delivery costs, or declining access costs, induce travellers to divert from local stations on the smaller network to more distant stations on the larger network. The effective catchment areas of the larger network increase relative to its natural

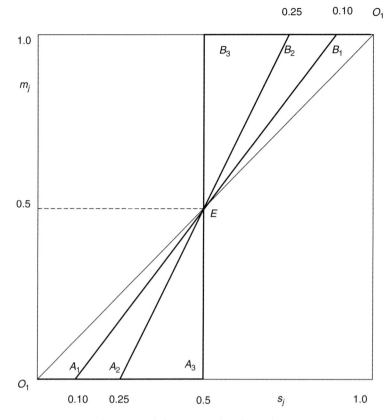

Figure A7.2. Mapping from capital share to market share: three cases

catchment areas, and those of the smaller network decline. As delivery costs become very large relative to access costs, h tends to infinity, and everyone uses the larger network.

The determination of market share is illustrated diagrammatically in Figure A7.2. Four special cases are illustrated, corresponding to different values of h and s_{j1}^*.

Case 1. $h = 1$; $s_{j1}^* = 0$: The mapping from relative size to market share in this case is indicated by the diagonal line O_1O_2. There is no minimum size for a firm's network: each firm shares the market in direct proportion to its number of stations. This case is analogous to the well-known 'tragedy of the commons' (Hardin 1968). Indeed, the present model may be seen as a generalization of the 'tragedy of the commons' model to the case where $s_{j1}^* > 0$. The analogy with the tragedy of the commons arises because the rival firms are both 'grazing' to obtain customers in the same way that animals graze on pasture to obtain food. Each firm invades territory currently occupied by the other firm by building a new station. It would pay the two firms to collude to restrict railway building to the level of capacity required to meet the available demand, but collusive agreements are not enforceable. While the firms collude over price, they cannot collude over new building projects. They cannot trust each other to refrain from new projects without a legally binding contract, and contracts cannot be made legally binding because the government will not approve them. If the value of the resource—the land required for railway building—were inflated to reflect the loss of profit incurred by the other firm when additional railway development took place then the inter-firm 'externality' would be internalized, but in the absence of binding agreements this internalization cannot take place.

Case 2. $h = 1.25$; $s_{j1}* = 0.1$ The mapping from capital share to market share is indicated by the line $O_1 A_1 B_1 O_2$. The mapping is only piece-wise linear, as it involves two kinks, at A_1 and B_1. The higher value of b is reflected in the fact that the segment $A_1 B_1$ is steeper than the diagonal $O_1 O_2$. Increasing the value of h increases the size of both networks, and causes profits to fall.

Case 3. $h = 2.0$; $s_{j1}* = 0.25$. The mapping from relative size to market share is indicated by the line $O_1 A_2 B_2 O_2$. The expansion of the network is such that super-normal profit is eliminated altogether.

Case 4. h is infinite; $s_{j1}* = 0.5$. The mapping from relative size to market share is indicated by the line $O_1 A_3 B_3 O_2$. In this case only the larger network is viable. Thus the networks can coexist only if they are of equal size.

Duopolistic Competition on Networks

Once market share has been related to relative size, it is possible to solve for a Cournot equilibrium of the entire system. Each firm decides the number of stations in response to the number of stations built by its rival, and an equilibrium prevails when, in the light of this, each rival is content with the number of stations that it has built.

There are three main stages in solving the Cournot model:

- Relate profit to the number of stations operated by the firm, n_j, and its rival, N_j. Maximize profit to determine a reaction curve showing how n_j responds to N_j.
- Find the intersection of the reaction curves. Because the two companies have identical costs, this intersection will occur where both companies are of equal size,

$$n_j = N_j \tag{13}$$

The solution of this equation determines the number of stations operated by each firm, and hence the total size of the network. The two companies will take equal shares of the national market. Once the number of stations and the market share are known, profitability can be calculated.

- Determine whether competitive responses will be constrained by a break-even condition, If so, calculate the number of stations from the break-even condition.

Stage 1

Substituting equation (11) into the profit equation (6) and applying equation (2) gives the profit expression

$$\pi_j = (P - w)qzhn_j/(n_j + N_j) - rn_j \tag{14}$$

where N_j represents the number of stations operated by firm j's rival. This equation is valid over the region $[s_{j1}*, 1 - s_{j1}*]$ in which a maximum of profit is sought.

Maximizing (14) with respect to n_j shows how the jth firm trades off the marginal revenue generated by increased market share against the marginal cost of operating additional stations. The first-order condition is

$$\partial v_j / \partial n_j = \left((P - w)qzhn_j/N_j^2 \right) - r = 0 \tag{15}$$

The first expression on the left-hand side is the marginal revenue product of a station and the second is its marginal cost.

Equation (15) is a quadratic in n_j, and the positive root corresponds to a maximum of profit. In the absence of a binding profit constraint, the solution determines a reaction curve which describes how firm j's investment in its network responds to the investment of the other firm:

$$n_j = ((P - w)qzh/r)^{1/2} N_j^{1/2} - N_j \tag{16}$$

This reaction curve is non-linear, with firm j's response steadily declining as the other firm's investment in stations increases.

Stage 2

Since both firms face identical conditions, their reaction curves will be mirror images of one another, and so their intersection will result in the same value of capital, n^*, for each. Setting $N_j = n_j = n_j^*$ in equation (7) gives the equilibrium number of stations for each firm:

$$n_j^* = (P - w)qzh/4r \quad j = 1,2 \tag{17}$$

Differentiation of equation (16) with respect to N_j shows that this is the critical value at which the reaction curve for n_j becomes horizontal. The reaction curves therefore intersect each other at right angles. Thus at the equilibrium, each firm makes no reaction to the other firm's change in the number of stations.

This property of the equilibrium is illustrated in Figure A7.3. The figure portrays the special case $h = 1$, $s_{j1}^* = 0$. The numbers of stations n_1, n_2 are measured along the vertical and horizontal axes, respectively. The reaction curves are OR_1, OR_2, respectively, and the equilibrium is at their intersection E.

Stage 3

Substituting (17) back into (6) and setting $m_j = 0.5$ gives equilibrium profit

$$\pi_j = (2 - h)(P - w)qz/4 \tag{18}$$

It can be seen that profitability declines as the sensitivity of market share to relative size, h, increases.

For $h > 2$ a break-even equilibrium exists in which the two firms share the market equally with a number of stations

$$n_j^{**} = (P - w)qz/2r \tag{19}$$

giving a total size of the system

$$n^{**} = 2n_j^{**} = (P - w)qz/r \tag{20}$$

Although both firms would like to increase their share of the market by increasing their number of stations, neither can afford to do so.

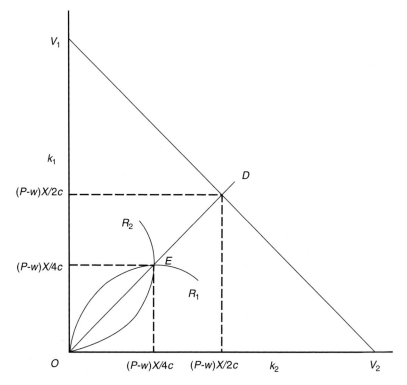

Figure A7.3. Industry equilibrium

Note: This figure illustrates the special case $h = 1$

Social Costs and Benefits

If the railway system were operated by a single operator with full inter-operability between routes the transport requirements could be met more efficiently. Each passenger could use their nearest station and, by making suitable connections, arrive at the closest station to their destination. Thus access and delivery costs would be eliminated. The only costs of using the system would be the cost of familiarization and the density-related cost of getting to and from the nearest station.

Recalling that all passengers receive the same benefit, v, from every trip, the aggregate social benefit, B, conferred by an integrated railway system would be

$$B = (v - (d/n))qz - fz \tag{21}$$

Since there are no supply-side economies of scale in network operation, cost is simply

$$C = wqz - rn \tag{22}$$

Maximizing net social benefit,

$$W = B - C \tag{23}$$

with respect to the size of the network, n, gives the optimal number of stations as

$$n^+ = (dqz/r)^{1/2} \tag{24}$$

Substituting (24) into (23) shows that the net benefit conferred by an integrated system of optimal size is

$$NB^+ = (v - w)qz - fz - 2(dqzr)^{1/2} \tag{25}$$

Because demand is price-inelastic, it does not require great skill to set the price at an appropriate level, P^+, in order to sustain this optimum. The price level is bounded from above by the net benefit per passenger per trip, and from below by the average cost per passenger per trip, both calculated for a system of optimal size:

$$w + (dr/qz)^{1/2} < P^+ < v - (f/q) - (dr/qz)^{1/2} \tag{26}$$

When there are positive access and delivery costs there is no way that the competitive system can match the performance of the integrated system. It is, however, possible to induce the rival companies to generate a national network of the same total size (i.e. with the same number of stations). Equating the equilibrium size of the competitive network, $n^* = 2n_j^*$ with the optimal size of the integrated network, n^+, and solving for the regulated price gives

$$P^* = (2/h)(dr/qz)^{1/2} + w \tag{27}$$

Equation (27) shows that for a given level of operating cost, w, the regulated price under competition should be lower, the higher the delivery cost, b, relative to the access cost, A, the higher the density premium, d, the lower the cost of capital, r, and the higher the level of population, z, and the frequency of trips, q.

Generalization to N Firms

Suppose now that there are $K \geq 2$ networks that make up the system, indexed $j = 1, \ldots, K$. The relative size of the jth network is measured in the same way as before, $s_j = n_j/n$. Each firm correctly conjectures that the other firms will all share the market in equal proportion, since they face similar demand and cost conditions. As before, each firm requires a minimum relative size s_{j1}^* to achieve a positive market share. It increases its market share linearly with respect to market size while other firms investments remain unchanged. It gains the whole market when the market shares of the remaining $N - 1$ firms have all been forced down to the critical size. At this point the remaining firms, being equal in scale, have surrendered in total $(K - 1) s_{j1}^*$ of the market. Thus when a firm achieves a relative size of $(K - 1) s_{j1}^*$ it has acquired the whole of the market. It follows that market share is a piece-wise linear function of the relative size of the networks:

$$m_j = \begin{cases} 0 & 0 < s_j < s_{j1}^* \\ h(s_j - s_{j1}^*) & s^* < s_j < 1 - s_{j1}^* \\ 1 & 1 - (K - 1)s_{j1}^* < s_j < 1 \end{cases} \tag{28}$$

where

$$h = 1/(1 - Ks_{j1}^{*}) \tag{29}$$

Equations (28) and (29) are natural generalizations of equations (11) and (12).

Once again, the firm's behaviour is governed by a reaction curve, which explains its optimal response to the investment decisions of all the other firms. Confining attention to an interior solution in the range $[s_{j1}^{*}, 1 - (K-1) s_{j1}^{*}]$ gives a natural generalization of the reaction curve (16):

$$n_j = ((P - w)qzh/r)^{1/2}N_j^{1/2} - N_j \tag{30}$$

where N_j now represents the total output of all firms other than firm j. Since all firms have the same reaction curves, $n_j = n_j^{*}$ for all j, and so

$$N_j = (K - 1)n_j^{*} \tag{31}$$

Substituting (31) into (30) gives

$$n_j^{*} = ((K - 1)/K^2)((P - w)qzh/r) \tag{32}$$

Profit in equilibrium is

$$v_j^{*} = ((P - w)qz/K)(1 - ((K - 1)/K)h) \tag{33}$$

Profit is therefore non-negative if and only if $h \le K/(K-1)$. For $h > K/(K-1)$ an equilibrium exists for which all firms share the market equally with a number of stations

$$n_j^{**} = (P - w)qzh/Kr \tag{34}$$

For $h \le K/(K-1)$ the total number of stations on the system is

$$n^{*} = Kn_j^{*} = ((K - 1)/K)((P - w)qzh/r) \tag{35}$$

It is easier for firms to gain the whole of the market when there are many rivals than when there is just a single rival, because with many rivals a small market share is sufficient to force the market shares of each of the other firms to below the critical level. On the other hand, the firm's return to increasing relative size is much greater as a result, and so firms have a greater incentive to increase relative size when there are many rival firms. But with many firms, a given increase in relative size requires a greater number of stations because the total number of stations owned by other firms is greater. This pushes investment to an even higher level than when only a single rival is involved.

Policy Implications for the Performance of the Victorian Railway System

The model explains very well the emergence of excess capacity in the Victorian railway system in Britain. In the period 1830–70 there was a substantial traffic demand which called for a significant amount of investment. The failure to complete many of the lines projected during the Railway Mania meant that it took a considerable time to meet these initial traffic requirements. As the density of the network increased during the 1860s, lines became closer to each other, and inter-firm competition began to intensify. It was at this stage that some of the major regional lines began to reveal national aspirations, and that network competition began to intensify. After 1870, traffic demand increased steadily, but network growth remained ahead of demand, creating a protracted period of excess capacity. There remained bottlenecks, which needed to be alleviated by improvements, but a significant amount of investment continued to go into new lines which were lightly used.

Railway rivals found it prohibitively costly to compete on price, as there was a tendency under competition for price to fall to the short-run variable cost given by the wage cost, w, thereby eliminating all operating profit. Although competition emerged for one-off sources of traffic, such as special excursions, fares for most major flows of traffic were regulated by informal inter-firm agreements. While reservation prices for many third-class travellers were relatively low, reservation prices for first class travellers were high, and so on average there was a substantial profit margin on the traffic carried. So far as freight was concerned, reservation prices for bulk traffic were relatively low, but those for time-sensitive traffic in parcels or perishables were high. Thus on average the operating profit margin was reasonably high.

Railways competed regularly on the basis of network size. The major companies all had pretensions to offer a national service. They expanded their networks both to invade other companies' territories, and to deter entry into their own territory by saturating it with lines. The implied level of b is therefore relatively high.

Note that this model predicts that a horizontal merger between two firms that creates a larger network will tend to provoke mergers between other firms. This can be observed in contemporary airline alliances and mobile telephone networks as well as in the railway system.

Conclusion

This paper has set out a new theory of regulation in network industries. The theory has been developed from an historical case study, based on the Victorian railway system in the UK. The theory is, however, a general theory, in the sense that it can, in principle, be applied to other network industries, in other countries and at other times, provided that the economic fundamentals are the same.

It has been argued that historical evidence supports both the *assumption* of this model, that private companies strove to build national networks, and the *implication* of the model, that excess capacity emerged as a result of the competitive pursuit of higher density. It has been argued that government policy was in error in condoning the development of rival private networks. Potential gains from competition were dissipated through wasteful excess capacity.

Parliament could have regulated railways better if they had taken a clearer view of the size of the railway network they required, in terms of the density of stations. Government should have imposed lower freight rates and passenger fares in order to eliminate the profits out of which the excess capacity was financed. Greater financial stringency would have encouraged companies to maximize the potential of their local and regional networks, and to cooperate more fully in the operation of the national network.

Even if they had achieved an optimal network density, however, they could not have achieved a high quality of service without promoting inter-operability between the companies. While some towns and cities showed initiative in promoting joint stations as hubs where connections could be made, companies could still frustrate these intentions by timing their trains so that key connections were missed. As a result, the network—though very extensive—never realized its full potential in terms of the quality of service it delivered.

Index

Index